1996 CASE SUPPLEMENT

to

LEGAL REGULATION

OF THE

COMPETITIVE PROCESS

Cases, Materials and Notes

on

*Unfair Business Practices, Trademarks,
Copyrights and Patents*

REVISED FOURTH EDITION

By

EDMUND W. KITCH
Joseph M. Hartfield Professor of Law
The University of Virginia

HARVEY S. PERLMAN
Dean and Professor of Law
The University of Nebraska

Westbury, New York
THE FOUNDATION PRESS, INC.
1996

COPYRIGHT © 1993, 1994, 1995 THE FOUNDATION PRESS, INC.

COPYRIGHT © 1996

By

THE FOUNDATION PRESS, INC.

All rights reserved

ISBN 1–56662–412–6

*TEXT IS PRINTED ON 10% POST
CONSUMER RECYCLED PAPER*

TABLE OF CONTENTS

[The page numbers on the left in bold are the page number in the casebook. The page numbers on the right are the page numbers in the supplement.]

CHAPTER I. THE PROBLEM OF ENTRY
   C. The Regulation of Public Goods

      Page 49.   Notes 1

   D. The Regulation of Advertising

      Page 64.   Notes 2
      Page 65.   Morales v. Trans World Airlines, Inc. 3
                     Notes 8
      Page 73.   Treaties and Intellectual Property 9

CHAPTER II. DECEPTIVE PRACTICES
   A. Competitors' Remedies
      (4) The Lanham Act

      Page 116.   Ortho Pharmaceutical Corp. v.
                          Copsprophar, Inc. 11
                     Notes 15
      Page 119.   Alpo Petfoods, Inc. v. Ralston Purina Co. ... 15
                     Note 19
      Page 122.   Johnson & Johnson * Merck Consumer
                        Pharmaceuticals Co. v. Smithkline
                        Beecham Corp. 19
                     Note 24
      Page 129.   Castrol, Inc. v. Quaker State Corp. 24
                     Note 28
      Page 137.   Note 29

      (5) Testing Agencies

      Page 155.   Turf Lawnmower Repair, Inc. v. Bergen
                        Record Corp. 31

   B.   Purchasers' Remedies

      Page 169.   Note (Serbin v. Ziebart Intern. Corp.) 33

   C. State Unfair Competition Statutes

iii

TABLE OF CONTENTS

        Page 193.   Champion Parts, Inc. v. Oppenheimer & Co. 35
                          Note 36

D. Federal Trade Commission
    (2) "Unfair and Deceptive" Practice

    Page 216.   Kraft, Inc. v. Federal Trade Commission ... 36
    Page 217.   Federal Trade Commission v. Pantron I Corporation 42

    (3) Private or Public Enforcement

    Page 239.   Federal Trade Commission v. Figgie International, Inc. 47

CHAPTER III. PRODUCT AND PRODUCER IDENTITY

A. The Fundamentals

    Page 249.   Note on Reverse Passing Off 53
    Page 253.   An Overview of National and International Protection of Trademarks 53

B. Problems of Validity
    (1) Distinctiveness

    Page 267.   Car-Freshner Corp. v. S.C. Johnson 58

    (2) Subject Matter

    Page 292.   Note on NAFTA and TRIPS 60
    Page 307.   Note on Color Depletion 61
    Page 312.   Romm Art Creations Ltd. v. Simcha International, Inc. 63
                  Notes 63
    Page 313.   Two Pesos, Inc. v. Taco Cabana, Inc. 64
                  Notes 72
    Page 313.   Krueger International, Inc. v. Nightingale Inc. 73
                  Notes 77
    Page 313.   Vornado Air Circulation Systems, Inc. v. Duracraft Corp. 80

C. Problems of Priority and Infringment
    (1) Adoption, Affixation, and Use

TABLE OF CONTENTS

Page 320.   Laureyssens v. Idea Group, Inc. 89
Page 321.   Problem 92

(2) Test for Infringement

Page 323.   Note. 92

(3) Incontestability

Page 328.   Shakespeare Co. v. Silstar Corp. 93

(4) Geographic Limitations

Page 348.   Problem 99

(5) Non-Competing Goods

Page 376.   Deere & Company v. MTD Products Inc. .. 100
                 Hormel Foods Corp. v. Jim Henson
                         Prod. Inc. 102
                 Notes 104

(6) Collateral Use

Page 380.   Matrix Essentials, Inc. v. Emporium Drug
                         Mart, Inc. 108
                 Note 112
Page 383.   New Kids on the Block v. News America
                         Publishing, Inc. 114
                 Notes 119

(7) Remedies

Page 385.   George Basch Co., Inc. v. Blue Coral, Inc. . 120
Page 388.   Sands, Taylor & Wood Co. v. The Quaker
                         Oats Co. 127
                 Sands, Taylor & Wood Co. v. The Quaker
                         Oats Co. 137
                 Notes 140

(9) Abandonment

Page 400.   Indianapolis Colts, Inc. v. Metropolitan
                         Football Club Ltd. Partnership 137
                 Note 140

TABLE OF CONTENTS

CHAPTER IV. PREDATORY PRACTICES
   A. Interference with Business Relations
      (2) Unfair Competition

Page 427.	Note	141

      (3) Interference with Contractual Relationships

Page 442.	Penna v. Toyota Motor Sales	142

   B. Appropriation
      (4) Trade Secrets

Page 475.	Phillips v. Frey	144
Page 482.	Omnitech International, Inc. v. The Clorox Co.	145
Page 483.	Note: Customer Lists	145
Page 485.	Note	147
Page 494.	Rockwell Graphic Systems, Inc. v. Dev Industries, Inc.	148
Page 494.	Amoco Production Co. v. Laird	153
Page 497.	Baxter International, Inc. v. Morris	157
	Pepsico v. Redmond	158
	Notes	160
Page 500.	G.S. Rasmussen & Associates, Inc. v. Kalitta Flying Service, Inc.	160
	Notes	166
Page 535.	Note	167

      (5) A Case Study: Exploitation of Characters and Personalities

Page 549.	Note	167
Page 564.	White v. Samsung Electronics America Inc.	168
	White v. Samsung Electronics America Inc.	174
	McFarland v. Miller	186
	Notes	187

CHAPTER V. COPYRIGHT

   An Overview of the Statute

Page 567.	New reference	190
Page 569.	Note on Deposits	190
Page 569.	Note on NAFTA and Mexican movies	

TABLE OF CONTENTS   vii

	in the public domain	190
Page 571.	Text on NAFTA and TRIPS	190
Page 572.	Note on TRIPS and Moral Rights	192

A. Copyrightable Subject Matter
(1) The Nature of the Material

Page 576.	Note on TRIPS and § 102(b)	193
Page 578.	Lotus Development Corp. v. Borland Int'l ..	193
Page 578.	Notes	207
Page 578.	Addition to Note	208
Page 585.	Note on NAFTA, TRIPS and Computer Programs	208
Page 596.	Note on NAFTA, TRIPS and Industrial Designs	208

(3) Originality

Page 601.	Feist Publications, Inc. v. Rural Telephone Service Company, Inc.	209
	Notes	209
Page 613.	Note on West Publishing Co. after Feist ...	210

B. Infringement
(1) The Exclusive Rights

Page 619.	Note on Digital Sound Recording Act	210
Page 622.	Lewis Galoob Toys, Inc. v. Nintendo of America, Inc.	211
	Note	215

(2) The Infringing Work

Page 667.	Beal v. Paramount Pictures Corporation ...	216
Page 672.	Computer Associates International v. Altai	227
	Notes	246

C. Fair Use

Page 710.	Note on Audio Home Recording Act	248
Page 711.	American Geophysical Union v. Texaco, Inc.	248
	Notes	285
Page 733.	Note on amendment to § 107	287

TABLE OF CONTENTS

(1) Parody

Page 733.	Campbell AKA Luke Skyywalker v. Acuff-Rose Music, Inc.	287
	Notes	302
Page 753.	Note on recent fair use cases	302

(3) Fair Use and Burden of Persuasion

Page 765.	Note on volume copying of class materials	303
Page 765.	Note on evidentiary burdens	303

D. Ownership of Copyright

Page 776.	Carter v. Helmsley-Spear, Inc.	304
Page 777.	Notes on computere software	316
Page 787.	Note on moral rights study	321
Page 787.	Noteon Rostropovichv.Koch Int'l	321
Page 788.	Copyright Royalty Tribunal Abolished	321
Page 791.	Note on criminal charges against student	322
Page 791.	Note on Enforcement Provisions of TRIPS	322

CHAPTER VI. PATENTS

Page 792.	New patent term	323
Page 794.	Brief Text on NAFTA and TRIPS	323

A. Patentable Subject Matter

Page 795.	Text on NAFTA, TRIPS and Patentable Subject Matter	323
Page 820.	Note	324
Page 821.	Note on Asgrow Seed case	324
Page 821.	TRIPS recognizes limits on medical patents	325
Page 831.	Note on patenting of animals	325
Page 840.	Arrhythmia Research Technology v. Corazonix Corp.	326
	Notes	333

B. Utility

Page 848.	Note on In re Brana	334

C. Nonobviousness

Page 853.	Note	334
Page 881.	Note	335
	Scripps Clinic & Research Fnd. v. Genentech, Inc.	336

EE. The Nonobvious Analysis of Chemical Inventions

Page 897.	Notes on biotechnological Patents Act	338
	In re Dillon	344
	In re Deul	354

F. Section 102
   (2) "Known or Used"

Page 933.	Envirotech Corporation v. Westech Engineering Inc.	364
	Note	370

H. First Inventor

Page 946.	Amended 104 and the National Treatment Clause of NAFTA and TRIPS	371
Page 947.	Scott v. Finney	371

   2(a) Conception

Page 958.	Burroughs Wellcome Co. v. Barr Laboratories, Inc.	375

I. Specification and Claims

Page 975.	Glaxo Inc.v. Novopharm Ltd.	384
	Note on Wahl Instruments, Inc. v. Acvious, Inc	393
	Note on Amegen, Inc. v. Chugai	394
	Amgen, Inc. v. Chugai Pharmaceutical Co., Ltd.	394

J. Scope of Patent Rights
   (2) Within the United States

Page 999.	TRIPS and Process Patents	398

   (3) Within the Term of the Patent

Page 1008.	Note on Joy Tech. v. Flakt Inc.	398

TABLE OF CONTENTS

  (4) Contributory Infringement

   Page 1025. Note on new antitrust guidelines 399

  (5) Construction of Claims

   Page 1037. Scripps Clinic & Research Foundation v.
          Genentech, Inc. 399
        Pennwalt Corporation v. Durand-Wayland,
           Inc 400
        Note 409

M. An Overview

   Page 1055. The Future of Patent and Copyright (J.H.
         Reichman, Charting the Collapse
         of the Patent-Copyright Dichotomy .. 410

TABLE OF CASES

Principal cases are in italic type. Non-principal cases are in roman type.
References are to Pages.

Abdul-Jabbar v. General Motors Corp.	19, 189
Abend v. MCA, Inc.	302
Advanced Computer Services of Michigan v. MAI Systems	321
Adray v. Adry-Mart, Inc.	136
Alappat, In re	333
Allen-Myland, Inc. v. International Business Machines Corp.	320
Alpo Petfoods, Inc., v. Ralston Purina Company	*15*
American Geophysical Union v. Texaco Inc.	248
Amgen, Inc. v. Chugai Pharmaceutical Co.	*324*, 394
Amoco Production Co. v. Laird	*153*
Anheuser-Busch Inc. v. L & L Wings Inc.	105
Anheuser-Busch Inc. v. Balducci Pub.	105
Animal Legal Defense Fund v. Quigg	325
Arrhythmia Research Technology, Inc. v. Corazonix Corp.	*325*
Asgrow Seed Co. v. Winterboer	324
Atari Games Corp. v. Nintendo	317
Autoskill, Inc. v. National Educational Support Systems, Inc.	247
Aymes v. Bonelli	215
Bateman v. Mnemonics, Inc.	167
Baxter International, Inc. v. Morris	*157*
Beal v. Paramount Pictures Corp.	*216*
Bellsouth Advertising & Pub. Corp. v. Donnelly Info. Pub. Inc.	210
Belmore v. City Pages Inc.	303
Brana, In re	*324*
Brooke Group Ltd. v. Brown & Williamson Tobacco Corp.	141
Brown Bag Software v. Symantec Corp.	247
Building Oficials & code Admin. Int'l Inc v. Code Tech. Inc.	*208*
Burroughs Wellcome Co. v. Barr Laboratories, Inc.	*375*
Cambell aka Luke Skyywalker v. Acuff Rose Music, Inc.	*287*, 302
Campbell v. Osmond	*89*
Carter v. Helmsley-Spear, Inc.	*304*
Car-Freshner Corp. v. S.C. Johnson & Son, Inc.	*58*
Castrol, Inc. v. Quaker State Corporation	*2*
CCC Information Services Inc. v. MacLean Hunter Market Reports Inc.	*210*
Central Point Software inc. v. Global Software & Accessories, Inc.	316
Champion Parts, Inc. v. Oppenheimer & Co.	*35*
Cipollone v. Liggett Group, Inc.	8
City of Cincinnati v. Discovery Network, Inc.	2
Computer Associates International v. Altai	209, 227

xi

TABLE OF CASES

Conopco, Inc. v. May Department Stores Co.	120
Data General Corp. v. Grumman Systems Support Corp.	321
Deere & Company v. MTD Products, Inc.	*100*
Deul, In re	*354*
Dillon, In re	*344*
Dowling v. United States	322
DSC Communications Corp. v. DGI Technologies, Inc.	318
Duraco Products, Inc. v. Joy Plastic Enterprises, LTD.	79
Durdon, In re	*339*
Eastman Kodak Co. v. Image Technical Services, Inc.	321
Elmer & HTH, Inc. v. ICC Fabricating, Inc.	87
Engineering Dynamics, Inc. v. Structural Software, Inc.	207
Escada AG v. The Limited, Inc.	88
Envirotech Corporation v. Westech Engineering Inc.	*364*
Ex parte Hibberd	325
Federal Trade Commission v. Figgie International, Inc.	*47*
Federal Trade Commission v. Pantron I Corporation	*42*
Feist Publications, Inc. v. Rural Telephone Service Company, Inc.	209
Ferrari S.P.A. Esercizio Fabrichre Automobili E. Corse v. Roberts	92
44 Liquormart, Inc. v. Rhode Island	2
Gates Rubber Co. v. Bando Chemical Indus.	247
General Electric Company v. R Squared Scan System, Inc.	320
George Basch Co., Inc. v. Blue Coral, Inc.	*120*
Glaxo Inc. v. Novopharm Ltd.	*384*
Gordon & Breach Science Publishers v. American Institute of Physics	29
Groden v. Random House, Inc.	30
Hilton Davis Chemical Co. v. Warner-Jenkinson Co.	409
Hormel Foods Corporation v. Jim Henson Productions, Inc.	*102*
Indianapolis Colts, Inc. v. Metropolitan Baltimore Football Club	*137*
Jeffrey Milstein, Inc. v. Greger, Lawlor, Roth, Inc.	63
*Johnson & Johnson * Merck Consumer Pharmaceuticals v. Smithkline Beecham Corp.*	*19*
Joy Technologics v. Flakt Inc.	398
K Mart Corp. v. Cartier, Inc.	99
Kohler Co. v. Moen Inc.	86
Kraft, Inc. v. Federal Trade Commission	*36*
Krueger International, Inc. v. Nightingale Inc.	*73*
Laureyssens v. Idea Group, Inc.	*89*
Lever Brothers Co. v. United States	99
Lewis Galoob Toys, Inc. v. Nintendo of America, Inc.	*211*
Lindy Pen Company Inc. v. Bic Pen Corp.	*136*

TABLE OF CASES

Case	Page
Lotus Development Corp. v. Borland Int'l Inc.	193
MAI Sys. Corp. v. Peak Computer	321
Major League Baseball Properties, Inc. v. Sed Non Olet Denarius, Ltd.	140
Manville Sales Corp. v. Paramount Systems	371
Markman v. Westview Instruments, Inc.	409
Master Distributors, Inc. v. Pako Corporation	61
Matrix Essentials, Inc. v. Emporium Drug Mart, Inc.	108
McFarland v. Miller	186
Midler v. Ford Motor Co.	167
Montana v. San Jose Mercury news, Inc.	188
Morales v. Trans World Airlines, Inc.'	3
National Rifle Ass'n v. Handgun Control Federation of Ohio	303
New Kids on the Block v. News America Publishing, Inc.	114
NutraSweet Co. v. Stadt Corp.	61
Omnitech International Inc. v. The Clorox Co.	145
Ortho Pharmaceutical Corp. v. Crosprophar, Inc.	11
Owens-Corning Fiberglas Corp.	61
The Paddington Corp. v. Attiki Importers & Distributors	77
Penna v. Toyota Motor Sales, U.S.A., Inc.	142
Pennwalt Corporation v. Durand-Wayland, Inc.	400
Pepsico, Inc. v. Redmond	158
Phillips v. Frey	144
Pleuddemann, In re	339
Practice Management Information Corp. v. American Medical Ass'n	208
Princeton University Press v. Michigan Document Services, Inc.	303
Qualitex Co. v. Jacobsen Products Co.	61
Rasmussen & Associates, Inc. v. Kalitta Flying Service, Inc.	160
Rockwell Graphic Systems, Inc. v. Dev Industries, Inc.	148
Romm Art Creations Ltd. v. Simcha International, Inc.	63
Rosemont Enterprises v. Random House	302
Rostropovich v. Koch Int'l	321
Rotbart v. J.R. O'Dwyer Co.	303
Rubin v. Coors Brewing Co.	2
Sands, Taylor & Wood Co. v. The Quaker Oats Company	127, 131, 134, 135
Scott v. Finney	371
Scripps Clinic & Research Foundation v. Genentech, Inc.	324, 336, 399
Sebastian International Inc. v. Longs Drug Stores Corp.	112
Sega Enterprises, Ltd. v. Accolade, Inc.	318
Semco, Inc. v. Amcast, Inc.	30
Serbin v. Ziebart International Corp.	33
Shakespeare Company v. Silstar Corp.	93
Shaw v. Dow Brands, Inc.	8

TABLE OF CASES

Stampede Tool Warehouse, Inc. v. May 146
State v. Synchronal Corp. 8
Summit Machine Tool Manufacturing Corp. v. Victor CNC Systems Inc. 53
Thomas & Betts Corp. v. Panduit Corp. 87
Town & Country properties, Inc. v. Riggins 188
Triad Systems Corp. v. Southeastern Express Co. 321
Trovato, In re 333
Turf Lawnmower Repair, Inc. v. Bergen Record Corp. *31*
Two Pesos, Inc. v. Taco Cabana, Inc. *64*
United States v. LaMacchia 322
Vault Corp. v. Quaid Software Ltd. *317*
Versa Products Company, Inc. v. Bifold Co. (Manufacturing) Ltd. *79*
Vornado Air Circulation Systems, Inc. v. Duracraft Corp. *80*
Wahl Instruments, Inc. v. Acvious, Inc. *393*
Waits v. Frito-Lay, Inc. 34, 167
Warmerdam, In re 333
WarnerVision Entertainment Inc. v. Empire of Carolina Inc. 92
Warren Publishing Inc. v. Microdos Data Corp 210
White v. Samsung Electronics America, Inc. *168, 174*
Williams & Wilkins Co. v. United States 285
Wolens v. American Airlines, Inc. 9
Zazú Designs v. L'Oréal S.A. 19

CHAPTER I

THE PROBLEM OF ENTRY

PAGE 49. Consider with existing notes.

NOTES

1. The drafters of the Restatement of Unfair Competition argue that the *INS* decision does not provide a general rule against misappropriation at common law. See Restatement (Third) of Unfair Competition § 38, Comment *b* (1995):

> The rule stated in this Section limits common law liability for appropriations of intangible trade values to cases involving an appropriation of trade secrets, an appropriation of the commercial value of another's identity, or an appropriation of a work of authorship that is not fixed in a tangible medium of expression and thus protectable under common law copyright. * * * Although courts have occasionally invoked the *INS* decision on an adhoc basis to grant relief against other commercial appropriations, they have not articulated coherent principles for its application. It is clear that no general rule of law prohibits the appropriation of a competitor's ideas, innovations, or other intangible assets once they become publicly known. In addition, the federal patent and copyright statutes now preempt a considerable portion of the domain in which the common law tort might otherwise apply. * * * The better approach, and the one most likely to achieve an appropriate balance between the competing interests, does not recognize a residual common law tort of misappropriation.

2. Recent articles relating to the *INS* case and the misappropriation doctrine include: Gordon, *On Owning Information: Intellectual Property and the Restitutionary Impulse*, 78 VA. L. REV. 149 (1992); Raskind, *The Misappropriation Doctrine as a Competitive Norm of Intellectual Property Law*, 75 MINN. L. REV. 875 (1991).

3. Two recent articles exploring the *Sears* and *Compco* preemption doctrine argue in favor of an expanded preemption doctrine. Joan Schaffner, *Patent Preemption UnLocked*, 1995 Wis. L. Rev. 1081 (1995) (trade secret law should be preempted); Theodore davis, Copying in the Shadow of the Constitution: The Rationale Limits of

Trade Dress Protection, 80 Minn. L. Rev. 595 (1996) (federal protection of functional trade dress is preempted).

PAGE 64. Add to Note 2.

In a concurring opinion in City of Cincinnati v. Discovery Network, Inc., 113 S. Ct. 1505 (1993), Justice Blackmun argued that once commercial speech is found to be about a lawful activity and not misleading, government regulations should be tested by the same level of scrutiny as non-commercial speech. The majority opinion did not reach the issue because the regulation at issue, a prohibition against distribution of "commercial handbills" from newsracks, was invalid even under the intermediate scrutiny standard of *Central Hudson*. In Rubin v. Coors Brewing Co., 115 S.Ct. 1585 (1995) the Court declared unconstitutional a federal regulation prohibiting disclosure of the alcoholic content of beer on labels, finding that the government's claimed justification that the regulation was needed to prevent beer manufacturers from competing by increasing alcholic content was not supported by the facts or the regulatory scheme. The Court reaffirmed *Central Hudson* but Justice Stevens concurred separately arguing that regulations of accurate and complete commercial speech is subject to the same scrutiny as non-commercial speech.

In 44 Liquormart, Inc. v. Rhode Island, 1996 WL 241709 (1996) the appropriate role of the *Central Hudson* test fractured the Court. Rhode Island prohibited advertising of the price of liquor, arguing that the prohibition was designed to discourage consumption by preventing sales and other methods of price competition. Justice Stevens writing for Justicies Kennedy and Ginsburg, held that where a state prohibits truthful speech about a lawful activity, the justification for the regulation must be evaluated in accordance wtih a stricter standard of review. These three justices believed that *Posadas* should be overruled. Justice Thomas would have gone further and invalidate any attempt to prohibit truthful speech about a lawful activity. Justice O'Connor writing for the Chief Justice and Justices Breyer and Souter found the Rhode Island statute unconstitutional under *Central Hudson*. Justice Scalia merely concurred in the judgment.

Thus, the deference to be paid to regulation of commercial speech, if any, remains unresolved but there appears to be growing skepticizm of asserted justifications for advertising prohibitions of lawful activity. Several Justices acknowledge that such regulations tend to shield from public scrutiny a governmental policy that would become obvious if regulated directly. A tax on liquor sales or a minimum price regulation would be more effective in discouraging price competition but would be more visible to the voting public. After *44 Liquormart*, can restrictions on cigarette advertising survive?

PAGE 65. Add prior to "The Economics of Advertising"

MORALES v. TRANS WORLD AIRLINES, INC.,
Supreme Court of the United States, 1992
504 U.S. 374

Justice SCALIA delivered the opinion of the Court.

The issue in this case is whether the Airline Deregulation Act of 1978, 49 U.S.C.App. § 1301 *et seq.*, preempts the States from prohibiting allegedly deceptive airline fare advertisements through enforcement of their general consumer protection statutes.

I

Prior to 1978, the Federal Aviation Act of 1958 (FAA), 72 Stat. 731, as amended, 49 U.S.C.App. § 1301 *et seq.*, gave the Civil Aeronautics Board (CAB) authority to regulate interstate air fares and to take administrative action against certain deceptive trade practices. It did not, however, expressly pre-empt state regulation, and contained a "saving clause" providing that "[n]othing ... in this chapter shall in any way abridge or alter the remedies now existing at common law or by statute, but the provisions of this chapter are in addition to such remedies." 49 U.S.C.App. § 1506. As a result, the States were able to regulate intrastate air fares (including those offered by interstate air carriers) and to enforce their own laws against deceptive trade practices.

In 1978, however, Congress, determining that "maximum reliance on competitive market forces" would best further "efficiency, innovation, and low prices" as well as "variety [and] quality ... of air transportation services," enacted the Airline Deregulation Act (ADA). 49 U.S.C.App. §§ 1302(a)(4), 1302(a)(9). To ensure that the States would not undo federal deregulation with regulation of their own, the ADA included a pre-emption provision, prohibiting the States from enforcing any law "relating to rates, routes, or services" of any air carrier. 49 U.S.C.App. § 1305(a)(1). The ADA retained the CAB's previous enforcement authority regarding deceptive trade practices (which was transferred to the Department of Transportation (DOT) when the CAB was abolished in 1985), and it also did not repeal or alter the saving clause in the prior law.

In 1987, the National Association of Attorneys General (NAAG), an organization whose membership includes the attorneys general of all 50 States, various Territories, and the District of Columbia, adopted Air Travel Industry Enforcement

Guidelines* containing detailed standards governing the content and format of airline advertising, the awarding of premiums to regular customers (so-called "frequent flyers"), and the payment of compensation to passengers who voluntarily yield their seats on overbooked flights. These guidelines do not purport to "create any new laws or regulations" applying to the airline industry; rather, they claim to "explain in detail how existing state laws apply to air fare advertising and frequent flyer programs." NAAG Guidelines, Introduction (1988).

[The DOT and Federal Trade Commission objected to enforcement of the NAAG Guidelines. Nonetheless the attorneys general threatened enforcement. The airlines then filed an action seeking a declaratory judgment that the guidelines were preempted. The district court found for the airlines and issued a permanent injunction against enforcement of the guidelines. The Court of Appeals affirmed.]

III

We now turn to the question whether enforcement of the NAAG guidelines on fare advertising through a State's general consumer protection laws is preempted by the ADA. As we have often observed, "[p]re-emption may be either express or implied, and is compelled whether Congress' command is explicitly stated in the statute's language or implicitly contained in its structure and purpose." FMC Corp. v. Holliday, 498 U.S. ----, ---- (1990) (internal quotation marks omitted); Shaw v. Delta Air Lines, Inc., 463 U.S. 85, 95 (1983). The question, at bottom, is one of statutory intent, and we accordingly "begin with the language employed by Congress and the assumption that the ordinary meaning of that language accurately expresses the legislative purpose." *Holliday, supra*, 498 U.S. ----, at ----; Park 'N Fly, Inc. v. Dollar Park and Fly, Inc., 469 U.S. 189, 194 (1985).

A

Section 1305(a)(1) expressly preempts the States from "enact[ing] or enforc[ing] any law, rule, regulation, standard, or other provision having the force and effect of law relating to rates, routes, or services of any air carrier...." For purposes of the present case, the key phrase, obviously, is "relating to." The ordinary meaning of these words is a broad one--"to stand in some relation; to have bearing or concern; to pertain; refer; to bring into association with or connection with," Black's Law Dictionary 1158 (5th ed. 1979)--and the words thus express a broad preemptive purpose. * * * [The Court held that (1) a general savings clause preserving "remedies now existing at common law or by statute" does not undermine a specific preemption provision, (2) the preemption provision applies not only to statutes directed specifically

---

* The court reproduced the NAAG Guidelines as an appendix to its opinion. That appendix is omitted here.

at the airline industry but also general regulatory statutes, and (3) that preemption applies even if the state regulation is consistent with federal regulation].

B

It is hardly surprising that petitioner rests most of his case on such strained readings of § 1305(a)(1), rather than contesting whether the NAAG guidelines really "relat[e] to" fares. They quite obviously do. Taking them seriatim: § 2.1, governing print advertisements of fares, requires "clear and conspicuous disclosure" [defined as the lesser of one-third the size of the largest typeface in the ad or ten-point type] of restrictions such as "limited time availability, limitations on refund or exchange rights, time-of-day or day-of-week restrictions, length-of-stay requirements, advance-purchase and round-trip-purchase requirements, variations in fares from or to different airports in the same metropolitan area, limitations on breaks or changes in itinerary, limits on fare availability," and "[a]ny other material restriction on the fare." Section 2.2 imposes similar, though somewhat less onerous, restrictions on broadcast advertisements of fares; and § 2.3 requires billboard fare ads to state clearly and conspicuously "Substantial restrictions apply" if there are any material restrictions on the fares' availability. The guidelines further mandate that an advertised fare be available in sufficient quantities to "meet reasonably foreseeable demand" on every flight on every day in every market in which the fare is advertised; if the fare will not be available on this basis, the ad must contain a "clear and conspicuous statement of the extent of unavailability." § 2.4. Section 2.5 requires that the advertised fare include all taxes and surcharges; round-trip fares, under § 2.6, must be disclosed at least as prominently as the one-way fare when the fare is only available on round trips; and § 2.7 prohibits use of the words " 'sale,' 'discount,' [or] 'reduced' " unless the advertised fare is available only for a limited time and is "substantially below the usual price for the same fare with the same restrictions."

One cannot avoid the conclusion that these aspects of the guidelines "relate to" airline rates. In its terms, every one of the guidelines enumerated above bears a "reference to" air fares. And, collectively, the guidelines establish binding requirements as to how tickets may be marketed if they are to be sold at given prices. Under Texas law, many violations of these requirements would give consumers a cause of action (for at least actual damages, see Tex. Bus. & Com. Code Ann. § 17.50 (1987 and Supp. 1991-1992)) for an airline's failure to provide a particular advertised fare-- effectively creating an enforceable right to that fare when the advertisement fails to include the mandated explanations and disclaimers. This case therefore appears to us much like *Pilot Life*, in which we held that a common-law tort and contract action seeking damages for the failure of an employee benefit plan to pay benefits "relate[d] to" employee benefit plans and was preempted by ERISA, 481 U.S., at 43-44, 47-48, 107 S.Ct., at 1550-1551, 1552-1553.

In any event, beyond the guidelines' express reference to fares, it is clear as an economic matter that state restrictions on fare advertising have the forbidden significant effect upon fares. Advertising "serves to inform the public of the ... prices of products and services, and thus performs an indispensable role in the allocation of resources." Bates v. State Bar of Arizona, 433 U.S. 350, 364 (1977). Restrictions on advertising "serv[e] to increase the difficulty of discovering the lowest cost seller ... and [reduce] the incentive to price competitively." Id., at 377. Accordingly, "where consumers have the benefit of price advertising, retail prices often are dramatically lower than they would be without advertising." Ibid. As Judge Easterbrook succinctly put it, compelling or restricting "[p]rice advertising surely 'relates to' price." Illinois Corporate Travel v. American Airlines, Inc., 889 F.2d 751, 754 (CA7 1989), cert. denied, 495 U.S. 919 (1990).

Although the State insists that it is not compelling or restricting advertising, but is instead merely preventing the market distortion caused by "false" advertising, in fact the dynamics of the air transportation industry cause the guidelines to curtail the airlines' ability to communicate fares to their customers. The expenses involved in operating an airline flight are almost entirely fixed costs; they increase very little with each additional passenger. The market for these flights is divided between consumers whose volume of purchases is relatively insensitive to price (primarily business travelers) and consumers whose demand is very price sensitive indeed (primarily pleasure travelers). Accordingly, airlines try to sell as many seats per flight as possible at higher prices to the first group, and then to fill up the flight by selling seats at much lower prices to the second group (since almost all the costs are fixed even a passenger paying far below average cost is preferable to an empty seat). In order for this marketing process to work, and for it ultimately to redound to the benefit of price-conscious travelers, the airlines must be able to place substantial restrictions on the availability of the lower priced seats (so as to sell as many seats as possible at the higher rate), and must be able to advertise the lower fares. The guidelines severely burden their ability to do both at the same time: The sections requiring "clear and conspicuous disclosure" of each restriction make it impossible to take out small or short ads, as does (to a lesser extent) the provision requiring itemization of both the one-way and round-trip fares. Since taxes and surcharges vary from State to State, the requirement that advertised fares include those charges forces the airlines to create different ads in each market. The section restricting the use of "sale," "discount," or "reduced" effectively prevents the airlines from using those terms to call attention to the fares normally offered to price-conscious travelers. As the FTC observed, "[r]equiring too much information in advertisements can have the paradoxical effect of stifling the information that customers receive." Letter from FTC to Christopher Ames, Deputy Attorney General of California, March 11, 1988, App. to Brief for Respondent Airlines 23a. Further, § 2.4, by allowing fares to be advertised only if sufficient seats are available to meet demand or if the extent of unavailability is disclosed, may make it impossible to use this marketing process at all. All in all, the obligations imposed by the guidelines would have a significant impact upon the airlines' ability to market their product, and hence a significant impact upon the fares they charge.

In concluding that the NAAG fare advertising guidelines are preempted, we do not, as Texas contends, set out on a road that leads to pre-emption of state laws against gambling and prostitution as applied to airlines. Nor need we address whether state regulation of the nonprice aspects of fare advertising (for example, state laws preventing obscene depictions) would similarly "relat[e] to" rates; the connection would obviously be far more tenuous. To adapt to this case our language in *Shaw*, "[s]ome state actions may affect [airline fares] in too tenuous, remote, or peripheral a manner" to have preemptive effect. 463 U.S., at 100, n. 21, 103 S.Ct., at 2901, n. 21. In this case, as in *Shaw*, "[t]he present litigation plainly does not present a borderline question, and we express no views about where it would be appropriate to draw the line." Ibid. Finally, we note that our decision does not give the airlines carte blanche to lie to and deceive consumers; the DOT retains the power to prohibit advertisements which in its opinion do not further competitive pricing.

* * *

We hold that the fare advertising provisions of the NAAG guidelines are preempted by the ADA, and affirm the judgment of the Court of Appeals insofar as it awarded injunctive and declaratory relief with respect to those provisions. Insofar as that judgment awarded injunctive relief directed at other matters, it is reversed and the injunction vacated.

It is so ordered.

Justice SOUTER took no part in the consideration or decision of this case.
* * *

Justice STEVENS, with whom THE CHIEF JUSTICE and Justice BLACKMUN join, dissenting.

* * *

IV

Even if I were to agree with the Court that state regulation of deceptive advertising could "relat[e] to rates" within the meaning of § 105(a) if it had a "significant impact" upon rates, * * * I would still dissent. The airlines' theoretical arguments have not persuaded me that the NAAG guidelines will have a significant impact upon the price of airline tickets. The airlines' argument (which the Court adopts, * * *) is essentially that (1) airlines must engage in price discrimination in order to compete and operate efficiently; (2) a modest amount of misleading price advertising may facilitate that practice; (3) thus compliance with the NAAG guidelines might increase the cost of price advertising or reduce the sales generated by the advertisements; (4) as the costs increase and revenues decrease, the airlines might purchase less price advertising; and (5) a reduction in price advertising might cause a reduction in price competition, which, in turn, might result in higher airline rates. This argument is not supported by any legislative or judicial findings.

Even on the assumption that the Court's economic reasoning is sound and restrictions on price advertising could affect rates in this manner, the airlines have not sustained their burden of proving that compliance with the NAAG guidelines would have a "significant" effect on their ability to market their product and, therefore, on their rates. Surely Congress could not have intended to pre-empt every state and local law and regulation that similarly increases the airlines' costs of doing business and, consequently, has a similar "significant impact" upon their rates.

For these reasons, I respectfully dissent.

NOTES

1. The question of preemption depends primarily on the extent to which Congress expresses a desire to preclude state law. See State v. Synchronal Corp., 800 F.Supp. 1456 (W.D.Tex. 1992) upholding application of the state consumer protection statutes to "infomercials" on cable television where Congress in regulating cable television adopted a savings provision for "any consumer protection law" and "criminal or civil liability . . . pursuant to the Federal, State, or local law of . . . false or misleading advertising . . . ."

2. The preemptive effect of Federal advertising regulation can become a significant issue in personal injury litigation. In Cipollone v. Liggett Group, Inc., 505 U.S. 504 (1992) the plaintiff sought recovery for personal injuries allegedly caused by cigarette smoking. The claims involved failure to warn, breach of express warranty, and fraudulent misrepresentation. The defendant cigarette manufacturers argued these causes of action were preempted by (1) the 1965 federal statute mandating warnings on cigarette packages which preempted the imposition of any other statement relating to smoking and health, and (2) the 1969 federal statute which prohibited any other "requirement or prohibition based on smoking and health . . . with respect to the advertising or promotion of cigarettes . . . ." A majority of the Court held the 1965 statute did not preempt tort claims for personal injury but merely prohibited state imposition of a different "statement" on cigarette packages. Justice Stevens in an opinion for four Justices held the 1969 statute preempted claims based on failure to warn and fraudulent misrepresentations based on advertising but not express warranty claims. Two other Justices argued the 1969 statute preempted all claims. See also Shaw v. Dow Brands, Inc., 994 F.2d 364 (7th Cir. 1993) holding the preemption clause of the Federal Insecticide, Fungicide and Rodenticide Act which prohibited any state "requirements for labeling or packaging in addition to or different from those required [by the Act]" preempted a personal injury claim based on strict liability and negligence for injuries caused by inhalation of a regulated substance.

3. In Wolens v. American Airlines, Inc., 115 S.Ct. 817 (1995), the plaintiff sued American Airlines seeking money damages for breach of contract and violation of the Illinois Consumer Fraud Act based on American's retroactive change in the criteria for use of its frequent flier miles. The Court found the claim under the Consumer Fraud Act preempted but allowed the breach of contract claim to proceed.

> We do not read the ADA's preemption clause, however, to shelter airlines from suits alleging no violation of state-imposed obligations, but seeking recovery solely for the airline's alleged breach of its own, self-imposed undertakings. As persuasively argued by the United States, terms and conditions airlines offer and passengers accept are privately ordered obligations "and thus do not amount to a State's 'enact[ment] or enforce[ment] [of] any law, rule, regulation, standard, or other provision having the force and effect of law' . . . . Cf. Cipollone v. Liggett Group, Inc., 505 U.S. ----, ----, 112 S.Ct. 2608, 2612, (1992) . . . . A remedy confined to a contract's terms simply holds parties to their agreements--in this instance, to business judgments an airline made public about its rates and services.

Page 73. Add.

TREATIES AND INTELLECTUAL PROPERTY

In December, 1993 the United States ratified the North American Free Trade Agreement ("NAFTA"), which became effective January 1, 1994. NAFTA established a free trade area made up of Canada, Mexico and the United States. Part Six of the agreement, titled Intellectual Property, contains extensive and detailed provisions relating to almost all of the subjects covered in this book. Similar provisions are contained in the revised General Agreement on Tariffs and Trade ("GATT") which has been signed by over one hundred countries, and was implemented by the United States in 1994. Pub. L. No. 103-465 (Dec. 8, 1994).

The new GATT agreement establishes that effective systems of trademark, trade secret, copyright and patent law are a basic international norm for capitalist economies participating in the world trading system. The intellectual property provisions of the GATT were not politically controversial in the implementation debates, not only because they are widely seen as being in the interest of the United States, but because the United States has already committed itself to similar provisions in the NAFTA.

U.S. adherence to these two agreements introduces new norms and sources of law, whose influence alongside the legacy of the common law and the sometimes distinctive U.S. statutory traditions, it is difficult to predict. At various points in this supplement, provisions of NAFTA and GATT relevant to issues in U.S. law are noted.

For background, see J.H. Reichman, *The TRIPS Component of the GATT's Uruguay Round: Competitive Prospects for Intellectual Property Owners in an Integrated World Market*, 4 FORDHAM INTELLECTUAL PROP., MEDIA & ENTERAINMENT L.J. 171 (1993).

CHAPTER II

DECEPTIVE PRACTICES

PAGE 116. Read after *Coca-Cola*

ORTHO PHARMACEUTICAL CORPORATION v. COSPROPHAR, INC.
United States Court of Appeals, Second Circuit, 1994
32 F. 3c 690

[Ortho manufacturers a drug called RETIN-A containing tretinoin, a retinoid of Vitamin A that the FDA classifies as a drug. The drug is obtainable by presciption and is approved only for the treatment of acne. Ortho may not promote the drug for other uses although physicians may lawfully prescribe the drug for "off-label" uses. After a 1988 article in the Journal of the American Medical Association advocating use of RETIN-A for treatment of photodamaged skin, "off-label" uses of RETIN-A increased significantly. Ortho developed a product called RENOVA, a cream identical to RETIN-A, and is seeking FDA approval to market RENOVA for treatment of photodamaged skin. Cosprophar, in 1988, introduced a line of cosmetics using the family name "ANTI-AGE" specifically advertised as beneficial for photodamaged or wrinkled skin. The advertisements claimed the products are associated with "retinol" and indicated that products based on tretinoin are less safe. Cosprophar's products were non-prescription but were marketed exclusively through pharmacies to give them credibility. Ortho brought this § 43(a) claim alleging that Cosprophar's advertisements were false. Cosprophar argued that Ortho had no standing under § 43(a).]

* * This appeal requires us to decide what evidence a plaintiff suing under § 43(a) of the Lanham Act must submit to demonstrate that its interests were or will likely be damaged by another business's allegedly false or misleading advertising. We hold that since Ortho's products are not obviously in competition with Cosprophar's, Ortho was required to submit proof demonstrating that consumers view Cosprophar's cosmetics as a comparable substitute for Ortho's drugs. Because Ortho failed to do so, and because Ortho failed to submit sufficient proof on its state law claims, we affirm the judgment of the district court.

* * *

* * * In order to establish standing to sue under [§ 43 (a)] a plaintiff must demonstrate a "reasonable interest to be protected" against the advertiser's false or misleading claims and a "reasonable basis" for believing that this interest is likely to be damaged by the false or misleading advertising, Coca-Cola Co. v. Tropicana Prods., Inc., 690

F.2d 312, 316 (2d Cir.1982). The "reasonable basis" prong embodies a requirement that the plaintiff show both likely injury and a causal nexus to the false advertising.

Although Judge Tenney ruled that Ortho had not satisfied its burden on either ground, we turn first to his decision that Ortho failed to demonstrate a "reasonable basis" to believe that it is likely to be injured by Cosprophar's advertising since we find this issue to be dispositive. We will assume for the purposes of our discussion that Ortho has a protectable interest in its off- label sales of RETIN-A and in its future sales of RENOVA.

This circuit has adopted a flexible approach toward the showing a Lanham Act plaintiff must make on the injury and causation component of its claim. We have held that, while a plaintiff must show more than a "subjective belief" that it will be damaged, it need not demonstrate that it is in direct competition with the defendant or that it has definitely lost sales because of the defendant's advertisements. However, we have also maintained that "[t]he likelihood of injury and causation will not be presumed, but must be demonstrated in some manner." The type and quantity of proof required to show injury and causation has varied from one case to another depending on the particular circumstances. On the whole, we have tended to require a more substantial showing where the plaintiff's products are not obviously in competition with defendant's products, or the defendant's advertisements do not draw direct comparisons between the two. * * *

Here, the district court found that "Ortho and Cosprophar are not in direct competition given the nature of their products: one is a drug requiring a doctor's prescription, the other is a cosmetic available in a pharmacy." Without disputing this finding, Ortho claims that it will be harmed by Cosprophar's advertising in three ways. First, it asserts that consumers who currently buy Cosprophar's cosmetics consequently will not buy RETIN-A. Second, it claims that consumers who are dissatisfied with Cosprophar's cosmetics will be discouraged from buying Ortho's products in the future. Third, it claims that consumers who like Cosprophar's cosmetics will continue to purchase them and will thus have no occasion to try either RETIN-A or RENOVA. As proof of this injury, Ortho relies solely on (a) Cosprophar's advertisements, and (b) statements made by a Cosprophar employee that its cosmetics were introduced to take advantage of the publicity surrounding transretinoic acid. The able district judge determined that this evidence was insufficient to establish that Ortho would likely be injured by Cosprophar's conduct. We agree.

The missing link in Ortho's proof is evidence that Cosprophar's advertising will have the effect on consumers that Ortho says it will--in other words, that consumers will see Cosprophar's cosmetics as substitutes for Ortho's drugs. In other cases, this link has been supplied by consumer surveys or consumer witnesses. For example, in *Johnson & Johnson,* a case upon which Ortho places much reliance, the plaintiff introduced market surveys indicating that some consumers thought they would not have to use the plaintiff's product (baby oil) if they used defendant's product (a depilatory which claimed to contain baby oil) and testimony from a consumer witness who stated that she switched from using plaintiff's baby oil to using defendant's depilatory because of defendant's advertisement.

The significance of this consumer evidence was highlighted in our subsequent *Coca-Cola* decision, where we observed that:

> Two recent decisions of this Court have examined the type of proof necessary to satisfy [the requirement that injury and causation must be demonstrated, not presumed. Vidal Sassoon, Inc. v. Bristol-Myers Co., 661 F.2d 272 (2d Cir.1981); Johnson & Johnson v. Carter-Wallace, Inc., 631 F.2d 186 (2d Cir.1980)]. ... In both decisions the Court reasoned that sales of the plaintiffs' products would probably be harmed if the competing products' advertising tended to mislead consumers in the manner alleged. Market studies were used as evidence that some consumers were in fact misled by the advertising in issue. Thus, the market studies supplied the causative link between the advertising and the plaintiffs' potential lost sales, and thereby indicated a likelihood of injury. 690 F.2d at 316-17 (footnotes omitted).

* * *

At trial, and again as part of its post-trial submissions, Ortho unsuccessfully attempted to introduce three market research surveys into evidence. Judge Tenney rejected this proffer because Ortho failed to show that the surveys were properly conducted and that they were business records within the meaning of Fed.R.Evid. 803(6). Judge Tenney further noted that even if admissible, the surveys did not establish a causal link between Cosprophar's advertisements and any damage claimed by Ortho because they merely corroborated the undisputed fact that consumers were aware of the alleged benefits of RETIN- A and did not address "alternative skin-care treatments, alternative products, or specifically, defendant's products."

Ortho does not challenge the district court's ruling excluding its surveys. Instead, it argues that it was not required to submit evidence of consumer perceptions because Cosprophar's advertisements draw comparisons to Ortho's drugs and therefore supply the necessary link between the two companies' products. Ortho points to excerpts from Cosprophar's advertisements which discuss the publicity regarding transretinoic acid and indicate that Cosprophar's retinol-based cosmetics are superior for the treatment of photoaged skin because they have no side effects. Specifically, Cosprophar's advertisements state that "interest in retinol in Europe reached very high levels after the discovery at a prominent University of the anti-wrinkle potential of transretinoic acid" with a citation to the 1988 JAMA article; that interest in anti-wrinkle products "is only partially met by two other products available on the market," one of which is "the dermatologist- prescribed anti-acne treatments based on retinoic acid"; and that "[u]sers of transretinoic acid ... complained of reddening and irritation while these effects have never been noted with the use of retinol in anti-wrinkle treatment." Ortho acknowledges that Cosprophar's advertisements refer to transretinoic acid, not specifically to RETIN-A or RENOVA, but argues that it is unnecessary to submit proof that consumers identify the ingredient in their products by its scientific name. Ortho also argues that a witness for Cosprophar admitted that the company tried to link its products to Ortho's drugs because she conceded that the ANTI-AGE RETARD line of cosmetics was introduced in 1988 in part "to tap into ... consumer interest in anti-aging products" and that Cosprophar took "advantage of the publicity, of the transretinoic acid."

For support of its advertisement-linkage analysis, Ortho relies on the decisions in Johnson & Johnson and Upjohn Co. v. Riahom Corp., 641 F.Supp. 1209 (D.Del.1986). However, both cases are distinguishable. In *Johnson & Johnson*, this court relied on the linkage in defendant's advertising between its product and plaintiff's product as proof that plaintiff had a "reasonable interest to be protected against the alleged false advertising." 631 F.2d at 190. In order to find that plaintiff had established a likelihood of injury, the court looked not only at the advertisements but also at plaintiff's market research indicating that the advertisements led consumers to believe that they would no longer need plaintiff's product. Thus, *Johnson & Johnson* does not establish that advertising-linkage alone is sufficient proof of injury.

The *Upjohn* case is no more helpful. In that case, the defendant's advertisements did not simply compare its products to plaintiff's products; they expressly incorporated materials relating to plaintiff and its research in such a manner as to suggest that defendant's product was associated with plaintiff. The court determined that this use of plaintiff's publicity was adequate proof of an injury because of the possibility of false attribution. Such a danger does not exist in this case. Ortho argues, however, that the Upjohn court also found injury based solely on the false claims in defendant's advertising without any reference to consumer research. To the extent this is true, the Upjohn court appeared to supply the missing link by presuming that defendant's false claims would adversely affect plaintiff's sales. See 641 F.Supp. at 1225 (stating that defendant's false claims "definitely tend to induce consumers to purchase their product, thereby depriving [plaintiff] of potential customers and sales"). While there may be room for such a presumption in cases where there is a question of false designation of goods, our circuit has expressly disfavored presumptions of harm in cases where the products are not obviously in competition or where the defendant's advertisements make no direct reference to any competitor's products.

Under the standards of this Circuit, Ortho has failed to present sufficient evidence to establish that it will likely be damaged by Cosprophar's conduct.

NOTES

1. In the District Court, Judge Tenney held that Ortho failed to show a reasonable interest to be protected because it could not, even if it wanted, market its product for photo-damaged skin because of the FDA's regulations. Why isn't it sufficient that physicians were able to, and did, prescribe RETIN-A for photodamaged skin and thus put Ortho in direct competition with Cosprophar?

2. Under what circumstances, if any, can a plaintiff assert standing under § 43(a) without introducing a consumer survey?

PAGE 119. Add after Court of Appeals decision in *ALPO*

ALPO PETFOODS, INC. v. RALSTON PURINA COMPANY
United States Court of Appeals, District of Columbia, 1993
997 F.2d. 949

D. H. GINSBURG, Circuit Judge:

[On remand from the Court of Appeals [ALPO Petfoods Inc. v. Ralston Purina Co., 778 F. Supp. 555 (D.D.C. 1991)], the district court awarded ALPO $12,140,356.50 and Ralston $53,434.86 in damages and awarded Ralston an additional $797,560 in attorneys fees. The court submitted the original trial record to expert witnesses from both parties and based on their testimony concluded that neither party could show lost profits caused by the respective false claims. However, the court awarded ALPO $3,585,610 to reimburse it for advertising and promotional expenses incurred in response to Ralston's false CHD campaign. The court found this award proper even though the responsive advertising did not refer specifically to Ralston or its false claims. The court found the additional advertising necessary for ALPO to retain its market share. The court also found that Ralston's false advertising delayed ALPO's plans to expand its puppy food market nationwide and awarded ALPO $4,507,961 representing the present value of the delayed income stream caused by this delay. The district court then enhanced the award by 50%. This decision was again appealed.

The Court of Appeals first upheld the award for responsive advertising even though the advertising did not refer specifically to Ralston's false claim. The Court observed that such a requirement would give broader circulation to the false claims. The Court recognized that directly responsive advertising might be necessary where there was consumer confusion of product or source. The Court then reviewed the calculation of damages:]

Third, Ralston attacks the district court's way of calculating the cost that ALPO incurred for responsive advertising. The court used ALPO's planned advertising budget for FY '86 as a baseline and assumed that ALPO's expenditures for FYs '86 and '87 would have been the same but for Purina's CHD campaign. The district court then subtracted what ALPO had planned to spend from what it actually spent for the two years, and treated the remainder as the cost of responding to Ralston's CHD campaign.

Ralston claims that for all its apparent precision the district court's approach is at bottom speculative. On the contrary, it seems to us that by using figures that ALPO had prepared in the ordinary course of business, the district court was able to start with an unusually solid foundation upon which to build its calculations.

* * *

Fifth, Ralston claims that the award should not stand because the amount ALPO spent on responsive advertisements was disproportionate to the amount Ralston spent on the CHD claims to which ALPO was responding. Ralston spent $2.2 million advertising its CHD claim in ALPO's marketing area; ALPO was awarded $3.6 million for responsive advertising. In view of the significance of Ralston's claims, however, it does not seem unreasonable for ALPO to have spent $3.6 million in order to rebut $2.2 million worth of false advertising; a consumer who heard the CHD claim would almost certainly conclude that Purina Puppy Chow was by far the superior product. Indeed, because Ralston's false claim was so bold and so specific, in comparison with which ALPO's reply was rather tepid and general, it stands to reason that ALPO's campaign may have been less persuasive dollar for dollar. In any event, ALPO's outspending Ralston by a ratio of little more than 1.5 to 1 is not so clearly disproportionate as to require any disallowance.

Sixth, The district court did not in fact award ALPO the full difference between its planned and its actual advertising expenditures, which came to $5.2 million. The court disallowed as unreasonable $1.6 million that ALPO had spent for a coupon campaign because "ALPO intentionally printed the false preference claim on a large number of its coupons." I.e., some of ALPO's responsive advertising was itself false and in violation of the Lanham Act.

Ralston alleges that the $3.6 million awarded still compensates ALPO for some expenditures it made in order to advertise its false claims. Unfortunately, the district court did not address this claim other than as noted above, and we cannot resolve it on the present record. The district court found, in resolving Ralston's counterclaim, that

ALPO did violate the Lanham Act. Over the relevant time period ALPO spent well in excess of $3.6 million on advertising, but ALPO may not have spent more than $3.6 million on non-false advertising. We cannot merely assume that the non-false advertisements run in FYs '86 and '87 were responsive to the CHD campaign (hence incremental and recoverable) while the false advertisements for which ALPO may not recover were part of the "baseline" expenditure (hence would have aired anyway and not recoverable). We must therefore remand this matter for the district court to determine in the first instance the percentage of ALPO's advertising expenses during the relevant period that were for false or misleading advertisements, and to reduce the $3.6 million award pro rata.

B. Delay of ALPO's Income Stream

Although the district court declined to speculate about the profits that either party lost on sales diverted to the other, the court did award ALPO the profits it lost due to the need, in view of Ralston's CHD campaign, to defer its national expansion. The court calculated ALPO's losses from the profits that ALPO had projected it would earn when it first decided to enter the national puppy food market. Early year losses and later year profits (projected into the indefinite future) were reduced to present value; the court then computed the present value of that same income stream assuming a five year delay in getting it started and awarded ALPO the difference, some $4.5 million.

Ralston argues that the delay in ALPO's receipt of income from a national rollout of ALPO Puppy Food is not a permissible category of damages, and is purely speculative. We disagree on both counts.

When we remanded this case earlier for the district court to recompute the damage award we noted that: [A]ctual damages under section 35(a) can include: profits lost by the plaintiff on sales actually diverted to the false advertiser, profits lost by the plaintiff on sales made at prices reduced as a demonstrated result of the false advertising, the costs of any completed advertising that actually and reasonably responds to the defendant's offending ads, and quantifiable harm to the plaintiff's good will, to the extent that completed corrective advertising has not repaired that harm. ALPO II, 913 F.2d at 969. While we did not specifically itemize a delay in the receipt of a stream of income as a compensable category of damages, the district court correctly understood that our list of such categories was illustrative, not exhaustive. The statute itself suggests as much, for it specifically authorizes the court, if it finds that a recovery based upon profits would be inadequate, "in its discretion [to] enter judgment for such sum as the court should find to be just," and to award the plaintiff what is in effect the time value of its deferred profits is hardly an abuse of discretion.

Nor do we view the award as unduly uncertain. The district court found that ALPO would have expanded nationally but was stymied by Ralston's false advertisements. The court therefore looked at ALPO's projections, prepared in the ordinary course of business and on the basis of which it was prepared to risk its own capital, in order to estimate the profits that ALPO would have reaped from that expansion. ALPO was not certain to succeed, of course, but the question is who is to bear the now-hypothetical risk that it would fail? We answered that question when we remanded this case to the district court: When assessing actual damages, the court may take into account the difficulty of proving an exact amount of damages from false advertising, as well as the maxim that "the wrongdoer shall bear the risk of uncertainty which his own wrong has created." That is what the district court has done--to Ralston's chagrin.

The district court erred, however, in refusing to reduce the award to reflect ALPO's alternative use of the funds it did not have to expend on a national rollout. In order to reflect economic reality, damages awarded in order to compensate for loss of a business opportunity should equal the plaintiff's " 'opportunity cost,' or the return it could have made on an alternative investment" of the funds not spent on the foregone opportunity.

ALPO retained the use of the funds it would have spent on a national rollout; presumably it did not put the money under a mattress but obtained some (albeit a second best) return on that capital. That ALPO may in fact have spent some or all of the money on a responsive advertising campaign, as the district court found, is beside the point. The responsive campaign itself constituted, in effect, an alternative investment, the return on which is the prejudgment interest to which ALPO is entitled.

To award ALPO prejudgment interest without reducing the award made in compensation for the loss of the future income stream would be double counting. The district court should therefore reduce the award for deferral of ALPO's future income stream in order to reflect the return on capital it presumably received from alternative investments, using the prejudgment interest rate as a measure of that return.

* * *

Section 35(a) of the Lanham Act authorizes the court to award up to three times a plaintiff's actual and proven damages so long as the result is compensatory, not punitive. The district court enhanced the award to ALPO by 50% in order to cover its lost profits (i.e., on sales diverted from ALPO to Ralston), compensate ALPO for a permanent distortion in the market for puppy food, and for interest and inflation. Ralston says the enhancement is speculative, punitive, and an indirect attempt to award attorneys' fees to ALPO notwithstanding our earlier reversal of such an award.

The last allegation is as unworthy of counsel as it is unnecessary to Ralston's cause. An enhancement is appropriate to compensate a Lanham Act plaintiff only for such adverse effects as can neither be dismissed as speculative nor precisely calculated. Interest and inflation are not such elusive quanta. Lost profits and market distortion are, however, appropriate bases for the catch-all enhancement contemplated by § 35(a). We thus remand this aspect of the award to the district court to compute the precise amounts to be awarded for interest and the effect of inflation, and to reconsider such enhancement as may be appropriate solely in order to compensate ALPO for its lost profits on sales diverted to Ralston and the continuing distortion of the market owing to Ralston's false advertising.

NOTE

The district court in Zazú Designs v. L'Oréal S.A., 979 F.2d 499 (7th Cir. 1992) had awarded the plaintiff $1,000,000 for the costs of corrective advertising where the defendant, knowing of plaintiff's intended but yet unsuccessful attempt to use the mark Zazú on hair care products, used the mark on its own hair cosmetics. The Seventh Circuit reversed, holding that corrective advertising is a method of repairing a damaged mark and in damage law the costs of repair cannot exceed the value of the asset. "To justify damages to pay for corrective advertising a plaintiff must show that the confusion caused by the defendant's mark injured the plaintiff and that 'repair' of the old trademark, rather than adoption of a new one, is the least expensive way to proceed." Here, the court found that the plaintiff's mark had no value because it had not yet been used extensively in the market."

In *Zazú*, the plaintiff had not yet actually undertaken any corrective advertising. Does the plaintiff face a real problem in asking for damages for planned future corrective advertising if it has not already undertaken to correct the defendant's infringement?

PAGE 122. Substitute for *American Home Products*

JOHNSON & JOHNSON * MERCK CONSUMER PHARMACEUTICALS COMPANY v. SMITHKLINE BEECHAM CORPORATION
United States Court of Appeals, Second Circuit, 1992
960 F.2d 294

WALKER, Circuit Judge.

[The parties are manufacturers of nonprescription antacids. The plaintiff, J & J * Merck, makes MYLANTA which contains aluminum and magnesium hydroxide. The defendant makes TUMS which uses calcium carbonate. Defendant produced two comparative commercials. In the first ("Ingredients") competing products including MYLANTA, ROLAIDS, and MAALOX appear on the screen with their ingredients, i.e., aluminum and magnesium. TUMS then appears with the voice-over stating it is "aluminum free" and that "only TUMS helps wipe out heartburn and gives you calcium you need every day." After complaints to the television networks, defendant withdrew "Ingredients" and began using "Ingredients-Revised". This second commercial listed the ingredients of the competing products but deleted all references to TUMS as "aluminum free". It continued to emphasized that TUMS contained calcium, which was good for users, and the others did not. A shorter version of this commercial compared TUMS only to MYLANTA. Plaintiff brought suit under § 43(a) of the Lanham Act alleging "Ingredients-Revised" was false and misleading in that it falsely represented that (1) TUMS had nutritional benefits, and (2) aluminum and magnesium were unsafe for human consumption. The district court found that plaintiff had failed to show that the assertion of nutritional benefits for TUMS was false. She also found that the commercials did not "communicate the message that aluminum or magnesium are harmful or unsafe." On appeal, plaintiff abandoned its attack on the calcium claim.]

J & J * Merck contends that, even though the content of the challenged commercials is literally true, Ingredients-Revised preys upon a publicly held misperception that the ingestion of aluminum causes Alzheimer's disease. According to J & J * Merck, the commercials accomplish this by repeatedly juxtaposing the absence of aluminum in TUMS with its presence in MYLANTA. In turn, this repetition supposedly links MYLANTA with an allegedly popularly held, yet unsubstantiated concern that aluminum is associated with Alzheimer's. Since the aluminum/Alzheimer's connection has not been scientifically established, J & J * Merck argues that Ingredients-Revised purposefully taps into a preexisting body of public misinformation in order to communicate the false and misleading message that aluminum-based antacids are harmful.

The gravamen of J & J * Merck's claim is that advertisers may be held liable for the knowing exploitation of public misperception. While this argument presents a novel theory of Lanham Act liability--one which we neither reject nor embrace--we note that, in any event, it would be unavailing in this case. Because J & J * Merck has failed to show that it has suffered any injury as a result of the challenged TUMS commercials, it cannot obtain relief under any theory of Lanham Act liability that is premised upon an implied falsehood.

I. *Liability for Implied Falsehoods*

* * *

The law governing false advertising claims under the Lanham Act is well settled in this circuit. In order to recover damages or obtain equitable relief, a plaintiff must show that either: 1) the challenged advertisement is literally false, or 2) while the advertisement is literally true it is nevertheless likely to mislead or confuse consumers.

Where, as here, a plaintiff's theory of recovery is premised upon a claim of implied falsehood, a plaintiff must demonstrate, by extrinsic evidence, that the challenged commercials tend to mislead or confuse consumers. It is not for the judge to determine, based solely upon his or her own intuitive reaction, whether the advertisement is deceptive. Rather, as we have reiterated in the past, "[t]he question in such cases is--what does the person to whom the advertisement is addressed find to be the message?" That is, what does the public perceive the message to be?

The answer to this question is pivotal because, where the advertisement is literally true, it is often the only measure by which a court can determine whether a commercial's net communicative effect is misleading. Thus, the success of a plaintiff's implied falsity claim usually turns on the persuasiveness of a consumer survey. * * *

[I]n attempting to show that the district court's findings on this point were clearly erroneous, J & J * Merck argues that Judge Cedarbaum failed sufficiently to consider factors other than consumer survey evidence, such as: 1) the general "commercial context" or sea of information in which consumers are immersed; 2) the defendant's intent to harness public misperception; 3) the defendant's prior advertising history; and 4) the sophistication of the advertising audience. This argument causes us some discomfort.

Appellant's criticism of the district court's findings misconstrues the proper role of consumer survey evidence in the analysis of implied falsehood claims. Generally, before a court can determine the truth or falsity of an advertisement's message, it must first determine what message was actually conveyed to the viewing audience. Consumer surveys supply such information.

Three of the factors listed by J & J * Merck, i.e., commercial context, defendant's prior advertising history, and sophistication of the advertising audience, only come into play, if at all, during the latter part of the court's analysis. In a particular case, these factors may shed some light on whether the challenged advertisement contributed to the meaning that was ultimately gleaned by the target audience. In other words, in determining whether an advertisement is likely to mislead or confuse, the district court may consider these factors after a plaintiff has established "that a not insubstantial number of consumers," *Coca-Cola Co.* [Coca-Cola Co. v. Tropicana Products Inc., 690 F.2d 312 (2d Cir. 1982)], 690 F.2d at 317, hold the false belief allegedly communicated in the ad.

Absent such a threshold showing, an implied falsehood claim must fail. This follows from the obvious fact that the injuries redressed in false advertising cases are the result of public deception. Thus, where the plaintiff cannot demonstrate that a statistically significant part of the commercial audience holds the false belief allegedly communicated by the challenged advertisement, the plaintiff cannot establish that it suffered any injury as a result of the advertisement's message. Without injury there can be no claim, regardless of commercial context, prior advertising history, or audience sophistication.

[The court acknowledged its rule that shifts the burden to the defendant to show an absence of consumer confusion "where a plaintiff adequately demonstrates that a defendant has intentionally set out to deceive the public," and the defendant's "deliberate conduct" in this regard is of an "egregious nature * * * ." Resource Developers, Inc. v. Statue of Liberty-Ellis Island Foundation, Inc., 926 F.2d 134, 140 (2d Cir.1991). However, the court held there was insufficient evidence of defendant's intent in this case.]

II. *The Bruno and Ridgway Survey*

At trial, J & J * Merck introduced the results of a consumer survey that it had conducted in conjunction with Bruno and Ridgway Research Associates, a marketing firm that conducts between 200-300 such surveys each year. According to Mr. Joseph Ridgway, the firm's president and J & J * Merck's expert witness, the survey was designed to assess what messages are communicated to consumers by Ingredients-Revised. In order to gain this information, 150 male and 150 female adult nonprescription antacid users were shown the commercial and interviewed in eight different shopping malls.

The aspects of the survey that are relevant to this appeal are those which concern the commercial's message regarding aluminum. Questions 8a and 8b asked: "Aside from trying to get you to buy the product, what are the main ideas the commercial communicates to you?" and "What other ideas does the commercial communicate to you?" Out of the 300 people surveyed, 18 people generally responded that "other antacids contain ingredients that are bad/harmful to you," only six of which specifically commented that "aluminum is not good for you." Two other responses were listed in the survey's tally as "aluminum is bad for brain/causes alzheimer's," and lastly, one additional response was recorded under the heading "miscellaneous negative aluminum comments." Questions 14a-c were asked of the 220 respondents who recalled Ingredients-Revised stating that MAALOX and MYLANTA contained aluminum and magnesium. They respectively inquired:

> 14a--What, if anything, does the commercial communicate to you about the aluminum and magnesium in Maalox and Mylanta?
>
> 14b--What else, if anything, does the commercial communicate to you about the aluminum and magnesium in Maalox and Mylanta?
>
> 14c--Based on the commercial you just saw, how do you feel about taking a product for heartburn that contains aluminum and magnesium?

Of the 220 people who responded to these questions, 83 answered with a comment classified as "not good for you/harmful/detrimental to your health." Three answered that aluminum causes Alzheimer's disease and, in addition, 38 responded that these ingredients are not needed by the body.

By adding up all negative comments made about either aluminum or magnesium in response to any of the survey questions, Mr. Ridgway concluded that Ingredients-Revised communicated to 45% of those surveyed that aluminum is either unhealthful or not good for you.

Smithkline and Jordan called Dr. Yoram Wind, a professor of marketing, as their expert witness to testify on nature of the messages communicated by Ingredients-Revised. Dr. Wind strongly criticized the Bruno and Ridgway study primarily on two grounds. First, he testified that, in his opinion, the survey was almost wholly comprised of leading questions. Second, he faulted the study for not taking into account the fact that respondents may have brought with them previously acquired information regarding calcium and aluminum, and for failing to adjust the survey accordingly. In his opinion, the study should have contained a control group--people who were asked similar questions that sought to elicit their beliefs regarding the safety of antacid ingredients, but who were not shown the challenged commercials beforehand.

The evidentiary value of a survey's results rests upon the underlying objectivity of the survey itself. This objectivity, in turn, "depends upon many factors, such as whether [the survey] is properly 'filtered' to screen out those who got no message from the advertisement, whether the questions are directed to the real issues, and whether the questions are leading or suggestive." American Home Products Corp. v. Johnson & Johnson, 654 F.Supp. 568, 590 (S.D.N.Y.1987); see also Weight Watchers Int'l, Inc. v. Stouffer Corp., 744 F.Supp. 1259, 1272 (S.D.N.Y.1990) (listing 7 criteria for survey trustworthiness).

Judge Cedarbaum's analysis of the Bruno and Ridgway survey was wholly in keeping with these principles. After hearing testimony from the parties' experts, and reviewing the results of the study itself, she specifically found that the study "did not show that 'Ingredients-Revised' communicates that the aluminum ... in Mylanta is harmful or unsafe." In her view, the responses to questions 8a and 8b, which elicited only nine anti-aluminum reactions from the 300 people surveyed, were "the most persuasive evidence of the message communicated by 'Ingredients-Revised.' " She attributed this to the fact that questions 8a and 8b were "open-ended," and, therefore, more objective.

On the other hand, Judge Cedarbaum discounted the value of the 86 anti-aluminum/magnesium responses obtained from the 220 people who answered questions 14a-c on the grounds that those questions ranged from being "somewhat leading" to "very leading." Accordingly, she rejected Mr. Ridgway's calculation that Ingredients-Revised communicated an anti-aluminum message to 45% of those surveyed--a figure largely based upon answers received to questions 14a-c.

* * *

The probative value of any given survey is a fact specific question that is uniquely contextual. While certain types of survey questions may be appropriate to discern the message of one advertisement, they may be completely inapposite with regard to another. * * * After reviewing the record in this case, we conclude that Judge Cedarbaum's evaluation of the survey questions is not clearly erroneous.

J & J * Merck also argues that the district court erroneously adopted Dr. Wind's opinion regarding the necessity of a controlled study. It contends that, "[t]he object of Mr. Ridgway's survey, like any advertising communication test, was to measure the impact of an ad upon consumers *in the real world*--not in some artificial or 'control[led]' environment." This contention lacks merit for two reasons. First, Judge Cedarbaum drew no conclusion from the fact that the survey lacked a control; indeed, her legal discussion makes no mention of it whatsoever. Second, we find J & J * Merck's opposition to a control study at odds with its own proposed theory of Lanham Act liability, i.e., that liability exists for exploiting publicly held misperceptions even where the challenged advertising is literally truthful. In these types of cases, the purpose of a control study is to identify the portion of the survey population that held extrinsic beliefs prior to viewing an advertisement--for example, the unsubstantiated belief that aluminum causes Alzheimer's disease. Thus, a control would likely be indispensable proof in an action premised on J & J * Merck's theory. After all, without such evidence it would be hard to imagine how a plaintiff could ever convincingly establish that there was, in the first instance, a public misperception for the defendant to exploit.

Since J & J * Merck did not submit persuasive extrinsic evidence that the challenged TUMS' commercials communicated a false message to consumers by implication or otherwise, we cannot say the district court was clearly erroneous in rejecting it. Accordingly, its false advertising claims must fail.

* * * . Affirmed.

NOTE

Don't consumers have a right to be informed by competitors that a product contains aluminum, whether or not their distaste for aluminum is rational?

PAGE 122. Substitute for *American Home Products*

CASTROL, INC. v. QUAKER STATE CORPORATION
United States Court of Appeals, Second Circuit, 1992
977 F.2d 57

WALKER, Circuit Judge:

* * *

The voiceover to Quaker State's 10W-30 motor oil commercial states:

> Warning: Up to half of all engine wear can happen when you start your car.
> At this critical time, tests prove Quaker State 10W-30 protects better than any other leading 10W-30 motor oil.
>
> In an overwhelming majority of engine tests, Quaker State 10W-30 flowed faster to all vital parts. In all size engines tested, Quaker State protected faster, so it protected better.
>
> Get the best protection against start up wear. Today's Quaker State! It's one tough motor oil.

[Castrol challenged the above advertisement under § 43(a) of the Lanham Act claiming it was literally false. Tests conducted by Rohm and Haas for Quaker State did show that its oil flowed faster to engine parts on start-up but failed to detect any evidence of improved engine wear. Experts introduced by Castrol testified that "the small amount of residual oil left from a prior running of an engine provides more than adequate lubrication at the next start-up."]

* * * Judge Haight credited the testimony of Castrol's three experts. In addition, he found their testimony corroborated by three key facts: (1) the failure of the 1987 Rohm and Haas tests to demonstrate reduced engine wear; (2) the Rohm and Haas technician's 1987 hypothesis that the presence of residual oil might be the reason for the failure to show better engine wear protection that is statistically significant; and (3) the virtual disappearance of catastrophic engine failure following the imposition of the J300 standards [industry standard to assure oil can flow at cold temperatures]. Judge Haight accordingly "accept[ed]" the residual oil theory put forth by these experts. The court explained that an engine is like "a fort besieged by an encircling and encroaching enemy." The enemy is engine wear; the fort's supplies are residual oil; and a relief column on its way to reinforce the fort is the new oil. "If that relief column does not reach the bearing surfaces before the residual oil is burned away, the engine will suffer not only wear but catastrophic failure.... [T]he Quaker State commercial is false because the evidence shows that during the time differentials demonstrated by the [Rohm and Haas] oiling tests, residual oil holds the fort."

Judge Haight concluded that because residual oil "holds the fort," Rohm and Haas' faster oiling time findings did not necessarily prove better protection. He consequently held that "Castrol has established the likelihood of proving at trial the falsity of Quaker State's claim that tests prove its oil protects better against start-up engine wear." On March 20, 1992, the district court entered an Order granting preliminary injunctive relief. Quaker State appeals.

* * *

To succeed under § 43(a), a plaintiff must demonstrate that "an advertisement is either literally false or that the advertisement, though literally true, is likely to mislead and confuse consumers.... Where the advertising claim is shown to be literally false, the court may enjoin the use of the claim 'without reference to the advertisement's impact on the buying public.' " McNeil- P.C.C., Inc. v. Bristol-Myers Squibb Co., 938 F.2d 1544, 1549 (2d Cir.1991) (quoting *Coca-Cola*, 690 F.2d at 317) (citations omitted). Here, Castrol contends that the challenged advertisement is literally false. It bears the burden of proving this to a "likelihood of success" standard.

As we have on two occasions explained, plaintiff bears a different burden in proving literally false the advertised claim that tests prove defendant's product superior, than it does in proving the falsity of a superiority claim which makes no mention of tests. In Procter & Gamble Co. v. Chesebrough- Pond's, Inc., 747 F.2d 114 (2d Cir.1984), for example, Chesebrough alleged the literal falsity of Procter's advertised claim that "clinical tests" proved its product superior. Id. at 116. Procter, in return, challenged as literally false a Chesebrough commercial which, making no mention of tests, asserted that its lotion was equal in effectiveness to any leading brand. Id. We explained that in order to prove literally false Procter's claim of "test- proven superiority," Chesebrough bore the burden of "showing that the tests referred to by P & G were not sufficiently reliable to permit one to conclude with reasonable certainty that they established the proposition for which they were cited." Id. at 119. We held that Procter could prove false Chesebrough's advertisement, however, "only upon adducing evidence" that affirmatively showed Chesebrough's claim of parity to be false. Id.

We drew this same distinction in McNeil-P.C.C., Inc. v. Bristol-Myers Squibb Co., 938 F.2d 1544 (2d Cir.1991). Bristol-Myers initially advertised to trade professionals that "clinical studies" had shown its analgesic provided better relief than McNeil's. Id. at 1546. Bristol-Myers' later televised commercial made the product superiority claim but "did not refer to clinical studies." Id. We held that, with respect to the initial trade advertising, "McNeil could ... meet its burden of proof by demonstrating that these studies did not establish that AF Excedrin provided superior pain relief." Id. at 1549. With respect to the televised commercial, however, McNeil bore the burden of generating "scientific proof that the challenged advertisement was false." Id.

A plaintiff's burden in proving literal falsity thus varies depending on the nature of the challenged advertisement. Where the defendant's advertisement claims that its product is superior, plaintiff must affirmatively prove defendant's product equal or inferior. Where, as in the current case, defendant's ad explicitly or implicitly represents that tests or studies prove its product superior, plaintiff satisfies its burden by showing that the tests did not establish the proposition for which they were cited. We have held that a plaintiff can meet this burden by demonstrating that the tests were not sufficiently reliable to permit a conclusion that the product is superior. The *Procter* "sufficiently reliable" standard of course assumes that the tests in question, if reliable, would prove the proposition for which they are cited. If the plaintiff can show that the tests, even if reliable, do not establish the proposition asserted by the defendant, the plaintiff has obviously met its burden. In such a case, tests which may or may not be "sufficiently reliable," are simply irrelevant.

The district court held that Castrol had met this latter burden, stating that "Castrol has established the likelihood of proving at trial the falsity of Quaker State's claim that tests prove its oil protects better...." * * *

[The Court upheld the district judge's acceptance of the "residual oil" theory to explain why the commercial's claim for improved engine wear resulting from faster oil flows was false.]

III. *Is the district court's injunction overly broad?*

In a March 20, 1992 memorandum opinion accompanying its simultaneously-issued Order of Preliminary Injunction, the district court explained its intent "to enjoin preliminarily Quaker State from claiming 'that tests prove its oil protects better against start-up engine wear.' " The injunction, however, goes beyond this limited intent. * * *

[Paragraph 2 of the injunction] enjoins Quaker State from distributing *any* advertisement claiming that its oil provides superior protection against engine wear at start-up, whether or not the ad claims test-proven superiority. As explained above, Castrol bears a different burden of proof with respect to this broader injunction than it does in seeking to enjoin only commercials which make the test-proven superiority claim.

The district court expressly found that Castrol had met its burden with respect to any test-proven superiority advertisement. It stated that "Castrol has established the likelihood of proving at trial the falsity of Quaker State's claim that tests prove its oil protects better...." Its injunction would be too broad, however, absent the additional finding that Castrol had met its burden with respect to superiority advertisements that omit the "tests prove" language. As we have noted above, Castrol meets this burden by adducing proof that Quaker State's oil is not, in fact, superior.

Judge Haight made this additional finding. Castrol submitted the report from the 1987 Rohm and Haas tests as proof that Quaker State's oil did not protect better. This submission was proper under our holding that "[plaintiff can] rel[y] on and analy[se] data generated by [defendant] as scientific proof that the challenged advertisement was false." *McNeil-P.C.C.*, 938 F.2d at 1549. The district court, referring to this document, stated that "the record makes it crystal clear that to the extent tests were performed to demonstrate better wear protection (as opposed to faster flowing), *the tests contradict, rather than support* the claim. I refer to the 1987 Rohm and Haas tests...." (emphasis added). The court went on to find that "Quaker State presents no convincing argument to counter the unequivocal conclusion of Roland [author of the 1987 report], a Rohm and Haas scientist, that the 1987 tests failed to demonstrate a superiority in protection against engine wear...." These statements amount to a finding that Castrol has met the additional burden. The injunction is not overly broad.

Quaker State also asks us to limit the injunction to advertisements based on the 1987 and 1991 Rohm and Haas tests. It contends that it should not be barred from advertising a superiority claim if later tests should support it.

Any time a court issues a preliminary injunction there is some chance that, after the issuance of the order but prior to a full adjudication on the merits, changes in the operative facts will undercut the court's rationale. We will not, however, require the district court to draft a technical and narrow injunction to address the possibility of additional tests which are, at this time, purely hypothetical. If tests supporting its claim do come to light, Quaker State may move to modify or dissolve the injunction.

NOTE

In BASF Corp. v. Old World Trading Co., Inc., 41 F.3d 1081 (7th Cir. 1994), Old World advertised that its antifreeze met all auto manufacturer's specifications. BASF challenged the claim under § 43(a) primarily by proving that Old World did not have adequate tests of its antifreeze to establish the claim. Old World argued that under *Castrol*, BASF had the burden of proving that in fact the antifreeze did not meet the specifications. BASF argued that a claim that a product "meets specifications" implies that it has been subjected to tests. If experts testify that a "meets specifications" claim is not truthful unless required tests have been passed, would that be sufficient proof of falsity or would BASF need a survey to show that consumers believed that a "meets specifications" claim means that tests have been passed? While adopting the *Castrol* logic, the Seventh Circuit held:

> The meaning of a given advertisement is a question of fact and the district court rejected Old World's interpretation. * * * Old World has not shown that this finding was clearly erroneous. * * * The district court found that meeting specifications means that all requisite tests were performed and passed. Since Old World did not perform the tests, its claim was literally false, and the district court did not err in finding Old World liable under the Lanham Act or state law.

In *BASF* what happened to the idea that it was the meaning of an advertisement to consumers that was relevant to the § 43(a) claim?

PAGE 137, Insert after *U.S. Healthcare.*

NOTE

The 1988 amendments to § 43(a) (see Casebook at page 109) limit the applicability of the false advertising provisions to statements made "in commercial advertising or promotion". In approving this language, Congress was apparently thinking about the applicability of First Amendment limitations and the greater scope of regulation permissible for "commercial" speech. Two recent cases interpreting the language highlight the problems.

1. Gordon & Breach Science Publishers v. American Institute of Physics, 859 F. Supp. 152 (S.D.N.Y. 1994). G & B is a commercial publisher of a scientific academic journal; AIP and APS are non-profit publishers of competing journals. Henry Barschall, a physics professor at the University of Wisconsin and an APS officer, conducted a survey to show that non-profit publisher's journals are more cost effective. The survey showed G & B to be among the least cost effective publishers and AIP to be among the best. Both AIP and APS published articles by Barschall containing the results of his survey along with his commentary suggesting that librarians should purchase more nonprofit publications. Reprints of the Barschall article were distributed at a librarians' conference. G & B, claiming the surveys misrepresented the facts, brought suit under § 43(a) of the Lanham Act.

After reviewing the legislative history and case law, the court concluded:

> The principles from the cases and legislative history may be summed up as follows: In order for representations to constitute "commercial advertising or promotion" under Section 43(a)(1)(B), they must be: (1) commercial speech; (2) by a defendant who is in commercial competition with plaintiff; (3) for the purpose of influencing consumers to buy defendant's goods or services. While the representations need not be made in a "classic advertising campaign," but may consist instead of more informal types of "promotion," the representations (4) must be disseminated sufficiently to the relevant purchasing public to constitute "advertising" or "promotion" within that industry.

The court held that publication of the articles themselves was not "commercial advertising or promotion" and "[t]o hold otherwise would be to squelch the expression of facts and opinions which might not otherwise find ready expression through commercial media." However, the court held that secondary uses of the surveys such as distribution of reprints of the articles at librarians' conferences and other disseminations of the survey results to librarians were actionable. See the court's subsequent opinion at 905 F. Supp. 169, 180 (1995): "Defendants' use of the surveys directly to target relevant consumers is precisely the type of promotional activity that the Lanham Act seeks to regulate. . . . This element of consumer-orientation -- of directly targeting relevant purchasers -- pervades virtually all of defendant's secondary uses. We find it dispositive."

See also, Semco, Inc. v. Amcast, Inc., 52 F.3d 108 (6th Cir. 1995). The editor of a trade journal requested the president of a company to submit for publication an article describing a manufacturing process. He complied but included self-serving statements about his company's own products. The court held the article was "commercial advertising or promotion" and could be constitutionally sanctioned if false.

2. Groden v. Random House, Inc., 61 F.3d 1045 (2d Cir. 1995). Gerald Posner wrote a book entitled "Case Closed" which refuted numerous conspiracy theories surrounding the Kennedy assassination, including that contained in Robert Groden's "High Treason". Random House placed an advertisement for Posner's book containing the names and photographs of the conspiracy theorists, including Groden, with a headline reading: "GUILTY OF MISLEADING THE AMERICAN PUBLIC". The ad concluded with a brief summary of Posner's thesis: "ONE MAN. ONE GUN. ONE INESCAPABLE CONCLUSION." Groden filed a Lanham Act § 43(a) claim arguing the "guilty of misleading" and the "one man-one gun" statements were false. The Second Circuit rejected the claims:

> In order to be actionable under the Lanham Act, a challenged advertisement must be literally false or, though literally true, likely to mislead or confuse consumers. However, statements of opinion are generally not the basis for Lanham Act liability. See Restatement (Third) of Unfair Competition § 3 cmt. d (1993). . . .
> Moreover, the statements "GUILTY OF MISLEADING THE AMERICAN PUBLIC" and "ONE MAN. ONE GUN. ONE INESCAPABLE CONCLUSION." are not literally false with respect to the work being advertised, because they accurately describe the thesis of *Case Closed*. The Lanham Act does not prohibit false statements generally. It prohibits only false or misleading descriptions or false or misleading representations of fact made about one's own or another's goods or services. No matter what the true facts might be concerning the Kennedy assassination, the ad's statements said nothing false about Posner's book.

> Although the District Court did not reach the argument, we also note . . . that any attempt to apply the Lanham Act to appellees' ad would raise substantial free speech issues. . . . In the context of expressive works, we have been careful not to permit overextension of the Lanham Act to intrude on First Amendment values. . . . With a subject of such manifest public interest as the Kennedy assassination,

ample leeway must be accorded to statements that advertise books by expressing opinions, no matter how extravagantly worded, about the merits of opposing viewpoints. Id. at 1552-53.

Page 155. Add after *Dairy Stores*.

TURF LAWNMOWER REPAIR, INC. v. BERGEN RECORD CORP., 139 N.J. 392, 655 A.2d 417 (Sup.Ct. N. J. 1995), cert. denied 116 S.Ct. 752 (1996). The New Jersey Supreme Court returned to the question of establishing the appropriate standard for defamation of a business. In *Turf* the defendant newspaper ran an investigative series which concluded that the plaintiff, a lawnmower repair shop, engaged in a systematic fraud on the consuming public by performing unnecessary or shoddy repairs on lawn mowers. The court posed the issue to be: "whether actual malice is the appropriate standard for all businesses, or whether negligence is the more appropriate standard of proof in defamation actions that involve businesses whose activities do not concern matters of public health or safety, do not constitute consumer fraud, or whose businesses are not subject to substantial government regulations." Adopting the latter view, the court reasoned:

> Like federal law and the vast majority of state law, the defamation law of our state holds the media responsible for libelous or defamatory statements about private citizens. Statements made by the media about public figures are treated differently from those of private citizens. Private persons are defined by their failure to thrust themselves voluntarily into the public limelight and by their inability to respond to criticism of them in the media. We find most ordinary businesses and their owners are like private persons, and therefore, generally, the defamation rules we apply to private persons are equally applicable to them.

> Many businesses are sole proprietorships or small individually-owned stores, like a local "mom and pop" stationery store, shoemaker, tailor, cleaner, or barber. Although those stores are important in the daily life of their communities, their owners are not "public figures." Nor do their activities involve "matters of public concern" that the United States Supreme Court and the vast majority of federal and state courts have made subject to the heightened actual-malice standard of proof. Neither the public nor the owners of those ordinary businesses see the owners in the vortex of a public controversy by selling their product or service to the public. Nor does our opinion change because those businesses do limited advertising. Most businesses do advertise if only in a local shopping flyer, to attract customers and to succeed. Such advertising is insufficient to thrust the business or its owner into the public spotlight.

> Moreover, most of those businesses and their owners have neither the financial resources nor "access to the channels of effective communication ... to counteract false statements" to protect their business and their livelihood from a defamatory newspaper report. They are neither traditional 'public figures' nor do they engage in activities that constitute traditional matters of public concern. Therefore, in respect of such prosaic and innocuous everyday businesses, we conclude that the negligence standard best balances the interests of the public in preserving an uninhibited, robust, and free press and the interests of a private individual and a business in preserving their reputation and good name.
>
> The public does, however, have a legitimate interest in any business charged with criminal fraud, a substantial regulatory violation, or consumer fraud that raises a matter of legitimate public concern. When the media addresses those issues of legitimate and compelling public concern, the actual-malice standard of proof will apply, regardless of the type of business involved. In so ruling, we seek a balance between a private person's right of privacy and the public's right to know of various dangers in our society.

The court ultimately found that the Bergen Record's article raised sufficient evidence of consumer fraud as to require plaintiff to prove actual malice, a burden unmet in this case.

Judge Pollock concurred:

> * * * My concern is that after today, notwithstanding the majority's protests to the contrary, reporting on matters in the public interest will be less "uninhibited, robust, and wide open."
>
> Furthermore, I would temper the majority's concern for the vulnerability of repair people, with some concern for the vulnerability of consumers. For me, the analogy of repair people to the "local 'mom and pop' stationery store, shoemaker, tailor, cleaner, or barber" does not work. Anyone who needs a repair person, unlike someone buying a newspaper or leaving a suit at the dry cleaners, is generally vulnerable. The motorist whose car breaks down on the highway is vulnerable to the demands of the tow truck operator and the service station. The individual with a broken washing machine does not enjoy equal bargaining power with the appliance repair person. And the homeowner with a broken lawn mower is open to exploitation.
>
> Unlike the majority, I would characterize as in the public interest articles about businesses that exploit vulnerable consumers.

Plaintiff had also filed a complaint against a competing lawnmower repair shop claiming it had cooperated with the Bergen Record in an attempt to destroy plaintiff's business. Should actual malice apply to this claim?

Can there be disparagement of services as distinct from defamation? Should the distinction Judge Pollock draws between goods and services influence the law of defamation or disparagement?

Page 169 Add to Note 1

The issue of consumer standing under § 43(a) was reviewed in an exhaustive opinion by Judge Pollak in Serbin v. Ziebart International Corp., 11 F.3d 1163 (3rd Cir. 1993). *Serbin* consolidated two classic consumer law suits: purchasers of a defendant's rust protection policy for automobiles claimed that the advertisements they relied upon were false and consumers of gasoline alleged advertising claims that defendant's gasoline provided more power and quicker acceleration were false. Acknowledging that the plain meaning of the statute would lead to incorporating consumer standing, the court concluded:

> The question of policy that underlies these appeals is not whether false advertising is a bad thing. It is, and consumers are victimized by it. The question of policy is what institution, or set of institutions, should be charged with identifying false advertising, ameliorating its malign consequences, and, in the long run, shrinking its dominion. State courts have substantial authority in this field by virtue of judge-made misrepresentation law, and some state legislatures have, through such legislation as the Uniform Deceptive Trade Practices Act, undertaken to widen that authority. Congress conferred a measure of public enforcement authority on the Federal Trade Commission and, through section 43(a) of the Lanham Act, has vested in the federal courts jurisdiction to entertain certain categories of private law suits predicated on claims of false advertising. Given this commitment of institutional resources to the cause of consumers injured by false advertising, if Congress had intended to make the additional commitment involved in recognizing a federal tort of misrepresentation and in bestowing access to federal fora without regard to the amount in issue, we are confident that the legislative history of the Lanham Act would have borne clear witness to that commitment. Because we find no clear indication of such an unusual commitment and because we are satisfied that section 43(a) had an important, though narrower and quite distinct purpose, we join the Second Circuit in holding that Congress, when authorizing federal courts to deal with claims of false advertising, did not contemplate that federal courts should entertain claims brought by consumers.

Although most courts agree that consumers do not have standing under the Lanham Act, there is less certainty as to what constitutes a commercial interest sufficient to invoke § 43(a). In Waits v. Frito-Lay, Inc., 978 F.2d 1093 (9th Cir. 1992) (singer permitted standing to sue under § 43(a) for unauthorized use of an imitation of the singer's voice in a radio commercial) the court tried to rationalize Smith v. Montoro and Halicki v. United Arts Communications (both cited in the Casebook, note 1). *Smith* permitted an actor to use § 43(a) to challenge failure of a film distributor to give the actor proper credit while *Halicki* denied standing to a movie producer who claimed theaters were attaching an improper rating to his movies.

> We have recognized that simple claims of false representations in advertising are actionable under section 43(a) when brought by competitors of the wrongdoer, even though they do not involve misuse of a trademark. The plaintiff's claim in *Halicki* was exclusively such a "false advertising" claim, for it sought redress for a simple misrepresentation as to a product's quality, the content of a movie. We were at pains to point out that the plaintiff's injury was not related to the Lanham Act's purpose of preventing the "deceptive and misleading use of marks," declaring that the statute's purposes with regard to the use of trademarks were irrelevant to his claim. Rather, where the misrepresentation simply concerns a product's qualities, it is actionable under section 43(a) only insofar the Lanham Act's other purpose of preventing "unfair competition" is served. * * *
>
> The plaintiff's claim in *Smith*, on the other hand, was a type of false association claim stemming from the misuse of a mark, for it alleged the wrongful removal of the plaintiff's name and the wrongful substitution of another's name. *Smith* teaches that where such a claim is presented, the plaintiff need not be a competitor, for the Lanham Act also grants a cause of action to certain noncompetitors who have been injured commercially by the "deceptive and misleading use of marks." Those with standing to bring such a claim include parties with a commercial interest in the product wrongfully identified with another's mark, as in *Smith*, or with a commercial interest in the misused mark.

PAGE 193. Add after *Jay's Foods*

CHAMPION PARTS, INC. v. OPPENHEIMER & CO.
United States Court of Appeals, Seventh Circuit, 1989
878 F.2d 1003

FLAUM, Circuit Judge.

This case involves an attempt by Champion Parts, Inc. ("Champion") to recover from the defendants the money it expended in a successful attempt to obtain equitable relief against a group of investors. The basis of Champion's action against the investors was that the investors failed to file proper disclosures under 15 U.S.C. § 78m(d) (1988) ("§ 13(d)") after they had accumulated greater than 5 percent of Champion's outstanding stock. The district court in the instant action held that Champion has no common law right to the recovery of its litigation expenses and therefore dismissed the action pursuant to Federal Rule of Civil Procedure 12(b)(6). We affirm.

[Champion first unsuccessfully asserted various common law tort causes of action as grounds for recovering its litigation expenses.]

Finally, Champion claims that it is entitled to damages because the actions of Oppenheimer violated both the Illinois Consumer Fraud and Business Practices Act and the New York Consumer Protection from Deceptive Acts and Practices Act. The unfair and deceptive practices of which Champion complains include, among other unstated actions, the stock parking and parallel buying employed by Russ and O'Neill in gathering Champion stock. Although its allegations are extremely vague, Champion apparently claims that it has standing to bring an action because it suffered some form of competitive injury as a result of Oppenheimer's activities.

The Illinois Consumer Fraud and Deceptive Business Practices Act (the "Illinois Act") is designed to protect consumers, borrowers and businessmen from "deceptive acts or practices in the conduct of any trade or commerce." Ill.Rev.Stat. ch. 121 1/2 (1973). The act has been interpreted to permit business competitors to sue to redress competitive injuries they suffer as a result of deceptive practices by other businesses. Newman-Green, Inc. v. Alfonzo-Larrain, 590 F.Supp. 1083, 1087 (N.D.Ill.1984). Assuming that the plaintiff and defendant businesses do in fact compete, the plaintiff competitor, to maintain such an action under the Illinois Act, must show that the practices of the defendant are of the type which affect consumers generally. The business competitors may also have to show that the public was injured by the deceptive practices, but this appears to be an open question. Although we believe that most of the cases which hold that public injury is not required are distinguishable, since they do not involve business plaintiffs alleging a competitive injury, we need not decide the issue to dispose of this case.

Oppenheimer's deceptive practices, "parking" and "side-by-side buying," are practices which affect consumers generally. The practices affect the market by withholding information about a possible change in control of a company. In fact, the whole idea behind the practices Oppenheimer allegedly engaged in is to deceive the market.

Still, Champion could not have suffered a competitive injury as a result of the deceptive practices because it was not a competitor of Oppenheimer with regard to the market that was affected by Oppenheimer's deceptive practices, i.e. the stock market. It would make no sense to permit a non-competitor to sue for damages under a theory of competitive injury and we do not believe Illinois has done so. Thus, Champion cannot maintain an action under the Illinois Act.

Champion also claims that Oppenheimer's actions violated New York's Consumer Protection from Deceptive Acts and Practices Act (the "New York Act"). The New York Act prohibits "[d]eceptive acts or practices in the conduct of any business, trade or commerce or in the furnishing of any service." N.Y. GEN.BUS. § 349 (McKinney 1984). Unlike the Illinois Act, no New York court, nor any federal court sitting in diversity, has interpreted this section of the New York act to permit business competitors to sue based on a claim of competitive injury. Indeed, the courts have limited standing to sue under the New York Act to "consumers," whether they be businesses or individuals. Champion does not bring this action as a corporate consumer and therefore cannot state a claim under the New York Act.

NOTE

Could other investors have sued Oppenheimer under the Illinois statute? Is this a possible method of recovering attorneys fees and other litigation expenses in pursuing federal remedies?

PAGE 216. Read in association with Note 4

KRAFT, INC. v. FEDERAL TRADE COMMISSION
United States Court of Appeals, Seventh Circuit, 1992
970 F.2d 311, cert. denied 113 S.Ct. 1254 (1993)

FLAUM, Circuit Judge.

Kraft, Inc. ("Kraft") asks us to review an order of the Federal Trade Commission ("FTC" or "Commission") finding that it violated §§ 5 and 12 of the Federal Trade Commission Act ("Act"), 15 U.S.C. §§ 45, 52. The FTC determined that Kraft, in an advertising campaign, had misrepresented information regarding the amount of calcium contained in Kraft Singles American Pasteurized Process Cheese

Food ("Singles") relative to the calcium content in five ounces of milk and in imitation cheese slices.

* The FTC ordered Kraft to cease and desist from making these misrepresentations and Kraft filed this petition for review. We enforce the Commission's order.

* * *

III.

Kraft makes numerous arguments on appeal, but its principal claim is that the FTC erred as a matter of law in not requiring extrinsic evidence of consumer deception. Without such evidence, Kraft claims (1) that the FTC had no objective basis for determining if its ads actually contained the implied claims alleged, and (2) that the FTC's order chills constitutionally protected commercial speech. Alternatively, Kraft contends that substantial evidence does not support the FTC's finding that the Class Picture ads contain the milk equivalency claim. Finally, Kraft maintains that even if it did make the alleged milk equivalency and imitation superiority claims, substantial evidence does not support the FTC's finding that these claims were material to consumers. We address each contention in turn.

A.

1.

In determining what claims are conveyed by a challenged advertisement, the Commission relies on two sources of information: its own viewing of the ad and extrinsic evidence. Its practice is to view the ad first and, if it is unable on its own to determine with confidence what claims are conveyed in a challenged ad, to turn to extrinsic evidence. The most convincing extrinsic evidence is a survey "of what consumers thought upon reading the advertisement in question," Thompson Medical, 104 F.T.C. at 788-89, but the Commission also relies on other forms of extrinsic evidence including consumer testimony, expert opinion, and copy tests of ads. FTC Policy Statement, 103 F.T.C. at 176 n. 8.

---

* The "milk equivalency" claim was a claim that Kraft singles had the same calcium as five ounces of milk when in fact the processing of the cheese destroyed some of the calcium. The administrative law judge found the claim in the advertisement's linking of calcium and milk and the express statement that a Kraft Single contained five ounces of milk. The "imitation superiority" claim was a claim that Kraft Singles had more calcium than imitation cheese slices. The administrative law judge found this claim implied from the fact that the advertisements stressed the importance of calcium and also indicated that imitation slices contained no milk. Footnote by editors.

Kraft has no quarrel with this approach when it comes to determining whether an ad conveys *express* claims, but contends that the FTC should be required, as a matter of law, to rely on extrinsic evidence rather than its own subjective analysis in all cases involving allegedly *implied* claims.[4] The basis for this argument is that implied claims, by definition, are not self-evident from the face of an ad. This, combined with the fact that consumer perceptions are shaped by a host of external variables--including their social and educational backgrounds, the environment in which they view the ad, and prior experiences with the product advertised, see Richard Craswell, Interpreting Deceptive Advertising, 65 B.U.L. Rev. 658, 672-74, 717 (1985); Richard Pollay, Deceptive Advertising and Consumer Behavior: A Case for Legislative and Judicial Reform, 17 U.Kan.L.Rev. 625, 629-31 (1969)--makes review of implied claims by a five-member commission inherently unreliable. The Commissioners, Kraft argues, are simply incapable of determining what implicit messages consumers are likely to perceive in an ad. Making matters worse, Kraft asserts that the Commissioners are predisposed to find implied claims because the claims have been identified in the complaint, rendering it virtually impossible for them to reflect the perceptions of unbiased consumers. * * *

Kraft buttresses its argument by pointing to the use of extrinsic evidence in an analogous context: cases brought under § 43(a) of the Lanham Act. 15 U.S.C. § 1125(a). Courts hearing deceptive advertising claims under that Act, which provides a private right of action for deceptive advertising, generally require extrinsic proof that an advertisement conveys an implied claim. Were this a Lanham Act case, a reviewing court in all likelihood would have relied on extrinsic evidence of consumer perceptions. While this disparity is sometimes justified on grounds of advertising "expertise"--the FTC presumably possesses more of it than courts--Kraft maintains this justification is an illusory one in that the FTC has no special expertise in discerning consumer perceptions. Indeed, proof of the FTC's inexpertise abounds: false advertising cases make up a small part of the Commission's workload, see Glen E. Weston, Deceptive Advertising and the Federal Trade Commission: Decline of Caveat Emptor, 24 Fed.B.J. 548, 571 (1964), most commissioners have little prior experience in advertising, see Paul H. LaRue, FTC Expertise: A Legend Examined, 16 Antitrust Bull. 1 (1971), and the average tenure of commissioners is very brief. See Richard A. Posner, The Federal Trade Commission, 37 U.Chi.L.Rev. 47, 86 (1969) (average tenure of four years). That evidence aside, no amount of expertise in Kraft's view can replace the myriad of external variables affecting consumer perceptions. Here, the

---

[4] Express claims directly represent the fact at issue while implied claims do so in an oblique or indirect way. *Thompson Medical,* 104 F.T.C. at 788. To illustrate, consider the following. Suppose a certain automobile gets poor gas mileage, say, 10 miles per gallon. One advertisement boasts that it gets 30 miles per gallon while another identifies the car as the "Miser," depicts it rolling through the countryside past one gas station after another, and proclaims that the car is inexpensive to operate. Both ads make deceptive claims: the first does so expressly, the second does so impliedly.

Commission found implied claims based solely on its own intuitive reading of the ads (although it did reinforce that conclusion by examining the proffered extrinsic evidence). Had the Commission fully and properly relied on available extrinsic evidence, Kraft argues it would have conclusively found that consumers do not perceive the milk equivalency and imitation superiority claims in the ads.

While Kraft's arguments may have some force as a matter of policy, they are unavailing as a matter of law. Courts, including the Supreme Court, have uniformly rejected imposing such a requirement on the FTC, see *Colgate-Palmolive*, 380 U.S. at 391-92, 85 S.Ct. at 1046 (FTC not required to conduct consumer surveys before determining that a commercial has a tendency to mislead) and we decline to do so as well. We hold that the Commission may rely on its own reasoned analysis to determine what claims, including implied ones, are conveyed in a challenged advertisement, so long as those claims are reasonably clear from the face of the advertisement.

Kraft's case for a *per se* rule has two flaws. First, it rests on the faulty premise that implied claims are inescapably subjective and unpredictable. In fact, implied claims fall on a continuum, ranging from the obvious to the barely discernible. The Commission does not have license to go on a fishing expedition to pin liability on advertisers for barely imaginable claims falling at the end of this spectrum. However, when confronted with claims that are implied, yet conspicuous, extrinsic evidence is unnecessary because common sense and administrative experience provide the Commission with adequate tools to makes its findings. The implied claims Kraft made are reasonably clear from the face of the advertisements, and hence the Commission was not required to utilize consumer surveys in reaching its decision.

Second, Kraft's reliance on Lanham Act decisions is misplaced. For one, not all courts applying the Lanham Act rely on extrinsic evidence when confronted with implied claims but more importantly, when they do, it is because they are ill equipped--unlike the Commission--to detect deceptive advertising. And the Commission's expertise in deceptive advertising cases, Kraft's protestations notwithstanding, undoubtedly exceeds that of courts as a general matter. That false advertising cases constitute a small percentage of the FTC's overall workload does not negate the fact that significant resources are devoted to such cases in absolute terms, nor does it account for the institutional expertise the FTC gains through investigations, rule-makings, and consent orders. The Commissioners' personal experiences quite obviously affect their perceptions, but it does not follow that they are incapable of predicting whether a particular claim is likely to be perceived by a reasonable number of consumers.

2.

The crux of Kraft's first amendment argument is that the FTC's current subjective approach chills some truthful commercial speech. Kraft acknowledges the novelty of its argument, but asserts that the issue warrants consideration in light of evolving commercial speech doctrine. * * *

Kraft contends that by relying on its own subjective judgment that an ad, while literally true, implies a false message, the FTC chills nonmisleading, protected speech because advertisers are unable to predict whether the FTC will find a particular ad misleading. Advertisers can run sophisticated pre-dissemination consumer surveys and find no implied claims present, only to have the Commission determine in its own subjective view that consumers would perceive an implied claim. Indeed, Kraft maintains that is precisely what happened here. Even more troubling, Kraft maintains that the ads most vulnerable to this chilling effect are factual, comparative ads, like the Five Ounces of Milk campaign, of greatest benefit to consumers. The net result of the Commission's subjective approach will be an influx of soft "feel good" ads designed to avoid unpredictable FTC decisions. See Richard M. Schmidt, Jr. & Robert C. Burns, Proof or Consequences: False Advertising and the Doctrine of Commercial Speech, 56 U.Cin.L.Rev. 1273, 1293 (1988); Note, The Risk of Chill: A Cost of the Standards Governing the Regulation of False Advertising Under Section 43(a) of the Lanham Act, 77 Va.L.Rev. 339, 349 (1991). The way to avoid this chilling effect, according to Kraft, is to require the Commission to rely on objective indicia of consumer perceptions in finding implied claims.

Kraft's first amendment challenge is doomed by the Supreme Court's holding in *Zauderer* [Zauderer v. Office of disciplinary Counsel of Supreme Court of Ohio, 471 U.S. 626 (1985)], which established that no first amendment concerns are raised when facially apparent implied claims are found without resort to extrinsic evidence. In *Zauderer*, a lawyer advertised that clients who retained him on a contingent-fee basis would not have to pay *legal fees* if their lawsuits were unsuccessful, without disclosing that these clients would be charged for *costs*, even though these are terms of art unknown to most laypersons; thus, the ad implied that hiring this lawyer was a no-lose proposition to potential clients. The state sanctioned Zauderer for engaging in misleading advertising, and he challenged that sanction on first amendment grounds. In approving the state's action, the Supreme Court declared, "When the possibility of deception is as self-evident as it is in this case, we need not require the State to 'conduct a survey of the ... public before it [may] determine that the [advertisement] had a tendency to mislead.'" *Zauderer*, 471 U.S. at 652-53 (quoting *Colgate-Palmolive*, 380 U.S. at 391-92).

Thus, *Zauderer* teaches that consumer surveys are not compelled by the first amendment when the alleged deception although implied, is conspicuous. In both *Zauderer* and here, an omitted piece of information--the definition of a key contractual term in *Zauderer*, the effect of processing on nutrient content here--led to potential consumer deception, and in both cases the ads were literally true, yet impliedly misleading. Kraft's implied claims were reasonably clear from the face of the ads and not unpredictable to Kraft. Our conclusion is strengthened by the fact that commercial speech is generally considered less susceptible to the chilling effect of regulation than other, more traditionally recognized forms of speech, such as political discourse. Because we conclude that the Commission was not required to rely on extrinsic evidence, we need not examine the extrinsic evidence proffered by Kraft that it says contravenes the Commission's findings. We note, however, that the Commission did thoroughly examine this evidence, albeit after the fact, and found that it did not refute the implied claim findings and that some of the evidence was based on unsound consumer testing methodologies.

Our holding does not diminish the force of Kraft's argument as a policy matter, and, indeed, the extensive body of commentary on the subject makes a compelling argument that reliance on extrinsic evidence should be the rule rather than the exception. Along those lines, the Commission would be well- advised to adopt a consistent position on consumer survey methodology-- advertisers and the FTC, it appears, go round and round on this issue--so that any uncertainty is reduced to an absolute minimum.

[The court found substantial evidence to support the Commission decision that the advertising contained the contested claims and that those claims were material to consumers.]

For the foregoing reasons, Kraft's petition to set-aside the order is DENIED and the Commission's order is ENFORCED.

MANION, concurring.

While I concur with the opinion of the court, I am concerned that the FTC can avoid extrinsic evidence by simply concluding that a deceptive, implied claim is facially apparent. While the FTC has expertise, consumer surveys provide at least some objective determination of what the purchaser thinks and should be considered since, after all, the consumer is among those we are trying to protect.

Moreover, the FTC's current procedure threatens to chill nonmisleading, protected speech. Although not all commercial speech has constitutional protection, the law has developed since this court decided that the FTC could rely on its own interpretation of ads * * *. The Supreme Court has recognized that a free flow of information is indispensable to decisionmaking in the free enterprise system. But the FTC jeopardizes this flow by relying on the FTC commissioners' subjective interpretation to determine whether an ad, while literally true, implies a false message. Advertisers will be unable to predict whether the FTC will find particular ads misleading. Pre- dissemination surveys showing consumers *are not* misled will be useless since the FTC is free to ignore any such extrinsic evidence and rely on its subjective judgment that consumers may be misled. Advertisers unwilling to gamble with a multi-million dollar ad campaign have essentially two choices: (1) submit every campaign to the FTC in advance or (2) disseminate ads that say little or nothing about a product or service. An advertiser will not want to risk producing comparative ads which the FTC may ultimately find to imply false, unintended messages.

* * * In both this case and *Zauderer*, an omitted piece of information led to an implication which turned an ad that was literally true into a potentially deceiving ad. But it is important to note that neither this case nor *Zauderer* gives the FTC leave to ignore extrinsic evidence in every case.

Unfortunately, judicial groping for a distinction between cases where extrinsic evidence is necessary and those where it is not is leaving both advertisers and the FTC uncertain. * * * Rather than leaving judges to hew the contours of this issue, the FTC would be well- advised to take this court's suggestion--apply its expertise and develop a consumer survey methodology that advertisers can use to ascertain whether their ads contain implied, deceptive messages.

PAGE 217. Add.

FEDERAL TRADE COMMISSION v. PANTRON I CORPORATION
United States Court of Appeals, 9th Circuit, 1994.
33 F.3d 1088, cert. denied 115 S.Ct. 1794 (1995)

REINHARDT, Circuit Judge:

These consolidated appeals require us to decide a previously unresolved question of federal consumer protection law: Whether it is lawful for a seller to represent a product as "effective" when its efficacy results solely from a "placebo effect." We conclude that the answer is no and that the representation constitutes a "false advertisement" under the Federal Trade Commission Act.

[Pantron markets a product known as the Helsinki Formula, consisting of polysorbate 60 and polysorbate 80, which supposedly arrests hair loss and stimulates hair regrowth in baldness sufferers. Advertisements for the Formula feature both the claim of reduced hair loss as well as the promotion of new hair. The F.T.C., to support its assertion of lack of effectiveness, introduced (1) expert testimony of doctors who stated there was "no reason to believe" the Formula was useful in treating hair loss; (2) the F.D.A.'s determination that polysorbate 60 does not affect hair growth; and (3) two placebo-controlled, double-blinded, randomized studies showing the polysorbate-based products to be ineffective. To prove effectiveness, Pantron introduced (1) live and deposition testimony of 18 users who had good results with the Formula; (2) a survey conducted by its own sales personnel which purported to show 70% of those who used the Formula for 6 months or more showed positive results; and (3) clinical studies by European doctors which were uncontrolled, unblinded, unrandomized and not peer reviewed which purported to show the products effective.]

In its own adjudications, the F.T.C. has to some extent clarified the legal standards which apply in section 12 cases. In Cliffdale Assocs., 103 F.T.C. 110 (1984), the Commission announced a three-part test for determining whether an advertisement is misleading and deceptive in violation of section 12. Under this test, the Commission will find an act or practice deceptive if, first, there is a representation, omission, or practice that, second, is likely to mislead consumers acting reasonably under the circumstances, and third, the representation, omission, or practice is material. The Commission has consistently adhered to the Cliffdale Associates standard. * * *

* * * Therefore, the only question before us is whether Pantron's representations regarding the product's effectiveness were likely to deceive or mislead consumers.

* * *

We hold that the district court erred in concluding that Pantron's representations regarding the Helsinki Formula's efficacy did not amount to false advertising. Although there was sufficient evidence in the record to support the district court's finding that use of the Helsinki Formula might arrest hair loss in some of the people some of the time, the overwhelming weight of the proof at trial made clear that any effectiveness is due solely to the product's placebo effect. As we explain infra, we conclude that a claim of product effectiveness is "false" for purposes of section 12 of the Federal Trade Commission Act if evidence developed under accepted standards of scientific research demonstrates that the product has no force beyond its placebo effect.

* * *

C.

Assessing this evidence, the district court concluded that the F.T.C. had failed to carry its burden of showing that the Helsinki Formula is "wholly ineffective." In essence, the district court held that, as a matter of law, a seller can represent that its product is effective even when this effectiveness is based solely on the placebo effect. We believe that the district court misapprehended the law.

* * * In essence, the F.T.C. urges that we should hold that contemporary standards of scientific evaluation-which preclude the consideration of the placebo effect-are the determinants of what is "true" and what is "false." In its view, when the application of these contemporary scientific standards would lead to the conclusion that a product is ineffective, any claim that the product is effective is "false" in an intrinsic, absolute sense. We disagree. Contemporary scientific standards obviously are not the definitive or sole measure of what is "true" or "false." Galileo's theories were contrary to then-contemporary scientific standards, but we treat as a given that these theories

were as essentially "true" when he explained them as they surely are today. Moreover, depending on our terms of reference, it may well not be incorrect to say that an efficacy representation is "true" when the product's effectiveness results solely from the placebo effect: for, in a certain sense, it would be "true" for a seller of sugar pills to represent that they relieve pain for some of the people some of the time, just as it would be "true" for Pantron to state that the Helsinki Formula sometimes arrests hair loss. Whether because of psychological factors or because of the physiological effects of regularly massaging any product into the scalp, the evidence makes clear that the Helsinki Formula does work to some extent to combat baldness in some people some of the time.

However, neither scientific standards on the one hand, nor the broadest possible definition of "truth" on the other, can determine what constitutes a "false advertisement" under section 12 of the Federal Trade Commission Act. Indeed, a "false advertisement" need not even be "false"; it need only be "misleading in a material respect." 15 U.S.C. § 55. We must read this definition of "false advertis[ing]" in light of the overriding purpose of the F.T.C. Act: "to protect the consumer from being misled by governing the conditions under which goods and services are advertised and sold to individual purchasers." National Petroleum Refiners Assoc. v. F.T.C., 482 F.2d 672, 685 (D.C. Cir. 1973)[.] The question we must face, then, is not whether Pantron's claims were "true" in some abstract epistemological sense, nor even whether they could conceivably be described as "true" in ordinary parlance. Rather, we must determine whether or not efficacy representations based solely on the placebo effect are "misleading in a material respect," and hence prohibited as "false advertis[ing]" under the Act.

Taking account of these principles, we hold that the Federal Trade Commission is not required to prove that a product is "wholly ineffective" in order to carry its burden of showing that the seller's representations of product efficacy are "false." Where, as here, a product's effectiveness arises solely as a result of the placebo effect, a representation that the product is effective constitutes a "false advertisement" even though some consumers may experience positive results. In such circumstances, the efficacy claim "is 'misleading' because the [product] is not inherently effective, its results being attributable to the psychosomatic effect produced by the advertising and marketing of the [product]," United States v. An Article ... Acu-Dot ..., 483 F. Supp. 1311, 1315 (N.D. Ohio 1980), as well as (in cases such as this one) the objective effects caused by the use of any product or even non-product in treating the condition in question. * * * In reasoning which fully applies to section 12 of the Federal Trade Commission Act, the court [in Acu-Dot] noted that "[a] kiss from mother on the affected area would serve just as well to relieve pain, if mother's kisses were marketed as effectively as the Acu-Dot device," id. at 1315, and that a consumer purchasing a pain-reliever would expect it to have more therapeutic value than such a kiss.

* * * Indeed, were we to hold otherwise, advertisers would be encouraged to foist unsubstantiated claims on an unsuspecting public in the hope that consumers would

believe the ads and the claims would be self-fulfilling. Bristol-Myers Co., 102 F.T.C. 21, 336 (1983). Moreover, allowing advertisers to rely on the placebo effect would not only harm those individuals who were deceived; it would create a substantial economic cost as well, by allowing sellers to fleece large numbers of consumers who, unable to evaluate the efficacy of an inherently useless product, make repeat purchases of that product.

* * *

In light of our conclusion, we instruct the district court to remove the portion of its injunction which allowed Pantron to "state that the Helsinki Formula is effective to some extent for some people." Such a representation- which, on the record before us, rests solely on the placebo effect-is misleading for the reasons set forth above. * * * On remand, the district court shall modify its injunction to prohibit the company from making any representations that the Helsinki Formula is effective in arresting hair loss or promoting hair regrowth.

III.

The F.T.C. argues that the district court erred in refusing to order Pantron or Lederman to pay restitution to consumers or disgorge their profits. Because the district court's refusal to award monetary equitable relief was based on the application of erroneous legal principles, we reverse. * * *

A.

Section 13(b) of the Federal Trade Commission Act provides "[t]hat in proper cases the Commission may seek, and after proper proof, the court may issue, a permanent injunction." 15 U.S.C. § 53(b). This provision gives the federal courts broad authority to fashion appropriate remedies for violations of the Act. As we explained in F.T.C. v. H.N. Singer, Inc., 668 F.2d 1107 (9th Cir.1982), the authority granted by section 13(b) is not limited to the power to issue an injunction; rather, it includes the "authority to grant any ancillary relief necessary to accomplish complete justice." This power includes the power to order restitution. A corporation is liable for monetary relief under section 13(b) if the F.T.C. shows that the corporation engaged in misrepresentations or omissions of a kind usually relied on by reasonably prudent persons and that consumer injury resulted.

Here, the district court concluded that Pantron had falsely claimed that the Helsinki Formula's effectiveness was supported by scientific proof. It also determined that these representations were material to consumers. Thus, the district court found the requisite material misrepresentations. Moreover, as we noted in the previous Part, Pantron's misrepresentations were even more extensive than the district court acknowledged. In any event, the district court refused to order the company to pay restitution or disgorge its profits because it concluded that the F.T.C. had not established any actual injury to consumers. In particular, it relied on the fact that "[a]ny individual injuries have been only economic and only in amounts less than $100--for which defendant had offered a reasonably adequate, albeit rarely exercised, remedy."

The district court's reasons for denying monetary equitable relief were inadequate as a matter of law. First, the district court erred when it relied on the fact that the consumer injuries have been only economic in nature. It is simply improper to treat this fact as a factor weighing against an award of monetary relief. The remedy of restitution seeks to correct unjust enrichment, and is therefore particularly suited to remedying economic injuries. Moreover, a major purpose of the Federal Trade Commission Act is to protect consumers from economic injuries. It would pervert the purposes of both the restitutionary remedy and the Act to deny monetary relief simply because the injury inflicted by the defendant is only economic in nature.

Second, the district court erred when it concluded that the modest amount of injury suffered by each individual consumer could preclude an order of restitution or disgorgement. Both the Commission and the courts have recognized that consumer injury is substantial when it is the aggregate of many small individual injuries. * * *

Finally, the existence of a money-back guarantee is insufficient reason as a matter of law to preclude a monetary remedy. As the Seventh Circuit recognized in Montgomery Ward & Co. v. F.T.C., 379 F.2d 666 (7th Cir.1967), allowing a seller to rely on a money-back guarantee as a defense to section 12 charges "would make the false advertising prohibitions of the Act a nullity. Anything might then be advertised as long as unsatisfied customers were returned their money." For the same reasons, allowing such a guarantee to bar monetary relief would make the broad equitable remedial power in section 13(b) a nullity. Because even many unsatisfied customers will not take advantage of a money-back guarantee, a company which has engaged in consumer fraud would be able to retain a significant portion of the proceeds simply by making a largely illusory money-back offer.

Because the district court's refusal to order monetary relief against the corporation was based on the application of erroneous legal principles, and because an application of the proper principles compels an order of monetary relief, we instruct the district court to order the Pantron Corporation to pay monetary equitable relief to the extent of its unjust enrichment.

PAGE 239. Read in association with Note 3

FEDERAL TRADE COMMISSION v. FIGGIE INTERNATIONAL, INC.
United States Court of Appeals, Ninth Circuit, 1993
994 F.2d 595, cert denied 114 S. Ct. 1051 (1994)

PER CURIAM:

Pursuant to Section 5 of the Federal Trade Commission ("FTC") Act, 15 U.S.C. § 45, Figgie International, Inc. ("Figgie") was ordered to cease and desist from the "unfair or deceptive" practices it used to market its Vanguard heat detectors. After the order became final, FTC sought consumer redress under section 19 of the FTC Act, 15 U.S.C. § 57b. The district court granted FTC's motions for summary judgment, finding Figgie liable for "dishonest or fraudulent" practices in its first judgment and setting the amount of liability at a minimum of $7.59 million and a maximum of $49.95 million (i.e. a range between the amount of Figgie's profits and the full amount spent by consumers) in the second. Figgie appeals both. We affirm as modified.

FACTS

[Figgie manufactured and sold heat detectors for home use beginning in 1959. For many years both heat and smoke detectors were recommended by the National Fire Prevention Association as a household fire warning system. However, a series of tests ("the Indiana Dunes" and "Cal Chiefs" tests) by fire-prevention experts in the mid-1970's showed that smoke detectors were superior and in most circumstances provided warnings several minutes earlier than heat detectors. NFPA changed its standards to recommend smoke detectors on each level of a home and additional smoke or heat detectors as required.]

Figgie knew of the results of the Indiana Dunes and Cal Chiefs tests and knew of the changes in the NFPA standards. However, its representations to consumers during the 1980's did not reflect them. The crux of Figgie's message was that heat detectors could be relied on as life-saving fire warning devices, and that the best protection for one's home is a combination of four or five heat detectors to one smoke detector. The ALJ's decision provides a thorough description of Figgie's promotional materials. He concluded that "every one of them clearly conveys" the claim that Vanguard heat detectors provide the necessary warning to allow safe escape from a residential fire. Similarly, "Virtually all of the promotional materials ... contain express and implied claims that the combination system combining Vanguard heat and smoke detectors significantly increase the level of fire warning protection than smoke detectors alone." * * *

Figgie sold its products to the public through at-home sales visits by distributors. This sales technique "heightened the impact of the materials because the captive consumer's attention is focussed for the duration of the sales presentation." In addition to the slide-tape shows, a sales presentation would often include a demonstration using a cardboard house with a tissue paper roof. The salesperson would place a lit candle inside the house while holding a heat detector directly over the tissue. The heat detector would alarm before the paper scorched. This dramatic and seemingly informative demonstration was in fact misleading. The cardboard house channelled hot air from the candle directly to the fuse, a situation that would be "completely fortuitous" under actual fire conditions. Also, given that the ignition temperature of paper is 450, the demonstration proved only that a heat detector held inches above a flame will activate sometime before the fuse reaches 450. Other forms of sales pressure could also be exerted in the home. Customers who bought less than the recommended number of the more expensive heat detectors were asked to sign a release acknowledging that only partial fire detection protection" had been purchased. Figgie's promotional techniques were very successful: its customers bought four or five heat detectors for every smoke detector.

The ALJ concluded that Figgie's representations were misleading and deceptive in the absence of an explanation of the limits of heat detectors and the comparative superiority of smoke detectors. [The Commission required a warning on all of Figgie's promotional material that read: "NOTICE: Smoke detectors give earlier warning than heat detectors in nearly all residential fires. That is because detectable amounts of smoke almost always develop before detectable levels of heat." The order also prohibited certain representations that were misleading.]

The Commission's cease and desist order was upheld on appeal. Figgie Int'l, Inc. v. FTC, 817 F.2d 102 (4th Cir. 1987). FTC then brought the current suit for consumer redress under Section 19 for the period between May 18, 1980 and July 20, 1987. * * * On February 9, 1990, the district court concluded that

> A reasonable man under the circumstances would have known that Figgie's representations that a) Vanguard heat detectors provide the necessary warning to allow safe escape in most residential fires, and b) a combined system of heat detectors and smoke detectors provides significantly greater warning than smoke detectors alone because heat detectors give earlier warning of hot, flaming fires were dishonest or fraudulent. Summary judgment was therefore granted to FTC on the issue of liability.

On January 14, 1991, the district court granted summary judgment on the amount of redress. The court found that Figgie received $7.59 million in gross revenues from sale of Vanguard heat detectors between the relevant dates, and that consumers paid $49.95 million for them (293,824 units @ $170). The court further concluded that "The Vanguard heat detector's value, given the misrepresentations recommended by Figgie and made by distributors to consumers, is de minimis." Therefore, the court ordered that Figgie pay $7.59 million into a fund which would refund the full purchase price of Vanguard heat detectors to customers. If aggrieved customers claim less than that amount, the balance is to be used for "indirect redress" in the form of corrective advertising or donations to non-profit fire safety organizations. If customers claim more, Figgie is to continue to add to the fund as necessary, to a maximum of $49.95 million.

Figgie timely appeals both summary judgment orders.

* * *

I. LIABILITY

Section 19(a)(2) of the FTC Act grants the Commission authority to bring a civil suit against any entity which engaged

> in any unfair or deceptive act or practice ... with respect to which the Commission has issued a final cease and desist order. If the Commission satisfies the court that the act or practice to which the cease and desist order relates is one which a reasonable man would have known under the circumstances was dishonest or fraudulent, the court may grant relief[.] 15 U.S.C. § 57b(a)(2).

The cease and desist order, affirmed by the Fourth Circuit, is final. Figgie mounts three challenges to the district court's judgment of liability based on its finding that a reasonable person would have known the act or practice was dishonest and fraudulent under the circumstances. (1) The district court erred in its characterization of the Commission's factual findings. (2) There was no evidence that Figgie had specific intent to defraud. (3) A reasonable person would not know that Figgie's practices were dishonest or fraudulent.

[The Court upheld the Commission's factual findings. As to specific intent, the Court interpreted the statute not to require a showing of specific intent to defraud on the part of Figgie. "Congress unambiguously referred the district court to the state of mind of a hypothetical reasonable person, not the knowledge of the defendant. The standard is objective, not subjective." The Court also found "ample evidence" that a reasonable person would have known Figgie's misrepresentations were "dishonest and fraudulent".]

II. REMEDY

The district court ordered that Figgie pay into an escrow account to be managed by the Commission. "These funds shall be used to provide direct redress to consumers who purchased Vanguard heat detectors during [the redress period] and who can make a valid claim for such redress through the plaintiff, including prejudgment interest from the date of purchase (and to pay any attendant expenses of administration)." At a minimum, Figgie would pay the amount of its profits, $7,590,000. At a maximum, Figgie would pay $49,950,000, the amount spent by consumers. Figgie challenges this order on several grounds.

A. Consumer Injury

* * *

The power bestowed is to "grant such relief as the court finds necessary to redress injury to consumers" resulting from dishonest or fraudulent trade practices. 15 U.S.C. § 57b(b). It follows, therefore, that there may be no redress without proof of injury caused by those practices. And the relief must be necessary to redress the injury.

1. Individual Reliance by Consumers

Figgie argues that because its liability is premised on certain misrepresentations or misleading statements, only those consumers that can prove that they purchased a Vanguard heat detector in reliance on those statements should be entitled to redress. As a factual matter, Figgie's argument that the district court had no proof of reliance is incorrect. Figgie's sales materials advocated the purchase of four or five heat detectors per smoke detector, and that matches Figgie's actual sales ratio. It is reasonable to conclude from the record evidence that consumers purchased Vanguard heat detectors in reliance upon respondent's express and implied claim that heat detectors "will provide necessary warning to allow a safe escape in most residential fires."

Figgie's claim is also incorrect as a matter of law. It is well established with regard to Section 13 of the FTC Act (which gives district courts the power to order equitable relief) that proof of individual reliance by each purchasing customer is not needed. Proof of reliance by the consumer upon the defendants' misrepresentations is a traditional element of recovery under common law fraud actions. Section 13 of the FTC Act differs from a private suit for fraud, however. Section 13 serves a public purpose by authorizing the Commission to seek redress on behalf of injured consumers. Requiring proof of subjective reliance by each individual consumer would thwart effective prosecutions of large consumer redress actions and frustrate the statutory goals of the section. A presumption of actual reliance arises once the Commission has proved that the defendant made material misrepresentations, that they were widely disseminated, and that consumers purchased the defendant's product. Some courts hold that at this point, the burden shifts to the defendant to prove the absence of reliance. The same reasoning is applicable to Section 19. Because Figgie has presented no evidence to rebut the presumption of reliance, injury to consumers has been established.

2. Amount of Refund Needed to Redress Injury

The Commission did not attempt to prove deaths or physical injuries resulting from the installation of Vanguard heat detectors rather than smoke detectors. The injury to consumers it sought to establish is the amount consumers spent on the heat detectors that would not have been spent absent Figgie's dishonest practices.

The district court ordered that consumers be allowed to receive full refunds for their Vanguard heat detectors, whose value, "given the misrepresentations recommended by Figgie and made by distributors to consumers, is de minimis." Figgie protests that the "de minimis" finding and the resulting full refund are inappropriate in light of the Commission's conclusive finding that heat detectors have some value. Although we agree with Figgie that the district court is not free to make this finding, we find the error harmless. Courts have previously rejected the contention "that restitution is available only when the goods purchased are essentially worthless." FTC v. International Diamond Corp., 1983-2 Trade Cases P 65,506, p. 68,459 (N.D. Cal. 1983) ("Diamond I").

* * *

The district court's order creates no windfall for Figgie's customers. Refunds are available to those buyers "who can make a valid claim for such redress." Those who paid less than the $170 figure challenged by Figgie (and discussed infra) will therefore obtain redress based on the lesser figure. Those consumers who decide, after advertising which corrects the deceptions by which Figgie sold them the heat detectors, that nevertheless the heat detectors serve their needs, may then make the informed choice to keep their heat detectors instead of returning them for refunds.

* * *

B. Minimum Redress

* * * The district court's judgment required that, at a minimum, Figgie be denied all of its profits from the redress period. Unclaimed money from the redress fund will be used for "indirect redress" in the form of corrective advertisements or donations to non-profit fire safety organizations. Figgie argues that the minimum redress provision amounts to an award of punitive damages forbidden by the statute.

Section 19(b) expressly contemplates corrective advertising in its "public notification" clause. The portion of the order that is questionable and could be barred as punitive is the provision for distributing unclaimed funds to non-profit fire safety organizations. We do find this portion in effect to be punitive. We can see no basis for allowing the Commission to keep money in excess of what it reasonably spends to find purchasers of the heat detectors, advertise to them the availability of the money and the importance of using smoke rather than heat detectors at appropriate locations, and process their claims and reimburse them. * * *

The district court's order provides that any unrefunded money be distributed by "donation to one or more nonprofit entities, at the discretion of the Commission, for the support of research, fellowships or consumer education in the field of fire safety." This extraordinary provision cannot be characterized as "redress." The word connotes making amends to someone who has been wronged. The nonprofit organizations, recipients of fellowships, researchers, and educators who might receive the money under this portion of the order were not wronged by Figgie's deceptive sales methods. Calling a fine "indirect redress" does not make it redress. * * *

* * *

Accordingly, the summary judgment on liability is AFFIRMED, but the summary judgment on damages is MODIFIED and the order VACATED for modification consistent with this opinion.

CHAPTER III

PRODUCT AND PRODUCER IDENTITY

PAGE 249. Add to the end of Note 2.

The limits of reverse passing off are illustrated in Summit Machine Tool Mfg. Corp. v. Victor CNC Systems, Inc., 7 F.3d 1434 (1993). Summit had a contract with ZMTW that gave Summit exclusive right to sell outside of China lathes manufactured by ZMTW to Summit's designs. Victor purchased seven lathes from ZMTW for resale in the United States. The designs were not protected by a copyright or patent. Thus, arguably if the lathes Victor purchased were actually "Summit lathes", Victor would be guilty of reverse passing off -- selling someone else's goods as your own. On the other hand Victor had the right to copy Summit's lathes and ZMTW had the right to manufacture and sell lathes other than those designed by Summit. Should the issue be whether the lathes Victor purchased were "substantially similar" to the lathes designed by Summit or should the courts require some evidence that Victor "bodily appropriated" one of Summit's lathes to sell under the Victor mark? The court holds that some "bodily appropriation" is required. Do *Sears* and *Compco* play a role in these cases?

PAGE 253. Substitute for existing "Overview"

AN OVERVIEW OF NATIONAL AND INTERNATIONAL PROTECTION OF TRADEMARKS

National Protection under the Lanham Act

The Lanham Act, 15 U.S.C. § 1051 et seq., enacts the federal regime of trademark registration. Administered by the Patent and Trademark Office (PTO) the Act creates two separate registers, the "Principal Register" (§ 1) and the "Supplemental Register" (§ 23).

The Principal Register is designed to affect trademark rights and controversies within the United States. Since 1947 the Act has provided that a "trademark owner" who has adopted and used a mark can apply for federal registration on the Principal Register. An application for registration is extensively examined by the PTO to determine if it qualifies for registration. This can delay registration for months or even years. If the PTO determines the application sets forth a mark entitled to be registered, the mark is published in the Official Gazette of the Patent and Trademark Office. Interested persons have 30 days after publication to file an opposition to registration (§ 13). If no opposition is filed, a registration is issued. A registration remains in force for 10 years provided the owner files an affidavit in the fifth year showing the mark is still in use (§ 8). The registration can be renewed for an unlimited number of additional 10 year terms by filing an affidavit within 6 months of expiration indicating the mark is still in use. (§ 9).

The Lanham Act as originally enacted required that a trademark owner first use the mark in commerce before applying for a registration. In 1988 amendments were adopted to permit trademark owners to apply for protection under the Lanham Act prior to actual use if they could demonstrate a bona fide intention to use the mark in the future. (§ 1(b)). Within six months after an intent to use application is filed, the trademark owner must file a statement that the mark has been actually used. The PTO can give an applicant additional time to demonstrate use, not to exceed 24 months after filing. (§ 1(d)). No actual registration issues until the mark is actually used but once use and registration occur, the owner's priority of use reverts back to the date of filing the application based on intent to use.

Controversies involving the validity of the application or registration of a mark may arise in a number of different contexts. An applicant may contest the denial of an application by the examiner (§ 20). Persons who might be injured by the registration may seek to oppose the registration prior to its issuance (§ 13) or may seek to cancel the registration after it is issued (§ 14). If the Commissioner believes the mark in an application resembles a registered mark or a mark in another pending application, the Commissioner can declare an interference proceeding which allows the owners of the two competing marks to litigate their respective rights. (§ 16).

Proceedings for all of the above disputes are heard by the PTO's Trademark Trial and Appeal Board (§ 17). Until 1982, appeals from the Board's decision were to the Court of Customs and Patent Appeals. In 1982 Congress created the United States Court of Appeals for the Federal Circuit (§ 21(a)) which hears direct appeals from the Board. A party may forego a direct appeal to the Federal Circuit and file a civil action in an appropriate federal district court (§ 21(b)).

International Protection of Trademarks

The Principal Register of the Lanham Act affects trademark rights within the United States. However, trademarked goods and services flow increasingly in a global economy. For more than a century, the countries of the world have struggled to provide an efficient mechanism for trademark owners to secure international protection of their trademarks. Although some international agreements have been negotiated, the United States has not participated. Thus, it remains largely true today that an American trademark owner interested in protecting a mark throughout the world must seek registration of the mark in each individual country. There have been renewed efforts at an agreement the United States could accept.

The protection of intellectual property, including trademarks, has become a major issue in efforts to implement freer trade policies among the nations of the world. Businesses in developed countries, such as the United States, have a comparative advantage in research and development activity that produces patented and copyrighted goods and also a significantly greater interest in the protection of famous brand names. In some developing countries, pirating of intellectual property has become an important industry, resulting in weak substantive laws or little actual enforcement of intellectual property rights.

The pressure for seeking international agreement on the proper scope of trademark protection and for establishing an efficient mechanism for international registration will play a significant role in the development of American domestic trademark law. Several past attempts at more sensible international trademark systems have been frustrated because the United States has been unwilling to change certain features of its domestic trademark law which are inconsistent with that of most other countries. For example, most countries do not require the trademark owner to actually use the mark prior to registration. Similarly most countries do not have an elaborate, time-consuming examination procedure prior to registration of a trademark. In the past few years, some changes in the Lanham Act have been adopted to bring it into conformity with the views of the international community. More such efforts are likely to occur in the near future.

The following is a very general outline of past and current developments in this area:

1. International Registration Systems

    a. International Convention for the Protection of Industrial Property (1883). The earliest international agreement aimed at multinational registration and protection of trademarks was the International Convention for the Protection of Industrial Property, signed in Paris in 1883. The principle underlying the Convention of Paris is that member states agree to confer on nationals of other member states the same entitlement relating to the protection of marks as are extended to their own citizens.

The Paris Convention provides that once a citizen obtains a trademark registration in the citizen's home country, every other signatory country must accept that registration for filing in its domestic system and to accord the owner the same rights it accords its own citizens. The scheme still requires the trademark owner to pursue registration in each country. The Supplemental Register of the Lanham Act is designed to allow an American company to satisfy the domestic registration requirement without the extended time period required for examination of the application under the Principal Register. The Supplemental Register, however, has little impact on domestic rights and, accordingly has few restrictions as to the marks that can be registered. Section 44 of the Lanham Act implements the Paris Convention by extending the benefits of Lanham Act registration to citizens of countries that provide reciprocal rights to American citizens.

A major feature of the Paris Convention, reflected in § 44, is that upon compliance with certain conditions the date of filing an application for registration in the applicant's home country becomes the date of filing in a foreign country for purposes of determining priority between competing marks in the foreign country. This constructive priority date applies as long as the foreign application is filed within 6 months of the filing of the domestic application. This feature causes some difficulty in the United States because the Lanham Act, unlike the law in most other countries, required, until the 1988 revisions, adoption and use of a mark prior to registration. Thus it was possible for a foreign national to register in its home country prior to using the mark, then register under the Lanham Act and claim priority in the United States over an American company who was the prior user of the mark in the United States.

b. Trademark Registration Treaty (1973). In Vienna in 1973 fourteen countries, including the United States, signed the Trademark Registration Treaty ("TRT"). This agreement provides for an international filing system administered by the World Intellectual Property Organization ("WIPO"). A trademark owner could file a single registration for a trademark with WIPO and designate the signatory countries in which actual registration is sought. The filing would then be automatically forwarded to those countries and reviewed under their respective domestic laws as though it were a domestic trademark application. Registration would follow in accordance with the domestic law of each country but the priority in each country would be the date of the international filing. The treaty provides that no member state can refuse trademark registration on grounds of non-use of the mark within three years of filing of the international application. Implementation in the United States would have required change in the Lanham Act. The treaty has not been ratified by the United States Senate.

c. The Madrid Registration of Marks Treaty (Madrid Agreement) (1890). The Madrid Agreement established a system for international registration of marks. Under the Agreement once a company obtained a registration under its own domestic law, it could register the mark with WIPO and designate those countries within the agreement in which protection was sought. The filing with WIPO automatically constituted an application for domestic registration in these designated foreign countries. Each country had 12 months to reject the application. If the application was not rejected, the company automatically obtained a registration in the foreign country, subject to that country's laws. This system facilitated foreign registrations for it required that a company only do two things: obtain a registration in its home country and file an application with WIPO. The agreement was signed by about thirty nations.

The United States did not join the Madrid Agreement because some of its components would place American companies at a disadvantage. First, the international registration was based on *registration* in the trademark owner's home country. Because of the delay caused by the examination procedures under the Lanham Act, American companies would run the risk that someone would obtain priority by obtaining an earlier registration under the laws of another country. Moreover, the PTO would have difficulty complying with the 12 month period for rejection of an international registration, given its workload. American companies also objected to the requirement that trademark applications under the Madrid Agreement were to be in the French language and to the doctrine of "central attack". Under this doctrine, if the trademark owner's domestic registration were cancelled within five years, it had the effect of also cancelling all of the other registrations obtained through the Agreement.

(d) The Madrid Protocol. The Madrid Protocol is a separate international agreement designed to respond to the concerns of the United States with the Madrid Agreement. Under the Protocol, the international filing could be based on a domestic *application* rather than an actual registration. A domestic application would support an international filing that would be automatically transmitted to each designated country for examination. Other countries would have up to 25 months to reject the international registration. The doctrine of "central attack" was abandoned so that if a domestic registration is cancelled, the international registrations are transformed into national applications with the same priority date. The Protocol also allowed applications to be in English. Legislation to permit the United States to join the Madrid Protocol has been introduced in Congress. See generally, Schechter, Facilitating Trademark Registration Abroad: The Implications of U.S. Ratification of the Madrid Protocol, 25 Geo. Wash. J. Int'l L & Econ. 419 (1991).

2. Intellectual Property and International Trade.

With the increased globalization of the economy, the countries of the world have undertaken considerable efforts to reduce tariffs and other barriers to world trade. The United States, Canada, and Mexico concluded the North American Free Trade Agreement ("NAFTA") designed to encourage unincumbered trade among the three countries. More broadly, the United States participates in the General Agreement on Tariffs and Trade ("GATT") which for many years has been the forum for trade discussions. In the most recent round of GATT negotiations, the Uruguay Round, the United States succeeded in placing the protection of intellectual property on the agenda. This was a recognition that failure of countries to protect intellectual property can have an inhibiting effect on trade.

The NAFTA agreement contains extensive provisions relating to intellectual property including trademarks in Part Six. The NAFTA provisions are similar to those contained in the GATT agreement, which in the GATT are called the Trade Related Aspects of Intellectual Property Rights, Including Trade in Counterfeit Goods

("TRIPS"). The United States Congress approved the NAFTA accord and the GATT agreement both of which required amendments to the Lanham Act.

The thrust of these agreements is to assure minimal standards of protection of intellectual property rights in the signatory countries. With regard to trademarks, the agreements address both the substantive rights to be accorded trademark owners as well as the procedural mechanisms required to enforce trademark rights. For example, Article 1708 of the NAFTA provides the minimum substantive law standards which, for the most part, are consistent with current United States law. Of particular significance is paragraph 6 which adopts Article 6*bis* of the Paris Convention relating to "well-known" marks. In most countries other than the United States, trademark rights are acquired by registration not by use. It was not uncommon for a local resident of a foreign country to register a well-known mark, i.e., FORD for automobiles, and thus demand payment before the mark owner could do business in that country. Article 6*bis* and now the NAFTA agreement require the signatory countries to refuse registration or to allow cancellation of registration of "well-known" marks. The GATT TRIPS contains similar provisions. See, Section 2, Article 16.

Other provisions of the agreements set out the minimum requirements for civil judicial procedures for enforcement of intellectual property rights and also provide for adoption of provisional remedies to prevent infringements, criminal penalties for "willful trademark counterfeiting", and enforcement of intellectual property rights at the border. The effect of these agreements will be to exert pressure to harmonize the domestic law of the affected nations.

PAGE 267. Read after Note 5

CAR-FRESHNER CORP. v. S.C. JOHNSON & SON, INC.
United States Court of Appeals for the Second Circuit, 1995
70 F.3d 267

LEVAL, Circuit Judge:

This action for trademark infringement involves the principle that the public's right to use language and imagery for descriptive purposes is not defeated by the claims of a trademark owner to exclusivity.

Plaintiff Car-Freshner Corporation sells air fresheners for cars in the shape of a pine tree. Over a number of years, Car-Freshner has sold millions of such pine-tree-shaped fresheners. Its air fresheners are made of flat scented cardboard and come in a variety of colors and odors, including a green pine-scented version. They have a string attached to the top of the tree, so that they can be hung from the rear-view mirror of an automobile. We assume that plaintiff has established trademark rights in the pine-tree shape of its product and in the name "Little Tree," which it uses on some of its products.

Defendant S.C. Johnson & Son, Inc., sells air fresheners under the trademark name "Glade." Johnson's "Glade" products include a line of air fresheners called "Plug-Ins," designed to be plugged into electrical outlets. Glade Plug-Ins have a plastic casing that holds a replaceable fragrance cartridge of scented gel. When the unit is plugged in, the electrical current warms the gel, causing release of the fragrance into the air. During the Christmas holiday season, Johnson sells a pine-tree-shaped, plug-in air freshener called "Holiday Pine Potpourri" under its Glade Plug-Ins trademark.

Car-Freshner brought this action against Johnson, claiming that Johnson's sale of its pine-tree-shaped plug-in freshener violates Car-Freshner's trademark rights in the pine-tree shape of its air fresheners and in its mark "Little Tree." * * *

It is a fundamental principle marking an outer boundary of the trademark monopoly that, although trademark rights may be acquired in a word or image with descriptive qualities, the acquisition of such rights will not prevent others from using the word or image in good faith in its descriptive sense, and not as a trademark. The principle is of great importance because it protects the right of society at large to use words or images in their primary descriptive sense, as against the claims of a trademark owner to exclusivity. This common-law principle is codified in the Lanham Act * * * 15 U.S.C. § 1115(b)(4).

The district court rejected Johnson's claim of fair use because it believed such a defense could be mounted only against a mark classed as "descriptive" in the four-tiered hierarchy of trademark law--generic, descriptive, suggestive, and arbitrary or fanciful. Although there is authority for that proposition, we believe that notion is misguided. It is true that the doctrine can apply only to marks consisting of terms or images with descriptive qualities. That is because only such terms or images are capable of being used by others in their primary descriptive sense. But it should make no difference whether the plaintiff's mark is to be classed on the descriptive tier of the trademark ladder (where protection is unavailable except on a showing of secondary meaning). What matters is whether the defendant is using the protected word or image descriptively, and not as a mark.

Whether the mark is classed as descriptive (and thus ineligible for protection without secondary meaning) depends on the relationship between the mark and the product described. Thus words like SWEET or CHEWY would be descriptive for a candy, but would be suggestive, or even arbitrary or fanciful, if used in connection with bed sheets, a computer, or an automobile. Regardless whether the protected mark is descriptive, suggestive, arbitrary, or fanciful as used in connection with the product or service covered by the mark, the public's right to use descriptive words or images in good faith in their ordinary descriptive sense must prevail over the exclusivity claims of the trademark owner. * * * If any confusion results to the detriment of the markholder, that was a risk entailed in the selection of a mark with descriptive attributes.

In short, fair use permits others to use a protected mark to describe aspects of their own goods, provided the use is in good faith and not as a mark. That is precisely the case here. Johnson's use of the pine-tree shape describes two aspects of its product. The pine tree refers to the pine scent of its air freshening agent. Furthermore, as a Christmas tree is traditionally a pine tree, the use of the pine-tree shape refers to the Christmas season, during which Johnson sells this item. Johnson's use of the pine-tree shape is clearly descriptive. There is no indication that Johnson uses its tree shape as a mark. Its pine-tree-shaped air fresheners come in boxes prominently bearing the "Glade Plug-Ins" trademark as well as Johnson's corporate logo. Each unit has "Glade" imprinted across the front of the product itself.

Car-Freshner contends that Johnson adopted the mark in bad faith and therefore cannot claim fair use. Car-Freshner bases its argument primarily on the fact that Johnson adopted its tree shape with knowledge of Car- Freshener's use of the tree shape and without consulting counsel. There is no merit to this argument. As Johnson was fully entitled to use a pine-tree shape descriptively notwithstanding Car-Freshener's use of a tree shape as a mark, the fact that it did so without consulting counsel has no tendency to show bad faith. * * *

We thus affirm the dismissal of Car-Freshner's complaint.

PAGE 292. Add after Note 2

2A. Article 1712 of the NAFTA agreement provides that "[e]ach party shall . . . refuse to register, or invalidate the registration of, a trademark containing or consisting of a geographical indication with respect to goods that do not originate in the indicated territory, region or locality, if use of the indication in the trademark for such goods is of such a nature as to mislead the public as to the geographical origin of the good." Marks that have been used continuously for 10 years or in good faith before the signature of the Agreement are exempt from the provision.

This provision required an amendment to § 1052 of the Lanham Act. Under the earlier version and under the common law a geographic term that misdescribed the origin of goods could be protected as a trademark if it acquired secondary meaning. Thus the mark "Mexico City Tacos" could be protected even though the tacos were made in Texas if consumers came to associate the mark with a common source. Under Article 1712 if some consumers are likely to believe that the mark suggests the tacos were made in Mexico, the mark would be invalid. Section 1052 was amended to provide that while geographically descriptive marks may be protected if distinctive, geographically *misdescriptive* marks may not be protected unless they had become distinctive prior to December 8, 1993.

Section 3 of the GATT TRIPS also addresses geographic designations in a similar fashion. However, Article 23 is a specific provision designed to protect geographical indications identifying wines and spirits. Article 23 requires a signatory to prevent use of a geographical indication for wines not originating in that location even if accompanied by the true origin. Thus if all burgundy wines are thought to come from a specific region in France, then the United States would be required to prevent California vintners from selling "California Burgundy". Again, an exception is provided for names used continuously for ten years or in good faith preceding the agreement.

PAGE 307. Substitute for Note 4

4. Whether color alone can be protected as a trademark has divided the courts. See, NutraSweet Co. v. Stadt Corp., 917 F.2d 1024 (7th Cir. 1990) (absolute bar to protecting color alone); In re Owens-Corning Fiberglas Corp., 774 F.2d 1116 (Fed. Cir. 1985) (registration of color pink for insulation approved); Master Distributors, Inc. v. Pako Corp., 986 F.2d 219 (8th Cir. 1993) (upheld protection for blue splicing tape known as "the blue tape." The issue was resolved in Qualitex Co. v. Jacobson Products Co., Inc., 115 S. Ct. 1300 (1995), where the Supreme Court in a unanimous opinion, protected the green-gold shade of Qualitex's press pads against use by a competitor of similarly colored pads and gave an encompassing interpretation to the Lanham Act's definition of a trademark:

> * * * Both the language of the Act and the basic underlying principles of trademark law would seem to include color within the universe of things that can qualify as a trademark. The language of the Lanham Act describes that universe in the broadest of terms. It says that trademarks "includ[e] any word, name, symbol, or device, or any combination thereof." § 1127. Since human beings might use as a "symbol" or "device" almost anything at all that is capable of carrying meaning, this language, read literally, is not restrictive. The courts and the Patent and Trademark Office have authorized for use as a mark a particular shape (of a Coca-Cola bottle), a particular sound (of NBC's three chimes), and even a particular scent (of plumeria blossoms on sewing thread). If a shape, a sound, and a fragrance can act as symbols why, one might ask, can a color not do the same?
>
> A color is also capable of satisfying the more important part of the statutory definition of a trademark, which requires that a person "us[e]" or "inten[d] to use" the mark "to identify and distinguish his or her goods, including a unique product, from those manufactured or sold by others and to indicate the source of the goods, even if that source is unknown." 15 U.S.C. § 1127. True, a product's color is unlike "fanciful," "arbitrary," or "suggestive" words or designs, which almost automatically tell a customer that they refer to a brand. But, over time, customers may come to treat a particular color on a product or its packaging (say, a color that in context seems unusual, such as

pink on a firm's insulating material or red on the head of a large industrial bolt) as signifying a brand. And, if so, that color would have come to identify and distinguish the goods -- i.e. "to "indicate" their "source" -- much in the way that descriptive words on a product (say, "Trim" on nail clippers or "Car-Freshner" on deodorizer) can come to indicate a product's origin. Again, one might ask, if trademark law permits a descriptive word with secondary meaning to act as a mark, why would it not permit a color, under similar circumstances, to do the same?

To the defendant's argument that courts would be unable to resolve disputes between different shades of the same color because of differences in lighting and consumer color perceptions, the Court responded: " We do not believe, however, that color, in this respect, is special. Courts traditionally decide quite difficult questions about whether two words or phrases or symbols are sufficiently similar, in context, to confuse buyers." And to the defendant's argument that colors were in limited supply and thus protection might give one competitor an unfair advantage, the Court observed:

> This argument is unpersuasive, however, largely because it relies on an occasional problem to justify a blanket prohibition. When a color serves as a mark, normally alternative colors will likely be available for similar use by others. Moreover, if that is not so -- if a "color depletion" or "color scarcity" problem does arise -- the trademark doctrine of "functionality" normally would seem available to prevent the anticompetitive consequences that Jacobson's argument posits, thereby minimizing that argument's practical force.

* * *

> The upshot is that, where a color serves a significant nontrademark function -- whether to distinguish a heart pill from a digestive medicine or to satisfy the "noble instinct for giving the right touch of beauty to common and necessary things," G.K. Chesterton, Simplicity and Tolstoy 61 (1912) -- courts will examine whether its use as a mark would permit one competitor (or a group) to interfere with legitimate (nontrademark-related) competition through actual or potential exclusive use of an important product ingredient. That examination should not discourage firms from creating aesthetically pleasing mark designs, for it is open to their competitors to do the same. But, ordinarily, it should prevent the anticompetitive consequences of Jacobson's hypothetical "color depletion" argument, when, and if, the circumstances of a particular case threaten "color depletion."

Under the Court's view of the Lanham Act, is there any limit to the subject matter capable of protection as a trademark? A reading of the Court's full opinion suggests that at least Justice Breyer, the opinion's author, found the argument against trademark protection for color somewhat incredulous: "It is the source-distinguishing ability of a mark -- not its ontological status as color, shape, fragrance, word, or sign -- that permits it to serve [the basic purposes of trademark law]." Would this same analysis apply to common law protection?

PAGE 312. Add after *Hartford House*

ROMM ART CREATIONS LTD. v. SIMCHA INTERNATIONAL, INC., 786 F.Supp. 1126 (E.D.N.Y. 1992). Romm Art obtained the exclusive right to distribute posters of the original art works of Itzchak Tarkay whose collection known as "Women and Cafes" had a distinctive style. The defendant, Asher Wainer ("Wainer") is president and sole owner of Simcha, which is the distributor of limited editions and posters of the art work of Patricia Govezensky -- the "Patricia" line which simulates the Tarkay style. Romm sued Wainer under § 43(a) of the Lanham Act for trade dress infringement. The court observed that "this suit falls within a rarely-tread area of the law, namely, the application of trade dress protection to works of art." However, the court applied traditional trade dress analysis finding that Tarkay had priority, that the style of the works had obtained secondary meaning, and that the Patricia works created a likelihood of confusion:

> Having examined the color patterns and shading of the Tarkay works, the placement of figures in each of the pictures examined, the physical attributes of his women, the depiction of women sitting and reclining, their characteristic clothing vis-a-vis those portrayed by Patricia, the Court concludes that there is "sufficient similarity between the products to scrutinize the evidence for proof of confusion." The test for determining similarity is whether the labels create the "same overall impression" when viewed separately. In light of the fact that the Tarkay and Patricia patterns are not dictated by function, and that a variety of patterns is possible, the similarity of the patterns is striking. When this striking similarity is factored into the likelihood of confusion analysis, in light of the strength of the Tarkay trade dress, consumer confusion is a likely result.

NOTES

1. Does this decision mean that all art works with an indentifiable style are protected by trademark law? If Patricia Govezensky's name had been prominently displayed on the defendant's prints, would the result have been different? If ordinary consumers could not tell the difference between some of the cubist works of George Braques and Pablo Picasso, would a court have to decide which artist had perfected the style first?

2. See Judge Newman's attempt to resolve these issues in Jeffrey Milstein, Inc. v. Greger, Lawlor, Roth, Inc. 58 F.3d 27 (2d Cir. 1995) where the plaintiff asserted

trade dress protection in greeting cards consisting of photographs die cut to the shape of the object in the photograph:

> Second, just as copyright law does not protect ideas but only their concrete expression, neither does trade dress law protect an idea, a concept, or a generalized type of appearance. See, e.g., Hartford House Ltd. v. Hallmark Cards, Inc. * * * . Examples of ideas or concepts too general to warrant protection are the "theme" of skeletons engaging in sexual activities, which plaintiff used in its t-shirt design, see Fashion Victim [v. Sunrise Turquoise, Inc., 785 F. Supp. 1302 (N.D. Ill. 1992)] and the "generalized concept" of grotesque figures in toys * * * . By contrast, the concrete expression of an idea in a trade dress has received protection. See, Hartford House * * * .
>
> Drawing the line between "ideas" or "concepts" on the one hand and "concrete expressions" on the other may sometimes present close questions. Often a helpful consideration will be the purpose of trade dress law: to protect an owner of a dress in informing the public of the source of its products, without permitting the owner to exclude competition from functionally similar products. * * * The level of generality at which a trade dress is described, as well as the fact that a similar trade dress is already being used by manufacturers of other kinds of products, may indicate that that dress is no more than a concept or idea to be applied to particular products.

3. How does copyright law relate to this decision? Could another author write a cold war spy thriller in the style of Tom Clancy without infringing Clancy's trademark? Can the *Romm* decision withstand a preemption analysis?

PAGE 313. Read in association with Note 3

TWO PESOS, INC. v. TACO CABANA, INC.
Supreme Court of the United States, 1992
112 S.Ct. 2753, rehearing denied, 113 S. Ct. 20

Justice WHITE delivered the opinion of the Court.

The issue in this case is whether the trade dress[1] of a restaurant may be protected under § 43(a) of the Trademark Act of 1946 (Lanham Act), 60 Stat. 441, 15 U.S.C. § 1125(a) (1982 ed.), based on a finding of inherent distinctiveness, without proof that the trade dress has secondary meaning.

I

Respondent Taco Cabana, Inc., operates a chain of fast-food restaurants in Texas. The restaurants serve Mexican food. The first Taco Cabana restaurant was opened in San Antonio in September 1978, and five more restaurants had been opened in San Antonio by 1985. Taco Cabana describes its Mexican trade dress as

> "a festive eating atmosphere having interior dining and patio areas decorated with artifacts, bright colors, paintings and murals. The patio includes interior and exterior areas with the interior patio capable of being sealed off from the outside patio by overhead garage doors. The stepped exterior of the building is a festive and vivid color scheme using top border paint and neon stripes. Bright awnings and umbrellas continue the theme." 932 F.2d 1113, 1117 (CA5 1991).

In December 1985, a Two Pesos, Inc., restaurant was opened in Houston. Two Pesos adopted a motif very similar to the foregoing description of Taco Cabana's trade dress. Two Pesos restaurants expanded rapidly in Houston and other markets, but did not enter San Antonio. In 1986, Taco Cabana entered the Houston and Austin markets and expanded into other Texas cities, including Dallas and El Paso where Two Pesos was also doing business.

In 1987, Taco Cabana sued Two Pesos in the United States District Court for the Southern District of Texas for trade dress infringement under § 43(a) of the Lanham Act, 15 U.S.C. § 1125(a) (1982 ed.), and for theft of trade secrets under Texas common law. The case was tried to a jury, which was instructed to return its

---

[1] The District Court instructed the jury: "'[T]rade dress' is the total image of the business. Taco Cabana's trade dress may include the shape and general appearance of the exterior of the restaurant, the identifying sign, the interior kitchen floor plan, the decor, the menu, the equipment used to serve food, the servers' uniforms and other features reflecting on the total image of the restaurant." 1 App. 83-84. The Court of Appeals accepted this definition and quoted from Blue Bell Bio- Medical v. Cin-Bad, Inc., 864 F.2d 1253, 1256 (CA5 1989): "The 'trade dress' of a product is essentially its total image and overall appearance." See 932 F.2d 1113, 1118 (CA5 1991). It "involves the total image of a product and may include features such as size, shape, color or color combinations, texture, graphics, or even particular sales techniques." John H. Harland Co. v. Clarke Checks, Inc., 711 F.2d 966, 980 (CA11 1983). Restatement (Third) of Unfair Competition § 16, Comment a (Tent.Draft No. 2, Mar. 23, 1990).

verdict in the form of answers to five questions propounded by the trial judge. The jury's answers were: Taco Cabana has a trade dress; taken as a whole, the trade dress is nonfunctional; the trade dress is inherently distinctive;[3] the trade dress has not acquired a secondary meaning[4] in the Texas market; and the alleged infringement creates a likelihood of confusion on the part of ordinary customers as to the source or association of the restaurant's goods or services. Because, as the jury was told, Taco Cabana's trade dress was protected if it either was inherently distinctive or had acquired a secondary meaning, judgment was entered awarding damages to Taco Cabana. In the course of calculating damages, the trial court held that Two Pesos had intentionally and deliberately infringed Taco Cabana's trade dress.[5]

The Court of Appeals ruled that the instructions adequately stated the applicable law and that the evidence supported the jury's findings. In particular, the Court of Appeals rejected petitioner's argument that a finding of no secondary meaning contradicted a finding of inherent distinctiveness.

In so holding, the court below followed precedent in the Fifth Circuit. In Chevron Chemical Co. v. Voluntary Purchasing Groups, Inc., 659 F.2d 695, 702 (CA5 1981), the court noted that trademark law requires a demonstration of secondary meaning only when the claimed trademark is not sufficiently distinctive of itself to identify the producer; the court held that the same principles should apply to protection of trade dresses. The Court of Appeals noted that this approach conflicts with decisions of other courts, particularly the holding of the Court of Appeals for the Second Circuit in Vibrant Sales, Inc. v. New Body Boutique, Inc., 652 F.2d 299 (1981), cert. denied, 455 U.S. 909 (1982), that § 43(a) protects unregistered trademarks or designs only where secondary meaning is shown. *Chevron, supra*, at 702. We granted certiorari to resolve the conflict among the Courts of Appeals on the question whether trade dress which is inherently distinctive is protectable under § 43(a)

---

[3] The instructions were that to be found inherently distinctive, the trade dress must not be descriptive.

[4] Secondary meaning is used generally to indicate that a mark or dress "has come through use to be uniquely associated with a specific source." Restatement (Third) of Unfair Competition § 13, Comment *e* (Tent.Draft No. 2, Mar. 23, 1990). "To establish secondary meaning, a manufacturer must show that, in the minds of the public, the primary significance of a product feature or term is to identify the source of the product rather than the product itself." Inwood Laboratories, Inc. v. Ives Laboratories, Inc., 456 U.S. 844, 851, n. 11 (1982).

[5] The Court of Appeals agreed: "The weight of the evidence persuades us, as it did Judge Singleton, that Two Pesos brazenly copied Taco Cabana's successful trade dress, and proceeded to expand in a manner that foreclosed several important markets within Taco Cabana's natural zone of expansion." 932 F.2d, at 1127, n. 20.

without a showing that it has acquired secondary meaning.[6] 502 U.S. ----, 112 S.Ct. 964 (1992). We find that it is, and we therefore affirm.

II

The Lanham Act[7] was intended to make "actionable the deceptive and misleading use of marks" and "to protect persons engaged in ... commerce against unfair competition." § 45, 15 U.S.C. § 1127. Section 43(a) "prohibits a broader range of practices than does § 32," which applies to registered marks, Inwood Laboratories, Inc. v. Ives Laboratories, Inc., 456 U.S. 844, 858 (1982), but it is common ground that § 43(a) protects qualifying unregistered trademarks and that the general principles qualifying a mark for registration under § 2 of the Lanham Act are for the most part applicable in determining whether an unregistered mark is entitled to protection under § 43(a). See, A.J. Canfield Co., v. Honickman, 808 F.2d 291, 299, n. 9 (CA3 1986); Thompson Medical Co. v. Pfizer Inc., 753 F.2d 208, 215-216 (CA2 1985).

A trademark is defined in 15 U.S.C. § 1127 as including "any word, name, symbol, or device or any combination thereof" used by any person "to identify and distinguish his or her goods, including a unique product, from those manufactured or sold by others and to indicate the source of the goods, even if that source is unknown." In order to be registered, a mark must be capable of distinguishing the applicant's goods from those of others. § 1052. Marks are often classified in categories of generally increasing distinctiveness; following the classic formulation set out by Judge Friendly, they may be (1) generic; (2) descriptive; (3) suggestive; (4) arbitrary; or (5) fanciful. The Court of Appeals followed this classification and petitioner accepts it. Brief for Petitioner 11-15. The latter three categories of marks, because their intrinsic nature serves to identify a particular source of a product, are deemed inherently distinctive and are entitled to protection. In contrast, generic marks--those that "refe[r] to the genus of which the particular product is a species," Park' N Fly, Inc. v. Dollar Park and Fly, Inc., 469 U.S. 189, 194 (1985), * * * are not registrable as trademarks.

Marks which are merely descriptive of a product are not inherently distinctive. When used to describe a product, they do not inherently identify a particular source,

---

[6] We limited our grant of certiorari to the above question on which there is a conflict. We did not grant certiorari on the second question presented by the petition, which challenged the Court of Appeals' acceptance of the jury's finding that Taco Cabana's trade dress was not functional.

[7] The Lanham Act, including the provisions at issue here, has been substantially amended since the present suit was brought. See Trademark Law Revision Act of 1988, 102 Stat. 3946, 15 U.S.C. § 1121.

and hence cannot be protected. However, descriptive marks may acquire the distinctiveness which will allow them to be protected under the Act. Section 2 of the Lanham Act provides that a descriptive mark that otherwise could not be registered under the Act may be registered if it "has become distinctive of the applicant's goods in commerce." §§ 2(e), (f), 15 U.S.C. §§ 1052(e), (f). This acquired distinctiveness is generally called "secondary meaning." The concept of secondary meaning has been applied to actions under § 43(a).

The general rule regarding distinctiveness is clear: an identifying mark is distinctive and capable of being protected if it either (1) is inherently distinctive or (2) has acquired distinctiveness through secondary meaning. Restatement (Third) of Unfair Competition, § 13, pp. 37-38, and Comment a (Tent. Draft No. 2, Mar. 23, 1990). It is also clear that eligibility for protection under § 43(a) depends on nonfunctionality. It is, of course, also undisputed that liability under § 43(a) requires proof of the likelihood of confusion.

The Court of Appeals determined that the District Court's instructions were consistent with the foregoing principles and that the evidence supported the jury's verdict. Both courts thus ruled that Taco Cabana's trade dress was not descriptive but rather inherently distinctive, and that it was not functional. None of these rulings is before us in this case, and for present purposes we assume, without deciding, that each of them is correct. In going on to affirm the judgment for respondent, the Court of Appeals, following its prior decision in *Chevron*, held that Taco Cabana's inherently distinctive trade dress was entitled to protection despite the lack of proof of secondary meaning. It is this issue that is before us for decision, and we agree with its resolution by the Court of Appeals. There is no persuasive reason to apply to trade dress a general requirement of secondary meaning which is at odds with the principles generally applicable to infringement suits under § 43(a).

Petitioner devotes much of its briefing to arguing issues that are not before us, and we address only its arguments relevant to whether proof of secondary meaning is essential to qualify an inherently distinctive trade dress for protection under § 43(a). Petitioner argues that the jury's finding that the trade dress has not acquired a secondary meaning shows conclusively that the trade dress is not inherently distinctive. Brief for Petitioner 9. The Court of Appeals' disposition of this issue was sound:

> "Two Pesos' argument--that the jury finding of inherent distinctiveness contradicts its finding of no secondary meaning in the Texas market--ignores the law in this circuit. While the necessarily imperfect (and often prohibitively difficult) methods for assessing secondary meaning address the empirical question of current consumer association, the legal recognition of an inherently distinctive trademark or trade dress acknowledges the owner's legitimate proprietary interest in its unique and valuable informational device, regardless of whether substantial

consumer association yet bestows the additional empirical protection of secondary meaning." 932 F.2d, at 1120, n. 7.

Although petitioner makes the above argument, it appears to concede elsewhere in its briefing that it is possible for a trade dress, even a restaurant trade dress, to be inherently distinctive and thus eligible for protection under § 43(a). Brief for Petitioner 10-11, 17-18; Reply Brief for Petitioner 10-14. Recognizing that a general requirement of secondary meaning imposes "an unfair prospect of theft [or] financial loss" on the developer of fanciful or arbitrary trade dress at the outset of its use, petitioner suggests that such trade dress should receive limited protection without proof of secondary meaning. Reply Brief for Petitioner 10. Petitioner argues that such protection should be only temporary and subject to defeasance when over time the dress has failed to acquire a secondary meaning. This approach is also vulnerable for the reasons given by the Court of Appeals. If temporary protection is available from the earliest use of the trade dress, it must be because it is neither functional nor descriptive but an inherently distinctive dress that is capable of identifying a particular source of the product. Such a trade dress, or mark, is not subject to copying by concerns that have an equal opportunity to choose their own inherently distinctive trade dress. To terminate protection for failure to gain secondary meaning over some unspecified time could not be based on the failure of the dress to retain its fanciful, arbitrary, or suggestive nature, but on the failure of the user of the dress to be successful enough in the marketplace. This is not a valid basis to find a dress or mark ineligible for protection. The user of such a trade dress should be able to maintain what competitive position it has and continue to seek wider identification among potential customers.

This brings us to the line of decisions by the Court of Appeals for the Second Circuit that would find protection for trade dress unavailable absent proof of secondary meaning, a position that petitioner concedes would have to be modified if the temporary protection that it suggests is to be recognized. * * * * The Second Circuit has nevertheless continued to deny protection for trade dress under § 43(a) absent proof of secondary meaning, despite the fact that § 43(a) provides no basis for distinguishing between trademark and trade dress.

The Fifth Circuit was quite right in *Chevron*, and in this case, to follow the *Abercrombie* classifications consistently and to inquire whether trade dress for which protection is claimed under § 43(a) is inherently distinctive. If it is, it is capable of identifying products or services as coming from a specific source and secondary meaning is not required. This is the rule generally applicable to trademark, and the protection of trademarks and trade dress under § 43(a) serves the same statutory purpose of preventing deception and unfair competition. There is no persuasive reason to apply different analysis to the two. * * * *

It would be a different matter if there were textual basis in § 43(a) for treating inherently distinctive verbal or symbolic trademarks differently from inherently distinctive trade dress. But there is none. The section does not mention trademarks or trade dress, whether they be called generic, descriptive, suggestive, arbitrary, fanciful, or functional. Nor does the concept of secondary meaning appear in the text of § 43(a). Where secondary meaning does appear in the statute, 15 U.S.C. § 1052 (1982 ed.), it is a requirement that applies only to merely descriptive marks and not to inherently distinctive ones. We see no basis for requiring secondary meaning for inherently distinctive trade dress protection under § 43(a) but not for other distinctive words, symbols, or devices capable of identifying a producer's product.

Engrafting onto § 43(a) a requirement of secondary meaning for inherently distinctive trade dress also would undermine the purposes of the Lanham Act. Protection of trade dress, no less than of trademarks, serves the Act's purpose to "secure to the owner of the mark the goodwill of his business and to protect the ability of consumers to distinguish among competing producers. National protection of trademarks is desirable, Congress concluded, because trademarks foster competition and the maintenance of quality by securing to the producer the benefits of good reputation." *Park' N Fly,* 469 U.S., at 198, 105 S.Ct., at 663, citing S.Rep. No. 1333, 79th Cong., 2d Sess., 3-5 (1946) (citations omitted). By making more difficult the identification of a producer with its product, a secondary meaning requirement for a nondescriptive trade dress would hinder improving or maintaining the producer's competitive position.

Suggestions that under the Fifth Circuit's law, the initial user of any shape or design would cut off competition from products of like design and shape are not persuasive. Only nonfunctional, distinctive trade dress is protected under § 43(a). The Fifth Circuit holds that a design is legally functional, and thus unprotectable, if it is one of a limited number of equally efficient options available to competitors and free competition would be unduly hindered by according the design trademark protection. See *Sicilia Di R. Biebow & Co. v. Cox,* 732 F.2d 417, 426 (CA5 1984). This serves to assure that competition will not be stifled by the exhaustion of a limited number of trade dresses.

On the other hand, adding a secondary meaning requirement could have anticompetitive effects, creating particular burdens on the start-up of small companies. It would present special difficulties for a business, such as respondent, that seeks to start a new product in a limited area and then expand into new markets. Denying protection for inherently distinctive nonfunctional trade dress until after secondary meaning has been established would allow a competitor, which has not adopted a distinctive trade dress of its own, to appropriate the originator's dress in other markets and to deter the originator from expanding into and competing in these areas.

As noted above, petitioner concedes that protecting an inherently distinctive trade dress from its inception may be critical to new entrants to the market and that withholding protection until secondary meaning has been established would be contrary to the goals of the Lanham Act. Petitioner specifically suggests, however, that the solution is to dispense with the requirement of secondary meaning for a reasonable, but brief period at the outset of the use of a trade dress. Reply Brief for Petitioner 11-12. If § 43(a) does not require secondary meaning at the outset of a business' adoption of trade dress, there is no basis in the statute to support the suggestion that such a requirement comes into being after some unspecified time.

III

We agree with the Court of Appeals that proof of secondary meaning is not required to prevail on a claim under § 43(a) of the Lanham Act where the trade dress at issue is inherently distinctive, and accordingly the judgment of that court is affirmed. It is so ordered.

Justice SCALIA, concurring.

I write separately to note my complete agreement with Justice THOMAS's explanation as to how the language of § 43(a) and its common-law derivation are broad enough to embrace inherently distinctive trade dress. Nevertheless, because I find that analysis to be complementary to (and not inconsistent with) the Court's opinion, I concur in the latter.

Justice STEVENS, concurring in the judgment.

As the Court notes in its opinion, the text of § 43(a) of the Lanham Act, 15 U.S.C. § 1125(a), "does not mention trademarks or trade dress." Nevertheless, the Court interprets this section as having created a federal cause of action for infringement of an unregistered trademark or trade dress and concludes that such a mark or dress should receive essentially the same protection as those that are registered. Although I agree with the Court's conclusion, I think it is important to recognize that the meaning of the text has been transformed by the federal courts over the past few decades. I agree with this transformation, even though it marks a departure from the original text, because it is consistent with the purposes of the statute and has recently been endorsed by Congress.

* * *

Justice THOMAS, concurring in the judgment.

Both the Court and Justice STEVENS decide today that the principles that qualify a mark for registration under § 2 of the Lanham Act apply as well to determining whether an unregistered mark is entitled to protection under § 43(a). The Court terms that view "common ground," though it fails to explain why that might be so, and Justice STEVENS decides that the view among the Courts of Appeals is textually insupportable, but worthy nonetheless of adherence. I see no need in answering the question presented either to move back and forth among the different sections of the Lanham Act or to adopt what may or may not be a misconstruction of the statute for reasons akin to stare decisis. I would rely, instead, on the language of § 43(a).

Section 43(a) made actionable (before being amended) "any false description or representation, including words or other symbols tending falsely to describe or represent," when "use[d] in connection with any goods or services." 15 U.S.C. § 1125(a) (1982 ed.). This language codified, among other things, the related common-law torts of technical trademark infringement and passing off, * * * which were causes of action for false descriptions or representations concerning a good's or service's source of production.

At common law, words or symbols that were arbitrary, fanciful, or suggestive (called "inherently distinctive" words or symbols, or "trademarks") were presumed to represent the source of a product, and the first user of a trademark could sue to protect it without having to show that the word or symbol represented the product's source in fact. That presumption did not attach to personal or geographic names or to words or symbols that only described a product (called "trade names"), and the user of a personal or geographic name or of a descriptive word or symbol could obtain relief only if he first showed that his trade name did in fact represent not just the product, but a producer (that the good or service had developed "secondary meaning"). Trade dress, which consists not of words or symbols, but of a product's packaging (or "image," more broadly), seems at common law to have been thought incapable ever of being inherently distinctive, perhaps on the theory that the number of ways to package a product is finite. Thus, a user of trade dress would always have had to show secondary meaning in order to obtain protection.

Over time, judges have come to conclude that packages or images may be as arbitrary, fanciful, or suggestive as words or symbols, their numbers limited only by the human imagination. A particular trade dress, then, is now considered as fully capable as a particular trademark of serving as a "representation or designation" of source under § 43(a). As a result, the first user of an arbitrary package, like the first user of an arbitrary word, should be entitled to the presumption that his package represents him without having to show that it does so in fact. This rule follows, in my view, from the language of § 43(a), and this rule applies under that section without regard to the rules that apply under the sections of the Lanham Act that deal with registration. Because the Court reaches the same conclusion for different reasons, I join its judgment.

NOTES

1. The original jury verdict against Two Pesos was for $3.7 million. After the Supreme Court's ruling, Taco Cabana filed a second suit seeking an additional $5 million. Subsequently Two Pesos signed a letter of intent to sell its 34 unit chain of restaurants to Taco Cabana. The Wall Street Journal, Pg. B8, Col. 1, January 14, 1993.

2. Does the *Two Pesos* decision improve the legal protection of trade dress? What factors will determine whether a trade dress is "inherently distinctive"? On your next visit to a supermarket, see if you can identify at least five products whose trade dress is inherently distinctive. If a client comes to you with an idea for a new trade dress, what will you look at to determine whether there is a risk of infringement?

PAGE 313. Read with *Two Pesos*, supra

KRUEGER INTERNATIONAL, INC. v. NIGHTINGALE INC.
915 F. Supp. 595
United States District Court, S.D. New York, 1996.

SOTOMAYOR, District Judge.

Plaintiff, a manufacturer of metal-frame stacking chairs, alleges that defendant, a competitor, has "slavishly copied" its chair design and thereby infringed its trade dress under s 43(a) of the Lanham Act, 15 U.S.C. s 1125(a). The plaintiff, Krueger International, Inc. ("KI"), moves for a preliminary injunction against the defendant, Nightingale Inc. ("NI"), on the grounds that the KI design is distinctive and that NI's design is confusingly similar. KI seeks to enjoin NI from advertising, manufacturing or selling copies of the KI chair. For the reasons discussed below, KI's motion is DENIED.

* * *

This case presents one of the most difficult analytical issues in all of trade dress law: how to determine whether a product design is "inherently distinctive." The issue is particularly pressing and unresolved in this circuit, whose rule for trade dress protection was upended three and a half years ago by the Supreme Court in Two Pesos, Inc. v. Taco Cabana, Inc., 505 U.S. 763, 112 S.Ct. 2753, 120 L.Ed.2d 615 (1992). Prior to Two Pesos, a plaintiff seeking trade dress protection in this circuit had to prove that the dress had acquired secondary meaning. *Two Pesos*, which unified the standard for trademark and trade dress law, held that protection for trade dress requires either inherent distinctiveness or secondary meaning, but not both.

* * *

The classic test for determining the distinctiveness of a trademark was outlined in Abercrombie & Fitch and the test has since been extended to trade dress as well. Under the *Abercrombie* test, marks are classified as either (1) generic, (2) descriptive, (3) suggestive, or (4) arbitrary or fanciful. Suggestive, arbitrary and fanciful marks and dresses are always considered inherently distinctive, in that their "intrinsic nature serves to identify a particular source of a product" or they are "capable of identifying a particular source of the product," whether or not the trade dress has acquired secondary meaning or a wide public association with the source. * * *

But as many courts have observed in varying degrees of frustration, the *Abercrombie* classifications do not translate easily to the trade dress context. The problem is not severe when the trade dress involves product packages and labels, which, like trademarks, at least have the advantage of using words and symbols independent of the product to convey information to consumers. The problem is often daunting, however, when it comes to product designs. Does the shape of a chair seat "suggest" a chair seat? Does it "describe" a chair seat? Or is it just a chair seat? No matter how beautifully designed, an industrial product is what it is. This conundrum recently led the Second Circuit in Knitwaves, Inc. v. Lollytogs Ltd., 71 F.3d 996 (2d Cir.1995), to abandon the Abercrombie test for product design and announce a new test. I believe, however, that this new test is not particularly helpful because it does not clearly address the standards in this area as set by the Supreme Court.

In *Knitwaves*, this circuit announced a departure from its earlier approach to trade dress law. *Knitwaves* involved the design of children's sweaters, particularly the use of "leaf" and "squirrel" designs placed on the sweaters. The court stated (1) that the Abercrombie classifications "make little sense when applied to product features" and were therefore "inapplicable" to product designs, and (2) that henceforth the new test for inherent distinctiveness is whether the manufacturer "used" or "intended to use" the design "to identify the source and distinguish his or her goods." In adopting this approach, the court cited approvingly to the Third Circuit decision in Duraco Prods., Inc. v. Joy Plastic Enterprises, Ltd., 40 F.3d 1431, 1440-41 (3d Cir.1994). The *Duraco* approach, however, leaves much to be desired. The Eighth Circuit instead has recently made a forceful and persuasive argument that the Supreme Court has not authorized us to abandon *Abercrombie*, no matter how much difficulty it causes. Stuart Hall Co. v. Ampad Corp., 51 F.3d 780, 788 (8th Cir.1995). As the Eighth Circuit reasoned, *Two Pesos* was clearly a case of product design and it expressly approved the application of the *Abercrombie* classifications to the design of a Mexican restaurant chain. Moreover, the entire thrust of *Two Pesos* was to unify the standards for trademark and trade dress, not to balkanize this complex field into yet more subcategories. I agree with the Eighth Circuit's conclusion that the Supreme Court envisions trade dress as a "single concept" with trademark law requiring a single test for inherent distinctiveness.

Further, I believe that *Knitwaves's* new test for inherent distinctiveness confuses the analytical requirements for inherent distinctiveness with those of secondary meaning. Inherent distinctiveness cannot hinge on how a producer intends to promote a design. If such were the case, the evidentiary requirements for inherent distinctiveness would be almost identical to those for secondary meaning, and there would be no point in having two categories. A producer could only prove "intent" by producing evidence of how he or she has advertised (or positioned) the product, and by producing consumer surveys showing how well the advertising worked. This is precisely the kind of evidence required for a showing of secondary meaning. * * *

Knitwaves, however, does provide some guidance for a workable approach to inherent distinctiveness, particularly when read in conjunction with efforts by other courts. The Fifth and Eighth Circuits offer particularly useful instruction. The Fifth Circuit's *Chevron* test, first developed for product packaging, states that "[i]f the features of the trade dress sought to be protected are arbitrary and serve no function either to describe the product or assist in its effective packaging," the dress is inherently distinctive. Chevron Chemical Co. v. Voluntary Purchasing Groups, Inc., 659 F.2d 695, 702 (5th Cir.1981) (packaging of lawn and garden products), cert. denied, 457 U.S. 1126, 102 S.Ct. 2947, 73 L.Ed.2d 1342 (1982). This is essentially a test of functionality. The Supreme Court explicitly approved the application of the *Chevron* test to product designs in its decision in *Two Pesos*.

The Eighth Circuit also emphasizes the issue of functionality, asking:

> whether, and how much, the trade dress is dictated by the nature of the product.... If the specific design of the trade dress is only tenuously connected with the nature of the product, then it is inherently distinctive.... If the design of the trade dress is dictated by the nature of the product, then secondary meaning must be proven.

A third test based on the *Abercrombie* classifications was developed 19 years ago by the Court of Customs and Patent Appeals:

> In determining whether a design is arbitrary or distinctive this court has looked to whether it was a 'common' basic shape or design, whether it was unique or unusual in a particular field, [or] whether it was a mere refinement of a commonly-adopted and well-known form of ornamentation for a particular class of goods view by the public as a dress or ornamentation for the goods.

Seabrook Foods, Inc. v. Bar-Well Foods Ltd., 568 F.2d 1342, 1344 (C.C.P.A.1977). The *Seabrook* test is the most useful of the three tests, in my view, because it clarifies the importance of market context. The Seabrook test asks "whether the design, shape or combination of elements is so unique, unusual or unexpected in this market that one can assume without proof that it will automatically be perceived by customers as an indici[um] of origin." * * * Any test of inherent distinctiveness must ask, "Inherently distinctive as compared to what?" The various tests of functionality, discussed in greater detail infra, serve much the same purpose; they ask whether a given design is functionally necessary in a given market (and therefore common) or whether it is more akin to a hood ornament. * * *

The *Seabrook* approach is fully consistent with the case law in the Second Circuit. Before *Two Pesos*, the question of market context generally arose in light of the so-called functionality defense. In the wake of *Two Pesos*, this circuit has continued to apply a Seabrook-type analysis to the puzzle of inherent distinctiveness. In *Knitwaves*, the court examined the clothing market and concluded that when people buy clothing, they do not tend to use overall design as an indicator of source. *Knitwaves* also quoted approvingly from the Restatement (Third) of Unfair Competition, which asks whether "because of the nature of the [design] and the context in which it is used, prospective purchasers are likely to perceive it" as a source-identifier. When considered in this light, *Knitwaves 's* emphasis on the producer's "intent" may be analogous to asking, "What is the custom in this industry?" Or: "How does this industry, including this claimant, use designs?"

Before applying these principles to the instant case, it is appropriate to address some common misconceptions about the interplay of patent law and trade dress law. The plaintiff in this case contends that because the Matrix chair has received a design patent, this patent constitutes proof of inherent distinctiveness. The defendant argues just the opposite: that KI is unlawfully seeking to extend its expired patent monopoly, and that patented designs can never claim the protection of trade dress law. Both arguments are incorrect. A design patent is analytically distinct from a protectable trade dress, and industrial products may qualify for both kinds of protection without violating the policy goals of either patent or trade dress law. * * * When a design patent expires, the design becomes copyable. It may not, however, be copied in such a way that customers are deceived about what they are buying.

The existence of a design patent, however, is relevant to the functionality defense. Because a design patent is granted only for non- functional designs, it can serve as evidence that a plaintiff's trade dress is not functional. This is not tantamount to saying, however, that a design patent always serves as a trademark. At best, a design patent can only help rebut the functionality defense; it cannot do the whole job of proving inherent distinctiveness. The plaintiff still needs to show that, in its market at the time of the alleged infringement, the design is both ornamental and deserving of trade dress protection.

The problem [of functionality], of course, is that a design feature may be both functional and pleasing. (Indeed, many industrial designs combine these two elements.) This has led the courts into a hopeless tangle about the difference between aesthetics and functionality. Some courts developed a doctrine of "aesthetic functionality" that was both unnecessary and illogical. If a pleasing design helped to sell a product, so the theory went, its aesthetic appeal became an "essential" competitive quality that could not in fairness be denied to others. Thus the doctrine of "aesthetic functionality" denied trade dress protection to design features whose only sin was to delight the senses. * * *

* * * *Knitwaves* seems to instruct that a design can serve only one primary purpose: either aesthetic or source-identifying, but not both. This approach is neither helpful nor logical. In the instant case, it would force me to determine whether the plaintiff chose its chair design because it was attractive or because it was meant to serve as a trademark (i.e., a source identifier). The likely answer is, both. Moreover, this plaintiff never had to choose between the two objectives because the design was patented and could not be copied. In more general terms, every producer hopes to create a design that is more pleasing than not and that that design will be associated with it. Every producer hopes that it and its trade dress will be remembered because its design is pleasing, not because it is ugly. * * *

Applying these principles to the facts before me, I conclude that plaintiff KI has a protectable trade dress in the overall look of its Matrix chair. Although each of the individual design elements serves both functional and aesthetic purposes, it is the overall look that I must consider. I base my following conclusions on the photographs of competing chairs submitted by the parties and the accompanying affidavits describing the high density stacking chair market. On this evidence, I find that the seat, the back and the Z- shaped connecting rods of the KI chair give the Matrix chair a distinctive overall look. Applying *Seabrook*, I find that this particular look is unique among high density stacking chairs and that manufacturers of these chairs generally seek unique designs as an important source identifier. Unlike the clothing industry, in which labels are prominent because designs change frequently, the chair industry does not rely heavily on labels to communicate with customers and its designs remain stable over time. Although the chair manufacturers' names appear prominently on shipping containers and hang tags, customers generally throw these away. The sole permanent label is molded into the plastic underneath the seat, where a sophisticated buyer would find it but a less sophisticated one might not. No consumer would see the label without looking for it.

* * *

To determine whether the design features at issue are functional, I must ask whether their shape is "dictated by the functions to be performed." The answer is clearly no. The function of a chair is to provide a place to sit. A stacking chair, in addition, must stack. On the evidence before me, many other designs serve these functions equally well. Therefore I find that the design features at issue are ornamental, not functional. Next I must address whether there are sufficient alternative arrangements to permit competition. I find that defendant has not met its burden of showing that the supply of alternative designs would be unduly limited if defendant could not replicate the Matrix chair.

NOTES

1. Shortly after the decision in *Two Pesos*, the Second Circuit confronted the test for inherent distinctiveness in The Paddington Corp. v. Attiki Importers &

Distributors, 996 F.2d 577 (2d Cir. 1993) which involved a contest between the appearance of two competing bottles of Ouzo, a Greek alcoholic beverage. The court held the *Abercrombie* classifications applicable to trade dress and found that a custom of an industry to package products in a particular way would make that packaging generic. As an example of a descriptive trade dress the court suggested an illustration of a shining car on a bottle of car wax. In *Knitwaves* referred to in the principal case, the Second Circuit held that *Paddington* was not applicable to trade dress consisting of product features as oppose to product packaging:

> Not only does the classification of marks into "generic," "descriptive," "suggestive," or "arbitrary or fanciful" make little sense when applied to product features, but it would have the unwelcome, and likely unintended, result of treating a class of product features as "inherently distinctive," and thus eligible for trade dress protection, even though they were never intended to serve a source-identifying function.

* * *

> As Knitwaves' objective in the two sweater designs was primarily aesthetic, the designs were not primarily intended as source identification. Those sweater designs therefore fail to qualify for protection of trade dress inherent in product design. Accordingly, the judgment in favor of Knitwaves on the Lanham Act claim is reversed.

Do you agree with Judge Sotomayor that the intention of the user is not an appropriate standard for inherent distinctiveness? Is it a precondition to a determination of distinctiveness. If a party does not use the mark as a trademark, can it become distinctive?

2. The Restatement (Third) of Unfair Competition § 16, Comment *b* (1995) acknowledges that "unique and prominent" trade dress may be inherently distinctive. However, the Restatement goes on to provide:

> As a practical matter, however, it is less common for consumers to recognize the design of a product or product feature as an indication of source. Product features are more likely to be seen merely as utilitarian or ornamental aspects of the goods. In addition, the competitive interest in copying product designs is more substantial than in the case of packaging, containers, labels, and related subject matter. Product designs are therefore not ordinarily considered inherently distinctive and are thus normally protected only upon proof of secondary meaning.

Arguably, the Supreme Court in *Two Pesos* did not address whether product designs should be considered differently from packaging and other forms of trade dress. In Duraco Products, Inc. v. Joy Plastic Enterprises, LTD., 40 F.3d 1431 (3rd Cir. 1994), cited in *Krueger* the focus was on Duraco's "Grecian Classics" plastic planters. The planters, although made of plastic, were constructed with a combination of features that created the illusion of marble, cement or stone construction. The defendant, Joy Plastic, produced a competing and similar planter. Claiming the design and "overall image" of the planter to be inherently distinctive trade dress, Duraco sued. The district court applying traditional trademark law, denied protection on the grounds that the trade dress was at best "descriptive", was without secondary meaning, and was functional.

Judge Becker affirmed but took a separate path. He found that the generic-descriptive-suggestive-arbitrary-fanciful classification applicable to trademarks was inappropriate in product configuration cases and suggested a new approach:

> Synthesizing the principles explored in the preceding sections, we think that there is a proper set of circumstances for treating a product configuration as inherently distinctive. These circumstances are characterized by a high probability that a product configuration serves a virtually exclusively identifying function for consumers -- where the concerns over "theft" of an identifying feature or combination or arrangement of features and the cost to an enterprise of gaining and proving secondary meaning outweigh concerns over inhibiting competition, and where consumers are especially likely to perceive a connection between the product's configuration and its source. In particular, we think that, to be inherently distinctive, a product configuration -- comprising a product feature or some particular combination or arrangement of product features -- for which Lanham Act protection is sought must be (i) unusual and memorable; (ii) conceptually separable from the product; and (iii) likely to serve primarily as a designator of origin of the product.

Does this formulation of inherent distinctiveness provide a better test than descriptiveness or is it the same thing? Can't a configuration describe a product? What about the horseshoe shape of a horseshoe? Isn't it descriptive if when seeing the particular shape and asked "what's that" most consumers would respond with the name of the product? And if not, isn't it probably unusual? Isn't this the same inquiry as whether the design is conceptually separate from the product?

3. Judge Becker took another swipe at product configuration protection in Versa Products Company, Inc. v. Bifold Co. (Manufacturing) Ltd., 50 F.3d 189 (3rd Cir. 1995). Here the controversy involved the configuration of a valve used in offshore oil drilling. Versa's B-316 valve dominated the market for some time before Bifold began competing with its Domino Junior valve. The district court found that the

two valves were "virtually identical in external design and visual appearance" and that Versa had shown its valve to be nonfunctional and distinctive. The district court, in assessing likelihood of confusion, applied a lower standard of "possibility of confusion" applicable when a second user intentionally infringes a long-established trade dress. The Third Circuit reversed, imposing a more stringent standard for proof of likelihood of confusion:

> In a product configuration trade dress infringement case, by contrast, consumers do not have to rely on a potentially distinctive configuration to identify the source of the product; rather, they can generally look to the packaging, trademarks, and advertising used to market the product, which are typically much less ambiguous. Consumers therefore have less need, and so are much less likely, to rely on a product configuration as an indicator of the product's source. Accordingly, they are less likely to be confused as to the sources of two products with substantially similar configurations. Thus, in trade dress infringement suits where the dress inheres in a product configuration, the primary factors to be considered in assessing likelihood of confusion are the product's labeling, packaging, and advertisements.

PAGE 313. Read in association with Note 5

VORNADO AIR CIRCULATION SYSTEMS, INC. v. DURACRAFT CORPORATION
United States Court of Appeals for the Tenth Circuit, 1995
58 F.3d 1498, cert. denied 116 S.Ct. 753 (1996)

STEPHEN H. ANDERSON, Circuit Judge.

This case presents an issue of first impression in our circuit concerning the intersection of the Patent Act and the Lanham Trade-Mark Act. We must decide whether a product configuration is entitled to trade dress protection when it is or has been a significant inventive component of an invention covered by a utility patent.

After expiration of any patents or copyrights on an invention, that invention normally passes into the public domain and can be freely copied by anyone. The district court found, however, that because the spiral structure of the household fan grill in question is "nonfunctional," a status largely determined by the availability of enough alternative grill designs so that other fan manufacturers can effectively compete without it, the grill can serve as trade dress. The court held that the grill could be protected under Lanham Act section 43(a) against copying by competitors, because that copying was likely to confuse consumers.

The court's injunction effectively prevents defendant Duracraft Corp. from ever practicing the full invention embodied in the patented fans of plaintiff Vornado Air Circulation Systems, Inc., after Vornado's utility patents expire. For the reasons discussed below, we find this result to be untenable. We hold that although a product configuration must be nonfunctional in order to be protected as trade dress under section 43(a), not every nonfunctional configuration is eligible for that protection. Where a product configuration is a significant inventive component of an invention covered by a utility patent, so that without it the invention cannot fairly be said to be the same invention, patent policy dictates that it enter into the public domain when the utility patents on the fans expire. To ensure that result, it cannot receive trade dress protection under section 43(a). The district court's order is reversed.

The product configurations at issue in this case are two household fan grills with spiral--or arcuate--vanes, produced by the plaintiff, Vornado, and the defendant, Duracraft.

The idea of using a spiral grill on a fan is not new. * * * Vornado began selling its fans with spiral grills in November 1988, at a time when it was the only fan company using that type of grill. On January 9, 1989, Vornado's founders, Donald J. Moore and Michael C. Coup, applied for a utility patent on their ducted fan with a spiral grill. They asserted, among other things, that their spiral grill produced an optimum air flow, although their own tests had shown that it performed about the same as the more common straight radial grill, and later tests suggested that some other grills worked better in some respects.

Their patent application claimed a fan with multiple features, including the spiral grill. The inventive aspect of Vornado's spiral grill was that the point of maximum lateral spacing between the curved vanes was moved inboard from the grill's outer radius, so that it was at the impeller blade's point of maximum power. Vornado emphasizes that its fan grill was not patentable by itself because a spiral grill per se was already in the public domain as "prior art," a patent law term for what was already known from previous patents or other sources.

On May 22, 1990, Messrs. Moore and Coup were issued a utility patent. They subsequently applied for and on February 22, 1994, were granted a reissue patent expanding their claims, including those that involved the arcuate-shaped grill vane structure.

Vornado advertised its grill as the "Patented AirTensity TM Grill," although the company had no separate patent on the grill. Between January 1989 and August 1990, Vornado sold about 135,000 fans. In its advertising, the company touted the grill as a "true achievement in aerodynamic efficiency," "the result of determinant ergonomic design," with "[u]nique AirTensity TM vortex action," accomplishing "a high degree of safety and functionality."

In August 1990, Duracraft began offering an inexpensive electric household fan called the Model DT-7 "Turbo Fan." The grill on Duracraft's Turbo Fan incorporated a spiral vane structure that was copied from Vornado's considerably more expensive fan models but was purposely designed not to infringe Vornado's patent. Apart from its look-alike grill and some aspects of the fan blade design, the Turbo Fan differed significantly from Vornado's fans in its overall configuration, its base and duct structure, its center knob, neon colors, packaging, labeling, and price. The box in which the Turbo Fan came had a circle cut out of the front so that the grill design showed through and was emphasized when the fan was displayed in its box.

By November 1992, Duracraft had sold nearly one million Turbo Fans in the United States. The Turbo Fan was the company's second-largest-selling household fan product.

Vornado sued, alleging that Duracraft had intentionally copied Vornado's grill design, but both sides agreed that the Turbo Fan did not infringe Vornado's patents. Vornado argued during the bench trial that the curved vanes in the "Patented AirTensity Grill" were legally nonfunctional, which they had to be in order to be protected as trade dress under section 43(a).

The district court found that the spiral grill was functional in a lay sense but not in a legal sense, based on our definition of trade dress functionality in terms of the competitive need to use a feature. The district court found that Vornado's grill did in fact perform a unique function in the way that it shaped the flow of air coming from the fan, but the difference in air flow produced by it as compared with other grill designs was not great enough for a customer to perceive, so it made no competitive difference. The court also noted that other feasible grill structures could easily do as well on other relevant performance tests, and the spiral grill was not shown to be cheaper to manufacture.

The district court did not find enough evidence to support a finding of aesthetic functionality, a type of functionality based on decorativeness or attractiveness, which we have previously recognized. Nor did the district court find that Duracraft would suffer a marketing disadvantage if it could not use the spiral grill. The court found that the grill's value lay not in its operational attributes but primarily in its appearance, which the court said suggests something about the fan's performance and creatively suggests Vornado's identity.

The court found that the grill design was nonfunctional and held that trade dress protection of nonfunctional product configurations under the Lanham Act was not incompatible with patent law. The court further found that the grill design was a suggestive symbol combined with a device, and thus inherently distinctive, so that no showing of secondary meaning was required. The court found that consumers were likely to be confused by Duracraft's use of a similar grill, and granted Vornado an injunction but no damages on the section 43(a) claim.

* * *

* * * Duracraft argues that *Bonito Boats* means that useful product features, which comprise utility patent subject matter, may not be protected as trademarks or trade dress and thereby be permanently monopolized by a single producer.

Vornado replies that there is no problem or inconsistency in its ability to obtain both patent protection for its fan in toto and trade dress protection for its spiral grill. Vornado argues 1) that of the main Supreme Court cases on which Duracraft relies, *Sears, Compco,* and *Bonito Boats* are all distinguishable, and *Kellogg* predates the Lanham Act; 2) that the Supreme Court and Congress both have said section 43(a) applies to product shapes; and 3) that the functionality doctrine properly reconciles the Patent Act with the Lanham Act, for if a product feature is not necessary to competition, no patent law purpose is served by allowing it to be copied.

We find each of these arguments wanting. At the same time, we need not rule as broadly as Duracraft would have us do either. We need not deal with whether every useful or potentially patentable product configuration is excluded from trade dress protection. Vornado does not argue that its grill was not a significant inventive component of its patented fans. Without that particular grill, the Vornado fan would not be the same invention that it is. We focus, therefore, on the law with regard to product configurations that are patented inventions or significant components thereof, and whether these product configurations can serve as trade dress.

[The court discussed the major Supreme Court preemption cases but held that notwithstanding some distinctions "we find it impossible to ignore the clear and continuing trend they collectively manifest in favor of the public's right to copy." The court also found nothing in the legislative history of § 43(a) or the patent act to help resolve the issue.]

Despite what appears to be a widespread perception that product configurations covered by utility patents are automatically functional for Lanham Act purposes, the district court in our case ably demonstrated that this is not so. Configurations can simultaneously be patentably useful, novel, and nonobvious and also nonfunctional, in trade dress parlance.

This is the case because to meet patent law's usefulness requirement, a product need not be better than other alternatives or essential to competition. To obtain a utility patent, an inventor need only show that an invention is 1) useful in the sense of serving some identified, beneficial purpose, and then-- much more difficult to prove--that it is 2) novel, i.e., not previously known, and 3) nonobvious, or sufficiently inventive, in light of prior art.

Functionality, by contrast, has been defined both by our circuit, and more recently by the Supreme Court, in terms of competitive need. If competitors need to be able to use a particular configuration in order to make an equally competitive product, it is functional, but if they do not, it may be nonfunctional. The availability of equally satisfactory alternatives for a particular feature, and not its inherent usefulness, is often the fulcrum on which Lanham Act functionality analysis turns.

As some courts have explained the competitive need test, it conceivably could allow one producer to permanently appropriate any distinctive patented invention for exclusive trademark or trade dress use as soon as its patent expired and sufficient alternatives became available to make the invention no longer one of a few superior designs.

Given that the functionality doctrine does not eliminate overlap between the Patent Act and the Lanham Act, we must decide whether Vornado is right that this doctrine nevertheless should be used to limit patent law's public domain.

Except to the extent that Congress has clearly indicated which of two statutes it wishes to prevail in the event of a conflict, we must interpret and apply them in a way that preserves the purposes of both and fosters harmony between them. Where, as here, both cannot apply, we look to their fundamental purposes to choose which one must give way.

Purposes of the Patent Act First, patent law seeks to foster and reward invention; second, it promotes disclosure of inventions to stimulate further innovation and to permit the public to practice the invention once the patent expires; third, the stringent requirements for patent protection seek to assure that ideas in the public domain remain there for the free use of the public.

* * *

In this respect, it is significant that the framers of the patent system did not require an inventor to demonstrate an invention's superiority to existing products in order to qualify for a patent. That they did not do so tells us that the patent system seeks not only superior inventions but also a multiplicity of inventions. A variety of choices is more likely to satisfy the desires of a greater number of consumers than is a single set of products deemed "optimal" in some average sense by patent examiners and/or judges. And the ability to intermingle and extrapolate from many inventors' solutions to the same problem is more likely to lead to further technological advances than is a single, linear approach seeking to advance one "superior" line of research and development. We conclude that patent law seeks the invention and the passing into the public domain of even what trade dress law would consider nonfunctional inventions.

Allowing an inventor both patent and trade dress protection in a configuration would not necessarily inhibit invention directly. Quite the opposite, this double benefit would probably increase an inventor's direct incentives to pursue an idea. But the inventor's supply of ideas itself and freedom to experiment with them might diminish if the inventor had to do a competitive market analysis before adopting useful features from others' inventions once their patents expired.

As to the second patent law objective, encouraging public disclosure of inventions, it is not immediately apparent what effect, if any, the trade dress protection in question would have. But this case clearly shows that trade dress protection can directly interfere with the public's ability to practice patented inventions after the patents have expired, and that it undermines the principle that ideas in the public domain should stay there. We conclude that the inability freely to copy significant features of patented products after the patents expire impinges seriously upon the patent system's core goals, even when those features are not necessary to competition.

* * *

The degree to which a producer's goodwill will be harmed by the copying of product configurations correlates with the degree of consumer confusion as to source or sponsorship that is likely to result from the copying. We do not doubt that at least some consumers are likely to ignore product labels, names, and packaging and look only to the design of product features to tell one brand from another. These consumers are likely to be confused by similar product designs, and to the degree that this confusion is tolerated, the goals of the Lanham Act will be undermined.

But the Lanham Act, like common-law unfair competition law and most state unfair competition statutes, has never provided absolute protection against all consumer confusion as to source or sponsorship.

* * *

We recognize also that consumer confusion resulting from the copying of product features is, in some measure, a self-fulfilling prophecy. To the degree that useful product configurations are protected as identifiers, consumers will come to rely on them for that purpose, but if copying is allowed, they will depend less on product shapes and more on labels and packaging.

We conclude that protecting against that degree of consumer confusion that may arise from the copying of configurations that are significant parts of patented inventions is, at best, a peripheral concern of section 43(a) of the Lanham Act.

Given, then, that core patent principles will be significantly undermined if we do not allow the copying in question, and peripheral Lanham Act protections will be denied if we do, our answer seems clear. Much has been said in this and other section 43(a) cases about whether a second competitor needs to use a particular product design to compete effectively. But where Lanham Act goals are not the only ones at stake, we must also examine the degree to which a first competitor needs to use a useful product feature instead of something else--a name, a label, a package--to establish its brand identity in the first place.

It would defy logic to assume that there are not almost always many more ways to identify a product than there are ways to make it.

We hold that where a disputed product configuration is part of a claim in a utility patent, and the configuration is a described, significant inventive aspect of the invention, so that without it the invention could not fairly be said to be the same invention, patent law prevents its protection as trade dress, even if the configuration is nonfunctional.

In future cases, the contribution of a particular configuration to the inventiveness of a patented product may not always be clear, and we do not wish to rule out the possibility that a court may appropriately conduct a factual inquiry to supplement its reading of the patent's claims and descriptions.

But in this case, we do not find it necessary to remand for such an inquiry. Vornado included the arcuate grill vane structure as an element of its patent claims and described the configuration as providing "an optimum air flow." Then, after the first patent issued and Vornado subsequently found evidence that other grill structures worked as well as or better than the spiral grill, Vornado did not repudiate or disclaim in any way the grill element of its patent. Instead, Vornado sought and received a reissue patent that expanded its claims with respect to the grill.

Even if we discount entirely Vornado's extensive advertising campaign emphasizing the importance of the "AirTensity Grill," this patent history on its face obviates any need for a remand on the question of inventive significance. We simply take Vornado at its word. Because the "Patented AirTensity Grill" is a significant inventive element of Vornado's patented fans, it cannot be protected as trade dress.

The district court's order is REVERSED.

NOTES

1. In Kohler Co. v. Moen Inc., 12 F.3d 632 (7th Cir. 1993) the Seventh Circuit considered whether in general trade dress protection for product configurations conflicted with the patent system and concluded it did not. Judge Cudahy dissented arguing that the Lanham Act federalized common law and thus was subject to the preemption arguments of *Sears, Compco,* and *Bonito Boats* and that the existence of both design and utility patent systems prevented common law (or Lanham Act) protection for product design.

Vornado was analyzed by the Seventh Circuit in Thomas & Betts Corp. v. Panduit Corp., 65 F.3d 654 (7th Cir. 1995) where Panduit claimed that any trade dress disclosed in an expired patent was ineligible for trade dress protection. The court did not have to decide whether to follow *Vornado* but nonetheless commented:

> Whether or not a feature [of a trade dress is claimed in a patent] is not necessarily, however, a good indicator of its relative importance to the invention as a whole. Additional elements in a claim narrow the scope of the patentee's monopoly since an infringing invention must contain each element of a claim or its equivalent. Therefore, a patent applicant seeks to draw his claims as broadly as possible with as few specific elements as he can get away with. The fact that Vornado included the spiral grill as an element of a claim likely means that it could not have received a patent on the rest of the invention without including the spiral grill limitation--not that the spiral grill itself was a "significant inventive aspect." This is particularly true in Vornado where the spiral grill itself was not independently claimed (that is why Duracraft's fan did not infringe the still valid patent) because it was disclosed in the prior art.
>
> Likewise, the fact that the Schwester patent includes the cable tie head as a required element without claiming a particular shape means that T & B was able to obtain a broader monopoly, i.e., they were able to exclude competitors from making metal barbed cable ties with any head shape. There is no reason, therefore, to infer from its absence as an element in a claim that the shape of the head is any less important to the two-piece cable tie than the spiral grill is to Vornado's fan. All one can infer is that because it was not separately claimed, the shape of the head, like the spiral grill, was not independently patentable.

2. The interaction of trade dress protection with the patent system was also considered, in part, in Elmer & HTH, Inc. v. ICC Fabricating, Inc., 67 F.3d 1571 (Fed. Cir. 1995). HTH claimed that ICC had copied its aerodynamic sign intended for use on automobiles. HTH had obtained both a utility and a design patent on the sign and sued for patent infringement and trade dress infringement. The court upheld the utility patent. The court noted that a design patent applied only to ornamental and not functional features. Focusing on the ornamental features, the court found that the two designs were not substantially similar and thus there was no infringement. On the trade dress claim, the court found that the design elements were functional and thus not protectable. The court observed the following relationship between trade dress and the utility patent law:

> Moreover, patent law, not trade dress law, is the principal means for providing exclusive rights in useful product features. As the

Court recognized in *Qualitex,* extending trademark/trade dress law to protect functional features might create perpetual, patent-like rights in unpatented or unpatentable items. Indeed, the district court's broad, functionally-defined injunction in this case has exactly that effect: it prevents ICC, indefinitely, from using any rigid, two-sided aerodynamic sign with a clear plastic window mount, the two sides extending vertically and parallel to the direction of vehicle travel. The injunction, in effect, broadens claim 1 of the '994 patent by protecting products lacking some of the limitations of the claim. HTH cannot, however, bypass the statutory requirements of the patent laws and obtain broadened patent protection under the guise of trade dress law.

Furthermore, once the '994 patent expires, the public will be entitled to practice the invention claimed in the patent. Enforcing a "trade dress" right defined, as it was here, to be essentially coextensive with, and in fact broader than, claim 1 of the '994 patent would frustrate that right because trade dress protection may last indefinitely and thus competitors could not effectively "copy and use" the invention after the patent expires. If the asserted trade dress had been narrowly defined to cover only one of the many product configurations within the scope of the claim, one might have a different case. In such case, upon expiration of the '994 patent competitors would be free to practice the '994 invention; they could sell "aerodynamic" vehicle-mounted signs. They simply could not choose a product configuration that would be confusingly similar to the trade dress of HTH's product. Here, however, the "trade dress" was broadly defined to be essentially coextensive with, and in fact broader than, the patent claim, and enforcing such a trade dress would effectively extend the life of the patent.

How do you think the court should evaluate the interaction between trade dress protection and the design patent law? The test for "substantial similarity" for purposes of design patent infringement is whether the patented and the infringing designs resemble each other enough to cause the ordinary observer to be deceived into purchasing "one supposing it to be the other." If this duplicates the likelihood of confusion test, should any trade dress protection be permitted?

3. Application of the New York dilution statute to the bottle design used for the sale of perfume was held preempted in Escada AG v. The Limited, Inc., 810 F. Supp. 571 (S.D.N.Y. 1993):

The Court [in *Bonito Boats],* however, did not prohibit all regulation of potentially patentable designs: it is permissible for states to require that goods be labeled, or that other precautionary steps, not directed to the copying or reproduction itself, be taken to prevent consumers from being misled as to the source of a product. Thus, a state may, without conflicting with patent law, protect trade secrets, and forbid industrial espionage. * * * In regulating unfair competition a state may also give limited protection to a particular design to prevent consumer confusion. However, one cannot argue that the New York dilution statute serves that purpose in this case, for the statute does not require any showing of consumer confusion as to the source of goods or services. Under the statute, plaintiffs attempt to enjoin defendants from making, using or selling bottle designs which allegedly mimic the Escada bottle design. Such an application of the dilution statute is not limited to a specific goal outside the contemplation of the federal patent scheme.

Were the statute to be so applied, a would-be inventor in New York would not have to meet the rigorous standards for obtaining a patent and his right to exclude copiers would not be confined to a design patent's 14 year limit. 35 U.S.C. §§ 171, 173. When the subject matter is potentially patentable the state interest in protecting the manufacturer from dilution must yield to the national interest in uniform patent law.

4. In Campbell v. Osmond, 917 F. Supp. 1574 (M.D.Fla. 1996) it was held that a Lanham Act claim for trade dress infringement was not preempted or subsumed by a copyright infringement claim. The case involved the appearance of collectable doll head sculptures and the copyright issue was whether the defendant's sculptures were "substantially similar" to the plaintiff's. Defendant argued that if the competing sculptures were not substantially similar, there could be no likelihood of confusion on the trade dress claim, and if they were substantially similar, the trade dress claim was subsumed under the copyright claim.

PAGE 320. Read in association with Note 3

LAUREYSSENS v. IDEA GROUP, INC.
United States Court of Appeals, Second Circuit, 1992
964 F.2d 131

OAKES, Chief Judge:

[Laureyssens sells puzzles under the name HAPPY CUBE which comes flat and can be assembled into a cube. They are marketed in their flat form in a clear plastic shrink-wrap with a cardboard insert. Idea Group began selling a similar competing puzzle in its flat form in a clear shrink-wrap with a cardboard insert. The parties' packaging were somewhat different in color and style. Laureyssens brought this claim, in part, for trade dress infringement.]

The district court found that there was no serious question whether *actual* secondary meaning exists in the HAPPY CUBE trade dress. We think this conclusion is sound given the weak sales of the HAPPY CUBE puzzles, low expenditures for advertising and promotion, minimal unsolicited media coverage, and the brief period of exclusive use of the HAPPY CUBE trade dress. And, while there was evidence of intentional imitation as to the puzzles themselves, there was no evidence of copying of the trade dress.

The district court concluded, however, that Laureyssens satisfied the requirement of secondary meaning by raising a serious question whether the flat-form, shrink-wrapped HAPPY CUBE trade dress should be protected under the doctrine of secondary meaning *in the making*.

In Metro Kane Imports, Ltd. v. Federated Dept. Stores, Inc., 625 F.Supp. 313, 316 (S.D.N.Y.1985), aff'd, 800 F.2d 1128 (2d Cir.1986), Judge Sweet explained that a trade dress will be "protected against intentional, deliberate attempts to capitalize on a distinctive product" where "secondary meaning is 'in the making' but not yet fully developed." See also Jolly Good Industries, Inc. v. Elegra, Inc., 690 F.Supp. 227, 230-31 (S.D.N.Y.1988) (indicating that the theory has been "well-received by commentators" and citing as an example, 3 R. Callman, The Law of Unfair Competition, Trademarks and Monopolies § 77.3, at 356 (3d ed.1971)).[5] The supposed doctrine seeks to prevent pirates from intentionally siphoning off another's nascent consumer recognition and goodwill.

* * *

We are, then, squarely presented for the first time with the question whether the doctrine of secondary meaning in the making should be recognized under the Lanham Act.

We begin our analysis with an examination of the text of section 43(a) * * * Two aspects of this statutory language lead us to believe that the theory of secondary meaning in the making should not be recognized under section 43(a). First, the statute prohibits only the use of any "word, term, name, symbol, or device, or any combination thereof" or "false designation of origin" which is likely to cause confusion, mistake, or deception as to the "origin, sponsorship, or approval" of goods. Where there is no actual secondary meaning in a trade dress, the purchasing public

---

[5] The subsequent edition of Callman's treatise, however, contains no language expressing approval for the doctrine of secondary meaning in the making. See 3 R. Callman, *The Law of Unfair Competition, Trademarks, and Monopolies* § 19.27 (4th Ed.1989).

simply does not associate the trade dress with a particular producer.[7] Therefore, a subsequent producer who adopts an imitating trade dress will not cause confusion, mistake, or deception as to the "origin, sponsorship, or approval" of the goods. Second, a junior producer's use of imitating trade dress bears no "false designation of origin" because, in the absence of secondary meaning in the senior producer's trade dress, the imitating trade dress suggests no particular origin to the consuming public.
* * *

Moreover, "[t]he doctrine, if taken literally, is inimical to the purpose of the secondary meaning requirement." *Restatement* [(Third) of Unfair Competition], *supra*, § 13 reporter's note, comment e at 53. The secondary meaning requirement exists to insure that something worth protecting exists--an association that has developed in the purchasing public's mind between a distinctive trade dress and its producer--before trademark law applies to limit the freedom of a competitor to compete by copying. As the drafters of the *Restatement, supra,* § 17 comment b at 104-05, explain:

> The freedom to copy product and packaging features is limited by the law of trademarks only when the copying is likely to confuse prospective purchasers as to the source or sponsorship of the goods. The imitation or even complete duplication of another's product or packaging creates no risk of confusion unless some aspect of the duplicated appearance is identified with a particular source. Unless a design is distinctive ... and thus distinguishes the goods of one producer from those of others, it is ineligible for protection as a trademark.

The so-called doctrine of secondary meaning in the making, by affording protection before prospective purchasers are likely to associate the trade dress with a particular sponsor, constrains unnecessarily the freedom to copy and compete.

* * *

The argument in favor of permitting development of a doctrine of secondary meaning in the making, offered by Laureyssens, rests principally on the supposition that, without such a doctrine, there will be strong incentives for pirates to capitalize on products that have not yet developed secondary meaning. This argument, however, underestimates the level of protection afforded under existing law to prevent piracy in the early stages of product development. * * * For example, intentional copying is "persuasive evidence" of secondary meaning. Furthermore, secondary meaning can develop quickly to preclude knock-off artists from infringing. Finally, under New York's common law of unfair competition, a producer's trade dress is protected without

---

[7] But see Taco Cabana Int'l, Inc. v. Two Pesos, Inc., 932 F.2d 1113, 1119-21 & n. 8 (5th Cir.1991), cert. granted, 112 S.Ct. 964 (1992).

proof of secondary meaning against practices imbued with an odor of bad faith. These practices include palming off, actual deception, appropriation of another's property or deliberate copying. Therefore, true innovators, at least under New York law, have adequate means of recourse against free-riders.

For these reasons, we reject the doctrine of secondary meaning in the making under section 43(a) of the Lanham Act. Accordingly, we reverse the district court's decision to grant a preliminary injunction against Idea Group based on section 43(a) of the Lanham Act. Given our holding, we need not address the likelihood of confusion which may have been created by the SNAFOOZ trade dress.

PAGE 321. Add to Note 4

Problem. Empire files an intent-to-use application for the trademark REAL WHEELS on September 23, 1994. WarnerVision adopts the mark and first uses it in January, 1995. When Empire begins to introduce its products under the mark, WarnerVision sues for a preliminary injunction alleging first use. Empire asserts that the constructive use provided by the intent-to-use registration gives it priority. WarnerVision argues that in accordance with the plain meaning of section 7(c) constructive use is "contingent on the registration of a mark on the principal register" and thus not applicable here. If WarnerVision's argument prevails, are there any advantages remaining to an intent-to-use registration? Any disadvantages? See WarnerVision Entertainment Inc. v. Empire of Carolina Inc., 919 F. Supp. 717 (S.D.N.Y. 1996).

PAGE 323. Add to Note 5

NOTE

Roberts makes fiberglass kits which can be installed on a standard automobile so that the exterior design is indistinguishable from that of a prestige automobile. At issue in Ferrari S.P.A. Esercizio Fabrichre Automobili E. Corse v. Roberts, 944 F.2d 1235 (6th Cir. 1991), cert. denied 112 S.Ct. 3028 (1992), is an $8500 kit capable of transforming a Pontiac into a Ferrari Testarossa. Assuming the design of the Testarossa is distinctive, can Ferrari win a trademark infringement claim? Who is likely to confuse an automobile selling for $230,000 with an $8500 fiberglass kit? The district court explained the basis for an injunction:

> If the country is populated with hundreds, if not thousands, of replicas of rare, distinct, and unique vintage cars, obviously they are no longer unique. Even if a person seeing one of these replicas driving down the road is not confused, Ferrari's exclusive association with this design has been diluted and eroded. If the replica Daytona looks cheap or in disrepair, Ferrari's reputation for rarity and quality would be damaged.

Does trademark infringement require confusion of purchasers? Can the injunction survive a preemption argument based on *Sears, Compco,* and *Bonito*?

PAGE 328. Read after *Park 'N Fly*

SHAKESPEARE COMPANY v. SILSTAR CORPORATION OF AMERICA, INC
United States Court of Appeals, Fourth Circuit, 1993
9 F.3d 1091, cert. denied, 114 S.Ct. 2134 (1994)

CHAPMAN, Senior Circuit Judge:

This appeal presents an issue of first impression for this court: whether a district court considering cancellation, pursuant to § 37 of the Lanham Act (15 U.S.C. § 1119 (1988)), of a trademark that has been registered more than five years, and is incontestable pursuant to 15 U.S.C. § 1065 (1988), can order cancellation on the ground that the trademark is found to be functional, even though functionality is not one of the grounds set forth in 15 U.S.C. § 1064. We hold that Congress adopted 15 U.S.C. § 1119 to give the district court power concurrent with, but not in excess of, the Patent and Trademark Review Board and that the district court is also limited by the language of the statutes controlling the Board. We therefore hold that the district court improperly canceled the registration on the ground of functionality because functionality is not one of the statutorily enumerated grounds upon which a trademark registered more than five years may be canceled.

[Shakespeare was first to manufacture a fishing rod with a clear, fiberglass tip attached to a graphite base giving the rod a two-toned color scheme. The use of a fiberglass tip added strength to the rod and the clear or translucent appearance resulted inevitably from the manufacturing process. Shakespeare obtained a patent on the method of attaching the tip to the base and thus was the only manufacturer of such rods. Shakespeare was able to secure a trademark registration on the Principal Register in 1983 by showing that it promoted the clear tip rod in its advertising and by introducing seven identical affidavits of buyers who claimed the clear tip "automatically" identified the rods as those of Shakespeare. The registration became incontestable in 1989. In 1990 Silstar began marketing rods with a clear tip similar to those sold by Shakespeare. Shakespeare filed suit under § 32(1) of the Lanham Act, § 43(a) of the Lanham Act, and the common law of unfair competition. The district court found for Silstar.]

The District Court's reasoning may be summarized as follows: that there was no dispute that Shakespeare's trademark on the clear tip had become "incontestable" pursuant to § 1065; that such status was conclusive evidence of Shakespeare's ownership of the trademark and its right to control it, pursuant to § 1115(b); that Silstar could defend by proving that its use of the mark was a fair use because the mark was merely descriptive of its product; that Silstar's use of the clear tip was a fair use because the court found the clear tip was merely descriptive of the contents of the product, namely fiberglass; that Silstar was not using the clear tip as a trademark or in bad faith; and that this determination rendered the trademark merely *prima facie* evidence of Shakespeare's right to own and control the clear tip. The court then found Silstar was entitled to raise equitable defenses to the infringement action under § 1115(a).

The court held that an element of a product that is functional is not subject to trademark protection, and that fiberglass was selected to compose the tip because it is the strongest, most practical material for the tip of a fishing rod. It found the clear tip to be functional because its very appearance communicates to the consumer that it is composed of fiberglass. Finding the clear tip to be functional and not intended to communicate a brand of origin, the district court concluded that it was required to cancel the trademark.

The district court's determination that there was no trademark infringement resulted in the dismissal of the dependent statutory claim for unfair competition, and the common law claims for trademark infringement and unfair competition.

The issue is whether a district court, pursuant to its power under § 1119, can cancel the registration of a trademark on grounds not enumerated in § 1064, namely "functionality," if the registration is more than five years old.

* * *

This is a novel question and we have not found a case that squarely addresses this precise issue. However, the Supreme Court has given some guidance in the only case in which it has discussed § 1119, Park 'N' Fly, Inc. v. Dollar Park and Fly, Inc., 469 U.S. 189 (1985). Though the central issue in Park 'N' Fly differs from that of the case at bar, we consider it to be analogous and therefore worthy of consideration.

* * *

The Court held that a district court, entertaining an action for cancellation of a mark, is obliged to consider the limits of the Lanham Act.

> [T]he power of the courts to cancel registrations and "to otherwise rectify the register," § 37, 15 U.S.C. § 1119, must be subject to the specific provisions concerning incontestability. In effect, both respondent and the dissent argue that these provisions offer insufficient protection against improper registration of a merely descriptive mark, and therefore the validity of petitioner's mark may be challenged notwithstanding its incontestable status. Our responsibility, however, is not to evaluate the wisdom of the legislative determinations reflected

in the statute, but instead to construe and apply the provisions that Congress enacted.

Park 'N' Fly, 469 U.S. at 203.

If the power of the district court under § 1119 is implicitly constrained by the specific provisions of one subsection of the Lanham Act, § 1115(b), it is reasonable to conclude that it is limited by another related subsection, § 1064. The Court states that § 1064 does limit cancellation of a registration more than five years old, 469 U.S. at 197, 105 S.Ct. at 663, and this would be cancellation pursuant to § 1119 because the Court's inquiry was rooted in that context.

We are persuaded that the rationale enunciated by Justice O'Connor in *Park 'N' Fly* would apply so as to limit cancellation under § 1119 to the grounds set forth in § 1064. Functionality is not one of such grounds and it may not be used as a basis for cancellation of a registration more than five years old.

We have considered the possibility that functionality invalidates a trademark at any stage of the process, and that registration offers no protection whatsoever to an invalid mark that should never have been registered in the first place. This is the position taken by Justice Stevens in his dissent in *Park 'N' Fly*, 469 U.S. at 206. Justice Stevens argued that mere descriptiveness, the quality at issue in that case, invalidated the registration, 469 U.S. at 206-07, and that incontestability could not be used as a shield behind which an invalid mark could hide. 469 U.S. at 211. We find these arguments unpersuasive.

Perhaps the provisions of the Lanham Act apply only to valid trademarks, and that a functional trademark is invalid, but it would seem anomalous for Congress to enumerate specific grounds for cancellation for a five-year-old registration, as it has done in § 1064, and not list functionality, if it intended functionality to serve as such a ground. * * *

In conclusion, we hold that the district court erred in canceling, pursuant to 15 U.S.C. § 1119, the trademark held by Shakespeare on the grounds that it is functional, because that is not an authorized ground for cancellation under 15 U.S.C. § 1064. Since no other ground enumerated under § 1064 was alleged by Silstar, the mark is valid as a matter of law. We therefore reverse the district court and remand the case for further consideration of Shakespeare's statutory and common law infringement and unfair competition claims. We further instruct the district court that any inquiry into an alleged "fair use" of the clear tip must be accompanied by an analysis of the likelihood of confusion among consumers that may be created by Silstar's use of the clear tip.

REVERSED.

NIEMEYER, Circuit Judge, dissenting:

While the majority treats this case as if it involved solely the cancellation of a trademark registration, I respectfully submit that such an analysis overlooks the antecedent issue of whether an enforceable trademark exists. Moreover, the question of whether Shakespeare's registration may be canceled is analytically distinct from the question of whether a defense to its enforcement exists, and the two are governed by different statutory provisions. The initial question, therefore, which is not addressed by the majority but which is dispositive of the case, is whether this court should enforce the trademark, not whether this court should cancel it (the relief prayed for in the counterclaim). When the doctrine of functionality, the full extent of which is not articulated in the majority's opinion, is applied, the judgment of the district court must be affirmed.

The doctrine of functionality is an extra-statutory doctrine, neither defined nor limited by the express provisions of the Lanham Trademark Act, which denies a perpetual monopoly of that which is functional. Despite the absence of a textual basis for this doctrine, it is integrated into the Act because of the presumption that Congress did not intend to upset the well-established principle that trademark protection is inapplicable to the functional. The doctrine of functionality is a public policy trump card that may be played against an otherwise valid trademark, not an element to be considered in determining a mark's validity. Even if every presumption is made in favor of the existence of a trademark--that the mark enables determination of source, that it distinguishes the relevant goods, and that it has secondary meaning-- these factors will not allow a functional feature to be monopolized beyond the limits imposed by the law of patents in compliance with the Constitution. See U.S. Const., art. I, § 8, cl. 8 (empowering Congress to grant exclusive rights to inventions only for "limited times"). * * *

* * *

The doctrine of functionality is well established and has long been applied, drawing its strength from constitutional underpinnings. Article I, section 8, clause 8 of the U.S. Constitution empowers Congress, "To Promote the Progress of Science and useful Arts, by securing for limited Times to Authors and Inventors the exclusive Right to their respective Writings and Discoveries." This formulation, stressing the limited time for which rights in discoveries are to be secured, was a direct response to the long history of British grants of private monopolies. The doctrine of functionality furthers this constitutional value, as well as conforming trademark law to Congress' statutory scheme set forth to govern patents. As the Supreme Court has explained, patent law has three goals:

> First, patent law seeks to foster and reward invention; second, it promotes disclosure of inventions to stimulate further innovation and to permit the public to practice the invention once the patent expires;

third, the stringent requirements for patent protection seek to assure that ideas in the public domain remain there for the free use of the public.

Aronson v. Quick Point Pencil Co., 440 U.S. 257, 262, 99 S.Ct. 1096, 1099, 59 L.Ed.2d 296 (1979). Two of these--the preservation of free use of functional ideas in the public domain and the passage of technology to the public sphere upon a patent's expiration--are potentially at odds with trademark law. Only through strict observation of the doctrine of functionality may the courts avoid frustration of the congressional policies underlying patent law, which provides for the passage of utilitarian product features into the public realm within a set time frame. Patent law was intended by Congress to be the sole source of protection for functional features. The three other areas of intellectual property law-- trademark, copyright, and design patent--share the basic policy of the functionality doctrine: that the public interest in free competition prohibits functional or utilitarian product features from achieving protection beyond that offered by the patent laws.

Three major Supreme Court cases have articulated the constitutional policy of denying perpetual protection to functional innovations, [*Sears*, *Compco*, and *Bonito Boats*]. In each of these cases the Court invalidated state-created grants of perpetual protection to functional designs under state unfair competition law, holding such grants inconsistent with the Supremacy Clause because of the manifested congressional intent to limit protection of such inventions to those protections provided in the patent law. Although the Sears-Compco-Bonito Boats trilogy does not directly control this case, it stands for the general principle that there is a strong federal policy against granting perpetual private rights in functional designs. In passing the Lanham Act, Congress intended neither to repudiate this policy nor to disturb the traditional exclusion from trademark protection of functional features.

* * *

The majority's focus on cancellation diverts attention to a non-determinative issue--whether the scope of the federal courts' power to cancel registrations is coterminous with that of the patent office. The federal courts are granted broad equitable powers over trademark registrations by 15 U.S.C. § 1119:

> In any action involving a registered mark the court may determine the right to registration, order the cancellation of registrations, in whole or in part, restore canceled registrations, and otherwise rectify the register with respect to the registrations of any party to the action. Decrees and orders shall be certified by the court to the Commissioner, who shall make appropriate entry upon the records of the Patent and Trademark Office, and shall be controlled thereby.

The majority cites many authorities for the proposition that this authority granted the courts is concurrent with that of the patent office. This may well be true as a general matter, but the present case involves a claim that that office has attempted an act beyond its power and undertaken actions repugnant to federal policy as expressed by the Constitution and statutory enactments. None of the authorities cited deals with such a situation, rendering their broad statements dicta insofar as they are phrased to seem relevant to this very different situation.

That the federal courts, in enforcing a trademark, are allowed to assess independently whether that trademark is permissible as a matter of law seems to me to flow from the judicial power described in Marbury v. Madison, 5 U.S. (1 Cranch) 137, 2 L.Ed. 60 (1803). As important, the doctrine of functionality, which goes to the question of whether an enforceable trademark ever existed, was never rejected by the Lanham Act. On the contrary, it is tacitly embraced, and every court that has considered the doctrine has so assumed. To conclude otherwise would imply that Congress intended to alter the underlying constitutional policies of restricting monopolies on function to promote copying and competition.

Whether this court should order cancellation of the plaintiff's trademark on the grounds of functionality is a secondary, not a dispositive, question. Even if the registration is allowed to stand, that does not preclude us from denying enforcement of a mark when such enforcement would be repugnant to the policies embodied in this nation's laws. I would affirm the district court's judgment on the grounds that because of its functionality, Shakespeare's trademark cannot be enforced.

For the reasons given, I respectfully dissent.

NOTE

On remand, Shakespeare Co. v. Silstar Corp., 906 F. Supp. 997 (D.S.C. 1995), Judge Shedd, found another way to use the functionality doctrine to deny Shakespeare relief.

> The panel majority's determination in Shakespeare II that Shakespeare's trademark may not be cancelled on the ground of functionality entitles the mark to remain on the Federal Register and, due to its incontestability, to be entitled to certain evidentiary benefits. This determination, which the Court fully respects, makes this case somewhat unique, since it removes Shakespeare's trademark from within the normal scope of the functionality rule. However, as addressed above, functionality is still a relevant factor and where, as here, a party (Silstar) seeks, in good faith and not as a means of source-identification, to use a functional feature of a product which another party (Shakespeare) has registered as a trademark, it is not unreasonable or unfair to allow even some residual confusion to occur. Under these circumstances, there could likely be no fairer use of a registered trademark. For these reasons, the Court concludes that Silstar must prevail on its fair-use defense.

PAGE 348. Add to "Parallel Imports" which begins on page 347

PROBLEM

Consider the facts of Lever Brothers Co. v. United States, 981 F.2d 1330 (D.C.Cir. 1993) and Lever Brothers Co. v. United States, 877 F.2d 101 (D.C.Cir. 1989). Lever Brothers manufacturers "Shield" hand soap for the United States market. An affiliated company manufactures "Shield" soap for the British market. The soaps are separately formulated to respond to the different tastes of British and American consumers. Should Lever Brothers be allowed to prevent a third party from importing British "Shield" soap into the United States? Would British "Shield" soap infringe the Lever Brothers trademark in the United States?

The Supreme Court decision in K Mart Corp. v. Cartier, Inc., 486 U.S. 281 (1988) upheld U.S. Customs regulations that permitted importation of trademarked goods by affiliated companies. Does the reformulation of the product make a difference?

See Restatement (Third) of Unfair Competition § 24, Comment *f* (1995):

In gray market contexts a factual question thus exists as to whether the trademark identifies the domestic trademark owner or the foreign manufacturer. To the extent that the trademark identifies to prospective purchasers the domestic owner as distinguished from the foreign manufacturer, imported gray market goods are not goods the source of which is accurately identified by the trademark . . . . The proper inquiry is whether the use of the trademark on the gray market goods is likely to confuse prospective purchasers, and the issue must be resolved on the basis of the particular circumstances of the case. For example, if the domestic and foreign companies are entirely separate entities and their respective goods are independently produced and marketed, the good will identified by the mark in the United States will be that of the domestic trademark owner. On the other hand, the nature of any on-going relationship between the foreign and domestic companies can affect whether consumers understand the mark to identify the domestic trademark owner as distinguished from the foreign manufacturer. . . . The issue is whether the domestic trademark owner can establish that the presence of the trademark on the imported goods creates a likelihood of confusion because the mark identifies to prospective purchasers the good will of the domestic owner.

How do you suppose the drafters of the Restatement would resolve the *Lever Brothers* problem?

PAGE 376. Add after *L.L.Bean*

DEERE & COMPANY v. MTD PRODUCTS, INC.
United States Court of Appeals, Second Circuit, 1994
41 F.3d 39

JON O. NEWMAN, Chief Judge.

[The parties are competing manufacturers of lawn tractors. Deere has used a deer design (Deere Logo) as a trademark for over 100 years on agricultural and lawn equipment and has registered different versions of the Deere Logo, all of which "depict a static, two-dimensional silhouette of a leaping male deer in profile." MTD developed an advertisement comparing its Yard-Man lawn tractor to that of Deere. As part of the advertisement MTD used an altered, animated form of the Deere Logo. "Specifically, the MTD deer looks over its shoulder, jumps through the logo frame (which breaks into pieces and tumbles to the ground), hops to a pinging noise, and, as a two-dimensional cartoon, runs, in apparent fear, as it is pursued by the Yard-Man lawn tractor and a barking dog." Deere filed a complaint under the Lanham Act for trademark infringement and under Section 368-d of the New York statutes for trademark dilution. The district court found no likelihood of confusion but did award a preliminary injunction on the dilution claim.]

Although a number of dilution cases in this Circuit have involved use of a trademark by a competitor to identify a competitor's products in comparative advertising, as well as use by a noncompetitor in a humorous variation of a trademark, we have not yet considered whether the use of an altered version of a distinctive trademark to identify a competitor's product and achieve a humorous effect can constitute trademark dilution. Though we find MTD's animated version of Deere's deer amusing, we agree with Judge McKenna that the television commercial is a likely violation of the anti-dilution statute. We therefore affirm the preliminary injunction.

[The court first described the two traditional categories of dilution, "blurring" and "tarnishment" articulated in Mead Data Central, Inc. v. Toyota Motor Sales (see, casebook at page 365).]

The District Court's analysis endeavored to fit the MTD commercial into one of the two categories we have recognized for a section 368-d claim. However, the MTD commercial is not really a typical instance of blurring, because it poses slight if any risk of impairing the identification of Deere's mark with its products. Nor is there tarnishment, which is usually found where a distinctive mark is depicted in a context of sexual activity, obscenity, or illegal activity. But the blurring/tarnishment dichotomy does not necessarily represent the full range of uses that can dilute a mark under New York law.

In giving content to dilution beyond the categories of blurring or tarnishment, however, we must be careful not to broaden section 368-d to prohibit all uses of a distinctive mark that the owner prefers not be made. Several different contexts may conveniently be identified. Sellers of commercial products may wish to use a competitor's mark to identify the competitor's product in comparative advertisements. As long as the mark is not altered, such use serves the beneficial purpose of imparting factual information about the relative merits of competing products and poses no risk of diluting the selling power of the competitor's mark. Satirists, selling no product other than the publication that contains their expression, may wish to parody a mark to make a point of social commentary, to entertain, or perhaps both to comment and entertain. Such uses risk some dilution of the identifying or selling power of the mark, but that risk is generally tolerated in the interest of maintaining broad opportunities for expression.

Sellers of commercial products who wish to attract attention to their commercials or products and thereby increase sales by poking fun at widely recognized marks of noncompeting products, risk diluting the selling power of the mark that is made fun of. When this occurs, not for worthy purposes of expression, but simply to sell their own products, that purpose can easily be achieved in other ways. The potentially diluting effect is even less deserving of protection when the object of the joke is the mark of a directly competing product. The line-drawing in this area becomes especially difficult when a mark is parodied for the dual purposes of making a satiric comment and selling a somewhat competing product.

Whether the use of the mark is to identify a competing product in an informative comparative ad, to make a comment, or to spoof the mark to enliven the advertisement for a noncompeting or a competing product, the scope of protection under a dilution statute must take into account the degree to which the mark is altered and the nature of the alteration. Not every alteration will constitute dilution, and more leeway for alterations is appropriate in the context of satiric expression and humorous ads for noncompeting products. But some alterations have the potential to so lessen the selling power of a distinctive mark that they are appropriately proscribed by a dilution statute. Dilution of this sort is more likely to be found when the alterations are made by a competitor with both an incentive to diminish the favorable attributes of the mark and an ample opportunity to promote its products in ways that make no significant alteration.

We need not attempt to predict how New York will delineate the scope of its dilution statute in all of the various contexts in which an accurate depiction of a distinctive mark might be used, nor need we decide how variations of such a mark should be treated in different contexts. Some variations might well be de minimis, and the context in which even substantial variations occur may well have such meritorious purposes that any diminution in the identifying and selling power of the mark need not be condemned as dilution.

Wherever New York will ultimately draw the line, we can be reasonably confident that the MTD commercial challenged in this case crosses it. The commercial takes a static image of a graceful, full-size deer--symbolizing Deere's substance and strength--and portrays, in an animated version, a deer that appears smaller than a small dog and scampers away from the dog and a lawn tractor, looking over its shoulder in apparent fear. Alterations of that sort, accomplished for the sole purpose of promoting a competing product, are properly found to be within New York's concept of dilution because they risk the possibility that consumers will come to attribute unfavorable characteristics to a mark and ultimately associate the mark with inferior goods and services.

* * *

The order of the District Court granting a preliminary injunction as to activities within New York State is affirmed. * * * .

HORMEL FOODS CORPORATION v. JIM HENSON PRODUCTIONS, INC.,

United States Court of Appeals, Second Circuit, 1996
73 F.3d 497

VAN GRAAFEILAND, Circuit Judge:

[The district court described the lawsuit as follows:

This lawsuit is sparked by the prospective appearance of a new Muppet who joins Kermit, Miss Piggy and others in the movie "Muppet Treasure Island," due to be released in about four months. The creators of the Muppets, Jim Henson Productions, Inc. ("Henson"), hope to provoke laughter by naming the new Muppet (an exotic, wild boar) "Spa'am"; they believe that the association between the exotic, wild boar and the tame, familiar luncheon meat, SPAM, will cause viewers to laugh. Hormel Foods Corporation ("Hormel") which manufactures SPAM, finds nothing humorous in the association, and fears that the use of the Spa'am character will cause a drop off in the consumption of SPAM, and a drop off in the consumption of SPAM tee-shirts and other SPAM-related merchandise. Although Henson has urged Hormel, effectively, to "lighten up," and to see the parody as a positive development for Hormel (especially in light of the fact that SPAM is regularly subjected to much more negative portrayals), Hormel insists on its right to a legal determination of whether Henson's use of the Spa'am character and name are lawful.

Hormel alleged trademark infringement, false advertisig, and dilution. As to the infringement claim, the Second Circuit found: "the clarity of Henson's parodic intent, the widespread familiarity with Henson's Muppet parodies, and the strength of Hormel's mark, all weigh strongly against the likelihood of confusion. . . ." Under the dilution claim, the court found that there was little likelihood that Henson's use would blur the association of the mark with Hormel's luncheon meat.]

Dilution may also occur by tarnishment. * * * Tarnishment can occur through a variety of uses. Some cases have found that a mark is tarnished when its likeness is placed in the context of sexual activity, obscenity, or illegal activity. However, tarnishment is not limited to seamy conduct. Hormel argues that the image of Spa'am, as a "grotesque," "untidy" wild boar will "inspire negative and unsavory associations with SPAM (R) luncheon meat." Both Hormel and Amicus Curiae rely heavily on our recent decision in *Deere* [Deere & Company v. MTD products, Inc., 41 F.3d 39 (2d Cir. 1994)] for the proposition that products that "pok[e] fun at widely recognized marks of non-competing products, risk diluting the selling power of the mark that is made fun of." Their reliance is misplaced.

In *Deere* we addressed the question "whether the use of an altered version of a distinctive trademark to identify a competitor's product and achieve a humorous effect can constitute trademark dilution." MTD produced a television commercial for its competing lawnmower tractor, altering the famous Deere trademark from a proud, majestic deer, to one that was cowardly and afraid. * * * We found a violation of the anti-dilution statute because "[a]lterations of that sort, accomplished for the sole purpose of promoting a competing product ... risk the possibility that consumers will come to attribute unfavorable characteristics to a mark and ultimately associate the mark with inferior goods and services." This holding mirrors the rationale of the tarnishment doctrine. Thus, although the court below understood *Deere* to create a new category of dilution, we find that our decision in *Deere* is better understood as a recognition of a broad view of tarnishment, where that doctrine had been sometimes narrowly confined.

The sine qua non of tarnishment is a finding that plaintiff's mark will suffer negative associations through defendant's use. Hormel claims that linking its luncheon meat with a wild boar will adversely color consumers' impressions of SPAM. However, the district court found that Spa'am, a likeable, positive character, will not generate any negative associations. Moreover, contrary to Hormel's contentions, the district court also found no evidence that Spa'am is unhygienic or that his character places Hormel's mark in an unsavory context. Indeed, many of Henson's own plans involve placing the Spa'am likeness on food products. In addition, the court also noted that a simple humorous reference to the fact that SPAM is made from pork is unlikely to tarnish Hormel's mark. Absent any showing that Henson's use will create negative associations with the SPAM mark, there was little likelihood of dilution.

Moreover, unlike *Deere*, Henson's merchandise will not be in direct competition with that of Hormel. This is an important, even if not determinative, factor. "Dilution of this sort is more likely to be found when the alterations are made by a competitor with both an incentive to diminish the favorable attributes of the mark and an ample opportunity to promote its products in ways that make no significant alteration." Here, Henson does not seek to ridicule SPAM in order to sell more of its competitive products; rather, the parody is part of the product itself. Without Spa'am, the joke is lost. Indeed, we were mindful of this problem in *Deere* when we noted that "[t]he line-drawing in this area becomes especially difficult when a mark is parodied for the dual purposes of making a satiric comment and selling a somewhat competing product." Thus, in *Deere* we did not proscribe any parody or humorous depiction of a mark. Overall, we took a cautious approach, stating that "we must be careful not to broaden section 368-d to prohibit all uses of a distinctive mark that the owner prefers not be made."

Therefore, in the instant case, where (1) there is no evidence that Henson's use will cause negative associations, (2) Henson is not a direct competitor, and (3) the parody inheres in the product, we find that there is no likelihood of dilution under a tarnishment theory.

NOTES

1. The district court enjoined MTD from using an animated or otherwise altered version of the deer trademark within the state of New York. The Second Circuit affirmed stating that the district court had the power to grant a broader injunction but "particularly at this early stage in the litigation" and where the issue is one of "first impression" it was appropriate to limit relief to New York state. Would you permit an injunction to extend into a state without a dilution statute? One with a dilution statute that has a judicial interpretation precluding relief in this type of case? On remand, the parties agreed to permit a final decision to be rendered on the record of the preliminary injunction hearing. Deere & Co. v. MTD Products, Inc., 1995 WL 81299 (S.D.N.Y. 1995). The court found the defendant had violated the New York anti-dilution statute and made the preliminary injunction permanent. Finding that it had the authority to issue a nation-wide injunction, the court refused to do so: "In making this decision, I am most persuaded by the fact that the injunction in this case is not based on common law unfair competition claims, which are more widely shared, but on New York's anti-dilution statute, which does not exist in at least half of the states, and which many states that did pass such legislation do not apply to competitors, and by the breadth of the injunction for which Deere seeks nationwide enforcement." The court had found that neither Illinois nor Ohio, where the parties had their principal place of business, would have upheld a dilution claim.

2. Does *Hormel* make clear that *Deere* is really a "tarnishment" case, in as much as the injury, from Deere's point of view, is the mockery of its deer logo? Can MTD run an advertisement where an announcer says: "Remember that little deer associated with the John Deere Company? When Yard-Man comes calling, that deer will scamper out of sight in fear?" Or an advertisement in which real deers are shown scampering away in fear on approach of the "Yard-Man"? Do you agree that *Hormel* is different because there the parties are not in direct competition? Aren't they competing in the merchandise (T-shirt, etc.) market?

3. A litigious target of attempted parodies is Anheuser-Busch, makers of Budweiser and other popular beers. Consider the following examples. Illustration 1 (below) was placed on T-shirts by a young entrepreneur and sold at retail beach stores at Myrle Beach, South Carolina. See Anheuser-Busch Inc. v. L & L Wings Inc., 962 F.2d 316, cert. denied 113 S.Ct. 206 (1992). Illustration 2 (below) represents the back cover of "Snicker", a humor magazine. See Anheuser-Busch, Inc. v. Balducci Pub., 28 F.3d 769 (8th Cir. 1994). Are either takeoffs of the Budweiser trademark actionable as trademark infringement or dilution?

Illustration 1:

APPENDIX
T-Shirt Design

Myrtle Beach

KING OF BEACHES

Myrtle Beach contains the Choicest Surf, Sun, and Sand

Myrtle Beach, S.C.

12 FL OZ. (355 ml)

This Beach is for You!

Venture Marketing, Inc.
1987 ALL RIGHTS RESERVED

Ch. 3   PRODUCT AND PRODUCER IDENTITY   107

Illustration 2:

APPENDIX A

Reduced-size reproduction. Original is on 11-1/4 x 17-1/2 inch page.

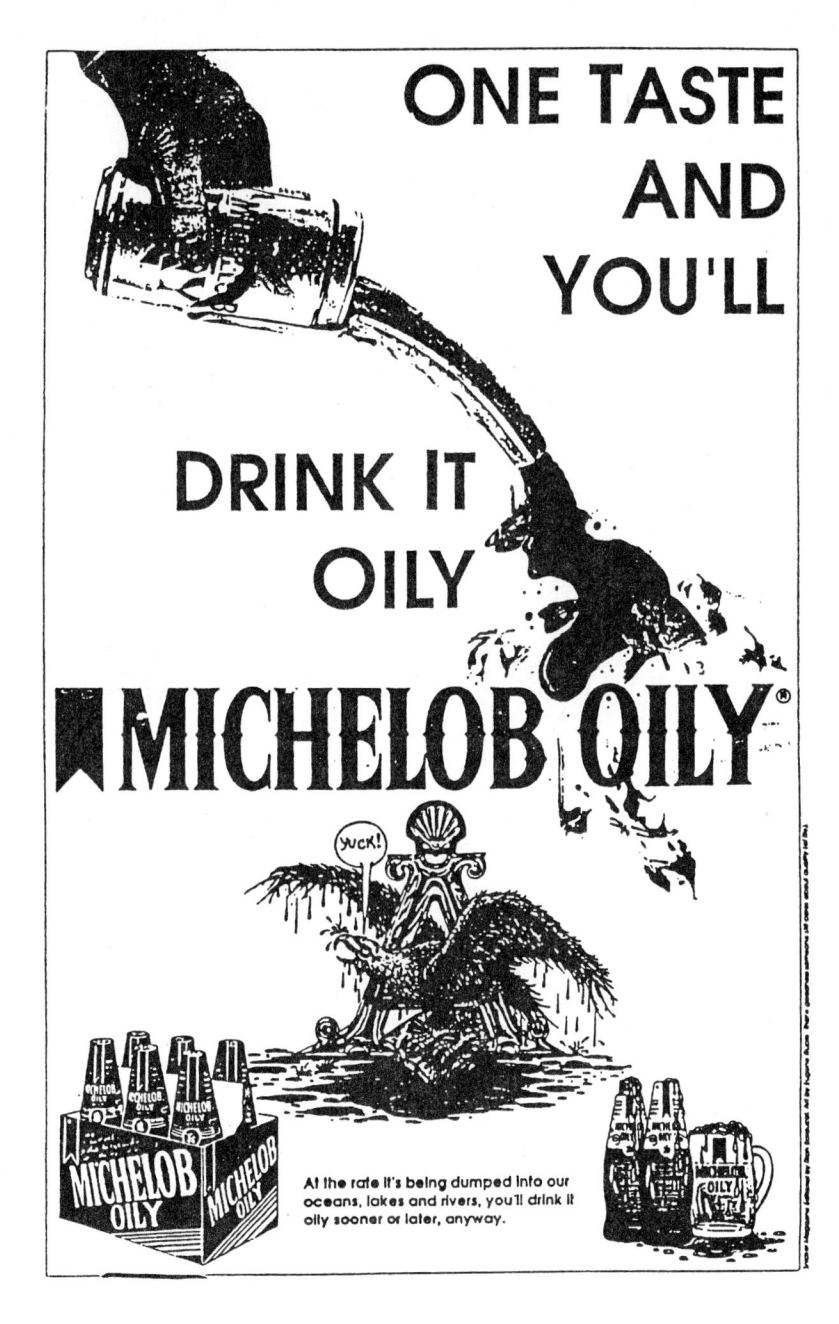

4. In the *Balducci* case, the court in assessing the likelihood of confusion made much of the fact that the Budweiser trademarks were unaltered and this was evidence that the plaintiff's use would not be regarded as a parody but rather be falsely attributable to Anheuser-Busch. Compare that with *Deere* in which the alteration of the trademark seems to make all the difference on the dilution claim.

5. What are the implications of Judge Newman's analysis in *Deere*? Can it withstand a First Amendment analysis? Why should I be able to mock my competitor's products but not my competitor's trademarks? Is the trademark more closely identified with the company? Presumably consumers can test a comparison of products by purchasing the products and experiencing them both, but how would Deere overcome the mocking of its trademark? Is it an answer that consumers may find the commercial amusing but will not hold it against Deere?

PAGE 380. Read in association with the Problem

MATRIX ESSENTIALS, INC. v. EMPORIUM DRUG MART, INC.,
United States Court of Appeals, Fifth Circuit, 1993
988 F.2d 587

GARWOOD, Circuit Judge:

[Matrix manufacturers specialty hair-care products which are distributed through wholesalers contractually bound to resell only to licensed cosmetologists. Matrix intends for consumers prior to purchase to consult with cosmetologists in order to obtain the appropriate product for their hair and scalp condition. Matrix spends millions of dollars training cosmetologists for this purpose although it does not monitor sales to consumers to insure consultation occurs. Emporium, a high-volume, over-the-counter retail drug store obtained a large quantity of genuine Matrix products and offered them for sale directly to consumers under the Matrix trademark. Some of the bottles were labeled "Sold Only in Professional Salons". Matrix sued Emporium for trademark infringement and under 43(a) of the Lanham Act. The district court granted Emporium's motion for summary judgment.]

There are no disputed issues of material fact here. * * * Taking the evidence in the light most favorable to Matrix, the non-moving party, Emporium purchased Matrix products and sold them without authorization by Matrix. Matrix has made no showing or allegation that the products are counterfeit, or that Emporium has tampered with them in any way. Matrix acknowledges that, at least physically, the products sold by Emporium are of the same origin and quality as those sold by salons.

Matrix bases its claim on two theories. The first theory is that Emporium is not selling "genuine" Matrix products, because it is selling them without the professional consultation that is supposed to be available when a consumer chooses a Matrix product to purchase. Thus, according to Matrix, Emporium is circumventing an important quality control function of Matrix's distribution system. The product that an Emporium customer buys, without this potential assistance in selection, is therefore not the full, complete, and genuine Matrix product.

Matrix's second theory is that by stocking Matrix products, Emporium is deceiving the public into believing that Matrix has authorized Emporium to do so. This, according to Matrix, "is likely to cause confusion, or to cause mistake, or to deceive as to the affiliation, connection, or association" of Emporium with Matrix "or as to the origin, sponsorship, or approval" by Matrix of Emporium's sale of Matrix products. 15 U.S.C. § 1125(a)(1).

Because liability under the Lanham Act is predicated on the use of a trademark in a way that is "likely to cause confusion," consumer confusion must be the linchpin of our analysis in this case. As recognized by the Fourth and Ninth Circuits (as well as various district courts), the general rule is that "trademark law does not apply to the sale of genuine goods bearing a true mark, even if the sale is without the mark owner's consent." Shell Oil Co. v. Commercial Petroleum, Inc., 928 F.2d 104, 107 (4th Cir.1991).

In *Shell, supra,* the defendant was prohibited from selling bulk oil under Shell trademarks because the distributor did not observe the strict tank and line cleaning requirements that Shell required of its authorized distributors. These requirements insured that pure Shell-trademarked oil was not subjected to residue impurities in the tanks and lines of the distributors as it made its way to customers.

In El Greco Leather Products Co., Inc. v. Shoe World, Inc., 806 F.2d 392 (2d Cir.1986), cert. denied, 484 U.S. 817 (1987), the defendant, a discount shoe retailer, bought shoes bearing the plaintiff's trademark from a Brazilian manufacturer that had manufactured the shoes pursuant to the plaintiff's order. The manufacturer sold the shoes to the defendant after the plaintiff cancelled the order because of late delivery. The Second Circuit held that, because the shoes imported by the defendant had not undergone the careful quality inspection by the plaintiff's Brazilian agent that was normally required by the plaintiff before it sold its shoes in the United States, the shoes imported by the defendant were not "genuine."

Similarly, in Adolph Coors Co. v. A. Genderson & Sons, Inc., 486 F.Supp. 131 (D.Colo.1980), the court found that the Coors beer sold by the defendant distributor was not "genuine" Coors beer (though it had been manufactured and labeled by Coors) because the defendant, an unauthorized distributor, did not maintain the careful refrigeration requirements in transporting and storing the beer mandated by Coors. Coors beer contained no preservatives, and if allowed to sit unrefrigerated for long periods of time could deteriorate. The district court therefore determined that the beer sold by the defendant was therefore not "genuine" Coors beer.

Not all value-added functions dictated by the manufacturer are required to insure a "genuine" product, however. In H.L. Hayden Co. of N.Y., Inc. v. Siemens Medical Systems, Inc., 879 F.2d 1005 (2d Cir.1989), the defendant imported and sold through its catalogue dental equipment manufactured by the plaintiff and bearing the plaintiff's trademarks. The defendant did not install the equipment sold, though the plaintiff required its authorized distributors to install the equipment they sold. The plaintiff argued that because its "product" was not merely what it manufactured, but rather what it manufactured and authorized its dealers to install, the defendant was not selling a genuine product. The Second Circuit rejected this contention, ruling that so long as customers knew that what they purchased from the defendant was only the plaintiff's manufactured product and did not include installation, no one was deceived and the product was genuine.

* * *

The critical element that is missing from Matrix's argument and from the facts of this case, however, is the element of consumer confusion. The common thread in all the above cited cases where trademark infringement was found is that each involved some defect (or potential defect) in the product itself that the customer would not be readily able to detect. The oil, shoes, and beer from *Shell*, *El Greco*, and *Coors* all contained or could potentially contain a latent product defect due to the unauthorized distributor's failure to observe the manufacturer and mark owner's rigorous quality control standards. Most importantly, a consumer would not necessarily be aware of the defective condition of the product and would thereby be confused or deceived.

Such was not the case with the medical equipment in *Siemens* * * * or the hair-care products here. No customer who went to Emporium to buy Matrix products was confused or deceived as to whether they were getting a cosmetologist's consultation with their purchase. Though Matrix claims that an uninformed customer could mistakenly have bought the wrong product for his or her hair or scalp conditions and that this could potentially have damaged Matrix's consumer goodwill, we will not find a cause of action under the Lanham Act where, as here, there is no evidence of consumer confusion or deception. We decline to expand the reach of the Lanham Act in a way that makes Matrix's complaint actionable thereunder.

We further note that Matrix's claim that having its products sold through Emporium would erode its goodwill does not even rest on a sound factual base. The evidence before the district court clearly establishes that, although Matrix spends a great deal of time and money educating cosmetologists in the use and sale of its products, it does not require, monitor, or otherwise attempt to insure that consumers who purchase Matrix products in salons are assisted by a cosmetologist in selecting the proper Matrix product. Matrix products may be purchased in a salon either with or without a cosmetologist's advice. We cannot ignore the fact that if a pre-sale consultation is a necessary part, in Matrix's opinion, of a "genuine" Matrix product, then many of the sales that occur in salons are not sales of "genuine" Matrix products either. Thus, Matrix's use of professional hair care salons as its exclusive distribution channel seems more marketing-related than quality-related. This fact makes this case even more analogous to *Siemens* than to *Coors, El Greco,* or *Shell*.[2]

The second theory under which Matrix argues its case is that by stocking Matrix products, Emporium is violating 15 U.S.C. § 1125(a) by misleading consumers into believing that it is an authorized retailer of Matrix products and that Matrix condones the sale of its products through ordinary retail drugstores. As with trademark infringement, the touchstone of a section 1125(a) unfair competition claim is whether the defendant's actions are "likely to cause confusion."

Here, Emporium's sale of Matrix products cannot cause confusion as to manufacture or sponsorship because the goods were manufactured and labeled by Matrix. Rather, the underlying assumption relied upon by Matrix to support this second theory is that consumers assume when they see a product on a store shelf that the manufacturer meant for it to be there. The alleged harm is that a customer seeing a Matrix product on an Emporium shelf will assume that Matrix has decided that salon consultation on the customer's choice of the appropriate Matrix product is unnecessary, since Matrix is allowing its products to be sold to the public in an environment where such consultation is not concurrently available.

* * *

---

[2] Nor do we consider Polymer Technology Corp. v. Mimran, 975 F.2d 58 (2d Cir.1992), recently cited to us by Matrix, as persuasive authority for a contrary result here. There two distinct lines of contact lens care products were involved. One line was packaged for retail sale, and contained Food and Drug Administration (FDA) required consumer labeling, warnings, and tamper-evident seals. The other line was distributed to professionals such as ophthalmologists and optometrists; the FDA regulations did not apply to this line and its packaging had not been submitted to the FDA for approval; it was frequently distributed in bulk, with individual items not having the labeling or warnings, and sometimes not the tamper-evident seals, required by the FDA for items sold at retail. The manufacturer and trademark owner, Polymer, claimed that the defendant sold professional kits at retail, and also broke them down and sold separately at retail the individual bottles of professional solutions. The district court denied a temporary injunction. On appeal, a divided Second Circuit panel remanded for reconsideration because the district court had apparently not considered evidence that the defendant broke the packaging on the professional kits and sold the individual items separately at retail. The majority noted Polymer's claim "that distribution of professional solutions in the retail market subjects it to criminal penalties, and creates a public hazard." The majority also stated, however, that on remand "Polymer must show more than its quality control efforts." Here there is no repackaging and no alteration of the contents labeling, use instructions, or warnings; nor is there any claim of FDA violation. We further note in respect to the claim of unauthorized distribution, the *Mimran* majority, citing *Hayden*, stated that "[t]he element of consumer confusion must also be present." There is no such showing here.

Though, as Matrix claims, a customer might well be confused as to whether Matrix believes a salon consultation is necessary in selecting its products, it is difficult to say that Emporium has made a "misleading representation of fact," which is the only language in the text of section 1125(a) that could possibly cover Emporium's acquisition and stocking of Matrix products. The parties have not directed this Court to any cases that have addressed this particular question.

* * *

We are not persuaded by Matrix's arguments to expand the reach of section 1125(a) to provide a cause of action merely for the unauthorized stocking and sale of a manufacturer's products. Absent more culpable conduct on the part of the seller, we are unwilling to find misrepresentation in the mere act of putting a manufacturer's product on one's shelf and offering it for sale. We therefore affirm the district court's grant of summary judgment in favor of Emporium on the trademark and unfair competition claims.

* * *

AFFIRMED.

NOTE

Compare with *Matrix*, Sebastian International Inc. v. Longs Drug Stores Corp., 30 U.S.P.Q.2d 1785 (C.D.Cal. 1994). Sebastian wanted to sell its hair care products only through professional salons. After experiencing diversions of its products to unauthorized retailers, it formed "The Sebastian Collective Membership Program" and registered the mark "Sebastian Collective Salon Member" as a collective membership and service mark. The mark was displayed on Sebastian's products. The defendant, Longs Drugs, obtained diverted Sebastian products and sold them at retail. The court granted Sebastian a preliminary injunction:

> Here, unlike *Matrix* and the other first sale doctrine cases, misrepresentations and likelihood of confusion are present. By selling products bearing the collective mark, Longs is arguably misrepresenting to consumers that it is affiliated with or authorized by Sebastian or the Collective. The survey results bear this out. In addition, apparently members of the Collective provide certain ancillary functions (namely, quality control, consultative services and charity contributions). The collective mark, more than a traditional trademark, indicates a closer connection to Sebastian and in turn could signal to customers the existence of these functions. Thus, Longs, by selling Sebastian products bearing the collective mark, is arguably misrepresenting that it provides these functions.

> Consumer confusion is also likely. The survey results indicate that a substantial number of consumers mistakenly perceived that a drug store selling goods bearing the collective mark must be authorized by or affiliated with Sebastian or the Collective. Evidence of actual consumer confusion, though not required, certainly tends to establish the likelihood of confusion.

Could it be that to get around the first sale doctrine (or the genuine goods doctrine) one merely could form a "membership club" and adopt a collective mark? The Ninth Circuit didn't think so, reversing the decision in Sebastian International, Inc. v. Longs Drug Stores Corp., 53 F.3d 1073 (9th Cir. 1995):

> Sebastian argues the "first sale" doctrine does not apply when resale by the first purchaser under the producer's trademark creates a likelihood of consumer confusion. Sebastian asserts that a survey it commissioned indicates that Longs's action of stocking and reselling Sebastian products bearing the collective mark has in fact confused consumers "into believing [falsely] that there is some type of affiliation, association, or approval between Longs and Sebastian...."
>
> Sebastian's premise is false. The "first sale" rule is not rendered inapplicable merely because consumers erroneously believe the reseller is affiliated with or authorized by the producer. It is the essence of the "first sale" doctrine that a purchaser who does no more than stock, display, and resell a producer's product under the producer's trademark violates no right conferred upon the producer by the Lanham Act. When a purchaser resells a trademarked article under the producer's trademark, and nothing more, there is no actionable misrepresentation under the statute.
>
> * * *
>
> Sebastian seeks to bootstrap its case over this obstacle by arguing that when Longs resold genuine Sebastian products in the original containers, the membership mark placed on the container by Sebastian itself became a misrepresentation by Longs that Longs was affiliated with Sebastian. If Sebastian were correct, a producer could avoid the "first sale" rule and invoke the assistance of the courts in controlling downstream distribution of its trademarked products simply by placing a statement on the container that the product was being resold only by affiliates of the producer. Because Sebastian itself placed the collective mark on its products, it is primarily responsible for any confusion that resulted from the mark's assertion of affiliation,

and that confusion cannot be used to support a charge of infringement against Longs.

PAGE 383. Add after *Smith v. Chanel*

NEW KIDS ON THE BLOCK v. NEWS AMERICA PUBLISHING, INC.
United States Court of Appeals, Ninth Circuit, 1991
971 F.2d 302

KOZINSKI, Circuit Judge.

The individual plaintiffs perform professionally as The New Kids on the Block, reputedly one of today's hottest musical acts. This case requires us to weigh their rights in that name against the rights of others to use it in identifying the New Kids as the subjects of public opinion polls.

Background

No longer are entertainers limited to their craft in marketing themselves to the public. This is the age of the multi-media publicity blitzkrieg: Trading on their popularity, many entertainers hawk posters, T-shirts, badges, coffee mugs and the like--handsomely supplementing their incomes while boosting their public images. The New Kids are no exception; the record in this case indicates there are more than 500 products or services bearing the New Kids trademark. Among these are services taking advantage of a recent development in telecommunications: 900 area code numbers, where the caller is charged a fee, a portion of which is paid to the call recipient. Fans can call various New Kids 900 numbers to listen to the New Kids talk about themselves, to listen to other fans talk about the New Kids, or to leave messages for the New Kids and other fans.

The defendants, two newspapers of national circulation, conducted separate polls of their readers seeking an answer to a pressing question: Which one of the New Kids is the most popular? *USA Today*'s announcement contained a picture of the New Kids and asked, "Who's the best on the block?" The announcement listed a 900 number for voting, noted that "any USA Today profits from this phone line will go to charity," and closed with the following:

> New Kids on the Block are pop's hottest group. Which of the five is your fave? Or are they a turn off? ... Each call costs 50 cents. Results in Friday's Life section.

The *Star*'s announcement, under a picture of the New Kids, went to the heart of the matter: "Now which kid is the sexiest?" The announcement, which appeared in the middle of a page containing a story on a New Kids concert, also stated:

> Which of the New Kids on the Block would you most like to move next door? STAR wants to know which cool New Kid is the hottest with our readers.

Readers were directed to a 900 number to register their votes; each call cost 95 cents per minute.

Fearing that the two newspapers were undermining their hegemony over their fans, the New Kids filed a shotgun complaint in federal court raising no fewer than ten claims: (1) common law trademark infringement; (2) Lanham Act false advertising; (3) Lanham Act false designation of origin; (4) Lanham Act unfair competition; (5) state trade name infringement; (6) state false advertising; (7) state unfair competition; (8) commercial misappropriation; (9) common-law misappropriation; and (10) intentional interference with prospective economic advantage. The two papers raised the First Amendment as a defense, on the theory that the polls were part and parcel of their "news- gathering activities." The district court granted summary judgment for defendants. 745 F.Supp. 1540 (C.D.Cal.1990).

Discussion

While the district court granted summary judgment on First Amendment grounds, we are free to affirm on any ground fairly presented by the record. Indeed, where we are able to resolve the case on nonconstitutional grounds, we ordinarily must avoid reaching the constitutional issue. Therefore, we consider first whether the New Kids have stated viable claims on their various causes of action.

I

A. * * *

Throughout the development of trademark law, the purpose of trademarks remained constant and limited: Identification of the manufacturer or sponsor of a good or the provider of a service. And the wrong protected against was traditionally equally limited: Preventing producers from free-riding on their rivals' marks. * * * The core protection of the Lanham Act remains faithful to this conception. * * *

A trademark is a limited property right in a particular word, phrase or symbol. And although English is a language rich in imagery, we need not belabor the point that some words, phrases or symbols better convey their intended meanings than others. Indeed, the primary cost of recognizing property rights in trademarks is the removal of words from (or perhaps non-entrance into) our language. Thus, the holder of a trademark will be denied protection if it is (or becomes) generic, i.e., if it does not relate exclusively to the trademark owner's product. This requirement allays fears that producers will deplete the stock of useful words by asserting exclusive rights in them. When a trademark comes to describe a class of goods rather than an individual product, the courts will hold as a matter of law that use of that mark does not imply sponsorship or endorsement of the product by the original holder.

A related problem arises when a trademark also describes a person, a place or an attribute of a product. If the trademark holder were allowed exclusive rights in such use, the language would be depleted in much the same way as if generic words were protectable. Thus trademark law recognizes a defense where the mark is used only "to describe the goods or services of [a] party, or their geographic origin." 15 U.S.C. § 1115(b)(4). "The 'fair- use' defense, in essence, forbids a trademark registrant to appropriate a descriptive term for his exclusive use and so prevent others from accurately describing a characteristic of their goods." Soweco, Inc. v. Shell Oil Co., 617 F.2d 1178, 1185 (5th Cir.1980). Once again, the courts will hold as a matter of law that the original producer does not sponsor or endorse another product that uses his mark in a descriptive manner.

With many well-known trademarks, such as Jell-O, Scotch tape and Kleenex, there are equally informative non-trademark words describing the products (gelatin, cellophane tape and facial tissue). But sometimes there is no descriptive substitute, and a problem closely related to genericity and descriptiveness is presented when many goods and services are effectively identifiable only by their trademarks. For example, one might refer to "the two-time world champions" or "the professional basketball team from Chicago," but it's far simpler (and more likely to be understood) to refer to the Chicago Bulls. In such cases, use of the trademark does not imply sponsorship or endorsement of the product because the mark is used only to describe the thing, rather than to identify its source.

Indeed, it is often virtually impossible to refer to a particular product for purposes of comparison, criticism, point of reference or any other such purpose without using the mark. For example, reference to a large automobile manufacturer based in Michigan would not differentiate among the Big Three; reference to a large Japanese manufacturer of home electronics would narrow the field to a dozen or more companies. Much useful social and commercial discourse would be all but impossible if speakers were under threat of an infringement lawsuit every time they made reference to a person, company or product by using its trademark.

* * *

The First Circuit confronted a similar problem when the holder of the trademark "Boston Marathon" tried to stop a television station from using the name:

[T]he words "Boston Marathon" ... do more than call attention to Channel 5's program; they also describe the event that Channel 5 will broadcast. Common sense suggests (consistent with the record here) that a viewer who sees those words flash upon the screen will believe simply that Channel 5 will show, or is showing, or has shown, the marathon, not that Channel 5 has some special approval from the [trademark holder] to do so. In technical trademark jargon, the use of words for descriptive purposes is called a "fair use," and the law usually permits it even if the words themselves also constitute a trademark.

WCVB-TV v. Boston Athletic Ass'n, 926 F.2d 42, 46 (1st Cir.1991). Similarly, competitors may use a rival's trademark in advertising and other channels of communication if the use is not false or misleading. See, e.g., Smith v. Chanel, Inc., 402 F.2d 562 (9th Cir.1968) (maker of imitation perfume may use original's trademark in promoting product).

* * * Indeed, we may generalize a class of cases where the use of the trademark does not attempt to capitalize on consumer confusion or to appropriate the cachet of one product for a different one. Such *nominative use* of a mark--where the only word reasonably available to describe a particular thing is pressed into service--lies outside the strictures of trademark law: Because it does not implicate the source-identification function that is the purpose of trademark, it does not constitute unfair competition; such use is fair because it does not imply sponsorship or endorsement by the trademark holder.

To be sure, this is not the classic fair use case where the defendant has used the plaintiff's mark to describe the defendant's *own* product. Here, the New Kids trademark is used to refer to the New Kids themselves. We therefore do not purport to alter the test applicable in the paradigmatic fair use case. If the defendant's use of the plaintiff's trademark refers to something other than the plaintiff's product, the traditional fair use inquiry will continue to govern. But, where the defendant uses a trademark to describe the plaintiff's product, rather than its own, we hold that a commercial user is entitled to a nominative fair use defense provided he meets the following three requirements: First, the product or service in question must be one not readily identifiable without use of the trademark; second, only so much of the mark or marks may be used as is reasonably necessary to identify the product or service; and third, the user must do nothing that would, in conjunction with the mark, suggest sponsorship or endorsement by the trademark holder.

B. The New Kids do not claim there was anything false or misleading about the newspapers' use of their mark. Rather, the first seven causes of action, while purporting to state different claims, all hinge on one key factual allegation: that the newspapers' use of the New Kids name in conducting the unauthorized polls somehow implied that the New Kids were sponsoring the polls. It is no more reasonably possible, however, to refer to the New Kids as an entity than it is to refer to the Chicago Bulls, Volkswagens or the Boston Marathon without using the trademark. Indeed, how could someone not conversant with the proper names of the individual New Kids talk about the group at all? While plaintiffs' trademark certainly deserves protection against copycats and those who falsely claim that the New Kids have endorsed or sponsored them, such protection does not extend to rendering newspaper articles, conversations, polls and comparative advertising impossible. The first nominative use requirement is therefore met.

Also met are the second and third requirements. Both *The Star* and *USA Today* reference the New Kids only to the extent necessary to identify them as the subject of the polls; they do not use the New Kids' distinctive logo or anything else that isn't needed to make the announcements intelligible to readers. Finally, nothing in the announcements suggests joint sponsorship or endorsement by the New Kids. The *USA Today* announcement implies quite the contrary by asking whether the New Kids might be "a turn off." *The Star*'s poll is more effusive but says nothing that expressly or by fair implication connotes endorsement or joint sponsorship on the part of the New Kids.

The New Kids argue that, even if the newspapers are entitled to a nominative fair use defense for the announcements, they are not entitled to it for the polls themselves, which were money-making enterprises separate and apart from the newspapers' reporting businesses. According to plaintiffs, defendants could have minimized the intrusion into their rights by using an 800 number or asking readers to call in on normal telephone lines which would not have resulted in a profit to the newspapers based on the conduct of the polls themselves.

The New Kids see this as a crucial difference, distinguishing this case from *Volkswagenwerk, WCBV-TV* and other nominative use cases. The New Kids' argument in support of this distinction is not entirely implausible: They point out that their fans, like everyone else, have limited resources. Thus a dollar spent calling the newspapers' 900 lines to express loyalty to the New Kids may well be a dollar not spent on New Kids products and services, including the New Kids' own 900 numbers. In short, plaintiffs argue that a nominative fair use defense is inapplicable where the use in question competes directly with that of the trademark holder.

We reject this argument. While the New Kids have a limited property right in their name, that right does not entitle them to control their fans' use of their own money. Where, as here, the use does not imply sponsorship or endorsement, the fact that it is carried on for profit and in competition with the trademark holder's business is beside the point. Voting for their favorite New Kid may be, as plaintiffs point out, a way for fans to articulate their loyalty to the group, and this may diminish the resources available for products and services they sponsor. But the trademark laws do not give the New Kids the right to channel their fans' enthusiasm (and dollars) only into items licensed or authorized by them. The New Kids could not use the trademark laws to prevent the publication of an unauthorized group biography or to censor all parodies or satires which use their name. We fail to see a material difference between these examples and the use here.

Summary judgment was proper as to the first seven causes of action because they all hinge on a theory of implied endorsement; there was none here as the uses in question were purely nominative.

* * *

The district court's judgment is

AFFIRMED.

NOTES

1. Is Judge Kozinski's elaboration of a new defense, the nominative fair use defense, necessary to resolve this case? Isn't the third element of that defense, that the defendant does nothing that suggests sponsorship or endorsement, merely a restatement of the traditional trademark rule that there is no infringement if there is no likelihood of confusion? Does Judge Kozinski's formulation shift the burden on the issue of likelihood of confusion to the defendant?

2. The defense was rejected in Abdul-Jabbar v. General Motors Corp., 75 F.3d 1391 (9th Cir. 1996) where Lew Alcindor's (now Kareem Abdul-Jabbar) record of winning the most valuable player award in the NCAA men's basketball tournament was referred to in a television advertisement for Oldsmobile. The court found a genuine issue of fact as to whether the use implied an endorsement by Abdul-Jabbar and distinguished *New Kids* because the "use of celebrity endorsements in television commercials is so well established by commercial custom that a jury might find an implied endorsement in General Motors' use of the celebrity's name in a commercial, which would not inhere in a newspaper poll."

PAGE 383. Add to Note 2.

A wide-spread practice in the over-the-counter drug and cosmetic industry is for larger retailers to market their own private labeled product side-by-side with the national branded product. Often the private labeled product mimics the trade dress, including container size and colors, of the better known national brand. The private labelers argue that the similarity of trade dress is not intended to confuse consumers but rather to inform consumers that the product is similar to and performs the same function as the national brand. Is this alone sufficient to overcome a claim of trademark infringement? What if, in addition, the private labeler adds to its label the phrase "Compare to [the national brand]"? A trip to any discount store will provide the student with numerous variations of this practice. In Conopco, Inc. v. May Department Stores Co., 46 F.3d 1556 (Fed. Cir. 1994) the court rejected a trademark infringement claim where the private label contained the "Compare to . . . " phrase and a black and white logo of the private labeler prominently displayed on the front of the package. The court observed: ". . . the marketing device employed by defendants in this case is neither new nor subtle. The cases have approved the general practice in a variety of settings, at least to the extent of not finding a violation of the Lanham Act absent a showing by the plaintiff that real consumers have real confusion or likelihood of it with regard to the origin of the products involved." The court discounted the testimony of one consumer who claimed to have been confused because her confusion arose "in part from her assumption * * * that national brand manufacturers secretly market private label brands. First, there is no evidence that this assumption is widely held by the relevant consumers * * *. Second, [where] the national brand is being sold side-by-side with the private label brand, the assumption is at best counter-intuitive -- it assumes that a national brand manufacturer would embark on a scheme to deliberately erode its sales of the national brand."

PAGE 385. Substitute for *Maier Brewing*.

GEORGE BASCH CO., INC. v. BLUE CORAL, INC.
United States Court of Appeals, Second Circuit, 1992
968 F.2d 1532, cert. denied 113 S.Ct. 510 (1992)

WALKER, Circuit Judge:

[Both parties sell metal polishes. After Blue Coral failed to reach an agreement with Basch to distribute, NEVR-DULL, a Basch product, it obtained a similar product from another manufacturer and marketed it under the mark EVER BRITE with a trade dress similar to that of Basch. Basch brought suit under the Lanham Act for trade dress infringement, misappropriation of confidential information, and tortious interference.]

The action was tried to a jury in July 1991. The district court directed a verdict in favor of Blue Coral with respect to Basch's claim for misappropriation of confidential business information. The court also ruled that, as a matter of law, Basch was precluded from receiving damages on its trade dress infringement claim because it had failed to produce any evidence regarding actual consumer confusion or that Blue Coral acted with intent to deceive the public.

The district court concluded, however, that despite Basch's failure to introduce evidence on either of these points, Basch could recover Blue Coral's profits if it succeeded on its trade dress infringement claim. The case was submitted to the jury by special verdict. The jury exonerated Blue Coral on the tortious interference count, but found against it on Basch's trade dress infringement claim. Accordingly, it awarded Basch $200,000 in Blue Coral's profits, allegedly stemming from Blue Coral's wrongful use of its EVER BRITE trade dress. [A judgment was entered against Blue Coral on the profits award.]

* * *

B. *Grounds for Awarding Profits*

We turn now to the issue of whether the district court correctly authorized an award of Blue Coral's profits. Section 35(a) of the Lanham Act generally provides that a successful plaintiff under the act shall be entitled, "subject to the principles of equity, to recover (1) defendant's profits, (2) any damages sustained by the plaintiff, and (3) costs of the action." 15 U.S.C. § 1117(a). Clearly, the statute's invocation of equitable principles as guideposts in the assessment of monetary relief vests the district court with some degree of discretion in shaping that relief. See id., (both damage and profit awards may be assessed "according to the circumstances of the case"). Nevertheless, that discretion must operate within legally defined parameters.

For example, it is well settled that in order for a Lanham Act plaintiff to receive an award of *damages* the plaintiff must prove either " 'actual consumer confusion or deception resulting from the violation,' " Getty Petroleum Corp. v. Island Transportation Corp., 878 F.2d 650, 655 (2d Cir. 1989) or that the defendant's actions were intentionally deceptive thus giving rise to a rebuttable presumption of consumer confusion. Here, Basch failed to present any evidence regarding consumer confusion or intentional deception. Accordingly, prior to the jury's deliberation, the district court correctly decided that damages were not an available form of relief. Basch does not appeal from this ruling.

However, with respect to authorizing an award of Blue Coral's profits, the district judge concluded that § 35(a) affords a wider degree of equitable latitude. In denying its j.n.o.v. motion, the district court rejected Blue Coral's position that, absent a finding of defendant's willfully deceptive conduct, a court may not award profits. Rather, it relied upon contrary dictum in Louis Vuitton S.A. v. Lee, 875 F.2d 584, 588-89 (7th Cir.1989), in determining that a Lanham Act plaintiff may be entitled to the profits of an innocent infringer, i.e., one who inadvertently misappropriates the plaintiff's trade dress. To the extent that the cases are ambiguous as to whether deceptive conduct is a necessary basis for an accounting, we take this opportunity to clarify the law.

The rule in this circuit has been that an accounting for profits is normally available "only if the 'defendant is unjustly enriched, if the plaintiff sustained damages from the infringement, or if the accounting is necessary to deter a willful infringer from doing so again.' " Burndy Corp. v. Teledyne Industries, Inc., 748 F.2d 767, 772 (2d Cir.1984). Courts have interpreted the rule to describe three categorically distinct rationales. *See e.g.,* Cuisinarts, Inc. v. Robot-Coupe Intern. Corp., 580 F.Supp. 634, 637 (S.D.N.Y.1984) ("These justifications are stated in the disjunctive. Any one will do.").

Thus, the fact that willfulness expressly defines the third rationale (deterrence) may suggest that the element of intentional misconduct is unnecessary in order to require an accounting based upon a theory of unjust enrichment or damages. However, the broad language contained in *Burndy Corp.* and *W.E. Bassett Co.* is in no way dispositive on this point. Indeed, a closer investigation into the law's historical development strongly supports our present conclusion that, under any theory, a finding of defendant's willful deceptiveness is a prerequisite for awarding profits.

Unjust Enrichment: The fact that an accounting may proceed on a theory of unjust enrichment is largely a result of legal institutional evolution. Prior to the fusion of law and equity under the Federal Rules of Civil Procedure, *see* Fed.R.Civ.P. 2, courts of law were the sole dispensary of damages, while the chancellor issued specific relief. However, in order to avoid piecemeal litigation, once a court of equity took jurisdiction over a case it would do complete justice--even if that entailed granting a monetary award. This resulted in the development of parallel remedial schemes.

Long ago, the Supreme Court explained the origin of profit awards in trademark infringement suits:

> The infringer is required in equity to account for and yield up his gains to the true owner [of the mark], upon a principle analogous to that which charges a trustee with the profits acquired by the wrongful use of the property of the cestui que trust. Not that equity assumes jurisdiction upon the ground that a trust exists.... [T]he jurisdiction must be rested upon some other equitable ground--in ordinary cases, as in the present, the right to an injunction--but the court of equity, having acquired jurisdiction upon such a ground, retains it for the purpose of administering complete relief, rather than send the injured party to a court of law for his damages. And profits are then allowed as an equitable measure of compensation, on the theory of a trust ex maleficio.

Hamilton-Brown Shoe Co. v. Wolf Brothers & Co., 240 U.S. 251, 259 (1916).

Thus, a defendant who is liable in a trademark or trade dress infringement action may be deemed to hold its profits in constructive trust for the injured plaintiff. However, this results only "when the defendant's sales 'were attributable to its infringing use' of the plaintiff's" mark, *Burndy Corp.*, 748 F.2d at 772 and when the infringing use was at the plaintiff's expense. In other words, a defendant becomes accountable for its profits when the plaintiff can show that, were it not for defendant's infringement, the defendant's sales would otherwise have gone to the plaintiff.

At bottom, this is simply another way of formulating the element of consumer confusion required to justify a damage award under the Lanham Act. As such, it follows that a profits award, premised upon a theory of unjust enrichment, requires a showing of actual consumer confusion--or at least proof of deceptive intent so as to raise the rebuttable presumption of consumer confusion.

Moreover, the doctrine of constructive trust has traditionally been invoked to defeat those gains accrued by wrongdoers as a result of fraud. * * *

The rationale underlying the Supreme Court's holding in *Hamilton-Brown Shoe Co.* reflects this purpose. There, the Court upheld a profits award for trademark infringement where the "imitation of complainant's mark was fraudulent, [and] the profits included in the decree [were] confined to such as accrued to the defendant through its persistence in the unlawful simulation...." 240 U.S. at 261. Thus, it would seem that for the defendant's enrichment to be "unjust" in terms of warranting an accounting, it must be the fruit of willful deception.

Where Plaintiff Sustains Damages: Historically, an award of defendant's profits has also served as a rough proxy measure of plaintiff's damages. Due to the inherent difficulty in isolating the causation behind diverted sales and injured reputation, damages from trademark or trade dress infringement are often hard to establish. Recognizing this, the Supreme Court has stated that, "[i]nfringement and damage having been found, the Act requires the trademark owner to prove only the sales of articles bearing the infringing mark." *Mishawaka Mfg. Co.*, 316 U.S. at 206.

Under this rule, profits from defendant's proven sales are awarded to the plaintiff unless the defendant can show "that the infringement had no relationship" to those earnings. Id. This shifts the burden of proving economic injury off the innocent party, and places the hardship of disproving economic gain onto the infringer. Of course, this "does not stand for the proposition that an accounting will be ordered merely because there has been an infringement." *Champion Plug Co.*, 331 U.S. at 131. Rather, in order to award profits there must first be "a basis for finding damage." Id.; *Mishawaka Mfg. Co.*, 316 U.S. at 206. While a plaintiff who seeks the defendant's profits may be relieved of certain evidentiary requirements otherwise carried by those trying to prove damages, a plaintiff must nevertheless establish its general right to damages before defendant's profits are recoverable.

Thus, under the "damage" theory of profits, a plaintiff typically has been required to show consumer confusion resulting from the infringement. Whether a plaintiff also had to show willfully deceptive conduct on the part of the defendant is not so clear. While some courts "rejected good faith as a defense to an accounting for profits," Burger King Corp. v. Mason, 855 F.2d 779, 781 (11th Cir.1988), others have concluded that a defendant's bad faith is the touchstone of accounting liability.

Deterrence: Finally, we have held that a court may award a defendant's profits solely upon a finding that the defendant fraudulently used the plaintiff's mark. The rationale underlying this holding is not compensatory in nature, but rather seeks to protect the public at large. By awarding the profits of a bad faith infringer to the rightful owner of a mark, we promote the secondary effect of deterring public fraud regarding the source and quality of consumer goods and services.

* * *

Although these three theories address slightly different concerns, they do share common ground. In varying degrees, a finding of defendant's intentional deceptiveness has always been an important consideration in determining whether an accounting was an appropriate remedy. In view of this, the American Law Institute has recently concluded that a finding of willful infringement is the necessary catalyst for the disgorgement of ill-gotten profits. *See Restatement* [(Third) of Unfair Competition, Tent. Draft No. 3, 1991], § 37(1)(a) ("One ... is liable for the net profits earned on profitable transactions resulting from [the infringement], if, but only if, the actor engaged in conduct with the intention of causing confusion or deception ...").

We agree with the position set forth in § 37 of the *Restatement* and therefore hold that, under § 35(a) of the Lanham Act, a plaintiff must prove that an infringer acted with willful deception before the infringer's profits are recoverable by way of an accounting. Along with the *Restatement* 's drafters, we believe that this requirement is necessary to avoid the conceivably draconian impact that a profits remedy might have in some cases. While damages directly measure the plaintiff's loss, defendant's profits measure the defendant's gain. Thus, an accounting may overcompensate for a plaintiff's actual injury and create a windfall judgment at the defendant's expense. See *Restatement*, § 37 at cmt. e. Of course, this is not to be confused with *plaintiff's* lost profits, which have been traditionally compensable as an element of plaintiff's damages.

So as to limit what may be an undue windfall to the plaintiff, and prevent the potentially inequitable treatment of an "innocent" or "good faith" infringer, most courts require proof of intentional misconduct before allowing a plaintiff to recover the defendant's profits. We underscore that in the absence of such a showing, a plaintiff is not foreclosed from receiving monetary relief. Upon proof of actual consumer confusion, a plaintiff may still obtain damages-- which, in turn, may be inclusive of plaintiff's own lost profits.

* * *

Having stated that a finding of willful deceptiveness is necessary in order to warrant an accounting for profits, we note that it may not be sufficient. While under certain circumstances, the egregiousness of the fraud may, of its own, justify an accounting, generally, there are other factors to be considered. Among these are such familiar concerns as: (1) the degree of certainty that the defendant benefited from the unlawful conduct; (2) availability and adequacy of other remedies; (3) the role of a particular defendant in effectuating the infringement; (4) plaintiff's laches; and (5) plaintiff's unclean hands. *See generally Restatement*, § 37(2) at cmt. f & cases cited in the reporter's notes. The district court's discretion lies in assessing the relative importance of these factors and determining whether, on the whole, the equities weigh in favor of an accounting. As the Lanham Act dictates, every award is "subject to equitable principles" and should be determined "according to the circumstances of the case." 15 U.S.C. § 1117.

In light of the foregoing legal analysis, the district court's error becomes apparent. To begin with, the district judge concluded that an accounting was warranted in order to prevent Blue Coral's unjust enrichment. However, as stated earlier, Basch produced no evidence to suggest that the infringement caused any sales diversion. As a result, there is nothing to suggest that Blue Coral's EVER BRITE sales were at Basch's expense. It follows that "an accounting based on unjust enrichment is precluded." *Burndy Corp.*, 748 F.2d at 773.

Secondly, even if Basch had shown loss of sales, it still would not have been entitled to an accounting for profits under a theory of unjust enrichment--or any other theory. The jury made no finding to the effect that Blue Coral was a bad faith infringer. Indeed, one reason why the judge refused to let the jury assess damages was the fact that Basch failed to present any evidence regarding bad faith infringement. Nevertheless, Basch argues that the court's jury instruction on liability--which suggested that the jury consider whether Blue Coral intended "to benefit" from Basch's NEVR-DULL trade dress--taken in conjunction with the special verdict finding that Blue Coral "intended to imitate Basch's NEVR-DULL trade dress," results in a constructive finding that Blue Coral engaged in intentionally deceptive conduct. We disagree.

There is an "essential distinction ... between a deliberate attempt to deceive and a deliberate attempt to compete. Absent confusion, imitation of certain successful features in another's product is not unlawful and to that extent a 'free ride' is permitted." Norwich Pharmacal Co. v. Sterling Drug, Inc., 271 F.2d 569, 572 (2d Cir.1959) (citation omitted). Of course, even when a likelihood of confusion does arise, that does not inexorably lead to the conclusion that the defendant acted with deliberate deceit. Depending upon the circumstances, consumer confusion might as easily result from an innocent competitor who inadvertently crosses the line between a "free ride" and liability, as it could from a defendant's intentionally fraudulent conduct.

Accordingly, we reverse the district court's denial of Blue Coral's j.n.o.v. motion, insofar as it related to the availability of an accounting in this case, and we vacate the jury's profits award. Because we hold that an accounting was not available in this case, we need not reach the issue of whether it was appropriate for the jury to calculate profits.

* * *

KEARSE, Circuit Judge, dissenting in part:

* * *

The jury was instructed, *inter alia*, that it could not find infringement of the NEVR-DULL trade dress simply on the basis that Blue Coral had intentionally copied it. Rather, it was told that if it found that Blue Coral had intentionally copied the NEVR-DULL trade dress, it could find infringement only if it also found a likelihood of confusion, which it might infer if it found "there was an intent to benefit from Basch's protectable right in its NEVR-DULL trade dress." The court also told the jury that the amount of monetary damages it could award for trade-dress infringement was "limited to what you find the defendant Blue Coral made as a result of the violation of Nevr-Dull trade dress." The court explained that the jury could properly award to Basch only the amount Blue Coral made that it would not be fair or equitable for Blue Coral to retain.

Having been thus instructed, the jury was asked the following questions and gave the following answers:

"Was Basch's trade dress for its NEVR-DULL product inherently distinctive? Yes."

"Did the trade dress for Basch's NEVR-DULL product acquire secondary meaning? Yes."

"Did defendants intend to imitate Basch's NEVR-DULL trade dress? Yes."

"Did defendants' use of its trade dress in marketing EVER BRITE create a likelihood of confusion among a substantial number of members of the consuming public as to the source of EVER BRITE, i.e., as to whether EVER BRITE was manufactured by the maker of NEVR-DULL? Yes."

"Did the violation of Basch's right(s) proximately cause damage to Basch? Yes."

The jury found that the "[p]rofits earned by Blue Coral due to trade dress infringement" totaled "$200,000."

These findings of Blue Coral's intentional copying of a distinctive trade dress that had acquired secondary meaning, thereby creating a likelihood of consumer confusion, in order to benefit from the breach of Basch's rights, and culminating in the unfair receipt by Blue Coral of $200,000 in profits due to the infringement, suffice, in my view, to support the conclusion that Blue Coral was unjustly enriched. I would affirm the district court's judgment that an award of profits was justified.

PAGE 388. Read with *George Basch, supra*

SANDS, TAYLOR & WOOD CO. v. The QUAKER OATS COMPANY
United States Court of Appeals, Seventh Circuit, 1992
978 F.2d 947, cert. denied 113 S.Ct. 1879 (1993)

CUDAHY, Circuit judge.

[From 1921 Middleby used the trademark "Thirst Aid" for soft drinks, ice cream toppings, and soda fountain syrups. In 1973 STW, a small Vermont-based company purchased Middleby and succeeded to the trademarks. In the late 1970's STW's sales of "Thirst Aid" declined. In 1980 Pet, Inc., negotiated a nationwide license to use the mark on an isotonic beverage intended to compete with the popular "Gatorade", an isotonic beverage produced by Stokely, but after a five month test marketing and after capturing 25% of the test markets, Pet withdrew. In 1981 STW sold the Middleby operation to Karp but obtained a license back for retail use of the "Thirst Aid" mark. In 1983 Stokely was acquired by Quaker Oats and shortly thereafter adopted the slogan "Gatorade is Thirst Aid for That Deep Down Body Thirst". Lawyers for Quaker concluded that the slogan was descriptive, that the use of "Thirst Aid" was not a use as a trademark, and that accordingly the slogan was a fair use and not an infringement. However, the district court granted summary judgment for STW and awarded it 10 percent of Quaker's pre-tax profits on Gatorade. That award including prejudgment interest and attorneys fees was $42,629,399.09. Quaker appealed.

The Court of Appeals upheld the district court's holdings that Quaker's use of "Thirst Aid" was as a trademark and not a fair use and that there was a likelihood of reverse confusion.]

V.

The district court awarded STW ten percent of Quaker's profits on sales of Gatorade for the period during which the "Thirst Aid" campaign ran-- $24,730,000-- based on its finding that Quaker had acted in bad faith. The court also ordered Quaker to pay STW's attorney's fees, again based on the finding of bad faith, as well as prejudgment interest on the award of profits beginning from May 12, 1984. Quaker challenges all three of these rulings.

A. *Profits*

Quaker argues that an award of its profits was inappropriate here because there was no evidence that Quaker intended to trade on STW's good will or reputation; indeed, such an intent is necessarily absent in a reverse confusion case. According to Quaker, an award of the defendant's profits is justified only where the defendant has been unjustly enriched by appropriating the plaintiff's good will. There is some support for this position in the case law. * * * The law of this circuit is not, however, so limited. As we stated in Roulo:

> The Lanham Act specifically provides for the awarding of profits in the discretion of the judge subject only to principles of equity. As stated by this Court, "The trial court's primary function is to make violations of the Lanham Act unprofitable to the infringing party." [citation omitted] Other than general equitable considerations, there is no express requirement that the parties be in direct competition or that the infringer wilfully infringe the trade dress to justify an award of profits. [citation omitted] Profits are awarded under different rationales including unjust enrichment, deterrence, and compensation.

886 F.2d at 941. This broader view seems to be more consistent with the language of the Lanham Act than is the narrower (though perhaps more logical) rule espoused by Quaker. We decline to adopt Quaker's restrictive interpretation in light of Seventh Circuit precedent.

Nevertheless, we are mindful of the fact that awards of profits are to be limited by "equitable considerations." The district court justified the award of profits based on its finding that Quaker acted in bad faith. The evidence of bad faith in this case, however, is pretty slim. The court based its finding on (1) Quaker's "failure to conduct a basic trademark search until days before the airing of the Thirst Aid commercial," and its "anonymous, cursory investigations" of Karp's use of the mark once it obtained such a search; (2) Quaker's decision to continue with the "Thirst Aid" campaign after it discovered Karp's registrations; (3) the fact that Quaker did not seek a formal legal opinion regarding potential trademark issues until after the first "Thirst Aid" commercials were aired; and (4) Quaker's failure to take "reasonable precautions" to avoid the likelihood of confusion.

None of these facts is particularly good evidence of bad faith. For example, Quaker's in-house counsel, Lannin, testified at trial that his review of the "Thirst Aid" campaign in February or March of 1984 did not include a trademark search because he concluded that the proposed advertisements used the words "Thirst Aid" descriptively, and not as a trademark, and therefore did not raise any trademark issues. The district court apparently accepted this testimony, but nonetheless found Quaker's failure to investigate indicative of bad faith. Further, the court stated that it is a "close question" whether "Thirst Aid" is a descriptive term. Indeed, this court has found that the district court erred in concluding that "Thirst Aid" was not descriptive as a matter of law. A party who acts in reasonable reliance on the advice of counsel regarding a close question of trademark law generally does not act in bad faith.

Nor does Quaker's decision to proceed with the "Thirst Aid" campaign once it learned of Karp's registrations necessarily show bad faith. Based both on his earlier conclusion that "Thirst Aid" was descriptive and on his investigation into Karp's use of the term, which revealed that Karp was not currently using the THIRST-AID mark on any products sold at retail, Lannin concluded that Quaker's ads did not infringe Karp's rights in its marks. That conclusion was confirmed by the opinion Quaker obtained a few weeks later from its outside counsel, which concluded that Quaker was making a fair use of "Thirst Aid" because " 'Thirst-Aid [sic] is not used as a trademark on the product but rather clearly as a positioning statement or claim in advertising. It is used descriptively to inform the purchaser that the product will aid your thirst, and as a play on the words 'First Aid.' " Mem. re Use of Term "Thirst-Aid" as Advertising Claim for Gatorade at 7-8 (undated). * * * Even the defendant's refusal to cease using the mark upon demand is not necessarily indicative of bad faith. * * *

Quaker's failure to obtain a formal legal opinion from outside counsel until after the "Thirst Aid" campaign began is similarly weak evidence of bad faith. Given Lannin's sincere, reasonable conclusion that Quaker's ads used "Thirst Aid" descriptively, so that no trademark issue was raised, Quaker had no reason to seek the opinion of outside trademark counsel. Similarly, Quaker had no reason to take any precautions to avoid likelihood of confusion; Quaker's research had revealed that there was no product about which people were likely to be confused.

A determination of bad faith is a finding of fact subject to the clearly erroneous standard of review. We cannot say on this record that the district court's conclusion was clearly erroneous. We do think, however, that the evidence of bad faith here is marginal at best. Further, this is not a case where the senior user's trademark is so well-known that the junior user's choice of a confusingly similar mark, out of the infinite number of marks in the world, itself supports an inference that the junior user acted in bad faith. There is no question that Quaker developed the "Thirst Aid" campaign entirely independently, with no knowledge of STW's marks. In such a case, an award of $24 million in profits is not "equitable"; rather, it is a windfall to the plaintiff. Quaker may have been unjustly enriched by using STW's mark without paying for it, but the award of profits bears no relationship to that enrichment. A reasonable royalty, perhaps related in some way to the fee STW was paid by Pet, would more accurately reflect both the extent of Quaker's unjust enrichment and the interest of STW that has been infringed. We therefore reverse the district court's award of profits and remand for a redetermination of damages. A generous approximation of the royalties Quaker would have had to pay STW for the use of the THIRST-AID mark had it recognized the validity of STW's claims seems to us an appropriate measure of damages, although perhaps not the only one. In any event, we can conceive of no rational measure of damages that would yield $24 million.[19]

* * *

VI.

For the foregoing reasons, the decision of the district court is AFFIRMED in part, REVERSED in part and REMANDED for further proceedings.

RIPPLE, Circuit Judge, concurring.

I join the judgment of the court and all but part V of Judge Cudahy's comprehensive and thoughtful opinion. In my view, Quaker's corporate conduct in this matter deserves a somewhat less charitable appraisal than that presented in part V. Therefore, in assessing damages, I believe the district court, in the exercise of its discretion, might well place substantial emphasis on deterrence. Therefore, I doubt very much that damages measured by a "reasonable royalty" --a speculative approximation itself-- necessarily would suffice in this case. Nevertheless, I agree with Judge Cudahy that the district court's use of a "percentage of profits" benchmark for the award of damages is difficult to sustain. I therefore concur in his conclusion that a more precise determination is appropriate.

FAIRCHILD, Senior Circuit Judge, dissenting in part.

Twenty-four million dollars ($24 million) is, indeed, a big number. It is, however, only 10% of the profit realized by Quaker out of the product it marketed by using STW's mark. We are affirming the finding that Quaker used the mark in bad faith. The real question, it seems to me, is one of causation. What portion of Quaker's profit resulted from its use of THIRST AID, and therefore constituted unjust

---

[19] Because neither Judge Ripple nor Judge Fairchild joins this part of the court's opinion, it expresses the individual views of Judge Cudahy. To enable this issue to be decided by majority vote, however, Judge Cudahy has no difficulty with deferring to Judge Ripple's view, expressed in his separate opinion, that the district court's award of damages should be reversed and remanded for "a more precise determination" not limited to a reasonable royalty. Thus, Judges Cudahy and Ripple agree that, in recalculating the award of damages, the district court should be guided by the following principles: (1) the court may not simply award STW a percentage of Quaker's profits; (2) the court should use a reasonable royalty as a baseline or starting point for determining the appropriate award; (3) in determining the appropriate award, the court may take into account the possible need for deterrence, which may involve consideration of the amount of Quaker's profits.

enrichment? I am unable to say that the district court's estimate of 10% was unreasonable or clearly erroneous. Quaker made no showing that it should have been a different number. The 90% ($216 million) of profit which Quaker retains is no paltry reward for everything it contributed to the success of the venture.

Therefore, I respectfully dissent from the decision to reverse the award.

SANDS, TAYLOR & WOOD CO. v. THE QUAKER OATS COMPANY
United States District Court, Northern District of Illinois, 1993
1993 WL 204092

Judge Marshall

* * *

Thus the Court of Appeals divided 1-1-1 on the subject of damages. Judge Cudahy thought $24 million was not equitable and was a "windfall"; Judge Ripple thought that there should be a "more precise determination" of damages but he doubted "very much that damages measured by a 'reasonable royalty'--a speculative approximation itself--necessarily would suffice in this case" and that the "district court, in the exercise of its discretion, might well place substantial emphasis on deterrence"; Judge Fairchild would have affirmed.

Judge Cudahy then added footnote 19 to his opinion * * * I regard footnote 19 as the mandate of the Court of Appeals, taking into account its judicial history. All that is before me is a recalculation of damages.

* * *

The Court of Appeals * * * has returned the case to me with instructions that I recalculate the award of damages using "a reasonable royalty as a baseline or starting point." Judge Cudahy suggests a "generous approximation." Judge Ripple "doubt[s] very much that damages measured by a 'reasonable royalty'--a speculative approximation itself-- necessarily would suffice in this case." However, Judge Cudahy admonishes "no rational measure of damages ... would yield $24 million." And Judge Ripple agrees that the original award of damages "is difficult to sustain." Thus the message appears to be: Be generous but not too generous, i.e., something less than $24 million.

* * *

The hypothetical determination of a reasonable royalty in a case such as this is a form of restitution designed to prevent unjust enrichment. * * * Determining a reasonable royalty is not a simple task. In Georgia-Pacific Corp. v. U.S. Plywood-Champion Papers, Inc., 318 F.Supp. 11 16 (S.D.N.Y.1970), modified and aff'd., 446 F.2d 295 (2d Cir.1971), cert. denied, 404 U.S. 870 (1971), the district court provided the following criteria for determining a reasonable royalty: (1) the royalty rates received in prior licenses by the licensor, (2) prior rates paid by the licensee, (3) the licensor's licensing policies, (4) the nature and scope of the infringer's infringing use, (5) the special value of the mark to the infringer, (6) the profitability of the infringer's use, (7) the lack of viable alternatives, (8) the opinion of expert witnesses, and (9) the amount that the licensor and licensee would have agreed upon in voluntary negotiations. These elements have received widespread acceptance and I apply them here. But the determination of a reasonable royalty remains a legal fiction, "created in an effort to 'compensate' when profits are not provable, a 'reasonable royalty' device conjures a 'willing' licensor and licensee, who like ghosts of Christmas Past are dimly seen as 'negotiating' a 'license.' There is, of course, no actual willingness on either side, and no license to do anything, the infringer being normally enjoined ... from further [use of the plaintiff's trademark]." Panduit Corp. v. Stahlin Bros. Fibre Works, Inc., [517 F.2d 1152 (2d Cir.1978)] at 1159.

So plaintiff sat at the hypothetical table with an incontestable registered mark of proven success in the isotonic beverage field while defendant was about to launch a new campaign in which THIRST-AID was its most attractive gambit. What royalty rate would a willing licensor and a willing licensee agree to? Plaintiff urges a running royalty of 1% of sales for the first year and .5% for each year thereafter. This rate is considerably less than plaintiff's witness Ralph Chapek's testimonial proposal of a $500,000 non-refundable fee, 2% of first year sales, 1.5% of second year sales, 1% of third through tenth year sales and .5% thereafter. Plaintiff's proposal is also less than its own 1% for King Arthur Flour, Chapek's Mrs. Fields/Sara Lee (5%), TGI Friday's/Stilwell Foods (24%), Ore/Ida (5%) and defendant's witnesses AAU (4- 7%) and Baseball Hall of Fame/Admiral Awards (4-10%). And while plaintiff's proposal is greater than its license to Pet of .5% and .33%, plaintiff's bargaining position in 1984 was much stronger than it was in 1980 and defendant's need for THIRST-AID in 1984 was greater than Pet's in 1980.

For its part defendant says a flat fee of $100,000 would exceed the fair valuation of THIRST-AID in 1984. Certainly that is not a "generous approximation." Indeed, it does not comport with defendant's earlier assertion that plaintiff's Pet agreement "establishes a royalty rate," or its assertion in its brief on the nature of the hearing on remand that "the Seventh Circuit remanded the case only for a more precise calculation of a royalty-based profit disgorgement."

I find that plaintiff's proposal of 1%-.5% of sales is reasonable and comports with the mandate of the Court of Appeals. In reaching this finding I have taken into account plaintiff's prior licenses, (defendant has declined to disclose its prior licenses), plaintiff's licensing policies, the nature and scope of defendant's infringing use (recounted in detail in my original decision and Judge Cudahy's opinion), the special value of THIRST-AID to defendant in 1984 (the huge increase in sales during infringement followed by a sharp decline after infringement ceased), the profitability of the defendant's infringement, the questionable attractiveness of defendant's alternatives, the expert opinions and defendant's persistent infringement in the face of the admonitions by its inside and outside counsel and my May 1985 ruling that it was infringing.

Applying this royalty rate to defendant's sales, less the $95 million in annual sales it enjoyed prior to its infringement, results in a royalty payment due plaintiff in the amount of $10,328,411 together with prejudgment interest (the award of which was affirmed by the Court of Appeals) in the amount of $5,431,413 for a total of $15,749,824.

Is this award adequate? Defendant knowingly and in bad faith infringed plaintiff's incontestable mark. Defendant knew of the mark. It knew of its registration. It knew it was incontestable. It knew that it had been used successfully by Pet. It was told immediately following its public use that it was infringing and would damage plaintiff's mark. It disregarded the advice of its outside trademark counsel to minimize the use of THIRST-AID in its advertising. It persisted for five years in its infringing use of plaintiff's THIRST-AID mark after I ruled in June, 1985 that its use was infringing. Will the imposition of a hypothetical licensing royalty deter predatory conduct such as defendant's? I doubt it. The royalty is nothing more than an approximation of what defendant would have paid plaintiff had defendant acted lawfully. "[An] infringer [has] nothing to lose, and everything to gain if [it] could count on paying only the normal, routine royalty, non-fringers might have paid ... [T]he infringer would be in a 'heads-I-win, tails-you-lose position.' " Panduit Corp. v. Stahlin Fibre Works, 575 F.2d 1152, 1158 (6th Cir.1978).

Plaintiff urges that I double or triple the royalty award. The Lanham Act provides for the trebling of damages in an appropriate case. * * *

* * *

After paying plaintiff a royalty of $10,328,411 defendant will realize a profit of $303,000,000 on its sales of GATORADE during the period of infringement. * * * Under the mandate in this case I "may take into account the possible need for deterrence, which may involve consideration of the amount of Quaker's profit." Indeed, Judge Ripple suggested a "substantial emphasis on deterrence."

I realize that the earlier award was large. Indeed, I am told by defendant it was the largest trademark award in history. But I know of no case in which an infringer has reaped the dollar benefits from infringement that defendant has here. To deter conduct such as defendant's, and in the exercise of my discretion under the Lanham Act, I double the amount of the hypothetical royalty to $20,656,822. However, prejudgment interest is applied only to the initial royalty award. Thus plaintiffs award of double royalty is $20,656,822 plus prejudgment interest of $5,431,413 for a total of $26,088,235.

NOTES

1. Judge Marshall's revised $26+million dollar award was appealed. The Seventh Circuit returned another 1-1-1 decision affirming in part and remanding in part. Sands, Taylor & Wood v. The Quaker Oats Co., 34 F.3d 1340 (7th Cir. 1994). All three judges approved of the calculation of the reasonable royalty of $10 million but could not agree on the appropriateness of the enhanced award. Judge Ripple emphasized the hypothetical nature of the royalty award:

> In our earlier opinion, we expressed concern that the mere award of a royalty would not be an adequate measure of damages. We noted that it is at best a rough approximation of the plaintiff's loss and therefore well might not compensate the victim fully for its loss. To ensure that any ambiguity with respect to the magnitude of that loss falls on the malefactor's shoulders and not on those of the injured party, the district court clearly had the authority to enhance the award. Indeed, when supported by the evidence, such an enhancement is necessary to deter adequately the wrongdoer.
>
> * * *
>
> As we have noted earlier, in making its determination of enhanced damages, the district court made reference to the hypothetical nature of the royalty calculation. We cannot determine, however, whether the entire enhancement was based upon this consideration or on an amorphous concern for deterrence unrelated to the initial calculation of the royalty. In directing the district court to use a royalty figure as a baseline, we contemplated that the enhancement would be tied to that determination. We are also concerned that, in calculating the hypothetical royalty based on the factors enumerated in [*Georgia-Pacific*] the district court relied on the same factors both to determine and to enhance the royalty. To the degree that those factors have been considered in the determination of the base figure, they should not be double-counted by using them to calculate an enhancement after they have been used to arrive at the base royalty.
>
> Although we regret the necessity of returning this case to the district court for further proceedings, we believe that it is necessary for the district court to state with more precision the basis for the enhancement. * * *

Judge Fairchild preferred to affirm the entire judgment but in order to form a majority joined Judge Ripple's opinion. Judge Cudahy dissented. Reaffirming his view that the evidence of bad faith in this case was "thin" and the royalty awarded "generous", he could find no basis for enhancing the award.

In Sands, Taylor & Wood Co. v. The Quaker Oats Co., 1995 WL 221871 (N.D. Ill. 1995), Judge Marshall, on remand, responded:

> In some respects I am called upon to justify my earlier judgment. I articulated the reasons for my decision in my memorandum opinion of June 7, 1993. Certainly I should not conjure up new reasons. I have somewhat the same apprehension as Job in his second dialogue with Bildad, "If I justify myself, mine own mouth shall condemn me." Job 9:20, King James Version. Or "If I would justify myself, my own mouth shall condemn me." Job 9:20, Douay Version.
>
> The royalty of $10,328,411, while substantial, was modest. It was based upon a running royalty of 1% of sales for the first year and .5% for each year thereafter. This was lower than testified to by any of plaintiff's or defendant's witnesses. Furthermore, I excluded from the gross sales to which the rates of 1% and .5% were applied amounts equal to defendant's gross sales prior to the period of infringement.
>
> The court of appeals in Sands I and Sands II agreed that defendant knowingly and in bad faith infringed plaintiff's mark. Defendant knew of the mark. It knew of its registration. It knew it was incontestable. It knew it had been used successfully by Pet under a license with plaintiff. Plaintiff immediately notified defendant following defendant's public use of THIRST-AID that defendant was infringing and would damage plaintiff's mark. Defendant disregarded the advice of its outside trademark counsel to minimize the use of THIRST-AID in its advertising. It persisted for five years in its infringing use of plaintiff's THIRST-AID mark after I had rejected its fair use defense.
>
> * * *
>
> The royalty which I awarded was 3.3% of defendant's profits during the period of infringement. In Sands I the court of appeals stated that my decision on remand could "involve consideration of the amount of Quaker's profits." 978 F.2d at 963 n. 19. Wouldn't Quaker, a profit-seeking person willing to violate federal law, pay 3.3 cents to make a dollar? Of course it would and did. Thus a base royalty would not make "the willful trademark infringement ... sufficiently unprofitable." Sands II at 1348. The post-infringement royalty "becomes for the malefactor simply the cost of doing business." Sands II at 1351.
>
> The enhancement is not a penalty. It reflects the inadequacy of the base royalty award in light of the "circumstances of the case,"

the extraordinary profits defendant realized as a consequence of its deliberate infringement. * * *

Furthermore, I assure the court of appeals that I did not "double-count" the factors which I used to determine the base royalty.

I can say no more.

Are you now in favor of the "reasonable royalty rate" to measure damages in trademark cases? Do you sense that Judge Marshall is somewhat frustrated about his task? Is there anything inherent in the nature of trademark litigation that inevitably leads to situations like this? What is the preferrable measure of damages in cases like this? Why would Congress include the enhancement remedy of increased damages and then require them to be compensatory?

2. In Lindy Pen Company Inc. v. Bic Pen Corp., 982 F.2d 1400 (9th Cir.), cert. denied, 114 S.Ct. 64 (1993) the Ninth Circuit held that an award of an accounting of the defendant's profits depended on "willful infringement" which "carries a connotation of deliberate intent to deceive." The fact that the defendant knew of the plaintiff's earlier use of the mark was not sufficient to show the infringement was willful. However, in Adray v. Adry-Mart, Inc., 68 F.3d 362 (9th Cir. 1995) the same court awarded plaintiff damages without a finding of willful infringement even though the damages were calculated as the defendant's profits attributable to the infringement. Can you rationalize the difference in these cases?

3. In the *Adray* case, *supra*, the plaintiff sought to recover its prospective corrective advertising costs -- the expenditures it would make in the future to correct the confusion created by the defendant's infringement. The district court refused, holding that prospective corrective advertising costs can only be recovered when plaintiff shows he was financially unable to conduct the advertising before trial. The Ninth Circuit reversed: "Prospective costs may be difficult to determine precisely and present a danger of overcompensation if they exceed the value of the mark; however, the burden of any uncertainty in the amount of damages should be borne by the wrongdoer and overcompensation can be avoided by appropriate limitation in the instruction." Do you see any reason why an award of prospective corrective advertising costs would not be appropriate in every infringement case?

PAGE 400. Add after *Exxon*.

INDIANAPOLIS COLTS, INC. v.
METROPOLITAN BALTIMORE FOOTBALL CLUB L. P.
United States Court of Appeals, Seventh Circuit, 1994
34 F.3d 410

POSNER, J.

The Indianapolis Colts and the National Football League, to which the Colts belong, brought suit for trademark infringement against the Canadian Football League's new team in Baltimore, which wants to call itself the "Baltimore CFL Colts." (Four of the Canadian Football League's teams are American.) The plaintiffs obtained a preliminary injunction against the new team's using the name "Colts," or "Baltimore Colts," or "Baltimore CFL Colts," in connection with the playing of professional football, the broadcast of football games, or the sale of merchandise to football fans and other buyers. The ground for the injunction was that consumers of "Baltimore CFL Colts" merchandise are likely to think, mistakenly, that the new Baltimore team is an NFL team related in some fashion to the Indianapolis Colts, formerly the Baltimore Colts. From the order granting the injunction the new team and its owners appeal to us. Since the injunction was granted, the new team has played its first two games-- without a name.

A bit of history is necessary to frame the dispute. In 1952, the National Football League permitted one of its teams, the Dallas Texans, which was bankrupt, to move to Baltimore, where it was renamed the "Baltimore Colts." Under that name it became one of the most illustrious teams in the history of professional football. In 1984, the team's owner, with the permission of the NFL, moved the team to Indianapolis, and it was renamed the "Indianapolis Colts." The move, sudden and secretive, outraged the citizens of Baltimore. The city instituted litigation in a futile effort to get the team back--even tried, unsuccessfully, to get the team back by condemnation under the city's power of eminent domain--and the Colts brought a countersuit that also failed.

Nine years later, the Canadian Football League granted a franchise for a Baltimore team. Baltimoreans clamored for naming the new team the "Baltimore Colts." And so it was named--until the NFL got wind of the name and threatened legal action. The name was then changed to "Baltimore CFL Colts" and publicity launched, merchandise licensed, and other steps taken in preparation for the commencement of play this summer.

* * *

They make a tremendous to-do over the fact that the district judge found that the Indianapolis Colts abandoned the trademark "Baltimore Colts" when they moved to Indianapolis. Well, of course; they were no longer playing football under the name "Baltimore Colts," so could not have used the name as the team's trademark; they could have used it on merchandise but chose not to, until 1991 (another story--and not one we need tell). When a mark is abandoned, it returns to the public domain, and is appropriable anew--in principle. In practice, because "subsequent use of [an] abandoned mark may well evoke a continuing association with the prior use, those who make subsequent use may be required to take reasonable precautions to prevent confusion." 2 McCarthy, supra, s 17.01[2], at p. 17-3. This precept is especially important where, as in this case, the former owner of the abandoned mark continues to market the same product or service under a similar name, though we cannot find any previous cases of this kind. No one questions the validity of "Indianapolis Colts" as the trademark of the NFL team that plays out of Indianapolis and was formerly known as the Baltimore Colts. If "Baltimore CFL Colts" is confusingly similar to "Indianapolis Colts" by virtue of the history of the Indianapolis team and the overlapping product and geographical markets served by it and by the new Baltimore team, the latter's use of the abandoned mark would infringe the Indianapolis Colts' new mark. The Colts' abandonment of a mark confusingly similar to their new mark neither broke the continuity of the team in its different locations--it was the same team, merely having a different home base and therefore a different geographical component in its name--nor entitled a third party to pick it up and use it to confuse Colts fans, and other actual or potential consumers of products and services marketed by the Colts or by other National Football League teams, with regard to the identity, sponsorship, or league affiliation of the third party, that is, the new Baltimore team.

* * *

A professional sports team is like Heraclitus's river: always changing, yet always the same. When Mr. Irsay transported his team, the Baltimore Colts, from Baltimore to Indianapolis in one night in 1984, the team remained, for a time anyway, completely intact: same players, same coaches, same front-office personnel. With the passage of time, of course, the team changed. Players retired or were traded, and were replaced. Coaches and other nonplaying personnel came and went. But as far as the record discloses there is as much institutional continuity between the Baltimore Colts of 1984 and the Indianapolis Colts of 1994 as there was between the Baltimore Colts of 1974 and the Baltimore Colts of 1984. Johnny Unitas, the Baltimore Colts' most famous player, swears in his affidavit that his old team has no connection with the Indianapolis Colts, and he has even asked the Colts to expunge his name from its record books. He is angry with Irsay for moving the team. He is entitled to his anger, but it has nothing to do with this lawsuit. The Colts were Irsay's team, it was moved intact, there is no evidence it has changed more since the move than it had in the years before. There is, in contrast, no continuity, no links contractual or otherwise, nothing but a geographical site in common, between the Baltimore Colts and the Canadian Football League team that would like to use its name. Any suggestion that there is such continuity is false and potentially misleading.

Potentially; for if everyone knows there is no contractual or institutional continuity, no pedigree or line of descent, linking the Baltimore-Indianapolis Colts and the new CFL team that wants to call itself the "Baltimore Colts" (or, grudgingly, the "Baltimore CFL Colts"), then there is no harm, at least no harm for which the Lanham Act provides a remedy, in the new Baltimore team's appropriating the name "Baltimore Colts" to play under and sell merchandise under. If not everyone knows, there is harm. Some people who might otherwise watch the Indianapolis Colts (or some other NFL team, for remember that the NFL, representing all the teams, is a coplaintiff) on television may watch the Baltimore CFL Colts instead, thinking they are the "real" Baltimore Colts, and the NFL will lose revenue. A few (doubtless very few) people who might otherwise buy tickets to an NFL game may buy tickets to a Baltimore CFL Colts game instead. Some people who might otherwise buy merchandise stamped with the name "Indianapolis Colts" or the name of some other NFL team may buy merchandise stamped "Baltimore CFL Colts," thinking it a kin of the NFL's Baltimore Colts in the glory days of Johnny Unitas rather than a newly formed team that plays Canadian football in a Canadian football league. It would be naive to suppose that no consideration of such possibilities occurred to the owners of the new Baltimore team when they were choosing a name, though there is no evidence that it was the dominant or even a major consideration.

Confusion thus is possible, and may even have been desired; but is it likely? There is great variance in consumer competence, and it would be undesirable to impoverish the lexicon of trade names merely to protect the most gullible fringe of the consuming public. The Lanham Act does not cast the net of protection so wide. The legal standard under the Act has been formulated variously, but the various formulations come down to whether it is likely that the challenged mark if permitted to be used by the defendant would cause the plaintiff to lose a substantial number of consumers. Pertinent to this determination is the similarity of the marks and of the parties' products, the knowledge of the average consumer of the product, the overlap in the parties' geographical markets, and the other factors that the cases consider. The aim is to strike a balance between, on the one hand, the interest of the seller of the new product, and of the consuming public, in an arresting, attractive, and informative name that will enable the new product to compete effectively against existing ones, and, on the other hand, the interest of existing sellers, and again of the consuming public, in consumers' being able to know exactly what they are buying without having to incur substantial costs of investigation or inquiry.

[The court examined the survey and other evidence and concluded that the district judge did not commit clear error in finding a likelihood of confusion if the defendant used the "Baltimore Colts" name.]

AFFIRMED.

NOTES

1. In Major League Baseball Properties, Inc. v. Sed Non Olet Denarius, Ltd., 817 F. Supp. 1103 (S.D.N.Y. 1993), vacated pursuant to settlement, 859 F. Supp. 80 (S.D.N.Y. 1994) the defendants opened a restaurant in 1987 in Brooklyn called the "Brooklyn Dodger Sports Bar and Restaurant". The plaintiffs, the owners of the old Brooklyn Dodgers baseball team who had moved the team to Los Angeles in 1958, objected to defendant's use. The evidence showed that the plaintiffs had not used the name from 1958 until 1981 and thereafter used it only on infrequent and sporadic uses. The court held the plaintiffs had abandoned the mark prior to 1981 and that their uses after 1981 entitled them only to limited protection for use on the "precise goods on or in connection with which the trademark was used since its resumption." As to the plaintiffs' argument that the term "Dodgers" remained protected throughout the period the court replied:

> Plaintiffs argue that their "Dodgers" mark without a geographical reference--that is, "Dodgers" alone--is a protected use infringed by defendants actions. However, in this context, "Brooklyn" is more than a geographic designation or appendage to the word "Dodgers." The "Brooklyn Dodgers" was a non-transportable cultural institution separate from the "Los Angeles Dodgers" or the "Dodgers" who play in Los Angeles. It is not simply the "Dodgers," (and certainly not the "Los Angeles Dodgers"), that defendants seek to invoke in their restaurant; rather defendants specifically seek to recall the nostalgia of the cultural institution that was the "Brooklyn Dodgers." It was the "Brooklyn Dodgers" name that had acquired secondary meaning in New York in the early part of this century, prior to 1958. It was that cultural institution that Los Angeles abandoned.

Would the plaintiffs have been assisted by a consumer survey that showed a significant percent of consumers surveyed associated the defendants' restaurant with the baseball team? If you were representing plaintiffs, how would you formulate the survey question?

2. Can you distinguish *Indianapolis Colts* from the Brooklyn Dodgers case?

CHAPTER IV

PREDATORY PRACTICES

PAGE 427. Read in association with *Utah Pie*

NOTE

The United States Supreme Court recently explained *Utah Pie* and the method of determining injury to primary line competition through predatory pricing in Brooke Group Ltd. v. Brown & Williamson Tobacco Corp., 113 S. Ct. 2578, reh. denied 114 S.Ct. 13 (1993). The case involved competition in the generic cigarette industry. Brooke Group (Liggett) introduced a generic cigarette selling for 30% below branded cigarettes and in response Brown & Williamson entered the market with substantial volume discounts. Liggett brought suit claiming that B & W was selling below cost to force Liggett to raise its price and thereby slow the growth of the generic cigarette industry. That growth, Liggett claimed, was injuring B & W's branded markets. The context of the case is an oligopolistic cigarette industry which for many years had lockstep price increases twice per year although presumably not as a result of unlawful conspiracy. The jury found in favor of Liggett. The Court of Appeals reversed. The Supreme Court affirmed the Court of Appeals.

The Court noted that the volume discounts were a violation of §2(a) of the Robinson-Patman Act because they were a "price difference". However, Liggett must show an injury to competition. As to *Utah Pie* the Court observed:

> *Utah Pie* has often been interpreted to permit liability for primary-line price discrimination on a mere showing that the defendant intended to harm competition or produced a declining price structure. The case has been criticized on the grounds that such low standards of competitive injury are at odds with the antitrust laws' traditional concern for consumer welfare and price competition. We do not regard the *Utah Pie* case itself as having the full significance attributed to it by its detractors. * * * As the law has been explored since *Utah Pie*, it has become evident that primary-line competitive injury under the Robinson-Patman Act is of the same general character as the injury inflicted by predatory pricing schemes actionable under § 2 of the Sherman Act. * * * but whatever additional flexibility the Robinson-Patman Act standard may imply, the essence of the claim under either statute is the same: A business rival has priced its products in an unfair manner with an object to eliminate or retard competition and thereby gain and exercise control over prices in the relevant market.

Accordingly, whether the claim alleges predatory pricing under § 2 of the Sherman Act or primary-line price discrimination under the Robinson-Patman Act, two prerequisites to recovery remain the same. First, a plaintiff seeking to establish competitive injury resulting from a rival's low prices must prove that the prices complained of are below an appropriate measure of a rival's costs. * * *

The second prerequisite to holding a competitor liable under the antitrust laws for charging low prices is a demonstration that the competitor had a reasonable prospect, or, under §2 of the Sherman Act, a dangerous probability, of recouping its investment in below-cost prices.

The Supreme Court went on to hold that the second prerequisite could not be shown here because the only way B & W could recoup its investment in below-cost prices was to force other members of the cigarette oligopoly to engage in supra-competitive prices. This, the Court believed was unlikely.

PAGE 442. Read after *Leigh Furniture*

PENNA v. TOYOTA MOTOR SALES, U.S.A., INC.
Supreme Court of California, 1995
45 Cal.Rptr.2d 436, 11 Cal.4th 376, 902 P.2d 740

ARABIAN, Justice

[Toyota Motors required their American Lexus dealers to sign "no export" clauses preventing them from selling Lexus automobiles to individuals intending to export them back to Japan. Penna purchased several automobiles from a dealer for export but Toyota applied pressure by, among other things, publishing an "offenders list" and threatening to reduce or eliminate supplies of automobiles to offenders. Penna sued Toyota for interfering with its source of Lexus to export. The California Supreme Court reviewed the history of the interference tort and noted the disarray of the California cases.]

IV

In searching for a means to recast the elements of the economic relations tort and allocate the associated burdens of proof, we are guided by an overmastering concern articulated by high courts of other jurisdictions and legal commentators: The need to draw and enforce a sharpened distinction between claims for the tortious disruption of an existing contract and claims that a prospective contractual or economic relationship has been interfered with by the defendant. Many of the cases do in fact acknowledge a greater array of justificatory defenses against claims of interference with prospective relations. Still, in our view and that of several other courts and commentators, the notion that the two torts are analytically unitary and derive from a common principle sacrifices practical wisdom to theoretical insight, promoting the idea that the interests invaded are of nearly equal dignity. They are not.

The courts provide a damage remedy against third party conduct intended to disrupt an existing contract precisely because the exchange of promises resulting in such a formally cemented economic relationship is deemed worthy of protection from interference by a stranger to the agreement. Economic relationships short of contractual, however, should stand on a different legal footing as far as the potential for tort liability is reckoned. Because ours is a culture firmly wedded to the social rewards of commercial contests, the law usually takes care to draw lines of legal liability in a way that maximizes areas of competition free of legal penalties.

A doctrine that blurs the analytical line between interference with an existing business contract and interference with commercial relations less than contractual is one that invites both uncertainty in conduct and unpredictability of its legal effect. The notion that inducing the breach of an existing contract is simply a subevent of the "more inclusive" class of acts that interfere with economic relations, while perhaps theoretically unobjectionable, has been mischievous as a practical matter. Our courts should, in short, firmly distinguish the two kinds of business contexts, bringing a greater solicitude to those relationships that have ripened into agreements, while recognizing that relationships short of that subsist in a zone where the rewards and risks of competition are dominant.

Beyond that, we need not tread today. It is sufficient to dispose of the issue before us in this case by holding that a plaintiff seeking to recover for alleged interference with prospective economic relations has the burden of pleading and proving that the defendant's interference was wrongful "by some measure beyond the fact of the interference itself." (Top Service, supra, 582 P.2d at p. 1371.) It follows that the trial court did not commit error when it modified BAJI No. 7.82 to require the jury to find that defendant's interference was "wrongful." And because the instruction defining "wrongful conduct" given the jury by the trial court was offered by plaintiff himself, we have no occasion to review its sufficiency in this case. The question of whether additional refinements to the plaintiff's pleading and proof burdens merit adoption by California courts--questions embracing the precise scope of "wrongfulness," or whether a "disinterested malevolence," in Justice Holmes's words (American Bank & Trust Co. v. Federal Reserve Bank (1921) 256 U.S. 350, 358, 41 S.Ct. 499, 500, 65 L.Ed. 983) is an actionable interference in itself, or whether the underlying policy justification for the tort, the efficient allocation of social resources, justifies including as actionable conduct that is recognized as anticompetitive under established state and federal positive law (see, e.g., Perlman, Interference with Contract and Other Economic Expectancies; A Clash of Tort and Contract Doctrine, supra, 49 U.Chi.L.Rev. 61) -- are matters that can await another day and a more appropriate case.

CONCLUSION

We hold that a plaintiff seeking to recover for an alleged interference with prospective contractual or economic relations must plead and prove as part of its case-in-chief that the defendant not only knowingly interfered with the plaintiff's expectancy, but engaged in conduct that was wrongful by some legal measure other than the fact of interference itself. The judgment of the Court of Appeal is reversed and the cause is remanded with directions to affirm the judgment of the trial court.

PAGE 475. Add after *Smith v. Snap-On*

PHILLIPS v. FREY
United States Court of Appeals, Fifth Circuit, 1994
20 F. 3d 623

REYNALDO G. GARZA, Circuit Judge:

[Phillips owned and operated Ambusher, Inc., which manufactured single pole deer stands for use by hunters. The defendants approaches Phillips about purchasing the business and Phillips mentioned a price of $140,000. To allow the defendants to evaluate the business, Phillips disclosed secret information regarding how the stands were manufactured. Shortly thereafter, defendants indicated they were having trouble arranging financing for the purchase and offered a lower price. Phillips refused. Seven months later defendants began marketing a similar deer stand.]

However, appellants deny that there was ever any confidential relationship established that would prevent them from using the information given to them. Appellants assert that the fact that a sale of Ambusher was contemplated does not create a per se confidential relationship between the parties.

* * *

* * * The proprietor of a trade secret may not unilaterally create a confidential relationship without the knowledge or consent of the party to whom he discloses the secret. However, no particular form of notice is needed; the question raised is whether the recipient of the information knew or should have known that the information was a trade secret and the disclosure was made in confidence.

The case before us is strikingly distinguishable [from *Smith v. Snap-On Tools Corp.*]. Even in *Snap-On* we implied that a manufacturer who has actively solicited disclosure from an inventor, and then used the disclosed material, would be liable for misappropriation of trade secrets even where the disclosure was made in the absence of any expressed understanding about confidentiality. Although Phillips never explicitly requested that the secret of his manufacturing process, which gave him a competitive advantage over competitors, be held in confidence, both parties mutually came to the negotiation table, and the disclosure was made within the course of negotiations for the sale of a business. The jury could validly accept such evidence that the defendants knew or should have known that the information was a trade secret and the disclosure was made in confidence.

PAGE 482. Add after *Metallurgic*.

Omnitech International Inc. v. The Clorox Co., 11 F.3d 1316 (5th Cir.), cert. denied 115 S.Ct. 71(1994). Clorox entered into a confidential relationship with Omnitech that permitted Clorox to evaluate Omnitech's "Dr. X" line of insecticides as part of Clorox's interest in entering the insecticide business. While the evaluation was being conducted, American Cyanamid announced the public auction of its Shulton Division which marketed "Combat" insecticides. Clorox ultimately purchased Shulton and broke off negotiations with Omnitech. Omnitech sued for misappropriation of its trade secrets. The court, holding that a cause of action for misappropriation of trade secrets requires proof that the defendant either disclosed or used the trade secret, found for Clorox:

> At best, and as Omnitech conceded at oral argument, Omnitech claims that its trade secrets made Clorox "smarter" about the market in investigating the potential Combat purchase. Certainly "misappropriation" of a trade secret means more than simply using knowledge gained through a variety of experiences, including analyses of possible target companies, to evaluate a potential purchase. To hold otherwise would lead to one of two unacceptable results: (i) every time a company entered into preliminary negotiations for a possible purchase of another company's assets in which the acquiring company was given limited access to the target's trade secrets, the acquiring party would effectively be precluded from evaluating other potential targets; or (ii) the acquiring company would, as a practical matter, be forced to make a purchase decision without the benefit of examination of the target company's most important assets its trade secrets.

PAGE 483. Substitute for Note 3

3. *Customer Lists.* One of the more troubling issues arising from the employment context is the protection afforded customer lists. Should an employee who learns the names and requirements of customers of his employer be entitled to use the information for a subsequent employer? The Restatement (Second) of Agency, § 396 (1958) proposed a test that prohibited a former employee from using or disclosing "written lists of names" although the agent "is entitled to use * * * names of the customers retained in his memory, if not acquired in violation of his duty as agent."

The memory rule has been controversial. Compare, Developments--Competitive Torts, 77 Harv. L. Rev. 888, 956 (1964) ("This 'memory' rule in most cases seems to have little merit other than as an arbitrary rule of thumb.") with Blake, Employee Agreements Not to Compete, 73 Harv. L. Rev. 625, 656 (1960) ("The explanation seems to be that the 'memory' rule of thumb, in application, allows the former employee to solicit those customers whom he has played some personal role in obtaining or retaining for the former employer, giving him the benefit of a rather wide margin of doubt."). The Restatement (Third) of Unfair Competition §42, comment *j* (1995) draws no absolute rule but suggests that the manner of taking by the employee may be evidence of the value or secrecy of the list. For a modern view see Stampede Tool Warehouse, Inc. v. May, 1995 WL 121439 (Ill.App. 1995):

> In determining whether information is a trade secret, the focus of both the common law and the ITSA [Illinois Trade Secret Act] is on the secrecy of the information sought to be protected. The key to secrecy is the ease with which information can be readily duplicated without involving considerable time, effort or expense.
>
> Under the ITSA, there are two requirements to consider: (1) whether the customer list is sufficiently secret to derive economic value, actual or potential, from not being generally known to other persons who can obtain economic value from its disclosure or use; and (2) whether the customer list is the subject of efforts that are reasonable under the circumstances to maintain its secrecy or confidentiality.
>
> Section 2(d)(1)(2) of the ITSA is similar to the following common law factors used in determining whether information is a trade secret, which include: (1) the extent to which the information is known outside the employer's business; (2) the extent to which it is known by employees and others involved in the business; (3) the extent of measures taken by the employer to guard the secrecy of the information; (4) the value of the information to the employer and his or her competitors; (5) the amount of effort or money expended by the employer in developing the information; and (6) the ease or difficulty with which the information could be properly acquired or duplicated by others.
>
> In this case, we find that the customer list is a trade secret. The customer list has been developed through the laborious method of prospecting, which requires a substantial amount of time, effort, and expense by Stampede. A list of jobbers is not readily available from any one public source. Instead, the salesmen obtain a list of end users through telephone books, catalogues, and other publicly available sources; then contact those people to get the names of jobbers, who

are the potential customers. The salesmen then develop a relationship with those potential customers.

In addition, we find that Stampede protects its customer list using reasonable efforts to maintain its secrecy and confidentiality. Moreover, both defendants signed employee confidentiality agreements that stated that the names of Stampede's customers could not be used or disclosed because they belonged to Stampede and were confidential. As a result, we conclude that Stampede's customer list is a trade secret that is protectable under the ITSA.

We must now consider whether defendants misappropriated the trade secret. * * *

Defendants assert that Stampede's customer list is not protectable because there was no physical taking of the list, but instead was committed to memory. Defendants contend that any general knowledge or information that they took with them when they left Stampede was not a misappropriation.

Although an employee may take general knowledge or information he or she has developed during their employment, he or she may not take any confidential information, including trade secrets. That taking does not have to be a physical taking by actually copying the names. A trade secret can be misappropriated by physical copying or by memorization.

There was substantial evidence that defendants misappropriated the customer list either through copying down names or through memorization. In fact, defendants admitted that they redeveloped their customer lists by remembering the names and locations of at least some of their Stampede customers. Using memorization to rebuild a trade secret does not transform that trade secret from confidential information into non-confidential information. The memorization is one method of misappropriation. Since the trial court's findings were not against the manifest weight of the evidence, we affirm the injunctions.

Can the list of customers on a delivery route be secret if one could acquire the list by following and openly observing the delivery truck?

PAGE 485. Add to Note 5

See Restatement (Third) of Unfair Competition § 41 (1995) for a restatement of the rule regarding confidential relationships.

PAGE 494. Add after *Christopher*

ROCKWELL GRAPHIC SYSTEMS, INC. v. DEV INDUSTRIES, INC.
United States Court of Appeals, Seventh Circuit, 1991
925 F.2d 174

POSNER, Circuit Judge.

This is a suit for misappropriation of trade secrets. Rockwell Graphic Systems, a manufacturer of printing presses used by newspapers, and of parts for those presses, brought the suit against DEV Industries, a competing manufacturer, and against the president of DEV, who used to be employed by Rockwell. * * *

When we said that Rockwell manufactures both printing presses and replacement parts for its presses--"wear parts" or "piece parts," they are called--we were speaking approximately. Rockwell does not always manufacture the parts itself. Sometimes when an owner of one of Rockwell's presses needs a particular part, or when Rockwell anticipates demand for the part, it will subcontract the manufacture of it to an independent machine shop, called a "vendor" by the parties. When it does this it must give the vendor a "piece part drawing" indicating materials, dimensions, tolerances, and methods of manufacture. Without that information the vendor could not manufacture the part. Rockwell has not tried to patent the piece parts. It believes that the purchaser cannot, either by inspection or by "reverse engineering" (taking something apart in an effort to figure out how it was made), discover how to manufacture the part; to do that you need the piece part drawing, which contains much information concerning methods of manufacture, alloys, tolerances, etc. that cannot be gleaned from the part itself. So Rockwell tries--whether hard enough is the central issue in the case--to keep the piece part drawings secret, though not of course from the vendors; they could not manufacture the parts for Rockwell without the drawings. * * *

Rockwell employed Fleck and Peloso in responsible positions that gave them access to piece part drawings. Fleck left Rockwell in 1975 and three years later joined DEV as its president. Peloso joined DEV the following year after being fired by Rockwell when a security guard caught him removing piece part drawings from Rockwell's plant. This suit was brought in 1984, and pretrial discovery by Rockwell turned up 600 piece part drawings in DEV's possession, of which 100 were Rockwell's. DEV claimed to have obtained them lawfully, either from customers of Rockwell or from Rockwell vendors, contrary to Rockwell's claim that either Fleck and Peloso stole them when they were employed by it or DEV obtained them in some other unlawful manner, perhaps from a vendor who violated his confidentiality agreement with Rockwell. Thus far in the litigation DEV has not been able to show which customers or vendors lawfully supplied it with Rockwell's piece part drawings.

The defendants persuaded the magistrate and the district judge that the piece part drawings weren't really trade secrets at all, because Rockwell made only perfunctory efforts to keep them secret. Not only were there thousands of drawings in the hands of the vendors; there were thousands more in the hands of owners of Rockwell presses, the customers for piece parts. The drawings held by customers, however, are not relevant. They are not piece part drawings, but assembly drawings. * * * An assembly drawing shows how the parts of a printing press fit together for installation and also how to integrate the press with the printer's other equipment. Whenever Rockwell sells a printing press it gives the buyer assembly drawings as well. These are the equivalent of instructions for assembling a piece of furniture. Rockwell does not claim that they contain trade secrets. It admits having supplied a few piece part drawings to customers, but they were piece part drawings of obsolete parts that Rockwell has no interest in manufacturing and of a safety device that was not part of the press as originally delivered but that its customers were clamoring for; more to the point, none of these drawings is among those that Rockwell claims DEV misappropriated.

The distinction between assembly and piece part drawings is not esoteric. * * * It is immaterial that Rockwell affixed the same legend enjoining the user to confidentiality to its assembly drawings as it did to its piece part drawings. Perhaps thinking of the doctrine of patent misuse DEV suggests that if a firm claims trade secret protection for information that is not really secret, the firm forfeits trade secret protection of information that is secret. There is no such doctrine--even the patent misuse doctrine does not decree forfeiture of the patent as the sanction for misuse--and it would make no sense. This is not only because there are any number of innocent explanations for Rockwell's action in "overclaiming" trade secret protection (if that is what it was doing)--such as an excess of caution, uncertainty as to the scope of trade secret protection, concern that clerical personnel will not always be able to distinguish between assembly and piece part drawings at a glance, and the sheer economy of a uniform policy--but also because it would place the owner of trade secrets on the razor's edge. If he stamped "confidential" on every document in sight, he would run afoul of what we are calling (without endorsing) the misuse doctrine. But if he did not stamp confidential on every document he would lay himself open to an accusation that he was sloppy about maintaining secrecy--and in fact DEV's main argument is that Rockwell *was* impermissibly sloppy in its efforts to keep the piece part drawings secret.

On this, the critical, issue, the record shows the following. (Because summary judgment was granted to DEV, we must construe the facts as favorably to Rockwell as is reasonable to do.) Rockwell keeps all its engineering drawings, including both piece part and assembly drawings, in a vault. Access not only to the vault, but also to the building in which it is located, is limited to authorized employees who display identification. These are mainly engineers, of whom Rockwell employs 200. They are required to sign agreements not to disseminate the drawings, or disclose their contents, other than as authorized by the company. An authorized employee who needs a drawing must sign it out from the vault and return it when he has finished with it. But he is permitted to make copies, which he is to destroy when he no longer needs them in his work. The only outsiders allowed to see piece part drawings are the vendors (who are given copies, not originals). They too are required to sign confidentiality agreements, and in addition each drawing is stamped with a legend stating that it contains proprietary material. Vendors, like Rockwell's own engineers, are allowed to make copies for internal working purposes, and although the confidentiality agreement that they sign requires the vendor to return the drawing when the order has been filled, Rockwell does not enforce this requirement. The rationale for not enforcing it is that the vendor will need the drawing if Rockwell reorders the part. Rockwell even permits unsuccessful bidders for a piece part contract to keep the drawings, on the theory that the high bidder this round may be the low bidder the next. But it does consider the ethical standards of a machine shop before making it a vendor, and so far as appears no shop has ever abused the confidence reposed in it.

The mere fact that Rockwell gave piece part drawings to vendors--that is, disclosed its trade secrets to "a limited number of outsiders for a particular purpose"--did not forfeit trade secret protection. On the contrary, such disclosure, which is often necessary to the efficient exploitation of a trade secret, imposes a duty of confidentiality on the part of the person to whom the disclosure is made. But with 200 engineers checking out piece part drawings and making copies of them to work from, and numerous vendors receiving copies of piece part drawings and copying them, tens of thousands of copies of these drawings are floating around outside Rockwell's vault, and many of these outside the company altogether. Although the magistrate and the district judge based their conclusion that Rockwell had not made adequate efforts to maintain secrecy in part at least on the irrelevant fact that it took no measures at all to keep its assembly drawings secret, DEV in defending the judgment that it obtained in the district court argues that Rockwell failed to take adequate measures to keep even the piece part drawings secret. Not only did Rockwell not limit copying of those drawings or insist that copies be returned; it did not segregate the piece part drawings from the assembly drawings and institute more secure procedures for the former. So Rockwell could have done more to maintain the confidentiality of its piece part drawings than it did, and we must decide whether its failure to do more was so plain a breach of the obligation of a trade secret owner to make reasonable efforts to maintain secrecy as to justify the entry of summary judgment for the defendants.

The requirement of reasonable efforts has both evidentiary and remedial significance, and this regardless of which of the two different conceptions of trade secret protection prevails. (Both conceptions have footholds in Illinois law, as we shall see.) The first and more common merely gives a remedy to a firm deprived of a competitively valuable secret as the result of an independent legal wrong, which might be conversion or other trespass or the breach of an employment contract or of a confidentiality agreement. Under this approach, because the secret must be taken by improper means for the taking to give rise to liability the only significance of trade secrecy is that it allows the victim of wrongful appropriation to obtain damages based on the competitive value of the information taken. The second conception of trade secrecy, illustrated by E.I. duPont de Nemours & Co. v. Christopher, 431 F.2d 1012 (5th Cir.1970), is that "trade secret" picks out a class of socially valuable information that the law should protect even against nontrespassory or other lawful conduct--in Christopher, photographing a competitor's roofless plant from the air while not flying directly overhead and hence not trespassing or committing any other wrong independent of the appropriation of the trade secret itself.

Since, however, the opinion in *Christopher* describes the means used by the defendant as "improper," which is also the key to liability under the first, more conventional conception of trade secret protection, it is unclear how distinct the two conceptions really are. It is not as if *Christopher* proscribes all efforts to unmask a trade secret. It specifically mentions reverse engineering as a proper means of doing so. This difference in treatment is not explained, but it may rest on the twofold idea that reverse engineering involves the use of technical skills that we want to encourage, and that anyone should have the right to take apart and to study a product that he has bought.

It should be apparent that the two different conceptions of trade secret protection are better described as different emphases. The first emphasizes the desirability of deterring efforts that have as their sole purpose and effect the redistribution of wealth from one firm to another. The second emphasizes the desirability of encouraging inventive activity by protecting its fruits from efforts at appropriation that are, indeed, sterile wealth-redistributive -- not productive -- activities. The approaches differ, if at all, only in that the second does not limit the class of improper means to those that fit a preexisting pigeonhole in the law of tort or contract or fiduciary duty--and it is by no means clear that the first approach assumes a closed class of wrongful acts, either.

Under the first approach, at least if narrowly interpreted so that it does not merge with the second, the plaintiff must prove that the defendant obtained the plaintiff's trade secret by a wrongful act, illustrated here by the alleged acts of Fleck and Peloso in removing piece part drawings from Rockwell's premises without authorization, in violation of their employment contracts and confidentiality agreements, and using them in competition with Rockwell. Rockwell is unable to prove directly that the 100 piece part drawings it got from DEV in discovery were stolen by Fleck and Peloso or obtained by other improper means. But if it can show that the probability that DEV could have obtained them otherwise--that is, without engaging in wrongdoing--is slight, then it will have taken a giant step toward proving what it must prove in order to recover under the first theory of trade secret protection. The greater the precautions that Rockwell took to maintain the secrecy of the piece part drawings, the lower the probability that DEV obtained them properly and the higher the probability that it obtained them through a wrongful act; the owner had taken pains to prevent them from being obtained otherwise.

Under the second theory of trade secret protection, the owner's precautions still have evidentiary significance, but now primarily as evidence that the secret has real value. For the precise means by which the defendant acquired it is less important under the second theory, though not completely unimportant; remember that even the second theory allows the unmasking of a trade secret by *some* means, such as reverse engineering. If Rockwell expended only paltry resources on preventing its piece part drawings from falling into the hands of competitors such as DEV, why should the law, whose machinery is far from costless, bother to provide Rockwell with a remedy? The information contained in the drawings cannot have been worth much if Rockwell did not think it worthwhile to make serious efforts to keep the information secret.

The remedial significance of such efforts lies in the fact that if the plaintiff has allowed his trade secret to fall into the public domain, he would enjoy a windfall if permitted to recover damages merely because the defendant took the secret from him, rather than from the public domain as it could have done with impunity. It would be like punishing a person for stealing property that he believes is owned by another but that actually is abandoned property. If it were true, as apparently it is not, that Rockwell had given the piece part drawings at issue to customers, and it had done so without requiring the customers to hold them in confidence, DEV could have obtained the drawings from the customers without committing any wrong. The harm to Rockwell would have been the same as if DEV had stolen the drawings from it, but it would have had no remedy, having parted with its rights to the trade secret. This is true whether the trade secret is regarded as property protected only against wrongdoers or (the logical extreme of the second conception, although no case--not even *Christopher*--has yet embraced it and the patent statute might preempt it) as property protected against the world. In the first case, a defendant is perfectly entitled to obtain the property by lawful conduct if he can, and he can if the property is in the hands of persons who themselves committed no wrong to get it. In the second case the defendant is perfectly entitled to obtain the property if the plaintiff has abandoned it by giving it away without restrictions.

* * *

But only in an extreme case can what is a "reasonable" precaution be determined on a motion for summary judgment, because the answer depends on a balancing of costs and benefits that will vary from case to case and so require estimation and measurement by persons knowledgeable in the particular field of endeavor involved. On the one hand, the more the owner of the trade secret spends on preventing the secret from leaking out, the more he demonstrates that the secret has real value deserving of legal protection, that he really was hurt as a result of the misappropriation of it, and that there really was misappropriation. On the other hand, the more he spends, the higher his costs. The costs can be indirect as well as direct. The more Rockwell restricts access to its drawings, either by its engineers or by the vendors, the harder it will be for either group to do the work expected of it. Suppose Rockwell forbids *any* copying of its drawings. Then a team of engineers would have to share a single drawing, perhaps by passing it around or by working in the same room, huddled over the drawing. And how would a vendor be able to make a piece part--would Rockwell have to bring all that work in house? Such reconfigurations of patterns of work and production are far from costless; and therefore perfect security is not optimum security.

There are contested factual issues here, bearing in mind that what is reasonable is itself a fact for purposes of Rule 56 of the civil rules. Obviously Rockwell took some precautions, both physical (the vault security, the security guards--one of whom apprehended Peloso *in flagrante delicto*) and contractual, to maintain the confidentiality of its piece part drawings. Obviously it could have taken more precautions. But at a cost, and the question is whether the additional benefit in security would have exceeded that cost. We do not suggest that the question can be answered with the same precision with which it can be posed, but neither can we say that no reasonable jury could find that Rockwell had done enough and could then go on to infer misappropriation from a combination of the precautions Rockwell took and DEV's inability to establish the existence of a lawful source of the Rockwell piece part drawings in its possession.

This is an important case because trade secret protection is an important part of intellectual property, a form of property that is of growing importance to the competitiveness of American industry. Patent protection is at once costly and temporary, and therefore cannot be regarded as a perfect substitute. If trade secrets are protected only if their owners take extravagant, productivity-impairing measures to maintain their secrecy, the incentive to invest resources in discovering more efficient methods of production will be reduced, and with it the amount of invention. And given the importance of the case we must record our concern at the brevity of the district court's opinion granting summary judgment (one and a half printed pages). Brevity is the soul of wit, and all that, and the district judge did have the benefit of a magistrate's opinion; but it is vital that commercial litigation not appear to be treated as a stepchild in the federal courts. The future of the nation depends in no small part on the efficiency of industry, and the efficiency of industry depends in no small part on the protection of intellectual property.

The judgment is reversed and the case remanded to the district court for further proceedings consistent with this opinion (including reinstatement of the pendent counts).

PAGE 494. Add after *Christopher.*

AMOCO PRODUCTION COMPANY v. LAIRD
Supreme Court of Indiana, 1993
622 N.E.2d 912

DICKSON, Justice.

[Amoco formed a team of experts to explore for oil in Southern Michigan and Northern Ohio and Indiana. They consulted published literature from the U.S. Geologic Survey, confidential information in Amoco's library, and eventually conducted microwave radar tests from over-flying aircraft. The microwave tests were protected by confidentiality agreements with independent contractors conducting the tests. Two sites were ultimately selected although drilling was deferred. John Clendenning, an Amoco geologist, provided his friend William Laird with a road atlas on which the two sites were marked. Laird immediately purchased oil and gas leases in the area, a fact Amoco discovered when they subsequently decided to pursue development of the sites. Amoco brings this suit against Laird under the Indiana Uniform Trade Secrets Act. The trial court issues a preliminary injunction against Laird; the Court of Appeals reversed.]

Amoco urges that the Court of Appeals distorted the clear meaning of "not being readily ascertainable" by endorsing a dual standard which requires the plaintiff to show that (1) it would be economically infeasible for the defendants to acquire the same information through other means and (2) there is evidence indicating that the information at issue could not have been created by any means other than plaintiff's business operations.

[The Supreme Court found the Court of Appeals reliance on Indiana precedent distorting of their content and also found no support in the statutory language for the economically infeasible standard.]

We also observe that in 1982, Indiana adopted the UTSA substantially as promulgated by the National Conference of Commissioners on Uniform State Laws. The Prefatory Note to the UTSA declares not only that the Act is a substitution of unitary definitions of trade secret, but that it "also codifies the results of the better reasoned cases concerning the remedies for trade secret misappropriation." 14 Uniform Laws Annotated, Uniform Trade Secrets Act With 1985 Amendments, Prefatory Note, 435 (1990). It is thus apparent that Indiana legislators, adopting the UTSA, sought the uniform application of UTSA definitions of trade secret consistent with the application of the act in other adopting jurisdictions. Therefore, case law from other UTSA jurisdictions becomes relevant authority for construction of trade secret law in Indiana.

* * *

In determining what information is "readily ascertainable," other jurisdictions have frequently looked to the degree of time, effort, and expense required of a defendant to acquire or reproduce the alleged trade secret information by other proper means. * * * Variation exists as to how much time, effort, and funding must be provided in duplicating information before such information is eligible for trade secret protection. Illinois, for example, has found that a trade secret may exist where the duplication of effort was time-consuming, relatively time-consuming and expensive, or producible "after significant time, effort, and expense." Similarly, [i]f the information can be readily duplicated without involving considerable time, effort or expense, then it is not secret. Conversely, information which can be duplicated only by an expensive and time-consuming method of reverse engineering, for instance, could be secret, and the ability to duplicate it would not constitute a defense. When information can be derived from research, "there must be at least a fair degree of inconvenient or difficult research required before trade secret status will be recognized." Even if information potentially could have been duplicated by other proper means, it is "no defense to claim that one's product could have been developed independently of plaintiff's, if in fact it was developed by using plaintiff's proprietary designs." That is, the mere availability of other proper means will not excuse a trade secret misappropriation. [citations for quotations omitted]

Alabama has held that information may not be protected as a trade secret where there is not a "substantial research investment" required to obtain such information. Similarly, under New York law, it has been recognized that information is a trade secret only when "discoverable with great effort ... through the expenditure of considerable time and money...." Thus, "[t]he more difficult, time consuming and costly it would be to develop the information, the less likely it is 'readily' ascertainable."

Although the standard utilized by other jurisdictions to determine "not being readily ascertainable" varies, we find no case holding that "not being readily ascertainable" adheres when measures required to duplicate or acquire information are so prohibitively burdensome as to be "economically infeasible". An economic infeasibility standard in trade secrets law not only would be unique to Indiana but also would be singularly extreme in its demand that the effort required to duplicate or acquire alleged trade secret information be not merely considerable or significant but so burdensome as to be a virtual economic impossibility.

* * *

We also address Laird's assertion that the alleged trade secret information is readily ascertainable because the discovery of the Indiana reserve sites was facilitated by an already-known process rather than by a procedure exclusively developed, owned, or controlled by Amoco. Laird contends that anyone could have contacted Airborne and hired it to perform the microwave radar survey. Laird also asserts that Amoco's claim must fail because Amoco failed to show that any other form of prospecting, such as satellite imaging, could not have generated the same information.

Other jurisdictions have held that a trade secret often may include elements which by themselves may be readily ascertainable in the public domain, but when viewed together may still qualify for trade secret protection. A trade secrets plaintiff need not prove that every element of an information compilation is unavailable elsewhere. Such a burden would be insurmountable since trade secrets frequently contain elements that by themselves may be in the public domain but taken together qualify as trade secrets. Thus, "the effort of compiling useful information is, of itself, entitled to protection even if the information is otherwise generally known."

Applying the foregoing to the facts of the present case, the Record reveals that, in its exploratory quest, Amoco utilized easily accessible information already within the public domain. United States Geologic Survey reports, as well as other data pertaining to geological fault lines and fracture swarms, are examples of information generally known, at least to those interested in the oil production marketplace, and utilized by Amoco in which Amoco cannot claim a proprietary interest. Similarly, Laird correctly asserts that microwave radar detection of potential oil reserve sites is not a technology which Amoco itself developed or to which it could claim ownership or exclusive access.

Notwithstanding Amoco's use of some information and technology residing in the public domain, Amoco's exploratory effort was nevertheless a unique undertaking. Amoco engaged in a considerable outlay of resources of time, effort, and funding preliminary to and culminating in its decision to utilize microwave radar and contact Airborne. Amoco initially conceived of the exploratory project in an area where 50-million-barrel production capacity was considered surprising. Prior to Laird's receipt of the map, Amoco had invested nearly seven months in project development, including the formation and supervision of an exploration team which included the full-time services of two highly trained employees as well as those efforts of other individuals assigned various tasks related to the project.

Amoco utilized its own proprietary, confidentially-stored information. The team consulted with other Amoco personnel who had previous geological experience with the territory under exploratory consideration. The team engaged in repeated statistical assessments of extensive areas, enabling it to narrow its exploratory focus. Only after allocation of considerable resources did Amoco contract with Airborne for $150,000 to conduct microwave radar surveys of the 13,000-square-mile area. Airborne was provided with an Amoco- generated grid pattern to guide Airborne's flyover procedure.

While some tools leading to Amoco's site discoveries were easily accessible within the public domain, such as U.S. Geological Survey data and the existence of microwave radar technology, we find that, taken together, the integration of pertinent site information and resultant projections as to potential oil reserves constitutes a unique compilation of information not previously known in the marketplace. We thus agree with the trial court's conclusion that the information generated by Amoco, later appearing on Clendenning's map, was not readily ascertainable.

PAGE 497. Add after *Brunswick Corp.*

BAXTER INTERNATIONAL, INC. v. MORRIS
United States Court of Appeals, Eighth Circuit, 1992
976 F.2d 1189

BEAM, Circuit Judge.

[Dr. Morris was a research scientist who was hired by Microscan, a division of Baxter. He signed an employment agreement providing he could not work for a competing company for one year after terminating his employment with Microscan. During his employment he became familiar with Microscan's trade secrets. On January 31, 1992, Morris quit Microscan's employ and began working for Vitek, Microscan's only competitor. Microscan sought an injunction to prohibit Morris from disclosing Microscan's trade secrets and to prohibit him from working for Vitek in any capacity for one year. The district court held that the noncompetition agreement was void. The court entered an order enjoining Morris from disclosing any of Microscan's trade secrets for one year but refused to prevent Morris from working for Vitek. Microscan appealed.]

Baxter argues on appeal that the district court's order erroneously permits inevitable disclosure of Microscan's trade secrets to Vitek. Baxter contends that the overlap between Microscan and Vitek in certain research and development areas makes disclosure of Microscan's technological and business planning trade secrets inevitable if Morris is allowed to work for Vitek.

The district court found that Morris is able to undertake employment with Vitek in a management capacity without divulging Microscan's trade secrets. The court noted that the evidence at trial indicated that Vitek does not intend to elicit trade secrets from Morris, and in fact that Vitek has no need for that information. After a careful review of the record, we cannot say that the district court's findings are clearly erroneous. There was testimony at trial that it is fairly common in the industry for employees to be hired away by competitors without disclosing trade secrets. In fact, Dr. Godsey, Morris's superior at Microscan, testified that he had been able to transfer from a competitor in the industry to Microscan without disclosing any confidential information. While some evidence at trial suggests that Microscan is ahead of Vitek in certain technologies, it is far from clear that Vitek will seek to develop products similar to Microscan's, or that Vitek could use Microscan's technology for its current purposes.

* * *

Baxter next argues that the district court erred as a matter of law in limiting the order enjoining Morris from disclosing trade secrets to the twelve-month period ending May 1, 1993. Baxter contends that the district court could not properly limit the injunction without making a finding of fact concerning the length of time in which Vitek could independently develop the information. * * *

In this case, the district court specifically found that no disclosure of trade secrets or proprietary information had occurred at the time of trial. Thus, Morris has not misappropriated Microscan's trade secrets. The court went on to find that Morris could fulfill his employment obligations at Vitek without disclosing trade secrets, that Vitek did not intend to elicit secret information from Morris, and that the secrets may be of no use in Vitek's products even if Vitek desired to know them. In light of these findings, the district court was under no obligation to make findings concerning the length of time necessary for Vitek to develop the information independently. The court properly considered the fact that the noncompete covenant drafted by Baxter to protect its trade secrets is limited to one year. We find that the district court did not err as a matter of law in concluding that limiting the injunction to one year adequately protects Baxter.

PEPSICO, INC. v. REDMOND
United States Court of Appeals, Seventh Circuit, 1995
54 F.3d 1262

[PepsiCo's "All Sport" and iced teas competed in the sports drink and new age drink markets with Quaker Oats' "Gatorade" and "Snapple" drinks. As a general manager of PepsiCo's Northern California unit (PCNA), Redmond learned of PepsiCo's operating and strategic plans, pricing architecture and innovations in its selling and delivery systems for 1995. Redmond hd signed a confidentiality agreement that stated he: "would not disclose at any time, to anyone . . . or make use of, confidential information relating to the business of [PepsiCo] . . . obtained while in the employ of [PepsiCo], which shall not be generally known or available to the public or recognized as standard practices." On November 8, 1994, Redmond accepted an offer to become Vice-President of Field Operations for Quaker. On November 16, 1994, PepsiCo filed suit for an injunction to prevent him from disclosing confidential information and from assuming his new duties at Quaker, arguing that Redmond's use of information regarding PepsiCo's confidential plans was inevitable. The district court, on December 15, 1994, issued an order enjoing Redmond from working for Quaker through May, 1995.]

The question of threatened or inevitable misappropriation in this case lies at the heart of a basic tension in trade secret law. Trade secret law serves to protect "standards of commercial morality" and "encourage [ ] invention and innovation" while maintaining "the public interest in having free and open competition in the manufacture and sale of unpatented goods." 2 Jager, [Trade Secrets Law] § IL.03 at IL-12. Yet that same law should not prevent workers from pursuing their livelihoods when they leave their current positions.

This tension is particularly exacerbated when a plaintiff sues to prevent not the actual misappropriation of trade secrets but the mere threat that it will occur. * * *

[The Illinois Trade Secret Act and prior cases] lead to the same conclusion: a plaintiff may prove a claim of trade secret misappropriation by demonstrating that defendant's new employment will inevitably lead him to rely on the plaintiff's trade secrets. * * *

PepsiCo presented substantial evidence at the preliminary injunction hearing that Redmond possessed extensive and intimate knowledge about PCNA's strategic goals for 1995 in sports drinks and new age drinks. The district court concluded on the basis of that presentation that unless Redmond possessed an uncanny ability to compartmentalize information, he would necessarily be making decisions about Gatorade and Snapple by relying on his knowledge of PCNA trade secrets. * * *

Admittedly, PepsiCo has not brought a traditional trade secret case, in which a former employee has knowledge of a special manufacturing process or customer list and can give a competitor an unfair advantage by transferring the technology or customers to that competitor. PepsiCo has not contended that Quaker has stolen the All Sport formula or its list of distributors. Rather PepsiCo has asserted that Redmond cannot help but rely on PCNA trade secrets as he helps plot Gatorade and Snapple's new course, and that these secrets will enable Quaker to achieve a substantial advantage by knowing exactly how PCNA will price, distribute, and market its sports drinks and new age drinks and being able to respond strategically. This type of trade secret problem may arise less often, but it nevertheless falls within the realm of trade secret protection under the present circumstances.

Quaker and Redmond assert that they have not and do not intend to use whatever confidential information Redmond has by virtue of his former employment. They point out that Redmond has already signed an agreement with Quaker not to disclose any trade secrets or confidential information gleaned from his earlier employment. They also note with regard to distribution systems that even if Quaker wanted to steal information about PCNA's distribution plans, they would be completely useless in attempting to integrate the Gatorade and Snapple beverage lines.

The defendants' arguments fall somewhat short of the mark. Again, the danger of misappropriation in the present case is not that Quaker threatens to use PCNA's secrets to create distribution systems or co-opt PCNA's advertising and marketing ideas. Rather, PepsiCo believes that Quaker, unfairly armed with knowledge of PCNA's plans, will be able to anticipate its distribution, packaging, pricing, and marketing moves. Redmond and Quaker even concede that Redmond might be faced with a decision that could be influenced by certain confidential information that he obtained while at PepsiCo. In other words, PepsiCo finds itself in the position of a coach, one of whose players has left, playbook in hand, to join the opposing team before the big game. Quaker and Redmond's protestations that their distribution systems and plans are entirely different from PCNA's are thus not really responsive.

* * *

For the foregoing reasons, we affirm the district court's order enjoining Redmond from assuming his responsibilities at Quaker through May, 1995, and preventing him forever from disclosing PCNA trade secrets and confidential information.

AFFIRMED.

NOTES

1. Does the nature of the trade secret make a difference as to whether the court should enjoin a person from accepting employment? If the concern is with a formula or some secret technology isn't it easier to determine subsequently whether the secret was actually used? How would you ever know whether Redmond used PepsiCo's secret plans?

2. Were you to advise Baxter in the future, how would you suggest structuring its employment agreements? Is a noncompetition agreement an effective device for protecting trade secrets? Are there advantages to the nondisclosure agreement PepsiCo secured from Redmond?

PAGE 500. Read in association with the "Interlude"

G.S. RASMUSSEN & ASSOCIATES, INC. v. KALITTA FLYING SERVICE, INC.
United States Court of Appeals, Ninth Circuit, 1992
958 F.2d 896, cert. denied 113 S. Ct. 2927 (1993)

KOZINSKI, Circuit Judge:

We shuttle back and forth between federal and state law in determining what legal protections--if any--are available to the holder of certain aircraft design permits issued by the Federal Aviation Administration.

[In order to adopt a change in the design of an airplane, a manufacturer must conduct extensive tests to demonstrate to the FAA that the design change is airworthy. If the safety of a design change is established the FAA issues a Supplemental Type Certificate (STC). Once an STC is issued, subsequent testing of each modified aircraft is unnecessary; the manufacturer need only show that the modification conforms to the STC. Rasmussen developed a modification for DC-8 cargo planes that significantly increased their cargo capacity and obtained an STC. To obtain a certificate of airworthiness for a DC-8 with Rasmussen's modifications, the owner must modify the aircraft by installing three instruments, provide a supplement to the flight manual instructing the pilot how to fly the modified aircraft, and show the FAA inspector an STC. An owner who did not have Rasmussen's STC would be required to conduct expensive tests in order to prove to the FAA that the modification was safe.]

Kalitta owns and operates cargo aircraft. In 1985, it bought a used DC-8 passenger airplane. It proceeded to convert the plane to cargo use, a use that would be uneconomical without the modification described in Rasmussen's STC. Rasmussen offered to license the STC to Kalitta for $95,000, but Kalitta declined. Instead, in the district court's words, "Kalitta decided to 'pirate' the Rasmussen STC." Kalitta copied the supplemental flight manual from a Rasmussen STC-equipped DC-8 it already owned, and obtained the three necessary instruments from sources other than Rasmussen. It installed them on the airplane and applied to the FAA for an airworthiness certificate; it typed the number of Rasmussen's STC on the appropriate line of the application, and included a photocopy of the certificate itself.[4] Kalitta's modification conformed with Rasmussen's validly issued STC. The FAA certified Kalitta's modified DC-8 as airworthy.

Taking the position that Kalitta was free-riding on his effort, Rasmussen sued for conversion of his STC and for unjust enrichment. The district court granted summary judgment for Kalitta, holding that Rasmussen had no protectable property interest in the STC and, in any event, that his action was preempted by the federal copyright and patent laws.

Discussion

A. *Is There a Property Right?*

How property rights in new goods and services are established and defined is a question of considerable significance in a society, such as ours, where private ownership is the principal incentive for the creation and maintenance of commodities, and for their efficient allocation. The failure or inability to recognize private property rights in certain types of goods often leads to a variety of adverse effects. One phenomenon, known as the tragedy of the commons, is the over-use of public goods because individual users do not suffer the full cost of their consumption. A related phenomenon is the free-rider problem, where third parties enjoy the benefits of a good

---

[4] It appears that the FAA does not require an original STC as part of the application process; indeed, because there is only a single original of any particular STC, airworthiness applications necessarily include only a copy of the certificate.

without having invested the time, money and effort of creating it. While the tragedy of the commons results in the overconsumption of existing goods, the free-rider problem discourages the creation of new goods. In order to avoid such inefficiencies, the law generally favors the establishment of property rights. See, for example, International News Service v. Associated Press, 248 U.S. 215 (1918).

Giving innovators the exclusive right to reap the benefits of their efforts compensates them for the costs of innovation, the risk of failure and the potential liability that can arise if the product proves defective.[6] If successful entrepreneurs are denied such exclusive rights, they will be less likely to invest the necessary time, money and energy into innovation.[7] It is with these considerations in mind that we turn to the unusual facts before us.

Rasmussen's interest is of a most interesting and peculiar sort, one that may become more prevalent as we continue to witness the expansion of the regulatory state: It has value *only* because it helps secure a government privilege to do something that would otherwise be forbidden. The time, money and effort Rasmussen devoted to obtaining his STC would largely be wasted but for the fact that they generated the data necessary to satisfy the requirements of the Federal Aviation Act and the Code of Federal Regulations.

Under the applicable FAA regulations, an STC is granted upon the presentation of certain documentation, which normally can be obtained only through expensive and time-consuming design, experimentation and testing. Moreover, an STC is issued to a particular individual and entitles the holder to specific privileges. The STC is transferable and it may be licensed, in accordance with FAA procedures.

That this enumeration of rights and privileges is insufficient, of itself, to establish property rights is clear from the facts of this case: Kalitta had no trouble obtaining the airworthiness certificate by filling in the number of Rasmussen's STC and

---

[6] Rasmussen, for example, could be held liable for huge damage awards if a plane modified pursuant to his STC crashes. This type of risk can be a substantial barrier to the production of new and useful products. See Peter W. Huber, *Liability: The Legal Revolution and its Consequences* 153-71 (1988).

[7] Of course, giving incentives to creative talent is not the only important consideration in determining the existence and extent of a property interest. Thus, granting patent rights for infinite duration might well result in an immediate increase in inventions, but would doubtless also impoverish the body of shared knowledge from which future inventors must draw in creating useful products in the future. The patent laws therefore grant protection for only a limited time. See 35 U.S.C. § 154 (seventeen years).

providing a photocopy thereof.[9] Whatever rights the regulations may provide, therefore, are not self-executing, and it is unclear whether Rasmussen could have challenged the FAA's action in issuing the airworthiness certificate to Kalitta.[10]

There are many reasons why a federal agency would choose not to police property rights that might be created incidental to its regulatory scheme. Here, for example, the purpose of the federal aviation statutes and regulations is to assure air safety. *Varig Airlines,* 467 U.S. at 804-05. The FAA may well have contemplated that holders of STCs would have the exclusive right to obtain airworthiness certificates, but the agency may deem it too burdensome to keep track of the hundreds, perhaps thousands, of STCs outstanding; it may lack the facilities and the expertise to adjudicate questions of joint ownership, transfer, license and the multitude of other issues that routinely arise when property rights are involved. The FAA may have decided it could best pursue its mission by granting airworthiness certificates to whoever can show compliance with a validly issued STC, leaving questions of property law to the courts. Cf. Wall St. J. B7 (Jan. 23, 1992) (discussing trademark dispute between two airlines, in federal court "because [in 1988] the Department of Transportation discontinued its decades-old practice of settling airline name disputes").

* * *

Because federal law plays a significant role in defining the right but provides no mechanism of private enforcement, we must turn to state law in determining whether Rasmussen's interest amounts to a property right. * * * The parties agree that the appropriate state law is that of California, which defines property very broadly: "The ownership of a thing is the right of one or more persons to possess and use it to the exclusion of others.... [T]he thing of which there may be ownership is called

---

[9] Why this is so is a mystery. A straightforward reading of the regulations would suggest that only a holder of an STC is entitled to an airworthiness certificate. See 14 CFR § 21.119(a). Kalitta did not hold the certificate either originally or as a transferee or licensee. Because the FAA did not participate in this case as a party or amicus, we have no authoritative way of determining whether issuance of the airworthiness certificate to Kalitta was a mistake, or whether the privilege granted by section 21.119 is narrower than it appears.

[10] Rasmussen might have been entitled to bring an APA action challenging the issuance of the STC, had he acted in a timely fashion. See *Oregon Environmental Council v. Kunzman,* 714 F.2d 901, 903 n. 2 (9th Cir.1983). We need not decide this issue because Rasmussen's failure to bring such an action is no bar to his bringing the current action under state law. The APA action would, in effect, be seeking to cancel what Rasmussen claims is an infringement of his exclusive privilege granted by the FAA regulations. The current action seeks a different remedy: compensation for the benefit bestowed upon Kalitta by use of the right Rasmussen claims was granted exclusively to him. Rasmussen was entitled to choose which of these remedies to pursue. See *Koratron Co. v. Deering Milliken Inc.,* 418 F.2d 1314, 1317-18 (9th Cir.1969), cert. denied, 398 U.S. 909 (1970).

property." Cal.Civil Code § 654. This somewhat tautological definition leaves unanswered the key question: How does one determine whether someone is entitled to exclusive use or possession of the thing in question?

Another provision of California law, giving examples of intangible property interests, is more helpful. The list includes the following: "[T]he composition of an author, the good-will of a business, trade-marks and signs, and ... rights created or granted by statute." Id. § 655. Also helpful are decisions of the California courts determining whether various interests amount to property. A state liquor license, for example, is property under California law. Golden v. State, 133 Cal.App.2d 640, 643-45, 285 P.2d 49 (1955). The *Golden* court found dispositive that the license was issued to a specific person and was transferable from one person to another. It is thus relevant that the STC involved in this case states on its face that "This certificate [is] issued to G.S. Rasmussen" and that "This certificate may be transferred."

That the interest in question is limited to obtaining a governmental privilege, and a federal one at that, does nothing to diminish its status as a property interest for purposes of state law. * * *

To the extent we can distill a principle on the basis of this somewhat amorphous body of law, three criteria must be met before the law will recognize a property right: First, there must be an interest capable of precise definition; second, it must be capable of exclusive possession or control;[12] and third, the putative owner must have established a legitimate claim to exclusivity.[13] The interest Rasmussen asserts here easily meets these criteria.

The nature and extent of the rights afforded by an STC are capable of precise definition: It enables an airplane owner to obtain an airworthiness certificate for a particular design modification without the delay, burden and expense of proving to the FAA that a plane so modified will be safe. Federal law also limits the interest in a significant way: The rights created by an STC are only applicable to airplanes within the safety jurisdiction of the FAA--"civil aircraft in air commerce." Thus, Kalitta is

---

[12] As the saying goes, some of the best things in life are free, and the reason may be that they cannot be reduced to possession: The air we breathe, scenic views, the night sky, the theory of relativity and the friendship of others cannot be reduced to possession and therefore cannot be the basis of property rights.

[13] Opinions defining property for takings purposes often use the phrase "reasonable investment-backed expectations" to describe such claims. The phrase aptly describes the nature of the interest needed to establish property rights for purposes of California law. The degree of investment--monetary or otherwise--is relevant, especially when dealing with intangibles, in determining whether the purported owner has developed a stake in the thing sufficient to warrant invoking the protections of the law of property.

free to make Rasmussen's modification on airplanes it flies entirely outside the United States.

Nor are there any conceptual or practical difficulties in restricting the right to the holder of the STC, or to someone who is a transferee or licensee. In fact, the federal regulations contemplate exactly that. Rasmussen's interest is thus precisely defined and capable of exclusive possession.

The final requirement--that Rasmussen have established a legitimate claim to exclusivity--is also amply met here. Rasmussen expended considerable time and effort in research and design; he conducted the appropriate tests and compiled the necessary data; he prepared an operations manual and lined up an instrument manufacturer; he convinced the FAA that the modification is safe; and he obtained a certificate which results in preferential rights in the issuance of airworthiness certificates by the FAA. Without Rasmussen's efforts, the STC Kalitta relied on simply would not exist. Rasmussen has the type of reasonable investment-backed expectations that give rise to a legitimate claim of exclusive control over the STC.

We therefore hold that Rasmussen has a property interest in his STC under California law, unless such an interest conflicts with federal law. We turn to that question now.

B. *Preemption*

[With respect to copyright preemption the court held: "* * * Were Rasmussen claiming an exclusive right to copy the manual, the drawings and plans or the STC itself, his claim would surely be preempted by the Copyright Act. * * *
Rasmussen claims a much different interest, however: The right to use the STC as a basis for obtaining an airworthiness certificate for an airplane that is modified in a particular way. Rasmussen thus complains not about the actual copying of the documents, but of their use as a shortcut in obtaining a valuable government privilege--the right to modify an airplane in a particular way without going to the trouble and expense of proving that the modification meets FAA standards. * * *
Federal copyright law governs only copying. Enforcement of Rasmussen's property right in his STC leaves Kalitta free to make as many copies of the certificate as it wishes; to the extent the manual supplement is not protected by the copyright laws, the same is true of it. That Kalitta is prevented from then using these copies to obtain an airworthiness certificate from the FAA does not interfere in any way with the operation of the copyright laws."]

[Regarding patent preemption the court held:

* * * The Supreme Court has summarized its preemption approach as follows: "States may not offer *patent-like protection* to intellectual creations which would otherwise remain unprotected as a matter of

federal law." *Bonito Boats*, 489 U.S. at 156, 109 S.Ct. at 980 (emphasis added). * * * The right involved here, however, is not "patent-like" at all. Rasmussen claims no exclusive right to modify DC-8s as described in his STC. Kalitta or anyone else may perform the necessary studies and obtain an STC from the FAA--even if the modification so certified is identical to Rasmussen's. * * * Granting Rasmussen a property right in his STC will serve many of the same purposes of the patent laws, because it will promote innovation in the field of aeronautics. * * * There is no patent law preemption."]

C. *State-Law Claims*

1. The Pirated STC

In California, conversion has three elements: ownership or right to possession of property, wrongful disposition of the property right and damages. Our earlier discussion establishes the first element: Rasmussen has an ownership interest in the use of his STC, which is property under California law. The second requirement is also satisfied: Kalitta photocopied the certificate, presented it to the FAA, and thereby obtained a valuable benefit as a consequence of using Rasmussen's STC without authorization or permission. Rasmussen has also suffered damages by being denied a return on his investment as a condition for granting Kalitta the right to use his STC. Thus, under California law, Kalitta tortiously converted Rasmussen's STC when it used the STC to obtain airworthiness certification for the modified DC-8.

Rasmussen also alleges that Kalitta has been unjustly enriched. Under California law, a contract will be implied when one party has something which "in equity and good conscience" it ought not. Kalitta has materially benefited from the pirated STC: Its DC-8 can now carry substantially more cargo, and the parties agree that use as a cargo plane would be economically infeasible without the modification. Conversely, Kalitta has been spared the delay and expense it would have had to incur in obtaining its own STC. This benefit is due solely to Rasmussen's STC, for which Kalitta has paid nothing. Confronted with such facts, the California courts would imply a contract between Rasmussen and Kalitta. On remand, the district court shall fix its terms based on further evidence.

* * *

AFFIRMED in part, REVERSED in part and REMANDED for further proceedings consistent with this opinion.

NOTES

1. Does the *Rasmussen* decision provide a sensible solution to the problem of use of information collected solely for purposes of governmental regulation? Are the

facts similar to *International News Service v. Associated Press*? Are any of Justice Brandeis's concerns expressed in his dissent in *INS* applicable here?

2. On remand how should the district court measure the damages? Under the claim for conversion, should it be the full fair market value of the STC or the value to Kalitta? Under the unjust enrichment claim, should the damages be the cost to Kalitta of independently testing the modifications?

3. Is there any social value in requiring Kalitta and others in its position to duplicate Rasmussen's tests?

4. In the absence of the regulatory framework, how would this situation be resolved? Assume Rasmussen develops a modification for DC-8s that is obvious upon inspection of a modified aircraft. Rasmussen advertises to the industry that it has undertaken extensive testing and has determined the modification to be safe. (If you were the owner of a DC-8, would you expect to see such testing before you adopted the modification?). Kalitta examines a modified aircraft to determine the nature of the modification and then incorporates the modification on its own aircraft, comforted by the knowledge that Rasmussen has tested the modification for safety. Would Kalitta face any liability?

PAGE 535. Add to Note 5

See Bateman v. Mnemonics, Inc., 79 F.3d 1532 (11th Cir. 1966): " We are wary of any trade secret claim predicated on the existence of an 'implied' confidential relationship, because we are aware that artful pleading and presentation of evidence seemingly may create a pendent state law claim that in actuality is nothing more than a dressed up version of a copyright infringement claim."

PAGE 549. Read with Note 3

NOTE

The United States Supreme Court denied certiorari in Midler v. Ford Motor Co., 849 F.2d 460, 463 (9th Cir.1988), cert. denied, 503 U.S. 951 (1992). The Ninth Circuit again considered a voice appropriation claim in Waits v. Frito-Lay, Inc., 978 F.2d 1093 (9th Cir. 1992) where it affirmed a jury award of $375,000 compensatory damages and $2 million punitive damages in favor of Tom Waits against Frito-Lay for broadcasting a radio commercial for its Salsorio Doritos using an imitation of Waits raspy singing voice. The court upheld a claim both for voice misappropriation under the common law right of publicity and a false endorsement claim under § 43(a) of the Lanham Act. Citing *Zacchini* (page 551 of the casebook) and limiting language in

Bonito Boats, the court rejected Frito-Lay's argument that the right of publicity was preempted by the patent and copyright statutes.

A false endorsement claim assumes that consumers will believe that Waits endorsed Frito-Lay's products. Such a claim is certainly a false representation under the Lanham Act and is analogous to trademark infringement. What injury does Waits suffer if Frito-Lay adequately informs the public in the commercial that the voice is an imitation of Tom Waits? What about a commercial that begins with a person imitating Tom Waits singing and then continues: "This is a man imitating Tom Waits. You might like his performance. But don't accept imitations of SalsoRio Doritos"?

How does such a commercial differ from one in which a man is shown eating from a bag of "TacoRight Corn Chips" and then a voice says, "This man is not smiling because he's eating the soggy chips. If you want crunch with your taste, eat Frito-Lay Corn Chips." Does the maker of TacoRight have a claim against Frito-Lay?

PAGE 564. Add after *Russen*.

WHITE v. SAMSUNG ELECTRONICS AMERICA, INC.
United States Court of Appeals, Ninth Circuit, 1992
971 F.2d 1395

GOODWIN, Senior Circuit Judge:

This case involves a promotional "fame and fortune" dispute. In running a particular advertisement without Vanna White's permission, defendants Samsung Electronics America, Inc. (Samsung) and David Deutsch Associates, Inc. (Deutsch) attempted to capitalize on White's fame to enhance their fortune. White sued, alleging infringement of various intellectual property rights, but the district court granted summary judgment in favor of the defendants. We affirm in part, reverse in part, and remand.

Plaintiff Vanna White is the hostess of "Wheel of Fortune," one of the most popular game shows in television history. An estimated forty million people watch the program daily. Capitalizing on the fame which her participation in the show has bestowed on her, White markets her identity to various advertisers.

The dispute in this case arose out of a series of advertisements prepared for Samsung by Deutsch. The series ran in at least half a dozen publications with widespread, and in some cases national, circulation. Each of the advertisements in the series followed the same theme. Each depicted a current item from popular culture and a Samsung electronic product. Each was set in the twenty-first century and conveyed the message that the Samsung product would still be in use by that time. By hypothesizing outrageous future outcomes for the cultural items, the ads created humorous effects. For example, one lampooned current popular notions of an unhealthy diet by depicting a raw steak with the caption: "Revealed to be health food. 2010 A.D." Another depicted irreverent "news"-show host Morton Downey Jr. in front of an American flag with the caption: "Presidential candidate. 2008 A.D."

The advertisement which prompted the current dispute was for Samsung video-cassette recorders (VCRs). The ad depicted a robot, dressed in a wig, gown, and jewelry which Deutsch consciously selected to resemble White's hair and dress. The robot was posed next to a game board which is instantly recognizable as the Wheel of Fortune game show set, in a stance for which White is famous. The caption of the ad read: "Longest-running game show. 2012 A.D." Defendants referred to the ad as the "Vanna White" ad. Unlike the other celebrities used in the campaign, White neither consented to the ads nor was she paid.

Following the circulation of the robot ad, White sued Samsung and Deutsch in federal district court under: (1) California Civil Code § 3344; (2) the California common law right of publicity; and (3) § 43(a) of the Lanham Act, 15 U.S.C. § 1125(a). The district court granted summary judgment against White on each of her claims. White now appeals.

[Section 3344 of the California Civil Code creates liability for using another person's "likeness" "for purposes of advertising or selling" without permission. The court held that the robot was not the "likeness" of Vanna White within the meaning of the statute.]

II. *Right of Publicity*

White next argues that the district court erred in granting summary judgment to defendants on White's common law right of publicity claim. In Eastwood v. Superior Court, 149 Cal.App.3d 409, 198 Cal.Rptr. 342 (1983), the California court of appeal stated that the common law right of publicity cause of action "may be pleaded by alleging (1) the defendant's use of the plaintiff's identity; (2) the appropriation of plaintiff's name or likeness to defendant's advantage, commercially or otherwise; (3) lack of consent; and (4) resulting injury." Id. at 417, 198 Cal.Rptr. 342 (citing Prosser, Law of Torts (4th ed. 1971) § 117, pp. 804-807). The district court dismissed White's claim for failure to satisfy *Eastwood*'s second prong, reasoning that defendants had not appropriated White's "name or likeness" with their robot ad. We agree that the robot ad did not make use of White's name or likeness. However, the common law right of publicity is not so confined.

The *Eastwood* court did not hold that the right of publicity cause of action could be pleaded only by alleging an appropriation of name or likeness. *Eastwood* involved an unauthorized use of photographs of Clint Eastwood and of his name. Accordingly, the *Eastwood* court had no occasion to consider the extent beyond the use of name or likeness to which the right of publicity reaches. That court held only that the right of publicity cause of action "may be" pleaded by alleging, *inter alia*, appropriation of name or likeness, not that the action may be pleaded *only* in those terms.

* * *

Since Prosser's early formulation [Prosser, *Privacy*, 48 Cal.L.Rev. 383 (1960)], the case law has borne out his insight that the right of publicity is not limited to the appropriation of name or likeness. In Motschenbacher v. R.J. Reynolds Tobacco Co., 498 F.2d 821 (9th Cir.1974), the defendant had used a photograph of the plaintiff's race car in a television commercial. Although the plaintiff appeared driving the car in the photograph, his features were not visible. Even though the defendant had not appropriated the plaintiff's name or likeness, this court held that plaintiff's California right of publicity claim should reach the jury.

In *Midler* [v. Ford Motor Co., 849 F.2d 460 (9th Cir.1988)], this court held that, even though the defendants had not used Midler's name or likeness, Midler had stated a claim for violation of her California common law right of publicity because "the defendants ... for their own profit in selling their product did appropriate part of her identity" by using a Midler sound-alike. Id. at 463-64.

In Carson v. Here's Johnny Portable Toilets, Inc., 698 F.2d 831 (6th Cir.1983), the defendant had marketed portable toilets under the brand name "Here's Johnny"--Johnny Carson's signature "Tonight Show" introduction--without Carson's permission. The district court had dismissed Carson's Michigan common law right of publicity claim because the defendants had not used Carson's "name or likeness." Id. at 835. In reversing the district court, the sixth circuit found "the district court's conception of the right of publicity ... too narrow" and held that the right was implicated because the defendant had appropriated Carson's identity by using, *inter alia*, the phrase "Here's Johnny." Id. at 835-37.

These cases teach not only that the common law right of publicity reaches means of appropriation other than name or likeness, but that the specific means of appropriation are relevant only for determining whether the defendant has in fact appropriated the plaintiff's identity. The right of publicity does not require that appropriations of identity be accomplished through particular means to be actionable. It is noteworthy that the *Midler* and *Carson* defendants not only avoided using the plaintiff's name or likeness, but they also avoided appropriating the celebrity's voice, signature, and photograph. The photograph in *Motschenbacher* did include the plaintiff, but because the plaintiff was not visible the driver could have been an actor or dummy and the analysis in the case would have been the same.

Although the defendants in these cases avoided the most obvious means of appropriating the plaintiffs' identities, each of their actions directly implicated the commercial interests which the right of publicity is designed to protect. As the *Carson* court explained:

> [t]he right of publicity has developed to protect the commercial interest of celebrities in their identities. The theory of the right is that a celebrity's identity can be valuable in the promotion of products, and the celebrity has an interest that may be protected from the unauthorized commercial exploitation of that identity.... If the celebrity's identity is commercially exploited, there has been an invasion of his right whether or not his "name or likeness" is used.

Carson, 698 F.2d at 835. It is not important how the defendant has appropriated the plaintiff's identity, but *whether* the defendant has done so. *Motschenbacher, Midler*, and *Carson* teach the impossibility of treating the right of publicity as guarding only against a laundry list of specific means of appropriating identity. A rule which says that the right of publicity can be infringed only through the use of nine different methods of appropriating identity merely challenges the clever advertising strategist to come up with the tenth.

Indeed, if we treated the means of appropriation as dispositive in our analysis of the right of publicity, we would not only weaken the right but effectively eviscerate it. The right would fail to protect those plaintiffs most in need of its protection. Advertisers use celebrities to promote their products. The more popular the celebrity, the greater the number of people who recognize her, and the greater the visibility for the product. The identities of the most popular celebrities are not only the most attractive for advertisers, but also the easiest to evoke without resorting to obvious means such as name, likeness, or voice.

* * *

Viewed separately, the individual aspects of the advertisement in the present case say little. Viewed together, they leave little doubt about the celebrity the ad is meant to depict. The female-shaped robot is wearing a long gown, blond wig, and large jewelry. Vanna White dresses exactly like this at times, but so do many other women. The robot is in the process of turning a block letter on a game-board. Vanna White dresses like this while turning letters on a game-board but perhaps similarly attired Scrabble-playing women do this as well. The robot is standing on what looks to be the Wheel of Fortune game show set. Vanna White dresses like this, turns letters, and does this on the Wheel of Fortune game show. She is the only one. Indeed, defendants themselves referred to their ad as the "Vanna White" ad. We are not surprised.

Television and other media create marketable celebrity identity value. Considerable energy and ingenuity are expended by those who have achieved celebrity value to exploit it for profit. The law protects the celebrity's sole right to exploit this value whether the celebrity has achieved her fame out of rare ability, dumb luck, or a combination thereof. We decline Samsung and Deutch's invitation to permit the evisceration of the common law right of publicity through means as facile as those in this case. Because White has alleged facts showing that Samsung and Deutsch had appropriated her identity, the district court erred by rejecting, on summary judgment, White's common law right of publicity claim.

[White also claimed that the Samsung ad also created a likelihood that consumers would believe she endorsed Samsung's products and this constituted a violation of § 43(a) of the Lanham Act. After reviewing the factors relative to proof of a likelihood of confusion the court concluded that it was error to grant Samsung a summary judgment on this issue. "First, construing the motion papers in White's favor, as we must, we hold only that White has raised a genuine issue of material fact concerning a likelihood of confusion as to her endorsement. Whether White's Lanham Act claim should succeed is a matter for the jury. Second, we stress that we reach this conclusion in light of the peculiar facts of this case. In particular, we note that the robot ad identifies White and was part of a series of ads in which other celebrities participated and were paid for their endorsement of Samsung's products."]

IV. *The Parody Defense*

In defense, defendants cite a number of cases for the proposition that their robot ad constituted protected speech. Those cases involved parodies of advertisements run for the purpose of poking fun at Jerry Falwell and L.L. Bean, respectively. This case involves a true advertisement run for the purpose of selling Samsung VCRs. The ad's spoof of Vanna White and Wheel of Fortune is subservient and only tangentially related to the ad's primary message: "buy Samsung VCRs." Defendants' parody arguments are better addressed to non-commercial parodies.[3] The difference between a "parody" and a "knock-off" is the difference between fun and profit.

---

[3] In warning of a first amendment chill to expressive conduct, the dissent reads this decision too broadly. This case concerns only the market which exists in our society for the exploitation of celebrity to sell products, and an attempt to take a free ride on a celebrity's celebrity value. Commercial advertising which relies on celebrity fame is different from other forms of expressive activity in two crucial ways. First, for celebrity exploitation advertising to be effective, the advertisement must evoke the celebrity's identity. The more effective the evocation, the better the advertisement. If, as Samsung claims, its ad was based on a "generic" game-show hostess and not on Vanna White, the ad would not have violated anyone's right of publicity, but it would also not have been as humorous or as effective. Second, even if some forms of expressive activity, such as parody, do rely on identity evocation, the first amendment hurdle will bar most right of publicity actions against those activities. In the case of commercial advertising, however, the first amendment hurdle is not so high. * * * Unless the first amendment bars all right of publicity actions--and it does not, see Zachini v. Scripps-Howard Broadcasting Co., 433 U.S. 562 (1977)--then it does not bar this case.

AFFIRMED IN PART, REVERSED IN PART, and REMANDED.

ALARCON, Circuit Judge, concurring in part, dissenting in part:

I must dissent from the majority's holding on Vanna White's right to publicity claim. The district court found that, since the commercial advertisement did not show a "likeness" of Vanna White, Samsung did not improperly use the plaintiff's identity. The majority asserts that the use of a likeness is not required under California common law. According to the majority, recovery is authorized if there is an appropriation of one's "identity." I cannot find any holding of a California court that supports this conclusion. Furthermore, the record does not support the majority's finding that Vanna White's "identity" was appropriated.

* * *

* * * The proper interpretation of *Motschenbacher*, *Midler*, and *Carson* is that where identifying characteristics unique to a plaintiff are the only information as to the identity of the person appearing in an ad, a triable issue of fact has been raised as to whether his or her identity as been appropriated.

The case before this court is distinguishable * * * . It is patently clear to anyone viewing the commercial advertisement that Vanna White was not being depicted. No reasonable juror could confuse a metal robot with Vanna White. * * * A recognition of the distinction between a performer and the part he or she plays is essential for a proper analysis of the facts of this case. As is discussed below, those things which Vanna White claims identify her are not unique to her. They are, instead, attributes of the role she plays. The representation of those attributes, therefore, does not constitute a representation of Vanna White.

Vanna White is a one-role celebrity. She is famous solely for appearing as the hostess on the "Wheel of Fortune" television show. There is nothing unique about Vanna White or the attributes which she claims identify her. * * *

The only characteristic in the commercial advertisement that is not common to many female performers or celebrities is the imitation of the "Wheel of Fortune" set. This set is the only thing which might possibly lead a viewer to think of Vanna White. The Wheel of Fortune set, however, is not an attribute of Vanna White's identity. It is an identifying characteristic of a television game show, a prop with which Vanna White interacts in her role as the current hostess. To say that Vanna White may bring an action when another blond female performer or robot appears on such a set as a hostess will, I am sure, be a surprise to the owners of the show.

[Judge Alarcon also argued there was no evidence of likelihood of confusion.]

* * *

The effect of the majority's holding on expressive conduct is difficult to estimate. The majority's position seems to allow any famous person or entity to bring suit based on any commercial advertisement that depicts a character or role performed by the plaintiff. Under the majority's view of the law, Gene Autry could have brought an action for damages against all other singing cowboys. Clint Eastwood would be able to sue anyone who plays a tall, soft-spoken cowboy, unless, of course, Jimmy Stewart had not previously enjoined Clint Eastwood. Johnny Weismuller would have been able to sue each actor who played the role of Tarzan. Sylvester Stallone could sue actors who play blue-collar boxers. Chuck Norris could sue all karate experts who display their skills in motion pictures. Arnold Schwarzenegger could sue body builders who are compensated for appearing in public.

* * *

I would affirm the district court's judgment in all respects.

WHITE v. SAMSUNG ELECTRONICS AMERICA, INC.
United States Court of Appeals, Ninth Circuit, 1993
989 F.2d 1512, cert. denied 113 S.Ct. 2443 (1993)

The petition for rehearing is DENIED and the suggestion for rehearing en banc is REJECTED.

KOZINSKI, Circuit Judge, with whom Circuit Judges O'SCANNLAIN and KLEINFELD join, dissenting from the order rejecting the suggestion for rehearing en banc.

I

Saddam Hussein wants to keep advertisers from using his picture in unflattering contexts.[1] Clint Eastwood doesn't want tabloids to write about him.[2] Rudolf Valentino's heirs want to control his film biography.[3] The Girl Scouts don't want

---

[1] See Eben Shapiro, *Rising Caution on Using Celebrity Images*, N.Y. Times, Nov. 4, 1992, at D20 (Iraqi diplomat objects on right of publicity grounds to ad containing Hussein's picture and caption "History has shown what happens when one source controls all the information").

[2] Eastwood v. Superior Court, 149 Cal.App.3d 409, 198 Cal.Rptr. 342 (1983).

[3] Guglielmi v. Spelling-Goldberg Prods., 25 Cal.3d 860, 160 Cal.Rptr. 352, 603 P.2d 454 (1979) (Rudolph Valentino); see also Maheu v. CBS, Inc., 201 Cal.App.3d 662, 668, 247

(continued...)

their image soiled by association with certain activities.[4] George Lucas wants to keep Strategic Defense Initiative fans from calling it "Star Wars."[5] Pepsico doesn't want singers to use the word "Pepsi" in their songs.[6] Guy Lombardo wants an exclusive

---

[3](...continued)
Cal.Rptr. 304 (1988) (aide to Howard Hughes).

[4] *Girl Scouts v. Personality Posters Mfg.*, 304 F.Supp. 1228 (S.D.N.Y.1969) (poster of a pregnant girl in a Girl Scout uniform with the caption "Be Prepared").

[5] *Lucasfilm Ltd. v. High Frontier*, 622 F.Supp. 931 (D.D.C.1985).

[6] Pepsico Inc. claimed the lyrics and packaging of grunge rocker Tad Doyle's "Jack Pepsi" song were "offensive to [it] and [...] likely to offend [its] customers," in part because they "associate [Pepsico] and its Pepsi marks with intoxication and drunk driving." Deborah Russell, *Doyle Leaves Pepsi Thirsty for Compensation*, Billboard, June 15, 1991, at 43. Conversely, the Hell's Angels recently sued Marvel Comics to keep it from publishing a comic book called "Hell's Angel," starring a character of the same name. Marvel settled by paying $35,000 to charity and promising never to use the name "Hell's Angel" again in connection with any of its publications. Marvel, *Hell's Angels Settle Trademark Suit*, L.A. Daily J., Feb. 2, 1993, § II, at 1.

Trademarks are often reflected in the mirror of our popular culture. See Truman Capote, *Breakfast at Tiffany's* (1958); Kurt Vonnegut, Jr., *Breakfast of Champions* (1973); Tom Wolfe, *The Electric Kool-Aid Acid Test* (1968) (which, incidentally, includes a chapter on the Hell's Angels); Larry Niven, *Man of Steel, Woman of Kleenex*, in *All the Myriad Ways* (1971); *Looking for Mr. Goodbar* (1977); *The Coca-Cola Kid* (1985) (using Coca-Cola as a metaphor for American commercialism); *The Kentucky Fried Movie* (1977); *Harley Davidson and the Marlboro Man* (1991); *The Wonder Years* (ABC 1988-present) ("Wonder Years" was a slogan of Wonder Bread); Tim Rice & Andrew Lloyd Webber, *Joseph and the Amazing Technicolor Dream Coat* (musical). Hear Janis Joplin, *Mercedes Benz*, on *Pearl* (CBS 1971); Paul Simon, *Kodachrome*, on *There Goes Rhymin' Simon* (Warner 1973); Leonard Cohen, *Chelsea Hotel*, on *The Best of Leonard Cohen* (CBS 1975); Bruce Springsteen, *Cadillac Ranch*, on *The River* (CBS 1980); Prince, *Little Red Corvette*, on *1999* (Warner 1982); dada, *Dizz Knee Land*, on *Puzzle* (IRS 1992) ("I just robbed a grocery store--I'm going to Disneyland / I just flipped off President George--I'm going to Disneyland"); Monty Python, *Spam*, on *The Final Rip Off* (Virgin 1988); Roy Clark, *Thank God and Greyhound [You're Gone]*, on *Roy Clark's Greatest Hits Volume I* (MCA 1979); Mel Tillis, *Coca-Cola Cowboy*, on *The Very Best of* (MCA 1981) ("You're just a Coca-Cola cowboy / You've got an Eastwood smile and Robert Redford hair ..."). Dance to Talking Heads, *Popular Favorites 1976-92: Sand in the Vaseline* (Sire 1992); Talking Heads, *Popsicle*, on id. Admire Andy Warhol, *Campbell's Soup Can.* Cf. REO Speedwagon, 38 Special, and Jello Biafra of the Dead Kennedys.

The creators of some of these works might have gotten permission from the trademark owners, though it's unlikely Kool-Aid relished being connected with LSD, Hershey with homicidal maniacs, Disney with armed robbers, or Coca-Cola with cultural imperialism. Certainly no free society can *demand* that artists get such permission.

property right to ads that show big bands playing on New Year's Eve.[7] Uri Geller thinks he should be paid for ads showing psychics bending metal through telekinesis.[8] Paul Prudhomme, that household name, thinks the same about ads featuring corpulent bearded chefs.[9] And scads of copyright holders see purple when their creations are made fun of.

Something very dangerous is going on here. Private property, including intellectual property, is essential to our way of life. It provides an incentive for investment and innovation; it stimulates the flourishing of our culture; it protects the moral entitlements of people to the fruits of their labors. But reducing too much to private property can be bad medicine. Private land, for instance, is far more useful if separated from other private land by public streets, roads and highways. Public parks, utility rights-of- way and sewers reduce the amount of land in private hands, but vastly enhance the value of the property that remains.

So too it is with intellectual property. Overprotecting intellectual property is as harmful as underprotecting it. Creativity is impossible without a rich public domain. Nothing today, likely nothing since we tamed fire, is genuinely new: Culture, like science and technology, grows by accretion, each new creator building on the works of those who came before. Overprotection stifles the very creative forces it's supposed to nurture.[11]

The panel's opinion is a classic case of overprotection. Concerned about what it sees as a wrong done to Vanna White, the panel majority erects a property right of remarkable and dangerous breadth: Under the majority's opinion, it's now a tort for advertisers to *remind* the public of a celebrity. Not to use a celebrity's name, voice, signature or likeness; not to imply the celebrity endorses a product; but simply to evoke the celebrity's image in the public's mind. This Orwellian notion withdraws far more from the public domain than prudence and common sense allow. It conflicts with the Copyright Act and the Copyright Clause. It raises serious First Amendment problems. It's bad law, and it deserves a long, hard second look.

II

---

[7] Lombardo v. Doyle, Dane & Bernbach, Inc., 58 A.D.2d 620, 396 N.Y.S.2d 661 (1977).

[8] Geller v. Fallon McElligott, No. 90-Civ-2839 (S.D.N.Y. July 22, 1991) (involving a Timex ad).

[9] Prudhomme v. Procter & Gamble Co., 800 F.Supp. 390 (E.D.La.1992).

[11] See Wendy J. Gordon, *A Property Right in Self Expression: Equality and Individualism in the Natural Law of Intellectual Property,* 102 Yale L.J. ----, Part IV(A) (forthcoming 1993).

Samsung ran an ad campaign promoting its consumer electronics. Each ad depicted a Samsung product and a humorous prediction: One showed a raw steak with the caption "Revealed to be health food. 2010 A.D." Another showed Morton Downey, Jr. in front of an American flag with the caption "Presidential candidate. 2008 A.D."[12] The ads were meant to convey--humorously--that Samsung products would still be in use twenty years from now.

The ad that spawned this litigation starred a robot dressed in a wig, gown and jewelry reminiscent of Vanna White's hair and dress; the robot was posed next to a Wheel-of-Fortune-like game board. See Appendix. The caption read "Longest-running game show. 2012 A.D." The gag here, I take it, was that Samsung would still be around when White had been replaced by a robot.

Perhaps failing to see the humor, White sued, alleging Samsung infringed her right of publicity by "appropriating" her "identity." Under California law, White has the exclusive right to use her name, likeness, signature and voice for commercial purposes. Cal.Civ.Code § 3344(a); Eastwood v. Superior Court, 149 Cal.App.3d 409, 417, 198 Cal.Rptr. 342, 347 (1983). But Samsung didn't use her name, voice or signature, and it certainly didn't use her likeness. The ad just wouldn't have been funny had it depicted White or someone who resembled her--the whole joke was that the game show host(ess) was a robot, not a real person. No one seeing the ad could have thought this was supposed to be White in 2012.

The district judge quite reasonably held that, because Samsung didn't use White's name, likeness, voice or signature, it didn't violate her right of publicity. 971 F.2d at 1396-97. Not so, says the panel majority: The California right of publicity can't possibly be limited to name and likeness. If it were, the majority reasons, a "clever advertising strategist" could avoid using White's name or likeness but nevertheless remind people of her with impunity, "effectively eviscerat[ing]" her rights. To prevent this "evisceration," the panel majority holds that the right of publicity must extend beyond name and likeness, to any "appropriation" of White's "identity"--anything that "evoke[s]" her personality. Id. at 1398-99.

III

But what does "evisceration" mean in intellectual property law? Intellectual property rights aren't like some constitutional rights, absolute guarantees protected against all kinds of interference, subtle as well as blatant. They cast no penumbras, emit no emanations: The very point of intellectual property laws is that they protect only against certain specific kinds of appropriation. I can't publish unauthorized copies of, say, *Presumed Innocent*; I can't make a movie out of it. But I'm perfectly free to

---

[12] I had never heard of Morton Downey, Jr., but I'm told he's sort of like Rush Limbaugh, but not as shy.

write a book about an idealistic young prosecutor on trial for a crime he didn't commit.[14] So what if I got the idea from *Presumed Innocent*? So what if it reminds readers of the original? Have I "eviscerated" Scott Turow's intellectual property rights? Certainly not. All creators draw in part on the work of those who came before, referring to it, building on it, poking fun at it; we call this creativity, not piracy.

The majority isn't, in fact, preventing the "evisceration" of Vanna White's existing rights; it's creating a new and much broader property right, a right unknown in California law. It's replacing the existing balance between the interests of the celebrity and those of the public by a different balance, one substantially more favorable to the celebrity. Instead of having an exclusive right in her name, likeness, signature or voice, every famous person now has an exclusive right to *anything that reminds the viewer of her*. After all, that's all Samsung did: It used an inanimate object to remind people of White, to "evoke [her identity]." 971 F.2d at 1399.[17]

Consider how sweeping this new right is. What is it about the ad that makes people think of White? It's not the robot's wig, clothes or jewelry; there must be ten million blond women (many of them quasi-famous) who wear dresses and jewelry like White's. It's that the robot is posed near the "Wheel of Fortune" game board. Remove the game board from the ad, and no one would think of Vanna White. See Appendix. But once you include the game board, anybody standing beside it--a brunette woman, a man wearing women's clothes, a monkey in a wig and gown--would evoke White's image, precisely the way the robot did. It's the "Wheel of Fortune" set, not the robot's face or dress or jewelry that evokes White's image. The panel is giving White an exclusive right not in what she looks like or who she is, but in what she does for a living.[18]

---

[14] It would be called "Burden of Going Forward with the Evidence," and the hero would ultimately be saved by his lawyer's adept use of Fed.R.Evid. 301.

[17] Some viewers might have inferred White was endorsing the product, but that's a different story. The right of publicity isn't aimed at or limited to false endorsements, Eastwood v. Superior Court, 149 Cal.App.3d 409, 419-20, 198 Cal.Rptr. 342, 348 (1983); that's what the Lanham Act is for.

Note also that the majority's rule applies even to advertisements that unintentionally remind people of someone. California law is crystal clear that the common-law right of publicity may be violated even by unintentional appropriations. *Id.* at 417 n. 6, 198 Cal.Rptr. at 346 n. 6; Fairfield v. American Photocopy Equipment Co., 138 Cal.App.2d 82, 87, 291 P.2d 194 (1955).

[18] Once the right of publicity is extended beyond specific physical characteristics, this will become a recurring problem: Outside name, likeness and voice, the things that most reliably remind the public of celebrities are the actions or roles they're famous for. A commercial with

(continued...)

This is entirely the wrong place to strike the balance. Intellectual property rights aren't free: They're imposed at the expense of future creators and of the public at large. Where would we be if Charles Lindbergh had an exclusive right in the concept of a heroic solo aviator? If Arthur Conan Doyle had gotten a copyright in the idea of the detective story, or Albert Einstein had patented the theory of relativity? If every author and celebrity had been given the right to keep people from mocking them or their work? Surely this would have made the world poorer, not richer, culturally as well as economically.[19]

This is why intellectual property law is full of careful balances between what's set aside for the owner and what's left in the public domain for the rest of us: The relatively short life of patents; the longer, but finite, life of copyrights; copyright's idea-expression dichotomy; the fair use doctrine; the prohibition on copyrighting facts; the compulsory license of television broadcasts and musical compositions; federal preemption of overbroad state intellectual property laws; the nominative use doctrine in trademark law; the right to make soundalike recordings. All of these diminish an intellectual property owner's rights. All let the public use something created by someone else. But all are necessary to maintain a free environment in which creative genius can flourish.

The intellectual property right created by the panel here has none of these essential limitations: No fair use exception; no right to parody; no idea-expression dichotomy. It impoverishes the public domain, to the detriment of future creators and the public at large. Instead of well-defined, limited characteristics such as name, likeness or voice, advertisers will now have to cope with vague claims of "appropriation of identity," claims often made by people with a wholly exaggerated sense of their own fame and significance. Future Vanna Whites might not get the chance to create their personae, because their employers may fear some celebrity will claim the persona is too similar to her own.[21] The public will be robbed of parodies of celebrities, and

---

[18](...continued)
an astronaut setting foot on the moon would evoke the image of Neil Armstrong. Any masked man on horseback would remind people (over a certain age) of Clayton Moore. And any number of songs--"My Way," "Yellow Submarine," "Like a Virgin," "Beat It," "Michael, Row the Boat Ashore," to name only a few--instantly evoke an image of the person or group who made them famous, regardless of who is singing. * * *.

[19] See generally Gordon, supra note 11; see also Michael Madow, *Private Ownership of Public Image: Popular Culture and Publicity Rights*, 81 Cal.L.Rev. 125, 201-03 (1993) (an excellent discussion).

[21] If Christian Slater, star of "Heathers," "Pump up the Volume," "Kuffs," and "Untamed Heart"--and alleged Jack Nicholson clone--appears in a commercial, can Nicholson sue? Of 54 stories on LEXIS that talk about Christian Slater, 26 talk about Slater's alleged similarities to
(continued...)

our culture will be deprived of the valuable safety valve that parody and mockery create.

Moreover, consider the moral dimension, about which the panel majority seems to have gotten so exercised. Saying Samsung "appropriated" something of White's begs the question: *Should* White have the exclusive right to something as broad and amorphous as her "identity"? Samsung's ad didn't simply copy White's schtick--like all parody, it created something new. True, Samsung did it to make money, but White does whatever she does to make money, too; the majority talks of "the difference between fun and profit," but in the entertainment industry fun *is* profit. Why is Vanna White's right to exclusive for-profit use of her persona--a persona that might not even be her own creation, but that of a writer, director or producer-- superior to Samsung's right to profit by creating its own inventions? Why should she have such absolute rights to control the conduct of others, unlimited by the idea-expression dichotomy or by the fair use doctrine?

* * *

IV

The panel, however, does more than misinterpret California law: By refusing to recognize a parody exception to the right of publicity, the panel directly contradicts the federal Copyright Act. Samsung didn't merely parody Vanna White. It parodied Vanna White appearing in "Wheel of Fortune," a copyrighted television show, and parodies of copyrighted works are governed by federal copyright law.

Copyright law specifically gives the world at large the right to make "fair use" parodies, parodies that don't borrow too much of the original. Federal copyright law also gives the copyright owner the exclusive right to create (or license the creation of) derivative works, which include parodies that borrow too much to qualify as "fair use."[24] When Mel Brooks, for instance, decided to parody *Star Wars*, he had two options: He could have stuck with his fair use rights under 17 U.S.C. § 107, or he could have gotten a license to make a derivative work under 17 U.S.C. § 106(b) from

---

[21](...continued)
Nicholson. Apparently it's his nasal wisecracks and killer smiles, St. Petersburg Times, Jan. 10, 1992, at 13, his eyebrows, Ottawa Citizen, Jan. 10, 1992, at E2, his sneers, Boston Globe, July 26, 1991, at 37, his menacing presence, USA Today, June 26, 1991, at 1D, and his sing-song voice, Gannett News Service, Aug. 27, 1990 (or, some say, his insinuating drawl, L.A. Times, Aug. 22, 1990, at F5). That's a whole lot more than White and the robot had in common.

[24] How much is too much is a hotly contested question, but one thing is clear: The right to make parodies belongs either to the public at large or to the copyright holder, not to someone who happens to appear in the copyrighted work.

the holder of the *Star Wars* copyright. To be safe, he probably did the latter, but once he did, he was guaranteed a perfect right to make his movie.[25]

The majority's decision decimates this federal scheme. It's impossible to parody a movie or a TV show without at the same time "evok[ing]" the "identit[ies]" of the actors. You can't have a mock *Star Wars* without a mock Luke Skywalker, Han Solo and Princess Leia, which in turn means a mock Mark Hamill, Harrison Ford and Carrie Fisher. You can't have a mock Batman commercial without a mock Batman, which means someone emulating the mannerisms of Adam West or Michael Keaton. See Carlos V. Lozano, *West Loses Lawsuit over Batman TV Commercial*, L.A. Times, Jan. 18, 1990, at B3 (describing Adam West's right of publicity lawsuit over a commercial produced under license from DC Comics, owner of the Batman copyright). The public's right to make a fair use parody and the copyright owner's right to license a derivative work are useless if the parodist is held hostage by every actor whose "identity" he might need to "appropriate."

Our court is in a unique position here. State courts are unlikely to be particularly sensitive to federal preemption, which, after all, is a matter of first concern to the federal courts. The Supreme Court is unlikely to consider the issue because the right of publicity seems so much a matter of state law. That leaves us. It's our responsibility to keep the right of publicity from taking away federally granted rights, either from the public at large or from a copyright owner. We must make sure state law doesn't give the Vanna Whites and Adam Wests of the world a veto over fair use parodies of the shows in which they appear, or over copyright holders' exclusive right to license derivative works of those shows. In a case where the copyright owner isn't even a party-- where no one has the interests of copyright owners at heart--the majority creates a rule that greatly diminishes the rights of copyright holders in this circuit.

V

The majority's decision also conflicts with the federal copyright system in another, more insidious way. Under the dormant Copyright Clause, state intellectual property laws can stand only so long as they don't "prejudice the interests of other States." Goldstein v. California, 412 U.S. 546, 558 (1973). A state law criminalizing record piracy, for instance, is permissible because citizens of other states would "remain free to copy within their borders those works which may be protected elsewhere." Id. But the right of publicity isn't geographically limited. A right of publicity created by one state applies to conduct everywhere, so long as it involves a celebrity domiciled in that state. If a Wyoming resident creates an ad that features a

---

[25] See *Spaceballs* (1987). Compare *Madonna: Truth or Dare* (1991) with *Medusa: Dare to Be Truthful* (1991); *Loaded Weapon I* (1993) *with Lethal Weapon* (1987); *Young Frankenstein* (1974) *with Bride of Frankenstein* (1935).

California domiciliary's name or likeness, he'll be subject to California right of publicity law even if he's careful to keep the ad from being shown in California.

The broader and more ill-defined one state's right of publicity, the more it interferes with the legitimate interests of other states. A limited right that applies to unauthorized use of name and likeness probably does not run afoul of the Copyright Clause, but the majority's protection of "identity" is quite another story. Under the majority's approach, any time anybody in the United States--even somebody who lives in a state with a very narrow right of publicity--creates an ad, he takes the risk that it might remind some segment of the public of somebody, perhaps somebody with only a local reputation, somebody the advertiser has never heard of. See note 17 *supra* (right of publicity is infringed by unintentional appropriations). So you made a commercial in Florida and one of the characters reminds Reno residents of their favorite local TV anchor (a California domiciliary)? Pay up.

This is an intolerable result, as it gives each state far too much control over artists in other states. No California statute, no California court has actually tried to reach this far. It is ironic that it is we who plant this kudzu in the fertile soil of our federal system.

VI

Finally, I can't see how giving White the power to keep others from evoking her image in the public's mind can be squared with the First Amendment. Where does White get this right to control our thoughts? The majority's creation goes way beyond the protection given a trademark or a copyrighted work, or a person's name or likeness. All those things control one particular way of expressing an idea, one way of referring to an object or a person. But not allowing *any* means of reminding people of someone? That's a speech restriction unparalleled in First Amendment law.

What's more, I doubt even a name-and-likeness-only right of publicity can stand without a parody exception. The First Amendment isn't just about religion or politics--it's also about protecting the free development of our national culture. Parody, humor, irreverence are all vital components of the marketplace of ideas. The last thing we need, the last thing the First Amendment will tolerate, is a law that lets public figures keep people from mocking them, or from "evok[ing]" their images in the mind of the public.[29]

---

[29] The majority's failure to recognize a parody exception to the right of publicity would apply equally to parodies of politicians as of actresses. Consider the case of Wok Fast, a Los Angeles Chinese food delivery service, which put up a billboard with a picture of then-L.A. Police Chief Daryl Gates and the text "When you can't leave the office. Or won't." (This was an allusion to Chief Gates's refusal to retire despite pressure from Mayor Tom Bradley.) Gates forced the restaurant to take the billboard down by threatening a right of publicity lawsuit.
(continued...)

The majority dismisses the First Amendment issue out of hand because Samsung's ad was commercial speech. *Id.* at 1401 & n. 3. So what? Commercial speech may be less protected by the First Amendment than noncommercial speech, but less protected means protected nonetheless. And there are very good reasons for this. Commercial speech has a profound effect on our culture and our attitudes. Neutral-seeming ads influence people's social and political attitudes, and themselves arouse political controversy. "Where's the Beef?" turned from an advertising catchphrase into the only really memorable thing about the 1984 presidential campaign. Four years later, Michael Dukakis called George Bush "the Joe Isuzu of American politics."

In our pop culture, where salesmanship must be entertaining and entertainment must sell, the line between the commercial and noncommercial has not merely blurred; it has disappeared. Is the Samsung parody any different from a parody on Saturday Night Live or in Spy Magazine? Both are equally profit-motivated. Both use a celebrity's identity to sell things--one to sell VCRs, the other to sell advertising. Both mock their subjects. Both try to make people laugh. Both add something, perhaps something worthwhile and memorable, perhaps not, to our culture. Both are things that the people being portrayed might dearly want to suppress.

Commercial speech is a significant, valuable part of our national discourse. The Supreme Court has recognized as much, and has insisted that lower courts carefully scrutinize commercial speech restrictions, but the panel totally fails to do this. The panel majority doesn't even purport to apply the *Central Hudson* test, which the Supreme Court devised specifically for determining whether a commercial speech restriction is valid. The majority doesn't ask, as *Central Hudson* requires, whether the speech restriction is justified by a substantial state interest. It doesn't ask whether the restriction directly advances the interest. It doesn't ask whether the restriction is narrowly tailored to the interest. These are all things the Supreme Court told us--in no uncertain terms--we must consider; the majority opinion doesn't even mention them.

* * *

VII

For better or worse, we *are* the Court of Appeals for the Hollywood Circuit. Millions of people toil in the shadow of the law we make, and much of their livelihood is made possible by the existence of intellectual property rights. But much of their livelihood--and much of the vibrancy of our culture--also depends on the existence of other intangible rights: The right to draw ideas from a rich and varied public domain, and the right to mock, for profit as well as fun, the cultural icons of our time.

---

[29](...continued)
Leslie Berger, *He Did Leave the Office--And Now Sign Will Go, Too*, L.A. Times, July 31, 1992, at B2.

In the name of avoiding the "evisceration" of a celebrity's rights in her image, the majority diminishes the rights of copyright holders and the public at large. In the name of fostering creativity, the majority suppresses it. Vanna White and those like her have been given something they never had before, and they've been given it at our expense. I cannot agree.

Ch. 4   *PREDATORY PRACTICES*   185

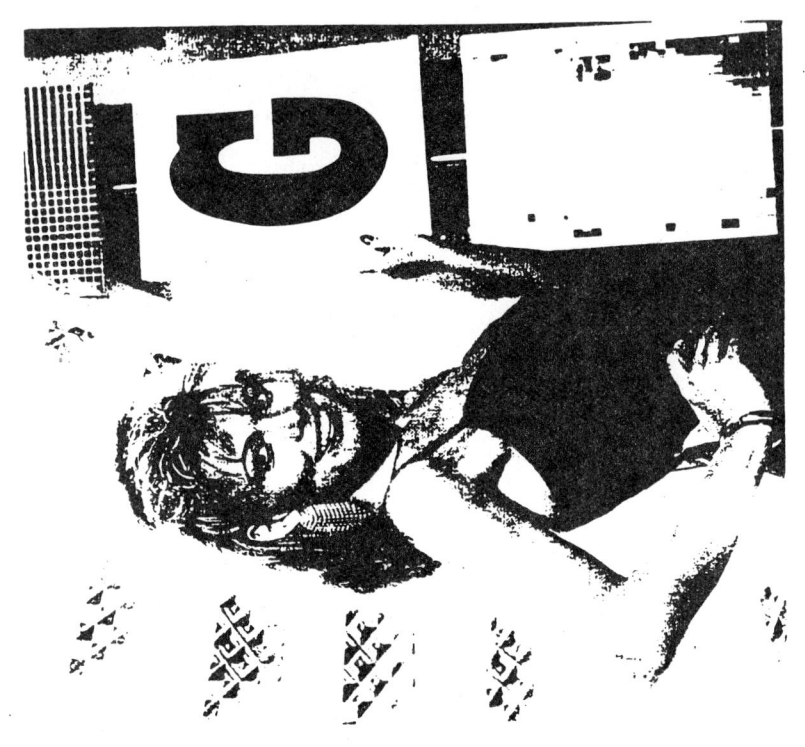

Ms. C3PO?

Vanna White

McFARLAND v. MILLER 14 F.3d 912 (3rd Cir. 1993). McFarland was the child actor who played "Spanky" in the movie and television series known as "Our Gang" and later as "Little Rascals". McFarland brought this action against Miller who opened a restaurant in New Jersey under the name "Spanky McFarland's". During the appeal from the district court's grant of Miller's motion for summary judgment, McFarland died. The Court of Appeals held that a person's right of publicity under New Jersey law survives the person's death and that the district court's grant of summary judgment was improper.

* * * Here, we are presented with two subtly different questions: Was there an identification of George McFarland with the character Spanky and, if so, does a right of publicity follow and vest in the performer with whom the character has become identified?

The district court saw this case as one in which George McFarland had been an actor playing the role of Spanky in the course of an employment relationship with the Studio that produced "Our Gang." Where an actor plays a well-defined part which has not become inextricably identified with his own person, it has been suggested the actor receives no right of exploitation in his portrayal of the character. * * *

In his concurrence in *Lugosi*, Justice Mosk recognized another distinct situation where the actor could obtain proprietary interests in a screen persona: "An original creation of a fictional figure played exclusively by its creator may well be protectible." Id. at 330, 603 P.2d at 432 (Mosk, J., concurring).[14] We are inclined to agree, but we think the difference between the two situations Justice Mosk contrasts is not wholly dependent on originality as his concurrence suggests. While originality plays a role, a court should also consider the association with the real life actor. Where an actor's screen persona becomes so associated with him that it becomes inseparable from the actor's own public image, the actor obtains an interest in the image which gives him standing to prevent mere interlopers from using it without authority.[15]

---

[14] Justice Mosk contrasted that case with Gregory Peck's role as General MacArthur, George C. Scott's role as General Patton, James Whitmore playing Will Rogers and Charlton Heston playing Moses, as well as Bela Lugosi as Dracula. Justice Mosk believed these actors had no proprietary interest in their roles.

[15] We think the case in which an actor becomes known for a single role such as Batman is different. See Carlos V. Lozano, West Loses Lawsuit Over Batman TV Commercial, (continued...)

In the current posture of this case, we do not have to decide whether Spanky McFarland was truly identical to George McFarland or whether Spanky was merely a character created by Hal Roach. Likewise, we do not have to determine whether McFarland had done a metamorphosis into Spanky McFarland over the years before or after the 1936 contract. The successor to the Studio is not before us. Therefore, we need not decide who would prevail in a contest between that entity and McFarland's estate. We hold only that there exists at least a triable issue of fact as to whether McFarland had become so inextricably identified with Spanky McFarland that McFarland's own identity would be invoked by the name Spanky. * * * On the record now before us, there is evidence of identification between the name Spanky and the actor McFarland sufficient to show that he, and now his estate, have a right of publicity superior to that of the interloper, Miller, in exploiting the name and image of Spanky McFarland. Accordingly, summary judgment was inappropriate. While others may be able to claim that they were entirely responsible for the value of the name and image or, by assignment, own the right to exploit the publicity value of the name and image of Spanky McFarland, Miller has no such claim or defense. George McFarland has alleged facts sufficient to support a right superior to that of Miller or Anaconda to exploit the items that invoke his own image.

NOTES

1. The Restatement (Third) of Unfair Competition §§ 46 - 49 (1995) limits the reach of the publicity right by attaching liability only to uses of another's identity "for purposes of trade". Id. at § 46. The phrase "purposes of trade" is limited to uses in advertising or on merchandise marketed by the user or in connection with services rendered by the user. Does this limitation answer the concerns expressed by Judges Alarcon and Kozinski in White?

2. The Restatement goes on to suggest that the publicity right "ordinarily" is not applicable to "news reporting, commentary, entertainment, works of fiction or nonfiction, or in advertising that is incidental to such uses." Id. at § 47, pg. 178. Does

---

[15](...continued)
L.A.Times, Jan.18, 1990, at B3 (Actor Adam West failing in bid to stop retail chain from using a Batman in a commercial that West argued invoked his portrayal). West's association with the role of Batman or Johnny Weismuller's with the role of Tarzan is different than McFarland's identification with Spanky. West's identity did not merge into Batman and Weismuller did not become indistinguishable from Tarzan. McFarland, like Groucho Marx, may have become indistinguishable in the public's eye from his stage persona of Spanky.

this reject the *Zacchini* and *Rusen* decisions? How would you articulate the constitutional limitations in this area? Consider the following recent decisions:

Case 1. As part of a divorce settlement John Riggins, a famous professional football player, gave his wife the former marital house. She, being a real estate agent and wanting to sell the house, produced a brochure for distribution to other real estate agents indicating that "John Riggins' Former Home" was for sale. Riggins sued his former wife and her real estate company under a Virginia statute prohibiting use of another's name for purposes of trade and won a jury verdict for compensatory and punitive damages. Does the First Amendment permit the defendants in this case to be liable for damages for what was the publication of truthful commercial speech? See, Town & Country Properties, Inc. v. Riggins, 457 S.E.2d 356(Va.Sup.Ct. 1995) ("Rather, the plaintiff's name was used strictly in a promotional sense to generate interest in the sale of real estate. The use was not relevant to dissemination of information to consumers about the physical condition, architectural features, or quality of the home. Simply, this is not the type of commercial speech accorded constitutional protection.")

Case 2. Joe Montana led the San Francisco 49'ers to four NFL championships between 1980 and 1990. The San Jose Mercury News, Inc., issued a special "Souvenir Section" devoted to the team. An artist's rendition of Montana graced the front page. Each page of the section was reproduced as a poster and sold to the general public. Montana sued claiming misappropriation of his name or likeness for advertising purposes. Does the First Amendment protect the newspaper in this instance? See, Montana v. San Jose Mercury News, Inc., 40 Cal. Rptr.2d 639 (Cal.App. 1995):

> At the hearing on the summary judgment motion in this case, SJMN submitted undisputed evidence that it sold the posters to advertise the quality and content of its newspaper. The posters were effective in this regard: they were exact reproductions of pages from the paper. They contained no additional information not included on the newspaper pages themselves, and they did not state or imply that Montana endorsed the newspaper. * * *
>
> In summary, the First Amendment protects the posters complained about here for two distinct reasons: first, because the posters themselves report newsworthy items of public interest, and second, because a newspaper has a constitutional right to promote itself by reproducing its originally protected articles or photographs.

Case 3. General Motors ran a television advertisement for Oldsmobile. A voice asks "How 'bout some trivia?" The voice then asks who holds the record for being most outstanding player during NCAA men's basketball tournament. The answer, Lew Alcindor" appears on the screen. The voice then asks whether any car had made Consumer Digest's Best Buy list more than once followed by the answer, "Oldsmobile". There follows 7 seconds of Oldsmobile advertising. Alcindor, now Kareem Abdul-Jabbar, sues GM for infringing his publicity right. Abdul-Jabbar v. General Motors Corp., 75 F.3d 1391 (9th Cir. 1996). Is Alcindor's record "newsworthy" and thus protected by the First Amendment or is this commercial exploitation subject to liability? The court, while recognizing his record to be newsworthy, held "its use is not automatically privileged. GMC used the information in the context of an automobile advertisement, not in a news or sports account."

2. Is there an interest on the part of the celebrity worth protecting in all of this? If the maker of a pole lamp has no protection against imitation, why should a television personality? If I can imitate a competitor's perfume and then advertise that my perfume smells the same, why can't I imitate Elvis Presley and advertise that my show is the same as his? On the other hand, should Vanna White have to endure a company exploiting her success to advertise their products without her permission? Is there any legitimate interest in a third party opening a restaurant using Spanky McFarland's name? Is there more of an interest now that the real McFarland is dead?

3. Was the persona of Vanna White appropriated or was it the persona of the show "Wheel of Fortune"? Does the *White* case stand for the proposition that as long as there is some recognition of the plaintiff, a cause of action arises? For an interesting extension of "name or likeness", see Cheatham v. Paisano Publications, Inc., 891 F. Supp. 381 (W.D. Kent. 1995) where the plaintiff claimed she created unique clothing designs which allowed a person's bottom to be displayed through fishnet fabric that replaced cut out portions of blue jeans. A picture of plaintiff wearing her creation was taken from behind (only from her waist to her thigh) and was used on defendant's T-shirts. The court overruled defendant's motion to dismiss arguing that if the clothing design were unique it would be possible to identify the plaintiff as the backside featured on the T-shirt.

4. The publicity right has become sufficiently important to have its own treatise. See McCarthy, The Rights of Publicity and Privacy (1993).

CHAPTER V

COPYRIGHT

PAGE 567. Add to Note 1.

Paul Goldstein, Copyright's Highway: From Gutenberg to the Celestial Jukebox (1994), is a short, lively and readable "behind the scenes" account of many of the issues and cases covered in this chapter.

PAGE 569. Add to Note 2.

The deposit requirements are simple enough to comply with for a single work. But suppose you are the regular publisher of a newspaper or other work published many times per year. The Copyright Office has adopted regulations easing the burden for certain kinds of serial publications such as newspapers and magazines, permitting a single deposit of separate issues. In 1995 the Registrar extended this procedure to certain kinds of newsletters. See 37 C.F.R. § 202.3.

PAGE 569. Add new Note 3.

3. The major impact of the notice requirement in U.S. copyright law prior to 1989 was to cause foreign works, published abroad without notice (in conformity with the requirements of the Berne Convention) to fall into the public domain. In Annex 1705.7 to the North American Free Trade Agreement ("NAFTA") the United States agreed to "provide protection to motion pictures produced in another Party's [party to NAFTA] territory that have been declared to be in the public domain pursuant to 17 U.S.C. section 405." This commitment was implemented by Public Law 103-182, signed December 8, 1993. That act to implement NAFTA added 17 U.S.C. § 104A, which provides such protection one year after the date of the coming into force of the agreement, provided certain conditions are met.

PAGE 571. Add.

THE NORTH AMERICAN FREE TRADE AGREEMENT ("NAFTA")
and
THE TRADE-RELATED ASPECTS OF INTELLECTUAL PROPERTY ("TRIPS")
of
THE GENERAL AGREEMENT ON TARIFFS AND TRADE ("GATT")

The United States has now implemented two international agreements which represent a significant departure from past international agreements such as the Berne Convention and the Universal Copyright Convention. The agreements are Part Six: Intellectual Property of the North American Free Trade Agreement (knows as "NAFTA") and the Agreement on Trade-Related Aspects of Intellectual Property Rights (known as the "TRIPS") of the General Agreement on Tariffs and Trade (known as the "GATT"). NAFTA has been approved by the United States, Canada and Mexico. GATT was signed by over 100 countries at Marrakesh, Morocco on April 15, 1994, and has been approved by the U.S. Congress.

These agreements are long and complex. They commit the signatories to adhere to the leading international intellectual property agreements and to accord to the citizens of all signatories national treatment. That much is in conformity with the received international standard of the developed world. But they go well beyond the existing international regime in two important ways. First, they contain provisions for enforcement of each party's obligations by the other parties to the agreement. And second, they contain extensive provisions designed to ensure that intellectual property rights are not only recognized in theory, but are actually enforceable through the provision of efficient and effective procedures and remedies.

It was at the insistence of the United States that the subject of intellectual property was placed on the free trade agenda. The argument of the United States was that it is increasingly a supplier of knowledge-based goods and services to the world, and that the value of such goods and services can only be obtained through market transactions which occur within the framework of effective intellectual property laws. Thus other countries, particularly the underdeveloped countries, should accord to the United States a commitment to recognize and enforce intellectual property rights in exchange for the right of the underdeveloped countries to have the right of access to the markets of the developed world. The U.S. negotiating leverage was enhanced by the use of Special 301 proceedings in which the U.S. threatened various countries such as Brazil, Taiwan, Korea and China with loss of access to U.S. markets if they did not revise their intellectual property laws.

There is considerable historic irony in this role for the United States. Reflecting its own historic role as a developing countries on the fringes of the more advanced European economies, the United States has traditionally been a non-participant in many of the major efforts to develop a coordinated system of effective intellectual property protection. Consider, for instance, its failure to join the Madrid Agreement on trademarks, and its long refusal to join the Berne Convention. The rhetoric of the U.S. initiative was that the agreements should require all signatories to come up to "our standard." But in fact, the U.S. standard is not the world "gold standard" for intellectual property protection. The European standard is. And once the U.S. sought allies for a uniform and effective commitment to intellectual property protection, it was inevitable that the emerging standard would be not a U.S. standard, but a European one. That means that various provisions of U.S. law may prove to be in violation of these agreements, and that other signatories can, if they wish, pursue remedies against the United States for these non-conforming provisions.

The U.S. agenda in the negotiations leading to NAFTA and the GATT TRIPS was controlled by the office of the Special Trade Representative in the White House, an office particularly concerned about the interests of U.S. multinationals with an interest in strong intellectual property protection. Thus these intellectual property provisions were not developed in an open, legislative process but rather in the context of international negotiations. Although the resulting provisions are in the interest of multinational businesses no matter in what nation they are headquartered, it is less clear that they provide a reasonable accommodation of the sometimes conflicting interests of consumers as well as producers.

For general background, see Marshall Leaffer, *Protecting United States Intellectual Property Abroad: Toward a New Multilateralism*, 76 IOWA LAW REV. 273 (1991). For a general discussion of NAFTA see Frank Garcia, *Protection of Intellectual Property Rights in the North American Free Trade Agreement: A Successful Case of Regional Trade Regulation*, 8 AM. U. J. INT'L L. & POL'Y 817 (1993) and George Gonzalez, *An Analysis of the Legal Implications of the Intellectual Property Provisions of the North American Free Trade Agreement*, 34 HARV. INT'L L.J. 305 (1993). For a discussion of the dispute resolution procedures of NAFTA, see David S. Huntington, Settling Disputes Under the North American Free Trade Agreement, 34 Harv. Int'l L.J. 407 (1993). For a discussion of TRIPS, see Monique Cordray, *GATT v. WIPO*, 76 J. PAT. & TRADEMARK OFF. SOC'Y 121 (1994).

Annex 2106 to NAFTA provides: "Notwithstanding any other provision of the Agreement, as between Canada and the United States, any measure adopted or maintained with respect to cultural industries, except as specifically provided in Article 302 (Market Access - Tariff Elimination), and any measure of equivalent commercial effect taken in response, shall be governed under this Agreement exclusively in accordance with the provisions of the *Canada - United States Free Trade Agreement*." This Annex has the effect of exempting "cultural industries" in Canada from the intellectual property provisions of NAFTA. Since copyright plays a central role in the "cultural industries" this is an important exception. Canada's concern is that the production of English language cultural works in the United States would overwhelm the cultural expression of English speaking Canada.

PAGE 572. New note 4.

4. Article 10.1, second sentence of the TRIPS provides: "However, Members shall not have rights or obligations under this Agreement in respect of the rights conferred under Article 6*bis* of that [the Berne] Convention or of the rights derived therefrom." One effect of this sentence is to protect the United States from the use

of the GATT process by Europeans or others who might claim that the United States does not provide sufficient recognition to moral rights.

PAGE 576. New note 1 after Baker v. Selden.

NOTE

Article 9.2 of TRIPS provides that "Copyright protection shall extend to expressions and not to ideas, procedures, methods of operation or mathematical concepts as such." Does this provision have the same meaning as 17 U.S.C. § 102(b)?

PAGE 578. Read after *Morrisey*.

LOTUS DEVELOPMENT CORP. v. BORLAND INTERNATIONAL, INC.

United States Court of Appeals for the First Circuit, 1995
49 F.3d 807, aff'd by an equally divided Court, 116 S.Ct. 804 (1996)

STAHL, Circuit Judge.

This appeal requires us to decide whether a computer menu command hierarchy is copyrightable subject matter. In particular, we must decide whether, as the district court held, plaintiff-appellee Lotus Development Corporation's copyright in Lotus 1-2-3, a computer spreadsheet program, was infringed by defendant-appellant Borland International, Inc., when Borland copied the Lotus 1-2-3 menu command hierarchy into its Quattro and Quattro Pro computer spreadsheet programs. * * *.

I.

Background

Lotus 1-2-3 is a spreadsheet program that enables users to perform accounting functions electronically on a computer. Users manipulate and control the program via a series of menu commands, such as "Copy," "Print," and "Quit." Users choose commands either by highlighting them on the screen or by typing their first letter. In all, Lotus 1-2-3 has 469 commands arranged into more than 50 menus and submenus.

Lotus 1-2-3, like many computer programs, allows users to write what are called "macros." By writing a macro, a user can designate a series of command choices with a single macro keystroke. Then, to execute that series of commands in multiple parts of the spreadsheet, rather than typing the whole series each time, the user only needs to type the single pre-programmed macro keystroke, causing the program to recall and perform the designated series of commands automatically. Thus, Lotus 1-2-3 macros shorten the time needed to set up and operate the program.

Borland released its first Quattro program to the public in 1987, after Borland's engineers had labored over its development for nearly three years. Borland's objective was to develop a spreadsheet program far superior to existing programs, including Lotus 1-2-3. In Borland's words, "[f]rom the time of its initial release ... Quattro included enormous innovations over competing spreadsheet products."

The district court found, and Borland does not now contest, that Borland included in its Quattro and Quattro Pro version 1.0 programs "a *virtually identical* copy of the entire 1-2-3 menu tree." ***. In so doing, Borland did not copy any of Lotus's underlying computer code; it copied only the words and structure of Lotus's menu command hierarchy. Borland included the Lotus menu command hierarchy in its programs to make them compatible with Lotus 1-2-3 so that spreadsheet users who were already familiar with Lotus 1-2-3 would be able to switch to the Borland programs without having to learn new commands or rewrite their Lotus macros.

In its Quattro and Quattro Pro version 1.0 programs, Borland achieved compatibility with Lotus 1-2-3 by offering its users an alternate user interface, the "Lotus Emulation Interface." By activating the Emulation Interface, Borland users would see the Lotus menu commands on their screens and could interact with Quattro or Quattro Pro as if using Lotus 1-2-3, albeit with a slightly different looking screen and with many Borland options not available on Lotus 1-2-3. In effect, Borland allowed users to choose how they wanted to communicate with Borland's spreadsheet programs: either by using menu commands designed by Borland, or by using the commands and command structure used in Lotus 1-2-3 augmented by Borland-added commands.

Lotus filed this action against Borland in the District of Massachusetts on July 2, 1990, four days after a district court held that the Lotus 1-2-3 "menu structure, taken as a whole--including the choice of command terms [and] the structure and order of those terms," was protected expression covered by Lotus's copyrights. Lotus Dev. Corp. v. Paperback Software Int'l, 740 F.Supp. 37, 68, 70 (D.Mass.1990) ("Paperback "). Three days earlier, on the morning after the Paperback decision, Borland had filed a declaratory judgment action against Lotus in the Northern District of California, seeking a declaration of non-infringement. On September 10, 1990, the district court in California dismissed Borland's declaratory judgment action in favor of this action.

Lotus and Borland filed cross motions for summary judgment; the district court denied both motions on March 20, 1992, concluding that "neither party's motion is supported by the record." Borland I, 788 F.Supp. at 80. The district court invited the parties to file renewed summary judgment motions that would "focus their arguments more precisely" in light of rulings it had made in conjunction with its denial of their summary judgment motions. *** Both parties filed renewed motions for summary judgment on April 24, 1992. In its motion, Borland contended that the Lotus 1-2-3 menus were not copyrightable as a matter of law and that no reasonable trier of fact could find that the similarity between its products and Lotus 1-2-3 was sufficient to sustain a determination of infringement. Lotus contended in its motion that Borland had copied Lotus 1-2-3's entire user interface and had thereby infringed Lotus's copyrights.

On July 31, 1992, the district court denied Borland's motion and granted Lotus's motion in part. The district court ruled that the Lotus menu command hierarchy was copyrightable expression because "[a] very satisfactory spreadsheet menu tree can be constructed using different commands and a different command structure from those of Lotus 1-2- 3. In fact, Borland has constructed just such an alternate tree for use in Quattro Pro's native mode. Even if one holds the arrangement of menu commands constant, it is possible to generate literally millions of satisfactory menu trees by varying the menu commands employed." ***. The district court demonstrated this by offering alternate command words for the ten commands that appear in Lotus's main menu. For example, the district court stated that "[t]he 'Quit' command could be named 'Exit' without any other modifications," and that "[t]he 'Copy' command could be called 'Clone,' 'Ditto,' 'Duplicate,' 'Imitate,' 'Mimic,' 'Replicate,' and 'Reproduce,' among others." Because so many variations were possible, the district court concluded that the Lotus developers' choice and arrangement of command terms, reflected in the Lotus menu command hierarchy, constituted copyrightable expression.

In granting partial summary judgment to Lotus, the district court held that Borland had infringed Lotus's copyright in Lotus 1-2-3:

> [A]s a matter of law, Borland's Quattro products infringe the Lotus 1-2-3 copyright because of (1) the extent of copying of the "menu commands" and "menu structure" that is not *genuinely* disputed in this case, (2) the extent to which the copied elements of the "menu commands" and "menu structure" contain expressive aspects separable from the functions of the "menu commands" and "menu structure," and (3) the scope of those copied expressive aspects as an integral part of Lotus 1-2-3.

***. The court nevertheless concluded that while the Quattro and Quattro Pro programs infringed Lotus's copyright, Borland had not copied the entire Lotus 1-2-3 user interface, as Lotus had contended. Accordingly, the court concluded that a jury trial was necessary to determine the scope of Borland's infringement, including whether Borland copied the long prompts of Lotus 1-2-3, whether the long prompts contained expressive elements, and to what extent, if any, functional constraints limited the number of possible ways that the Lotus menu command hierarchy could have been arranged at the time of its creation. ***. Additionally, the district court granted Lotus summary judgment on Borland's affirmative defense of waiver, but not on its affirmative defenses of laches and estoppel. ***.

Immediately following the district court's summary judgment decision, Borland removed the Lotus Emulation Interface from its products. Thereafter, Borland's spreadsheet programs no longer displayed the Lotus 1-2-3 menus to Borland users, and as a result Borland users could no longer communicate with Borland's programs as if they were using a more sophisticated version of Lotus 1-2-3. Nonetheless, Borland's programs continued to be partially compatible with Lotus 1-2-3, for Borland retained what it called the "Key Reader" in its Quattro Pro programs. Once turned on, the Key Reader allowed Borland's programs to understand and perform some Lotus 1-2-3 macros. With the Key Reader on, the Borland programs used Quattro Pro menus for display, interaction, and macro execution, except when they encountered a slash ("/") key in a macro (the starting key for any Lotus 1-2-3 macro), in which case they interpreted the macro as having been written for Lotus 1-2-3. Accordingly, people who wrote or purchased macros to shorten the time needed to perform an operation in Lotus 1-2-3 could still use those macros in Borland's programs. The district court permitted Lotus to file a supplemental complaint alleging that the Key Reader infringed its copyright.

The parties agreed to try the remaining liability issues without a jury. The district court held two trials, the Phase I trial covering all remaining issues raised in the original complaint (relating to the Emulation Interface) and the Phase II trial covering all issues raised in the supplemental complaint (relating to the Key Reader). At the Phase I trial, there were no live witnesses, although considerable testimony was presented in the form of affidavits and deposition excerpts. The district court ruled upon evidentiary objections counsel interposed. At the Phase II trial, there were two live witnesses, each of whom demonstrated the programs for the district court.

After the close of the Phase I trial, the district court permitted Borland to amend its answer to include the affirmative defense of "fair use." Because Borland had presented all of the evidence supporting its fair-use defense during the Phase I trial, but Lotus had not presented any evidence on fair use (as the defense had not been raised before the conclusion of the Phase I trial), the district court considered Lotus's motion for judgment on partial findings of fact. See Fed.R.Civ.P. 52(c). The district court held that Borland had failed to show that its use of the Lotus 1-2-3 menu command hierarchy in its Emulation Interface was a fair use. ***.

In its Phase I-trial decision, the district court found that "each of the Borland emulation interfaces contains a virtually identical copy of the 1-2-3 menu tree and that the 1-2-3 menu tree is capable of a wide variety of expression." ***. The district court also rejected Borland's affirmative defenses of laches and estoppel. ***.

In its Phase II-trial decision, the district court found that Borland's Key Reader file included "a virtually identical copy of the Lotus menu tree structure, but represented in a different form and with first letters of menu command names in place of the full menu command names." ***. In other words, Borland's programs no longer included the Lotus command terms, but only their first letters. The district court held that "the Lotus menu structure, organization, and first letters of the command names ... constitute part of the protectable expression found in [Lotus 1-2-3]." ***. Accordingly, the district court held that with its Key Reader, Borland had infringed Lotus's copyright. ***. The district court also rejected Borland's affirmative defenses of waiver, laches, estoppel, and fair use. ***. The district court then entered a permanent injunction against Borland *** from which Borland appeals.

This appeal concerns only Borland's copying of the Lotus menu command hierarchy into its Quattro programs and Borland's affirmative defenses to such copying. Lotus has not cross-appealed; in other words, Lotus does not contend on appeal that the district court erred in finding that Borland had not copied other elements of Lotus 1-2-3, such as its screen displays.

II.

Discussion

On appeal, Borland does not dispute that it factually copied the words and arrangement of the Lotus menu command hierarchy. Rather, Borland argues that it "lawfully copied the unprotectable menus of Lotus 1-2-3." Borland contends that the Lotus menu command hierarchy is not copyrightable because it is a system, method of operation, process, or procedure foreclosed from protection by 17 U.S.C. § 102(b). Borland also raises a number of affirmative defenses.

A. Copyright Infringement Generally

In this appeal, we are faced only with whether the Lotus menu command hierarchy is copyrightable subject matter in the first instance, for Borland concedes that Lotus has a valid copyright in Lotus 1-2-3 as a whole and admits to factually copying the Lotus menu command hierarchy. As a result, this appeal is in a very different posture from most copyright-infringement cases, for copyright infringement generally turns on whether the defendant has copied protected expression as a factual matter. Because of this different posture, most copyright-infringement cases provide only limited help to us in deciding this appeal. This is true even with respect to those copyright- infringement cases that deal with computers and computer software.

B. Matter of First Impression

Whether a computer menu command hierarchy constitutes copyrightable subject matter is a matter of first impression. * * *. Thus we are navigating in uncharted waters.

Borland vigorously argues, however, that the Supreme Court charted our course more than 100 years ago when it decided Baker v. Selden, 101 U.S. 99 (1879).

The facts of *Baker v. Selden*, and even the arguments advanced by the parties in that case, are identical to those in this case. The only difference is that the "user interface" of Selden's system was implemented by pen and paper rather than by computer. To demonstrate that *Baker v. Selden* and this appeal both involve accounting systems, Borland even supplied this court with a video that, with special effects, shows Selden's paper forms "melting" into a computer screen and transforming into Lotus 1-2-3.

We do not think that Baker v. Selden is nearly as analogous to this appeal as Borland claims. Of course, Lotus 1-2-3 is a computer spreadsheet, and as such its grid of horizontal rows and vertical columns certainly resembles an accounting ledger or any other paper spreadsheet. Those grids, however, are not at issue in this appeal for, unlike Selden, Lotus does not claim to have a monopoly over its accounting system. Rather, this appeal involves Lotus's monopoly over the commands it uses to operate the computer. Accordingly, this appeal is not, as Borland contends, "identical" to Baker v. Selden.

C. * * *.

D. The Lotus Menu Command Hierarchy: A "Method of Operation"

Borland argues that the Lotus menu command hierarchy is uncopyrightable because it is a system, method of operation, process, or procedure foreclosed from copyright protection by 17 U.S.C. § 102(b).

We think that "method of operation," as that term is used in § 102(b), refers to the means by which a person operates something, whether it be a car, a food processor, or a computer. Thus a text describing how to operate something would not extend copyright protection to the method of operation itself; other people would be free to employ that method and to describe it in their own words. Similarly, if a new method of operation is used rather than described, other people would still be free to employ or describe that method.

We hold that the Lotus menu command hierarchy is an uncopyrightable "method of operation." The Lotus menu command hierarchy provides the means by which users control and operate Lotus 1-2-3. If users wish to copy material, for example, they use the "Copy" command. If users wish to print material, they use the "Print" command. Users must use the command terms to tell the computer what to do. Without the menu command hierarchy, users would not be able to access and control, or indeed make use of, Lotus 1-2-3's functional capabilities.

The Lotus menu command hierarchy does not merely explain and present Lotus 1-2-3's functional capabilities to the user; it also serves as the method by which the program is operated and controlled. The Lotus menu command hierarchy is different from the Lotus long prompts, for the long prompts are not necessary to the operation of the program; users could operate Lotus 1-2-3 even if there were no long prompts. The Lotus menu command hierarchy is also different from the Lotus screen displays, for users need not "use" any expressive aspects of the screen displays in order to operate Lotus 1-2-3; because the way the screens look has little bearing on how users control the program, the screen displays are not part of Lotus 1-2-3's "method of operation." The Lotus menu command hierarchy is also different from the underlying computer code, because while code is necessary for the program to work, its precise formulation is not. In other words, to offer the same capabilities as Lotus 1-2-3, Borland did not have to copy Lotus's underlying code (and indeed it did not); to allow users to operate its programs in substantially the same way, however, Borland had to copy the Lotus menu command hierarchy. Thus the Lotus 1-2-3 code is not a uncopyrightable "method of operation."

The district court held that the Lotus menu command hierarchy, with its specific choice and arrangement of command terms, constituted an "expression" of the "idea" of operating a computer program with commands arranged hierarchically into menus and submenus. *** Under the district court's reasoning, Lotus's decision to employ hierarchically arranged command terms to operate its program could not foreclose its competitors from also employing hierarchically arranged command terms to operate their programs, but it did foreclose them from employing the specific command terms and arrangement that Lotus had used. In effect, the district court limited Lotus 1-2-3's "method of operation" to an abstraction.

Accepting the district court's finding that the Lotus developers made some expressive choices in choosing and arranging the Lotus command terms, we nonetheless hold that that expression is not copyrightable because it is part of Lotus 1-2-3's "method of operation." We do not think that "methods of operation" are limited to abstractions; rather, they are the means by which a user operates something. If specific words are essential to operating something, then they are part of a "method of operation" and, as such, are unprotectable. This is so whether they must be highlighted, typed in, or even spoken, as computer programs no doubt will soon be controlled by spoken words.

The fact that Lotus developers could have designed the Lotus menu command hierarchy differently is immaterial to the question of whether it is a "method of operation." In other words, our initial inquiry is not whether the Lotus menu command hierarchy incorporates any expression. Rather, our initial inquiry is whether the Lotus menu command hierarchy is a "method of operation." Concluding, as we do, that users operate Lotus 1-2-3 by using the Lotus menu command hierarchy, and that the entire Lotus menu command hierarchy is essential to operating Lotus 1-2-3, we do not inquire further whether that method of operation could have been designed differently. The "expressive" choices of what to name the command terms and how to arrange them do not magically change the uncopyrightable menu command hierarchy into copyrightable subject matter.

Our holding that "methods of operation" are not limited to mere abstractions is bolstered by Baker v. Selden. In Baker, the Supreme Court explained that the teachings of science and the rules and methods of useful art have their final end in application and use; and this application and use are what the public derive from the publication of a book which teaches them.... The description of the art in a book, though entitled to the benefit of copyright, lays no foundation for an exclusive claim to the art itself. The object of the one is explanation; the object of the other is use. The former may be secured by copyright. The latter can only be secured, if it can be secured at all, by letters-patent. Baker v. Selden, 101 U.S. at 104-05. Lotus wrote its menu command hierarchy so that people could learn it and use it. Accordingly, it falls squarely within the prohibition on copyright protection established in Baker v. Selden and codified by Congress in § 102(b).

In many ways, the Lotus menu command hierarchy is like the buttons used to control, say, a video cassette recorder ("VCR"). A VCR is a machine that enables one to watch and record video tapes. Users operate VCRs by pressing a series of buttons that are typically labelled "Record, Play, Reverse, Fast Forward, Pause, Stop/Eject." That the buttons are arranged and labeled does not make them a "literary work," nor does it make them an "expression" of the abstract "method of operating" a VCR via a set of labeled buttons. Instead, the buttons are themselves the "method of operating" the VCR.

When a Lotus 1-2-3 user chooses a command, either by highlighting it on the screen or by typing its first letter, he or she effectively pushes a button. Highlighting the "Print" command on the screen, or typing the letter "P," is analogous to pressing a VCR button labeled "Play."

Just as one could not operate a buttonless VCR, it would be impossible to operate Lotus 1-2-3 without employing its menu command hierarchy. Thus the Lotus command terms are not equivalent to the labels on the VCR's buttons, but are instead equivalent to the buttons themselves. Unlike the labels on a VCR's buttons, which merely make operating a VCR easier by indicating the buttons' functions, the Lotus menu commands are essential to operating Lotus 1-2-3. Without the menu commands, there would be no way to "push" the Lotus buttons, as one could push unlabeled VCR buttons. While Lotus could probably have designed a user interface for which the command terms were mere labels, it did not do so here. Lotus 1-2-3 depends for its operation on use of the precise command terms that make up the Lotus menu command hierarchy.

One might argue that the buttons for operating a VCR are not analogous to the commands for operating a computer program because VCRs are not copyrightable, whereas computer programs are. VCRs may not be copyrighted because they do not fit within any of the § 102(a) categories of copyrightable works; the closest they come is "sculptural work." Sculptural works, however, are subject to a "useful-article" exception whereby "the design of a useful article ... shall be considered a pictorial, graphic, or sculptural work only if, and only to the extent that, such design incorporates pictorial, graphic, or sculptural features that can be identified separately from, and are capable of existing independently of, the utilitarian aspects of the article." 17 U.S.C. § 101. A "useful article" is "an article having an intrinsic utilitarian function that is not merely to portray the appearance of the article or to convey information." Id. Whatever expression there may be in the arrangement of the parts of a VCR is not capable of existing separately from the VCR itself, so an ordinary VCR would not be copyrightable.

Computer programs, unlike VCRs, are copyrightable as "literary works." 17 U.S.C. § 102(a). Accordingly, one might argue, the "buttons" used to operate a computer program are not like the buttons used to operate a VCR, for they are not subject to a useful-article exception. The response, of course, is that the arrangement of buttons on a VCR would not be copyrightable even without a useful-article exception, because the buttons are an uncopyrightable "method of operation." Similarly, the "buttons" of a computer program are also an uncopyrightable "method of operation."

That the Lotus menu command hierarchy is a "method of operation" becomes clearer when one considers program compatibility. Under Lotus's theory, if a user uses several different programs, he or she must learn how to perform the same operation in a different way for each program used. For example, if the user wanted the computer to print material, then the user would have to learn not just one method of operating the computer such that it prints, but many different methods. We find this absurd. The fact that there may be many different ways to operate a computer program, or even many different ways to operate a computer program using a set of hierarchically arranged command terms, does not make the actual method of operation chosen copyrightable; it still functions as a method for operating the computer and as such is uncopyrightable.

Consider also that users employ the Lotus menu command hierarchy in writing macros. Under the district court's holding, if the user wrote a macro to shorten the time needed to perform a certain operation in Lotus 1-2-3, the user would be unable to use that macro to shorten the time needed to perform that same operation in another program. Rather, the user would have to rewrite his or her macro using that other program's menu command hierarchy. This is despite the fact that the macro is clearly the user's own work product. We think that forcing the user to cause the computer to perform the same operation in a different way ignores Congress's direction in § 102(b) that "methods of operation" are not copyrightable. That programs can offer users the ability to write macros in many different ways does not change the fact that, once written, the macro allows the user to perform an operation automatically. As the Lotus menu command hierarchy serves as the basis for Lotus 1-2-3 macros, the Lotus menu command hierarchy is a "method of operation."

* * *.

We also note that in most contexts, there is no need to "build" upon other people's expression, for the ideas conveyed by that expression can be conveyed by someone else without copying the first author's expression. In the context of methods of operation, however, "building" requires the use of the precise method of operation already employed; otherwise, "building" would require dismantling, too. Original developers are not the only people entitled to build on the methods of operation they create; anyone can. Thus, Borland may build on the method of operation that Lotus designed and may use the Lotus menu command hierarchy in doing so.

Our holding that methods of operation are not limited to abstractions goes against Autoskill, 994 F.2d at 1495 n. 23, in which the Tenth Circuit rejected the defendant's argument that the keying procedure used in a computer program was an uncopyrightable "procedure" or "method of operation" under § 102(b). The program at issue, which was designed to test and train students with reading deficiencies, id. at 1481, required students to select responses to the program's queries "by pressing the 1, 2, or 3 keys." Id. at 1495 n. 23. The Tenth Circuit held that, "for purposes of the preliminary injunction, ... the record showed that [this] keying procedure reflected at least a minimal degree of creativity," as required by Feist for copyright protection. Id. As an initial matter, we question whether a programmer's decision to have users select a response by pressing the 1, 2, or 3 keys is original. More importantly, however, we fail to see how "a student select[ing] a response by pressing the 1, 2, or 3 keys," id., can be anything but an unprotectable method of operation.

III.

Conclusion

Because we hold that the Lotus menu command hierarchy is uncopyrightable subject matter, we further hold that Borland did not infringe Lotus's copyright by copying it. Accordingly, we need not consider any of Borland's affirmative defenses. The judgment of the district court is Reversed.

BOUDIN, Circuit Judge, concurring.

The importance of this case, and a slightly different emphasis in my view of the underlying problem, prompt me to add a few words to the majority's tightly focused discussion.

I.

Most of the law of copyright and the "tools" of analysis have developed in the context of literary works such as novels, plays, and films. In this milieu, the principal problem--simply stated, if difficult to resolve--is to stimulate creative expression without unduly limiting access by others to the broader themes and concepts deployed by the author. The middle of the spectrum presents close cases; but a "mistake" in providing too much protection involves a small cost: subsequent authors treating the same themes must take a few more steps away from the original expression.

The problem presented by computer programs is fundamentally different in one respect. The computer program is a means for causing something to happen; it has a mechanical utility, an instrumental role, in accomplishing the world's work. Granting protection, in other words, can have some of the consequences of patent protection in limiting other people's ability to perform a task in the most efficient manner. Utility does not bar copyright (dictionaries may be copyrighted), but it alters the calculus.

Of course, the argument for protection is undiminished, perhaps even enhanced, by utility: if we want more of an intellectual product, a temporary monopoly for the creator provides incentives for others to create other, different items in this class. But the "cost" side of the equation may be different where one places a very high value on public access to a useful innovation that may be the most efficient means of performing a given task. Thus, the argument for extending protection may be the same; but the stakes on the other side are much higher.

It is no accident that patent protection has preconditions that copyright protection does not--notably, the requirements of novelty and non-obviousness-- and that patents are granted for a shorter period than copyrights. This problem of utility has sometimes manifested itself in copyright cases, such as Baker v. Selden, 101 U.S. 99 (1879), and been dealt with through various formulations that limit copyright or create limited rights to copy. But the case law and doctrine addressed to utility in copyright have been brief detours in the general march of copyright law.

Requests for the protection of computer menus present the concern with fencing off access to the commons in an acute form. A new menu may be a creative work, but over time its importance may come to reside more in the investment that has been made by users in learning the menu and in building their own mini- programs--macros--in reliance upon the menu. Better typewriter keyboard layouts may exist, but the familiar QWERTY keyboard dominates the market because that is what everyone has learned to use. See P. David, CLIO and the Economics of QWERTY, 75 Am.Econ.Rev. 332 (1985). The QWERTY keyboard is nothing other than a menu of letters.

Thus, to assume that computer programs are just one more new means of expression, like a filmed play, may be quite wrong. The "form"--the written source code or the menu structure depicted on the screen--look hauntingly like the familiar stuff of copyright; but the "substance" probably has more to do with problems presented in patent law or, as already noted, in those rare cases where copyright law has confronted industrially useful expressions. Applying copyright law to computer programs is like assembling a jigsaw puzzle whose pieces do not quite fit.

All of this would make no difference if Congress had squarely confronted the issue, and given explicit directions as to what should be done. The Copyright Act of 1976 took a different course. While Congress said that computer programs might be subject to copyright protection, it said this in very general terms; and, especially in § 102(b), Congress adopted a string of exclusions that if taken literally might easily seem to exclude most computer programs from protection. The only detailed prescriptions for computers involve narrow issues (like back-up copies) of no relevance here.

Of course, one could still read the statute as a congressional command that the familiar doctrines of copyright law be taken and applied to computer programs, in cookie cutter fashion, as if the programs were novels or play scripts. Some of the cases involving computer programs embody this approach. It seems to be mistaken on two different grounds: the tradition of copyright law, and the likely intent of Congress.

The broad-brush conception of copyright protection, the time limits, and the formalities have long been prescribed by statute. But the heart of copyright doctrine--what may be protected and with what limitations and exceptions--has been developed by the courts through experience with individual cases. B. KAPLAN, AN UNHURRIED VIEW OF COPYRIGHT 40 (1967). Occasionally Congress addresses a problem in detail. For the most part the interstitial development of copyright through the courts is our tradition.

Nothing in the language or legislative history of the 1976 Act, or at least nothing brought to our attention, suggests that Congress meant the courts to abandon this case-by-case approach. Indeed, by setting up § 102(b) as a counterpoint theme, Congress has arguably recognized the tension and left it for the courts to resolve through the development of case law. And case law development is adaptive: it allows new problems to be solved with help of earlier doctrine, but it does not preclude new doctrines to meet new situations.

II.

In this case, the raw facts are mostly, if not entirely, undisputed. Although the inferences to be drawn may be more debatable, it is very hard to see that Borland has shown any interest in the Lotus menu except as a fall-back option for those users already committed to it by prior experience or in order to run their own macros using 1-2-3 commands. At least for the amateur, accessing the Lotus menu in the Borland Quattro or Quattro Pro program takes some effort.

Put differently, it is unlikely that users who value the Lotus menu for its own sake--independent of any investment they have made themselves in learning Lotus' commands or creating macros dependent upon them--would choose the Borland program in order to secure access to the Lotus menu. Borland's success is due primarily to other features. Its rationale for deploying the Lotus menu bears the ring of truth.

Now, any use of the Lotus menu by Borland is a commercial use and deprives Lotus of a portion of its "reward," in the sense that an infringement claim if allowed would increase Lotus' profits. But this is circular reasoning: broadly speaking, every limitation on copyright or privileged use diminishes the reward of the original creator. Yet not every writing is copyrightable or every use an infringement. The provision of reward is one concern of copyright law, but it is not the only one. If it were, copyrights would be perpetual and there would be no exceptions.

The present case is an unattractive one for copyright protection of the menu. The menu commands (e.g., "print," "quit") are largely for standard procedures that Lotus did not invent and are common words that Lotus cannot monopolize. What is left is the particular combination and sub-grouping of commands in a pattern devised by Lotus. This arrangement may have a more appealing logic and ease of use than some other configurations; but there is a certain arbitrariness to many of the choices.

If Lotus is granted a monopoly on this pattern, users who have learned the command structure of Lotus 1-2-3 or devised their own macros are locked into Lotus, just as a typist who has learned the QWERTY keyboard would be the captive of anyone who had a monopoly on the production of such a keyboard. Apparently, for a period Lotus 1-2-3 has had such sway in the market that it has represented the de facto standard for electronic spreadsheet commands. So long as Lotus is the superior spreadsheet--either in quality or in price--there may be nothing wrong with this advantage.

But if a better spreadsheet comes along, it is hard to see why customers who have learned the Lotus menu and devised macros for it should remain captives of Lotus because of an investment in learning made by the users and not by Lotus. Lotus has already reaped a substantial reward for being first; assuming that the Borland program is now better, good reasons exist for freeing it to attract old Lotus customers: to enable the old customers to take advantage of a new advance, and to reward Borland in turn for making a better product. If Borland has not made a better product, then customers will remain with Lotus anyway.

Thus, for me the question is not whether Borland should prevail but on what basis. Various avenues might be traveled, but the main choices are between holding that the menu is not protectable by copyright and devising a new doctrine that

Borland's use is privileged. No solution is perfect and no intermediate appellate court can make the final choice.

To call the menu a "method of operation" is, in the common use of those words, a defensible position. After all, the purpose of the menu is not to be admired as a work of literary or pictorial art. It is to transmit directions from the user to the computer, i.e., to operate the computer. The menu is also a "method" in the dictionary sense because it is a "planned way of doing something," an "order or system," and (aptly here) an "orderly or systematic arrangement, sequence or the like." RANDOM HOUSE WEBSTER'S COLLEGE DICTIONARY 853 (1991).

A different approach would be to say that Borland's use is privileged because, in the context already described, it is not seeking to appropriate the advances made by Lotus' menu; rather, having provided an arguably more attractive menu of its own, Borland is merely trying to give former Lotus users an option to exploit their own prior investment in learning or in macros. The difference is that such a privileged use approach would not automatically protect Borland if it had simply copied the Lotus menu (using different codes), contributed nothing of its own, and resold Lotus under the Borland label.

The closest analogue in conventional copyright is the fair use doctrine. E.g., Harper & Row, Publishers, Inc. v. Nation Enters., 471 U.S. 539 (1985). Although invoked by Borland, it has largely been brushed aside in this case because the Supreme Court has said that it is "presumptively" unavailable where the use is a "commercial" one. See id. at 562. But see Campbell v. Acuff-Rose Music, Inc., 114 S.Ct. 1164 (1994). In my view, this is something less than a definitive answer; "presumptively" does not mean "always" and, in any event, the doctrine of fair use was created by the courts and can be adapted to new purposes.

But a privileged use doctrine would certainly involve problems of its own. It might more closely tailor the limits on copyright protection to the reasons for limiting that protection; but it would entail a host of administrative problems that would cause cost and delay, and would also reduce the ability of the industry to predict outcomes. Indeed, to the extent that Lotus' menu is an important standard in the industry, it might be argued that any use ought to be deemed privileged.

In sum, the majority's result persuades me and its formulation is as good, if not better, than any other that occurs to me now as within the reach of courts. Some solutions (e.g., a very short copyright period for menus) are not options at all for courts but might be for Congress. In all events, the choices are important ones of policy, not linguistics, and they should be made with the underlying considerations in view.

NOTES

1. The Supreme Court granted certiorari, received briefs and heard oral argument, but then affirmed without opinion because the Court was equally divided. Mr. Justice Stevens did not participate in the case, leaving the Court with eight members.

2. Does the approach of the Court in *Lotus* raise questions about the early computer software cases such as Apple Computer, Inc. v. Formula Int'l, Inc., casebook page 580, that held that operating systems were copyrightable? For example, an operating system will usually contain a command such as copy, which enables the user to copy a file. Or is the point that the computer code in Lotus was entirely different, only the command was the same? In the early operating system cases the infringer had copied the computer code directly.

3. In Engineering Dynamics, Inc. v. Structural Software, Inc., 26 F.3d 1335 (5th Cir. 1994), the court held that the data input formats for a statistical analysis program used in designing offshore oil platforms are copyrightable, relying extensively on the district court opinion in *Lotus*, reversed in the principal case. The court, however, qualified its conclusion in the following way:

> Based upon the nature of the offshore structural engineering marketplace, SSI contends, EDI had to use the same or similar formats to those it chose in order to provide a compatible, standardized and efficient product for its customers. In other words, *scenes a faire* dictated EDI's choice of input formats and output reports in the same way that the external requirements of the cotton market dictated the program in *Plains Cotton*, [Coop. Ass'n. v. Goodpasture Computer Serv., Inc., 807 F.2d 1256, 1260 (5th Cir.), cert. denied, 484 U.S. 821 (1987)], leading to a rejection of copyright protection in that case.
>
> Although the parties disagree over application of the doctrine in this case, neither side cites any evidence to support its position. On remand, the district court must consider whether or to what extent industry demand and practice in the offshore engineering market dictated the SACS IV input and output formats.

Is industry or user demand really the point of the First Circuit in the principal case? Or are *Lotus* and *Engineering Dynamics* in conflict?

4. *Symposium: Toward a Third Intellectual Property Paradigm*, 94 COLUM. L. REV. No. 8, pp. 2307-2747 (1994), contains much useful material on the intellectual property protection of software. The central paper of this symposium is Pamela Samulelson et. al., *A Manifesto Concerning the Legal Protection of Computer Programs*, 94 COLUM. L. REV. 2308 (1994), which argues for the creation a specialized form of protection for software innovations. The *Manifesto* argues that both copyright and patent are a poor fit for software innovations, with both over and under protection. This inherent misfit, the *Manifesto* argues, makes the law inherently

unstable. The rest of the symposium consists of comments on the *Manifesto* by Jane C. Ginsburg, Paul Goldstein, Wendy J. Gordon, Dennis S. Karjala, Zentaro Kitagawa, Michael Lehmann, Ejan Mackaay, Peter S. Menell, Robert P. Merges and Richard R. Nelson.

PAGE 578. Add to note 2.

Is there copyright protection in privately drafted laws, such as the model laws of the Commissioners on Uniform State Laws or the American Law Institute? In Practice Management Information Corp. v. American Medical Ass'n, 877 F. Supp. 1386 (C.D. Cal. 1994), the court held that the AMA's coding system for medical services required for Medicare and Medicaid reimbursements is protected by copyright. The court pointed out that the coding system is not "law" since it does not alter substantive rights and may cease to be required upon 90 days written notice of termination to the AMA. The Court distinguished Building Officials & Code Administrators Int'l Inc. v. Code Technology Inc., 628 F2d 730 (1st Cir. 1980), on the ground that the building codes held not to be protected by copyright in that case were actually adopted as binding laws.

PAGE 585. New note 6.

6. Article 10.1 of TRIPS provides that "Computer programs, whether in source or object code, shall be protected as literary works under the Berne Convention (1971)."

PAGE 596. New Note 3.

3. Articles 25 and 26 of the GATT TRIPS, Section 4 of Part II, provide:

1. Members shall provide for the protection of independently created industrial designs that are new or original. Members may provide that designs are not new or original if they do not significantly differ from known designs or combinations of known design features. Members may provide that such protection shall not extend to designs dictated essentially by technical or functional considerations.

2. Each Member shall ensure that requirements for securing protection for textile designs, in particular in regard to any cost, examination or publication, do not unreasonably impair the opportunity to seek and obtain such protection. Members shall be free to meet this obligation through industrial design law or through copyright law.

Does U.S. copyright law meet these requirements?

PAGE 601. Read in addition to or in place of *Financial Information, Inc.*

FEIST PUBLICATIONS, INC. v. RURAL TELEPHONE SERVICE COMPANY, INC.
Supreme Court of the United States, 1991
499 U.S. 340, 111 S.Ct. 1282, 113 L.Ed.2d 358

[The text of the case is set out in Supplement A, at pages 1057 to 1071 of the casebook.]

NOTES

1. Can Feist now copy Rural's white pages by use of a photocopy process and sell it? Is this true even if Rural has placed dummy entries in its phone book?

2. Wasn't the question for the court really whether Feist's conduct infringed Rural's copyright, not whether Rural has any copyright protection? Certiorari was granted in the case limited to the question of the validity of the copyright. 111 S. Ct. 40 (1990).

3. There was no need for the Court to address the question of whether originality is a constitutional requirement since the case was fully resolved on statutory grounds. The usual rule is that the Court will not consider a constitutional question unless it is necessary to do so in order to decide the case. Why did the Court insist on addressing it here?

4. The language of the decision has affected questions far removed from the scope of the copyright protection to be accorded to information in compilations of facts. The Court's criticism of the "sweat of the brow" theory has focused the attention of the lower courts on whether or not the infringing works appropriates protected expression. See, *e.g.*, Computer Associates v. Altai, 982 F.2d 693, 711-12 (2d Cir. 1992).

5. Article 10.2 of the GATT TRIPS, Part II, Section 1, provides:

"[C]ompilations of data or other material, whether in machine readable or other form, which by reason of the selection or arrangement of their contents constitute intellectual creations, shall be protected as such."

Is *Feist* consistent with these provisions?

5. After *Feist* the lower courts have been faced with the problem of separating works that are original from works that are not original. Some early results:

In CCC Information Services Inc. v. Maclean Hunter Market Reports Inc., 44 F.3d 61 (2d Cir. 1994), the Second Circuit held that a compilation of predicted used car prices was sufficiently original to be protected by copyright, reversing the district court. The alleged infringer in that case was copying the prices into a computer data base for sale to subscribers.

In Warren Publishing Inc. v. Microdos Data Corp., 52 F.3rd 950 (11th Cir. 1995), the court held that the selection of communities for inclusion in a directory of cable systems is a copyrightable element of a compilation that was infringed by a virtually identical selection of communities in a software package of cable information. The court distinguished Bellsouth Advertising & Publishing Corp. v. Donnelly Information Publishing Inc., 999 F.2d 1436 (11th Cir. 1993), which held that there was no creative originality in a "yellow pages."

See, Tracy Lea Meade, *Note, Ex-post Feist: Applications of a Landmark Copyright Decision*, 2 J. INTELL. PROP. L. 245-278 (1994). William S. Strong, *Database Protection after Feist v. Rural Telephone Company*, 42 J. COPYRIGHT SOC'Y U.S.A. 39 (1994).

PAGE 613. New Note 9.

9. Does the *West Publishing Co.* decision remain good law after *Feist*?

PAGE 619. Before the *Mirage Editions* case.

Under § 114(a) of the Copyright Act the rights of the owner of the copyright in a sound recording to not include an exclusive right of public performance. Thus a radio station, for instance, can play a sound recording on the air without obtaining permission from the owner of the copyright in the sound recording (as opposed to the owner of any copyright to any musical or other work performed on the sound recording). The Registrar of Copyrights and others have long urged that the copyright in a sound recording should include a right of public performance, a position opposed by broadcasters and others who would have to pay to use the expanded right.

Techological change led Congress to act in 1995, resulting in Public Law 104-39, the Digital Sound Recordings Act, Nov. 1, 1995. The technology now exists to broadcast sound recordings digitally (the same technology used in making compact discs) with a sound quality as good as that of the original recording. It is also not unlikely that within a short time there may be interactive services in which material can be broadcast on request. For instance, a cable subscriber may be able to call an 800 number and order up particular music on request to be transmitted to the subscriber over the cable system. This raises the possibility that the purchase of recordings will become obsolete. Instead of owning compact disc collections whose individual discs can be manufactured only with the consent of the owner of the copyright in the sound recording, customers will simply order up the music they want to hear from a central broadcast facility. The purpose of the Digital Sound Recordings Act is to enable the owners of the copyright in the sound recording to share in this market without disrupting the arrangements that have developed in reliance on existing law.

The Act basically extends a public performance right in sound recordings to digital (not analog) transmissions on a system that is a subscription system that charges. The Act accomplishes this by adding a new § 106(6) which adds to the list of exclusive rights, in the case of sound recordings, the exclusive right "to perform the copyrighted work publicly by means of a digital audio transmission." This new exclusive right is then limited by a new § 114(d). In order to extend the existing system that has applied to the manufacture of sound recordings, the compulsory license system that has existed for phonorecords is also extended to this new regime by amendments to § 115, mostly in a new § 115(c)(3).

PAGE 622. Read after *Mirage Editions, Inc.*

LEWIS GALOOB TOYS, INC. v. NINTENDO OF AMERICA, INC.
United States Court of Appeals for the Ninth Circuit, 1992
964 F. 2d 965, certiorari denied 113 Sup. Ct. 1382 (1993)

FARRIS, Circuit Judge:

Nintendo of America appeals the district court's judgment following a bench trial (1) declaring that Lewis Galoob Toys' Game Genie does not violate any Nintendo copyrights and dissolving a temporary injunction and (2) denying Nintendo's request for a permanent injunction enjoining Galoob from marketing the Game Genie. Lewis Galoob Toys, Inc. v. Nintendo of America, Inc., 780 F.Supp. 1283 (N.D.Cal.1991). * * *. We affirm.

FACTS

The Nintendo Entertainment System is a home video game system marketed by Nintendo. To use the system, the player inserts a cartridge containing a video game that Nintendo produces or licenses others to produce. By pressing buttons and manipulating a control pad, the player controls one of the game's characters and progresses through the game. The games are protected as audiovisual works under 17 U.S.C. § 102(a)(6).

The Game Genie is a device manufactured by Galoob that allows the player to alter up to three features of a Nintendo game. For example, the Game Genie can increase the number of lives of the player's character, increase the speed at which the character moves, and allow the character to float above obstacles. The player controls the changes made by the Game Genie by entering codes provided by the Game Genie Programming Manual and Code Book. The player also can experiment with variations of these codes.

The Game Genie functions by blocking the value for a single data byte sent by the game cartridge to the central processing unit in the Nintendo Entertainment System and replacing it with a new value. If that value controls the character's strength, for example, then the character can be made invincible by increasing the value sufficiently. The Game Genie is inserted between a game cartridge and the Nintendo Entertainment System. The Game Genie does not alter the data that is stored in the game cartridge. Its effects are temporary.

DISCUSSION

1. Derivative work

The Copyright Act of 1976 confers upon copyright holders the exclusive right to prepare and authorize others to prepare derivative works based on their copyrighted works. See 17 U.S.C. § 106(2). * * *.

A derivative work must incorporate a protected work in some concrete or permanent "form." The Copyright Act defines a derivative work as follows: A "derivative work" is a work based upon one or more preexisting works, such as a translation, musical arrangement, dramatization, fictionalization, motion picture version, sound recording, art reproduction, abridgment, condensation, or any other *form* in which a work may be recast, transformed, or adapted. A work consisting of editorial revisions, annotations, elaborations, or other modifications which, as a whole, represent an original work of authorship, is a "derivative work." 17 U.S.C. § 101 (emphasis added). The examples of derivative works provided by the Act all physically incorporate the underlying work or works. The Act's legislative history similarly indicates that "the infringing work must incorporate a portion of the copyrighted work in some form." 1976 U.S.Code Cong. & Admin.News 5659, 5675. See also Mirage Editions, Inc. v. Albuquerque A.R.T. Co., 856 F.2d 1341, 1343-44 (9th Cir.1988) (discussing same), *cert. denied*, 489 U.S. 1018 (1989).

Our analysis is not controlled by the Copyright Act's definition of "fixed." The Act defines copies as "material objects, other than phonorecords, in which a work is *fixed* by any method." 17 U.S.C. § 101 (emphasis added). The Act's definition of "derivative work," in contrast, lacks any such reference to fixation. See *id*. Further, we have held in a copyright infringement action that "[i]t makes no difference that the derivation may not satisfy certain requirements for statutory copyright registration itself." Lone Ranger Television v. Program Radio Corp., 740 F.2d 718, 722 (9th Cir.1984). See also Paul Goldstein, Derivative Rights and Derivative Works in Copyright, 30 J. Copyright Soc'y U.S.A. 209, 231 n. 75 (1983) ("the Act does not require that the derivative work be protectable for its preparation to infringe"). Cf. Kalem Co. v. Harper Bros., 222 U.S. 55, 61, 32 S.Ct. 20, 21, 56 L.Ed. 92 (1911) (finding the movie "Ben Hur" infringed copyright in the book Ben Hur even though Copyright Act did not yet include movies as protectable works). A derivative work must be fixed to be protected under the Act, see 17 U.S.C. § 102(a), but not to infringe.

The argument that a derivative work must be fixed because "[a] 'derivative work' is a work," 17 U.S.C. § 101, and "[a] work is 'created' when it is fixed in a copy or phonorecord for the first time," id., relies on a misapplication of the Copyright Act's definition of "created": A work is 'created' when it is fixed in a copy or phonorecord for the first time; where a work is prepared over a period of time, the portion of it that has been fixed at any particular time constitutes the work as of that time, and where the work has been prepared in different versions, each version constitutes a separate work. Id. The definition clarifies the time at which a work is created. If the provision were a definition of "work," it would not use that term in such a casual manner. The Act does not contain a definition of "work." Rather, it contains specific definitions: "audiovisual works," "literary works," and "pictorial, graphic and sculptural works," for example. The definition of "derivative work" does not require fixation.

The district court's finding that no independent work is created, see Galoob, 780 F.Supp. at 1291, is supported by the record. The Game Genie merely enhances the audiovisual displays (or underlying data bytes) that originate in Nintendo game cartridges. The altered displays do not incorporate a portion of a copyrighted work in some concrete or permanent form. Nintendo argues that the Game Genie's displays are as fixed in the hardware and software used to create them as Nintendo's original displays. Nintendo's argument ignores the fact that the Game Genie cannot produce an audiovisual display; the underlying display must be produced by a Nintendo Entertainment System and game cartridge. Even if we were to rely on the Copyright Act's definition of "fixed," we would similarly conclude that the resulting display is not "embodied," see 17 U.S.C. § 101, in the Game Genie. It cannot be a derivative work.

Mirage Editions is illustrative. Albuquerque A.R.T. transferred artworks from a commemorative book to individual ceramic tiles. See *Mirage Editions*, 856 F.2d at 1342. We held that "[b]y borrowing and mounting the preexisting, copyrighted individual art images without the consent of the copyright proprietors ... [Albuquerque A.R.T.] has prepared a derivative work and infringed the subject copyrights." Id. at 1343. The ceramic tiles physically incorporated the copyrighted works in a form that could be sold. Perhaps more importantly, sales of the tiles supplanted purchasers' demand for the underlying works. Our holding in *Mirage Editions* would have been much different if Albuquerque A.R.T. had distributed lenses that merely enabled users to view several artworks simultaneously.

Nintendo asserted at oral argument that the existence of a $150 million market for the Game Genie indicates that its audiovisual display must be fixed. We understand Nintendo's argument; consumers clearly would not purchase the Game Genie if its display was not "sufficiently permanent or stable to permit it to be perceived ... for a period of more than transitory duration." 17 U.S.C. § 101. But, Nintendo's reliance on the Act's definition of "fixed" is misplaced. Nintendo's argument also proves too much; the existence of a market does not, and cannot, determine conclusively whether a work is an infringing derivative work. For example, although there is a market for kaleidoscopes, it does not necessarily follow that kaleidoscopes create unlawful derivative works when pointed at protected artwork. The same can be said of countless other products that enhance, but do not replace, copyrighted works.

Nintendo also argues that our analysis should focus exclusively on the audiovisual displays created by the Game Genie, *i.e.*, that we should compare the altered displays to Nintendo's original displays. Nintendo emphasizes that " '[a]udiovisual works' are works that consist of a series of related images ... regardless of the nature of the material objects ... in which the works are embodied." 17 U.S.C. § 101 (emphasis added). The Copyright Act's definition of "audiovisual works" is inapposite; the only question before us is whether the audiovisual displays created by the Game Genie are "derivative works." The Act does not similarly provide that a work can be a derivative work regardless of the nature of the material objects in which the work is embodied. A derivative work must incorporate a protected work in some concrete or permanent form. We cannot ignore the actual source of the Game Genie's display.

Nintendo relies heavily on Midway Mfg. Co. v. Artic Int'l, Inc., 704 F.2d 1009 (7th Cir.), cert. denied, 464 U.S. 823 (1983). Midway can be distinguished. The defendant in Midway, Artic International, marketed a computer chip that could be inserted in Galaxian video games to speed up the rate of play. The Seventh Circuit held that the speeded-up version of Galaxian was a derivative work. Id. at 1013-14. Artic's chip substantially copied and replaced the chip that was originally distributed by Midway. Purchasers of Artic's chip also benefited economically by offering the altered game for use by the general public. The Game Genie does not physically incorporate a portion of a copyrighted work, nor does it supplant demand for a component of that work. The court in Midway acknowledged that the Copyright Act's definition of "derivative work" "must be stretched to accommodate speeded-up video games." Id. at 1014. Stretching that definition further would chill innovation and fail to protect "society's competing interest in the free flow of ideas, information, and commerce." Sony Corp. of America v. Universal Studios, Inc., 464 U.S. 417, 429 (1984).

In holding that the audiovisual displays created by the Game Genie are not derivative works, we recognize that technology often advances by improvement rather than replacement. See Christian H. Nadan, Note, A Proposal to Recognize Component Works: How a Teddy Bears on the Competing Ends of Copyright Law, 78 Cal.L.Rev. 1633, 1635 (1990). Some time ago, for example, computer companies began marketing spell-checkers that operate within existing word processors by signalling the writer when a word is misspelled. These applications, as well as countless others, could not be produced and marketed if courts were to conclude that the word processor and spell-checker combination is a derivative work based on the word processor alone. The Game Genie is useless by itself, it can only enhance, and cannot duplicate or recaste, a Nintendo game's output. It does not contain or produce a Nintendo game's output in some concrete or permanent form, nor does it supplant demand for Nintendo game cartridges. Such innovations rarely will constitute infringing derivative works under the Copyright Act. See generally Nadan, *supra*, at 1667-72.

2. Fair use

[The court also affirmed the district court's conclusion that if the audiovisual displays created by the Game Genie are derivative works, they are fair use.]

* * *

AFFIRMED.

NOTE

It is possible to argue that the scope of the § 106(2) exclusive right to prepare derivative works is narrowed by § 117(1) which permits the owner of a computer program to make an adaptation "created as an essential step in the utilization of the computer program in conjunction with a machine." The Nintendo game cartridges are of course computer programs. Does the fact that they are also audiovisual works make § 117(1) unavailable? Are not most computer programs audiovisual works, so such a reading would surprisingly narrow § 117(1), would it not? Of course, the owner who makes an adaptation under § 117(1) can only use the adaptation "in conjunction with a machine," he cannot sell it. But the argument can be made that the "Game Genie" is not the adaptation, the performance by the owner of the Nintendo machine using the Game Genie is the adaptation.

In Aymes v. Bonelli, 47 F.3d 23 (2d Cir. 1995), the court addressed the issue of whether and how much adaptation is permitted under §117(1). Aymes had written a program for Bonelli for use in his swimming pool business in 1980. Subsequently, Aymes hired other programmers to modify the program to adapt to new business needs and to enable the program to run on new computers. Aymes sued for infringement in 1985, and argued that these modifications were infringing derivative works. The court held that they were not infringing under § 117(1). The court said:

> According to the Contu Report, copyright laws should reflect the fact that transactions involving computer programs are entered into with "full awareness that users will modify their copies to suit their own needs." Foresight Resources Corp. v. Pfortmiller, 719 F.Supp. 1006, 1009 (D.Kan.1989) (quoting Contu Report). This right of adaption includes "the right to add features to the program that were not present at the time of rightful acquisition", id., and was intended to apply to modifications for internal use, as long as the adapted

program is not distributed in an unauthorized manner. See *id.* at 1009-10; Apple Computer, Inc. v. Formula Int'l, Inc., 594 F.Supp. 617, 621 (C.D.Cal.1984). The district court found that Island used the program for internal purposes only and did not distribute the program to its subsidiaries.

Nor does it appear that the modifications to the program were for any purpose other than Island's internal business needs. The original program made provisions for late charges, and Island did alter CSALIB to keep it current from year to year and to maintain the viability of the original software when Island upgraded its computer to accommodate successive generations of IBM systems. In this connection, the Contu Report also comments: "The conversion of a program from one higher-level language to another to facilitate use would fall within this right [of adaption], *as would the right to add features to the program that were not present at the time of rightful acquisition* .... Again, it is likely that many transactions involving copies of programs are entered into with *full awareness that users will modify their copies to suit their own needs*, and this should be reflected in the law.... Should proprietors feel strongly that they do not want rightful possessors of copies of their programs to prepare such adaptations, they could, of course, make such desires a contractual matter." Contu Report at 13-14 (emphasis added) quoted in, Foresight Resources, 719 F.Supp. at 1009.

PAGE 667. Add or Read in place of the other principal infringement cases.

BEAL v. PARAMOUNT PICTURES CORPORATION
United States Court of Appeals for the Eleventh Circuit, 1994
20 F.3d 454, certiorari denied 115 S. Ct. 675 (1994)

ANDERSON, Circuit Judge:

In this copyright infringement case, Alveda King Beal appeals the district court's grant of summary judgment in favor of the defendants below, Paramount Pictures Corp. and Eddie Murphy. The court rejected the claim that the movie "Coming to America" violated the copyright in Beal's adventure novel The Arab Heart. 806 F.Supp. 963 (N.D. Ga.1992). Because we agree with the district court's conclusions, we affirm.

I. THE WORKS

When called upon to adjudicate a copyright dispute, a court must compare the works in question. See Autoskill, Inc. v. National Educ. Support Sys., Inc., 994 F.2d

1476, 1490 (10th Cir.), cert. denied, 126 L.Ed.2d 254 (1993). With that in mind, we have independently reviewed the book and the motion picture involved in this lawsuit, and will begin by briefly summarizing them.

A. The Arab Heart

Plaintiff-Appellant Alveda King Beal is the author of The Arab Heart, a novel she describes as a "historical tale of romance and adventure." The book's protagonist is Sharaf Ammar Hakim Riad, prince and sole heir to the sheikdom of Whada, a fictitious Arabian nation. As the book begins, Sharaf has reluctantly agreed with the plan of his grandfather, Sheik Hussein, to send Sharaf to the United States. Hussein believes the heir would benefit from a year of technical training that would enable Sharaf to improve Whada's oil production. Although initially resisting the plan, Sharaf agrees to attend the Georgia Institute of Technology (Georgia Tech), as long as he is allowed to live as a normal college student.

As Beal contends, The Arab Heart has two main plotlines. One involves the political unrest in Whada, manifested by the efforts of Hussein's half-brother, Mansur, to take over the throne by means of force. As heir, Sharaf plays a prominent role in these events, though they may be characterized as centering on Hussein. For example, before Sharaf leaves for America, Mansur's forces carry out an unsuccessful assassination attempt at the palace involving both Hussein and Sharaf. The other plot involves Sharaf's adventures in America, which soon focus on his romantic exploits. It is this plotline that Beal contends was infringed by "Coming to America."

Upon his arrival in Atlanta, Sharaf and his two bodyguards take up residence in a boarding house near campus. Sharaf shares his apartment with Mark Anderson, a black graduate student who initially harbors a dislike of those from different racial or ethnic groups. As the book progresses, however, Mark begins to appreciate cultures other than his own; this type of enlightenment is a major theme of the book. Through Mark and his girlfriend, Ebony, Sharaf is introduced to Flora Johnston. Flora is a shy college student and songwriter, the daughter of a well-to-do white man and black woman from Savannah. Sharaf is immediately interested in her. However, his attention also is drawn to Claire Eastman, a beautiful but opportunistic white woman from Boston. This "romantic triangle" plays a large role in the book. For example, Sharaf is invited to a Halloween party at the home of Flora's parents in Savannah. At the party, Flora performs a sensual belly dance for Sharaf, and Ebony sings a song Flora has written for him. However, Sharaf has brought Claire to the party as his guest. Although harboring feelings for Flora, Sharaf pursues his romance with Claire and the two become intimate.

During this time, the book also develops the plot regarding unrest in Whada. Hussein travels to Georgia to meet with a financier and arrange the purchase of weapons. At semester break, Sharaf and Mark travel to Whada, where Sharaf undergoes training to prepare him to take over the throne should Hussein die. Hussein, recovering from an attempted poisoning, arranges a dinner at which Sharaf meets Kauthar, the daughter of Hussein's ally. The sheik hopes Sharaf will make Kauthar one of his wives, but Sharaf resists. In the spring, Sharaf returns to Whada to quell an uprising by Mansur's forces; one of Mansur's sons is killed in the fight. During this visit, Sharaf tells Hussein that he is thinking of marrying both Claire and Kauthar. However, he also is influenced by his parents' atypical (for Whada) monogamous marriage and his attraction to Flora; he returns to Atlanta to finish school unsure of whom he should marry (and of how many wives he should have).

Upon his return, Sharaf overhears Claire's conversation with a friend that reveals her prejudice and her intolerance of Arab customs. This ends any interest Sharaf had in marrying Claire. He rekindles his romance with Flora, and the two are married a few weeks later at her parents' home. Sharaf tells Flora and her father that he will try living with only one wife, although he is entitled to more. After the marriage, the book skips forward a year, with Sharaf and Flora living in Whada. Hussein does not fully accept Flora, largely because she has failed to give Sharaf a son. When Flora finally does become pregnant, she finds her husband in bed with a servant, which causes a strain in the marriage. The couple eventually reconciles, with an implicit understanding that Sharaf will continue his occasional infidelities but will be more discreet. Flora delivers a son, and exerts her influence to convince Sharaf to give more help to the needy of Whada. In a final battle, both Hussein and Mansur are killed. Sharaf becomes ruler of Whada, with Hussein's dying wish that Sharaf seek and value Flora's opinion.

B. "Coming to America"

"Coming to America" is a romantic comedy released by defendant Paramount Pictures. The film begins on the twenty-first birthday of Akeem, Prince of Zamunda (portrayed by defendant Eddie Murphy). Although little detail is given regarding the country, Zamunda is an African nation with a lavish royal palace situated in what appears to be a lush tropical forest. Akeem's father states that the time has come for the prince to take a bride; following Zamundan custom, a wife has been chosen for Akeem. The prospective bride is introduced at an elaborate ceremony. Akeem speaks with her in private; it becomes clear that she has been raised to show total subservience to her husband. After commanding her to do several demeaning acts, and her ready compliance, Akeem decides he would prefer an independent wife with her own opinion. He seeks his father's permission to search for such a bride in America. The king resists, but finally allows Akeem to go to the United States for forty days to "sow his royal oats," after which time he shall return and marry his arranged bride. Akeem accepts this arrangement, but secretly plans to find a wife of his choice in America.

Akeem is accompanied to America by his friend and companion Semmi. The prince concludes that the logical place to search for a future queen of Zamunda is Queens, New York. Throughout his sojourn in America, Akeem is determined to find a woman who values him for himself, not for his wealth or position. To this end, he goes to great lengths to hide his true identity. His luggage and fine clothes are stolen, but Akeem does not mind. Akeem and Semmi take a dilapidated apartment in a tenement. The pair initially searches for suitable brides in a nightclub, but finds only comically inappropriate women. Neighborhood residents tell Akeem that he may have more luck at a black awareness rally. At the rally, Akeem first sees Lisa McDowell, a community activist and daughter of the owner of a fast-food restaurant. He is immediately attracted to Lisa; Akeem and Semmi take jobs in the restaurant so Akeem can get to know Lisa. Akeem soon learns that Lisa has a boyfriend, Darryl, the son of a family that owns a line of hair-care products. The Akeem-Lisa-Darryl triangle plays a major role in the movie. Lisa attempts to get Akeem interested in her sister Patrice, but Akeem continues to pursue Lisa.

Several comic episodes take place with Akeem and Semmi in the restaurant, including the foiling--with a mop handle--of an armed robbery. Other scenes focus on the developing Akeem-Lisa relationship. During a party at Lisa's parents' house, Lisa becomes angry with Darryl for announcing their engagement without first asking her. Akeem comforts Lisa and the two begin to date. Akeem continues to hide his true identity. However, Semmi tires of living the "common" life and wires Akeem's parents for more money. This request brings the king and queen to America, where the king tells Lisa that she would be an inappropriate bride for Akeem. Stung by the king's comments and Akeem's dishonesty in hiding his identity, Lisa rebuffs Akeem's proposal of marriage. Akeem returns to Zamunda, apparently to enter into the arranged marriage. However, when he lifts the bride's veil, he sees that it is Lisa. The movie ends immediately after the couple's marriage, when Akeem says he is willing to give up his kingdom for Lisa and she replies that the sacrifice won't be necessary.

II. THE PROCEEDINGS

Although not directly relevant to this case, we note that the movie "Coming to America" has been the subject of another lawsuit that drew a good deal of attention. We mention this because the differences between the cases highlight the issues in this case. In the previous lawsuit, humorist and author Art Buchwald sued Paramount and others in an action for breach of contract, claiming that "Coming to America" was based on a film proposal written and submitted by Buchwald. Buchwald v. Paramount Pictures Corp., 13 U.S.P.Q.2d 1497 (Cal.Super.Ct.1990). It is crucial to note that Buchwald was not a copyright infringement suit. The court found that a contract existed between Buchwald and the defendants, and that "Coming to America" was "based upon" Buchwald's proposal, which entitled Buchwald to payment pursuant to a contract between the parties. See Buchwald, 13 U.S.P.Q.2d at 1501-02, 1506. The court was careful to emphasize that its finding that "Coming to America" was "based upon" Buchwald's proposal was premised on much different ground than a copyright claim. See id. at 1502- 03. In essence, liability was found because Paramount had used Buchwald's idea as a basis for the movie. Id. at 1503.[3]

On the other hand, a basic premise of copyright law is that, while expression is protected, ideas are not the proper subject of copyright. 17 U.S.C. § 102(b); Baker v. Selden, 101 U.S. 99, 103 (1880). Therefore, copyright infringement exists only if protected expression is wrongfully appropriated. To prevail in the present case, Beal must show more than Buchwald was required to prove. Moreover, while the defendants here may have appropriated Buchwald's ideas, that would not necessarily preclude appropriation also of Beal's expression.

The district court, after summarizing the works and surveying the law, found that summary judgment for the defendants was supported on two grounds: that any similarity between The Arab Heart and "Coming to America" concerned only noncopyrightable elements of the book, and that no reasonable jury, properly instructed, would find the two works to be substantially similar. 806 F.Supp. at 967. The court based this conclusion upon consideration of the works' plots, characterizations, mood, pace, and settings. Id. Beal then brought this appeal, alleging various errors of law and fact.

III. LEGAL ANALYSIS

A. Summary Judgment Standards

Summary judgment is proper when there is no genuine issue of material fact and the moving party is entitled to judgment as a matter of law. Fed.R.Civ.P. 56(c). Evidence is viewed in a light most favorable to the nonmoving party, United States v. Four Parcels of Real Property, 941 F.2d 1428, 1437 (11th Cir.1991) (en banc); this, however, does not mean that we are constrained to accept all the nonmovant's factual characterizations and legal arguments. If no reasonable jury could return a verdict in favor of the nonmoving party, there is no genuine issue of material fact and summary judgment will be granted. Anderson v. Liberty Lobby, Inc., 477 U.S. 242, 248, 106 S.Ct. 2505, 2510, 91 L.Ed.2d 202 (1986). We review the district court's grant of summary judgment de novo. Vernon v. FDIC, 981 F.2d 1230, 1232, reh'g en banc denied, 990 F.2d 1270 (11th Cir.1993).

Some courts have observed that summary judgment is peculiarly inappropriate in copyright infringement cases due to their inherent subjectivity. See Hoehling v. Universal City Studios, Inc., 618 F.2d 972, 977 (2d Cir.), cert. denied, 449 U.S. 841

---

[3] Another unreported decision rejected a copyright infringement claim brought by parties unrelated to Buchwald and Beal against Paramount, Murphy, and others regarding "Coming to America." Gregory v. Murphy, Copyright L.Rep. (CCH) ¶ 26,707, reported as table case, 928 F.2d 1136 (9th Cir.1991).

(1980). Beal's reply brief states this premise, although it also notes that there is no issue in this case regarding the propriety of summary judgment. In any event, courts have been willing to grant summary judgment in infringement cases when it is clear that the moving party is entitled to judgment as a matter of law. See, e.g., *Hoehling*, 618 F.2d at 979; Evans v. Wallace Berrie & Co., 681 F.Supp. 813 (S.D.Fla.1988).

B. Test for Determination of Infringement

To establish copyright infringement, two elements must be proven: ownership of a valid copyright, and copying of constituent elements of the work that are original. Feist Publications, Inc. v. Rural Telephone Service Co., 499 U.S. 340 (1991); Bellsouth Advertising & Publishing Corp. v. Donnelley Info. Publishing, Inc., 999 F.2d 1436, 1440 (11th Cir.1993) (en banc). For purposes of its motion for summary judgment, Paramount concedes that Beal holds a valid copyright in The Arab Heart; therefore, only copying is contested.

In recognizing that plaintiffs rarely have direct evidence on this issue, courts have developed methods by which copying can be proven indirectly. The approach applied in this Circuit involves a two-part test for indirect proof of copying. The plaintiff is first required to show that the defendant had access to the plaintiff's work; second, the plaintiff must show that the defendant's work is substantially similar to the plaintiff's protected expression. Original Appalachian Artworks, Inc. v. Toy Loft, Inc., 684 F.2d 821, 829 & n. 11 (11th Cir.1982). A court may grant summary judgment for a defendant if the similarity between the works concerns only noncopyrightable elements, or if no reasonable jury upon proper instruction would find that the two works are substantially similar. Warner Bros., Inc. v. American Broadcasting Cos., 720 F.2d 231, 240 (2d Cir.1983). Because the Copyright Act protects "original works of authorship," 17 U.S.C. § 102(a), the "sine qua non of copyright is originality." Feist Publications, supra, 499 U.S. at 345. Material that is not original cannot be copyrighted. In addition to broad ideas, noncopyrightable material includes "scenes a faire" --stock scenes that naturally flow from a common theme. See, e.g., Walker v. Time Life Films, Inc., 784 F.2d 44, 50 (2d Cir.) (no protection for common elements in police fiction, such as "drunks, prostitutes, vermin and derelict cars" and "foot chases and the morale problems of policemen, not to mention the familiar figure of the Irish cop"), cert. denied, 476 U.S. 1159 (1986); Evans v. Wallace Berrie & Co., 681 F.Supp. at 817 ("Such similarities as using a sand dollar as currency, foods made of seaweed, seahorses for transportation and plates made of oysters or mother of pearl are not protected similarities of expression, but are more accurately characterizations that naturally follow from the common theme of an underwater civilization.").

C. Application of Law to Facts

In the present case, Paramount concedes access for purposes of the summary judgment motion only. This leaves "substantial similarity" as the crucial issue. The district court found that no reasonable jury, properly instructed, could find The Arab

Heart and "Coming to America" substantially similar, and also found that any similarities involve noncopyrightable elements. 806 F.Supp. at 967. We agree that although there are a few broad similarities between the works, they involve ideas and other general themes that are not susceptible to copyright protection.

Beal argues that because there is clear and convincing proof of access, she should be required to prove a degree of similarity lesser in quantum than the standard "substantial similarity." We first note that this contention, known as the inverse-ratio rule, see Shaw v. Lindheim, 919 F.2d 1353, 1361 (9th Cir.1990), was raised for the first time in Beal's reply brief and therefore should be deemed to be waived. See Jackson v. United States, 976 F.2d 679, 680 (11th Cir.1992). In addition, the inverse-ratio rule has never been applied in this Circuit. Finally, even though Paramount conceded access for purposes of the summary judgment motion, even convincing proof of access does not do away with the necessity of finding similarity. See Shaw, 919 F.2d at 1361 ("[A]ccess without similarity cannot create an inference of copying.").

The district court noted that the book and the motion picture do share a few general similarities. Both involve young crown princes from wealthy royal families coming to America, where they meet the women they will marry. Both feature a strong ruler who (with varying degrees of intensity) initially prefers that the prince enter into an arranged marriage. However, as the court noted, these generalized themes are in the realm of ideas, which are not protected by copyright. 806 F.Supp. at 967. In addition, the book and the movie diverge sharply from these broad similarities. Id. Both before the district court and this court, Beal has presented lengthy lists of elements she claims were appropriated by Paramount. The district court correctly noted that such lists are " 'inherently subjective and unreliable,' particularly where the list contains random similarities. Many such similarities could be found in very dissimilar works." Id. at 967 n. 2 (citation omitted). Contrary to Beal's assertion, the district court did not ignore these other claimed similarities. The court's subsequent analysis amply demonstrates that some of the similarities consist of noncopyrightable elements, while others cannot fairly be considered similarities. Although we have examined all of Beal's claimed similarities, it would be neither useful nor judicious to detail each and every one. Our analysis will make use of a few of the claimed similarities that we consider representative. See Wavelength Film Co. v. Columbia Pictures Indus., 631 F.Supp. 305, 306 (N.D.Ill.1986).

In evaluating claims of substantial similarity, courts have examined different aspects of the work in question. The district court specifically enumerated plot, mood, characterization, pace, and setting as relevant factors. 806 F.Supp. at 967 (citing Walker v. Time Life Films, 784 F.2d at 49, and Litchfield v. Spielberg, 736 F.2d 1352, 1357 (9th Cir.1984)). Beal contends that the district court erred in finding insufficient similarities in these aspects. We will examine each aspect independently, adding sequence of events, which Beal argues is also relevant. We keep in mind the practical difficulty of drawing a bright line between idea and expression, see Peter Pan

Ch. 5   INFRINGEMENT   223

Fabrics, Inc. v. Martin Weiner Corp., 274 F.2d 487, 489 (2d Cir. 1960) (L. Hand, J.), and recognize that a genuine issue of material fact would preclude summary judgment.

    1. Plot.--The similarity in plot between the two works is only on the most basic level. As we have observed, both involve a prince coming to the United States, where he meets a woman he will marry. Beyond the broad similarity in ideas, however, we find great differences in expression, as well as differences in ideas. Akeem in "Coming to America" wants to make the journey to find an independent wife who values him for himself, not his wealth and position. Sharaf in The Arab Heart initially resists going to America, finally giving in to his grandfather's wish that he receive technical training. Thus the purposes of the journeys were entirely different. Akeem went to great lengths to conceal his identity, living in a tenement and working in a fast-food restaurant. In contrast, although Sharaf's expressed intent at the outset was to live as other students do and not be handicapped by the royal wealth, and although he made some modest steps in that direction, living for example in a normal student apartment, Sharaf made his lineage and status known to all and did not hesitate to openly give expensive gifts. Sharaf aggressively pursued both Claire and Flora, who were interested in him almost immediately, while Akeem quietly courted Lisa's favor.

    Beal argues that Akeem's quest for a wife parallels Sharaf's voluntary return to America in the spring, when he became intent on marrying either Claire or Flora. This cannot reasonably be seen as a similarity. By the spring, Sharaf had become involved with two American women. His return is prompted by his attraction to Claire and Flora specifically, along with his desire to finish his classes at Georgia Tech. This is very different from Akeem's unguided voyage to America to find a wife. In addition, Sharaf still was considering marriage to Kauthar, the arranged bride, in addition to one of his American women. Akeem, on the other hand, conclusively rejected the idea of an arranged marriage.

    Although both works feature a romantic triangle, the mere existence of this device is unoriginal and noncopyrightable. The book's triangle involves Sharaf, Flora, and Claire; the points of the movie's triangle are Akeem, Lisa, and Darryl. Beal argues that the movie has a second triangle involving Akeem, Lisa, and Lisa's sister, Patrice, that is similar to the book's. However, Akeem dates Patrice only once (and agrees to the date unwittingly, at that), whereas Sharaf was intimately involved with both women in his triangle. Beal also maintains that the book features a second triangle with Sharaf, Claire, and Claire's once and future boyfriend, Raymond. However, Raymond plays only the smallest of roles in the book.

    Additionally, there is the entire second plot of the book, dealing with the internal problems in Whada. Beal maintains that this plot is irrelevant because Paramount appropriated only the romantic plot. In other words, she claims that most (if not all) of the movie is derived from the book, although not all of the book is in the movie; therefore we should disregard the book's second plot. Beal cites no authority for this proposition. We think that the existence of the second plot is relevant because it greatly influences the mood of the book. Even if we accept Beal's argument, however, we would reach the same conclusion. The plots regarding the princes' adventures in America contain basic similarities that are not subject to copyright protection. Beyond that, they differ enough to preclude a finding of substantial similarity.

2. Mood.--The general mood of the two works differs greatly. The Arab Heart is a serious work with few lighter overtones, whereas "Coming to America" is a quintessential light romantic comedy. Sharaf's relationships with Claire and Flora are much more physical than that of Akeem and Lisa. The book includes several episodes of political violence, while the movie features only a foiled robbery attempt with something of a humorous slant. "Coming to America" draws much humor from the situation of having a wealthy prince masquerade as an impoverished visitor to this country, whereas Sharaf's interactions with Americans focus on exchanges of culture and tradition. There are a very few isolated instances of comedy relief in the book, but they are largely dissimilar to those in the film. The similarities that Beal attempts to highlight--for example, both works feature dogs whose names begin with the letter D--cannot reasonably be considered substantial.[6]

The Arab Heart has as one of its underlying themes the resolution of tensions caused by racial, ethnic, and cultural differences. This theme, which contributes much to the book's mood, is displayed in many ways: the depiction of interracial couples (Flora's parents; Sharaf's Arab father and Egyptian mother; Sharaf and Flora), Mark's changing attitudes, and frequent references to Dr. Martin Luther King, Jr. This theme is notably absent from "Coming to America." Although a black awareness rally takes place and characters briefly discuss Dr. King, these features are used only for comic effect and to advance the romantic plot. Both princes are subjected to a small amount of taunting regarding their national origin, but the scenes are not substantially similar. In any event, showings of prejudice and ignorance toward those from other continents are scenes a faire in stories of foreigners abroad.

3. Characterization.--The protagonists of the two works share one broad similarity: they are crown princes and sole heirs to the thrones of foreign nations who have come to America. From this point, the characterizations of Sharaf and Akeem vary greatly. Both show some degree of rebellion from tradition, but this rebellion is manifested in different ways. Sharaf, often described as a "young lion," tends to be brash and impetuous. He wishes to bring social change to Whada by achieving greater equity in wealth distribution, but he accepts many of the harsh (by Western standards) traditional customs, such as notion that women are to be subservient to a degree and

---

[6] To illustrate this point, we note that the dogs appear in entirely dissimilar circumstances. In the book, the dog is owned by the proprietor of Sharaf's boarding house and does little. In the movie, the dog is owned by Lisa's parents and is ordered to attack Darryl, Lisa's would-be fiance. Moreover, the role of the dog is insignificant in both works.

men are not expected to be totally monogamous. Akeem primarily rebels against a single tradition, that of arranged marriage. He also shows distaste for some of the more ostentatious traditions regarding Zamundan royalty (for example, the spreading of rose petals where royals walk). This, however, has little in common with Sharaf's character. Sharaf does refuse to live lavishly in Atlanta, but he certainly allows himself more creature comforts that Akeem.

A marked disparity exists between the general attitudes of Sharaf and Akeem. Sharaf is aggressive and imperious at times, as evidenced by his conduct during college registration (when he becomes angry because he has not been given a private suite), when approached by a woman on a bus (when he tells her she should be glad she "still [has] the skin on [her] back"), and when called "olive skin" by a football player (where he says he has decided to spare the athlete's life). His treatment of women, although perhaps progressive by Whadan standards, clearly displays his belief in their subservient role. Sharaf's sexual encounters are marked by physical aggressiveness; he treats his partners other than Claire and Flora with an attitude bordering on disdain. Akeem, on the other hand, courts Lisa quietly and nonaggressively, although with some persistence. He does not show Sharaf's short temper and refrains from striking out when others do not treat him with a measure of respect. In total, as the district court observed, Akeem is humble, kind, gentle, and seemingly innocent. His foiling of the armed robbery shows some aggressiveness, but it is totally unlike the aggressive nature of Sharaf's personality. When Akeem requests his intended arranged bride to hop on one foot and bark like a dog, it is not evidence of his view of women; rather, it shows the type of spouse he wishes to avoid.

Beal asserts that both protagonists wanted wives with similar qualities. While Sharaf finally decides to have only Flora for a wife, he is constantly concerned about the ability of an American woman to adapt to Arab customs. A dying Hussein does tell Sharaf to listen to Flora's opinion, but this comes late in the book. Akeem's stated purpose for coming to America was to find a wife who thinks for herself. From the start Akeem wants a bride who is nontraditional for Zamundan royalty, whereas Sharaf finally concludes that Flora reminds him of his mother.

Beal argues that Akeem's companion Semmi is a composite of Sharaf's bodyguards and Mark, his roommate (in addition to Sharaf's horse, Samir). Semmi, however, is a comic character who quickly tires of living the common life and passes himself off as the prince; these are characteristics wholly absent from any character in The Arab Heart. Other characters in the two works are likewise dissimilar.

4. Pace.--"Coming to America" is fast paced, covering Akeem's forty days in Queens and ending with his marriage to Lisa, presumably shortly thereafter. The Arab Heart takes place over two years. Beal contends that the relevant time frame for the book is Sharaf's nine months in Atlanta. Even if Beal's argument is accepted, the time frame of the book is several times that of the movie. Although both works are

relatively quick in pace, any similarity is not sufficient to weigh heavily in Beal's favor.

5. Setting.--The district court considered setting broadly, comparing Whada with Zamunda and Akeem's living conditions in Queens with those of Sharaf in Atlanta. Beal contends that an examination of setting should encompass any identifiable location where a significant scene takes place, but cites no authority for this proposition. Our independent research has not given a definitive answer. Although we believe the settings analyzed by the district court obviously are relevant, we will examine Beal's alleged similarities on a more specific level as well.

Both works begin in or near a palace. Beal argues that the film's palace appears similar to the palace on the book's cover. However, the idea of a mosque-style palace with minarets is a scene a faire in a story about Arabian or African royalty. The fact that both palaces are lavish and contain private quarters and baths also is not copyrightable expression. Although both works include scenes in which male characters are bathed by females, such scenes naturally follow in works focusing on wealthy men in countries where women are in a subservient role. These scenes, in addition, play relatively small roles in both the book and movie.

The living quarters of Sharaf are modest but comfortable, in a pleasant neighborhood near Georgia Tech; the one-room apartment shared by Akeem and Semmi is in an extremely rundown area of Queens (in fact, a blind man and his dog had been murdered in the apartment before Akeem's arrival). Both works include visits to fast-food restaurants and nightclub sequences, but such broad similarities are merely scenes a faire without a showing of more specific resemblances. For example, Sharaf first sees Claire in a brief visit to a fast-food establishment and thinks of taking a job there, but this thought is never pursued and the restaurant plays a minor role in the story. Akeem, however, does take a job in a restaurant--which is owned by Lisa's father-- primarily for the purpose of getting to know Lisa. A good portion of the film takes place in the restaurant. Similarly, the presence of hotels, dining in a restaurant near a window, festivities at a palace, and parties at a private home are not copyrightable elements. As a final illustration, Beal draws a parallel between the Halloween party at Flora's parents' house and the party that Lisa's father throws. However, Sharaf is the guest of honor at the first, while Akeem works as a servant at the latter. The parties themselves are not expression, and the details surrounding the party scenes differ widely in elements of expression.

6. Sequence of events.--The similarity in the sequence of events also is insufficient to show infringement. Any work in which the protagonist is royalty visiting America will naturally move from a palace to an airport to some form of lodging. Likewise, all works involving courtship and marriage will feature a wedding, usually near the end of the story. Beyond common elements of the broadest nature, the works have no similarities of detail.

7. Other claims of similarity.--In her reply brief, Beal sets out other attributes--theme and dialogue--that she argues must be considered when evaluating substantial similarity. Analysis of these attributes overlaps to a significant extent with those we have examined (for example, theme is similar to plot and mood). Further, an examination of these additional factors would lead to the same conclusion we have already reached: no reasonable factfinder could conclude that "Coming to America" is substantially similar to the copyrightable elements of The Arab Heart.

IV. CONCLUSION

Beal has failed to show genuine issues of material fact regarding substantial similarity between the works in question. If the similarities in general ideas and scenes a faire serve to show anything at all, perhaps it is only that "in Hollywood, as in [life] generally, there is only rarely anything new under the sun." Berkic v. Crichton, 761 F.2d 1289, 1294 (9th Cir.1985). See also Ecclesiastes 1:9 ("[T]here is no new thing under the sun."). The district court's entry of summary judgment for Paramount and Murphy is AFFIRMED.

PAGE 672. Read in addition to or in place of *Whelan Associates, Inc.*

COMPUTER ASSOCIATES INTERNATIONAL v. ALTAI
United States Court of Appeals for the Second Circuit, 1992
982 F. 2d 693

Before ALTIMARI, MAHONEY and WALKER, Circuit Judges.

* * *

* * *[T]his case deals with the challenging question of whether and to what extent the "non-literal" aspects of a computer program, that is, those aspects that are not reduced to written code, are protected by copyright. While a few other courts have already grappled with this issue, this case is one of first impression in this circuit. As we shall discuss, we find the results reached by other courts to be less than satisfactory. Drawing upon long-standing doctrines of copyright law, we take an approach that we think better addresses the practical difficulties embedded in these types of cases. In so doing, we have kept in mind the necessary balance between creative incentive and industrial competition.

This appeal comes to us from the United States District Court for the Eastern District of New York, the Honorable George C. Pratt, Circuit Judge, sitting by designation. By Memorandum and Order entered August 12, 1991, Judge Pratt found that defendant Altai, Inc.'s ("Altai"), OSCAR 3.4 computer program had infringed plaintiff Computer Associates' ("CA"), copyrighted computer program entitled CA-SCHEDULER. Accordingly, the district court awarded CA $364,444 in actual damages and apportioned profits. Altai has abandoned its appeal from this award. With respect to CA's second claim for copyright infringement, Judge Pratt found that Altai's OSCAR 3.5 program was not substantially similar to a portion of CA-SCHEDULER called ADAPTER, and thus denied relief. * * *.

Because we are in full agreement with Judge Pratt's decision and in substantial agreement with his careful reasoning regarding CA's copyright infringement claim, we affirm the district court's judgment on that issue.

* * *

I. COMPUTER PROGRAM DESIGN

* * *

The first step in * * * [computer programming] is to identify a program's ultimate function or purpose. An example of such an ultimate purpose might be the creation and maintenance of a business ledger. Once this goal has been achieved, a programmer breaks down or "decomposes" the program's ultimate function into "simpler constituent problems or 'subtasks,' " Englund, [Note, Idea, Process, or Protected Expression?: Determining the Scope of Copyright Protection of the Structure of Computer Programs, 88 Mich.L.Rev. 866, 867-73 (1990)] at 870, which are also known as subroutines or modules. See Spivack,[Comment, Does Form Follow Function? The Idea/Expression Dichotomy In Copyright Protection of Computer Software, 35 U.C.L.A.L.Rev. 723 (1988)] at 729. In the context of a business ledger program, a module or subroutine might be responsible for the task of updating a list of outstanding accounts receivable. Sometimes, depending upon the complexity of its task, a subroutine may be broken down further into sub-subroutines.

Having sufficiently decomposed the program's ultimate function into its component elements, a programmer will then arrange the subroutines or modules into what are known as organizational or flow charts. Flow charts map the interactions between modules that achieve the program's end goal. See Kretschmer, [Note, Copyright Protection For Software Architecture: Just Say No!, 1988 Colum.Bus.L.Rev. 823 (1988)] at 826.

In order to accomplish these intra-program interactions, a programmer must carefully design each module's parameter list. A parameter list, according to the expert appointed and fully credited by the district court, Dr. Randall Davis, is "the information sent to and received from a subroutine." See Report of Dr. Randall Davis, at 12. The term "parameter list" refers to the form in which information is passed between modules (e.g. for accounts receivable, the designated time frame and particular customer identifying number) and the information's actual content (e.g. 8/91-7/92; customer No. 3). Id. With respect to form, interacting modules must share similar parameter lists so that they are capable of exchanging information.

"The functions of the modules in a program together with each module's relationships to other modules constitute the 'structure' of the program." Englund, at 871. Additionally, the term structure may include the category of modules referred to as "macros." A macro is a single instruction that initiates a sequence of operations or module interactions within the program. Very often the user will accompany a macro with an instruction from the parameter list to refine the instruction (e.g. current total of accounts receivable (macro), but limited to those for 8/91 to 7/92 from customer No. 3 (parameters)).

In fashioning the structure, a programmer will normally attempt to maximize the program's speed, efficiency, as well as simplicity for user operation, while taking into consideration certain externalities such as the memory constraints of the computer upon which the program will be run. See id.; Kretschmer, at 826; Menell [Peter S. Menell, An Analysis of the Scope of Copyright Protection for Application Programs, 41 Stan.L.Rev. 1045, (1989)], at 1052. "This stage of program design often requires the most time and investment." Kretschmer, at 826.

Once each necessary module has been identified, designed, and its relationship to the other modules has been laid out conceptually, the resulting program structure must be embodied in a written language that the computer can read. This process is called "coding," and requires two steps. Whelan, 797 F.2d at 1230. First, the programmer must transpose the program's structural blue-print into a source code. This step has been described as "comparable to the novelist fleshing out the broad outline of his plot by crafting from words and sentences the paragraphs that convey the ideas." Kretschmer, at 826. The source code may be written in any one of several computer languages, such as COBAL, FORTRAN, BASIC, EDL, etc., depending upon the type of computer for which the program is intended. * * *. Once the source code has been completed, the second step is to translate or "compile" it into object code. Object code is the binary language comprised of zeros and ones through which the computer directly receives its instructions. * * *.

After the coding is finished, the programmer will run the program on the computer in order to find and correct any logical and syntactical errors. This is known as "debugging" and, once done, the program is complete. See Kretschmer, at 826-27.

II. FACTS

* * *

The subject of this litigation originates with one of CA's marketed programs entitled CA-SCHEDULER. CA-SCHEDULER is a job scheduling program designed for IBM mainframe computers. Its primary functions are straightforward: to create a schedule specifying when the computer should run various tasks, and then to control the computer as it executes the schedule. CA-SCHEDULER contains a sub-program entitled ADAPTER, also developed by CA. ADAPTER is not an independently marketed product of CA; it is a wholly integrated component of CA-SCHEDULER and has no capacity for independent use.

Nevertheless, ADAPTER plays an extremely important role. It is an "operating system compatibility component," which means, roughly speaking, it serves as a translator. An "operating system" is itself a program that manages the resources of the computer, allocating those resources to other programs as needed. The IBM System 370 family of computers, for which CA-SCHEDULER was created, is, depending upon the computer's size, designed to contain one of three operating systems: DOS/VSE, MVS, or CMS. As the district court noted, the general rule is that "a program written for one operating system, e.g., DOS/VSE, will not, without modification, run under another operating system such as MVS." Computer Assocs., 775 F.Supp. at 550. ADAPTER's function is to translate the language of a given program into the particular language that the computer's own operating system can understand.

The district court succinctly outlined the manner in which ADAPTER works within the context of the larger program. In order to enable CA-SCHEDULER to function on different operating systems, CA divided the CA-SCHEDULER into two components: --a first component that contains only the task-specific portions of the program, independent of all operating system issues, and --a second component that contains all the interconnections between the first component and the operating system. In a program constructed in this way, whenever the first, task-specific, component needs to ask the operating system for some resource through a "system call", it calls the second component instead of calling the operating system directly. The second component serves as an "interface" or "compatibility component" between the task-specific portion of the program and the operating system. It receives the request from the first component and translates it into the appropriate system call that will be recognized by whatever operating system is installed on the computer, e.g., DOS/VSE, MVS, or CMS. Since the first, task- specific component calls the adapter component rather than the operating system, the first component need not be customized to use any specific operating system. The second, interface, component insures that all the system calls are performed properly for the particular operating system in use. Id. at 551. ADAPTER serves as the second, "common system interface" component referred to above.

A program like ADAPTER, which allows a computer user to change or use multiple operating systems while maintaining the same software, is highly desirable. It saves the user the costs, both in time and money, that otherwise would be expended in purchasing new programs, modifying existing systems to run them, and gaining familiarity with their operation. The benefits run both ways. The increased compatibility afforded by an ADAPTER-like component, and its resulting popularity among consumers, makes whatever software in which it is incorporated significantly more marketable.

Starting in 1982, Altai began marketing its own job scheduling program entitled ZEKE. The original version of ZEKE was designed for use in conjunction with a VSE operating system. By late 1983, in response to customer demand, Altai decided to rewrite ZEKE so that it could be run in conjunction with an MVS operating system.

At that time, James P. Williams ("Williams"), then an employee of Altai and now its President, approached Claude F. Arney, III ("Arney"), a computer programmer who worked for CA. Williams and Arney were longstanding friends, and had in fact been co-workers at CA for some time before Williams left CA to work for Altai's predecessor. Williams wanted to recruit Arney to assist Altai in designing an MVS version of ZEKE.

At the time he first spoke with Arney, Williams was aware of both the CA-SCHEDULER and ADAPTER programs. However, Williams was not involved in their development and had never seen the codes of either program. When he asked Arney to come work for Altai, Williams did not know that ADAPTER was a component of CA-SCHEDULER.

Arney, on the other hand, was intimately familiar with various aspects of ADAPTER. While working for CA, he helped improve the VSE version of ADAPTER, and was permitted to take home a copy of ADAPTER'S source code. This apparently developed into an irresistible habit, for when Arney left CA to work for Altai in January, 1984, he took with him copies of the source code for both the VSE and MVS versions of ADAPTER. He did this in knowing violation of the CA employee agreements that he had signed.

Once at Altai, Arney and Williams discussed design possibilities for adapting ZEKE to run on MVS operating systems. Williams, who had created the VSE version of ZEKE, thought that approximately 30% of his original program would have to be modified in order to accommodate MVS. Arney persuaded Williams that the best way to make the needed modifications was to introduce a "common system interface" component into ZEKE. He did not tell Williams that his idea stemmed from his familiarity with ADAPTER. They decided to name this new component-program OSCAR.

Arney went to work creating OSCAR at Altai's offices using the ADAPTER source code. The district court accepted Williams' testimony that no one at Altai, with the exception of Arney, affirmatively knew that Arney had the ADAPTER code, or that he was using it to create OSCAR/VSE. However, during this time period, Williams' office was adjacent to Arney's. Williams testified that he and Arney "conversed quite frequently" while Arney was "investigating the source code of ZEKE" and that Arney was in his office "a number of times daily, asking questions." In three months, Arney successfully completed the OSCAR/VSE project. In an additional month he developed an OSCAR/MVS version. When the dust finally settled, Arney had copied approximately 30% of OSCAR's code from CA's ADAPTER program.

The first generation of OSCAR programs was known as OSCAR 3.4. From 1985 to August 1988, Altai used OSCAR 3.4 in its ZEKE product, as well as in programs entitled ZACK and ZEBB. In late July 1988, CA first learned that Altai may have appropriated parts of ADAPTER. After confirming its suspicions, * * *[,] CA * * * brought this copyright and trade secret misappropriation action against Altai.

Apparently, it was upon receipt of the summons and complaint that Altai first learned that Arney had copied much of the OSCAR code from ADAPTER. After Arney confirmed to Williams that CA's accusations of copying were true, Williams immediately set out to survey the damage. Without ever looking at the ADAPTER code himself, Williams learned from Arney exactly which sections of code Arney had taken from ADAPTER.

Upon advice of counsel, Williams initiated OSCAR's rewrite. The project's goal was to save as much of OSCAR 3.4 as legitimately could be used, and to excise those portions which had been copied from ADAPTER. Arney was entirely excluded from the process, and his copy of the ADAPTER code was locked away. Williams put eight other programmers on the project, none of whom had been involved in any way in the development of OSCAR 3.4. Williams provided the programmers with a description of the ZEKE operating system services so that they could rewrite the appropriate code. The rewrite project took about six months to complete and was finished in mid-November 1989. The resulting program was entitled OSCAR 3.5.

From that point on, Altai shipped only OSCAR 3.5 to its new customers. Altai also shipped OSCAR 3.5 as a "free upgrade" to all customers that had previously purchased OSCAR 3.4. While Altai and Williams acted responsibly to correct Arney's literal copying of the ADAPTER program, copyright infringement had occurred.

* * *

DISCUSSION

* * *

* * *. CA contends that the district court applied an erroneous method for determining whether there exists substantial similarity between computer programs, and thus, erred in determining that OSCAR 3.5 did not infringe the copyrights held on the different versions of its CA- SCHEDULER program. CA asserts that the test applied by the district court failed to account sufficiently for a computer program's non-literal elements. * * *.

I. COPYRIGHT INFRINGEMENT

* * *

For the purpose of analysis, the district court assumed that Altai had access to the ADAPTER code when creating OSCAR 3.5. See Computer Assocs., 775 F.Supp. at 558. Thus, in determining whether Altai had unlawfully copied protected aspects of CA's ADAPTER, the district court narrowed its focus of inquiry to ascertaining whether Altai's OSCAR 3.5 was substantially similar to ADAPTER. Because we approve Judge Pratt's conclusions regarding substantial similarity, our analysis will proceed along the same assumption.

* * *

A. Copyright Protection for the Non-literal Elements of Computer Programs

* * *

CA argues that, despite Altai's rewrite of the OSCAR code, the resulting program remained substantially similar to the structure of its ADAPTER program. As discussed above, a program's structure includes its non-literal components such as general flow charts as well as the more specific organization of inter-modular relationships, parameter lists, and macros. In addition to these aspects, CA contends that OSCAR 3.5 is also substantially similar to ADAPTER with respect to the list of services that both ADAPTER and OSCAR obtain from their respective operating systems. We must decide whether and to what extent these elements of computer programs are protected by copyright law.

* * *

1) Idea vs. Expression Dichotomy

It is a fundamental principle of copyright law that a copyright does not protect an idea, but only the expression of the idea. * * *. [§ 102(b)] * * *.

* * *

The essentially utilitarian nature of a computer program further complicates the task of distilling its idea from its expression. See SAS Inst., 605 F.Supp. at 829; cf. Englund, at 893. In order to describe both computational processes and abstract ideas, its content "combines creative and technical expression." See Spivack, at 755. The variations of expression found in purely creative compositions, as opposed to those contained in utilitarian works, are not directed towards practical application. For example, a narration of Humpty Dumpty's demise, which would clearly be a creative composition, does not serve the same ends as, say, a recipe for scrambled eggs--which is a more process oriented text. Thus, compared to aesthetic works, computer programs hover even more closely to the elusive boundary line described in § 102(b).

To the extent that an accounting text [such as that involved in *Baker v. Selden*] and a computer program are both "a set of statements or instructions ... to bring about a certain result," 17 U.S.C. § 101, they are roughly analogous. In the former case, the processes are ultimately conducted by human agency; in the latter, by electronic means. In either case, as already stated, the processes themselves are not protectable. But the holding in *Baker* goes farther. The Court concluded that those aspects of a work, which "must necessarily be used as incident to" the idea, system or process that the work describes, are also not copyrightable. 101 U.S. at 104. Selden's ledger sheets, therefore, enjoyed no copyright protection because they were "necessary incidents to" the system of accounting that he described. Id. at 103. From this reasoning, we conclude that those elements of a computer program that are necessarily incidental to its function are similarly unprotectable.

While *Baker v. Selden* provides a sound analytical foundation, it offers scant guidance on how to separate idea or process from expression, and moreover, on how to further distinguish protectable expression from that expression which "must necessarily be used as incident to" the work's underlying concept. In the context of computer programs, the Third Circuit's noted decision in *Whelan* has, thus far, been the most thoughtful attempt to accomplish these ends.

The court in *Whelan* faced substantially the same problem as is presented by this case. There, the defendant was accused of making off with the non-literal structure of the plaintiff's copyrighted dental lab management program, and employing it to create its own competitive version. In assessing whether there had been an infringement, the court had to determine which aspects of the programs involved were ideas, and which were expression. In separating the two, the court settled upon the following conceptual approach: [T]he line between idea and expression may be drawn with reference to the end sought to be achieved by the work in question. In other words, the purpose or function of a utilitarian work would be the work's idea, and everything that is not necessary to that purpose or function would be part of the expression of the idea.... Where there are various means of achieving the desired purpose, then the particular means chosen is not necessary to the purpose; hence, there is expression, not idea. 797 F.2d at 1236 (citations omitted). The "idea" of the program at issue in *Whelan* was identified by the court as simply "the efficient management of a dental laboratory." Id. at n. 28.

So far, in the courts, the *Whelan* rule has received a mixed reception. While some decisions have adopted its reasoning, * * * [cites], others have rejected it, * * * [cites].

Whelan has fared even more poorly in the academic community, where its standard for distinguishing idea from expression has been widely criticized for being conceptually overbroad. * * * [cites]. The leading commentator in the field has stated that "[t]he crucial flaw in [*Whelan's*] reasoning is that it assumes that only one 'idea,' in copyright law terms, underlies any computer program, and that once a separable idea can be identified, everything else must be expression." 3 Nimmer § 13.03(F), at 13-62.34. This criticism focuses not upon the program's ultimate purpose but upon the reality of its structural design. As we have already noted, a computer program's ultimate function or purpose is the composite result of interacting subroutines. Since each subroutine is itself a program, and thus, may be said to have its own "idea," *Whelan's* general formulation that a program's overall purpose equates with the program's idea is descriptively inadequate.

* * *

2) Substantial Similarity Test for Computer Program Structure: Abstraction-Filtration-Comparison

We think that *Whelan's* approach to separating idea from expression in computer programs relies too heavily on metaphysical distinctions and does not place enough emphasis on practical considerations. * * *.

As discussed herein, we think that district courts would be well-advised to undertake a three-step procedure, based on the abstractions test utilized by the district court, in order to determine whether the non-literal elements of two or more computer programs are substantially similar. This approach breaks no new ground; rather, it draws on such familiar copyright doctrines as merger, *scenes a faire*, and public domain. In taking this approach, however, we are cognizant that computer technology is a dynamic field which can quickly outpace judicial decisionmaking. Thus, in cases where the technology in question does not allow for a literal application of the procedure we outline below, our opinion should not be read to foreclose the district courts of our circuit from utilizing a modified version.

In ascertaining substantial similarity under this approach, a court would first break down the allegedly infringed program into its constituent structural parts. Then, by examining each of these parts for such things as incorporated ideas, expression that is necessarily incidental to those ideas, and elements that are taken from the public domain, a court would then be able to sift out all non-protectable material. Left with a kernel, or possible kernels, of creative expression after following this process of elimination, the court's last step would be to compare this material with the structure of an allegedly infringing program. The result of this comparison will determine whether the protectable elements of the programs at issue are substantially similar so as to warrant a finding of infringement. It will be helpful to elaborate a bit further.

Step One: Abstraction

As the district court appreciated * * * the theoretic framework for analyzing substantial similarity expounded by Learned Hand in the *Nichols* case is helpful in the present context. In *Nichols*, we enunciated what has now become known as the "abstractions" test for separating idea from expression * * *.

* * *

As applied to computer programs, the abstractions test will comprise the first step in the examination for substantial similarity. Initially, in a manner that resembles reverse engineering on a theoretical plane, a court should dissect the allegedly copied program's structure and isolate each level of abstraction contained within it. This process begins with the code and ends with an articulation of the program's ultimate function. Along the way, it is necessary essentially to retrace and map each of the designer's steps--in the opposite order in which they were taken during the program's creation. * * *.

As an anatomical guide to this procedure, the following description is helpful: At the lowest level of abstraction, a computer program may be thought of in its entirety as a set of individual instructions organized into a hierarchy of modules. At a higher level of abstraction, the instructions in the lowest- level modules may be replaced conceptually by the functions of those modules. At progressively higher levels of abstraction, the functions of higher-level modules conceptually replace the implementations of those modules in terms of lower-level modules and instructions, until finally, one is left with nothing but the ultimate function of the program.... A program has structure at every level of abstraction at which it is viewed. At low levels of abstraction, a program's structure may be quite complex; at the highest level it is trivial. * * *.

Step Two: Filtration

Once the program's abstraction levels have been discovered, the substantial similarity inquiry moves from the conceptual to the concrete. Professor Nimmer suggests, and we endorse, a "successive filtering method" for separating protectable expression from non-protectable material. See generally 3 Nimmer § 13.03[F]. This process entails examining the structural components at each level of abstraction to determine whether their particular inclusion at that level was "idea" or was dictated by considerations of efficiency, so as to be necessarily incidental to that idea; required by factors external to the program itself; or taken from the public domain and hence is nonprotectable expression. See also Kretschmer, at 844-45 (arguing that program features dictated by market externalities or efficiency concerns are unprotectable). The structure of any given program may reflect some, all, or none of these considerations. Each case requires its own fact specific investigation.

* * *

(a) Elements Dictated by Efficiency

The portion of *Baker v. Selden*, discussed earlier, which denies copyright protection to expression necessarily incidental to the idea being expressed, appears to be the cornerstone for what has developed into the doctrine of merger. * * *. The doctrine's underlying principle is that "[w]hen there is essentially only one way to express an idea, the idea and its expression are inseparable and copyright is no bar to copying that expression." Concrete Machinery Co. v. Classic Lawn Ornaments, Inc., 843 F.2d 600, 606 (1st Cir.1988). Under these circumstances, the expression is said to have "merged" with the idea itself. In order not to confer a monopoly of the idea upon the copyright owner, such expression should not be protected. * * *.

CONTU recognized the applicability of the merger doctrine to computer programs. In its report to Congress it stated that: [C]opyrighted language may be copied without infringing when there is but a limited number of ways to express a given idea.... In the computer context, this means that when specific instructions, even though previously copyrighted, are the only and essential means of accomplishing a given task, their later use by another will not amount to infringement. CONTU Report, at 20. While this statement directly concerns only the application of merger to program code, that is, the textual aspect of the program, it reasonably suggests that the doctrine fits comfortably within the general context of computer programs.

Furthermore, when one considers the fact that programmers generally strive to create programs "that meet the user's needs in the most efficient manner," Menell, at 1052, the applicability of the merger doctrine to computer programs becomes compelling. In the context of computer program design, the concept of efficiency is akin to deriving the most concise logical proof or formulating the most succinct mathematical computation. Thus, the more efficient a set of modules are, the more closely they approximate the idea or process embodied in that particular aspect of the program's structure.

While, hypothetically, there might be a myriad of ways in which a programmer may effectuate certain functions within a program,--i.e., express the idea embodied in a given subroutine--efficiency concerns may so narrow the practical range of choice as to make only one or two forms of expression workable options. See 3 Nimmer § 13.03[F][2], at 13-63; see also Whelan, 797 F.2d at 1243 n. 43 ("It is true that for certain tasks there are only a very limited number of file structures available, and in such cases the structures might not be copyrightable...."). Of course, not all program structure is informed by efficiency concerns. See Menell, at 1052 (besides efficiency, simplicity related to user accommodation has become a programming priority). It follows that in order to determine whether the merger doctrine precludes copyright protection to an aspect of a program's structure that is so oriented, a court must inquire "whether the use of this particular set of modules is necessary efficiently to implement that part of the program's process" being implemented. Englund, at 902. If the answer is yes, then the expression represented by the programmer's choice of a specific module or group of modules has merged with their underlying idea and is unprotected. Id. at 902-03.

* * *

Efficiency is an industry-wide goal. Since, as we have already noted, there may be only a limited number of efficient implementations for any given program task, it is quite possible that multiple programmers, working independently, will design the identical method employed in the allegedly infringed work. Of course, if this is the case, there is no copyright infringement. * * *.

Under these circumstances, the fact that two programs contain the same efficient structure may as likely lead to an inference of independent creation as it does to one of copying. See 3 Nimmer § 13.03[F][2], at 13-65; cf. *Herbert Rosenthal Jewelry Corp.*, 446 F.2d at 741 (evidence of independent creation may stem from defendant's standing as a designer of previous similar works). Thus, since evidence of similarly efficient structure is not particularly probative of copying, it should be disregarded in the overall substantial similarity analysis. See 3 Nimmer § 13.03[F][2], at 13-65.

* * *

In Manufacturers Technologies, Inc. v. Cams, Inc., 706 F.Supp. 984, 995-99 (D.Conn.1989), the infringement claims stemmed from various alleged program similarities "as indicated in their screen displays." Id. at 990. Stressing efficiency concerns in the context of a merger analysis, the court determined that the program's method of allowing the user to navigate within the screen displays was not protectable because, in part, "the process or manner of navigating internally on any specific screen displays ... is limited in the number of ways it may be simply achieved to facilitate user comfort." Id. at 995.

The court also found that expression contained in various screen displays (in the form of alphabetical and numerical columns) was not the proper subject of copyright protection because it was "necessarily incident to the idea[s]" embodied in the displays. Id. at 996-97. Cf. Digital Communications, 659 F.Supp. at 460 (finding no merger and affording copyright protection to program's status screen display because "modes of expression chosen ... are clearly not necessary to the idea of the status screen").

We agree with the approach taken in these decisions, and conclude that application of the merger doctrine in this setting is an effective way to eliminate non-protectable expression contained in computer programs.

(b) Elements Dictated By External Factors

We have stated that where "it is virtually impossible to write about a particular historical era or fictional theme without employing certain 'stock' or standard literary devices," such expression is not copyrightable. Hoehling v. Universal City Studios, Inc., 618 F.2d 972, 979 (2d Cir.), cert. denied, 449 U.S. 841 (1980). For example, the *Hoehling* case was an infringement suit stemming from several works on the Hindenberg disaster. There we concluded that similarities in representations of German beer halls, scenes depicting German greetings such as "Heil Hitler," or the singing of certain German songs would not lead to a finding of infringement because they were "'indispensable, or at least standard, in the treatment of'" life in Nazi Germany. Id. (quoting Alexander v. Haley, 460 F.Supp. 40, 45 (S.D.N.Y.1978)). This is known as the *scenes a faire* doctrine, and like "merger," it has its analogous application to computer programs. Cf. *Data East USA*, 862 F.2d at 208 (applying *scenes a faire* to a home computer video game).

Professor Nimmer points out that "in many instances it is virtually impossible to write a program to perform particular functions in a specific computing environment without employing standard techniques." 3 Nimmer § 13.03[F][3], at 13-65. This is a result of the fact that a programmer's freedom of design choice is often circumscribed by extrinsic considerations such as (1) the mechanical specifications of the computer on which a particular program is intended to run; (2) compatibility requirements of other programs with which a program is designed to operate in conjunction; (3) computer manufacturers' design standards; (4) demands of the industry being serviced; and (5) widely accepted programming practices within the computer industry. Id. at 13-66-71.

Courts have already considered some of these factors in denying copyright protection to various elements of computer programs. In the *Plains Cotton* case, the Fifth Circuit refused to reverse the district court's denial of a preliminary injunction against an alleged program infringer because, in part, "many of the similarities between the ... programs [were] dictated by the externalities of the cotton market." 807 F.2d at 1262.

In *Manufacturers Technologies*, the district court noted that the program's method of screen navigation "is influenced by the type of hardware that the software is designed to be used on." 706 F.Supp. at 995. Because, in part, "the functioning of the hardware package impact[ed] and constrain[ed] the type of navigational tools used in plaintiff's screen displays," the court denied copyright protection to that aspect of the program. Id.; cf. Data East USA, 862 F.2d at 209 (reversing a district court's finding of audiovisual work infringement because, inter alia, "the use of the Commodore computer for a karate game intended for home consumption is subject to various constraints inherent in the use of that computer").

Finally, the district court in Q-Co Industries rested its holding on what, perhaps, most closely approximates a traditional *scenes a faire* rationale. There, the court denied copyright protection to four program modules employed in a teleprompter program. This decision was ultimately based upon the court's finding that "the same modules would be an inherent part of any prompting program." 625 F.Supp. at 616.

Building upon this existing case law, we conclude that a court must also examine the structural content of an allegedly infringed program for elements that might have been dictated by external factors.

(c) Elements taken From the Public Domain

Closely related to the non-protectability of *scenes a faire*, is material found in the public domain. Such material is free for the taking and cannot be appropriated by a single author even though it is included in a copyrighted work. See E.F. Johnson Co. v. Uniden Corp. of America, 623 F.Supp. 1485, 1499 (D.Minn.1985); see also Sheldon, 81 F.2d at 54. We see no reason to make an exception to this rule for elements of a computer program that have entered the public domain by virtue of freely accessible program exchanges and the like. See 3 Nimmer § 13.03[F][4]; see also Brown Bag Software, 960 F.2d at 1473 (affirming the district court's finding that " '[p]laintiffs may not claim copyright protection of an ... expression that is, if not standard, then commonplace in the computer software industry.' "). Thus, a court must also filter out this material from the allegedly infringed program before it makes the final inquiry in its substantial similarity analysis.

Step Three: Comparison

The third and final step of the test for substantial similarity that we believe appropriate for non-literal program components entails a comparison. Once a court has sifted out all elements of the allegedly infringed program which are "ideas" or are dictated by efficiency or external factors, or taken from the public domain, there may remain a core of protectable expression. In terms of a work's copyright value, this is the golden nugget. See Brown Bag Software, 960 F.2d at 1475. At this point, the court's substantial similarity inquiry focuses on whether the defendant copied any aspect of this protected expression, as well as an assessment of the copied portion's relative importance with respect to the plaintiff's overall program. See 3 Nimmer § 13.03[F][5]; Data East USA, 862 F.2d at 208 ("To determine whether similarities result from unprotectable expression, analytic dissection of similarities may be performed. If ... all similarities in expression arise from use of common ideas, then no substantial similarity can be found.").

3) Policy Considerations

We are satisfied that the three step approach we have just outlined not only comports with, but advances the constitutional policies underlying the Copyright Act.

Since any method that tries to distinguish idea from expression ultimately impacts on the scope of copyright protection afforded to a particular type of work, "the line [it draws] must be a pragmatic one, which also keeps in consideration 'the preservation of the balance between competition and protection....' " Apple Computer, 714 F.2d at 1253 (citation omitted).

CA and some amici argue against the type of approach that we have set forth on the grounds that it will be a disincentive for future computer program research and development. At bottom, they claim that if programmers are not guaranteed broad copyright protection for their work, they will not invest the extensive time, energy and funds required to design and improve program structures. While they have a point, their argument cannot carry the day. The interest of the copyright law is not in simply conferring a monopoly on industrious persons, but in advancing the public welfare through rewarding artistic creativity, in a manner that permits the free use and development of non-protectable ideas and processes.

* * *

Recently, the Supreme Court has emphatically reiterated that "[t]he primary objective of copyright is not to reward the labor of authors...." Feist Publications, Inc. v. Rural Tel. Serv. Co., 111 S.Ct. 1282, 1290 (1991) (emphasis added). While the *Feist* decision deals primarily with the copyrightability of purely factual compilations, its underlying tenets apply to much of the work involved in computer programming. *Feist* put to rest the "sweat of the brow" doctrine in copyright law. 111 S.Ct. at 1295. The rationale of that doctrine "was that copyright was a reward for the hard work that went into compiling facts." 111 S.Ct. at 1291. The Court flatly rejected this justification for extending copyright protection, noting that it "eschewed the most fundamental axiom of copyright law--that no one may copyright facts or ideas." Id.

Feist teaches that substantial effort alone cannot confer copyright status on an otherwise uncopyrightable work. As we have discussed, despite the fact that significant labor and expense often goes into computer program flow- charting and debugging, that process does not always result in inherently protectable expression. Thus, *Feist* implicitly undercuts the *Whelan* rationale, "which allow[ed] copyright protection beyond the literal computer code ... [in order to] provide the proper incentive for programmers by protecting their most valuable efforts...." Whelan, 797 F.2d at 1237 (footnote omitted). We note that *Whelan* was decided prior to *Feist* when the "sweat of the brow" doctrine still had vitality. In view of the Supreme Court's recent holding, however, we must reject the legal basis of CA's disincentive argument.

Furthermore, we are unpersuaded that the test we approve today will lead to the dire consequences for the computer program industry that plaintiff and some amici predict. To the contrary, serious students of the industry have been highly critical of the sweeping scope of copyright protection engendered by the *Whelan* rule, in that it "enables first comers to 'lock up' basic programming techniques as implemented in programs to perform particular tasks." Menell, at 1087; see also Spivack, at 765 (*Whelan* "results in an inhibition of creation by virtue of the copyright owner's quasi-monopoly power").

To be frank, the exact contours of copyright protection for non-literal program structure are not completely clear. We trust that as future cases are decided, those limits will become better defined. Indeed, it may well be that the Copyright Act serves as a relatively weak barrier against public access to the theoretical interstices behind a program's source and object codes. This results from the hybrid nature of a computer program, which, while it is literary expression, is also a highly functional, utilitarian component in the larger process of computing.

Generally, we think that copyright registration--with its indiscriminating availability--is not ideally suited to deal with the highly dynamic technology of computer science. Thus far, many of the decisions in this area reflect the courts' attempt to fit the proverbial square peg in a round hole. The district court, see Computer Assocs., 775 F.Supp. at 560, and at least one commentator have suggested that patent registration, with its exacting up-front novelty and non-obviousness requirements, might be the more appropriate rubric of protection for intellectual property of this kind. See Randell M. Whitmeyer, Comment, A Plea for Due Processes: Defining the Proper Scope of Patent Protection for Computer Software, 85 Nw.U.L.REV. 1103, 1123-25 (1991); see also Lotus Dev. Corp. v. Borland Int'l, Inc., 788 F.Supp. 78, 91 (D.Mass.1992) (discussing the potentially supplemental relationship between patent and copyright protection in the context of computer programs). In any event, now that more than 12 years have passed since CONTU issued its final report, the resolution of this specific issue could benefit from further legislative investigation--perhaps a CONTU II.

In the meantime, Congress has made clear that computer programs are literary works entitled to copyright protection. Of course, we shall abide by these instructions, but in so doing we must not impair the overall integrity of copyright law. While incentive based arguments in favor of broad copyright protection are perhaps attractive from a pure policy perspective, see Lotus Dev. Corp., 740 F.Supp. at 58, ultimately, they have a corrosive effect on certain fundamental tenets of copyright doctrine. If the test we have outlined results in narrowing the scope of protection, as we expect it will, that result flows from applying, in accordance with Congressional intent, long-standing principles of copyright law to computer programs. Of course, our decision is also informed by our concern that these fundamental principles remain undistorted.

B. The District Court Decision

We turn now to our review of the district court's decision in this particular case. At the outset, we must address CA's claim that the district court erred by relying too heavily on the court appointed expert's "personal opinions on the factual and legal issues before the court."

1) Use of Expert Evidence in Determining Substantial Similarity Between Computer Programs

Pursuant to Fed.R.Evid. 706, and with the consent of both Altai and CA, Judge Pratt appointed and relied upon Dr. Randall Davis of the Massachusetts Institute of Technology as the court's own expert witness on the issue of substantial similarity. Dr. Davis submitted a comprehensive written report that analyzed the various aspects of the computer programs at issue and evaluated the parties' expert evidence. At trial, Dr. Davis was extensively cross-examined by both CA and Altai.

The well-established general rule in this circuit has been to limit the use of expert opinion in determining whether works at issue are substantially similar. As a threshold matter, expert testimony may be used to assist the fact finder in ascertaining whether the defendant had copied any part of the plaintiff's work. See Arnstein v. Porter, 154 F.2d 464, 468 (2d Cir.1946). To this end, "the two works are to be compared in their entirety ... [and] in making such comparison resort may properly be made to expert analysis...." 3 Nimmer § 13.03[E][2], at 13-62.16.

However, once some amount of copying has been established, it remains solely for the trier of fact to determine whether the copying was "illicit," that is to say, whether the "defendant took from plaintiff's works so much of what is pleasing to [lay observers] who comprise the audience for whom such [works are] composed, that defendant wrongfully appropriated something which belongs to the plaintiff." Arnstein, 154 F.2d at 473. Since the test for illicit copying is based upon the response of ordinary lay observers, expert testimony is thus "irrelevant" and not permitted. Id. at 468, 473. We have subsequently described this method of inquiry as "merely an alternative way of formulating the issue of substantial similarity." Ideal Toy Corp. v. Fab-Lu Ltd. (Inc.), 360 F.2d 1021, 1023 n. 2 (2d Cir.1966).

Historically, *Arnstein's* ordinary observer standard had its roots in "an attempt to apply the 'reasonable person' doctrine as found in other areas of the law to copyright." 3 Nimmer § 13.03[E][2], at 13-62.10-11. That approach may well have served its purpose when the material under scrutiny was limited to art forms readily comprehensible and generally familiar to the average lay person. However, in considering the extension of the rule to the present case, we are reminded of Holmes' admonition that, "[t]he life of the law has not been logic: it has been experience." O.W. Holmes, Jr., THE COMMON LAW 1 (1881).

Thus, in deciding the limits to which expert opinion may be employed in ascertaining the substantial similarity of computer programs, we cannot disregard the highly complicated and technical subject matter at the heart of these claims. Rather, we recognize the reality that computer programs are likely to be somewhat impenetrable by lay observers--whether they be judges or juries--and, thus, seem to fall outside the category of works contemplated by those who engineered the *Arnstein* test. * * *

* * * [W]e leave it to the discretion of the district court to decide to what extent, if any, expert opinion, regarding the highly technical nature of computer programs, is warranted in a given case.

In this case, Dr. Davis' opinion was instrumental in dismantling the intricacies of computer science so that the court could formulate and apply an appropriate rule of law. While Dr. Davis' report and testimony undoubtedly shed valuable light on the subject matter of the litigation, Judge Pratt remained, in the final analysis, the trier of fact. The district court's use of the expert's assistance, in the context of this case, was entirely appropriate.

2) Evidentiary Analysis

The district court had to determine whether Altai's OSCAR 3.5 program was substantially similar to CA's ADAPTER. We note that Judge Pratt's method of analysis effectively served as a road map for our own, with one exception-- Judge Pratt filtered out the non-copyrightable aspects of OSCAR 3.5 rather than those found in ADAPTER, the allegedly infringed program. We think that our approach--i.e., filtering out the unprotected aspects of an allegedly infringed program and then comparing the end product to the structure of the suspect program--is preferable, and therefore believe that district courts should proceed in this manner in future cases.

We opt for this strategy because, in some cases, the defendant's program structure might contain protectable expression and/or other elements that are not found in the plaintiff's program. Since it is extraneous to the allegedly copied work, this material would have no bearing on any potential substantial similarity between the two programs. Thus, its filtration would be wasteful and unnecessarily time consuming. Furthermore, by focusing the analysis on the infringing rather than on the infringed material, a court may mistakenly place too little emphasis on a quantitatively small misappropriation which is, in reality, a qualitatively vital aspect of the plaintiff's protectable expression.

The fact that the district court's analysis proceeded in the reverse order, however, had no material impact on the outcome of this case. Since Judge Pratt determined that OSCAR effectively contained no protectable expression whatsoever, the most serious charge that can be levelled against him is that he was overly thorough in his examination.

The district court took the first step in the analysis set forth in this opinion when it separated the program by levels of abstraction. The district court stated: As applied to computer software programs, this abstractions test would progress in order of "increasing generality" from object code, to source code, to parameter lists, to services required, to general outline. In discussing the particular similarities, therefore, we shall focus on these levels. *Computer Assocs.*, 775 F.Supp. at 560. While the facts of a different case might require that a district court draw a more particularized blueprint of a program's overall structure, this description is a workable one for the case at hand.

Moving to the district court's evaluation of OSCAR 3.5's structural components, we agree with Judge Pratt's systematic exclusion of non-protectable expression. With respect to code, the district court observed that after the rewrite of OSCAR 3.4 to OSCAR 3.5, "there remained virtually no lines of code that were identical to ADAPTER." Id. at 561. Accordingly, the court found that the code "present[ed] no similarity at all." Id. at 562.

Next, Judge Pratt addressed the issue of similarity between the two programs' parameter lists and macros. He concluded that, viewing the conflicting evidence most favorably to CA, it demonstrated that "only a few of the lists and macros were similar to protected elements in ADAPTER; the others were either in the public domain or dictated by the functional demands of the program." Id. As discussed above, functional elements and elements taken from the public domain do not qualify for copyright protection. With respect to the few remaining parameter lists and macros, the district court could reasonably conclude that they did not warrant a finding of infringement given their relative contribution to the overall program. See Warner Bros., Inc. v. American Broadcasting Cos., Inc., 720 F.2d 231, 242 (2d Cir.1983) (discussing de minimis exception which allows for literal copying of a small and usually insignificant portion of the plaintiff's work); 3 Nimmer § 13.03[F][5], at 13-74. In any event, the district court reasonably found that, for lack of persuasive evidence, CA failed to meet its burden of proof on whether the macros and parameter lists at issue were substantially similar. See *Computer Assocs.*, 775 F.Supp. at 562.

The district court also found that the overlap exhibited between the list of services required for both ADAPTER and OSCAR 3.5 was "determined by the demands of the operating system and of the applications program to which it [was] to be linked through ADAPTER or OSCAR...." Id. In other words, this aspect of the program's structure was dictated by the nature of other programs with which it was designed to interact and, thus, is not protected by copyright.

Finally, in his infringement analysis, Judge Pratt accorded no weight to the similarities between the two programs' organizational charts, "because [the charts were] so simple and obvious to anyone exposed to the operation of the program[s]." Id. CA argues that the district court's action in this regard "is not consistent with copyright law"--that "obvious" expression is protected, and that the district court erroneously failed to realize this. However, to say that elements of a work are "obvious," in the manner in which the district court used the word, is to say that they "follow naturally from the work's theme rather than from the author's creativity." 3 Nimmer § 13.03

[F][3], at 13-65. This is but one formulation of the *scenes a faire* doctrine, which we have already endorsed as a means of weeding out unprotectable expression.

* * *

[The court affirmed the district court's judgment that OSCAR 3.5 did not infringe the copyright in CA-SCHEDULER.]

NOTES

1. For all the differences in approach between *Whelan* and *Computer Associates*, are they not easily reconcilable on their facts? The infringing Dentcom program in *Whelan* was simply a translation of the Dentalab program from the EDL computer language to the BASIC computer language. That is clearly a violation of both 17 U.S.C. §§ 106(1) and (2), is it not? The non-infringing program, OSCAR 3.5, in *Computer Associates* was written in a highly constraining technological environment. The task of the program was to interface between the application program (ZEKE) and the computer's operating system. In this environment the structure of OSCAR will be determined by the design of the operating system and the way in which it requires other programs to communicate with it, and by the design of ZEKE, and the demands it makes on the operating system. The programmer simply needs to inventory the demands which ZEKE makes on the operating system, and develop routines that can translate the ZEKE demands into the form required by the operating system. This technological environment means that almost all of the content of both OSCAR and ADAPTER are functional, doesn't it? Therefore, infringement (absent the slavish copying present in OSCAR 3.4) is very unlikely. For a recent article by a member of CONTU taking the general position that the cases are consistent and that the courts have implemented the CONTU recommendations in a satisfactory manner, see Arthur Miller, Copyright Protection for Computer Programs, Databases, and Computer-generated Works: Is Anything New Since CONTU?, 106 Harv. L. Rev. 977, 1001-1002 (1993): "Unfortunately, some observers have tended to overstate the differences between the approach of *Altai* and that of *Whelan* and *Paperback*, perhaps, in part, because the *Altai* opinion presented itself as a significant break with the Third Circuit. On close examination, however, it seems more accurate to view *Altai* as adopting a series of modifications of *Whelan's* generalized statements and as using different terminology without deviating markedly from the *Whelan* court's fundamental reliance on the idea-expression dichotomy. But there is no question that the gestalt of the Second Circuit's opinion is more grudging toward software protection than that of the Third Circuit."

2. Note how the opinion in *Computer Associates*, just like the opinion in *Whelan*, gets confused about whether the question is (1) whether there is sufficient similarity to support an inference of copying or (2) whether there is taking of the

protectible elements of the copyrighted program. It as if the judges become so focused on the problem of dealing with computer technology that they forget basic copyright law. But while this was simply an analytic error in *Whelan*, it is actually an important problem in *Computer Associates*. In *Whelan* it was clear that the defendants had copied, the only question was whether they had copied program elements protected by copyright. But in *Computer Associates* it was an important question whether Altai had copied at all.

OSCAR 3.5 was, according to the undisputed testimony summarized by the court, created through the use of what is called a "clean room" procedure. The program was written by programmers who had not seen the code for ADAPTER. Instead, they were provided with information about the calls which ZEKE needed to make to the operating system, and information about the form in which the operating systems needed to have the calls passed to it (and of course, vice versa --how the operating system could pass information back to ZEKE and how ZEKE could receive the information). Provided with these basic, functional specifications, they then wrote a program to provide the necessary interface. Thus Altai could argue that there was no taking of any protected expression, and with no taking there is no infringement. See the Casebook, page 613.

The court doesn't address the argument. The Court assumes access, presumably because Altai's employee Claude F. Arney, III who wrote OSCAR 3.4 had access to the ADAPTER source code. But access plus similarity only shifts the burden of persuasion on the issue of copying. See the Casebook, page 623. Thus Altai could have still won by showing the absence of copying, which it apparently did. Why doesn't the court address this argument? Is it because OSCAR 3.4 did infringe and therefore Altai faces an unusually demanding burden of persuasion to show that OSCAR 3.5 is "clean"? Is it because Arney, an employee of Altai, had the code, and therefore knowledge of the code is imputed to every employee of Altai? Or is the court so eager to write an opinion on the broader question that it overlooks the issue?

3. What would you have advised if James P. Williams had shown up in your law office with the newly discovered problem that OSCAR 3.4 infringed ADAPTER? What options would you discuss with Williams? Would Altai have been in a stronger position if it had hired an outside, independent programming firm to write an interface between ZEKE and the operating system?

4. What now seems to be called the "abstraction-filtration-comparison method" is sweeping the circuits. See Kepner-Tregoe, Inc. v. Leadership Software Inc., 12 F.3d 527 (5th Cir.1994); Brown Bag Software v. Symantec Corp., 960 F.2d 1465 (9th Cir. 1992); Autoskill, Inc. v. National Educational Support Systems, Inc., 994 F.2d 1476 (10th Cir. 1993) and Gates Rubber Co. v. Bando Chemical Indus., 9 F.3d 823 (10th Cir. 1993).

PAGE 710. Add to Text on Audio Taping.

In the Audio Home Recording Act of 1992, P.L. 106-563 (1992), Congress added a new Chapter 10 to Title 17, 17 U.S.C. §§ 1001-1010. That act requires that importers and manufacturers of digital audio recording devices and media pay a royalty of 2 percent, and that digital audio recording devices include a serial copy management system. The purpose of the serial copy management system is to prevent devices that can make copies of copies.

In addition, 17 U.S.C. § 1008 provides that "No action may be brought under this title alleging infringement of copyright based on the manufacture, importation, or distribution of a digital audio recording device, a digital audio recording medium, an analog recording device, or an analog recording medium, or based on the noncommercial use by a consumer of such a device or medium for making digital musical recordings or analog musical recordings."

Note that the form of § 1008 permitted Congress to authorize home recording without taking a position on whether or not the recording was otherwise infringement under the statute.

PAGE 711. Read in addition to or in place of *Williams & Wilkins Co.*

AMERICAN GEOPHYSICAL UNION v. TEXACO INC.
United States Court of Appeals for the Second Circuit, 1994 and 1995
60 F. 3d 913

[Editor's Note: The opinion in this case was first issued in 1994 and is printed at 37 F.3d 881. A petition for certiorari to the United States Supreme Court was filed in 1995. While the petition was pending the parties settled the case for an agreement by Texaco to pay the Copyright Clearance Center and sum reputed to be in excess of "seven figures." After the tentative settlement but before the petition for certiorari was dismissed the opinion was amended in significant ways. In the following text material deleted from the 1994 opinon is indicated by strikeout, material added is indicated by background shading. Although the amount of new text in the 1995 opinion is small, the result of the changes was to significantly narrow the precedential importance of the decision.]

Jon O. Newman, Chief Judge:

This interlocutory appeal presents the issue of whether, under the particular circumstances of this case, the fair use defense to copyright infringement applies to the photocopying of articles in a scientific journal. This issue arises on the appeal of defendant Texaco Inc. from the July 23, 1992, order of the United States District Court for the Southern District of New York (Pierre N. Leval, Judge) holding, after a limited-issue bench trial, that the photocopying of eight articles from the *Journal of Catalysis* for use by one of Texaco's researchers was not fair use. See American Geophysical Union v. Texaco Inc., 802 F.Supp. 1 (S.D.N.Y.1992). Though not for precisely the same reasons, we agree with the District Court's conclusion that this particular copying was not fair use and therefore affirm.

Background

The District Court Proceedings. Plaintiffs American Geophysical Union and 82 other publishers of scientific and technical journals (the "publishers") brought a class action claiming that Texaco's unauthorized photocopying of articles from their journals constituted copyright infringement. Among other defenses, Texaco claimed that its copying was fair use under section 107 of the Copyright Act, 17 U.S.C. § 107 (1988). Since it appeared likely that the litigation could be resolved once the fair use defense was adjudicated, the parties agreed that an initial trial should be limited to whether Texaco's copying was fair use, and further agreed that this issue would be submitted for decision on a written record.

Although Texaco employs 400 to 500 research scientists, of whom all or most presumably photocopy scientific journal articles to support their Texaco research, the parties stipulated—in order to spare the enormous expense of exploring the photocopying practices of each of them—that one scientist would be chosen at random as the representative of the entire group. The scientist chosen was Dr. Donald H. Chickering, II, a scientist at Texaco's research center in Beacon, New York. For consideration at trial, the publishers selected from Chickering's files photocopies of eight particular articles from the *Journal of Catalysis*.

In a comprehensive opinion, reported at 802 F.Supp. 1, the District Court considered the statutory fair use factors identified in section 107, weighed other equitable considerations, and held that Texaco's photocopying, as represented by Chickering's copying of these eight articles did not constitute fair use. The District Court certified its ruling for interlocutory appeal under 28 U.S.C. § 1292(b) (1988).

Essential Facts. Employing between 400 and 500 researchers nationwide, Texaco conducts considerable scientific research seeking to develop new products and technology primarily to improve its commercial performance in the petroleum industry. As part of its substantial expenditures in support of research activities at its Beacon facility, Texaco subscribes to many scientific and technical journals and maintains a sizable library with these materials. Among the periodicals that Texaco receives at its

Beacon research facility is the *Journal of Catalysis* ("*Catalysis*"), a monthly publication produced by Academic Press, Inc., a major publisher of scholarly journals and one of the plaintiffs in this litigation. Texaco had initially purchased one subscription to *Catalysis* for its Beacon facility, and increased its total subscriptions to two in 1983. Since 1988, Texaco has maintained three subscriptions to *Catalysis*.

Each issue of *Catalysis* contains articles, notes, and letters (collectively "articles"), ranging in length from two to twenty pages. All of the articles are received by the journal's editors through unsolicited submission by various authors. Authors are informed that they must transfer the copyright in their writings to Academic Press if one of their articles is accepted for publication, and no form of money payment is ever provided to authors whose works are published. Academic Press typically owns the copyright for each individual article published in *Catalysis*, and every issue of the journal includes a general statement that no part of the publication is to be reproduced without permission from the copyright owner. The average monthly issue of *Catalysis* runs approximately 200 pages and comprises 20 to 25 articles.

Chickering, a chemical engineer at the Beacon research facility, has worked for Texaco since 1981 conducting research in the field of catalysis, which concerns changes in the rates of chemical reactions. To keep abreast of developments in his field, Chickering must review works published in various scientific and technical journals related to his area of research. Texaco assists in this endeavor by having its library circulate current issues of relevant journals to Chickering when he places his name on the appropriate routing list.

The copies of the eight articles from *Catalysis* found in Chickering's files that the parties have made the exclusive focus of the fair use trial were photocopied in their entirety by Chickering or by other Texaco employees at Chickering's request. Chickering apparently believed that the material and data found within these articles would facilitate his current or future professional research. The evidence developed at trial indicated that Chickering did not generally use the *Catalysis* articles in his research immediately upon copying, but placed the photocopied articles in his files to have them available for later reference as needed. Chickering became aware of six of the photocopied articles when the original issues of *Catalysis* containing the articles were circulated to him. He learned of the other two articles upon seeing a reference to them in another published article. As it turned out, Chickering did not have occasion to make use of five of the articles that were copied.

Discussion

I. The Nature of the Dispute

The parties and many of the amici curiae have approached this case as if it concerns the broad issue of whether photocopying of scientific articles is fair use, or at least the only slightly more limited issue of whether photocopying of such articles is fair use when undertaken by a research scientist employed at a for-profit corporation engaged in his own research. Such broad issues are not before us. Rather, we consider whether Texaco's photocopying by 400 or 500 scientists, as represented by Chickering's example, is fair use. This includes the question whether such institutional, systematic copying increases the number of copies available to scientists while avoiding the necessity of paying for license fees or for additional subscriptions. We do not deal with the question of copying by an individual, for personal use in research or otherwise (not for resale), recognizing that under the fair use doctrine or the de minimis doctrine, such a practice by an individual might well not constitute an infringement. In other words, our opinion does not decide the case that would arise if Chickering were a professor or an independent scientist engaged in copying and creating files for independent research, as opposed to being employed by an institution in the pursuit of his research on the institution's behalf.

Fair use is a doctrine the application of which always depends on consideration of the precise facts at hand, see Campbell v. Acuff-Rose Music, Inc., 510 U.S. 569, ----, 114 S.Ct. 1164, 1170 (1994); Harper & Row, Publishers, Inc. v. Nation Enterprises, 471 U.S. 539, 549 (1985); Wright v. Warner Books, Inc., 953 F.2d 731, 740 (2d Cir.1991); H.R.Rep. No. 1476, 94th Cong., 2d Sess. 65-66 (1976) ("no generally applicable definition [of fair use] is possible, and each case raising the question must be decided on its own facts"), and in this case the parties have helpfully circumscribed the scope of the issue to be decided by tendering for the District Court's decision the facts concerning the copying of eight particular articles. Our concern is whether the copying of these eight articles, as representative of the systematic copying that Texaco encouraged, was properly determined not to be fair use. Thus, the many background details stressed by each side are of only limited relevance in resolving this specific case.[1]

A. Fair Use and Photocopying

---

[1] Texaco, for example, uses a significant portion of its initial brief to expound on photocopying activities in various industries. Similarly, a large part of the publishers' statement of facts is devoted to a broad discussion of Texaco's photocopying practices, the social importance of academic and scientific journals, and the economics of journal publication and photocopying. These and other details presented by the parties are discussed in the District Court's opinion, 802 F.Supp. at 4-9.

We consider initially the doctrine of fair use and its application to photocopying of documents. Seeking "to motivate the creative activity of authors ... by the provision of a special reward," Sony Corporation of America v. Universal City Studios, Inc., 464 U.S. 417 (1984), copyright law grants certain exclusive rights in original works to authors, see 17 U.S.C. §§ 102(a), 106, 201(a). However, the fair use doctrine "tempers the protection of copyright by allowing ... [the] use [of] a limited amount of copyrighted material under some circumstances." Twin Peaks Productions, Inc. v. Publications International, Ltd., 996 F.2d 1366, 1373 (2d Cir.1993). Traditionally conceived as based on authors' implied consent to reasonable uses of their works, see Harper & Row, 471 U.S. at 549-50, or on an exception to authors' monopoly privileges needed in order to fulfill copyright's purpose to promote the arts and sciences, see Campbell, 114 S.Ct. at 1169, the fair use doctrine has a lengthy and rich common-law history, see William F. Patry, The Fair Use Privilege in Copyright Law 1-63 (1985) [hereinafter Patry, The Fair Use Privilege], and is now codified in section 107 of the Copyright Act, 17 U.S.C. § 107.

As with the development of other easy and accessible means of mechanical reproduction of documents, the invention and widespread availability of photocopying technology threatens to disrupt the delicate balances established by the Copyright Act. See 3 Melville B. Nimmer & David Nimmer, Nimmer on Copyright § 13.05[E][1], at 13-225 to 13-226 (1994) [hereinafter Nimmer on Copyright] (noting that "unrestricted photocopying practices could largely undercut the entire law of copyright") . . . . As a leading commentator astutely notes, the advent of modern photocopying technology creates a pressing need for the law "to strike an appropriate balance between the authors' interest in preserving the integrity of copyright, and the public's right to enjoy the benefits that photocopying technology offers." 3 Nimmer on Copyright § 13.05 [E][1], at 13-226.

Indeed, if the issue were open, we would seriously question whether the fair use analysis that has developed with respect to works of authorship alleged to use portions of copyrighted material is precisely applicable to copies produced by mechanical means. The traditional fair use analysis, now codified in section 107, developed in an effort to adjust the competing interests of authors--the author of the original copyrighted work and the author of the secondary work that "copies" a portion of the original work in the course of producing what is claimed to be a new work. Mechanical "copying" of an entire document, made readily feasible and economical by the advent of xerography, see SCM Corp. v. Xerox Corp., 463 F.Supp. 983, 991-94 (D.Conn.1978), aff'd, 645 F.2d 1195 (2d Cir.1981), cert. denied, 455 U.S. 1016 (1982), is obviously an activity entirely different from creating a work of authorship. Whatever social utility copying of this sort achieves, it is not concerned with creative authorship.

Though we have been instructed to defer to Congress "when major technological innovations alter the market for copyrighted materials," Sony, 464 U.S. at 431, Congress has thus far provided scant guidance for resolving fair use issues involving photocopying, legislating specifically only as to library copying, see 17 U.S.C. § 108, and providing indirect advice concerning classroom copying. * * *. However, we learn from the Supreme Court's consideration of copying achieved by use of a videotape recorder that mechanical copying is to be assessed for fair use purposes under the traditional mode of analysis, including the four statutory factors of section 107. See Sony, 464 U.S. at 447-56. We therefore are obliged to apply that analysis to the photocopying that occurred in this case.

B. The Precise Copyrights at Issue

We must first identify precisely the copyrighted works alleged to be infringed, since certain arguments made on appeal seem to focus on different works. The publishers typically hold two separate sets of copyrights in their journal publications. As a consequence of the publishers' requirement that authors transfer their copyrights when their articles are accepted for publication, the publishers usually possess the copyrights that subsist in each individual article appearing within their journals.[4] For various reasons, for example, because certain articles are the work of the United States Government (which makes copyright protection unavailable, see 17 U.S.C. § 105), the publishers do not always possess the copyrights for all articles within each journal. Moreover, to the extent that the compilation of a journal issue involves an original work of authorship, the publishers possess a distinct copyright in each journal issue as a collective work, * * *.

From the outset, this lawsuit concerned alleged infringement of the copyrights in individual journal articles, copyrights assigned by the authors to the publishers. More specifically, by virtue of the parties' stipulation, this case now concerns the copyrights in the eight articles from *Catalysis* found in Chickering's files, copyrights now owned by Academic Press. There are no allegations that raise questions concerning Academic Press's potential copyrights in whole issues or annual volumes of *Catalysis* as collective works.

C. Burdens of Proof and Standard of Review

Fair use serves as an affirmative defense to a claim of copyright infringement, and thus the party claiming that its secondary use of the original copyrighted work constitutes a fair use typically carries the burden of proof as to all issues in the dispute. See Campbell, 114 S.Ct. at 1177. Moreover, since fair use is a "mixed question of law and fact," Harper & Row, 471 U.S. at 560, we review the District Court's

---

[4] For various reasons, for example, because certain articles are the work of the United States Government (which makes copyright protection unavailable, see 17 U.S.C. § 105), the publishers do not always possess the copyrights for all articles within each journal.

conclusions on this issue de novo, though we accept its subsidiary findings of fact unless clearly erroneous, see Twin Peaks, 996 F.2d at 1374.

II. The Enumerated Fair Use Factors of Section 107

Section 107 of the Copyright Act identifies four non-exclusive factors that a court is to consider when making its fair use assessment, see 17 U.S.C. § 107(1)-(4). The District Court concluded that three of the four statutory factors favor the publishers. As detailed below, our analysis of certain statutory factors differs somewhat from that of the District Court, though we are in agreement on the ultimate determination. Our differences stem primarily from the fact that, unlike the District Court, we have had the benefit of the Supreme Court's important decision in Campbell, decided after Judge Leval issued his opinion.

A. First Factor: Purpose and Character of Use

The first factor listed in section 107 is "the purpose and character of the use, including whether such use is of a commercial nature or is for nonprofit educational purposes." 17 U.S.C. § 107(1). Especially pertinent to an assessment of the first fair use factor are the precise circumstances under which copies of the eight *Catalysis* articles were made. After noticing six of these articles when the original copy of the journal issue containing each of them was circulated to him, Chickering had them photocopied, at least initially, for the same basic purpose that one would normally seek to obtain the original--to have it available on his shelf for ready reference if and when he needed to look at it. The library circulated one copy and invited all the researchers to make their own photocopies. It is a reasonable inference that the library staff wanted each journal issue moved around the building quickly and returned to the library so that it would be available for others to look at. Making copies enabled all researchers who might one day be interested in examining the contents of an article in the issue to have the ~~issue~~ article readily available in their own offices. In Chickering's own words, the copies of the articles were made for "my personal convenience," since it is "far more convenient to have access in my office to a photocopy of an article than to have to go to the library each time I wanted to refer to it." Affidavit of Donald Chickering at 11 (submitted as direct trial testimony) [hereinafter Chickering testimony]. Significantly, Chickering did not even have occasion to use five of the photocopied articles at all, further revealing that the photocopies of the eight *Catalysis* articles were primarily made just for "future retrieval and reference." Id.

It is true that photocopying these articles also served other purposes. The most favorable for Texaco is the purpose of enabling Chickering, if the need should arise, to go into the lab with pieces of paper that (a) were not as bulky as the entire issue or a bound volume of a year's issues, and (b) presented no risk of damaging the original by exposure to chemicals. And these purposes might suffice to tilt the first fair use factor in favor of Texaco if these purposes were dominant. For example, if Chickering had asked the library to buy him a copy of the pertinent issue of *Catalysis* and had placed it on his shelf, and one day while reading it had noticed a chart, formula, or other material that he wanted to take right into the lab, it might be a fair use for him to make a photocopy, and use that copy in the lab (especially if he did not retain it and build up a mini-library of photocopied articles). This is the sort of "spontaneous" copying that is part of the test for permissible nonprofit classroom copying. See Agreement on Guidelines for Classroom Copying in Not-For-Profit Educational Institutions, quoted in Patry, The Fair Use Privilege, at 308.[5] But that is not what happened here as to the six items copied from the circulated issues.

As to the other two articles, the circumstances are not quite as clear, but they too appear more to serve the purpose of being additions to Chickering's office "library" than to be spontaneous copying of a critical page that he was reading on his way to the lab. One was copied apparently when he saw a reference to it in another article, which was in an issue circulated to him. The most likely inference is that he decided that he ought to have copies of both items--again for placement on his shelf for later use if the need arose. The last article was copied, according to his affidavit, when he saw a reference to it "elsewhere." Chickering testimony at 22. What is clear is that this item too was simply placed "on the shelf." As he testified, "I kept a copy to refer to in case I became more involved in support effects research." Id.

The photocopying of these eight *Catalysis* articles may be characterized as "archival"--i.e., done for the primary purpose of providing numerous Texaco scientists (for whom Chickering served as an example) each with his or her own personal copy of each article without Texaco's having to purchase another original journal.[6] The

---

[5] These guidelines were included in the legislative history of the 1976 revision of the Copyright Act, see H.R.Rep. No. 1476, 94th Cong., 2d Sess. 68-71 (1976), U.S.Code Cong. & Admin.News 1976, p. 5659 and were endorsed by the House Judiciary Committee as "a reasonable interpretation of the minimum standards of fair use." Id. at 72, U.S. Code Cong. & Admin. News 1976, at 5686. Though these guidelines are not considered necessarily binding on courts, see Marcus v. Rowley, 695 F.2d 1171, 1178 (9th Cir.1983), they exist as a persuasive authority marking out certain minimum standards for educational fair uses, see Basic Books, Inc. v. Kinko's Graphics Corp., 758 F.Supp. 1522-36 (S.D.N.Y.1991). See generally 3 Nimmer on Copyright § 13.05[E][3][a], at 13-226.1 to 13-226.2 (discussing nature and impact of guidelines); Patry, The Fair Use Privilege, at 307-09, 404-07 (same).

[6] In this regard, the District Court's conclusion that the "primary aspect" of Texaco's copying was to multiply copies is accurate, see 802 F.Supp. at 14-15, irrespective of the evidence (or lack of evidence) concerning the nature and scope of Texaco's photocopying activity for its entire population of scientists. Even if the photocopies of the *Catalysis* articles in Chickering's files were the only copies ever made by Texaco-- which, as Texaco stresses, is all that the evidence developed below conclusively showed--the primary objective in making these single copies was to provide Chickering with his own, additional, readily accessible copy of the original article. As the District Court noted, "[I]f Chickering were the subscriber and sole user of the subscription to *Catalysis*, and he made an extra copy of an article for use in the

photocopying "merely 'supersede[s]' the objects' of the original creation," Campbell, 114 S.Ct. at 1171 (quoting Folsom v. Marsh, 9 F.Cas. 342, 348 (No. 4,901) (C.C.D.Mass.1841)), and tilts the first fair use factor against Texaco. We do not mean to suggest that no instance of archival copying would be fair use, but the first factor tilts against Texaco in this case because the making of copies to be placed on the shelf in Chickering's office is part of a systematic process of encouraging employee researchers to copy articles so as to multiply available copies while avoiding payment.

Texaco criticizes three aspects of the District Court's analysis of the first factor. Relying largely on the Supreme Court's discussion of fair use in Sony, the District Court suggested that a secondary user will "win" this first factor by showing a "transformative (or productive) nonsuperseding use of the original, or [a] noncommercial use, generally for a socially beneficial or widely accepted purpose." 802 F.Supp. at 12. The District Court then concluded that Texaco's copying is "neither transformative nor noncommercial," id. at 13: not transformative because Texaco "simply makes mechanical photocopies of the entirety of relevant articles" and the "primary aspect" of Texaco's photocopying is to multiply copies, see id. at 13-15; and not noncommercial because, though it facilitates research, this research is conducted solely for commercial gain, see id. at 15-16.

Texaco asserts that the District Court mischaracterized the inquiry under the first factor and overlooked several relevant considerations. First, Texaco contends that the District Court inappropriately focussed on the character of the user rather than the nature of the use in labeling Texaco's copying as commercial. Texaco claims that its status as a for-profit corporation has no bearing on the fair use analysis, and that its use should be considered noncommercial since it photocopied articles in order to aid Chickering's research. Texaco emphasizes that "research" is explicitly listed in the preamble of section 107, a circumstance that Texaco contends should make its copying favored under the first factor and throughout the entire fair use analysis.[7]

Second, Texaco contends that the District Court put undue emphasis on whether its use was "transformative," especially since the Supreme Court appears to have rejected the view that a use must be transformative or productive to be a fair use. See

---

lab or for marking with scratch notes, the argument [for a transformative" fair use] might have considerable force." 802 F.Supp. at 14.

[7] Though Texaco claims that its copying is for "research" as that term is used in the preamble of section 107, this characterization might somewhat overstate the matter. Chickering has not used portions of articles from *Catalysis* in his own published piece of research, nor has he had to duplicate some portion of copyrighted material directly in the course of conducting an experiment or investigation. Rather, entire articles were copied as an intermediate step that might abet Chickering's research.

Sony, 464 U.S. at 455 n. 40 ("The distinction between 'productive' and 'unproductive' uses may be helpful in calibrating the balance [of interests], but it cannot be wholly determinative."). Texaco asserts that the "transformative use" concept is valuable only to the extent that it focusses attention upon whether a second work unfairly competes with the original. Texaco states that in this case, where the photocopies it made were not sold or distributed in competition with the original, the nontransformative nature of its copying should not prevent a finding of fair use. Texaco also suggests that its use should be considered transformative: photocopying the article separated it from a bulky journal, made it more amenable to markings, and provided a document that could be readily replaced if damaged in a laboratory, all of which "transformed" the original article into a form that better served Chickering's research needs.

Finally, Texaco claims that it should prevail on the first factor because, as the District Court acknowledged, the type of photocopying it conducted is widespread and has long been considered reasonable and customary. Texaco stresses that some courts and commentators regard custom and common usage as integral to the fair use analysis. See, e.g., Williams & Wilkins Co. v. United States, 487 F.2d 1345, 1353-56 (Ct. Claims 1973), aff'd by equally divided Court, 420 U.S. 376 (1975); Lloyd L. Weinreb, Fair's Fair: A Comment on the Fair Use Doctrine, 103 Harv.L.Rev. 1137, 1140 (1990) [hereinafter Weinreb, Fair's Fair]. We consider these three lines of attack separately.

1. Commercial use. We generally agree with Texaco's contention that the District Court placed undue emphasis on the fact that Texaco is a for-profit corporation conducting research primarily for commercial gain. Since many, if not most, secondary users seek at least some measure of commercial gain from their use, unduly emphasizing the commercial motivation of a copier will lead to an overly restrictive view of fair use. See Campbell, 114 S.Ct. at 1174; see also Maxtone-Graham v. Burtchaell, 803 F.2d 1253, 1262 (2d Cir.1986) (noting that if "commercial" nature of a secondary use is over-emphasized in the analysis, "fair use would be virtually obliterated"), cert. denied, 481 U.S. 1059 (1987). See generally 3 Nimmer on Copyright § 13.05[A][1][c], at 13-162 to 13-163 (categorical rule against commercial uses unwarranted since this "would cause the fair use analysis to collapse in all but the exceptional case of nonprofit exploitation"). Though the Supreme Court had stated in Sony that every commercial use was "presumptively" unfair, see 464 U.S. at 451 that Court and lower courts have come to explain that the commercial nature of a secondary use simply " 'tends to weigh against a finding of fair use.' " Campbell, 114 S.Ct. at 1174 (quoting Harper & Row, 471 U.S. at 562); accord Rogers v. Koons, 960 F.2d 301, 309 (2d Cir.), cert. denied, 113 S.Ct. 365 (1992); Sega Enterprises Limited v. Accolade, Inc., 977 F.2d 1510, 1522 (9th Cir.1992); Maxtone-Graham, 803 F.2d at 1262.

"Indeed, Campbell warns against 'elevat[ing] ... to a per se rule' Sony's language about a presumption against fair use arising from commercial use. 114 S.Ct. at 1174. Campbell discards that language in favor of a more subtle, sophisticated approach, which recognizes that 'the more transformative the new work, the less will be the significance of other factors, like commercialism, that may weigh against a finding of fair use.' Id. at 1171. The Court states that 'the commercial or nonprofit educational purpose of a work is only one element of the first factor enquiry,' id. at 1174, and points out that '[i]f, indeed, commerciality carried presumptive force against a finding of fairness, the presumption would swallow nearly all of the illustrative uses listed in the preamble paragraph of § 107....' Id."

We do not mean to suggest that the District Court overlooked these principles; in fact, the Court discussed them insightfully, see 802 F.Supp. at 12-13. Rather, our concern here is that the Court let the for-profit nature of Texaco's activity weigh against Texaco without differentiating between a direct commercial use and the more indirect relation to commercial activity that occurred here. Texaco was not gaining direct or immediate commercial advantage from the photocopying at issue in this case--i.e., Texaco's profits, revenues, and overall commercial performance were not tied to its making copies of eight *Catalysis* articles for Chickering. Cf. Basic Books, Inc. v. Kinko's Graphics Corp., 758 F.Supp. 1522 (S.D.N.Y.1991) (revenues of reprographic business stemmed directly from selling unauthorized photocopies of copyrighted books). Rather, Texaco's photocopying served, at most, to facilitate Chickering's research, which in turn might have led to the development of new products and technology that could have improved Texaco's commercial performance. Texaco's photocopying is more appropriately labeled an "intermediate use." See Sega Enterprises, 977 F.2d at 1522-23 (labeling secondary use "intermediate" and finding first factor in favor of for-profit company, even though ultimate purpose of copying was to develop competing commercial product, because immediate purpose of copying computer code was to study idea contained within computer program).

We do not consider Texaco's status as a for-profit company irrelevant to the fair use analysis. Though Texaco properly contends that a court's focus should be on the use of the copyrighted material and not simply on the user, it is overly simplistic to suggest that the "purpose and character of the use" can be fully discerned without considering the nature and objectives of the user.[8]

Ultimately, the somewhat cryptic suggestion in section 107(1) to consider whether the secondary use "is of a commercial nature or is for nonprofit educational purposes" connotes that a court should examine, among other factors, the value

---

[8] See Patry, The Fair Use Privilege, at 416-17 (noting that the nature of person or entity engaging in use affects the character of the use); Report of the Register of Copyrights--Library Reproduction of Copyrighted Works (17 U.S.C. 108) 85 (1983) (explaining that though a scientist in a for-profit firm and a university student may engage in the same photocopying of scholarly articles to facilitate their research, "the copyright consequences are different: [the scientist's] copying is of a clearly commercial nature, and less likely to be fair use") quoted in Patry, The Fair Use Privilege, at 417 n. 307.

obtained by the secondary user from the use of the copyrighted material. See Rogers, 960 F.2d at 309 ("The first factor ... asks whether the original was copied in good faith to benefit the public or primarily for the commercial interests of the infringer."); MCA, Inc. v. Wilson, 677 F.2d 180, 182 (2d Cir.1981) (court is to consider "whether the alleged infringing use was primarily for public benefit or for private commercial gain"). The commercial/nonprofit dichotomy concerns the unfairness that arises when a secondary user makes unauthorized use of copyrighted material to capture significant revenues as a direct consequence of copying the original work. See Harper & Row, 471 U.S. at 562 ("The crux of the profit/nonprofit distinction is ... whether the user stands to profit from exploitation of the copyrighted material without paying the customary price.").

Consistent with these principles, courts will not sustain a claimed defense of fair use when the secondary use can fairly be characterized as a form of "commercial exploitation," i.e., when the copier directly and exclusively acquires conspicuous financial rewards from its use of the copyrighted material. See Harper & Row, 471 U.S. at 562-63; Twin Peaks, 996 F.2d at 1375; Rogers, 960 F.2d at 309; Iowa State University Research Foundation, Inc. v. American Broadcasting Companies, Inc., 621 F.2d 57, 61 (2d Cir.1980); Meeropol v. Nizer, 560 F.2d 1061, 1069 (2d Cir.1977) (examining whether use was "predominantly for commercial exploitation"), cert. denied, 434 U.S. 1013 (1978). Conversely, courts are more willing to find a secondary use fair when it produces a value that benefits the broader public interest. See Twin Peaks, 996 F.2d at 1375; Sega Enterprises, 977 F.2d at 1523; Rosemont Enterprises, Inc. v. Random House, Inc., 366 F.2d 303, 307-09 (2d Cir. 1966), cert. denied, 385 U.S. 1009 (1967). The greater the private economic rewards reaped by the secondary user (to the exclusion of broader public benefits), the more likely the first factor will favor the copyright holder and the less likely the use will be considered fair.

As noted before, in this particular case the link between Texaco's commercial gain and its copying is somewhat attenuated: the copying, at most, merely facilitated Chickering's research that might have led to the production of commercially valuable products. Thus, it would not be accurate to conclude that Texaco's copying of eight particular *Catalysis* articles amounted to "commercial exploitation," especially since the immediate goal of Texaco's copying was to facilitate Chickering's research in the sciences, an objective that might well serve a broader public purpose. See Twin Peaks, 996 F.2d at 1375; Sega Enterprises, 977 F.2d at 1522. Still, we need not ignore the for-profit nature of Texaco's enterprise, especially since we can confidently conclude that Texaco reaps at least some indirect economic advantage from its photocopying. As the publishers emphasize, Texaco's photocopying for Chickering could be regarded simply as another "factor of production" utilized in Texaco's efforts to develop profitable products. Conceptualized in this way, it is not obvious why it is fair for Texaco to avoid having to pay at least some price to copyright holders for the right to photocopy the original articles.

2. Transformative Use. The District Court properly emphasized that Texaco's photocopying was not "transformative." After the District Court issued its opinion, the Supreme Court explicitly ruled that the concept of a "transformative use" is central to a proper analysis under the first factor, see Campbell, 114 S.Ct. at 1171-73. The Court explained that though a "transformative use is not absolutely necessary for a finding of fair use, ... the more transformative the new work, the less will be the significance of other factors, like commercialism, that may weigh against a finding of fair use." Id. at 1171.

The "transformative use" concept is pertinent to a court's investigation under the first factor because it assesses the value generated by the secondary use and the means by which such value is generated. To the extent that the secondary use involves merely an untransformed duplication, the value generated by the secondary use is little or nothing more than the value that inheres in the original. Rather than making some contribution of new intellectual value and thereby fostering the advancement of the arts and sciences, an untransformed copy is likely to be used simply for the same intrinsic purpose as the original, thereby providing limited justification for a finding of fair use. See Weissmann v. Freeman, 868 F.2d 1313, 1324 (2d Cir.) (explaining that a use merely for the same "intrinsic purpose" as original "moves the balance of the calibration on the first factor against" secondary user and "seriously weakens a claimed fair use"), cert. denied, 493 U.S. 883 (1989).[9]

In contrast, to the extent that the secondary use "adds something new, with a further purpose or different character," the value generated goes beyond the value that inheres in the original and "the goal of copyright, to promote science and the arts, is generally furthered." Campbell, 114 S.Ct. at 1171; see also Pierre N. Leval, Toward a Fair Use Standard, 103 Harv.L.Rev. 1105, 1111 (1990) [hereinafter Leval, Toward a Fair Use Standard]. It is therefore not surprising that the "preferred" uses illustrated in the preamble to section 107, such as criticism and comment, generally involve some transformative use of the original work. See 3 Nimmer on Copyright § 13.05[A][1][b], at 13-160.

Texaco suggests that its conversion of the individual *Catalysis* articles through photocopying into a form more easily used in a laboratory might constitute a transformative use. However, Texaco's photocopying merely transforms the material object embodying the intangible article that is the copyrighted original work. See 17 U.S.C. ss 101, 102 (explaining that copyright protection in literary works subsists in

---

[9] See also Marcus v. Rowley, 695 F.2d at 1175 (emphasizing that "a finding that the alleged infringers copied the material to use it for the same intrinsic purpose for which the copyright owner intended it to be used is strong indicia of no fair use."). See generally Leon E. Seltzer, Exemptions and Fair Use in Copyright 24 (1978) (noting traditional limit on the applicability of fair use doctrine when reproduction of original work is done "in order to use it for its intrinsic purpose--to make what might be called the 'ordinary' use of it").

the original work of authorship "regardless of the nature of the material objects ... in which they are embodied"). Texaco's making of copies cannot properly be regarded as a transformative use of the copyrighted material. See Steven D. Smit, "Make a Copy for the File ...": Copyright Infringement by Attorneys, 46 Baylor L.Rev. 1, 15 & n. 58 (1994); see also Basic Books, 758 F.Supp. at 1530-31 (repackaging in anthology form of excerpts from copyrighted books not a transformative use).

Even though Texaco's photocopying is not technically a transformative use of the copyrighted material, we should not overlook the significant independent value that can stem from conversion of original journal articles into a format different from their normal appearance. See generally Sony, 464 U.S. at 454, 455 n. 40, (acknowledging possible benefits from copying that might otherwise seem to serve "no productive purpose"); Weinreb, Fair's Fair, at 1143 & n. 29 (discussing potential value from non- transformative copying). As previously explained, Texaco's photocopying converts the individual *Catalysis* articles into a useful format. Before modern photocopying, Chickering probably would have converted the original article into a more serviceable form by taking notes, whether cursory or extended;[10] today he can do so with a photocopying machine. Nevertheless, whatever independent value derives from the more usable format of the photocopy does not mean that every instance of photocopying wins on the first factor. In this case, the predominant archival purpose of the copying tips the first factor against the copier, despite the benefit of a more usable format.

3. Reasonable and Customary Practice. Texaco contends that Chickering's photocopying constitutes a use that has historically been considered "reasonable and customary." We agree with the District Court that whatever validity this argument might have had before the advent of the photocopying licensing arrangements discussed below in our consideration of the fourth fair use factor, the argument today is insubstantial. As the District Court observed, "To the extent the copying practice was 'reasonable' in 1973 [when *Williams & Wilkins* was decided], it has ceased to be 'reasonable' as the reasons that justified it before [photocopying licensing] have ceased to exist." 802 F.Supp. at 25.

In amplification of Texaco's arguments, our dissenting colleague makes two further points about the first factor analysis that merit a response. First, the dissent

---

[10] In stating that a handwritten copy would have been made, we do not mean to imply that such copying would necessarily have been a fair use. Despite the 1973 dictum in Williams & Wilkins asserting that "it is almost unanimously accepted that a scholar can make a handwritten copy of an entire copyrighted article for his own use ...," 487 F.2d at 1350, the current edition of the Nimmer treatise reports that "[t]here is no reported case on the question of whether a single handwritten copy of all or substantially all of a book or other protected work made for the copier's own private use is an infringement or fair use." 3 Nimmer on Copyright s 1305[E][4][a], at 13-229.

disputes our characterization of Chickering's use as "archival" on the ground that such a use would occur in an institutional setting, whereas Chickering copied for his personal use. Second, the dissent contends that Chickering's use is transformative because it is an important step in the process of doing research. We think the proper response to these observations emerges from considering how they would fare if the Texaco library had sent around entire books, rather than issues of a journal. Clearly, Chickering (and all the other researchers at the Beacon facility) would be making archival use of the circulating books if they made photocopies of the books for their individual offices and thereby spared Texaco the expense of buying them all individual volumes. An individual copies for archival purposes even if the resulting archive remains in a private office. When a corporation invites such archival copying by circulating items likely to be worth copying (whether articles or entire books), any distinction between individual and institutional archiving loses all significance.

Moreover, the concept of a "transformative" use would be extended beyond recognition if it was applied to Chickering's copying simply because he acted in the course of doing research. The purposes illustrated by the categories listed in section 107 refer primarily to the work of authorship alleged to be a fair use, not to the activity in which the alleged infringer is engaged. Texaco cannot gain fair use insulation for Chickering's archival photocopying of articles (or books) simply because such copying is done by a company doing research. It would be equally extravagant for a newspaper to contend that because its business is "news reporting" it may line the shelves of its reporters with photocopies of books on journalism or that schools engaged in "teaching" may supply its faculty members with personal photocopies of books on educational techniques or substantive fields. Whatever benefit copying and reading such books might contribute to the process of "teaching" would not for that reason satisfy the test of a "teaching" purpose.

On balance, we agree with the District Court that the first factor favors the publishers, primarily because the dominant purpose of the use is "archival" to assemble a set of papers for future reference systematic institutional policy of multiplying the available number of copies of pertinent copyrighted articles by circulating the journals among employed scientists for them to make copies, thereby serving the same purpose for which additional subscriptions are normally sold, or, as will be discussed, for which photocopying licenses may be obtained.

B. Second Factor: Nature of Copyrighted Work

The second statutory fair use factor is "the nature of the copyrighted work." 17 U.S.C. § 107(2). In assessing this factor, the District Court noted that the articles in *Catalysis* "are created for publication with the purpose and intention of benefiting from the protection of the copyright law," and that copyright protection "is vitally necessary to the dissemination of scientific articles of the sort that are at issue." 802 F.Supp. at 16. Nevertheless, the Court ultimately concluded that this factor favored Texaco because the photocopied articles were essentially factual in nature and the " 'scope of fair use is greater with respect to factual than nonfactual works.'" Id. at 16-17 (quoting New Era Publications International, ApS v. Carol Publishing Group, 904 F.2d 152, 157 (2d Cir.), cert. denied, 498 U.S. 921 (1990)).

On appeal, the publishers stress the District Court's comments concerning the importance of broad copyright protection for journal publications in order to foster journal production. Further, citing Harper & Row for the proposition that the creativity of an original work weighs against finding fair use, see 471 U.S. at 563, the publishers also point out that "the journal articles are expressions of highly original, creative and imaginative thinking."

Though a significant measure of creativity was undoubtedly used in the creation of the eight articles copied from *Catalysis*, even a glance at their content immediately reveals the predominantly factual nature of these works.[11] Moreover, though we have previously recognized the importance of strong copyright protection to provide sufficient incentives for the creation of scientific works, see Weissmann, 868 F.2d at 1325, nearly every category of copyrightable works could plausibly assert that broad copyright protection was essential to the continued vitality of that category of works.

Ultimately, then, the manifestly factual character of the eight articles precludes us from considering the articles as "within the core of the copyright's protective purposes," Campbell, 114 S.Ct. at 1175; see also Harper & Row, 471 U.S. at 563 ("The law generally recognizes a greater need to disseminate factual works than works of fiction or fantasy."). Thus, in agreement with the District Court, we conclude that the second factor favors Texaco.

C. Third Factor: Amount and Substantiality of Portion Used

The third statutory fair use factor is "the amount and substantiality of the portion used in relation to the copyrighted work as a whole." 17 U.S.C. § 107(3). The District Court concluded that this factor clearly favors the publishers because Texaco copied the eight articles from *Catalysis* in their entirety.

Texaco makes various responses to the District Court's straightforward conclusion. First, Texaco claims that this factor is significant only as a means to determine whether a copy unfairly supersedes demand for the original and should be considered "largely irrelevant" where, as here, a copy is not sold or distributed. Second, Texaco claims that, rather than focus on Texaco's copying of entire articles,

---

[11] Not only are the *Catalysis* articles essentially factual in nature, but the evidence suggests that Chickering was interested exclusively in the facts, ideas, concepts, or principles contained within the articles. Though scientists surely employ creativity and originality to develop ideas and obtain facts and thereafter to convey the ideas and facts in scholarly articles, it is primarily the ideas and facts themselves that are of value to other scientists in their research.

it is more appropriate to consider that Texaco copied only a very small portion of any particular issue or volume of *Catalysis*. Finally, Texaco cites Sony and Williams & Wilkins for the proposition that the copying of entire copyrighted works can still constitute fair use. See Sony, 464 U.S. at 449-50; Williams & Wilkins, 487 F.2d at 1353.

Texaco's suggestion that we consider that it copied only a small percentage of the total compendium of works encompassed within *Catalysis* is superficially intriguing, especially since *Catalysis* is traditionally marketed only as a periodical by issue or volume. However, as the District Court recognized, each of the eight articles in *Catalysis* was separately authored and constitutes a discrete "original work[ ] of authorship," 17 U.S.C. § 102. As we emphasized at the outset, each article enjoys independent copyright protection, which the authors transferred to Academic Press, and what the publishers claim has been infringed is the copyright that subsists in each individual article--not the distinct copyright that may subsist in each journal issue or volume by virtue of the publishers' original compilation of these articles. The only other appellate court to consider the propriety of photocopying articles from journals also recognized that each article constituted an entire work in the fair use analysis. See Williams & Wilkins, 487 F.2d at 1353.

Despite Texaco's claims that we consider its amount of copying "minuscule" in relation to the entirety of *Catalysis*, we conclude, as did the District Court, that Texaco has copied entire works. Though this conclusion does not preclude a finding of fair use, it militates against such a finding, see Sony, 464 U.S. at 449-50, and weights the third factor in favor of the publishers.

Finally, though we are sensitive to Texaco's claim that the third factor serves merely as a proxy for determining whether a secondary use significantly interferes with demand for the original--a concern echoed by some commentators, see William W. Fisher III, Reconstructing the Fair Use Doctrine, 101 Harv.L.Rev. 1661, 1678 (1988) [hereinafter Fisher, Reconstructing Fair Use]--we think this factor serves a further end that advances the fair use analysis. Specifically, by focussing on the amount and substantiality of the original work used by the secondary user, we gain insight into the purpose and character of the use as we consider whether the quantity of the material used was "reasonable in relation to the purpose of the copying." See Campbell, 114 S.Ct. at 1175. In this case, the fact that Texaco photocopied the eight *Catalysis* articles in their entirety weakens its assertion that the over-riding purpose and character of its use was to enable the immediate use of the article in the laboratory and strengthens our view that the predominant purpose and character of the use was to establish a personal library of pertinent articles for Chickering. Cf. id. at 1176 (intimating that extent of copying can provide insight into primary purpose of copying).

D. Fourth Factor: Effect Upon Potential Market or Value

The fourth statutory fair use factor is "the effect of the use upon the potential market for or value of the copyrighted work." 17 U.S.C. § 107(4). Assessing this factor, the District Court detailed the range of procedures Texaco could use to obtain authorized copies of the articles that it photocopied and found that "whatever combination of procedures Texaco used, the publishers' revenues would grow significantly." 802 F.Supp. at 19. The Court concluded that the publishers "powerfully demonstrated entitlement to prevail as to the fourth factor," since they had shown "a substantial harm to the value of their copyrights" as the consequence of Texaco's copying. See id. at 18-21.

Prior to Campbell, the Supreme Court had characterized the fourth factor as "the single most important element of fair use," Harper & Row, 471 U.S. at 566; accord 3 Nimmer on Copyright s 13.05[A][4], at 13- 183. However, Campbell's discussion of the fourth factor conspicuously omits this phrasing. Apparently abandoning the idea that any factor enjoys primacy, Campbell instructs that "[a]ll [four factors] are to be explored, and the results weighed together, in light of the purposes of copyright." 114 S.Ct. at 1171.

In analyzing the fourth factor, it is important (1) to bear in mind the precise copyrighted works, namely the eight journal articles, and (2) to recognize the distinctive nature and history of "the potential market for or value of" these particular works.[12] Specifically, though there is a traditional market for, and hence a clearly defined value of, journal issues and volumes, in the form of per-issue purchases and journal subscriptions, there is neither a traditional market for, nor a clearly defined value of, individual journal articles. As a result, analysis of the fourth factor cannot proceed as simply as would have been the case if Texaco had copied a work that carries a stated or negotiated selling price in the market.

Like most authors, writers of journal articles do not directly seek to capture the potential financial rewards that stem from their copyrights by personally marketing copies of their writings. Rather, like other creators of literary works, the author of a journal article "commonly sells his rights to publishers who offer royalties in exchange for their services in producing and marketing the author's work." Harper & Row, 471

---

[12] We focus on the eight articles to emphasize the special characteristics of articles as distinguished from journal issues or bound volumes. In doing so, we recognize, as did the District Court, see 802 F.Supp. at 18 n. 15, that the fourth factor is concerned with the category of a defendant's conduct, not merely the specific instances of copying. See 3 Nimmer on Copyright s 13.05[A][4], at 13-183 to 13-184 ("[I]t is a mistake to view [the fourth] factor ... as merely raising the question of the extent of damages to plaintiff caused by the particular activities of the defendant. This factor rather poses the issue of whether unrestricted and widespread conduct of the sort engaged in by the defendant ... would result in a substantially adverse impact on the potential market for or value of the plaintiff's present work.") (emphasis added).

U.S. at 547. In the distinctive realm of academic and scientific articles, however, the only form of royalty paid by a publisher is often just the reward of being published, publication being a key to professional advancement and prestige for the author, see Weissmann, 868 F.2d at 1324 (noting that "in an academic setting, profit is ill-measured in dollars. Instead, what is valuable is recognition because it so often influences professional advancement and academic tenure."). The publishers in turn incur the costs and labor of producing and marketing authors' articles, driven by the prospect of capturing the economic value stemming from the copyrights in the original works, which the authors have transferred to them. Ultimately, the monopoly privileges conferred by copyright protection and the potential financial rewards therefrom are not directly serving to motivate authors to write individual articles; rather, they serve to motivate publishers to produce journals, which provide the conventional and often exclusive means for disseminating these individual articles. It is the prospect of such dissemination that contributes to the motivation of these authors.

Significantly, publishers have traditionally produced and marketed authors' individual articles only in a journal format, i.e., in periodical compilations of numerous articles. In other words, publishers have conventionally sought to capture the economic value from the "exclusive rights" to "reproduce" and "distribute copies" of the individual articles, see 17 U.S.C. § 106(1) & (3), solely by compiling many such articles together in a periodical journal and then charging a fee to subscribe. Publishers have not traditionally provided a simple or efficient means to obtain single copies of individual articles; reprints are usually available from publishers only in bulk quantities and with some delay.

This marketing pattern has various consequences for our analysis of the fourth factor. First, evidence concerning the effect that photocopying individual journal articles has on the traditional market for journal subscriptions is of somewhat less significance than if a market existed for the sale of individual copies of articles. Second, this distinctive arrangement raises novel questions concerning the significance of the publishers' establishment of an innovative licensing scheme for the photocopying of individual journal articles.

1. *Sales of Additional Journal Subscriptions, Back Issues, and Back Volumes.* Since we are concerned with the claim of fair use in copying the eight individual articles from *Catalysis*, the analysis under the fourth factor must focus on the effect of Texaco's photocopying upon the potential market for or value of these individual articles. Yet, in their respective discussions of the fourth statutory factor, the parties initially focus on the impact of Texaco's photocopying of individual journal articles upon the market for *Catalysis* journals through sales of *Catalysis* subscriptions, back issues, or back volumes.

As a general matter, examining the effect on the marketability of the composite work containing a particular individual copyrighted work serves as a useful means to gauge the impact of a secondary use "upon the potential market for or value of" that individual work, since the effect on the marketability of the composite work will frequently be directly relevant to the effect on the market for or value of that individual work.[13] Quite significantly, though, in the unique world of academic and scientific articles, the effect on the marketability of the composite work in which individual articles appear is not obviously related to the effect on the market for or value of the individual articles. Since (1) articles are submitted unsolicited to journals, (2) publishers do not make any payment to authors for the right to publish their articles or to acquire their copyrights, and (3) there is no evidence in the record suggesting that publishers seek to reprint particular articles in new composite works, we cannot readily conclude that evidence concerning the effect of Texaco's use on the marketability of journals provides an effective means to appraise the effect of Texaco's use on the market for or value of *individual journal articles*.

These considerations persuade us that evidence concerning the effect of Texaco's photocopying of individual articles within *Catalysis* on the traditional market for *Catalysis* subscriptions is of somewhat limited significance in determining and evaluating the effect of Texaco's photocopying "upon the potential market for or value of" the individual articles. We do not mean to suggest that we believe the effect on the marketability of journal subscriptions is completely irrelevant to gauging the effect on the market for and value of individual articles. Were the publishers able to demonstrate that Texaco's type of photocopying, if widespread,[14] would impair the marketability of journals, then they might have a strong claim under the fourth factor. Likewise, were Texaco able to demonstrate that its type of photocopying, even if widespread, would have virtually no effect on the marketability of journals, then it might have a strong claim under this fourth factor.

On this record, however, the evidence is not resounding for either side. The District Court specifically found that, in the absence of photocopying, (1) "Texaco would not ordinarily fill the need now being supplied by photocopies through the

---

[13] One reason that the effect on the marketability of the composite work is typically relevant is because the strength of the market for the composite work will influence the payment producers will be willing to give to the author of the individual work for permission to include that individual work. For example, if a secondary use of a copyrighted story adversely affects purchases of a collection of short stories in which this story appears, then other producers of short story collections will less likely seek to have, or will pay less to have, that story as part of their collections. In this way, the market for or value of the story has clearly been affected by the secondary use.

[14] Properly applied, the fourth factor requires a court to consider "not only ... particular actions of the alleged infringer, but also 'whether unrestricted and widespread conduct of the sort engaged in by the defendant ... would result in a substantially adverse impact on the potential market' for the original." Campbell, 114 S.Ct. at 1177 (quoting 3 Nimmer on Copyright s 13.05[A][4]). Accord Harper & Row, 471 U.S. at 568-69; Rogers, 960 F.2d at 312.

purchase of back issues or back volumes ... [or] by enormously enlarging the number of its subscriptions," but (2) Texaco still "would increase the number of subscriptions somewhat." 802 F.Supp. at 19.[15] This moderate conclusion concerning the actual effect on the marketability of journals, combined with the uncertain relationship between the market for journals and the market for and value of individual articles, leads us to conclude that the evidence concerning sales of additional journal subscriptions, back issues, and back volumes does not strongly support either side with regard to the fourth factor. Cf. Sony, 464 U.S. at 451-55 (rejecting various predictions of harm to value of copyrighted work based on speculation about possible consequences of secondary use). At best, the loss of a few journal subscriptions tips the fourth factor only slightly toward the publishers because evidence of such loss is weak evidence that the copied articles themselves have lost any value., 104 S.Ct. at 792

2. Licensing Revenues and Fees. The District Court, however, went beyond discussing the sales of additional journal subscriptions in holding that Texaco's photocopying affected the value of the publishers' copyrights. Specifically, the Court pointed out that, if Texaco's unauthorized photocopying was not permitted as fair use, the publishers' revenues would increase significantly since Texaco would (1) obtain articles from document delivery services (which pay royalties to publishers for the right to photocopy articles), (2) negotiate photocopying licenses directly with individual publishers, and/or (3) acquire some form of photocopying license from the Copyright Clearance Center Inc. ("CCC").[16] See 802 F.Supp. at 19. Texaco claims that the

---

[15] Texaco assails the conclusion that, without photocopying, it would increase subscriptions "somewhat" as an improper inference unsupported by the evidence. Though we accept Texaco's assertion that additional subscriptions provide an imperfect substitute for the copies of individual articles that scientists need and prefer, we cannot conclude that the District Court's factual finding that "Texaco would add at least a modest number of subscriptions," 802 F.Supp. at 19, is clearly erroneous.

First, though Texaco claims that there is no reliable evidence suggesting that photocopying served to facilitate journal circulation, the evidence concerning Texaco's routing practices supports the District Court's inference that, without photocopying, Texaco will need a greater number of subscriptions to insure the prompt circulation of journals. Second, as discussed in connection with the first statutory factor, the dominant reason for, and value derived from, the copying of the eight particular *Catalysis* articles was to make them available on Chickering's shelf for ready reference when he needed to look at them. Thus, it is reasonable to conclude that Texaco would purchase at least a few additional subscriptions to serve this purpose, i.e., to provide certain researchers with personal copies of particular articles in their own offices.

[16] The CCC is a central clearing-house established in 1977 primarily by publishers to license photocopying. The CCC offers a variety of licensing schemes; fees can be paid on a per copy basis or through blanket license arrangements. Most publishers are registered with the CCC, but the participation of for-profit institutions that engage in photocopying has been limited, largely because of uncertainty concerning the legal questions at issue in this lawsuit. The CCC

District Court's reasoning is faulty because, in determining that the value of the publishers' copyrights was affected, the Court assumed that the publishers were entitled to demand and receive licensing royalties and fees for photocopying. Yet, continues Texaco, whether the publishers can demand a fee for permission to make photocopies is the very question that the fair use trial is supposed to answer.

It is indisputable that, as a general matter, a copyright holder is entitled to demand a royalty for licensing others to use its copyrighted work, see 17 U.S.C. § 106 (copyright owner has exclusive right "to authorize" certain uses), and that the impact on potential licensing revenues is a proper subject for consideration in assessing the fourth factor, see, e.g., Campbell, 114 S.Ct. at 1178; Harper & Row, 471 U.S. at 568-69; Twin Peaks, 996 F.2d at 1377; DC Comics Inc. v. Reel Fantasy, Inc., 696 F.2d 24, 28 (2d Cir.1982); United Telephone Co. of Missouri v. Johnson Publishing Co., Inc., 855 F.2d 604, 610 (8th Cir.1988).

However, not every effect on potential licensing revenues enters the analysis under the fourth factor.[17] Specifically, courts have recognized limits on the concept of "potential licensing revenues" by considering only traditional, reasonable, or likely to be developed markets when examining and assessing a secondary use's "effect upon the potential market for or value of the copyrighted work." See Campbell, 114 S.Ct. at 1178 ("The market for potential derivative uses includes only those that creators of original works would in general develop or license others to develop."); Harper & Row, 471 U.S. at 568, 105 S.Ct. at 2234 (fourth factor concerned with "use that supplants *any part* of the normal market for a copyrighted work") (emphasis added) (quoting S.Rep. No. 473, 94th Cong., 1st Sess. 65 (1975)); see also Mathieson v. Associated Press, 23 U.S.P.Q.2d 1685, 1690-91, 1992 WL 164447 (S.D.N.Y.1992) (refusing to find fourth factor in favor of copyright holder because secondary use did not affect any aspect of the normal market for copyrighted work).

---

is fully described in the District Court's opinion. 802 F. Supp. at 7-9. A more extended discussion of the formation, development, and effectiveness of the CCC and its licensing schemes is contained in Stanley M. Besen & Sheila Nataraj Kirby, Compensating Creators of Intellectual Property: Collectives that Collect (1989).

[17] As Texaco notes and others have recognized, a copyright holder can always assert some degree of adverse affect on its potential licensing revenues as a consequence of the secondary use at issue simply because the copyright holder has not been paid a fee to permit that particular use. See Leval, Toward a Fair Use Standard, at 1124 ("By definition every fair use involves some loss of royalty revenue because the secondary user has not paid royalties."); Fisher, Reconstructing Fair Use, at 1671 (noting that in almost every case "there will be some material adverse impact on a 'potential market'" since the secondary user has not paid for the use). Thus, were a court automatically to conclude in every case that potential licensing revenues were impermissibly impaired simply because the secondary user did not pay a fee for the right to engage in the use, the fourth fair use factor would always favor the copyright holder. See Leval, Toward a Fair Use Standard, at 1125; Fisher, Reconstructing Fair Use, at 1672.

For example, the Supreme Court recently explained that because of the "unlikelihood that creators of imaginative works will license critical reviews or lampoons" of their works, "the law recognizes no derivative market for critical works," Campbell, 114 S.Ct. at 1178. Similarly, other courts have found that the fourth factor will favor the secondary user when the only possible adverse effect occasioned by the secondary use would be to a potential market or value that the copyright holder has not typically sought to, or reasonably been able to, obtain or capture. See Twin Peaks, 996 F.2d at 1377 (noting that fourth factor will favor secondary user when use "filled a market niche that the [copyright owner] simply had no interest in occupying"); Pacific and Southern Co. v. Duncan, 744 F.2d 1490, 1496 (11th Cir.1984) cert. denied, 471 U.S. 1004 (1985) (noting that the fourth factor may not favor copyright owner when the secondary user "profits from an activity that the owner could not possibly take advantage of").[18]

Thus, Texaco is correct, at least as a general matter, when it contends that it is not always appropriate for a court to be swayed on the fourth factor by the effects on potential licensing revenues. Only an impact on potential licensing revenues for traditional, reasonable, or likely to be developed markets should be legally cognizable when evaluating a secondary use's "effect upon the potential market for or value of the copyrighted work."

Though the publishers still have not established a conventional market for the direct sale and distribution of individual articles, they have created, primarily through the CCC, a workable market for institutional users to obtain licenses for the right to produce their own copies of individual articles via photocopying. The District Court found that many major corporations now subscribe to the CCC systems for photocopying licenses. 802 F.Supp. at 25. Indeed, it appears from the pleadings, especially Texaco's counterclaim, that Texaco itself has been paying royalties to the CCC. See Complaint ¶ 38; First Counterclaim ¶ 71. Since the Copyright Act explicitly provides that copyright holders have the "exclusive rights" to "reproduce" and "distribute copies" of their works, see 17 U.S.C. § 106(1) & (3), and since there currently exists a viable market for licensing these rights for individual journal articles, it is appropriate that potential licensing revenues for photocopying be considered in a fair use analysis.

---

[18] The Supreme Court's holding in Sony implicitly recognizes limits on the concept of "potential market for or value of the copyrighted work." Despite Justice Blackmun's dissenting view that the copying of television programs to enable private viewing at a more convenient time, i.e., "time- shifting," deprived copyright holders of the ability to exploit the "sizable market" of persons who "would be willing to pay some kind of royalty" for the "privilege of watching copyrighted work at their convenience," Sony, 464 U.S. at 485, the majority found that the copyright holders "failed to demonstrate that time-shifting would cause any likelihood of non-minimal harm to the potential market for, or the value of, their copyrighted works." Id. at 456. The Court thus implicitly ruled that the potential market in licensing royalties enunciated by Justice Blackmun should be considered too insubstantial to tilt the fourth fair use factor in favor of the copyright holder.

Despite Texaco's claims to the contrary, it is not unsound to conclude that the right to seek payment for a particular use tends to become legally cognizable under the fourth fair use factor when the means for paying for such a use is made easier. This notion is not inherently troubling: it is sensible that a particular unauthorized use should be considered "more fair" when there is no ready market or means to pay for the use, while such an unauthorized use should be considered "less fair when there is a ready market or means to pay for the use. The vice of circular reasoning arises only if the availability of payment is conclusive against fair use. Whatever the situation may have been previously, before the development of a market for institutional users to obtain licenses to photocopy articles, see Williams & Wilkins, 487 F.2d at 1357-59, it is now appropriate to consider the loss of licensing revenues in evaluating "the effect of the use upon the potential market for or value of" journal articles. It is especially appropriate to do so with respect to copying of articles from *Catalysis*, a publication as to which a photocopying license is now available. We do not decide how the fair use balance would be resolved if a photocopying license for *Catalysis* articles were not currently available.

In two ways, Congress has impliedly suggested that the law should recognize licensing fees for photocopying as part of the "potential market for or value of" journal articles. First, section 108 of the Copyright Act narrowly circumscribes the conditions under which libraries are permitted to make copies of copyrighted works. See 17 U.S.C. § 108. Though this section states that it does not in any way affect the right of fair use, see id. § 108(f)(4), the very fact that Congress restricted the rights of libraries to make copies implicitly suggests that Congress views journal publishers as possessing the right to restrict photocopying, or at least the right to demand a licensing royalty from nonpublic institutions that engage in photocopying. Second, Congress apparently prompted the development of CCC by suggesting that an efficient mechanism be established to license photocopying, see S.Rep. No. 983, 93d Cong., 2d Sess. 122 (1974); S.Rep. No. 473, 94th Cong., 1st Sess. 70-71 (1975); H.R.Rep. No. 83, 90th Cong., 1st Sess. 33 (1968). It is difficult to understand why Congress would recommend establishing such a mechanism if it did not believe that fees for photocopying should be legally recognized as part of the potential market for journal articles.

Primarily because of lost licensing revenue, and to a minor extent because of lost subscription revenue, we agree with the District Court that "the publishers have demonstrated a substantial harm to the value of their copyrights through [Texaco's] copying," 802 F.Supp. at 21, and thus conclude that the fourth statutory factor favors the publishers.

E. Aggregate Assessment

We conclude that three of the four statutory factors, including the important first and fourth factors, favor the publishers. We recognize that the statutory factors provide a nonexclusive guide to analysis, see Harper & Row, 471 U.S. at 560, but to whatever extent more generalized equitable considerations are relevant, we are in agreement with the District Court's analysis of them. See 802 F.Supp. at 21-27. We therefore agree with the District Court's conclusion that Texaco's photocopying of eight particular articles from the *Journal of Catalysis* was not fair use.

Though we recognize the force of many observations made in Judge Jacobs's dissenting opinion, we are not dissuaded by his dire predictions that our ruling in this case "has ended fair-use photocopying with respect to a large population of journals," 60 F.3d at 938-39, or, to the extent that the transactional licensing scheme is used, "would seem to require that an intellectual property lawyer be posted at each copy machine," id. at 937-38. Our ruling does not consider photocopying for personal use by an individual. Our ruling is confined to the institutional, systematic, archival multiplication of copies revealed by the record—the precise copying that the parties stipulated should be the basis for the District Court's decision now on appeal and for which licenses are in fact available. And the claim that lawyers need to be stationed at copy machines is belied by the ease with which music royalties have been collected and distributed for performances at thousands of cabarets, without the attendance of intellectual property lawyers in any capacity other than as customers. If Texaco wants to continue the precise copying we hold not to be a fair use, it can either use the licensing schemes now existing or some variant of them, or, if all else fails, purchase one more subscription for each of its researchers who wish to keep issues of *Catalysis* on the office shelf.

The order of the District Court is affirmed.[19]

JACOBS, Circuit Judge, dissenting:

The stipulated facts crisply present the fair use issues that govern the photocopying of entire journal articles for a scientist's own use, either in the laboratory

---

[19] Though neither the limited trial nor this appeal requires consideration of the publishers' remedy if infringement is ultimately found, we note that the context of this dispute appears to make ill-advised an injunction, which, in any event, has not been sought. If the dispute is not now settled, this appears to be an appropriate case for exploration of the possibility of a court-imposed compulsory license. See Campbell, 114 S.Ct. at 1171 n. 10; 3 Nimmer on Copyright s 13.05[E][4][e], at 13-241 to 13-242.

or as part of a personal file assisting that scientist's particular inquiries. I agree with much in the majority's admirable review of the facts and the law. Specifically, I agree that, of the four nonexclusive considerations bearing on fair use enumerated in section 107, the second factor (the nature of the copyrighted work) tends to support a conclusion of fair use, and the third factor (the ratio of the copied portion to the whole copyrighted work) militates against it. I respectfully dissent, however, in respect of the first and fourth factors. As to the first factor: the purpose and character of Dr. Chickering's use is integral to transformative and productive ends of scientific research. As to the fourth factor: the adverse effect of Dr. Chickering's use upon the potential market for the work, or upon its value, is illusory. For these reasons, and in light of certain equitable considerations and the overarching purpose of the copyright laws, I conclude that Dr. Chickering's photocopying of the *Catalysis* articles was fair use.

A. Purpose and Character of the Use

The critical facts adduced by the majority are that Dr. Chickering is a chemical engineer employed at a corporate research facility who keeps abreast of developments in his field by reviewing specialized scientific and technical journals, and who photocopies individual journal articles in the belief that doing so will facilitate his current or future professional research. 60 F.3d at 915. I agree with the majority that the immediate goal of the photocopying was "to facilitate Chickering's research in the sciences, an objective that might well serve a broader public purpose." 60 F.3d at 922-23. The photocopying was therefore integral to ongoing research by a scientist. In my view, all of the statutory factors organize themselves around this fact. The four factors listed in section 107 (and reviewed one by one in the majority opinion) are considerations that bear upon whether a particular use is fair; but those factors are informed by a preamble sentence in section 107 that recites in pertinent part that "the fair use of a copyrighted work, including such use by reproduction in copies ... for purposes such as ... scholarship, or research, is not an infringement of copyright."

"[T]here is a strong presumption that factor one favors the defendant if the allegedly infringing work fits the description of uses described in section 107." Wright v. Warner Books, Inc., 953 F.2d 731, 736 (2d Cir.1991). Much of our fair use case law has been generated by the use of quotation in biographies, a practice that fits "'comfortably within' the[ ] statutory categories 'of uses illustrative of uses that can be fair.'" New Era Publications Int'l, ApS v. Carol Pub. Group (New Era II), 904 F.2d 152, 156 (2d Cir.) (quoting Salinger v. Random House, Inc., 811 F.2d 90, 96 (2d Cir.), cert. denied, 484 U.S. 890 (1987)), cert. denied, 498 U.S. 921(1990)). The photocopying of journal articles as part of ongoing scientific research fits just as squarely within the scope of these illustrative fair uses. This court has stated on several occasions: "'[I]f a book falls into one of these categories [i.e., criticism, scholarship or research], assessment of the first fair use factor should be at an end....'" Wright, 953 F.2d at 736 (quoting New Era II, 904 F.2d at 156 (quoting New Era Publications Int'l, ApS v. Henry Holt & Co., 884 F.2d 659, 661 (2d Cir.1989) (Miner, J., concurring in denial of rehearing in banc))). This is so "even though, as will often be the case," the copyist "'anticipates profits.'" Wright, 953 F.2d at 736-37 (quoting New Era II, 904 F.2d at 156 (quoting Salinger, 811 F.2d at 96)).

The majority recognizes that photocopying puts the articles into a "a useful format," 60 F.3d at 923, for use in a laboratory, where the bound volume or whole journal would be cumbersome and subject to damage, and that "these purposes might suffice to tilt the first fair use factor in favor of Texaco if these purposes were dominant." 60 F.3d at 919. This view modifies the district court's conclusion that fair use might allow the photocopying of whole articles for use in the laboratory "if the original were copied onto plastic paper so that it could be used in a wet environment, onto metal so that it would resist extreme heat, onto durable archival paper to prevent deterioration, or onto microfilm to conserve space...." American Geophysical Union v. Texaco Inc. 802 F.Supp. 1, 14 (1992). The majority notes, however, that Dr. Chickering "did not even have occasion to use five of the photocopied articles at all," 60 F.3d at 919, and emphasizes that Dr. Chickering's photocopying was done to assemble a personal file used, in Dr. Chickering's phrase, for "future retrieval and reference." 60 F.3d at 919. The majority calls this a the "predominant[ly] archival purpose of the copying," 60 F.3d at 924, and therefore not in the nature of research. In my view, the research function is far broader than the majority opinion and the district court opinion contemplate.

Replication of laboratory experiments is of course a form of scientific research, but it is not the whole or main part of it. Often, a researcher needs to know what others have thought and done in order to steer clear of repetition and dead ends, to evaluate theories and hypotheses for possible theoretical development or commercial application, to give credit to others, and much else. None of this requires a scientist to enter a laboratory. In any event, to describe Dr. Chickering's file as "archival," as the majority does, is a misnomer: an archive is ordinarily a bulk of documents accumulated by a bureaucratic process and serving as a resource for public or institutional reference. By contrast, Dr. Chickering's personal file contains articles available for reference to assist the memory, curiosity and ongoing inquiries of a single researcher. As such, it is part of a transformative process of scientific research that has a long history.

The majority concludes that the photocopying was "done for the primary purpose of providing Chickering with his own personal copy of each article," dismissively rejecting (in a footnote) Texaco's argument that the true, and fundamental, purpose for the photocopying was research: Though Texaco claims that its copying is for "research" as that term is used in the preamble of section 107, this characterization might somewhat overstate the matter. Chickering has not used portions of articles from *Catalysis* in his own published piece of research, nor has he had to duplicate some portion of copyrighted material directly in the course of conducting an experiment or investigation. Rather, entire articles were copied as an intermediate step that might abet Chickering's research. 60 F.3d at 920 n. 7. In my view, it is no overstatement to call this process research. I have difficulty thinking of anything else to call it.

The scientific method, properly conceived, is much more than a system of repeated laboratory experimentation. Rather, it is a dynamic process of "planned co-operation of scientists, each of whom uses and continues the investigations of his predecessors...." Edgar Zilsel, "The Sociological Roots of Science," in Hugh F. Kearney, ed. *Origins of the Scientific Revolution*, 97 (1968). The scientific journal is an essential tool in this incremental, ongoing, transformative process. The physicist Peter L. Kapitza has noted the central role that journals play in it:

> [T]he fundamental factor determining the collective work of scientists is the organization of information exchange. The more effectively this is carried out, the greater its scale and the more intensively science develops. The most effective method of scientific information up to date [sic] appears to be its dissemination through periodicals, since one can most widely and quickly communicate the scientific achievements in this way to a large number of interested scientists.

Peter L. Kapitza, Experiment, Theory, Practice, 173 (1980). Today there are some 200,000 scientific journals published worldwide. Id. at 174.

A use that is reasonable and customary is likely to be a fair one. See Harper & Row Publishers, Inc. v. Nation Enterprises, 471 U.S. 539, 550, 105 S.Ct. 2218, 2225, 85 L.Ed.2d 588 (1985) ("the fair use doctrine was predicated on the author's implied consent to 'reasonable and customary' use"). The district court, the majority and I start from the same place in assessing whether Dr. Chickering's photocopying is a reasonable and customary use of the material: making single photocopies for research and scholarly purposes has been considered both reasonable and customary for as long as photocopying technology has been in existence. See Williams & Wilkins Co. v. United States, 487 F.2d 1345, 1355-56 (Ct. Cl. 1973), aff'd by an equally divided court, 420 U.S. 376 (1976). The majority quotes the district court's short answer to this important insight: "To the extent the copying practice was 'reasonable' in 1973 [when Williams v. Wilkins was decided], it has ceased to be 'reasonable' as the reasons that justified it before [photocopying licensing] have ceased to exist." 802 F.Supp. at 25. I do not agree at all that a reasonable and customary use becomes unfair when the copyright holder develops a way to exact an additional price for the same product. Moreover, I view the advent of the CCC as an event that bears analytically upon the distinct question of whether Dr. Chickering's use supersedes the original (the fourth factor). I therefore reach an issue--reasonable and customary use--not explored by the district court or by the majority.

Consider what Dr. Chickering actually does with scientific journals. As a research scientist, he routinely sifts through the latest research done by his peers, much of which is printed in journals such as *Catalysis*. He determines which articles potentially assist his specific trains of thought and lines of inquiry, and he photocopies them. Relative to the volume of articles in each issue, his photocopying is insubstantial. He then files the articles for possible future use or study. As the majority observes, "[b]efore modern photocopying, Chickering probably would have converted the original article into a more serviceable form by taking notes, whether cursory or extended; today he can do so with a photocopying machine." 60 F.3d at 923-24. The majority's footnote 10, appended to this passage, questions whether or not a scholar's handwritten copy of a full work is "necessarily" a fair use. As the majority adds, however, *Williams & Wilkins* says it is: [I]t is almost unanimously accepted that a scholar can make a handwritten copy of an entire copyrighted article for his own use, and in the era before photoduplication it was not uncommon (and not seriously questioned) that he could have his secretary make a typed copy for his personal use and files. These customary facts of copyright-life are among our givens. Williams & Wilkins, 487 F.2d at 1350. What Dr. Chickering does is simply a technologically assisted form of note-taking, such as has long been customary among researchers: the photocopy machine saves Dr. Chickering the toil and time of recording notes on index cards or in notebooks, and improves the accuracy and range of the data, charts, and formulas he can extract from the passing stream of information; but the note-taking purpose remains the same.

The anthropologist Bruno Latour spent two years studying scientists at the Salk Institute for Biological Sciences. During the course of his study, he conducted anthropological observations of a neurobiologist working on an article for a journal. This scientist's desk was littered with copies of journal articles authored by other scientists: Xeroxed copies of articles, with words underlined and exclamation marks in the margins, are everywhere. Drafts of articles in preparation intermingle with diagrams scribbled on scrap paper, letters from colleagues and reams of paper spewed out by the computer in the next room; pages cut from articles are glued to other pages; excerpts from draft paragraphs change hands between colleagues while more advanced drafts pass from office to office being altered constantly, retyped, recorrected, and eventually crushed into the format of this or that journal. Bruno Latour and Steve Woolgar, Laboratory Life: The Social Construction of Scientific Facts, 49 (1979). One essential step toward this drafting process is the accumulation over time of the journal articles that reflect the current state of knowledge that the journal author seeks to advance. Latour confirms that the photocopying of journal articles, and the use of them, is customary and integral to the creative process of science.

The majority emphasizes that, as it happened, Dr. Chickering did not "use" the photocopied articles because, in five out of eight instances, he filed them away. There is nothing odd about making notes one does not immediately use, or that one may never consult again. Photocopies, which to Dr. Chickering are the functional counterpart of notes, are used (or not, as the case may be) in the same way. Dr. Chickering's filing away of these photocopies does not subvert his claim of fair use. Like the majority, I am convinced that his deposit of the photocopied articles in his personal file, pending his personal use of them in the future, is an important fact bearing upon fair use; but the dominant significance of that fact, under the first factor of section 107, is that (whether he "uses" them or files them) the articles are not re-sold or retailed in any way. If the copies were sold by Dr. Chickering, that would be a telling--possibly determinative--fact. What Dr. Chickering has done reinforces the view that his photocopying was not commercial in purpose or character.

The majority recognizes that, while the photocopying of the *Catalysis* articles was "not technically a transformative use," there is "significant independent value" in converting the articles to a photocopied format. 37 F.3d at 891. Nevertheless, the majority concludes that this transformative process does not militate in favor of fair use because of the "predominant archival purpose". In my view, however, the "archival purpose" is just a step in the process of taking and keeping notes, which should ordinarily entail no transformation of the material. Good notes, being as precise and copious as time allows, do not aspire to transform the original text, but are useful in research only to the extent that they faithfully record the original. ~~Accordingly~~Such notes, ~~I find the nature and purpose of the use to be fully transformative, and therefore find that this factor weighs clearly~~however, are important raw material in ~~favor of Texaco~~the synthesis of new ideas. Accordingly, I find the nature and purpose of the use to be fully transformative.

The majority emphasizes passim that the photocopying condemned here is "systematic" and "institutional". These terms furnish a ground for distinguishing this case from the case that the majority expressly does not reach: the copying of journal articles by an individual researcher outside an institutional framework. For all the reasons adduced above, I conclude that the institutional environment in which Dr. Chickering works does not alter the character of the copying done by him or at his instance, and that the selection by an individual scientist of the articles useful to that scientist's own inquiries is not systematic copying, and does not become systematic because some number of other scientists in the same institution--four hundred or four-- are doing the same thing.

First, the majority's reliance on Texaco's institutional framework does not limit the potentially uncontrolled ramifications of the result. Research is largely an institutional endeavor nowadays, conducted by employees pursuing the overall goals of corporations, university laboratories, courts and law firms, governments and their agencies, think-tanks, publishers of newspapers and magazines, and other kinds of institutions. The majority's limitation of its holding to institutional environments may give comfort to inventors in bicycle shops, scientists in garage laboratories, freelance book reviewers, and solo conspiracy theorists, but it is not otherwise meaningful.

The majority's reliance on the systematic character of the photocopying here also seems to me erroneous. The majority deems Texaco's photocopying systematic because Texaco uses circulation lists to route a copy of each journal issue to the scientists interested in the field. The majority, however, ignores the one determinative issue: whether the decision to photocopy individual articles is made by the individual researcher, as Dr. Chickering did here. Journal issues may be systematically circulated to all scientists in a given group, rather than (say) at random, but the circulation of journal issues is not photocopying, systematic or otherwise. The journal issues circulated by Texaco are procured by subscription. Once Texaco receives the subscription copies from the publisher, Texaco is free to circulate them in-house so that they can be seen by as many scientists as can lay eyes on them. This circulation of copies allows individual scientists to select individual articles for copying. The majority opinion, which leaves open the idea that this practice may comport with copyright law if done by an individual scientist, does not explain why it is impermissible when done by more than one.

The nature and purpose of the use is not affected by Texaco's size or institutional nature, or by Texaco's circulation of its subscription journals to its scientists. I therefore find that this factor weighs clearly in favor of Texaco.

B. Effect Upon Potential Market or Value

In gauging the effect of Dr. Chickering's photocopying on the potential market or value of the copyrighted work, the majority properly considers two separate means of marketing: (1) journal subscriptions and sales, and (2) licensing revenues and fees.

(1) Subscriptions and sales. The majority makes clear that, considered solely in terms of journal subscriptions and sales, this factor is a toss-up that may tip in the publisher's favor, but only after teetering for a while: "At best, the loss of a few journal subscriptions tips the fourth factor only slightly toward the publishers because evidence of such loss is weak evidence that the copied articles themselves have lost any value." 37 F.3d at 896-97. The majority pointedly observes that no evidence is offered that the photocopying at issue here, "if widespread, would impair the marketability of journals...." 37 F.3d at 896. Since Dr. Chickering's use maximizes the utility of a *Catalysis* subscription for the only audience it is ever likely to capture, I do not consider that the failure of proof in this respect is an oversight by the publishers or their able counsel.

As to the individual articles photocopied by Dr. Chickering, I agree with the majority--as I read the opinion--that one cannot put a finger on any loss suffered by the publishers in the value of the individual articles or in the traditional market for subscriptions and back issues. The district court found that Texaco would not purchase back-issues or back volumes in the numbers needed to supply individual copies of articles to individual scientists.

Finally, the circulation of *Catalysis* among a number of Texaco scientists can come as no surprise to the publisher of *Catalysis*, which charges double the normal subscription rate to institutional subscribers. The publisher must therefore assume that, unless they are reading *Catalysis* for pleasure or committing it to memory, the scientists will extract what they need and arrange to copy it for personal use before passing along the institutional copies.

(2) Licensing Revenues and Fees. The majority states that "[o]nly an impact on potential licensing revenues for traditional, reasonable, or likely to be developed markets should be legally cognizable when evaluating a secondary use's 'effect upon the potential market for or value of the copyrighted work.' " 37 F.3d at 897-98. That statement of the law, with which I fully agree, supports the conclusion that the availability of a CCC license has little to do with fair use. The Supreme Court, in *Harper & Row*, held that this fourth factor addresses " 'use that supplants any part of the normal market for a copyrighted work....' " 471 U.S. at 568 (quoting S.Rep. No. 473, 94th Cong., 1st Sess. 65 (1975)). The Court has more recently declared, in considering the fair use ramifications of parody, that "[t]he market for potential derivative uses includes only those that creators of original works would in general develop or license others to develop." Campbell v. Acuff-Rose Music, Inc., 114 S.Ct. 1164, 1178 (1994). One factor deemed to make parody eligible for treatment as a fair use is that copyright holders do not ordinarily license artistic criticisms of their own works. However, even if authors were to seek to license these secondary works, it is not clear that they would succeed, because the Court found the secondary works to be a fair use: "when ... the second use is transformative, market substitution is at least less certain, and market harm may not be so readily inferred." Id. at 1177.

In this case the only harm to a market is to the supposed market in photocopy licenses. The CCC scheme is neither traditional nor reasonable; and its development into a real market is subject to substantial impediments. There is a circularity to the problem: the market will not crystallize unless courts reject the fair use argument that Texaco presents; but, under the statutory test, we cannot declare a use to be an infringement unless (assuming other factors also weigh in favor of the secondary user) there is a market to be harmed. At present, only a fraction of journal publishers have sought to exact these fees. I would hold that this fourth factor decisively weighs in favor of Texaco, because there is no normal market in photocopy licenses, and no real consensus among publishers that there ought to be one.

The majority holds that photocopying journal articles without a license is an infringement. Yet it is stipulated that (a) institutions such as Texaco subscribe to numerous journals, only 30 percent of which are covered by a CCC license; (b) not all publications of each CCC member are covered by the CCC licenses; and (c) not all the articles in publications covered by the CCC are copyrighted. It follows that no CCC license can assure a scientist that photocopying any given article is legal. I will separately consider the Transactional Reporting Service (the per-copy transactional license) and the Annual Authorization Service (the blanket license). I confine my discussion here to scientists, although I note that the record reflects CCC's intention to pursue licensing arrangements in other sectors as well.

Under a transactional license, the user must undertake copyright research every time an article is photocopied. First, one must consult a directory to determine whether or not the publisher of the journal is a member of the CCC. If it is, one must ascertain whether the particular publication is one that is covered by the CCC arrangement, because not all publications of participating publishers are covered. Then one must somehow determine whether the actual article is one in which the publisher actually holds a copyright, since there are many articles that, for such reasons as government sponsorship of the research, are not subject to copyright. The production director of plaintiff Springer-Verlag testified at trial that it is almost impossible to tell which articles might be covered by a copyright. Since even an expert has difficulty making such a determination, the transactional scheme would seem to require that an intellectual property lawyer be posted at each copy machine. Finally, once it is determined that the specific article is covered, the copyist will need to record in a log the date, name of publication, publisher, title and author of article, and number of pages copied.

It may be easier to hand copy the material. The transactions costs alone would compel users to purchase a blanket license. However, if (as the majority holds) three of the fair use factors tip in favor of the publishers even without considering the market for license fees, a blanket license is offers Texaco no safe harbor. Individual publishers remain free to stand upon the rights conferred in this Court's opinion, and negotiate separate licenses with separate terms, or sell offprints and refuse any license at all. Unless the each publisher's licensing rights are made to depend upon whether or not the that publisher participates in the CCC, we have the beginnings of a total market failure: with many thousands of scientific publications in circulation, a user cannot negotiate licensing fees individually with numerous publishers--unless it does nothing else. For many publications, licenses are simply not available. As to those, Dr. Chickering has the choice of hand copying, typescript, or the photocopying of selected pages only.

The blanket license fares no better. The CCC license cannot confer absolution for the photocopying of articles published by non-members of the CCC. Nor can the participating publishers properly collect fees for the photocopying of articles for which they do not hold the copyright. The district court found that there is currently a viable market for licensing, chiefly for the following reasons: (a) "[M]any of the largest corporations involved in research have become licensees under a CCC Annual Authorization." 802 F.Supp. at 24. However, until this case is decided, companies have had little choice but to become licensees or defendants. (b) The CCC has developed an Annual Authorization arrangement that "permits free copying without any administrative burden of record-keeping or reporting." Id. That system works, however, only if one ignores the rights of publishers who are non-members of the CCC. (c) "[P]ublishers and individual users have ... developed private annual licensing agreements. For example, AT & T Bell Labs, in addition to its membership in the CCC, has over 200 agreements with publishers covering photocopying with respect to some 350 journals that are not registered with the CCC. Furthermore, publishers have extended photocopying licenses to document delivery services." Id. at 24-25. These developments "(and the other parallel steps taken by the owner-user communities)", satisfy the district court that "[r]easonably priced, administratively tolerable licensing procedures are available...." Id. at 25.

It is hard to escape the conclusion that the existence of the CCC--or the perception that the CCC and other schemes for collecting license fees are or may become "administratively tolerable"--is the chief support for the idea that photocopying scholarly articles is unfair in the first place. The majority finds it "sensible" that a use "should be considered 'less fair' when there is a ready market or means to pay for the use." 60 F.3d at 931. That view is sensible only to a point. There is no technological or commercial impediment to imposing a fee for use of a work in a parody, or for the quotation of a paragraph in a review or biography. Many publishers could probably unite to fund a bureaucracy that would collect such fees. The majority is sensitive to this problem, but concludes that "[t]he vice of circular reasoning arises only if the availability of payment is conclusive against fair use." 60 F.3d at 931. That vice is not avoided here. The majority expressly declines to "decide how the fair use balance would be resolved if a photocopying license for *Catalysis* articles were not currently available." 60 F.3d at 931. Moreover, the "important" fourth factor, 60 F.3d at 931, tips in favor of the publishers (according to the majority) "[p]rimarily because of lost licensing revenue" and only "to a minor extent" on the basis of journal sales and subscriptions. 60 F.3d at 931.

I do not agree with the majority that the publishers "have created, primarily through the CCC, a workable market for institutional users to obtain licenses for the right to produce their own copies of individual articles via photocopying." 60 F.3d at 930. By the CCC's admission, in its correspondence with the Antitrust Division of the Justice Department, "the mechanism for the negotiation of a photocopy license fee is often not even in place.... Nor can it be said that CCC's current licensing programs have adequately met the market's needs."[1] There is nothing workable, and there is no market.

Even if the CCC is or becomes workable, the holder of a CCC blanket license is not thereby privileged to photocopy journal articles published by non-members of the CCC, as to which articles there is no "ready market or means to pay for the fair use". See 60 F.3d at 931. This Court has ended fair-use photocopying with respect to a large population of journals, but the CCC mechanism allows fair-use photocopying only of some of them. The facts before us demonstrate that the holder of a blanket license must still deal separately with CCC-member Bell Labs as to certain hundreds of its publications. With respect to the journals for which the publishers do not market licenses, users will either (a) research which publications are in this category and copy them longhand, in typescript or in partial photocopy, or (b) ignore our fair-use doctrine as unworkable. Neither option serves scientific inquiry or respect for copyright. In any event, it seems to me that when a journal is used in a customary way--a way that the authors uniformly intend and wish--the user should not be subjected on a day to day

---

[1] Letter from R. Bruce Rich, Weil, Gotshal & Manges (as counsel to CCC) to Thomas H. Liddle, Antitrust Division, United States Department of Justice (February 2, 1992) (filed as part of supplementation of record, pursuant to motion granted on October 12, 1993).

basis to burdens that cannot be satisfied without a team of intellectual property lawyers and researchers.

The fourth factor tips decidedly in Texaco's favor because there is no appreciable impairment of the publishing revenue from journal subscriptions and sales; because the publisher captures additional revenue from institutional users by charging a double subscription price (and can presumably charge any price the users will pay); and because the market for licensing is cumbersome and unrealized.

C. Equitable Considerations

The fair use doctrine is an "equitable rule of reason." Sony Corp. of America v. Universal City Studios, 464 U.S. 417, 448 & n. 31 (1984). Applying the doctrine requires a case-by-case review that includes the four factors listed in section 107; but the statutory list is not exhaustive or exclusive. See Harper & Row, 471 U.S. at 549. The purpose of this equitable rule is " 'to avoid rigid application of the copyright statute when, on occasion, it would stifle the very creativity which that law is designed to foster.' " Harper & Row, 471 U.S. at 550 n. 3 (quoting Iowa State University Research Foundation, Inc. v. American Broadcasting Cos., 621 F.2d 57, 60 (2d Cir.1980)).

" '[T]he author's consent to a reasonable use of his copyrighted works ha[s] always been implied by the courts as a necessary incident of the constitutional policy of promoting the progress of science and the useful arts, since a prohibition of such use would inhibit subsequent writers from attempting to improve upon prior works and thus ... frustrate the very ends sought to be attained.' " Harper & Row, 471 U.S. at 549 (quoting H. Ball, Law of Copyright and Literary Property 260 (1944)). "[T]he fair use doctrine [is] predicated on the author's implied consent to 'reasonable and customary' use when he release[s] his work for public consumption...." Id. at 550. All facts bearing upon the terms of that consent are germane to this analysis.

The single fact that evidences the fair use expectation of the people whose creativity Congress seeks to stimulate, is that they give away their copyright in order to promote their work, their ideas and their reputations. The district court found that the "publishers do not pay authors money to publish their articles...." American Geophysical, 802 F.Supp. at 26. The majority finds, "[n]o form of money payment is ever provided to authors whose works are published." 37 F.3d at 883-84; see also id. at 896 ("[P]ublishers do not make any payment to authors for the right to publish their articles or to acquire their copyrights....").

This is not to say, however, that the authors derive no benefit from the use of their works. To the contrary: "[T]he authors derive benefit from the publication of their works far more important than any small royalty the traffic might bear." American Geophysical, 802 F.Supp. at 26. The authors of scientific articles work and publish in order to gain distinction, appointment, resources, tenure. But they seek and derive absolutely no direct cash benefit from publication. It seems to me that this fact is of great importance: it means that, so long as the copyright system assures sufficient revenue to print and distribute scientific journals, the level of copyright revenue is not among the incentives that drive the authors to the creative acts that the copyright laws are intended to foster.

As to this issue, the majority adopts the district court's view that it is "irrelevant" because the authors have assigned the copyright to publishers who risk capital to achieve the wide dissemination of the articles that the authors want and need. 802 F.Supp. at 27. The district court greatly overstates the case in concluding that "[o]nce an author has assigned her copyright, her approval or disapproval of photocopying is of no further relevance." Id. As a commercial proposition, that is unassailable. But equitable considerations under the copyright law justify an inquiry into the incentives for creating the work--here, the scientific journal articles. See Harper & Row, 471 U.S. at 550 n. 3 (equitable rule of reason permits inquiry into whether "rigid application of the copyright statute ... would stifle the very creativity which that law is designed to foster."). " 'The immediate effect of our copyright law is to secure a fair return for an 'author's' creative labor. But the ultimate aim is, by this incentive, to stimulate artistic creativity for the general public good.' " Fogerty v. Fantasy, Inc., 114 S.Ct. 1023, 1029 (1994) (quoting Twentieth Century Music Corp. v. Aiken, 422 U.S. 151, 156 (1975)). To that end, we are reminded that: "The primary objective of copyright is not to reward the labor of authors, but '[t]o promote the Progress of Science and useful Arts.' To this end, copyright assures authors the right to their original expression, but encourages others to build freely upon the ideas and information conveyed by a work." Id. at 1030 (quoting Feist Publications, Inc. v. Rural Telephone Service Co., 499 U.S. 340, 349-50 (1991)).

The CCC's licensing fees unquestionably benefit the copyright holders, but no argument has been made that this additional revenue will fuel scientific creativity. According to Kapitza, "[e]very 10-15 years, the number of journals doubles and it has now reached the imposing number of 200,000." Experiment, Theory, Practice at 174. This proliferation of journals has been accomplished through sales and subscriptions. Clearly, the incentives currently in place for journal publishing assure a fair return, or else we would not see the exponential growth in scientific journals reported by Kapitza. Under the current system, publishers sell journals and subscriptions. They can, and do, charge institutional users more money, and are free to charge what they like.

Since the copyright laws seek to stimulate creativity, we should consider the incentives chiefly from the perspective of the authors and scientists. It has been recognized by this Court that in the scientific community, "what is valuable [to the authors] is recognition because it so often influences professional advancement and academic tenure." Weissmann v. Freeman, 868 F.2d 1313, 1324 (2d Cir.), cert. denied, 493 U.S. 883 (1989). From their point of view, then, what is truly important is the wide dissemination of their works to their colleagues.

The incentives for scientific publication have been in place since the project of science began to be perceived as a cooperative venture more than three centuries ago. See E. Zilsel, "The Sociological Roots of Science," in Hugh F. Kearney, ed., Origins of the Scientific Revolution, at 97 (1968) ("In his Nova Atlantis Bacon depicted an ideal state in which technological and scientific progress is reached by planned co-operation of scientists, each of whom uses and continues the investigations of his predecessors and fellow workers.").[2] Scientists communicate through journals, and use them to stake claims to new ideas, disseminate their ideas, and advance their careers and reputations. These "authors have a far greater interest in the wide dissemination of their work than in royalties...." American Geophysical, 802 F.Supp. at 27. That, evidently, is why they do not seek or expect royalties, and that is why licensing fees cannot be expected to increase or diminish their creativity or their drive to publish. The majority's ruling on fair use will add to the cost, time and effort that scientists spend to scan, keep and use journal articles, and will therefore tend to diminish the only reward that the authors seek from publication.

Nowhere in the case law is there support for the proposition that the monopoly granted by copyright is designed to ensure the holder a maximum economic return; rather, the law's purpose is to balance competing interests-- assuring the author a fair return, while permitting creative uses that build upon the author's work. See, e.g., Fogerty, 114 S.Ct. at 1029 ("While it is true that one of the goals of the Copyright Act is to discourage infringement, it is by no means the only goal of that Act.... 'The immediate effect of our copyright law is to secure a fair return for an 'author's' creative labor. But the ultimate aim is, by this incentive, to stimulate artistic creativity....'") (quoting Twentieth Century Music, 422 U.S. at 156 (1975)); Harper & Row, 471 U.S. at 546 ("The rights conferred by copyright are designed to assure contributors to the store of knowledge a fair return for their labors."). More fundamentally, Dr. Chickering's photocopying is part of a creative enterprise that Dr.

---

[2] The Royal Society of London, founded in 1662, was the first to give institutional validity to the Baconian principles of verified experimentation and public reporting of theories and experimental results. See William Eamon, "From the Secrets of Nature to Public Knowledge," reprinted in David C. Lindberg and Robert S. Westman, eds. Reappraisals of the Scientific Revolution, at 349-57 (1991). The "ideal of cooperative research" allowed scientists to approach their work more methodically, and the project of science evolved into the system of experimentation, reporting, verification, and modification that is the scientific method. Id. The first scientific journal, Philosophical Transactions, was published in London in the 1660s. A. Rupert Hall, The Revolution in Science, 1500-1700, 230-31 (1983). The publisher, Henry Oldenburg, "created the scientific journal and the scientific paper as a means of communication," providing a vehicle for international communication between scientists about the results of their experiments. Id. at 231. In Philosophical Transactions, "[f]requent controversies over moot theoretical issues directed experimental interest to the testing of the conflicting theories; new hypotheses were broadcast; recent scientific works were critically reviewed; and plans for initiating research along certain lines were made public." Robert K. Merton, Science, Technology & Society in Seventeenth Century England, 224 (1978).

Chickering conducts in common with the authors of the articles. For that reason, and the others stated in this dissent, I conclude that Dr. Chickering's photocopying of isolated journal articles to assist his own research inquiries is fair use.

NOTES

1. A factor in the settlement of the *Texaco* case may have been the appointment to the Court in 1994 of Justice Stephen Breyer. As a younger law professor Breyer wrote the law review article cited in the casebook at page 567, The Uneasy Case for Copyright: A Study of Copyright in Books, Photocopies, and Computer Programs, 84 Harv. L. Rev. 281 (1970). The article is deeply skeptical of copyright. As an articulate and able Justice with skeptical attitude about copyright, he might be expected to influence the Court in favor of a broad fair use priviledge.

2. The *Texaco* case was a test case. The precedent that results from the litigation will have an important influence on thousands of users of copyrighted works, large and small. Is Texaco, Inc., a large oil company, an adequate representative for the smaller copyright users? Texaco has already registered with the Copyright Clearance Center, along with other large oil companies. Large oil companies can reason that a fair use defense is unlikely to be available to them, or at least that they will make ideal test case defendants. But once they have registered with the Center, isn't their interest in insuring that everyone else has to register too? And isn't the burden of the clearance mechanism substantially less, proportionally, for large companies with substantial research budgets than it is for small ones? The CCC system may be easy enough for Texaco, AT&T and other large companies to comply with, but what about small businesses and individuals that may copy, for example, ten or fewer times a year?

Did the 1995 changes in the opinion address this issue by confining it to systematic copying by a large commercial firm?

What can be concluded about Texaco's suitability as a representative of the public when it settles the case on the brink of obtaining a hearing before the U.S. Supreme Court? Is it possible that the CCC hopes to use the Second Circuit decision to persuade most entities to sign up, so that when and if the issue ever reaches the Court payment of CCC fees will be a well-established practice?

The trial record in Williams & Wilkins Co. v. United States, 487 F.2d 1345, discussed casebook page 711, was far more extensive than the trial record in *Texaco*. See Paul Goldstein, Copyright's Highway 93-104 (1994) for a description of the trial in *Williams & Wilkins*. The record in *Williams & Wilkins*, for instance, contained the information that the authors of the articles copied received no compensation for the articles, that in many cases they paid publication fees, that they had no objection to the copying, and that in many cases their work had been supported by government grants.

One wonders by whom and under what conditions the articles in the JOURNAL OF CATALYSIS were written.

Isn't it odd that the question of whether the use is copyright infringement should turn on whether or not the owners of the copyrights have created an institution like the CCC? Does that mean that the practice of copying for the file was fair use before the CCC existed, but then ceased to be fair use? Does it mean that it is fair use to copy a work whose copyright owner is not a member of the CCC?

The CCC is, of course, based upon the successful example of ASCAP. There is one important difference, however. Musical copyrights are infringed only by *public* performances, and it is possible for ASCAP investigators to locate and observe public performances. Copying, however, can occur anywhere. With increasingly cheap, portable and fast copying machines available, how is the CCC going to achieve reasonable compliance levels?

3. What is the status of the type of copying described in *Texaco* in universities and other non-profit institutions. How about in the government? Are not many students, for instance, seeking to increase their knowledge so that they can command larger salaries in the market place? The Court explicitly recognizes that academic professionals receive benefits from their research activities. Would you advise a university to sign up with the Copyright Clearance Center?

4. Do the court's observations about § 108 mean that individuals and small businesses can go to libraries and make whatever copies they need for themselves, even if the result is that hundreds if not thousands of copies are made at the library? Could the scientists at Texaco go across the street one by one and copy the articles from volumes in a library independent of Texaco? What if Texaco supported the library though donations?

5. If the research scientists are not separate individuals for purposes of § 108 when they use the Texaco in-house library, what about the students and faculty at a university using the library of the university?

6. Could Judge Leval have reached any other result given the precedents? Is the argument that copying for the file is just another form of *Sony* time shifting plausible? Note that in *Sony* the viewers had not even purchased a single copy (or anything else for that matter). They only had the right to watch the program because a non-public performance is not infringing.

8. Note the high subscription price to *Catalysis*. During the 1960's and 70's a number of businessmen discovered that the publication of academic journals could be very profitable in spite of their small circulation by charging very high prices to the small number of research libraries who felt that they had to have a subscription. Robert Maxwell (now notorious because his suicide led to the discovery of a massive

financial fraud) made a fortune through his ownership of Pergamon Press, a publisher of academic journals based in Oxford, U.K., because of this strategy. The court notes Texaco's evidence that Academic Press is the crown jewel of Harcourt, Brace, Jovanovich Inc. In what other business is the raw material (the articles and the editing) provided free of charge? Isn't it likely that the willingness of libraries to pay the high subscription fees was related to the fact that once they had a copy they could make additional copies from it? Why does Academic Press charge less for a "personal" subscription? Now are the libraries to pay both high subscription fees and additional fees for copying?

PAGE 733. Add to Notes.

10. After *Nation* and the Second Circuit cases discussed in note 9, Congress considered at length and finally passed an amendment to § 107. The amendment added the final paragraph which provides: "The fact that a work is unpublished shall not itself bar a finding of fair use if such finding is made upon consideration of all the above factors." Pub.L. 102-492, Oct. 24, 1992, 106 Stat. 3145. What difference does the final paragraph make?

PAGE 733. Read in place of *Benny v. Loew's Incorporated*.

CAMPBELL AKA LUKE SKYYWALKER v. ACUFF-ROSE MUSIC, INC.
Supreme Court of the United States, 1994
510 U.S. 569, 114 Sup. Ct. 1164, 127 L.Ed. 2d 500 (1994)

JUSTICE SOUTER delivered the opinion of the Court.

We are called upon to decide whether 2 Live Crew's commercial parody of Roy Orbison's song, "Oh, Pretty Woman," may be a fair use within the meaning of the Copyright Act of 1976, 17 U. S. C. § 107. Although the District Court granted summary judgment for 2 Live Crew, the Court of Appeals reversed, holding the defense of fair use barred by the song's commercial character and excessive borrowing. Because we hold that a parody's commercial character is only one element to be weighed in a fair use enquiry, and that insufficient consideration was given to the nature of parody in weighing the degree of copying, we reverse and remand.

I

In 1964, Roy Orbison and William Dees wrote a rock ballad called "Oh, Pretty Woman" and assigned their rights in it to respondent Acuff-Rose Music, Inc. See Appendix A, infra [p. 289]. Acuff-Rose registered the song for copyright protection.

Petitioners Luther R. Campbell, Christopher Wongwon, Mark Ross, and David Hobbs, are collectively known as 2 Live Crew, a popular rap music group.[1] In 1989, Campbell wrote a song entitled "Pretty Woman," which he later described in an affidavit as intended, "through comical lyrics, to satirize the original work...." App. to Pet. for Cert. 80a. On July 5, 1989, 2 Live Crew's manager informed Acuff-Rose that 2 Live Crew had written a parody of "Oh, Pretty Woman," that they would afford all credit for ownership and authorship of the original song to Acuff-Rose, Dees, and Orbison, and that they were willing to pay a fee for the use they wished to make of it. Enclosed with the letter were a copy of the lyrics and a recording of 2 Live Crew's song. See Appendix B, infra, at [p. 289]. Acuff-Rose's agent refused permission, stating that "I am aware of the success enjoyed by 'The 2 Live Crews', but I must inform you that we cannot permit the use of a parody of 'Oh, Pretty Woman.'" App. to Pet. for Cert. 85a. Nonetheless, in June or July 1989, 2 Live Crew released records, cassette tapes, and compact discs of "Pretty Woman" in a collection of songs entitled "As Clean As They Wanna Be." The albums and compact discs identify the authors of "Pretty Woman" as Orbison and Dees and its publisher as Acuff-Rose.

Almost a year later, after nearly a quarter of a million copies of the recording had been sold, Acuff-Rose sued 2 Live Crew and its record company, Luke Skyywalker Records, for copyright infringement. The District Court granted summary judgment for 2 Live Crew, reasoning that the commercial purpose of 2 Live Crew's song was no bar to fair use; that 2 Live Crew's version was a parody, which "quickly degenerates into a play on words, substituting predictable lyrics with shocking ones" to show "how bland and banal the Orbison song" is; that 2 Live Crew had taken no more than was necessary to "conjure up" the original in order to parody it; and that it was "extremely unlikely that 2 Live Crew's song could adversely affect the market for the original." 754 F. Supp. 1150, 1154-1155, 1157-1158 (M.D. Tenn. 1991). The District Court weighed these factors and held that 2 Live Crew's song made fair use of Orbison's original. Id., at 1158-1159.

The Court of Appeals for the Sixth Circuit reversed and remanded. 972 F. 2d 1429, 1439 (1992). Although it assumed for the purpose of its opinion that 2 Live Crew's song was a parody of the Orbison original, the Court of Appeals thought the District Court had put too little emphasis on the fact that "every commercial use ... is presumptively ... unfair," Sony Corp. of America v. Universal City Studios, Inc., 464

---

[1] Rap has been defined as a "style of black American popular music consisting of improvised rhymes performed to a rhythmic accompaniment." The Norton/Grove Concise Encyclopedia of Music 613 (1988). 2 Live Crew plays "[b]ass music," a regional, hip-hop style of rap from the Liberty City area of Miami, Florida. Brief for Petitioners 34.

U. S. 417, 451 (1984), and it held that "the admittedly commercial nature" of the parody "requires the conclusion" that the first of four factors relevant under the statute weighs against a finding of fair use. 972 F. 2d, at 1435, 1437. Next, the Court of Appeals determined that, by "taking the heart of the original and making it the heart of a new work," 2 Live Crew had, qualitatively, taken too much. Id., at 1438. Finally, after noting that the effect on the potential market for the original (and the market for derivative works) is "undoubtedly the single most important element of fair use," Harper & Row, Publishers, Inc. v. Nation Enterprises, 471 U. S. 539, 566 (1985), the Court of Appeals faulted the District Court for "refus[ing] to indulge the presumption" that "harm for purposes of the fair use analysis has been established by the presumption attaching to commercial uses." 972 F. 2d, at 1438-1439. In sum, the court concluded that its "blatantly commercial purpose ... prevents this parody from being a fair use." Id., at 1439.

We granted certiorari, 507 U. S. (1993), to determine whether 2 Live Crew's commercial parody could be a fair use.

II

It is uncontested here that 2 Live Crew's song would be an infringement of Acuff-Rose's rights in "Oh, Pretty Woman," under the Copyright Act of 1976, 17 U. S. C. § 106, but for a finding of fair use through parody.[2] From the infancy of copyright protection, some opportunity for fair use of copyrighted materials has been thought necessary to fulfill copyright's very purpose, "[t]o promote the Progress of Science and useful Arts...." U. S. Const., Art. I, § 8, cl. 8. For as Justice Story explained, "[i]n truth, in literature, in science and in art, there are, and can be, few, if any, things, which in an abstract sense, are strictly new and original throughout. Every book in literature, science and art, borrows, and must necessarily borrow, and use much which was well known and used before." Emerson v. Davies, 8 F. Cas. 615, 619 (No. 4,436) (C.C.D. Mass. 1845). Similarly, Lord Ellenborough expressed the inherent tension in the need simultaneously to protect copyrighted material and to allow others to build upon it when he wrote, "while I shall think myself bound to secure every man in the enjoyment of his copyright, one must not put manacles upon science." Carey v. Kearsley, 4 Esp. 168, 170, 170 Eng. Rep. 679, 681 (K.B. 1803). In copyright cases brought under the Statute of Anne of 1710, English courts held that in some instances "fair abridgements" would not infringe an author's rights, see W. Patry, The Fair Use Privilege in Copyright Law 6-17 (1985) (hereinafter Patry); Leval, Toward a Fair Use Standard, 103 Harv. L. Rev. 1105, 1105 (1990) (hereinafter Leval), and although the First Congress enacted our initial copyright statute, Act of

---

[2] * * *. 2 Live Crew concedes that it is not entitled to a compulsory license under § 115 because its arrangement changes "the basic melody or fundamental character" of the original. § 115(a)(2).

May 31, 1790, 1 Stat. 124, without any explicit reference to "fair use," as it later came to be known, the doctrine was recognized by the American courts nonetheless.

* * * *

Congress meant § 107 "to restate the present judicial doctrine of fair use, not to change, narrow, or enlarge it in any way" and intended that courts continue the common law tradition of fair use adjudication. H. R. Rep. No. 94-1476, p. 66 (1976) (hereinafter House Report); S. Rep. No. 94-473, p. 62 (1975) (hereinafter Senate Report). The fair use doctrine thus "permits [and requires] courts to avoid rigid application of the copyright statute when, on occasion, it would stifle the very creativity which that law is designed to foster." Stewart v. Abend, 495 U. S. 207, 236 (1990) (internal quotation marks and citation omitted).

The task is not to be simplified with bright-line rules, for the statute, like the doctrine it recognizes, calls for case-by-case analysis. Harper & Row, 471 U. S., at 560; Sony, 464 U. S., at 448, and n. 31; House Report, pp. 65-66; Senate Report, p. 62. The text employs the terms "including" and "such as" in the preamble paragraph to indicate the "illustrative and not limitative" function of the examples given, § 101; see Harper & Row, supra, at 561, which thus provide only general guidance about the sorts of copying that courts and Congress most commonly had found to be fair uses. Nor may the four statutory factors be treated in isolation, one from another. All are to be explored, and the results weighed together, in light of the purposes of copyright. See Leval 1110-1111; Patry & Perlmutter, Fair Use Misconstrued: Profit, Presumptions, and Parody, 11 Cardozo Arts & Ent. L. J. 667, 685-687 (1993) (hereinafter Patry & Perlmutter).[10]

A

---

[10] Because the fair use enquiry often requires close questions of judgment as to the extent of permissible borrowing in cases involving parodies (or other critical works), courts may also wish to bear in mind that the goals of the copyright law, "to stimulate the creation and publication of edifying matter," Leval 1134, are not always best served by automatically granting injunctive relief when parodists are found to have gone beyond the bounds of fair use. See 17 U. S. C. § 502(a) (court "may ... grant ... injunctions on such terms as it may deem reasonable to prevent or restrain infringement") (emphasis added); Leval 1132 (while in the "vast majority of cases, [an injunctive] remedy is justified because most infringements are simple piracy," such cases are "worlds apart from many of those raising reasonable contentions of fair use" where "there may be a strong public interest in the publication of the secondary work [and] the copyright owner's interest may be adequately protected by an award of damages for whatever infringement is found"); Abend v. MCA, Inc., 863 F. 2d 1465, 1479 (CA9 1988) (finding "special circumstances" that would cause "great injustice" to defendants and "public injury" were injunction to issue), aff'd sub nom. Stewart v. Abend, 495 U. S. 207 (1990).

The first factor in a fair use enquiry is "the purpose and character of the use, including whether such use is of a commercial nature or is for nonprofit educational purposes." § 107(1). * * *. The enquiry here may be guided by the examples given in the preamble to § 107, looking to whether the use is for criticism, or comment, or news reporting, and the like, see § 107. The central purpose of this investigation is to see, in Justice Story's words, whether the new work merely "supersede[s] the objects" of the original creation, Folsom v. Marsh, [9 F. Cas. 342, 348 (No. 4,901) (C.C.D. Mass. 1841)] * * * ; it asks, in other words, whether and to what extent the new work is "transformative." Leval 1111. Although such transformative use is not absolutely necessary for a finding of fair use, *Sony,* supra, at 455, n. 40,[11] the goal of copyright, to promote science and the arts, is generally furthered by the creation of transformative works. Such works thus lie at the heart of the fair use doctrine's guarantee of breathing space within the confines of copyright, see, e.g., *Sony,* supra, at 478-480 (Blackmun, J., dissenting), and the more transformative the new work, the less will be the significance of other factors, like commercialism, that may weigh against a finding of fair use.

This Court has only once before even considered whether parody may be fair use, and that time issued no opinion because of the Court's equal division. Benny v. Loew's Inc., 239 F. 2d 532 (9th Cir. 1956), aff'd sub nom. Columbia Broadcasting System, Inc. v. Loew's Inc., 356 U. S. 43 (1958). Suffice it to say now that parody has an obvious claim to transformative value, as Acuff-Rose itself does not deny. Like less ostensibly humorous forms of criticism, it can provide social benefit, by shedding light on an earlier work, and, in the process, creating a new one. We thus line up with the courts that have held that parody, like other comment or criticism, may claim fair use under § 107. See, e.g., Fisher v. Dees, 794 F. 2d 432 (9th Cir. 1986) ("When Sonny Sniffs Glue," a parody of "When Sunny Gets Blue," is fair use); Elsmere Music, Inc. v. National Broadcasting Co., 482 F. Supp. 741 (S.D.N.Y.), aff'd, 623 F. 2d 252 (2nd Cir. 1980) ("I Love Sodom," a "Saturday Night Live" television parody of "I Love New York" is fair use); see also House Report, p. 65; Senate Report, p. 61 ("[U]se in a parody of some of the content of the work parodied" may be fair use).

The germ of parody lies in the definition of the Greek parodeia, quoted in Judge Nelson's Court of Appeals dissent, as "a song sung alongside another." 972 F. 2d, at 1440, quoting 7 Encyclopedia Britannica 768 (15th ed. 1975). Modern dictionaries accordingly describe a parody as a "literary or artistic work that imitates the characteristic style of an author or a work for comic effect or ridicule,"[12] or as a "composition in prose or verse in which the characteristic turns of thought and phrase

---

[11] The obvious statutory exception to this focus on transformative uses is the straight reproduction of multiple copies for classroom distribution.

[12] The American Heritage Dictionary 1317 (3d ed. 1992).

in an author or class of authors are imitated in such a way as to make them appear ridiculous."[13] For the purposes of copyright law, the nub of the definitions, and the heart of any parodist's claim to quote from existing material, is the use of some elements of a prior author's composition to create a new one that, at least in part, comments on that author's works. * * *. If, on the contrary, the commentary has no critical bearing on the substance or style of the original composition, which the alleged infringer merely uses to get attention or to avoid the drudgery in working up something fresh, the claim to fairness in borrowing from another's work diminishes accordingly (if it does not vanish), and other factors, like the extent of its commerciality, loom larger.[14] Parody needs to mimic an original to make its point, and so has some claim to use the creation of its victim's (or collective victims') imagination, whereas satire can stand on its own two feet and so requires justification for the very act of borrowing.[15] * * *.

The fact that parody can claim legitimacy for some appropriation does not, of course, tell either parodist or judge much about where to draw the line. Like a book review quoting the copyrighted material criticized, parody may or may not be fair use, and petitioner's suggestion that any parodic use is presumptively fair has no more justification in law or fact than the equally hopeful claim that any use for news reporting should be presumed fair, see Harper & Row, 471 U. S., at 561. The Act has no hint of an evidentiary preference for parodists over their victims, and no workable presumption for parody could take account of the fact that parody often shades into satire when society is lampooned through its creative artifacts, or that a work may contain both parodic and non-parodic elements. Accordingly, parody, like any other use, has to work its way through the relevant factors, and be judged case by case, in light of the ends of the copyright law.

---

[13] 11 The Oxford English Dictionary 247 (2d ed. 1989).

[14] A parody that more loosely targets an original than the parody presented here may still be sufficiently aimed at an original work to come within our analysis of parody. If a parody whose wide dissemination in the market runs the risk of serving as a substitute for the original or licensed derivatives (see infra, discussing factor four), it is more incumbent on one claiming fair use to establish the extent of transformation and the parody's critical relationship to the original. By contrast, when there is little or no risk of market substitution, whether because of the large extent of transformation of the earlier work, the new work's minimal distribution in the market, the small extent to which it borrows from an original, or other factors, taking parodic aim at an original is a less critical factor in the analysis, and looser forms of parody may be found to be fair use, as may satire with lesser justification for the borrowing than would otherwise be required.

[15] Satire has been defined as a work "in which prevalent follies or vices are assailed with ridicule," 14 The Oxford English Dictionary 500 (2d ed. 1989), or are "attacked through irony, derision, or wit," The American Heritage Dictionary 1604 (3d ed. 1992).

Here, the District Court held, and the Court of Appeals assumed, that 2 Live Crew's "Pretty Woman" contains parody, commenting on and criticizing the original work, whatever it may have to say about society at large. As the District Court remarked, the words of 2 Live Crew's song copy the original's first line, but then "quickly degenerat[e] into a play on words, substituting predictable lyrics with shocking ones ... [that] derisively demonstrat[e] how bland and banal the Orbison song seems to them." 754 F. Supp., at 1155 (footnote omitted). Judge Nelson, dissenting below, came to the same conclusion, that the 2 Live Crew song "was clearly intended to ridicule the white-bread original" and "reminds us that sexual congress with nameless streetwalkers is not necessarily the stuff of romance and is not necessarily without its consequences. The singers (there are several) have the same thing on their minds as did the lonely man with the nasal voice, but here there is no hint of wine and roses." 972 F. 2d, at 1442. Although the majority below had difficulty discerning any criticism of the original in 2 Live Crew's song, it assumed for purposes of its opinion that there was some. Id., at 1435-1436, and n. 8.

We have less difficulty in finding that critical element in 2 Live Crew's song than the Court of Appeals did, although having found it we will not take the further step of evaluating its quality. The threshold question when fair use is raised in defense of parody is whether a parodic character may reasonably be perceived.[16] Whether, going beyond that, parody is in good taste or bad does not and should not matter to fair use. As Justice Holmes explained, "[i]t would be a dangerous undertaking for persons trained only to the law to constitute themselves final judges of the worth of [a work], outside of the narrowest and most obvious limits. At the one extreme some works of genius would be sure to miss appreciation. Their very novelty would make them repulsive until the public had learned the new language in which their author spoke." Bleistein v. Donaldson Lithographing Co., 188 U. S. 239, 251 (1903) (circus posters have copyright protection); cf. Yankee Publishing Inc. v. News America Publishing, Inc., 809 F. Supp. 267, 280 (S.D.N.Y. 1992) (Leval, J.) ("First Amendment protections do not apply only to those who speak clearly, whose jokes are funny, and whose parodies succeed") (trademark case).

While we might not assign a high rank to the parodic element here, we think it fair to say that 2 Live Crew's song reasonably could be perceived as commenting on the original or criticizing it, to some degree. 2 Live Crew juxtaposes the romantic musings of a man whose fantasy comes true, with degrading taunts, a bawdy demand for sex, and a sigh of relief from paternal responsibility. The later words can be taken

---

[16] The only further judgment, indeed, that a court may pass on a work goes to an assessment of whether the parodic element is slight or great, and the copying small or extensive in relation to the parodic element, for a work with slight parodic element and extensive copying will be more likely to merely "supersede the objects" of the original. See infra, at, discussing factors three and four.

as a comment on the naivete of the original of an earlier day, as a rejection of its sentiment that ignores the ugliness of street life and the debasement that it signifies. It is this joinder of reference and ridicule that marks off the author's choice of parody from the other types of comment and criticism that traditionally have had a claim to fair use protection as transformative works.

The Court of Appeals, however, immediately cut short the enquiry into 2 Live Crew's fair use claim by confining its treatment of the first factor essentially to one relevant fact, the commercial nature of the use. The court then inflated the significance of this fact by applying a presumption ostensibly culled from *Sony*, that "every commercial use of copyrighted material is presumptively ... unfair...." *Sony*, 464 U. S., at 451. In giving virtually dispositive weight to the commercial nature of the parody, the Court of Appeals erred.

The language of the statute makes clear that the commercial or nonprofit educational purpose of a work is only one element of the first factor enquiry into its purpose and character. Section 107(1) uses the term "including" to begin the dependent clause referring to commercial use, and the main clause speaks of a broader investigation into "purpose and character." As we explained in *Harper & Row*, Congress resisted attempts to narrow the ambit of this traditional enquiry by adopting categories of presumptively fair use, and it urged courts to preserve the breadth of their traditionally ample view of the universe of relevant evidence. 471 U. S., at 561; House Report, p. 66. Accordingly, the mere fact that a use is educational and not for profit does not insulate it from a finding of infringement, any more than the commercial character of a use bars a finding of fairness. If, indeed, commerciality carried presumptive force against a finding of fairness, the presumption would swallow nearly all of the illustrative uses listed in the preamble paragraph of § 107, including news reporting, comment, criticism, teaching, scholarship, and research, since these activities "are generally conducted for profit in this country." *Harper & Row*, supra, at 592 (Brennan, J., dissenting). Congress could not have intended such a rule, which certainly is not inferable from the common-law cases, arising as they did from the world of letters in which Samuel Johnson could pronounce that "[n]o man but a blockhead ever wrote, except for money." 3 Boswell's Life of Johnson 19 (G. Hill ed. 1934).

Sony itself called for no hard evidentiary presumption. There, we emphasized the need for a "sensitive balancing of interests," 464 U. S., at 455, n. 40, noted that Congress had "eschewed a rigid, bright-line approach to fair use," id., at 449, n. 31, and stated that the commercial or nonprofit educational character of a work is "not conclusive," id., at 448-449, but rather a fact to be "weighed along with other[s] in fair use decisions." Id., at 449, n. 32 (quoting House Report, p. 66). The Court of Appeals's elevation of one sentence from *Sony* to a per se rule thus runs as much counter to Sony itself as to the long common-law tradition of fair use adjudication. Rather, as we explained in *Harper & Row*, *Sony* stands for the proposition that the "fact that a publication was commercial as opposed to nonprofit is a separate factor that tends to weigh against a finding of fair use." 471 U. S., at 562. But that is all, and the fact that even the force of that tendency will vary with the context is a further reason against elevating commerciality to hard presumptive significance. The use, for example, of a copyrighted work to advertise a product, even in a parody, will be entitled to less indulgence under the first factor of the fair use enquiry, than the sale of a parody for its own sake, let alone one performed a single time by students in school.

B

The second statutory factor, "the nature of the copyrighted work," § 107(2), draws on Justice Story's expression, the "value of the materials used." *Folsom v. Marsh*, 9 F. Cas., at 348. This factor calls for recognition that some works are closer to the core of intended copyright protection than others, with the consequence that fair use is more difficult to establish when the former works are copied. See, e.g., *Stewart v. Abend*, 495 U. S., at 237-238 (contrasting fictional short story with factual works); *Harper & Row*, 471 U. S., at 563-564 (contrasting soon-to-be-published memoir with published speech); Sony, 464 U. S., at 455, n. 40 (contrasting motion pictures with news broadcasts); *Feist*, 499 U. S., 348-351 (contrasting creative works with bare factual compilations); 3 M. Nimmer & D. Nimmer, Nimmer on Copyright s 13.05[A][2] (1993) (hereinafter Nimmer); Leval 1116. We agree with both the District Court and the Court of Appeals that the Orbison original's creative expression for public dissemination falls within the core of the copyright's protective purposes. 754 F. Supp., at 1155-1156; 972 F. 2d, at 1437. This fact, however, is not much help in this case, or ever likely to help much in separating the fair use sheep from the infringing goats in a parody case, since parodies almost invariably copy publicly known, expressive works.

C

The third factor asks whether "the amount and substantiality of the portion used in relation to the copyrighted work as a whole," § 107(3) (or, in Justice Story's words, "the quantity and value of the materials used," *Folsom v. Marsh,* supra, at 348) are reasonable in relation to the purpose of the copying. Here, attention turns to the persuasiveness of a parodist's justification for the particular copying done, and the enquiry will harken back to the first of the statutory factors, for, as in prior cases, we recognize that the extent of permissible copying varies with the purpose and character of the use. See *Sony*, 464 U. S., at 449-450 (reproduction of entire work "does not have its ordinary effect of militating against a finding of fair use" as to home videotaping of television programs); *Harper & Row*, 471 U. S., at 564 ("[E]ven substantial quotations might qualify as fair use in a review of a published work or a news account of a speech" but not in a scoop of a soon-to-be-published memoir). The facts bearing on this factor will also tend to address the fourth, by revealing the degree to which the parody may serve as a market substitute for the original or potentially licensed derivatives. See Leval 1123.

The District Court considered the song's parodic purpose in finding that 2 Live Crew had not helped themselves overmuch. 754 F. Supp., at 1156-1157. The Court of Appeals disagreed, stating that "[w]hile it may not be inappropriate to find that no more was taken than necessary, the copying was qualitatively substantial.... We conclude that taking the heart of the original and making it the heart of a new work was to purloin a substantial portion of the essence of the original." 972 F. 2d, at 1438.

The Court of Appeals is of course correct that this factor calls for thought not only about the quantity of the materials used, but about their quality and importance, too. In *Harper & Row*, for example, the Nation had taken only some 300 words out of President Ford's memoirs, but we signalled the significance of the quotations in finding them to amount to "the heart of the book," the part most likely to be newsworthy and important in licensing serialization. 471 U. S., at 564-566, 568 (internal quotation marks omitted). We also agree with the Court of Appeals that whether "a substantial portion of the infringing work was copied verbatim" from the copyrighted work is a relevant question, see id., at 565, for it may reveal a dearth of transformative character or purpose under the first factor, or a greater likelihood of market harm under the fourth; a work composed primarily of an original, particularly its heart, with little added or changed, is more likely to be a merely superseding use, fulfilling demand for the original.

Where we part company with the court below is in applying these guides to parody, and in particular to parody in the song before us. Parody presents a difficult case. Parody's humor, or in any event its comment, necessarily springs from recognizable allusion to its object through distorted imitation. Its art lies in the tension between a known original and its parodic twin. When parody takes aim at a particular original work, the parody must be able to "conjure up" at least enough of that original to make the object of its critical wit recognizable. See, e.g., Elsmere Music, 623 F. 2d, at 253, n. 1; Fisher v. Dees, 794 F. 2d, at 438-439. What makes for this recognition is quotation of the original's most distinctive or memorable features, which the parodist can be sure the audience will know. Once enough has been taken to assure identification, how much more is reasonable will depend, say, on the extent to which the song's overriding purpose and character is to parody the original or, in contrast, the likelihood that the parody may serve as a market substitute for the original. But using some characteristic features cannot be avoided.

We think the Court of Appeals was insufficiently appreciative of parody's need for the recognizable sight or sound when it ruled 2 Live Crew's use unreasonable as a matter of law. It is true, of course, that 2 Live Crew copied the characteristic opening bass riff (or musical phrase) of the original, and true that the words of the first line copy the Orbison lyrics. But if quotation of the opening riff and the first line may be said to go to the "heart" of the original, the heart is also what most readily conjures up the song for parody, and it is the heart at which parody takes aim. Copying does not become excessive in relation to parodic purpose merely because the portion taken was the original's heart. If 2 Live Crew had copied a significantly less memorable part of the original, it is difficult to see how its parodic character would have come through. See Fisher v. Dees, 794 F. 2d, at 439.

This is not, of course, to say that anyone who calls himself a parodist can skim the cream and get away scot free. In parody, as in news reporting, see Harper & Row, supra, context is everything, and the question of fairness asks what else the parodist did besides go to the heart of the original. It is significant that 2 Live Crew not only copied the first line of the original, but thereafter departed markedly from the Orbison lyrics for its own ends. 2 Live Crew not only copied the bass riff and repeated it,[19] but also produced otherwise distinctive sounds, interposing "scraper" noise, overlaying the music with solos in different keys, and altering the drum beat. See 754 F. Supp., at 1155. This is not a case, then, where "a substantial portion" of the parody itself is composed of a "verbatim" copying of the original. It is not, that is, a case where the parody is so insubstantial, as compared to the copying, that the third factor must be resolved as a matter of law against the parodists.

Suffice it to say here that, as to the lyrics, we think the Court of Appeals correctly suggested that "no more was taken than necessary," 972 F. 2d, at 1438, but just for that reason, we fail to see how the copying can be excessive in relation to its parodic purpose, even if the portion taken is the original's "heart." As to the music, we express no opinion whether repetition of the bass riff is excessive copying, and we remand to permit evaluation of the amount taken, in light of the song's parodic purpose and character, its transformative elements, and considerations of the potential for market substitution sketched more fully below.

D

The fourth fair use factor is "the effect of the use upon the potential market for or value of the copyrighted work." § 107(4). It requires courts to consider not only the extent of market harm caused by the particular actions of the alleged infringer, but also "whether unrestricted and widespread conduct of the sort engaged in by the defendant ... would result in a substantially adverse impact on the potential market" for the original. Nimmer § 13.05[A] [4], p. 13-102.61 (footnote omitted); accord *Harper & Row*, 471 U. S., at 569; Senate Report, p. 65; Folsom v. Marsh, 9 F. Cas., at

---

[19] This may serve to heighten the comic effect of the parody, as one witness stated, App. 32a, Affidavit of Oscar Brand; see also Elsmere Music, Inc. v. National Broadcasting Co., 482 F. Supp. 741, 747 (S.D.N.Y. 1980) (repetition of "I Love Sodom"), or serve to dazzle with the original's music, as Acuff-Rose now contends.

349. The enquiry "must take account not only of harm to the original but also of harm to the market for derivative works." Harper & Row, supra, at 568.

Since fair use is an affirmative defense,[20] its proponent would have difficulty carrying the burden of demonstrating fair use without favorable evidence about relevant markets.[21] In moving for summary judgment, 2 Live Crew left themselves at just such a disadvantage when they failed to address the effect on the market for rap derivatives, and confined themselves to uncontroverted submissions that there was no likely effect on the market for the original. They did not, however, thereby subject themselves to the evidentiary presumption applied by the Court of Appeals. In assessing the likelihood of significant market harm, the Court of Appeals quoted from language in *Sony* that " '[i]f the intended use is for commercial gain, that likelihood may be presumed. But if it is for a noncommercial purpose, the likelihood must be demonstrated.' " 972 F. 2d, at 1438, quoting *Sony*, 464 U. S., at 451. The court reasoned that because "the use of the copyrighted work is wholly commercial, ... we presume a likelihood of future harm to Acuff-Rose exists." 972 F. 2d, at 1438. In so doing, the court resolved the fourth factor against 2 Live Crew, just as it had the first, by applying a presumption about the effect of commercial use, a presumption which as applied here we hold to be error.

No "presumption" or inference of market harm that might find support in *Sony* is applicable to a case involving something beyond mere duplication for commercial purposes. *Sony*'s discussion of a presumption contrasts a context of verbatim copying of the original in its entirety for commercial purposes, with the non-commercial context of *Sony* itself (home copying of television programming). In the former circumstances, what Sony said simply makes common sense: when a commercial use amounts to mere duplication of the entirety of an original, it clearly "supersede[s] the objects," *Folsom v. Marsh*, 9 F. Cas., at 348, of the original and serves as a market replacement for it, making it likely that cognizable market harm to the original will occur. *Sony*, 464 U. S., at 451. But when, on the contrary, the second use is transformative, market substitution is at least less certain, and market harm may not be so readily inferred. Indeed, as to parody pure and simple, it is more likely that the new work will not affect the market for the original in a way cognizable under this factor, that is, by acting as a substitute for it ("supersed[ing][its] objects"). See Leval 1125; Patry & Perlmutter

---

[20] Harper & Row, 471 U. S., at 561; H. R. Rep. No. 102-836, p. 3, n. 3 (1992).

[21] Even favorable evidence, without more, is no guarantee of fairness. Judge Leval gives the example of the film producer's appropriation of a composer's previously unknown song that turns the song into a commercial success; the boon to the song does not make the film's simple copying fair. Leval 1124, n. 84. This factor, no less than the other three, may be addressed only through a "sensitive balancing of interests." Sony, 464 U. S., at 455, n. 40. Market harm is a matter of degree, and the importance of this factor will vary, not only with the amount of harm, but also with the relative strength of the showing on the other factors.

692, 697- 698. This is so because the parody and the original usually serve different market functions. * * *.

We do not, of course, suggest that a parody may not harm the market at all, but when a lethal parody, like a scathing theater review, kills demand for the original, it does not produce a harm cognizable under the Copyright Act. Because "parody may quite legitimately aim at garroting the original, destroying it commercially as well as artistically," B. Kaplan, An Unhurried View of Copyright 69 (1967), the role of the courts is to distinguish between "[b]iting criticism [that merely] suppresses demand [and] copyright infringement[, which] usurps it." *Fisher v. Dees*, 794 F. 2d, at 438.

This distinction between potentially remediable displacement and unremediable disparagement is reflected in the rule that there is no protectable derivative market for criticism. The market for potential derivative uses includes only those that creators of original works would in general develop or license others to develop. Yet the unlikelihood that creators of imaginative works will license critical reviews or lampoons of their own productions removes such uses from the very notion of a potential licensing market. "People ask ... for criticism, but they only want praise." S. Maugham, Of Human Bondage 241 (Penguin ed. 1992). Thus, to the extent that the opinion below may be read to have considered harm to the market for parodies of "Oh, Pretty Woman," see 972 F. 2d, at 1439, the court erred. Accord, Fisher v. Dees, 794 F. 2 d, at 437; Leval 1125; Patry & Perlmutter 688-691.[22]

In explaining why the law recognizes no derivative market for critical works, including parody, we have, of course, been speaking of the later work as if it had nothing but a critical aspect (i.e., ½parody pure and simple," supra, at 22). But the later work may have a more complex character, with effects not only in the arena of criticism but also in protectable markets for derivative works, too. In that sort of case, the law looks beyond the criticism to the other elements of the work, as it does here. 2 Live Crew's song comprises not only parody but also rap music, and the derivative market for rap music is a proper focus of enquiry, see *Harper & Row*, 471 U. S., at 568; Nimmer § 13.05[B]. Evidence of substantial harm to it would weigh against a finding of fair use, because the licensing of derivatives is an important economic incentive to the creation of originals. * * *. Of course, the only harm to derivatives that need concern us, as discussed above, is the harm of market substitution. The fact that a parody may impair the market for derivative uses by the very effectiveness of its

---

[22] We express no opinion as to the derivative markets for works using elements of an original as vehicles for satire or amusement, making no comment on the original or criticism of it.

critical commentary is no more relevant under copyright than the like threat to the original market.[24]

Although 2 Live Crew submitted uncontroverted affidavits on the question of market harm to the original, neither they, nor Acuff-Rose, introduced evidence or affidavits addressing the likely effect of 2 Live Crew's parodic rap song on the market for a non-parody, rap version of "Oh, Pretty Woman." And while Acuff-Rose would have us find evidence of a rap market in the very facts that 2 Live Crew recorded a rap parody of "Oh, Pretty Woman" and another rap group sought a license to record a rap derivative, there was no evidence that a potential rap market was harmed in any way by 2 Live Crew's parody, rap version. The fact that 2 Live Crew's parody sold as part of a collection of rap songs says very little about the parody's effect on a market for a rap version of the original, either of the music alone or of the music with its lyrics. The District Court essentially passed on this issue, observing that Acuff-Rose is free to record "whatever version of the original it desires," 754 F. Supp., at 1158; the Court of Appeals went the other way by erroneous presumption. Contrary to each treatment, it is impossible to deal with the fourth factor except by recognizing that a silent record on an important factor bearing on fair use disentitled the proponent of the defense, 2 Live Crew, to summary judgment. The evidentiary hole will doubtless be plugged on remand.

III

It was error for the Court of Appeals to conclude that the commercial nature of 2 Live Crew's parody of "Oh, Pretty Woman" rendered it presumptively unfair. No such evidentiary presumption is available to address either the first factor, the character and purpose of the use, or the fourth, market harm, in determining whether a transformative use, such as parody, is a fair one. The court also erred in holding that 2 Live Crew had necessarily copied excessively from the Orbison original, considering the parodic purpose of the use. We therefore reverse the judgment of the Court of Appeals and remand for further proceedings consistent with this opinion.

It is so ordered.

Appendix A

"Oh, Pretty Woman" by Roy Orbison and William Dees Pretty Woman, walking down the street, **Pretty Woman, the kind I like to meet,**
Pretty Woman, I don't believe you, you're not the truth,

---

[24] In some cases it may be difficult to determine whence the harm flows. In such cases, the other fair use factors may provide some indicia of the likely source of the harm. A work whose overriding purpose and character is parodic and whose borrowing is slight in relation to its parody will be far less likely to cause cognizable harm than a work with little parodic content and much copying.

No one could look as good as you
Mercy
Pretty Woman, won't you pardon me,
Pretty Woman, I couldn't help but see,
Pretty Woman, that you look lovely as can be
Are you lonely just like me?
Pretty Woman, stop a while,
Pretty Woman, talk a while,
Pretty Woman give your smile to me
Pretty woman, yeah, yeah, yeah
Pretty Woman, look my way,
Pretty Woman, say you'll stay with me
'Cause I need you, I'll treat you right
Come to me baby, Be mine tonight
Pretty Woman, don't walk on by,
Pretty Woman, don't make me cry,
Pretty Woman, don't walk away,
Hey, O. K.
If that's the way it must be, O. K.
I guess I'll go on home, it's late
There'll be tomorrow night, but wait!
What do I see
Is she walking back to me?
Yeah, she's walking back to me!
Oh, Pretty Woman.

Appendix B
"Pretty Woman" as Recorded by 2 Live Crew

Pretty woman walkin' down the street **Pretty woman girl you look so sweet**
Pretty woman you bring me down to that knee
Pretty woman you make me wanna beg please
Oh, pretty woman
Big hairy woman you need to shave that stuff
Big hairy woman you know I bet it's tough
Big hairy woman all that hair it ain't legit
'Cause you look like 'Cousin It'
Big hairy woman
Bald headed woman girl your hair won't grow
Bald headed woman you got a teeny weeny afro
Bald headed woman you know your hair could look nice
Bald headed woman first you got to roll it with rice
Bald headed woman here, let me get this hunk of biz for ya
Ya know what I'm saying you look better than rice a roni

Oh bald headed woman
Big hairy woman come on in
And don't forget your bald headed friend
Hey pretty woman let the boys
Jump in
Two timin' woman girl you know you ain't right
Two timin' woman you's out with my boy last night
Two timin' woman that takes a load off my mind
Two timin' woman now I know the baby ain't mine
Oh, two timin' woman
Oh pretty woman

NOTES

1. The most important part of the *Acuff-Rose* opinion may prove to be footnote 10, which explicitly recognizes the possibility of a class of infringements for which no injunction will issue, thus creating the nucleus of what may become a compulsory licensing system for infringements which are close to, but not quite, fair use. The court cited Abend v. MCA, Inc., 863 F. 2d 1465 (9th Cir. 1988), discussed in the casebook at note 4, p. 774, in support of this practice. Another example would be Rosemont Enterprises v. Random House, 366 F.2d 303 (2d Cir. 1966), discussed in the casebook at note 1, p. 729.

2. The Court accepted 2 Live Crew's concession that it was not entitled to a compulsory license because its parody changes "the basic melody or fundamental character" of the original. 17 U.S.C. § 115(a)(2). See note 4 of the opinion, supra page 278. House Report 94-1476, p. 109 says that "The second clause of subsection (a) is intended to recognize the practical need for a limited privilege to make arrangements of music being used under a compulsory license, but without allowing the music to be perverted, distorted, or travestied." Webster's Ninth New Collegiate Dictionary defines the verb to travesty as to parody. If Congress explicitly provided that a parody was not entitled to a compulsory license, isn't it a clear inference from the statute that a parody infringes?

3. Assume you were to represent one of the parties on remand. How would you formulate the instructions to the jury? What evidence would you present to the jury? If you were a member of the jury, would you find the instructions understandable?

4. Which party do you think is likely to win on remand?

PAGE 753. Add new Note.

6. Courts continue to be faced with claims of fair use many different situations.

In Rotbart v. J.R. O'Dwyer Co., 34 U.S.P.Q. 2d 1085 (S.D.N.Y. 1995), the plaintiff, publisher of a newsletter and a person who also gives seminars and workshops to public relations professionals, delivered a talk to over 200 persons at the national conference of the Public Relations Society of America. The defendant attended the talk, took detailed hand-written notes, and recorded the talk on a tape recorder. The defendant published stories about the talk in his own newsletter which were critical, and when members of the media asked about the context of quoted excerpts, circulated transcripts of the talk made from the tape recording. Rotbart sued for copyright infringement. The court held fair use.

In National Rifle Ass'n v. Handgun Control Federation of Ohio, 15 F.3rd 559 (6th Cir. 1994), the NRA sued for copyright infringement after the Handgun Control Federation made copies of a list of state legislators from a NRA newsletter. The Sixth Circuit held the copying fair use.

In Belmore v. City Pages Inc., 880 F. Supp. 673 (D. Minn. 1995), a police officer had written a short story whose point was unflattering to welfare recipients. It appeared in the September 1993 issue of a newsletter published by the Police Officers' Federation of Minneapolis. A local weekly paper reprinted the story in full in a column entitled "Hooligan's Island," and an introductory comment which stated that the tale "is beyond description, so I'll just reprint the whole thing." The policeman sued for copyright infringement. The court held fair use in spite of the fact that the entire story was copied.

PAGE 765. Add new Note.

Copying services that prepare course packs consisting of selections from various copyrighted material at the request of instructors continue to argue that their service is a fair use. The courts reject this argument in the context of high-volume, organized and repetitive copying where the course packs take the place of text books or other printed material. See Princeton University Press v. Michigan Document Services Inc., 855 F. Supp. 905 (E.D. Mich. 1994), rev'd 74 F.3d 1512 (6th Cir. 1996), petition for rehearing granted and decision vacated, 74 F.3d 1524 (6th Cir. 1996); Basic Books Inc. v. Kinko's Graphics Corp., 758 F. Supp. 1522 (S.D.N.Y. 1991).

PAGES 765 to 766. Add.

In *Acuff-Rose Music*, supra page 276, the Court says: "Since fair use is an affirmative defense, its proponent would have difficulty carrying the burden of demonstrating fair use without favorable evidence about relevant markets." Supra, page 286. The Court does not say whether this affirmative defense simply places the burden of going forward on the proponent of the defense, or also places the burden of persuasion on the proponent. The Court does make it clear that there is no presumption that a commercial use is not fair use, as had been suggested in *Sony*. And the Court is uninterested in any possible negative inference from 17 U.S.C. § 115(a)(2). See supra note 2, page 290.

PAGE 776. Add after Note 5.

CARTER V. HELMSLEY-SPEAR, INC.
United States Court of Appeals for the Second Circuit, 1995
71 F.3d 77, certiorari denied 1996 WL 106140 (1996)

CARDAMONE, Circuit Judge:

Defendants 474431 Associates and Helmsley-Spear, Inc. (defendants or appellants), as the owner and managing agent respectively, of a commercial building in Queens, New York, appeal from an order of the United States District Court for the Southern District of New York (Edelstein, J.), entered on September 6, 1994 following a bench trial. The order granted plaintiffs, who are three artists, a permanent injunction that enjoined defendants from removing, modifying or destroying a work of visual art that had been installed in defendants' building by plaintiffs-artists commissioned by a former tenant to install the work. See Carter v. Helmsley-Spear, Inc., 861 F.Supp. 303 (S.D.N.Y.1994). Defendants also appeal from the dismissal by the trial court of their counterclaim for waste. Plaintiffs cross-appeal from the dismissal of their cause of action for tortious interference with contractual relations and from the denial of their requests to complete the work and for an award of attorney's fees and costs.

On this appeal we deal with an Act of Congress that protects the rights of artists to preserve their works. One of America's most insightful thinkers observed that a country is not truly civilized "where the arts, such as they have, are all imported, having no indigenous life." 7 Works of Ralph Waldo Emerson, Society and Solitude, Chapt. II Civilization 34 (AMS. ed. 1968). From such reflection it follows that American artists are to be encouraged by laws that protect their works. Although Congress in the statute before us did just that, it did not mandate the preservation of art at all costs and without due regard for the rights of others.

For the reasons that follow, we reverse and vacate the grant of injunctive relief to plaintiffs and affirm the dismissal by the district court of plaintiffs' other claims and its dismissal of defendants' counterclaim for waste.

BACKGROUND

Defendant 474431 Associates (Associates) is the owner of a mixed use commercial building located at 47-44 31st Street, Queens, New York, which it has owned since 1978. Associates is a New York general partnership. The general partners are Alvin Schwartz and Supervisory Management Corp., a wholly-owned subsidiary of Helmsley Enterprises, Inc. Defendant Helmsley-Spear, Inc. is the current managing agent of the property for Associates.

On February 1, 1990 Associates entered into a 48-year net lease, leasing the building to 47-44 31st Street Associates, L.P. (Limited Partnership), a Delaware limited partnership. From February 1, 1990 until June 1993, Irwin Cohen or an entity under his control was the general partner of the Limited Partnership, and managed the property through Cohen's SIG Management Company (SIG). Corporate Life Insurance Company (Corporate Life) was a limited partner in the Limited Partnership. In June 1993 SIG ceased its involvement with the property and Corporate Life, through an entity controlled by it, became the general partner of the Limited Partnership. The property was then managed by the Limited Partnership, through Theodore Nering, a Corporate Life representative. See 861 F.Supp. at 312. There is no relationship, other than the lease, between Associates, the lessor, and the Limited Partnership, the lessee.

Plaintiffs John Carter, John Swing and John Veronis (artists or plaintiffs) are professional sculptors who work together and are known collectively as the "Three-J's" or "Jx3." On December 16, 1991 SIG entered into a one-year agreement with the plaintiffs "engag[ing] and hir[ing] the Artists ... to design, create and install sculpture and other permanent installations" in the building, primarily the lobby. Under the agreement plaintiffs had "full authority in design, color and style," and SIG retained authority to direct the location and installation of the artwork within the building. The artists were to retain copyrights to their work and SIG was to receive 50 percent of any proceeds from its exploitation. On January 20, 1993 SIG and the artists signed an agreement extending the duration of their commission for an additional year. When Corporate Life became a general partner of the Limited Partnership, the Limited Partnership assumed the agreement with plaintiffs and in December 1993 again extended the agreement.

The artwork that is the subject of this litigation is a very large "walk-through sculpture" occupying most, but not all, of the building's lobby. The artwork consists of a variety of sculptural elements constructed from recycled materials, much of it metal, affixed to the walls and ceiling, and a vast mosaic made from pieces of recycled glass embedded in the floor and walls. Elements of the work include a giant hand fashioned from an old school bus, a face made of automobile parts, and a number of interactive components. These assorted elements make up a theme relating to environmental concerns and the significance of recycling.

The Limited Partnership's lease on the building was terminated on March 31, 1994. It filed for bankruptcy one week later. The property was surrendered to defendant Associates on April 6, 1994 and defendant Helmsley-Spear, Inc. took over management of the property. Representatives of defendants informed the artists that they could no longer continue to install artwork at the property, and instead had to vacate the building. These representatives also made statements indicating that defendants intended to remove the artwork already in place in the building's lobby.

As a result of defendants' actions, artists commenced this litigation. On April 26, 1994 the district court issued a temporary restraining order enjoining defendants from taking any action to alter, deface, modify or mutilate the artwork installed in the building. In May 1994 a hearing was held on whether a preliminary injunction should issue. The district court subsequently granted a preliminary injunction enjoining defendants from removing the artwork pending the resolution of the instant litigation. See Carter v. Helmsley-Spear, Inc., 852 F.Supp. 228 (S.D.N.Y.1994).

A bench trial was subsequently held in June and July 1994, at the conclusion of which the trial court granted the artists the permanent injunction prohibiting defendants from distorting, mutilating, modifying, destroying and removing plaintiffs' artwork. Carter v. Helmsley-Spear, Inc., 861 F.Supp. 303, 337 (S.D.N.Y.1994). The injunction is to remain in effect for the lifetimes of the three plaintiffs. Plaintiffs' other claims, including their cause of action for tortious interference and a request for an award of costs and attorney's fees and that they be allowed to continue to add to the artwork in the lobby, as well as defendants' counterclaim for waste, were all dismissed with prejudice. This appeal and cross-appeal followed.

DISCUSSION

I Artists' Moral Rights

A. History of Artists' Moral Rights

Because it was under the rubric of the Visual Artists Rights Act of 1990 that plaintiffs obtained injunctive relief in the district court, we must explore, at least in part, the contours of that Act. In doing so it is necessary to review briefly the concept of artists' moral rights and the history and development of those rights in American jurisprudence, which led up to passage of the statute we must now examine.

The term "moral rights" has its origins in the civil law and is a translation of the French le droit moral, which is meant to capture those rights of a spiritual, non-economic and personal nature. The rights spring from a belief that an artist in the process of creation injects his spirit into the work and that the artist's personality, as well as the integrity of the work, should therefore be protected and preserved. See Ralph E. Lerner & Judith Bresler, Art Law 417 (1989) (Art Law). Because they are personal to the artist, moral rights exist independently of an artist's copyright in his or her work. See, e.g., 2 Nimmer on Copyright 8D-4 & n. 2 (1994) (Nimmer).

While the rubric of moral rights encompasses many varieties of rights, two are protected in nearly every jurisdiction recognizing their existence: attribution and integrity. See Art Law at 420. The right of attribution generally consists of the right of an artist to be recognized by name as the author of his work or to publish anonymously or pseudonymously, the right to prevent the author's work from being attributed to someone else, and to prevent the use of the author's name on works created by others, including distorted editions of the author's original work. See, e.g., id. at 419-20; Nimmer at 8D-5. The right of integrity allows the author to prevent any deforming or mutilating changes to his work, even after title in the work has been transferred. See, e.g., Art Law at 420.

In some jurisdictions the integrity right also protects artwork from destruction. Whether or not a work of art is protected from destruction represents a fundamentally different perception of the purpose of moral rights. If integrity is meant to stress the public interest in preserving a nation's culture, destruction is prohibited; if the right is meant to emphasize the author's personality, destruction is seen as less harmful than the continued display of deformed or mutilated work that misrepresents the artist and destruction may proceed. See Art Law at 421; see also 2 William F. Patry, Copyright Law and Practice 1044 n. 128 (1994) (Copyright Law) (noting the different models but suggesting that "destruction of a work shows the utmost contempt for the artist's honor or reputation").

Although moral rights are well established in the civil law, they are of recent vintage in American jurisprudence. Federal and state courts typically recognized the existence of such rights in other nations, but rejected artists' attempts to inject them into U.S. law. See, e.g., Vargas v. Esquire, Inc., 164 F.2d 522, 526 (7th Cir.1947); Crimi v. Rutgers Presbyterian Church, 194 Misc. 570, 573-76 (N.Y.Sup.Ct.1949). Nonetheless, American courts have in varying degrees acknowledged the idea of moral rights, cloaking the concept in the guise of other legal theories, such as copyright, unfair competition, invasion of privacy, defamation, and breach of contract. See Nimmer at 8D-10; Art Law at 423.

In the landmark case of Gilliam v. American Broadcasting Companies, Inc., 538 F.2d 14 (2d Cir.1976), we relied on copyright law and unfair competition principles to safeguard the integrity rights of the "Monty Python" group, noting that although the law "seeks to vindicate the economic, rather than the personal rights of authors ... the economic incentive for artistic ... creation ... cannot be reconciled with the inability of artists to obtain relief for mutilation or misrepresentation of their work to the public on which the artists are financially dependent." Id. at 24. Because decisions protecting artists rights are often "clothed in terms of proprietary right in one's creation," we continued, "they also properly vindicate the author's personal right to prevent the presentation of his work to the public in a distorted form." Id.

Artists fared better in state legislatures than they generally had in courts. California was the first to take up the task of protecting artists with the passage in 1979 of the California Art Preservation Act, Cal.Civ.Code § 987 et seq. (West 1982 & Supp.1995), followed in 1983 by New York's enactment of the Artist's Authorship

Rights Act, N.Y.Arts & Cult. Aff. Law § 14.03 (McKinney Supp.1995). Nine other states have also passed moral rights statutes, generally following either the California or New York models. See generally Art Law at 430-35; id. at 301-09 (Supp.1992) (describing the different states' laws).

B. Visual Artists Rights Act of 1990

Although bills protecting artists' moral rights had first been introduced in Congress in 1979, they had drawn little support. See Copyright Law at 1018 n. 1. The issue of federal protection of moral rights was a prominent hurdle in the debate over whether the United States should join the Berne Convention, the international agreement protecting literary and artistic works. Article 6bis of the Berne Convention protects attribution and integrity, stating in relevant part: Independently of the author's economic rights, and even after the transfer of the said rights, the author shall have the right to claim authorship of the work and to object to any distortion, mutilation or other modification of, or other derogatory action in relation to, the said work, which would be prejudicial to his honor or reputation. Berne Convention for the Protection of Literary and Artistic Works, September 9, 1886, art. 6bis, S.Treaty Doc. No. 27, 99th Cong., 2d Sess. 41 (1986).

The Berne Convention's protection of moral rights posed a significant difficulty for U.S. adherence. See Copyright Law at 1022 ("The obligation of the United States to provide droit moral ... was the single most contentious issue surrounding Berne adherence."); Nimmer at 8D-15 ("During the debate over [the Berne Convention Implementation Act], Congress faced an avalanche of opposition to moral rights, including denunciations of moral rights by some of the bill's most vociferous advocates."); H.R.Rep. No. 514, 101st Cong., 2d Sess. 7 (1990), reprinted in 1990 U.S.C.C.A.N. 6915, 6917 ("After almost 100 years of debate, the United States joined the Berne Convention.... [C]onsensus over United States adherence was slow to develop in large part because of debate over the requirements of Article 6bis.").

Congress passed the Berne Convention Implementation Act of 1988, Pub.L. No. 100-568, 102 Stat. 2853 (1988), and side-stepped the difficult question of protecting moral rights. It declared that the Berne Convention is not self-executing, existing law satisfied the United States' obligations in adhering to the Convention, its provisions are not enforceable through any action brought pursuant to the Convention itself, and neither adherence to the Convention nor the implementing legislation expands or reduces any rights under federal, state, or common law to claim authorship of a work or to object to any distortion, mutilation, or other modification of a work. See id. §§ 2, 3; see also S.Rep. No. 352, 100th Cong., 2d Sess. 9-10 (1988), reprinted in 1988 U.S.C.C.A.N. 3706, 3714-15.

Two years later Congress enacted the Visual Artists Rights Act of 1990 (VARA or Act), Pub.L. No. 101-650 (tit. VI), 104 Stat. 5089, 5128-33 (1990). Construing this Act constitutes the subject of the present appeal. The Act protects both the reputations of certain visual artists and the works of art they create. It provides these artists with the rights of "attribution" and "integrity." ... These rights are analogous to those protected by Article 6bis of the Berne Convention, which are commonly known as "moral rights." The theory of moral rights is that they result in a climate of artistic worth and honor that encourages the author in the arduous act of creation. H.R.Rep. No. 514 at 5 (internal quote omitted). The Act brings to fruition Emerson's insightful observation.

Its principal provisions afford protection only to authors of works of visual art--a narrow class of art defined to include paintings, drawings, prints, sculptures, or photographs produced for exhibition purposes, existing in a single copy or limited edition of 200 copies or fewer. 17 U.S.C. § 101. With numerous exceptions, VARA grants three rights: the right of attribution, the right of integrity and, in the case of works of visual art of "recognized stature," the right to prevent destruction. 17 U.S.C. § 106A. For works created on or after June 1, 1991--the effective date of the Act--the rights provided for endure for the life of the author or, in the case of a joint work, the life of the last surviving author. The rights cannot be transferred, but may be waived by a writing signed by the author. Copyright registration is not required to bring an action for infringement of the rights granted under VARA, or to secure statutory damages and attorney's fees. 17 U.S.C. §§ 411, 412. All remedies available under copyright law, other than criminal remedies, are available in an action for infringement of moral rights. 17 U.S.C. § 506. With this historical background in hand, we pass to the merits of the present litigation.

II Work of Visual Art

Because VARA is relatively new, a fuller explication of it is helpful. In analyzing the Act, therefore, we will follow in order the definition set forth in § 101, as did the district court when presiding over this litigation. The district court determined that the work of art installed in the lobby of Associates' building was a work of visual art as defined by VARA; that distortion, mutilation, or modification of the work would prejudice plaintiffs' honor and reputations; that the work was of recognized stature, thus protecting it from destruction (including removal that would result in destruction); and that Associates consented to or ratified the installation of the work in its building. The result was that defendants were enjoined from removing or otherwise altering the work during the lifetimes of the three artists.

A. Singleness of the Work

As a preliminary matter, we must determine whether the trial court correctly found that the work is a single piece of art, to be analyzed under VARA as a whole, rather than separate works to be considered individually. This finding was a factual one reviewed under the clearly erroneous standard. For purposes of framing the issues at trial the parties entered into a joint stipulation relating to numerous facts, including a definition of "the Work." This stipulated definition contained a long, detailed list of all the sculptural elements contained in the building's lobby. The district court found that, with a few precise exceptions determined to be separate works of art, the artwork created by plaintiffs in the lobby was a single work. See 861 F.Supp. at 314-15. This finding was based on testimony, credited by the trial judge, of the artists themselves and of their expert witnesses.

The trial court found further support for its conclusion in the method by which the artists created the work--each additional element of the sculpture was based on the element preceding it so that they would mesh together. The result was a thematically consistent, inter-related work whose elements could not be separated without losing continuity and meaning. See id. at 315. The record evidence of singleness was confirmed at the request of the parties by the district court's own inspection of the work.

Appellants' primary contention is that the finding of singleness is inconsistent with a finding that certain works of art were separate from the work that is the subject of this appeal. This assertion rests on the mistaken belief that the parties' joint stipulation to a definition of "the Work" precluded an ultimate determination by the factfinder that most but not all of the work installed in the lobby was a single artwork. In other words, according to appellants, either every component in the stipulated definition is part of a single work or every component is an individual work; there is no middle ground. Appellants' goal is to have VARA applied to each element of the sculpture individually, so that components that may not be visual art standing alone cannot be considered visual art when they are combined by the artists to create a whole that has a nature different than the mere sum of its parts.

Appellants' goal is not attainable. The parties stipulated that when they used the term "the Work" it included a list of sculptural components. The result was that during the trial there was no dispute as to the parties' meaning when referring to "the Work." The trial court was free to find that a few items of "the Work" were separate works of art, while the remainder of "the Work" was a single, interrelated, indivisible work of art. The finding of singleness was based on determinations of witness credibility as well as the district court's own inspection of the artwork. We cannot say that such a finding was clearly erroneous.

B. The Statutory Definition

A "work of visual art" is defined by the Act in terms both positive (what it is) and negative (what it is not). In relevant part VARA defines a work of visual art as "a painting, drawing, print, or sculpture, existing in a single copy" or in a limited edition of 200 copies or fewer. 17 U.S.C. § 101. Although defendants aver that elements of the work are not visual art, their contention is foreclosed by the factual finding that the work is a single, indivisible whole. Concededly, considered as a whole, the work is a sculpture and exists only in a single copy. Therefore, the work satisfies the Act's positive definition of a work of visual art. We next turn to the second part of the statutory definition--what is not a work of visual art.

The definition of visual art excludes "any poster, map, globe, chart, technical drawing, diagram, model, applied art, motion picture or other audio- visual work." 17 U.S.C. § 101. Congress meant to distinguish works of visual art from other media, such as audio-visual works and motion pictures, due to the different circumstances surrounding how works of each genre are created and disseminated. See H.R.Rep. No. 514 at 9. Although this concern led to a narrow definition of works of visual art, [t]he courts should use common sense and generally accepted standards of the artistic community in determining whether a particular work falls within the scope of the definition. Artists may work in a variety of media, and use any number of materials in creating their works. Therefore, whether a particular work falls within the definition should not depend on the medium or materials used. Id. at 11.

"Applied art" describes "two- and three-dimensional ornamentation or decoration that is affixed to otherwise utilitarian objects." Carter, 861 F.Supp. at 315, citing Kieselstein-Cord v. Accessories By Pearl, Inc., 632 F.2d 989, 997 (2d Cir.1980). Defendants' assertion that at least parts of the work are applied art appears to rest on the fact that some of the sculptural elements are affixed to the lobby's floor, walls, and ceiling--all utilitarian objects. Interpreting applied art to include such works would render meaningless VARA's protection for works of visual art installed in buildings. A court should not read one part of a statute so as to deprive another part of meaning. ***.

Appellants do not suggest the entire work is applied art. The district court correctly stated that even if components of the work standing alone were applied art, "nothing in VARA proscribes protection of works of visual art that incorporate elements of, rather than constitute, applied art." 861 F.Supp. at 315. VARA's legislative history leaves no doubt that "a new and independent work created from snippets of [excluded] materials, such as a collage, is of course not excluded" from the definition of a work of visual art. H.R.Rep. No. 514 at 14. The trial judge correctly ruled the work is not applied art precluded from protection under the Act.

III Work Made for Hire

Also excluded from the definition of a work of visual art is any work made for hire. 17 U.S.C. § 101. A "work made for hire" is defined in the Copyright Act, in relevant part, as "a work prepared by an employee within the scope of his or her employment." Id. § 101(1). Appellants maintain the work was made for hire and therefore is not a work of visual art under VARA. The district court held otherwise, finding that the plaintiffs were hired as independent contractors.

A. Reid Tests

The Copyright Act does not define the terms "employee" or "scope of employment." In Community for Creative Non-Violence v. Reid, 490 U.S. 730 (1989), the Supreme Court looked to the general common law of agency for guidance. It held that a multi-factor balancing test was required to determine if a work was produced for hire (by an employee) or was produced by an independent contractor. Reid, 490 U.S. at 751. The Court elaborated 13 specific factors: the hiring party's right to control the manner and means by which the product is accomplished.... the skill required; the source of the instrumentalities and tools; the location of the work; the duration of the relationship between the parties; whether the hiring party has the right to assign additional projects to the hired party; the extent of the hired party's discretion over when and how long to work; the method of payment; the hired party's role in hiring and paying assistants; whether the work is part of the regular business of the hiring party; whether the hiring party is in business; the provision of employee benefits; and the tax treatment of the hired party. Reid, 490 U.S. at 751-52. While all of these factors are relevant, no single factor is determinative. Id. at 752. ***.

The district court determined that the sculpture was not "work for hire" and therefore not excluded from the definition of visual art. The Reid test is a list of factors not all of which may come into play in a given case. ***. The Reid test is therefore easily misapplied. We are usually reluctant to reverse a district court's factual findings as to the presence or absence of any of the Reid factors and do so only when the district court's findings are clearly erroneous. By contrast, the ultimate legal conclusion as to whether or not the sculpture is "work for hire" is reviewed de novo. The district court correctly stated the legal test. But some of its factual findings, we think, were clearly erroneous.

B. Factors Applied

The district court properly noted that Aymes [v. Bonelli, 980 F.2d 857, 861 (2d Cir.1992)] established five factors which would be relevant in nearly all cases: the right to control the manner and means of production; requisite skill; provision of employee benefits; tax treatment of the hired party; whether the hired party may be assigned additional projects. See 980 F.2d at 861. Analysis begins with a discussion of these factors.

First, plaintiffs had complete artistic freedom with respect to every aspect of the sculpture's creation. Although the artists heeded advice or accepted suggestions from building engineers, architects, and others, such actions were not a relinquishment of their artistic freedom. The evidence strongly supports the finding that plaintiffs controlled the work's "manner and means." This fact, in turn, lent credence to their contention that they were independent contractors. ***. While artistic freedom remains a central factor in our inquiry, the Supreme Court has cautioned that "the extent of control the hiring party exercises over the details of the product is not dispositive." Reid, 490 U.S. at 752. Hence, resolving the question of whether plaintiffs had artistic freedom does not end the analysis.

The district court also correctly found the artists' conception and execution of the work required great skill in execution. Appellants' contention that the plaintiffs' reliance on assistants in some way mitigates the skill required for this work is meritless, particularly because each of the plaintiffs is a professional sculptor and the parties stipulated that professional sculpting is a highly skilled occupation. The right to control the manner and means and the requisite skill needed for execution of this project were both properly found by the district court to weigh against "work for hire" status.

The trial court erred, however, when it ruled that the defendants could not assign the artists additional projects. First, the employment agreement between SIG Management Company and the artists clearly states that the artists agreed not only to install the sculpture but also to "render such other related services and duties as may be assigned to [them] from time to time by the Company." By the very terms of the contract the defendants and their predecessors in interest had the right to assign other related projects to the artists. The district court incorrectly decided that this language supported the artists' claim to be independent contractors. While the artists' obligations were limited to related services and duties, the defendants nonetheless did have the right to assign to plaintiffs work other than the principal sculpture.

Further, the defendants did, in fact, assign such other projects. The district court concedes as much, explaining that "plaintiffs did create art work on the property other than that in the Lobby." Carter, 861 F.Supp. at 319. The record shows the artists performed projects on the sixth floor of the building, on the eighth floor, and in the boiler room. Thus, on at least three different occasions the plaintiffs were assigned additional projects, which they completed without further compensation. The trial court suggests this fact "does not undermine plaintiffs' contention that they were hired solely to install art work on the Property." Id. We disagree. If the artists were hired to perform work other than the sculpture (as both their employment agreement and their actual practice suggests) then they were not hired solely to install the sculpture. It makes no difference that all work performed by the plaintiffs was artistic in nature. The point is that the performance of other assigned work not of the artists' choosing supports a conclusion that the artists were not independent contractors but employees.

We must also consider factors the district court correctly found to favor finding the sculpture to be work for hire. Specifically, the provision of employee benefits and the tax treatment of the plaintiffs weigh strongly in favor of employee status. The defendants paid payroll and social security taxes, provided employee benefits such as life, health, and liability insurance and paid vacations, and contributed to unemployment insurance and workers' compensation funds on plaintiffs' behalf. Moreover, two of the three artists filed for unemployment benefits after their positions were terminated, listing the building's management company as their former employer. Other formal indicia of an employment relationship existed. For instance, each plaintiff was paid a weekly salary. The artists also agreed in their written contract that they would work principally for the defendants for the duration of their agreement on a 40-hour per week basis and they would only do other work to the extent that it would not "interfere with services to be provided" to the defendants. All of these facts strongly suggest the artists were employees.

Some of the other Reid factors bolster this view. The artists were provided with many (if not most) of the supplies used to create the sculpture. This factor was not, as the district court found, "inconclusive." The court also wrongly ruled that plaintiffs were hired for a "finite term of engagement." In fact, they were employed for a substantial period of time, their work continuing for over two years with no set date of termination (other than the sculpture's completion). Nor was the fact that the artists could not hire paid assistants without the defendants' approval "inconclusive" as the trial court erroneously found. Instead, this and the other just enumerated factors point towards an employer-employee relationship between the parties.

In reaching its conclusion, the district court also relied partly on the artists' copyright ownership of the sculpture, viewing such ownership as a "plus factor." We are not certain whether this element is a "plus factor," and therefore put off for another day deciding whether copyright ownership is probative of independent contractor status. Even were it to be weighed as a "plus factor," it would not change the outcome in this case.

C. Employee Status

Our review of the legal conclusion drawn from balancing the various Reid factors persuades us that the factors that weigh in favor of finding the artists were employees outweigh those factors supporting the artists' claim that they were independent contractors. One of the factors that did not persuade us was the appellants' simplistic contention that usage of the words "employ" or "employment" in the agreements between the artists and SIG or the Limited Partnership establishes that the plaintiffs were employees. The use of these terms does not transform them into "magic words" imbued with legally controlling significance.

Again, we emphasize that despite the conclusion reached we do not intend to marginalize factors such as artistic freedom and skill, making them peripheral to the status inquiry. The fact that artists will always be retained for creative purposes cannot serve to minimize this factor of the Reid test, even though it will usually favor VARA protection. Also, that the work was produced on the employer's premises is a necessary incident to all nonremovable art and therefore should not carry great weight. Similarly, we were not swayed by the boilerplate contract language or the accounting decision to deduct FICA taxes. To so read § 101 runs against the broad remedial purposes of VARA. As discussed earlier, the moral rights of the artist whose artistic work comes under VARA's umbrella are to be protected, not ignored, in light of Congress' pathbreaking legislation.

Moreover, because the Reid test is fact-dependent, future cases involving the work for hire question will not always fit neatly into an employee or independent contractor category. We also recognize that by counting indicia such as health insurance and paid vacations against the artists' independent contractor status, it may appear that artists regrettably are being forced to choose between the personal benefits inuring in an employment relationship and VARA's protection of the artists' work afforded only to independent contractors. Of course, when an employer today denies an artist "basic attributes of employment" like vacation time or health benefits, such denial will be wholly inconsistent with a "work for hire" defense. See Aymes, 980 F.2d at 862-63.

Consequently, while the existence of payroll formalities alone would not be controlling, see Reid, 490 U.S. at 743 n. 8, in combination with other factors, it may lead to a conclusion that a given work is one made for hire. Such other factors include: plaintiffs under their contract could be and were in fact assigned projects in addition to the work in the lobby; they were paid a weekly salary for over two years for a contracted 40 hours of work per week; they were furnished many of the needed supplies necessary to create the work; and plaintiffs could not hire paid assistants without defendants' consent. These factors, properly considered and weighed with the employee benefits granted plaintiffs and the tax treatment accorded them, are more than sufficient to demonstrate that the artists were employees, and the sculpture is therefore a work made for hire as a matter of law.

IV Defendants' Counterclaim and Plaintiffs' Cross-appeal

Finally, since we have determined that the work is one made for hire and therefore outside the scope of VARA's protection, we need not discuss that Act's broad protection of visual art and the protection it affords works of art incorporated into a building. Also, as plaintiffs' sculpture was not protected from removal because the artists were employees and not independent contractors, we need not reach the defendants' Fifth Amendment takings argument.

Moreover, because the sculpture is not protected by VARA from removal resulting in its destruction or alteration, we do not address plaintiffs' contentions that VARA entitles them to complete the "unfinished" portion of the work, that they are entitled to reasonable costs and attorney's fees, and that appellants tortiously interfered with the artists' contract with SIG and the Limited Partnership. Finally, the district court dismissed defendants' counterclaim against the artists for waste, finding, inter alia, that such a cause of action under New York law may only be brought by a landlord against a tenant. See 861 F.Supp. at 334-36. Appellants have failed to persuade us that it was error to dismiss this counterclaim.

CONCLUSION

Accordingly, the district court's order insofar as it held the work was one not made for hire is reversed and the injunction vacated. In all other respects, the order of the district court is affirmed. Each party to bear its own costs.

PAGE 777. Add to Notes.

8. Under § 109(a) the owner of a copy is entitled "to sell or otherwise dispose of the possession of that copy or phonorecord." This includes rental or lending, which is why libraries are able to lend out the books they own. In recent years some businesses took advantage of the ubiquity of copying equipment to open stores that rented sound recordings. Patrons could rent the recording, take it home, make a copy, and return it. This became a sufficient economic threat to the industry that Congress amended the statute to provide that disposal by rental, lease or lending for direct or indirect commerical advantage is infringement. § 109(b). These provisions were subsequently extended to computer programs. Some stores have attempted to evade this prohibition by offering to buy back recordings they have sold, or by offering "deferred billing." This has required the courts to determine whether the store is engaging in a sham, and actually renting, or not. See Central Point Software Inc. v. Global Software & Accessories Inc., 880 F. Supp. 957 (E.D.N.Y. 1995).

9. The unfamiliar fit between traditional notions of copyright and the extension of copyright protection to computer software continues to present new problems to the producers and users of software, and to the courts. CONTU recognized that it is impossible to even use a piece of software without making a copy of it, because in order for the machine to run the software it has to copy it from a storage medium such as a hard disk into the volatile memory which can be accessed by the machine's processor. Although the copy in the computer's volatile memory is temporary --it is destroyed, for instance, whenever the power is turned off to the computer-- it fits within the definition of copy in the 1976 Act. CONTU recognized this, and thus recommended that § 117 permit the owner to make a new copy or adaptation "as an essential step in the utilization of the computer program in conjunction with a machine and that it is used in no other manner."

Many owners of the copyright on computer programs find the § 117 right can be read more broadly than they would like. Most customers, of course, will buy and use the program in the way the seller intended. But some "customers" (i.e., anyone who buys a copy of the program) might, for instance, like to learn more about the program. They might want to learn more about the program in order to get ideas about programming techniques and strategies, to help design a competitive program, drawing upon the unprotected ideas embodied in the program, or to design a program that compliments, enhances, or interfaces with the program.

In order to defeat the application of § 117 (and the doctrine of exhaustion under § 109), most sellers of software provide that the software is licensed, not sold. Title remains with the seller, and the buyer is not an owner. The reasons why such license agreements are likely to be viewed as a sham and unenforceable in the mass marketing context are spelled out in David Rice, Licensing the Use of Computer Program Copies and the Copyright Act First Sale Doctrine, 30 Jurimetrics 157 (1990), cited in note 6 at page 777 of the casebook. Such agreements are, however, probably enforceable outside the mass market context, i.e. a specialized program sold for a high price to a few buyers for a particular purpose on individually negotiated terms.

As additional protection for the program, sellers of software distribute only the compiled object code --the 1's and 0's that the computer understands-- and keep the source code from which the program was compiled to themselves. In order to understand the program it is necessary to use a decompiler program. A decompiler will convert the object code back into source code. But of course, to decompile the program it is necessary to load it in the computer and make a copy.

A relatively early case involving the scope of § 117 was Vault Corp. v. Quaid Software Ltd., 847 F.2d 255 (5th Cir. 1988), briefly described in note 5, page 623 of the casebook. That case involved Quaid's product RAMKEY, designed to defeat Vault's product, PROLOK, a program designed to prevent consumers from making copies of software. Vault's software was sold with the usual licensing agreement, and in the context of the case the force of the agreement was strengthened by a Louisiana statute specifically providing that such a license agreement was enforceable. The Fifth Circuit held the agreement preempted by § 301 and treated Quaid (who had purchased a copy in order to figure out how to defeat it) as an owner. One problem in the case was that Quaid had run the program in order to figure out how to defeat it, in violation of the licensing agreement. Quaid argued that this was permitted by § 117(1). Vault argued that the "essential step in the utilization of the computer program" permitted by § 117 had to be a step that the seller of the software contemplated the user would take. The court rejected Vault's proffered reading, holding that § 117 should be read broadly to cover any utilization in conjunction with a machine.

Two cases involving computer games have involved the same basic problem. Nintendo markets its highly successful game consoles with a lock code designed to keep cartridges from unauthorized manufacturers from running when inserted in the console. Atari, whose once very successful game system lost out to Nintendo, undertook to market game cartridges that consumers could play on their Nintendo consoles. To do this, Atari had to "peel" the chip in the Nintendo console that contained the lock out program, read the program off of the chip, and then figure out how to program its cartridges to fool the lock out program into treating the Atari cartridges as if they were authorized. Atari did this, and marketed the cartridges. Nintendo, of course, sued for copyright infringement. In Atari Games Corp. v. Nintendo, 975 F.2d 832 (Fed. Cir. 1992), the court (applying the law of the Ninth Circuit) held that such reverse engineering was fair use. The court affirmed the preliminary injunction in that case, however, because Atari's reverse engineering was facilitated by a copy of the program obtained from the copyright office by means of a false representation that there was litigation between the parties. The Ninth Circuit also held that reverse engineering is fair use in a similar situation, Sega Enterprises, Ltd. v. Accolade, Inc., 977 F.2d 1510 (9th Cir. 1993), and noted its agreement with *Nintendo*. [This fair use approach of the Ninth Circuit was foreshadowed in a deleted portion of the *Lewis Galoob* opinion above, which held that if the Game Genie did create a derivative work, that the derivative work was fair use.]

In *Sega*, the court described the reverse engineering procedure which it held to be fair use as follows:

> "Accolade used a two-step process to render its video games compatible with the Genesis console. First, it 'reverse engineered' Sega's video game programs in order to discover the requirements for compatibility with the Genesis console. As part of the reverse engineering process, Accolade transformed the machine-readable object code contained in commercially available copies of Sega's game cartridges into human-readable source code using a process called 'disassembly' or 'decompilation'. Accolade purchased a Genesis console and three Sega game cartridges, wired a decompiler into the console circuitry, and generated printouts of the resulting source code. Accolade engineers studied and annotated the printouts in order to identify areas of commonality among the three game programs. They then loaded the disassembled code back into a computer, and experimented to discover the interface specifications for the Genesis console by modifying the programs and studying the results. At the end of the reverse engineering process, Accolade created a development manual that incorporated the information it had discovered about the requirements for a Genesis-compatible game. According to the Accolade employees who created the manual, the manual contained only functional descriptions of the interface requirements and did not include any of Sega's code." 977 F.2d 1514-15.

Why doesn't this reverse engineering fall within § 117(1)?

In DSC Communications Corp. v. DGI Technologies, Inc., 81 F.3d 597 (5th Cir. 1996), the court held that a license restriction which purported to prevent the operation of the plaintiff's software on any machine other than its own was likely to be copyright misusue, rendering the copyright unenforceable, because of the effect of the restriction was to turn copyright protection into patent-like protection.

10. In order to highlight the unusual status of computer programs under the copyright statute, it is helpful to contrast the way copyright protection of computer programs works with the way it works for books, the paradigm for copyright. It is, of course, possible to write a book and keep it secret. There is, under the 1976

Copyright Act, copyright protection of unpublished books (and before the 1976 act there was common law copyright protection of unpublished books). However, for an author to enjoy any economic benefit from the book it must be published, and (for a U.S. author) to enjoy the right to enforce the copyright (or at the request of the Library of Congress) it must deposited with the Registrar of Copyrights, who will place it on the shelves of the Library of Congress where it can be read and examined by anyone. It is true that a book could be translated into an unintelligible code and then published, [*] but there would be no demand for such a book. And once the book is published and available, the act of reading, analyzing, using, and thinking about the book is not infringing. Although the act of reading a book may result in the formation of a visual image on the reader's retina, that image is not a copy because the work cannot be further perceived, reproduced, or otherwise communicated.

Computer programs, on the other hand, are regularly published in object code form, which is an unintelligible code. The intelligible source code is kept secret, and even the object code is distributed under license provisions that are the equivalent of "DO NOT READ THIS BOOK." Not only that, the Registrar requires deposit of only a few pages of a print out of the code, not wanting to fill government warehouses with meaningless paper. And the program cannot be used without making another copy when the program is loaded into the computer. The owner of the program can only use it because of the exception from infringement liability in § 117(1).

As a result of the way computer programs are protected under the copyright statute, it is possible for the owner of a computer program to enjoy copyright protection for the long copyright term on any original program and never give access to anyone else to information about the structure of the program, its creative elements, or even what parts of it are unprotectable because either in the public domain, not original, functional, or unprotected under § 102(b).[**] The fair use decisions in *Nintendo* and *Sega* can be seen as an effort by the courts to address this situation.

---

[*] Should a court deny copyright protection to a book not written in a known language on the grounds that it is not a work of authorship fixed in a tangible medium of expression from which it can be perceived?

[**] Another odd consequence of this intersection between books and computer programs is that when Congress came to consider amendments to § 107 in the aftermath of the *Nation* decision designed to make it clear that fair use is available in the case of unpublished works, it was the computer software industry that had the strongest objections. Since the source code remains unpublished under the standard publication practices, the software producers saw an amendment relating to unpublished works as affecting their interests. Thus an issue of policy about the appropriate use of unpublished manuscripts accessible in research libraries and elsewhere was entangled with issues about the protection of computer software.

11. The protection of computer programs now has implications for the purchase, use and servicing of many machines other than computers. As the prices of computer chips have fallen, built-in, special purpose computers are becoming an important component of many machines. For instance, the devices which control the fuel and ignition on internal combustion engines are increasingly electronic. A cellular telephone includes computer programs to enable it to interface with the cellular system. In addition, a car may be equipped with electronic sensors and a special wiring harness which enable it to be hooked up to a diagnostic computer that speedily locates any malfunction. Large special purpose electronic machines such as imaging machines or copying machines increasingly have their diagnostics built in so that the machine can identify and report any malfunctioning part.

All of these electronic devices contain specialized computer chips which are programmed with computer programs protected by the copyright statute. If the seller of the machine owns the copyright on the embedded programs and retains ownership of the program after the sale, then the seller can continue to retain ownership of much of the machine. For instance, any modification of the program by the machine owner to change the characteristics of the program could be viewed as an adaptation. More likely, the machine seller could restrict use of the diagnostic programs to its own service organization, meaning, as a practical matter, that the machine purchaser would be limited to using the seller's service organization for the life of the machine.

The most important practical consequence of this is that it is important for the purchaser of a machine incorporating computer programs to address at the time of purchase what rights the purchaser has in the computer program. For instance, can the owner of the machine authorize an independent serviceman to use the machine diagnostics? Can the owner provide his own or a third-party service organization with copies of the diagnostic program? Will the owner have access to enhancements and improvements to the programs embedded in the machine, which can often be installed simply by replacing a chip?

The initial reported litigation of these issues has involved an IBM mainframe computer. Allen-Myland, Inc.[*] v. International Business Machines Corp., 746 F. Supp. 520, 533 (E.D. Pa. 1990), involved a suit for copyright infringement against an independent service organization that copied and altered machine microcode in order to implement changes in the machine hardware made by the independent service organization at the request of the machine owner. The court held the procedures followed there to be copyright infringement. The litigation is spreading beyond computers. See, for instance, the litigation described in General Electric Company v.

---

[*] Edmund W. Kitch filed an appearance for AMI in that case. Arthur Miller, author of Arthur R. Miller, Copyright Protection for Computer Programs, Databases, and Computer-Generated Works: Is Anything New Since CONTU, 106 Harv. L. Rev. 977 (1993), testified as an expert witness on copyright law for IBM.

Ch. 5								FAIR USE								321

R Squared Scan System, Inc., 1990 WL 7186 (N.D.Ill. 1990), involving third-party service on a CAT scanner; MAI Sys. Corp. v. Peak Computer, 991 F.2d 511 (9th Cir.1993); and Advanced Computer Services of Michigan v. MAI Systems, 845 F. Supp. 356 (E.D. Va. 1994). In Triad Systems Corp. v. Southeastern Exp. Co., 64 F.3d 1330 (9th Cir. 1995), certiorari denied 116 S.Ct. 1015 (1996), the Ninth Circuit affirmed an injunction against a third-party service provider who loaded the operating system and diagnostic programs in order to service the computer.

A further complication in this situation is that seller policies that link purchasers to continuing use of the seller's repair and maintenance services involve antitrust issues. See Eastman Kodak Co. v. Image Technical Services, Inc., 501 U.S. 1216 (1992). In Data General Corp. v. Grumman Systems Support Corp., 36 F.3d 1147 (1st Cir. 1994), the court rejected the argument that a refusal to license to third party service organizations software necessary to provide computer maintenance services is copyright misuse, making the copyright in the software unenforceable.

12. Does footnote 10 of *Acuff-Rose* suggest another way to address these problems?

PAGE 787. Add to Note 8.

The Copyright Office study has now been completed. It does not recommend adoption of the right in the United States.

PAGE 787. New Note 9.

9. In Rostropovich v. Koch Int'l Corp., 34 U.S.P.Q. 2d 1609 (S.D.N.Y. 1995), reargument denied 36 U.S.P.Q. 2d 1383 (1996), Mstislav Rostropovich sued the American distributor of compact discs of recordings made when Rostropovich was a cellist with Russian symphonies during the 1960's. Most of the compact discs have a picture of Rostropovich with his name prominently displayed. Rostropovich was a Russian national who fled the Soviet Union in 1974. Since 1977 he has been Music Director of the National Symphony Orchestra in Washington, D.C. The distributor claimed a license from a private Rusian organization, a successor to the rights of the All Union Recording Studio, an agency of the Russian government which owned all recording rights of Russian orchestras. Rostropovich sued under § 43(a) of the Lanham Act, § 51 of the New York Civil Rights Law, and unjust enrichment. The principal defense was that the U.S. distribution of the recordings was properly authorized. The court granted in part a summary judgment for the defendants.

PAGES 788 to 789. Add to the discussion of the Copyright Royalty Tribunal.

The Copyright Royalty Tribunal was abolished by Public Law 103-198, signed by the President on December 17, 1993. Its functions are now to be performed by copyright arbitration royalty panels. In the event of a dispute, the Librarian of Congress selects two members of the panel, and the two members select a third. See new 17 U.S.C. §§ 801-803.

PAGE 791. Add to Note 4.

David LaMacchia, a twenty-one year old student at the Massacusetts Institute of Technology set up a computer bulletin board on MIT's computer network and accessible from the internet. He encouraged others to download copies of popular software applications and games to the bulletin board, and made them accessible to others for uploading. When the volume of world-wide internet traffic attracted to his bulletin board was noticed by authorities, he was indicted for wire fraud, in violation of 18 U.S.C. § 1343. The district court dismissed the indictment, relying by analogy on Dowling v. United States, 473 U.S. 207 (1985). United States v. LaMaccchia, 871 F. Supp. 535 (1994).

PAGE 791. New Note 5.

5. The GATT TRIPS contain extensive provisions as to the procedures and remedies for enforcing intellectual property rights. See Articles 41 to 62. So does NAFTA, Articles 1714-1718.

CHAPTER VI

PATENTS

PAGE 792. Add to text on patent term.

As part of the legislation implementing the GATT TRIPS, The Uruguay Round Agreements Act, P.L. 103-465, amended 35 U.S.C. § 154 to provide that the term of all utility and plant patents ends 20 years from filing. This applies to all patents with application dates on or after June 8, 1995 (six months after the passage of the act). 35 U.S.C. § 154(a)(2). Patents with filing dates before that date are entitled to the longer of either 20 years from filing or 17 years from issue. 35 U.S.C. § 154(c)(1). There is protection for infringing acts which were commenced or for which substantial investment was made before June 8, 1995 and which are infringement only because of an effective extension of their term resulting from the operation of § 154(c)(1).

These amendments conform the U.S. patent term to the international norm. An advantage of a patent term defined from the date of filing is that it removes the incentive for applicants to delay the processing of their applications by the patent office. A disadvantage of a patent term defined from the date of filing is that delays by the patent office shorten the length of the effective patent term. To deal with this problem, term extensions are permitted for certain delays caused by the patent office. § 154(b).

PAGE 794. Add to Text.

The GATT TRIPS (and NAFTA) contain extensive provisions relating to minimum standards for patent protection and the procedures by which patent rights are asserted and enforced. The background of those agreements has been briefly essayed elsewhere in this supplement, and will not be repeated here. See pages 8-9, 49-54, 181-183. Some of the provisions of the agreements relevant to the issues covered in the chapter will be noted.

PAGE 795. Add to text before *O'Reilly v. Morse*.

Article 27 of the GATT TRIPS provides:

Article 27
Patentable Subject Matter

1. Subject to the provisions of paragraphs 2 and 3, patents shall be available for any inventions, whether products or processes, in all fields of technology, provided that they are new, involve an inventive step and are capable of industrial application. Subject to paragraph 4 of Article 65, paragraph 8 of Article 70 [paragraphs relating to

transitional issues] and paragraph 3 of this Article, patents shall be available and patent rights enjoyable without discrimination as to the place of invention, the field of technology and whether products are imported or locally produced.

2. Members may exclude from patentability inventions, the prevention within their territory of the commercial exploitation of which is necessary to protect *ordre public* or morality, including to protect human, animal or plant life or health or to avoid serious prejudice to the environment, provided that such exclusion is not made merely because the exploitation is prohibited by their law.

3. Members may also exclude from patentability:
(a) diagnostic, therapeutic and surgical methods for the treatment of humans or animals;
(b) plants and animals other than micro-organisms, and essentially biological processes for the production of plants or animals other than non-biological and microbiological processes. However, Members shall provide for the protection of plant varieties either by patents or by an effective *sui generis* system or by any combination thereof. The provisions of this subparagraph shall be reviewed four years after the date of entry into force of the WTO Agreement.

PAGE 820. Add to note 3.

The Factor VIII:C patent litigation has continued. In Scripps Clinic and Research Foundation v. Genentech, Inc., 707 F. Supp. 1547 (N.D. Cal. 1989) and 724 F. Supp. 690 (N.D. Cal. 1989), the court granted summary judgment for Genentech on the ground that the patent applicant had engaged in inequitable conduct before the patent office and failed to properly disclose the best mode. The Federal Circuit reversed and remanded for trial, 927 F.2d 1565 (Fed. Cir. 1991), but reversed a finding that the patent, if valid, was infringed, invoking the reverse doctrine of equivalents. Id. at 1581. See casebook, page 1037, note 2, and material in this supplement keyed to that page.

PAGE 821. Add to note 5.

In Asgrow Seed Co. v. Winterboer, 115 S.Ct. 788 (1995), the Court held that a farmer may sell under the Plant Variety Protection Act only seed that has been saved to replant the farmer's own acreage.

PAGE 821. Add to note 8.

In connection with the discussion of the use of depositories, see the discussion of the depository practice in Amgen, Inc. v. Chugai Pharmaceutical Co., 927 F.2d

Ch. 6 PATENTABLE SUBJECT MATTER 325

1200, 1209-12 (Fed. Cir. 1991), excerpted in this supplement in connection with the discussion of the best mode requirement, casebook page 973-75.

PAGE 822. Add note 9.

Article 27.3 of the GATT TRIPS, quoted above page 311, recognizes that limitation can be placed on the patentability of "diagnostic, therapeutic and surgical methods for the treatment of humans or animals."

PAGE 831. Add to note 1.

The notice issued by the PTO on April 21, 1987, read as follows: "A decision by the Board of Patent Appeals and Interferences in Ex parte Allen, [2 USPQ2d 1425] (Bd.App. & Int. April 3, 1987), held that claimed polyploid oysters are nonnaturally occurring manufactures or compositions of matter within the meaning of 35 U.S.C. 101. The Board relied upon the opinion of the Supreme Court in Diamond v. Chakrabarty, 447 U.S. 303 (1980) as it had done in Ex parte Hibberd, 227 USPQ 443 (Bd.App. & Int., 1985), as controlling authority that Congress intended statutory subject matter to 'include anything under the sun that is made by man.' The Patent and Trademark Office now considers nonnaturally occurring non-human multicellular living organisms, including animals, to be patentable subject matter within the scope of 35 U.S.C. 101. The Board's decision does not affect the principle and practice that products found in nature will not be considered to be patentable subject matter under 35 U.S.C. 101 and/or 102. An article of manufacture or composition of matter occurring in nature will not be considered patentable unless given a new form, quality, properties or combination not present in the original article existing in nature in accordance with existing law. [Citations omitted]. A claim directed to or including within its scope a human being will not be considered to be patentable subject matter under 35 U.S.C. 101. The grant of a limited, but exclusive property right in a human being is prohibited by the Constitution. Accordingly, it is suggested that any claim directed to a non-plant multicellular organism which would include a human being within its scope include the limitation 'non-human' to avoid this ground of rejection. The use of a negative limitation to define the metes and bounds of the claimed subject matter is a permissible form of expression. In re Wakefield, 422 F.2d 897 (CCPA 1970). Accordingly, the Patent and Trademark Office is now examining claims directed to multicellular living organisms, including animals. To the extent that the claimed subject matter is directed to a non-human 'nonnaturally occurring manufacture or composition of matter--a product of human ingenuity' (Diamond v. Chakrabarty), such claims will not be rejected under 35 U.S.C. 101 as being directed to nonstatutory subject matter."

In Animal Legal Defense Fund v. Quigg, 932 F.2d 920 (Fed.Cir. 1991), animal rights groups challenged the legality of the notice. The Federal Circuit held that the complaint was properly dismissed for lack of standing.

The Harvard mouse patent was issued in 1988. No further animal patents issued until December 1992 when the PTO issued patents on three more mice: a virus-resistant mouse strain, a strain that fails to develop a functional immune system, and a strain whose males develop enlarged prostate glands.

PAGE 840. Read after *Diamond v. Diehr*.

ARRHYTHMIA RESEARCH TECHNOLOGY, INC. v. CORAZONIX CORPORATION
United States Court of Appeals for the Federal Circuit, 1992
958 F.2d 1053

PAULINE NEWMAN, Circuit Judge.

Arrhythmia Research Technology, Inc. appeals the grant of summary judgment by the United States District Court for the Northern District of Texas declaring United States Patent No. 4,422,459 to Michael B. Simson (the '459 or Simson patent) invalid for failure to claim statutory subject matter under 35 U.S.C. § 101. The court did not decide the question of infringement.

We conclude that the claimed subject matter is statutory in terms of section 101. The judgment of invalidity on this ground is reversed.

The Simson Invention

The invention claimed in the '459 patent is directed to the analysis of electrocardiographic signals in order to determine certain characteristics of the heart function. In the hours immediately after a heart attack (myocardial infarction) the victim is particularly vulnerable to an acute type of heart arrhythmia known as ventricular tachycardia. Ventricular tachycardia leads quickly to ventricular fibrillation, in which the heart ceases effectively to pump blood through the body. Arrhythmia Research states that 15-25% of heart attack victims are at high risk for ventricular tachycardia. It can be treated or prevented with certain drugs, but these drugs have undesirable and sometimes dangerous side effects. Dr. Simson, a cardiologist, sought a solution to the problem of determining which heart attack victims are at high risk for ventricular tachycardia, so that these persons can be carefully monitored and appropriately treated.

Heart activity is monitored by means of an electrocardiograph device, whereby electrodes attached to the patient's body detect the heart's electrical signals in accordance with the various phases of heart activity. The signals can be displayed in wave form on a monitor and/or recorded on a chart. It was known that in patients subject to ventricular tachycardia certain anomalous waves having very low amplitude and high frequency, known as "late potentials," appear toward the end of the QRS[2] segment of the electrocardiographic signal, that is, late in the ventricular contraction cycle. Dr. Simson's method of detecting and measuring these late potentials in the QRS complex, and associated apparatus, are the subject of the '459 patent.

The '459 patent specification describes these procedures. Certain of the heart attack patient's electrocardiographic signals, those obtained from electrodes designated as X, Y, and Z leads, are converted from analog to digital values, and a composite digital representation of the QRS segment is obtained by selecting and averaging a large number of the patient's QRS waveforms. The anterior portion of the composite QRS waveform is first isolated, and then processed by a digital high pass filter in reverse time order; that is, backwards. This step of reverse time order filtering is described as the critical feature of the Simson invention, in that it enables detection of the late potentials by eliminating certain perturbations that obscure these signals. The root mean square of the reverse time filtered output is then calculated, as described in the specification, to determine the average magnitude of the anterior portion of the QRS complex. Comparison of the output, which is measured in microvolts, with a predetermined level of high frequency energy, indicates whether the patient is subject to ventricular tachycardia. That is, if the root mean square magnitude is less than the predetermined level, then low amplitude, high frequency late potentials have been shown to be present, indicating a higher risk of ventricular tachycardia. If the root mean square value is greater than the predetermined level, high risk for ventricular tachycardia is not indicated.

Certain steps of the invention are described as conducted with the aid of a digital computer, and the patent specification sets forth the mathematical formulae that are used to configure (program) the computer. The specification states that dedicated, specific purpose equipment or hard wired logic circuitry can also be used.

The district court held that the method and apparatus claims of the Simson patent are directed to a mathematical algorithm, and thus do not define statutory subject matter. Claim 1 is the broadest method claim: 1. A method for analyzing electrocardiograph signals to determine the presence or absence of a predetermined level of high frequency energy in the late QRS signal, comprising the steps of: converting a series of QRS signals to time segments, each segment having a digital value equivalent to the analog value of said signals at said time; applying a portion of said time segments in reverse time order to high pass filter means; determining an arithmetic value of the amplitude of the output of said filter; and comparing said value with said predetermined level. Claim 7 is a representative apparatus claim: 7. Apparatus for analyzing electrocardiograph signals to determine the level of high frequency energy in the late QRS signal comprising: means for converting X, Y, and Z lead electrocardiographic input signals to digital valued time segments; means for

---

[2] According to Arrhythmia Research, the QRS complex lasts about one tenth of a second and arises from the depolarization of the ventricles prior to contraction.

examining said X, Y, and Z digital valued time segments and selecting therefrom the QRS waveform portions thereof; means for signal averaging a multiplicity of said selected QRS waveforms for each of said X, Y, and Z inputs and providing composite, digital X, Y, and Z QRS waveforms; high pass filter means; means for applying to said filter means, in reverse time order, the anterior portion of each said digital X, Y, and Z waveform; and means for comparing the output of said filter means with a predetermined level to obtain an indication of the presence of a high frequency, low level, energy component in the filter output of said anterior portions. The Patent and Trademark Office had granted the patent without questioning that its claims were directed to statutory subject matter under § 101.

35 U.S.C. § 101

Whether a claim is directed to statutory subject matter is a question of law. Although determination of this question may require findings of underlying facts specific to the particular subject matter and its mode of claiming, in this case there were no disputed facts material to the issue. Thus we give plenary review to the question, with appropriate recognition of the burdens on the challenger of a duly issued United States patent. * * *.

* * *

[The court discussed *Diamond v. Chakrabarty*, casebook page 822, *Gottschalk v. Benson*, described in *Chakrabarty*, casebook page 823, *Diamond v. Diehr*, casebook page 832, and *Parker v. Flook*, described in *Chakrabarty*, casebook page 824.]

The Court thus placed the patentability of computer-aided inventions in the mainstream of the law. The ensuing mode of analysis of such inventions was summarized in In re Meyer, 688 F.2d 789, 795 (CCPA 1982): In considering a claim for compliance with 35 USC § 101, it must be determined whether a scientific principle, law of nature, idea, or mental process, which may be represented by a mathematical algorithm, is included in the subject matter of the claim. If it is, it must then be determined whether such principle, law, idea, or mental process is applied in an invention of a type set forth in 35 USC § 101. The law crystallized about the principle that claims directed solely to an abstract mathematical formula or equation, including the mathematical expression of scientific truth or a law of nature, whether directly or indirectly stated, are nonstatutory under section 101; whereas claims to a specific process or apparatus that is implemented in accordance with a mathematical algorithm will generally satisfy section 101.

In applying this principle to an invention whose process steps or apparatus elements are described at least in part in terms of mathematical procedures, the mathematical procedures are considered in the context of the claimed invention as a whole. *Diehr*, 450 U.S. at 188. Determination of statutory subject matter has been conveniently conducted in two stages, following a protocol initiated by the Court of

Customs and Patent Appeals in In re Freeman, 573 F.2d 1237 (CCPA 1978); modified after the Court's *Flook* decision by In re Walter, 618 F.2d 758 (CCPA 1980); and again after the Court's *Diehr* decision by In re Abele, 684 F.2d 902 (CCPA 1982).

This analysis has been designated the *Freeman-Walter-Abele* test for statutory subject matter. It is first determined whether a mathematical algorithm is recited directly or indirectly in the claim. If so, it is next determined whether the claimed invention as a whole is no more than the algorithm itself; that is, whether the claim is directed to a mathematical algorithm that is not applied to or limited by physical elements or process steps. Such claims are nonstatutory. However, when the mathematical algorithm is applied in one or more steps of an otherwise statutory process claim, or one or more elements of an otherwise statutory apparatus claim, the requirements of section 101 are met. The court explained in *Abele*, 684 F.2d at 907: "[P]atentable subject matter [is not limited] to claims in which structural relationships or process steps are defined, limited or refined by the application of the algorithm. Rather, Walter should be read as requiring no more than that the algorithm be "applied in any manner to physical elements or process steps," provided that its application is circumscribed by more than a field of use limitation or non- essential post-solution activity. As summarized by the PTO in Ex Parte Logan, 20 USPQ2d 1465, 1468 (PTO Bd.Pat.App. and Interf.1991), the emphasis is "on *what* the claimed method steps do rather than *how* the steps are performed". (Emphases in original).

Although the *Freeman-Walter-Abele* analysis is not the only test for statutory subject matter, *Meyer*, 688 F.2d at 796, and this court has stated that failure to meet that test may not always defeat the claim, In re Grams, 888 F.2d 835, 839 (Fed.Cir.1989), this analytic procedure is conveniently applied to the Simson invention.

Analysis

Arrhythmia Research states that the district court erred in law, and that the combination of physical, mechanical, and electrical steps that are described and claimed in the '459 patent constitutes statutory subject matter. Arrhythmia Research stresses that the claims are directed to a process and apparatus for detecting and analyzing a specific heart activity signal, and do not preempt the mathematical algorithms used in any of the procedures. Arrhythmia Research states that the patentability of such claims is now well established by law, precedent, and practice.

Corazonix states that the claims define no more than a mathematical algorithm that calculates a number. Corazonix states that in Simson's process and apparatus claims mathematical algorithms are merely presented and solved, and that Simson's designation of a field of use and post-solution activity are not essential to the claims and thus do not cure this defect. Thus, Corazonix states that the claims are not directed to statutory subject matter, and that the district court's judgment was correct.

A. The Process Claims

Although mathematical calculations are involved in carrying out the claimed process, Arrhythmia Research argues that the claims are directed to a method of detection of a certain heart condition by a novel method of analyzing a portion of the electrocardiographically measured heart cycle. This is accomplished by procedures conducted by means of electronic equipment programmed to perform mathematical computation.

Applying the *Freeman-Walter-Abele* protocol, we accept for the purposes of this analysis the proposition that a mathematical algorithm is included in the subject matter of the process claims in that some claimed steps are described in the specification by mathematical formulae. See In re Johnson, 589 F.2d 1070, 1078 (CCPA 1979) ("Reference to the specification must be made to determine whether [claimed] terms indirectly recite mathematical calculations, formulae, or equations.") We thus proceed to the second stage of the analysis, to determine whether the claimed process is otherwise statutory; that is, we determine what the claimed steps do, independent of how they are implemented.

Simson's process is claimed as a "method for analyzing electrocardiograph signals to determine the presence or absence of a predetermined level of high-frequency energy in the late QRS signal". This claim limitation is not ignored in determining whether the subject matter as a whole is statutory, for all of the claim steps are in implementation of this method. The electrocardiograph signals are first transformed from analog form, in which they are obtained, to the corresponding digital signal. These input signals are not abstractions; they are related to the patient's heart function. The anterior portion of the QRS signal is then processed, as the next step, by the procedure known as reverse time order filtration. The digital filter design selected by Dr. Simson for this purpose, known as the Butterworth filter, is one of several known procedures for frequency filtering of digital waveforms. The filtered signal is further analyzed to determine its average magnitude, as described in the specification, by the root mean square technique. Comparison of the resulting output to a predetermined level determines whether late potentials reside in the anterior portion of the QRS segment, thus indicating whether the patient is at high risk for ventricular tachycardia. The resultant output is not an abstract number, but is a signal related to the patient's heart activity.

These claimed steps of "converting", "applying", "determining", and "comparing" are physical process steps that transform one physical, electrical signal into another. The view that "there is nothing necessarily physical about 'signals'" is incorrect. In re Taner, 681 F.2d 787, 790 (CCPA 1982) (holding statutory claims to a method of seismic exploration including the mathematically described steps of "summing" and "simulating from"). The *Freeman-Walter-Abele* standard is met, for the steps of Simson's claimed method comprise an otherwise statutory process whose mathematical procedures are applied to physical process steps.

It was undisputed that the individual mathematical procedures that describe these steps are all known in the abstract. The method claims do not wholly preempt these procedures, but limit their application to the defined process steps. In answering the question "What did the applicant invent?", *Grams*, 888 F.2d at 839, the Simson method is properly viewed as a method of analyzing electrocardiograph signals in order to determine a specified heart activity. Like the court in *Abele*, which was "faced simply with an improved CAT-scan process", 684 F.2d at 909, the Simson invention is properly viewed as an electrocardiograph analysis process. The claims do not encompass subject matter transcending what Dr. Simson invented, as in O'Reilly v. Morse, 56 U.S. (15 How.) at 113 (claims covered any use of electric current to transmit characters at a distance); or in Benson, 409 U.S. at 68 (use of claimed process could "vary from the operation of a train to verification of driver's licenses to researching the law books for precedents"); or in *Grams*, 888 F.2d at 840 (invention had application to "any complex system, whether it be electrical, mechanical, chemical or biological, or combinations thereof.")

The Simson claims are analogous to those upheld in *Diehr*, wherein the Court remarked that the applicants "do not seek to patent a mathematical formula.... they seek only to foreclose from others the use of that equation in conjunction with all of the other steps in their claimed process". 450 U.S. at 187. Simson's claimed method is similarly limited. The process claims comprise statutory subject matter.

B. The Apparatus Claims

The Simson apparatus for analyzing electrocardiographic signals is claimed in the style of 35 U.S.C. § 112, paragraph 6, whereby functionally described claim elements are "construed to cover the corresponding structure, material, or acts described in the specification and equivalents thereof". Thus the statutory nature vel non of Simson's apparatus claims is determined with reference to the description in the '459 patent specification. In re Iwahashi, 888 F.2d 1370, 1375 (Fed.Cir.1989).

The apparatus claims require a means for converting the electrocardiograph signals from the analog form in which they are generated into digital form. This means is described in the specification as a specific electronic device, a conventional analog-to-digital converter. A minicomputer, configured as described in the specification, is the means of calculating composite digital time segments of the QRS waveform. The product is stored, as stated in the specification, in the form of electrical signals. The high pass filter means is described in the specification as the minicomputer configured to perform the function of reverse time order filtration of the anterior portion of the QRS waveform. The specification and drawings show a disc memory unit to store the composite QRS signals, and associated connecting leads to the computer's processing unit. The comparing means is the processing unit configured to perform the specified function of root mean square averaging of the anterior portion of the QRS complex, and comparison of the resulting output with a predetermined level to provide an indication of the presence of late potentials in the electrocardiograph signal.

The Simson apparatus claims thus define "a combination of interrelated means" for performing specified functions. *Iwahashi*, 888 F.2d at 1375. The computer-performed operations transform a particular input signal to a different output signal, in accordance with the internal structure of the computer as configured by electronic instructions. "The claimed invention ... converts one physical thing into another physical thing just as any other electrical circuitry would do". In re Sherwood, 613 F.2d 809, 819 (CCPA 1980), cert. denied, 450 U.S. 994 (1981) (holding statutory claims to an apparatus for analyzing seismic signals including mathematically described means for "sonogramming", "dividing", and "plotting").

The use of mathematical formulae or relationships to describe the electronic structure and operation of an apparatus does not make it nonstatutory. Iwahashi, 888 F.2d at 1375. When mathematical formulae are the standard way of expressing certain functions or apparatus, it is appropriate that mathematical terms be used. See W.L. Gore & Assoc., Inc. v. Garlock, Inc., 721 F.2d 1540, 1556 (Fed.Cir.1983), cert. denied, 469 U.S. 851 (1984) (patents are directed to those of skill in the art). See also In re Bernhart, 417 F.2d 1395, 1399 (CCPA 1969) ("all machines function according to the laws of physics which can be mathematically set forth if known.") That Simson's claimed functions could not have been performed effectively without the speed and capability of electronic devices and components does not determine whether the claims are statutory.

Corazonix argues that the final output of the claimed apparatus (and process) is simply a number, and that Benson and Flook support the position that when the end product is a number, the claim is nonstatutory and can not be saved by claim limitations of the use to which this number is put. However, the number obtained is not a mathematical abstraction; it is a measure in microvolts of a specified heart activity, an indicator of the risk of ventricular tachycardia. That the product is numerical is not a criterion of whether the claim is directed to statutory subject matter. See Meyer, 688 F.2d at 796 n. 4 (explaining that so-called "negative rules" of patentability "were not intended to be separate tests for determining whether a claim positively recites statutory subject matter.")

The Simson apparatus claims satisfy the criteria for statutory subject matter. They are directed to a specific apparatus of practical utility and specified application, and meet the requirements of 35 U.S.C. § 101.

Conclusion

The judgment of invalidity on the ground that the claimed method and apparatus do not define statutory subject matter is reversed. The cause is remanded for resolution of remaining issues.

Taxable costs in favor of Arrhythmia Research.

REVERSED AND REMANDED.

NOTES

1. The Patent Office and the Federal Circuit have for perfectly understandable reasons had some difficulty in applying the teachings of the Supreme Court in *Diamond v. Chakrabarty*, casebook page 822, *Gottschalk v. Benson*, described in *Chakrabarty*, casebook page 823, *Diamond v. Diehr*, casebook page 832, and *Parker v. Flook*, described in *Chakrabarty*, casebook page 824.

The court considered the case of In re Alappat, 33 F.3d 1526 (Fed. Cir. 1994) in banc, leading to hopes that the Court might use the case as a vehicle for announcing clearer guidelines for patentable subject matter including mathematical alogrithms processed by a digital computer. In *Alappat* the Patent Office had rejected an application on a patent for a method (and an apparatus that implemented the method) of smoothing the waveform on an oscilloscope. The technique made use of a procedure expressed in terms of mathematical equations, and implemented through the circuitry of the oscilloscope. The implementation was straight-forward for one skilled in the art once the equations were specified. The court reversed, holding that the process claim was for a useful process and that the apparatus claim was for a machine, i.e. an improved oscilloscope. The opinion, written by Judge Rich, was consistent with the line of precedents discussed in the principal case.

However, the opinion was less definitive than it might have been because the issue of § 101 subject matter was combined with an issue of the legality of the composition of the Board of Patent Appeals and Interferences that issued the decsion under review. The court concluded that this question affected its own jurisdiction. Of the ten members of the court sitting in banc, four judges (and Judge Rich) concurred in the opinion of the court, two dissented, and three declined to express an opinon on the ground that the court lacked jurisdiction.

Recent cases involving these issues are In re Trovato, 42 F.3d 1376 (Fed. Cir. 1994) (procedure for finding the optimal path between two points unpatentable subject matter), vacated and remanded 60 F.3d 807 (Fed. Cir. 1995); In re Warmerdam, 33 F.3d 1354 (Fed. Cir. 1994) (claim for collision avoidance procedure for robots unpatentable subject matter). In In re Warmerdam, Judge Plager remarked of the Freeman-Walter-Abele test that "The difficulty is that there is no clear agreement as to what is a 'mathematical algorithm', which makes rather dicey the determination of whether the claim as a whole is no more than that." 33 F.3d 1359.

3. Although the Supreme Court decided in 1981 (in Diamond v. Diehr, casebook page 832) that some software was patentable, cases involving claims of exclusive right to software continued to be almost exclusively copyright cases. This was because after the Supreme Court decision the firms in the industry had to devise a strategy for using patent protection, prepare applications and submit them to the PTO. The PTO in turn had to hire examiners and process the applications. Significant

software patents began to trickle out in the late 1980's. Two events in 1994 brought home the importance that software patents are likely to have in the future.

In February, 1994 Stac Electronics won a jury verdict against Microsoft for $120,000,000 for infringement of its patent on a data compression system. Stac had developed and marketed a program, "Stacker," that would double the amount of storage space available on a hard disk. Microsoft decided to build a similar feature into Microsoft DOS 6.0, an upgrade for the popular operating system used on IBM-style personal computers. It first approached Stac for a license to use its software, but when negotiations broke down it developed its own system. The system was not a copy of Stacker, and hence not copyright infringement, but it employed some of the same techniques. The parties settled the litigation on June 21, 1994, agreeing to cross-license their disk compression technology and Microsoft agreeing to pay royalties of $1,000,0000 a month for 43 months and buy $39.9 million of non-voting convertible preferred Stac stock. 48 BNA Patent Trademark & Copyright Journal 193.

An event that attracted even more attention, although it was ultimately less important, was the issuance to Compton's NewMedia of Patent No. 5,241,671 on a "Multimedia Search System Using a Plurality of Entry Path Means Which Indicate Interrelatedness of Information." The patent was issued on August 31, 1993 on an application filed on October 26, 1989. Compton's announced the issuance of the patent to it in November, 1993 at the COMDEX trade show, the big personal computer trade show held in Las Vegas, and that it planned to collect reasonable royalties from all sellers of multimedia products. The industry and the specialized journalists that cover the industry reacted with astonishment and hostility. In their view, it was as if Compton's had been granted a patent on the technique of providing an index with a book. The PTO responded to the furor by proceeding on its own motion to re-examine the patent and ultimately, in October, 1994, to deny the claims. This information was drawn from various LEXIS-NEXIS files.

PAGE 848. Add to note 5.

In In re Brana, 51 F.3d 1560 (Fed. Cir. 1995), the court reversed a rejection by the PTO of an application for a patent on a chemical compound shown to have superior anti-tumor properties in mice. The PTO rejected the application on the ground that this was an insufficient showing of utility. It objected, for instance, that the tests involved injecting tumor-causing cells into the mice, rather than demonstrating the efficacy of the compound against an actual disease. The court reversed on the groundsthat in light of the art this was a sufficient showing of utility. The court did not discuss the Brenner v. Manson opinion.

PAGE 853. Add new note 12.

12. The National Institutes of Health and the Energy Department of the U.S. Government are engaged (at great expense) in the "National Genome Project," a multi-year effort to locate and decode all of the genetic information stored in the DNA of every cell and passed on from one generation to another. The history of the project

is described in Robert M. Cook-Deegan, The Gene Wars : Science, Politics, and the Human Genome (New York: W.W. Norton & Co., 1994).

In 1992 NIH began filing patent applications on behalf of its researchers for hundreds of complementary cDNA fragments or "express sequence tags" to be used to identify full gene sequences. Although it is believed this information will ultimately lead to useful therapies, the present applications simply disclose the structure of the cDNA fragments. The PTO has rejected these applications for failure to demonstrate novelty, nonobviousness and usefulness. That rejection is correct, is it not?

One concern of the NIH is that private firms will be able to develop patentable discoveries based on the information gathered in the National Genome Project to make patentable inventions which would be privately owned, even though the National Genome Project is publicly funded. Are patent applications the way to solve this problem. What other approaches could be used? Another concern was that publication of the results of the project would raise the level of ordinary skill in the art such that subsequent useful inventions resulting from the foundational work of the project would be unpatentable, with the possible result that they might not be commercialized.

PAGE 881. Add to note 4.

Section 251 of the patent statute, 35 U.S.C. § 251, first sentence, provides: "Whenever any patent is, through error without any deceptive intention, deemed wholly or partly inoperative or invalid, by reason of a defective specification or drawing, or by reason of the patentee claiming more or less than he had a right to claim in the patent, the Commissioner shall, on the surrender of such patent and the payment of the fee required by the law, reissue the patent for the invention disclosed in the original patent, and in accordance with a new and amended application, for the unexpired part of the term of the original patent."

In Scripps Clinic and Research Foundation v. Genentech, Inc., 927 F.2d 1565 (Fed. Cir. 1991), involving the patent on Factor VIII:C, the original patent owned by Scripps based on the extraction of purified Factor VIII:C from plasma contained process claims and product by process claims, but no straight product claims. The defendant produced its Factor VIII:C through biological manipulations not involving purification, and argued that its Factor VIII:C did not infringe the Scripps patent. Scripps sought reissue of its patent to include product claims, and the PTO granted the reissue. Genentech challenged the reissue as inappropriate. The Federal Circuit discussed the scope of the reissue procedure as follows:

SCRIPPS CLINIC & RESEARCH FOUNDATION v. GENENTECH, INC.
United States Court of Appeals for the Federal Circuit, 1991.
927 F. 2d 1565

* * *

II

35 U.S.C. § 251

A

The R'011 patent is a reissue of Patent No. 4,361,509 ("the '509 patent"), granted on November 20, 1982. Genentech challenged the adequacy of the patentee's reason for seeking reissue, stating that this reason was insufficient in terms of 35 U.S.C. § 251. On this ground the district court granted Genentech's motion for partial summary judgment of invalidity of claims 17, 18, 24-29, and 34 [the reissue claims].

Although there were factual aspects debated by the parties, they are not material to the question of the legal adequacy of the patentee's reason for requesting reissue. That is a question of law, and the facts material to that question were not in dispute. The matter could have been, and was, decided summarily. * * *. However, the district court erred in its conclusion of law.

* * *

The principal error that the inventors sought to cure was the claiming of "less than [they] had a right to claim in the patent" due to the omission of product claims. The '509 patent contained only process and product-by-process claims.[7] In the reissue application inventors Zimmerman and Fulcher declared that they had always viewed the Factor VIII:C product as their invention, pointing out that the '509 specification stated that it was an object of their invention to produce highly purified Factor VIII:C.

An error of law is not excluded from the class of error subject to correction in accordance with the reissue statute. Although attorney error is not an open invitation to reissue in every case in which it may appear, see In re Weiler, 790 F.2d 1576, 1579 (Fed.Cir.1986) ("not every event or circumstance that might be labeled 'error' is correctable by reissue"), the purpose of the reissue statute is to avoid forfeiture of substantive rights due to error made without intent to deceive. See generally Ball Corp. v. United States, 729 F.2d 1429, 1939 n. 28 (Fed.Cir.1984) (the reissue statute "is based on fundamental principles of equity and fairness").

---

[7] Broadened claims by reissue must be applied for within two years of grant of the original patent. 35 U.S.C. § 251. This requirement was met.

When the statutory requirements are met, reissuance of the patent is not discretionary with the Commissioner; it is mandatory ("shall"). See In re Handel, 312 F.2d 943, 948 (CCPA 1963) ("the whole purpose of the statute, so far as claims are concerned, is to permit limitations to be added to claims that are too broad or to be taken from claims that are too narrow").

Genentech does not dispute that error was made, and does not challenge the principle of the availability of product claims to the purified Factor VIII:C. Further, Genentech does not assert that the attorneys' initial view of the unavailability of product claims involved any deceptive intention. The district court, holding that there was insufficient reason for reissue, appeared to interpret § 251 as requiring a showing that the error in claiming the product could not have been avoided, in order to be eligible for cure. This is not the framework of the reissue statute.

The law does not require that no competent attorney or alert inventor could have avoided the error sought to be corrected by reissue. Failure of the attorney to claim the invention sufficiently broadly is "one of the most common sources of defects". In re Wilder, 736 F.2d 1516 (Fed.Cir.1984), cert. denied, 469 U.S. 1209 (1985): An attorney's failure to appreciate the full scope of the invention is one of the most common sources of defects in patents. The fact that the error could have been discovered at the time of prosecution with a more thorough patentability search or with improved communication between the inventors and the attorney does not, by itself, preclude a patent owner from correcting defects through reissue. Id. at 1519.

Subjective intent is not determinative of whether the applicants erred in claiming less than they had a right to claim. In re Mead, 581 F.2d 251, 255 (CCPA 1978). "Intent to claim" is not the criterion for reissue, and has been well described as "but judicial shorthand, signifying a means of measuring whether the statutorily required error is present." In re Weiler, 790 F.2d 1576, 1581 (Fed.Cir.1986) (emphasis in original). The statutory standard of reissuable error is objective, and does not require proof of subjective state of mind: Determining what protection [an inventor] intended to secure by [an] original patent for the purposes of § 251 is an essentially factual inquiry confined to the *objective* intent manifested by the original patent. In re Rowand, 526 F.2d 558, 560 (CCPA 1975) (emphasis in original).

On undisputed facts, the inventors established that they had claimed less than they had a right to claim, that they had done so in error, and that there was not deceptive intention. The application for reissue fully complied with the statutory and regulatory requirements.

As a matter of law, reissue claims 17, 18, 24-29, and 34 are not invalid on this ground. The grant of partial summary judgment is reversed. On remand, partial summary judgment shall be entered for Scripps on this ground.

PAGE 897. Add.

EE. The Nonobviousness Analysis of Chemical and Biotechnological Inventions

Public Law 104-41, Biotechnological Process Patents, Nov. 1, 1995, added new § 103(b)(1) and a new third sentence to the first paragraph of § 282.

The purpose of the law was described in House Rep. No. 104-178, 1995 U.S. Code Cong. & Admin. News vol. 2, p. 395, 396-400 as follows:

Patents can be granted on any invention that is included within the statutory subject matter provisions, including processes under 35 U.S.C. § 101. A patent on an invention gives the patent owner the right to exclude others from making, using or selling that invention. A process patent may be obtained for a new method of use or new method of making a product. A process patent can be infringed if the process is used in making any product or used in any manner covered by the process patent. If a patent is obtained on a product, the owner of the patent can prevent the manufacture, the sale or the importation of that particular product in the United States. The owner of a United States patent cannot prevent the manufacture or sale of that patented product in another country, unless a patent is obtained in that country.

It is not uncommon to seek a product patent with process claims relating to the same invention. A process can be described in simple terms such as a new method of draining swamps to more complex processes detailing the exact steps that take place when a starting material is pasteurized, pressurized, radiated or subjected to other procedures. Product and process patents claims are each subject to examination under the same principles of patent law, including examining criteria such as novelty, nonobviousness, and usefulness.

If a patent containing process claims is granted on the manufacturing process or development process of a particular product, then the owner of the patent also can prevent the manufacture or sale of a product made using that process. Under the provisions of the Process Patent Amendments Act of 1988, the process owner also can prevent importation of the product if the product is made overseas using the patented process [under § 271(g)]. A patent may be obtained on the starting materials or materials used in a process but unless a patent on the process is obtained (or a patent on the final product), the final product could be produced overseas and imported back into the United States for sale without infringing the patent on the materials used in the process.

A problem arises in those situations in which the final product produced by a process may not be patentable. Without a patent on the final product or a patent on the process, the original developer of the product cannot take advantage either of basic product patent protection or the process patent protection permitted under the Process Patent Amendments Act of 1988.

Under present patent law, an owner of a product patent can prevent others in the United States from using or making a patented product even in the absence of a process patent. The value of the process patent is the ability to prevent others from importing a non-patentable product that was made by use of a protected process. The value of the process patent is the ability to prevent others from importing a non-patentable product that was made by use of a protected process.

H.R. 587 and related predecessor bills were developed as a result of two conflicting and irreconcilable decisions issued by the Court of Appeals for the Federal Circuit, In re Durden, 763 F. 2d 1406 (Fed. Cir. 1985) and In re Pleuddemann, 910 F. 2d 823 (Fed. Cir. 1990).

In re Durden concerned a process patent claim which had been rejected by the PTO. The case involved a chemical process. The applicants for the patent argued on appeal that while individual process steps were obvious, the use of a novel and nonobvious starting material and the production of a new and nonobvious product meant that the process should be patentable. The Court concluded that the use of a new starting material and/or the development of a patented product did not automatically ensure the nonobviousness of a process or the grant of a process patent. The Court noted that if every process using a new or novel material was granted a patent, then simple processes such as dissolving or heating would be patentable when using a new compound.

Following this case, there were complaints from various industry groups that the PTO was automatically rejecting process claims under circumstances similar to *In re Durden*. In the subsequent case of *In re Pleuddemann*, the Court emphasized that *In re Durden* was not to be read as a "per se" rule against patenting old processes using new starting materials or producing new products. The Court stated that each invention had to be viewed as a whole and considered on its individual facts.

In holding of *In re Pleuddemann*, the Court distinguished *In re Durden* on the grounds that the fact situation there involved a process of "making", and *In re Pleuddemann* involved a process of "using." The Court did not specifically overrule *In re Durden* but relied on the distinction of "using" versus "making." The distinction between the two types of processes was lost on many and caused others to manipulate phrasing in developing patent applications to ensure that processes were "using" instead of "making." At two different hearings during the 103d Congress of the then Subcommittee on Intellectual Property and Judicial Administration, testimony was provided which indicated that in several cases the patent applicant had originally written a claim as a "making" process. After the examiner rejected the claims on the basis of

In re Durden, the claims were rewritten as a "using" claim and were approved by the examiner.

The holdings in *In re Durden* and *In re Pleuddemann* have led to inconsistent practices by the PTO in the examination of applications for process patents. The result has been that some process patents have been granted without any delay or controversy while other applications, similar in nature, have been rejected or required to be defended at length with the patent examiner.

Legislation was developed as a response to a perceived failure on the part of PTO to grant process patents based on the *In re Durden* decision and the resulting importation problem due to the inability of inventors to obtain process patents. While the holdings of *In re Durden* and *In re Pleuddemann* have been applied generally, the resulting problems were considered to affect particularly biotechnology applications because of the nature of the products produced. In the case of biotechnology products, the final product is a naturally occurring substance despite the fact that it has never been able to be produced before in commercially viable quantities.

The final unpatentable product is often developed or synthesized through the use of a "host cell" that has been genetically altered in a way to produce the final product in large quantities. The host cell is usually patentable. The issue is whether the process, by which the final product is produced, also can be patented.

Since the host cell is patented, the host cell cannot be used in the United States without the patent owner's permission and no products can be produced in the United States from that host cell. Without a United States process patent, however, the host cell can be taken offshore and used to make the final product. The final product produced from the host cell can be imported back into the United States for commercial sale. The owner of the patented host cell has no recourse because there is no "use" of the patented host cell in the United States and thus no infringement. Since there is no patent on the process by which the final product was produced, the importation of the product cannot be challenged.

Clearly, obtaining a process patent could solve the importation problem for the biotechnology industry. H.R. 587 is necessitated by the difficulty of obtaining timely and adequate process patent protection under present court rulings and PTO interpretation.

The approach taken in H.R. 587 is industry specific, as were some prior bills designed to take care of the problem. Although industry specific legislation, particularly in the context of patent law, is generally not favored, considerable opposition to a more comprehensive solution proposed by other predecessor bills, such as H.R. 4307, made their enactment unlikely. As a result of concerns raised by certain industries as to the impact of a broad change in patent law, the applicability of H.R. 587 has been limited to biotechnological processes only. The computer industry, the electronics industry and others previously raised questions as to the ability of certain patent owners to secure patents that would have such extensive coverage that public domain processes would be combined with new products to obtain patent coverage to the detriment of the industry. The chemical industry also raised questions as to the scope and potential infringement of patents issued under the revised examination process proposed in H.R. 4307, as introduced, and as amended.

The legislation impacts only one element of patentability of biotechnological processes-the element of nonobviousness. There is no guarantee of patentability if the process claim satisfies the special nonobviousness provisions of the revised § 103. The process must still satisfy all other requirements of patentability, including the utility requirement under 35 U.S.C. § 101 and the enabling provisions of 35 U.S.C. § 112 which require sufficient description provisions of the invention and claims, described in "full, clear and concise, and exact terms," so that other skilled in the art can use the process. Process claims patented pursuant to the proposed revisions of § 103 would not enjoy greater protection than process claims granted under present law.

Resolution of this problem will provide both certainty for patent applicants in the field of biotechnology and protection against foreign competition. Once process patents are awarded, foreign companies will not be able to take advantage of the inability of the United States manufacturer to obtain a product patent. There is no question, as some opponents have argued, that, in many cases, a product patent provides better protection than a process patent against foreign manufacture and importation of the product into the United States. However, if a product patent is unobtainable because of the nature of the final product, it is essential that some other protection be afforded. In the opinion of the Committee, the appropriate protection is a process patent and the infringement protection pursuant to 35 U.S.C. § 271(g) against importation of products resulting from foreign use of the patented process.

The unpredictability of the patent examination process has become a critical problem for development of new technologies, such as biotechnology. With a mitigation of uncertainty, that industry can now better assess the chances and risks associated with the patent application process. The granting of a process patent will no longer depend on the chance of the wording of a claim or the preference of an examiner in applying the holding of *In re Durden* versus the holding of *In re Pleuddemann*.

H.R. 587 is in no way intended to reduce or eliminate any requirements of the patent laws of the United States other than providing, upon election of an applicant, that a biotechnological process using or resulting in a composition of matter found upon examination to be novel and nonobvious, shall likewise be found nonobvious. It is intended that biotechnological processes using or resulting in a composition of matter, otherwise patentable to the applicant, be entitled to full patent protection including the benefits of enforcement, specifically of 35 U.S.C. § 271(g).

It is not intended by this bill that applicants be given the right to extend patent claims to all upstream or downstream processes leading to or resulting from use of the patented composition of matter in a way that would create infringement liability on parties not making or using the patented composition of matter, except as is already provided under existing law for infringement.

There are presently two cases being considered by the U.S. Court of Appeals for the Federal Circuit which may have a bearing on the matter considered in H.R. 587.[12] The Court still has not issued opinions in these cases which might resolve the perceived inconsistencies of the two previous opinions of the Court, *In re Durden* and *In re Pleuddemann*. The two cases were argued in November 1992. There has been no indication when the Court might issue the decisions. In any event, it is by no means certain that the two cases will resolve the underlying issues. On the other hand, because H.R. 587 is restricted to biotechnological processes, its enactment would not moot these cases, as they involve chemical processes.

The PTO testified before the Subcommittee that it does not believe it can resolve the problem administratively because of the two seemingly conflicting Court opinions.

NOTE

The *Ochiai* and *Brouwer* cases mentioned in footnote 12 to the House Report have been decided. In re Ochiai, 71 F.3d 1565 (Fed. Cir. 1995) and In re Brouwer, 77 F.3d 422 (Fed. Cir. 1996). The opinions were joined by only two members of the court, Judges Archer and Michel, the third member of the panel, a district judge on assignment, had resigned from the bench. Both opinions deny that the case law of the federal circuit is in conflict. For instance, in Ochiai, 71 F.3d 1572-73, the Court said:

Both the Solicitor and Ochiai devote substantial portions of their briefs to purported demonstrations that our precedents on the obviousness vel non of chemical processes are, if not in conflict, at least in severe tension with one another and thus create unnecessary confusion. Both parties identify the same two sets of three cases as presenting the conflict: *Larsen*, *Albertson*, and *Durden*, upholding rejections on appeal, are said to be inconsistent with *Kuehl*, *Mancy*, and *Pleuddemann*, reversing rejections on appeal. While we agree that some generalized commentary found within several of these decisions may present minor tensions, both Ochiai and the Solicitor draw far too bleak a picture of the state of our case law. Other language in these cases, like their actual holdings, obviates any real inconsistency.

---

[12] In re Ochiai, No. 92-1446 (Fed. Cir. filed July 22, 1992); In re Brouwer, No. 92-1225 (Fed. Cir. filed March 11, 1992).

In *Albertson*, the court "reiterate[d] that all of the evidence must be considered on the 'subject matter as a whole,' from the viewpoint of one skilled in the art, in the determination of obviousness, and not simply the patentability of one of the starting reactants in a process." Albertson, 332 F.2d at 382. Thus, the Board in this case looked to the general result in Albertson while ignoring the Albertson court's explicit methodology. Every subsequent case that the parties discuss has been grounded on the same analytic principle: namely, that section 103 requires a fact-intensive comparison of the claimed process with the prior art rather than the mechanical application of one or another per se rule. See Pleuddemann, 910 F.2d at 827 ("We repeat that the controlling law is in § 103 of the statute, which must be applied to the facts of this case."); Durden, 763 F.2d at 1411 ("Our function is to apply, in each case, § 103 as written to the facts of disputed issues, not to generalize or make rules for other cases which are unforeseeable."); Mancy, 499 F.2d at 1292, ("[T]he statutory standard of § 103 for determining obviousness of an invention is whether in view of the prior art the invention as a whole would have been obvious at the time it was made."); Kuehl, 475 F.2d at 665 ("The test of unobviousness is a statutory test and requires comparison of the invention with the prior art in each case...."). As a consequence, these cases do not--indeed, cannot--present or create conflicting legal rules. They present, instead, applications of a unitary legal regime to different claims and fields of art to yield particularized results. It is thus surprising that the Board relies on *Durden* for a general rule when the *Durden* court expressly cautioned the bar "not to generalize or make rules for other cases."

Because the regime of section 103, much like the Fourth Amendment proscriptions against "unreasonable" searches and warrants issued upon less than "probable cause," mandates that legal outcomes turn on the close analysis of facts, reasonable persons may well disagree about the outcome of a given obviousness determination. These disagreements over the application of a legal rule can, however, be transformed into perceived "irreconcilable conflicts" between legal rules only when, as occurred here, examiners, members of the Board, and patent lawyers purport to find competing per se rules in our precedents and argue for rejection or allowance of a particular claim accordingly. We acknowledge that some generalized commentary found in these cases reviewing rejections of claims directed to chemical processes may, if viewed in isolation, have inadvertently provided encouragement to those who desire per se rules in this area. For example, one case includes an extensive discussion of the conceptual link between the obviousness vel non of a chemical composition and the obviousness vel non of a process for making the composition.[6] Such discussion, while

---

[6] See *Pleuddemann*, 910 F.2d at 827, ("'From the standpoint of patent law, a compound and all of its properties are inseparable; they are one and the same thing.' In re Papesch, 315 F.2d 381, 391 (1963). It is the properties of appellant's compounds as bonding/priming agents for certain polymers and fillers or support surfaces that give them their utility. As stated above, the compounds and their use are but different aspects of, or ways of looking at, the same invention and consequently that invention is capable of being claimed both as new compounds

entirely accurate, may have contributed to the erroneous view that one may determine the obviousness of a chemical process merely by determining whether it is a process for making a composition. As the cases noted above make clear, however, this is not and has never been the law of section 103. Indeed, *Durden*, the very case relied on by the examiner and the Board for a purported per se rule, clearly states that there are no such per se rules.

The use of per se rules, while undoubtedly less laborious than a searching comparison of the claimed invention--including all its limitations-- with the teachings of the prior art, flouts section 103 and the fundamental case law applying it. Per se rules that eliminate the need for fact-specific analysis of claims and prior art may be administratively convenient for PTO examiners and the Board. Indeed, they have been sanctioned by the Board as well. But reliance on per se rules of obviousness is legally incorrect and must cease. Any such administraconvenience is simply inconsistent with section 103, which, according to *Graham* and its progeny, entitles an applicant to issuance of an otherwise proper patent unless the PTO establishes that the invention as claimed in the application is obvious over cited prior art, based on the specific comparison of that prior art with claim limitations. We once again hold today that our precedents do not establish any per se rules of obviousness, just as those precedents themselves expressly declined to create such rules. Any conflicts as may be perceived to exist derive from an impermissible effort to extract per se rules from decisions that disavow precisely such extraction.

In sum, as we clearly indicated in *In re Dillon*, a recent in banc decision, "[w]hen any applicant properly presents and argues suitable method claims, they should be examined in light of all ... relevant factors, free from any presumed controlling effect of *Durden*" or any other precedent. 919 F.2d 688, 695 (Fed.Cir.1990) (in banc), cert. denied, 500 U.S. 904 (1991). Having compared Ochiai's claims, limited as they are to the use of a particular nonobvious starting material for making a particular nonobvious end product, to the prior art of record, we reverse the rejection of claims 6 through 10 as an incorrect conclusion reached by incorrect methodology.

In re DILLON
United States Court of Appeals for the Federal Circuit (in banc), 1990.
919 F.2d 688.

---

or as a new method or process of bonding/priming. On the other hand, a process or method of making the compounds is a quite different thing; they may have been made by a process which was new or old, obvious or nonobvious. In this respect, therefore, there is a real difference between a process of making and a process of using and the cases dealing with one involve different problems from the cases dealing with the other.").

LOURIE, Circuit Judge.

Diane M. Dillon, assignor to Union Oil Company of California, appeals the November 25, 1987, decision of the Board of Patent Appeals and Interferences (Board) of the United States Patent and Trademark Office (PTO), Appeal No. 87-0944, rejecting claims 2-14, 16-22, and 24-37, all the remaining claims of patent application Serial No. 671,570 entitled "Hydrocarbon Fuel Composition." We affirm the rejection of all of the claims.[7]

The Invention

Dillon's patent application describes and claims her discovery that the inclusion of certain tetra-orthoester compounds in hydrocarbon fuel compositions will reduce the emission of solid particulates (i.e., soot) during combustion of the fuel. In this appeal Dillon asserts the patentability of claims to hydrocarbon fuel compositions containing these tetra-orthoesters, and to the method of reducing particulate emissions during combustion by combining these esters with the fuel before combustion.

Claim 2 is the broadest composition claim:

2. A composition comprising: a hydrocarbon fuel; and a sufficient amount of at least one orthoester so as to reduce the particulate emissions from the combustion of the hydrocarbon fuel, wherein the orthoester is of the formula:

$$R_3-O-\underset{\underset{O-R_5}{|}}{\overset{\overset{O-R_7}{|}}{C}}-O-R_6$$

wherein R, R, R, and R, are the same or different monovalent organic radical comprising 1 to about 20 carbon atoms.

The broadest method claim is claim 24:

---

[7] A panel of this court heard this appeal and reversed the Board on December 29, 1989. 892 F.2d 1554. The PTO petitioned for rehearing and suggested rehearing in banc on February 12, 1990. Rehearing in banc was ordered on May 21, 1990, and the judgment which was entered on December 29, 1989, was vacated, the accompanying opinion being withdrawn.

24. A method of reducing the particulate emissions from the combustion of a hydrocarbon fuel comprising combusting a mixture of the hydrocarbon fuel and a sufficient amount of at least one orthoester so as to reduce the particulate emissions, wherein the orthoester is of the formula:

$$R_3-O-\underset{\underset{O-R_5}{|}}{\overset{\overset{O-R_7}{|}}{C}}-O-R_5$$

wherein R, R, R, and R, are the same or different monovalent organic radical comprising 1 to about 20 carbon atoms.

The other claims contain additional limitations and thus are narrower in scope.

The tetra-orthoesters are a known class of chemical compounds. It is undisputed that their combination with hydrocarbon fuel, for any purpose, is not shown in the prior art, and that their use to reduce particulate emissions from combustion of hydrocarbon fuel is not shown or suggested in the prior art.

The Rejection

The Board held all of the claims to be unpatentable on the ground of obviousness, 35 U.S.C. § 103, in view of certain primary and secondary references. As primary references the Board relied on two Sweeney U.S. patents, 4,390,417 ('417) and 4,395,267 ('267). Sweeney '417 describes hydrocarbon fuel compositions containing specified chemical compounds, viz., ketals, acetals, and tri-orthoesters,[8] used for "dewatering" the fuels, particularly diesel oil. Sweeney '267 describes three-component compositions of hydrocarbon fuels heavier than gasoline, immiscible alcohols, and tri-orthoesters, wherein the tri-orthoesters serve as cosolvents to prevent phase separation between fuel and alcohol. The Board explicitly found that the Sweeney patents do not teach the use of the tetra-orthoesters recited in appellant's claims.

---

[8] Tri-orthoesters have three -OR groups bonded to a central carbon atom, and the fourth carbon bond is to hydrogen or a hydrocarbon group (-R); they are represented as C(R)(OR). Tetra-orthoesters have four -OR groups bonded to a central carbon atom, and are represented as C(OR); see Dillon's claims, supra.

The Board cited Elliott U.S. Patent 3,903,006 and certain other patents, including Howk U.S. Patent 2,840,613, as secondary references. Elliott describes tri-orthoesters and tetra-orthoesters for use as water scavengers in hydraulic (non-hydrocarbon) fluids. The Board stated that the Elliott reference shows equivalence between tetra-orthoesters and tri-orthoesters, and that "it is clear from the combined teachings of these references ... that [Dillon's tetra-orthoesters] would operate to remove water from non-aqueous liquids by the same mechanism as the orthoesters of Sweeney."

The Board stated that there was a "reasonable expectation" that the tri- and tetra-orthoester fuel compositions would have similar properties, based on "close structural and chemical similarity" between the tri- and tetra-orthoesters and the fact that both the prior art and Dillon use these compounds as "fuel additives." The Commissioner argues on appeal that the claimed compositions and method "would have been prima facie obvious from combined teachings of the references." On this reasoning, the Board held that unless Dillon showed some unexpected advantage or superiority of her claimed tetra-orthoester fuel compositions as compared with tri-orthoester fuel compositions, Dillon's new compositions as well as her claimed method of reducing particulate emissions are unpatentable for obviousness. It found that no such showing was made.

The Issue

The issue before this court is whether the Board erred in rejecting as obvious under 35 U.S.C. § 103 claims to Dillon's new compositions and to the new method of reducing particulate emissions, when the additives in the new compositions are structurally similar to additives in known compositions, having a different use, but the new method of reducing particulate emissions is neither taught nor suggested by the prior art.

The Broad Composition Claims

Claim 2, the broadest composition claim, comprises a hydrocarbon fuel and an amount of tetra-orthoester sufficient to reduce the particulate emissions from the combustion of the hydrocarbon fuel. The other composition claims contain various limitations including a minimum amount of emission reduction to be achieved (claim 3), percentages of ester in the fuel (claims 4, 5, 16, 20, 21), use of different esters (claims 6-10, 17-19), use of different fuels (claims 11-14, 22), and the requirement that the composition be essentially free of alcohol (claims 36, 37).

* * *

The Board found that the claims to compositions of a hydrocarbon fuel and a tetra-orthoester were prima facie obvious over Sweeney '417 and '267 in view of Elliott and Howk. We agree. Appellant argues that none of these references discloses or suggests the new use which she has discovered. That is, of course, true, but the composition claims are not limited to this new use; i.e., they are not physically or structurally distinguishable over the prior art compositions except with respect to the orthoester component. We believe that the PTO has established, through its combination of references, that there is a sufficiently close relationship between the tri-orthoesters and tetra-orthoesters (see the cited Elliott and Howk references) in the fuel oil art to create an expectation that hydrocarbon fuel compositions containing the tetra-esters would have similar properties, including water scavenging, to like compositions containing the tri-esters, and to provide the motivation to make such new compositions. Howk teaches use of both tri- and tetra-orthoesters in a similar type of chemical reaction. Elliott teaches their equivalence for a particular practical use.

* * *

Appellant cites In re Wright, 848 F.2d 1216, 1219 (Fed.Cir.1988), for the proposition that a prima facie case of obviousness requires that the prior art suggest the claimed compositions' properties and the problem the applicant attempts to solve. The earlier panel opinion in this case, In re Dillon, 892 F.2d 1554 (now withdrawn), in fact stated "a *prima facie* case of obviousness is not deemed made unless both (1) the new compound or composition is structurally similar to the reference compound or composition and (2) there is some suggestion or expectation *in the prior art* that the new compound or composition will have the *same or a similar utility as that discovered by the applicant.*" Id. at 1560 (emphasis added).

This court, in reconsidering this case in banc, reaffirms that structural similarity between claimed and prior art subject matter, proved by combining references or otherwise, where the prior art gives reason or motivation to make the claimed compositions, creates a *prima facie* case of obviousness, and that the burden (and opportunity) then falls on an applicant to rebut that *prima facie* case. Such rebuttal or argument can consist of a comparison of test data showing that the claimed compositions possess unexpectedly improved properties or properties that the prior art does not have ([cites]* * *), that the prior art is so deficient that there is no motivation to make what might otherwise appear to be obvious changes ([cites]* * *), or any other argument or presentation of evidence that is pertinent. There is no question that all evidence of the properties of the claimed compositions and the prior art must be considered in determining the ultimate question of patentability, but it is also clear that the discovery that a claimed composition possesses a property not disclosed for the prior art subject matter, does not by itself defeat a prima facie case. [cite]* * *. Each situation must be considered on its own facts, but it is not necessary in order to establish a *prima facie* case of obviousness that both a structural similarity between a claimed and prior art compound (or a key component of a composition) be shown and that there be a suggestion in or expectation from *the prior art* that the claimed compound or composition will have the same or a similar utility *as one newly discovered by applicant*. To the extent that *Wright* suggests or holds to the contrary, it is hereby overruled. In particular, the statement that a *prima facie* obviousness rejection is not supported if no reference shows or suggests the newly-discovered properties and results of a claimed structure is not the law.[9]

Under the facts we have here, as described above, we have concluded that a *prima facie* case has been established. The art provided the motivation to make the claimed compositions in the expectation that they would have similar properties. Appellant had the opportunity to rebut the prima facie case. She did not present any showing of data to the effect that her compositions had properties not possessed by the prior art compositions or that they possessed them to an unexpectedly greater degree. She attempted to refute the significance of the teachings of the prior art references. She did not succeed and we do not believe the PTO was in error in its decision.

Appellant points out that none of the references relates to the problem she confronted, citing *In re Wright*, and that the combination of references is based on hindsight. It is clear, however, that appellant's claims have to be considered as she has drafted them, i.e., as compositions consisting of a fuel and a tetra-orthoester, and that Sweeney '417 and '267 describe the combination of a liquid fuel with a related compound, a tri-orthoester. While Sweeney does not suggest appellant's use, her composition claims are not limited to that use;[10] the claims merely recite compositions analogous to those in the Sweeney patents, and appellant has made no showing overcoming the *prima facie* presumption of similar properties for those analogous compositions. The mention in the appealed claims that the amount of orthoester must be sufficient to reduce particulate emissions is not a distinguishing limitation of the claims, unless that amount is different from the prior art and critical to the use of the claimed composition. * * *. That is not the case here. The amount of ester recited in the dependent claims can be from 0.05-49%, a very broad range; a preferred range is .05-9%, compared with a percentage in Sweeney '417 approximately equimolar to the amounts of water in the fuel which the ester is intended to remove (.01-5%).

---

[9] The earlier, now-withdrawn *Dillon* opinion, this opinion, and the dissent cite and rely on cases involving claims to chemical compounds, whereas this case involves compositions. The reason for this reliance is that, in this case, the principal difference between the claimed and prior art compositions is the difference between chemical compounds, viz., tri- orthoesters and tetra-orthoesters. Cases dealing with chemical compounds are therefore directly analogous here and, in view of the history of this case and its in banc status, we will make much comment on these cases in this opinion. We do not, however, intend to imply that in all cases involving claimed compositions, structural obviousness between involved chemical compounds necessarily makes the claimed compositions prima facie obvious.

[10] The dissent misinterprets this comment as indicating that claims to new compounds and compositions must contain a limitation to a specific use, and states that past cases have rejected this proposition. Our comment only points out that the composition claims on appeal are not structurally or physically distinguishable from the prior art compositions by virtue of the recitation of their newly-discovered use.

Appellant attacks the Elliott patent as non-analogous art, being in the field of hydraulic fluids rather than fuel combustion. We agree with the PTO that the field of relevant prior art need not be drawn so narrowly. As this court stated in In re Deminski, 796 F.2d 436, 442 (Fed.Cir.1986) (quoting In re Wood, 599 F.2d 1032, 1036 (CCPA 1979)):

> [t]he determination that a reference is from a nonanalogous art is therefore two-fold. First, we decide if the reference is within the field of the inventor's endeavor. If it is not, we proceed to determine whether the reference is reasonably pertinent to the particular problem with which the inventor was involved.

Following that test, one concerned with the field of fuel oils clearly is chargeable with knowledge of Sweeney '417, which discloses fuel compositions with tri-orthoesters for dewatering purposes, and chargeable with knowledge of other references to tri--orthoesters, including for use as dewatering agents for fluids, albeit other fluids. These references are "within the field of the inventor's endeavor." Moreover, the statement of equivalency between tri- and tetra-orthoesters in Elliott is not challenged. We therefore conclude that Elliott is not excludable from consideration as non-analogous art. It is evidence that supports the Board's holding that the prior art makes the claimed compositions obvious, a conclusion that appellant did not overcome.

Appellant urges that the Board erred in not considering the unexpected results produced by her invention and in not considering the claimed invention as a whole. The Board found, on the other hand, that no showing was made of unexpected results for the claimed compositions compared with the compositions of Sweeney. We agree. Clearly, in determining patentability the Board was obligated to consider all the evidence of the properties of the claimed invention as a whole, compared with those of the prior art. However, after the PTO made a showing that the prior art compositions suggested the claimed compositions, the burden was on the applicant to overcome the presumption of obviousness that was created, and that was not done. For example, she produced no evidence that her compositions possessed properties not possessed by the prior art compositions. Nor did she show that the prior art compositions and use were so lacking in significance that there was no motivation for others to make obvious variants. There was no attempt to argue the relative importance of the claimed compositions compared with the prior art. * * *.

Appellant's patent application in fact included data showing that the prior art compositions containing tri-orthoesters had equivalent activity in reducing particulate emissions (she apparently was once claiming such compositions with either tri--orthoesters or tetra-orthoesters). She asserts that the examiner used her own showing of equivalence against her in violation of the rule of In re Ruff, 256 F.2d 590, 596 (CCPA 1958). While we caution against such a practice, it is clear to us that references by the PTO to the comparative data in the patent application were not employed as evidence of equivalence between the tri- and tetra-orthoesters; the PTO was simply pointing out that the applicant did not or apparently could not make a showing of superiority for the claimed tetra-ester compositions over the prior art tri-ester compositions.

Other Claims

* * * *

Regarding the method claims, the Commissioner urges affirmance, citing In re Durden, 763 F.2d 1406 (Fed.Cir.1985), for the proposition that even "substitution of an unobvious starting material into an old process does not necessarily result in an unobvious process." The PTO has, as the Commissioner urges here, applied *Durden* regularly to claims to processes of making and processes of using, on the ground that the type of step involved in the claimed process is not novel.[11]

We make no judgment as to the patentability of claims that Dillon might have made and properly argued to a method directed to the novel aspects of her invention, except to question the lack of logic in a claim to a method of reducing particulate emissions by combusting. Suffice it to say that we do not regard *Durden* as authority to reject as obvious every method claim reading on an old *type of process*, such as mixing, reacting, reducing, etc. The materials used in a claimed process as well as the result obtained therefrom, must be considered along with the specific nature of the process, and the fact that new or old, obvious or nonobvious, materials are used or result from the process are only factors to be considered, rather than conclusive indicators of the obviousness or nonobviousness of a claimed process. When any applicant properly presents and argues suitable method claims, they should be examined in light of all these relevant factors, free from any presumed controlling effect of *Durden*. *Durden* did not hold that all methods involving old process steps are obvious; the court in that case concluded that the particularly claimed process was obvious; it refused to adopt an unvarying rule that the fact that nonobvious starting materials and nonobvious products are involved *ipso facto* makes the process nonobvious. Such an invariant rule always leading to the opposite conclusion is also not the law. Thus, we reject the Commissioner's argument that we affirm the rejection of the method claims under the precedent of *Durden*.

However, appellant did not argue in her brief the separate patentability of her method claims. The statement in her brief to the Board that "the invention 'as a whole' includes the property of the claimed compositions--which property is taken advantage of in the method claims" (Brief at 22, J.App. at 112) is not such a separate argument, since it implies more an added argument for the patentability of the composition claims than an argument that, even if the claimed compositions are found to have been

---

[11] See M.A. Litman, Obvious Process Rejections Under 35 USC 103, 71 JPTOS 775 (1989); H.C. Wegner, Much Ado About Durden, 71 JPTOS 785 (1989).

obvious, the claimed methods were nonobvious for particularly stated reasons. Moreover, no such reasons were particularly stated by Dillon. We will therefore not analyze these claims separately and affirm the Board's rejection on that basis.

The Dissent

The strong assertions by the dissent [the dissent is not reprinted here] and its treatment of some of the case law impel us to make the following comments:

The dissent argues that our decision is "contrary to the weight and direction of ... precedent, as embodied in over three decades of decision"; that we are resurrecting the "Hass-Henze" Doctrine, which was "discarded thirty years ago"; and that our holding today "changes what must be proved in order to patent a new chemical compound and composition and its new use, and thus changes what is patentable." We have done none of the above.

What we have done is to decide the case before us on the basis of long-established principles which had provided a stable understanding of the chemical patent law until the issuance of the original panel opinion in this case which we have now vacated. Our intent is to restore the law to its state existing before that panel opinion.

The length of the dissent and the number of cases it discusses may convey the impression that the weight of past jurisprudence is contrary to our holding today. That is not the case. The cited cases are simply not controlling on the facts of the present case or they are not contrary. Many do not deal with the requirements of a *prima facie* case. Some involve process claims, not compound or composition claims. Others are not pertinent for other reasons.

In brief, the cases establish that if an examiner considers that he has found prior art close enough to the claimed invention to give one skilled in the relevant chemical art the motivation to make close relatives (homologs, analogs, isomers, etc.) of the prior art compound(s), then there arises what has been called a presumption of obviousness or a *prima facie* case of obviousness. In re Henze, 181 F.2d 196 (CCPA 1950); In re Hass, 141 F.2d 122, 127, 130 (CCPA 1944). The burden then shifts to the applicant, who then can present arguments and/or data to show that what appears to be obvious, is not in fact that, when the invention is looked at as a whole. In re Papesch, 315 F.2d 381 (CCPA 1963). The cases of *Hass* and *Henze* established the rule that, unless an applicant showed that the prior art compound lacked the property or advantage asserted for the claimed compound, the presumption of unpatentability was not overcome.

Exactly what facts constituted a *prima facie* case varied from case to case, but it was not the law that, where an applicant asserted that an invention possessed properties not known to be possessed by the prior art, no *prima facie* case was established unless the reference also showed the novel activity. There are cases, cited in the dissent, in which a prima facie case was not established based on lack of structural similarity. * * * [cites]. Some of the cited cases also contained language suggesting that the fact that the claimed and the prior art compounds possessed the same activity were added factors in the establishment of the *prima facie* case. * * *[Cites]. Those cases did not say, however, as the dissent asserts, that, in the absence of the similarity of activities, there would have been no *prima facie* case.

* * *

We will not review all the cases cited in the dissent, but [In re] *Stemniski*[, 444 F.2d 581 (CCPA 1971)] is an important case, for it overruled *Henze* and In re Riden, 318 F.2d 761 (CCPA 1963) (a case similar to Henze), "to the extent that [they] are inconsistent with the views expressed herein." 444 F.2d at 587. The views that were expressed therein were that: [w]here the prior art reference neither discloses nor suggests a utility for certain described compounds, why should it be said that a reference makes obvious to one of ordinary skill in the art an isomer, homolog or analog or related structure, when that mythical, but intensely practical, person knows of no "practical" reason to make the reference compounds, much less any structurally related compounds? Id. at 586. Thus, *Stemniski*, rather than destroying the established practice of rejecting closely-related compounds as *prima facie* obvious, qualified it by holding that a presumption is not created when the reference compound is so lacking in any utility that there is no motivation to make close relatives.

Albrecht followed this line of thinking when it held that the prior art compound so irritated the skin that it could not be regarded as useful and therefore did not create a motivation to make related compounds. 514 F.2d at 1392.

Properties, therefore, *are* relevant to the creation of a *prima facie* case in the sense of affecting the motivation of a researcher to make compounds closely related to or suggested by a prior art compound, but it is not required, as stated in the dissent, that the prior art disclose or suggest the properties newly-discovered by an applicant in order for there to be a prima facie case of obviousness.

The dissent cites the seminal case of *Papesch*, suggesting that it rejected the principle that we now "adopt," thereby implying that we are weakening *Papesch*. We are doing nothing of the sort. *Papesch* indeed stated that a compound and all of its properties are inseparable and must be considered in the determination of obviousness. We heartily agree and intend not to retreat from *Papesch* one inch. *Papesch*, however, did not deal with the requirements for establishing a *prima facie* case, but whether the examiner had to consider the properties of an invention at all, when there was a presumption of obviousness. 315 F.2d at 391. The reference disclosed a lower homolog of the claimed compounds, so it was clear that impliedly a *prima facie* case existed; the question was whether, under those circumstances, the biological data were admissible at all. The court ruled that they were, id. at 391 and we agree with that result. The dissent quotes the brief passage at the end of the *Papesch* opinion to the effect that the prior art must "at least to a degree" disclose the applicant's desired property, id. at 392, but this brief mention was not central to the decision in that case and did not refer to the requirements of a *prima facie* case. *Papesch* is irrelevant to the question of the requirements for a prima facie case, which is the question we have here.

* * *

Properties must be considered in the overall evaluation of obviousness, and the lack of any disclosure of useful properties for a prior art compound may indicate a lack of motivation to make related compounds, thereby precluding a *prima facie* case, but it is not correct that similarity of structure and a suggestion of *the activity of an applicant's compounds* in the prior art are necessary before a *prima facie* case is established.

Conclusion

We affirm the Board's decision rejecting claims 2-14, 16-22, and 24-37.

In re DEUEL
United States Court of Appeals for the Federal Circuit, 1995
51 F.3d 1552

LOURIE, Circuit Judge.

Thomas F. Deuel, Yue-Sheng Li, Ned R. Siegel, and Peter G. Milner (collectively "Deuel") appeal from the November 30, 1993 decision of the U.S. Patent and Trademark Office Board of Patent Appeals and Interferences affirming the examiner's final rejection of claims 4-7 of application Serial No. 07/542,232, entitled "Heparin-Binding Growth Factor," as unpatentable on the ground of obviousness under 35 U.S.C. § 103 (1988). ***. Because the Board erred in concluding that Deuel's claims 5 and 7 directed to specific cDNA molecules would have been obvious in light of the applied references, and no other basis exists in the record to support the rejection with respect to claims 4 and 6 generically covering all possible DNA molecules coding for the disclosed proteins, we reverse.

BACKGROUND

The claimed invention relates to isolated and purified DNA and cDNA molecules encoding heparin-binding growth factors ("HBGFs").[12] HBGFs are proteins that stimulate mitogenic activity (cell division) and thus facilitate the repair or replacement of damaged or diseased tissue. DNA (deoxyribonucleic acid) is a generic term which encompasses an enormous number of complex macromolecules made up of nucleotide units. DNAs consist of four different nucleotides containing the nitrogenous bases adenine, guanine, cytosine, and thymine. A sequential grouping of three such nucleotides (a "codon") codes for one amino acid. A DNA's sequence of codons thus determines the sequence of amino acids assembled during protein synthesis. Since there are 64 possible codons, but only 20 natural amino acids, most amino acids are coded for by more than one codon. This is referred to as the "redundancy" or "degeneracy" of the genetic code.

DNA functions as a blueprint of an organism's genetic information. It is the major component of genes, which are located on chromosomes in the cell nucleus. Only a small part of chromosomal DNA encodes functional proteins.

Messenger ribonucleic acid ("mRNA") is a similar molecule that is made or transcribed from DNA as part of the process of protein synthesis. Complementary DNA ("cDNA") is a complementary copy ("clone") of mRNA, made in the laboratory by reverse transcription of mRNA. Like mRNA, cDNA contains only the protein-encoding regions of DNA. Thus, once a cDNA's nucleotide sequence is known, the amino acid sequence of the protein for which it codes may be predicted using the genetic code relationship between codons and amino acids. The reverse is not true, however, due to the degeneracy of the code. Many other DNAs may code for a particular protein. The functional relationships between DNA, mRNA, cDNA, and a protein may conveniently be expressed as follows:

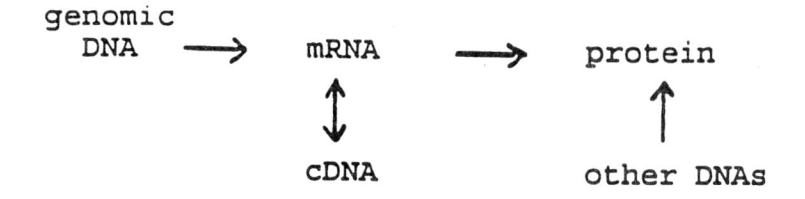

```
genomic
  DNA    ──→   mRNA    ──→   protein
               ↕↓             ↑
               cDNA          other DNAs
```

---

[12] For a more extensive discussion of recombinant DNA technology, see In re O'Farrell, 853 F.2d 894, 895-99 (Fed.Cir.1988); Amgen Inc. v. Chugai Pharmaceutical Co., 927 F.2d 1200 (Fed.Cir.), cert. denied, 502 U.S. 856 (1991).

Collections ("libraries") of DNA and cDNA molecules derived from various species may be constructed in the laboratory or obtained from commercial sources. Complementary DNA libraries contain a mixture of cDNA clones reverse-transcribed from the mRNAs found in a specific tissue source. Complementary DNA libraries are tissue-specific because proteins and their corresponding mRNAs are only made ("expressed") in specific tissues, depending upon the protein. Genomic DNA ("gDNA") libraries, by contrast, theoretically contain all of a species' chromosomal DNA. The molecules present in cDNA and DNA libraries may be of unknown function and chemical structure, and the proteins which they encode may be unknown. However, one may attempt to retrieve molecules of interest from cDNA or gDNA libraries by screening such libraries with a gene probe, which is a synthetic radiolabelled nucleic acid sequence designed to bond ("hybridize") with a target complementary base sequence. Such "gene cloning" techniques thus exploit the fact that the bases in DNA always hybridize in complementary pairs: adenine bonds with thymine and guanine bonds with cytosine. A gene probe for potentially isolating DNA or cDNA encoding a protein may be designed once the protein's amino acid sequence, or a portion thereof, is known.

As disclosed in Deuel's patent application, Deuel isolated and purified HBGF from bovine uterine tissue, found that it exhibited mitogenic activity, and determined the first 25 amino acids of the protein's N-terminal sequence.[13] Deuel then isolated a cDNA molecule encoding bovine uterine HBGF by screening a bovine uterine cDNA library with an oligonucleotide probe designed using the experimentally determined N-terminal sequence of the HBGF. Deuel purified and sequenced the cDNA molecule, which was found to consist of a sequence of 1196 nucleotide base pairs. From the cDNA's nucleotide sequence, Deuel then predicted the complete amino acid sequence of bovine uterine HBGF disclosed in Deuel's application.

Deuel also isolated a cDNA molecule encoding human placental HBGF by screening a human placental cDNA library using the isolated bovine uterine cDNA clone as a probe. Deuel purified and sequenced the human placental cDNA clone, which was found to consist of a sequence of 961 nucleotide base pairs. From the nucleotide sequence of the cDNA molecule encoding human placental HBGF, Deuel predicted the complete amino acid sequence of human placental HBGF disclosed in Deuel's application. The predicted human placental and bovine uterine HBGFs each have 168 amino acids and calculated molecular weights of 18.9 kD. Of the 168 amino acids present in the two HBGFs discovered by Deuel, 163 are identical. Deuel's application does not describe the chemical structure of, or state how to isolate and purify, any DNA or cDNA molecule except the disclosed human placental and bovine uterine cDNAs, which are the subject of claims 5 and 7.

---

[13] Deuel determined that the N-terminal sequence of bovine uterus HBGF is Gly-Lys-Lys-Glu-Lys-Pro-Glu-Lys-Lys-Val-Lys-Lys-Ser-Asp-Cys-Gly-Glu-Trp- Gln-- Trp-Ser-Val-Cys-Val-Pro.

Claims 4-7 on appeal are all independent claims and read, in relevant part, as follows:

> 4. A purified and isolated DNA sequence consisting of a sequence encoding human heparin binding growth factor of 168 amino acids having the following amino acid sequence: Met Gln Ala ... [remainder of 168 amino acid sequence].
> 5. The purified and isolated cDNA of human heparin-binding growth factor having the following nucleotide sequence: GTCAAAGGCA ... [remainder of 961 nucleotide sequence].
> 6. A purified and isolated DNA sequence consisting of a sequence encoding bovine heparin binding growth factor of 168 amino acids having the following amino acid sequence: Met Gln Thr ... [remainder of 168 amino acid sequence].
> 7. The purified and isolated cDNA of bovine heparin-binding growth factor having the following nucleotide sequence: GAGTGGAGAG ... [remainder of 1196 nucleotide sequence].

Claims 4 and 6 generically encompass all isolated/purified DNA sequences (natural and synthetic) encoding human and bovine HBGFs, despite the fact that Deuel's application does not describe the chemical structure of, or tell how to obtain, any DNA or cDNA except the two disclosed cDNA molecules. Because of the redundancy of the genetic code, claims 4 and 6 each encompass an enormous number of DNA molecules, including the isolated/purified chromosomal DNAs encoding the human and bovine proteins. Claims 5 and 7, on the other hand, are directed to the specifically disclosed cDNA molecules encoding human and bovine HBGFs, respectively.

During prosecution, the examiner rejected claims 4-7 under 35 U.S.C. § 103 as unpatentable over the combined teachings of Bohlen[14] and Maniatis.[15] The Bohlen reference discloses a group of protein growth factors designated as heparin-binding brain mitogens ("HBBMs") useful in treating burns and promoting the formation, maintenance, and repair of tissue, particularly neural tissue. Bohlen isolated three such HBBMs from human and bovine brain tissue. These proteins have respective molecular weights of 15 kD, 16 kD, and 18 kD. Bohlen determined the first 19 amino acids of the proteins' N-terminal sequences, which were found to be identical for human and

---

[14] European Patent Application No. 0326075, naming Peter Bohlen as inventor, published August 2, 1989.

[15] Maniatis et al., Molecular Cloning: A Laboratory Manual, "Screening Bacteriophage [lambda] Libraries for Specific DNA Sequences by Recombination in Escherichia coli," Cold Spring Harbor Laboratory, New York, 1982, pp. 353-361.

bovine HBBMs.[16] Bohlen teaches that HBBMs are brain-specific, and suggests that the proteins may be homologous between species. The reference provides no teachings concerning DNA or cDNA coding for HBBMs.

Maniatis describes a method of isolating DNAs or cDNAs by screening a DNA or cDNA library with a gene probe. The reference outlines a general technique for cloning a gene; it does not describe how to isolate a particular DNA or cDNA molecule. Maniatis does not discuss certain steps necessary to isolate a target cDNA, e.g., selecting a tissue-specific cDNA library containing a target cDNA and designing an oligonucleotide probe that will hybridize with the target cDNA.

The examiner asserted that, given Bohlen's disclosure of a heparin-binding protein and its N-terminal sequence and Maniatis's gene cloning method, it would have been prima facie obvious to one of ordinary skill in the art at the time of the invention to clone a gene for HBGF.[17] According to the examiner, Bohlen's published N-terminal sequence would have motivated a person of ordinary skill in the art to clone such a gene because cloning the gene would allow recombinant production of HBGF, a useful protein. The examiner reasoned that a person of ordinary skill in the art could have designed a gene probe based on Bohlen's disclosed N-terminal sequence, then screened a DNA library in accordance with Maniatis's gene cloning method to isolate a gene encoding an HBGF. The examiner did not distinguish between claims 4 and 6 generically directed to all DNA sequences encoding human and bovine HBGFs and claims 5 and 7 reciting particular cDNAs.

In reply, Deuel argued, inter alia, that Bohlen teaches away from the claimed cDNA molecules because Bohlen suggests that HBBMs are brain-specific and, thus, a person of ordinary skill in the art would not have tried to isolate corresponding cDNA clones from human placental and bovine uterine cDNA libraries. The examiner made the rejection final, however, asserting that [t]he starting materials are not relevant in this case, because it was well known in the art at the time the invention was made that proteins, especially the general class of heparin binding proteins, are highly homologous between species and tissue type. It would have been entirely obvious to attempt to isolate a known protein from different tissue types and even different species. No prior art was cited to support the proposition that it would have been obvious to screen human placental and bovine uterine cDNA libraries for the claimed cDNA clones. Presumably, the examiner was relying on Bohlen's suggestion that HBBMs may be

---

[16] Bohlen's disclosed N-terminal sequence for human and bovine HBBMs is Gly-Lys-Lys-Glu-Lys-Pro-Glu-Lys-Lys-Val-Lys-Lys-Ser-Asp-Cys-Gly-Glu-Trp-Gln. This sequence matches the first 19 amino acids of Deuel's disclosed N-terminal sequence.

[17] The examiner and the Board apparently used the term "gene" to refer both to natural (chromosomal) DNA and synthetic cDNA. We will use the several terms as appropriate.

homologous between species, although the examiner did not explain how homology between species suggests homology between tissue types.

The Board affirmed the examiner's final rejection. In its opening remarks, the Board noted that it is "constantly advised by the patent examiners, who are highly skilled in this art, that cloning procedures are routine in the art." According to the Board, "the examiners urge that when the sequence of a protein is placed into the public domain, the gene is also placed into the public domain because of the routine nature of cloning techniques." Addressing the rejection at issue, the Board determined that Bohlen's disclosure of the existence and isolation of HBBM, a functional protein, would also advise a person of ordinary skill in the art that a gene exists encoding HBBM. The Board found that a person of ordinary skill in the art would have been motivated to isolate such a gene because the protein has useful mitogenic properties, and isolating the gene for HBBM would permit large quantities of the protein to be produced for study and possible commercial use. Like the examiner, the Board asserted, without explanation, that HBBMs are the same as HBGFs and that the genes encoding these proteins are identical. The Board concluded that "the Bohlen reference would have suggested to those of ordinary skill in this art that they should make the gene, and the Maniatis reference would have taught a technique for 'making' the gene with a reasonable expectation of success." Responding to Deuel's argument that the claimed cDNA clones were isolated from human placental and bovine uterine cDNA libraries, whereas the combined teachings of Bohlen and Maniatis would only have suggested screening a brain tissue cDNA library, the Board stated that "the claims before us are directed to the product and not the method of isolation. Appellants have not shown that the claimed DNA was not present in and could not have been readily isolated from the brain tissue utilized by Bohlen." Deuel now appeals.[18]

DISCUSSION

Obviousness is a question of law, which we review de novo, though factual findings underlying the Board's obviousness determination are reviewed for clear error. ***. The examiner bears the burden of establishing a prima facie case of obviousness. ***. Only if this burden is met does the burden of coming forward with rebuttal argument or evidence shift to the applicant. ***. When the references cited by the examiner fail to establish a prima facie case of obviousness, the rejection is improper and will be overturned. ***.

---

[18] Deuel is supported in its appeal by an amicus curiae brief submitted by the Biotechnology Industry Organization and the Bay Area Science Center. Amici urge that, contrary to controlling precedent, the PTO has unlawfully adopted a per se rule that a gene is prima facie obvious when at least part of the amino acid sequence of the protein encoded by the gene is known in the prior art.

On appeal, Deuel challenges the Board's determination that the applied references establish a prima facie case of obviousness. In response, the PTO maintains that the claimed invention would have been prima facie obvious over the combined teachings of Bohlen and Maniatis. Thus, the appeal raises the important question whether the combination of a prior art reference teaching a method of gene cloning, together with a reference disclosing a partial amino acid sequence of a protein, may render DNA and cDNA molecules encoding the protein prima facie obvious under § 103.

Deuel argues that the PTO failed to follow the proper legal standard in determining that the claimed cDNA molecules would have been prima facie obvious despite the lack of structurally similar compounds in the prior art. Deuel argues that the PTO has not cited a reference teaching cDNA molecules, but instead has improperly rejected the claims based on the alleged obviousness of a method of making the molecules. We agree.

Because Deuel claims new chemical entities in structural terms, a prima facie case of unpatentability requires that the teachings of the prior art suggest the claimed compounds to a person of ordinary skill in the art. Normally a prima facie case of obviousness is based upon structural similarity, i.e., an established structural relationship between a prior art compound and the claimed compound. Structural relationships may provide the requisite motivation or suggestion to modify known compounds to obtain new compounds. For example, a prior art compound may suggest its homologs because homologs often have similar properties and therefore chemists of ordinary skill would ordinarily contemplate making them to try to obtain compounds with improved properties. Similarly, a known compound may suggest its analogs or isomers, either geometric isomers (cis v. trans) or position isomers (e.g., ortho v. para).

In all of these cases, however, the prior art teaches a specific, structurally-definable compound and the question becomes whether the prior art would have suggested making the specific molecular modifications necessary to achieve the claimed invention. See In re Jones, 958 F.2d 347, 351(Fed.Cir.1992); In re Dillon, 919 F.2d 688, 692 (Fed.Cir.1990) (en banc) ("structural similarity between claimed and prior art subject matter, ... where the prior art gives reason or motivation to make the claimed compositions, creates a prima facie case of obviousness"), cert. denied, 500 U.S. 904 (1991); In re Grabiak, 769 F.2d 729, 731-32 (Fed.Cir.1985) ("[I]n the case before us there must be adequate support in the prior art for the [prior art] ester/[claimed] thioester change in structure, in order to complete the PTO's prima facie case and shift the burden of going forward to the applicant."); In re Lalu, 747 F.2d 703, 705 (Fed.Cir.1984) ("The prior art must provide one of ordinary skill in the art the motivation to make the proposed molecular modifications needed to arrive at the claimed compound.").

Here, the prior art does not disclose any relevant cDNA molecules, let alone close relatives of the specific, structurally-defined cDNA molecules of claims 5 and 7 that might render them obvious. Maniatis suggests an allegedly obvious process for trying to isolate cDNA molecules, but that, as we will indicate below, does not fill the gap regarding the subject matter of claims 5 and 7. Further, while the general idea of the claimed molecules, their function, and their general chemical nature may have been obvious from Bohlen's teachings, and the knowledge that some gene existed may have been clear, the precise cDNA molecules of claims 5 and 7 would not have been obvious over the Bohlen reference because Bohlen teaches proteins, not the claimed or closely related cDNA molecules. The redundancy of the genetic code precluded contemplation of or focus on the specific cDNA molecules of claims 5 and 7. Thus, one could not have conceived the subject matter of claims 5 and 7 based on the teachings in the cited prior art because, until the claimed molecules were actually isolated and purified, it would have been highly unlikely for one of ordinary skill in the art to contemplate what was ultimately obtained. What cannot be contemplated or conceived cannot be obvious.

The PTO's theory that one might have been motivated to try to do what Deuel in fact accomplished amounts to speculation and an impermissible hindsight reconstruction of the claimed invention. It also ignores the fact that claims 5 and 7 are limited to specific compounds, and any motivation that existed was a general one, to try to obtain a gene that was yet undefined and may have constituted many forms. A general motivation to search for some gene that exists does not necessarily make obvious a specifically-defined gene that is subsequently obtained as a result of that search. More is needed and it is not found here.

The genetic code relationship between proteins and nucleic acids does not overcome the deficiencies of the cited references. A prior art disclosure of the amino acid sequence of a protein does not necessarily render particular DNA molecules encoding the protein obvious because the redundancy of the genetic code permits one to hypothesize an enormous number of DNA sequences coding for the protein. No particular one of these DNAs can be obvious unless there is something in the prior art to lead to the particular DNA and indicate that it should be prepared. We recently held in In re Baird, 16 F.3d 380 (Fed.Cir.1994), that a broad genus does not necessarily render obvious each compound within its scope. Similarly, knowledge of a protein does not give one a conception of a particular DNA encoding it. Thus, a fortiori, Bohlen's disclosure of the N-terminal portion of a protein, which the PTO urges is the same as HBGF, would not have suggested the particular cDNA molecules defined by claims 5 and 7. This is so even though one skilled in the art knew that some DNA, albeit not in purified and isolated form, did exist. The compounds of claims 5 and 7 are specific compounds not suggested by the prior art. A different result might pertain, however, if there were prior art, e.g., a protein of sufficiently small size and simplicity, so that lacking redundancy, each possible DNA would be obvious over the protein. See In re Petering, 301 F.2d 676 (CCPA 1962) (prior art reference disclosing limited genus of 20 compounds rendered every species within the genus unpatentable). That is not the case here.

The PTO's focus on known methods for potentially isolating the claimed DNA molecules is also misplaced because the claims at issue define compounds, not methods. See In re Bell, 991 F.2d 781, 785 (Fed.Cir.1993). In Bell, the PTO asserted a rejection based upon the combination of a primary reference disclosing a protein (and its complete amino acid sequence) with a secondary reference describing a general method of gene cloning. We reversed the rejection, holding in part that "[t]he PTO's focus on Bell's method is misplaced. Bell does not claim a method. Bell claims compositions, and the issue is the obviousness of the claimed compositions, not of the method by which they are made." Id.

We today reaffirm the principle, stated in Bell, that the existence of a general method of isolating cDNA or DNA molecules is essentially irrelevant to the question whether the specific molecules themselves would have been obvious, in the absence of other prior art that suggests the claimed DNAs. A prior art disclosure of a process reciting a particular compound or obvious variant thereof as a product of the process is, of course, another matter, raising issues of anticipation under 35 U.S.C. § 102 as well as obviousness under § 103. Moreover, where there is prior art that suggests a claimed compound, the existence, or lack thereof, of an enabling process for making that compound is surely a factor in any patentability determination. See In re Brown, 329 F.2d 1006 (CCPA 1964) (reversing rejection for lack of an enabling method of making the claimed compound). There must, however, still be prior art that suggests the claimed compound in order for a prima facie case of obviousness to be made out; as we have already indicated, that prior art was lacking here with respect to claims 5 and 7. Thus, even if, as the examiner stated, the existence of general cloning techniques, coupled with knowledge of a protein's structure, might have provided motivation to prepare a cDNA or made it obvious to prepare a cDNA, that does not necessarily make obvious a particular claimed cDNA. "Obvious to try" has long been held not to constitute obviousness. In re O'Farrell, 853 F.2d 894, 903 (Fed.Cir.1988). A general incentive does not make obvious a particular result, nor does the existence of techniques by which those efforts can be carried out. Thus, Maniatis's teachings, even in combination with Bohlen, fail to suggest the claimed invention.

The PTO argues that a compound may be defined by its process of preparation and therefore that a conceived process for making or isolating it provides a definition for it and can render it obvious. It cites Amgen Inc. v. Chugai Pharmaceutical Co., 927 F.2d 1200 (Fed.Cir.), cert. denied, 502 U.S. 856 (1991), for that proposition. We disagree. The fact that one can conceive a general process in advance for preparing an undefined compound does not mean that a claimed specific compound was precisely envisioned and therefore obvious. A substance may indeed be defined by its process of preparation. That occurs, however, when it has already been prepared by that process and one therefore knows that the result of that process is the stated compound. The process is part of the definition of the compound. But that is not possible in advance, especially when the hypothetical process is only a general one. Thus, a conceived method of preparing some undefined DNA does not define it with the precision necessary to render it obvious over the protein it encodes. We did not state otherwise in Amgen. See Amgen, 927 F.2d at 1206-9 (isolated/purified human gene held nonobvious; no conception of gene without envisioning its precise identity despite conception of general process of preparation).

We conclude that, because the applied references do not teach or suggest the claimed cDNA molecules, the final rejection of claims 5 and 7 must be reversed. See also Bell, 991 F.2d at 784-85 (human DNA sequences encoding IGF proteins nonobvious over asserted combination of references showing gene cloning method and complete amino acid sequences of IGFs).

Claims 4 and 6 are of a different scope than claims 5 and 7. As is conceded by Deuel, they generically encompass all DNA sequences encoding human and bovine HBGFs. Written in such a result-oriented form, claims 4 and 6 are thus tantamount to the general idea of all genes encoding the protein, all solutions to the problem. Such an idea might have been obvious from the complete amino acid sequence of the protein, coupled with knowledge of the genetic code, because this information may have enabled a person of ordinary skill in the art to envision the idea of, and, perhaps with the aid of a computer, even identify all members of the claimed genus. The Bohlen reference, however, only discloses a partial amino acid sequence, and thus it appears that, based on the above analysis, the claimed genus would not have been obvious over this prior art disclosure. We will therefore also reverse the final rejection of claims 4 and 6 because neither the Board nor the patent examiner articulated any separate reasons for holding these claims unpatentable apart from the grounds discussed above.

One further matter requires comment. Because Deuel's patent application does not describe how to obtain any DNA except the disclosed cDNA molecules, claims 4 and 6 may be considered to be inadequately supported by the disclosure of the application. See generally Amgen Inc. v. Chugai Pharmaceutical Co., 927 F.2d 1200, 1212-14 (Fed.Cir.) (generic DNA sequence claims held invalid under 35 U.S.C. § 112, first paragraph), cert. denied, 502 U.S. 856 (1991); In re Fisher, 427 F.2d 833, 839 (CCPA 1970) (Section 112 "requires that the scope of the claims must bear a reasonable correlation to the scope of enablement provided by the specification to persons of ordinary skill in the art."). As this issue is not before us, however, we will not address whether claims 4 and 6 satisfy the enablement requirement of § 112, first paragraph, but will leave to the PTO the question whether any further rejection is appropriate.

***. The Board's decision affirming the final rejection of claims 4-7 is reversed.

PAGE 933. Add after note 4.

ENVIROTECH CORPORATION v. WESTECH ENGINEERING INCORPORATED
United States Court of Appeals for the Federal Circuit, 1990.
904 F.2d 1571

MAYER, Circuit Judge.

Envirotech Corporation appeals the judgment of the United States District Court for the District of Utah, 713 F.Supp. 372 (1989), holding U.S. Patent No. 4,391,705 (Cook) invalid under 35 U.S.C. § 102(b) (1982). We reverse and remand.

Background

The patented invention is a ballasted digester cover for use in wastewater treatment plants. Dubbed a "hydroballaster" by its inventors, Envirotech employees Lynn Cook and David Brown, the invention is a floating (as opposed to fixed) cover-type digester consisting of a circular steel top with cylindrical sidewalls that slide up and down telescopically inside a large cylindrical steel tank. The tank contains sewage sludge that, when digested by microorganisms, supplies a large volume of methane and other gases on which the cover "floats." Appropriately ballasting the lower rim of the cover enables it to maintain these gases at a predetermined and constant design pressure, making the gas available to fuel other components of the treatment facility.

Archimedes' Principle--that an object wholly or partially submerged in fluid is buoyed up by a force equal to the weight of the fluid displaced--dictates the ballast design of all floating cover digesters. The Cook invention implements this principle by attaching tub-shaped concrete blocks to the bottom of the cylindrical sidewalls of the floating cover. When submerged, these "hydroballast" blocks displace the same amount of sludge and therefore weigh the same as traditional, solid concrete blocks composed of an equal volume of concrete. Thus, because pressure is directly proportional to weight, the Cook invention achieves the same gas operating pressure as a traditionally ballasted digester when their respective ballasts are submerged. However, when a hydroballast block is emerged it outweighs an equal volume traditional block by the weight of the sludge filling the block cavity. Accordingly, the Cook invention can achieve a specified gas operating pressure using significantly less concrete than--or, conversely, attain a higher gas operating pressure using the same amount of concrete as--a cover ballasted only with traditional blocks when their respective ballasts are emerged.

It is principally the Cook invention's ability to attain a higher pressure differential between its submerged and emerged positions that makes it superior to a traditionally ballasted digester. Prior to the Cook invention, engineers using traditional ballast blocks resorted to various techniques to increase the achievable pressure differential. One technique was to construct the blocks of low-density concrete: the additional concrete volume necessary to equal the weight of an emerged, traditional density block displaced proportionately more sludge when submerged, thereby creating a larger weight differential between the emerged and submerged blocks and, thus, a larger pressure differential. A second technique, relevant here, combined traditional ballast blocks with an air-filled steel buoyancy ring. This technique allowed a higher pressure differential because of the increased buoyant force the ring provided when submerged.

Envirotech Corporation (Envirotech) is engaged in the design and sale of ballasted digester covers for use in municipal wastewater treatment plants. In response to a December 1979 invitation to bid on an addition to the Nine Springs Wastewater Treatment Plant in Madison, Wisconsin (Madison project), Envirotech submitted proposals for a digester cover to all general contractors bidding the mechanical portion of the project. In these February 21, 1980 proposals, Envirotech offered to provide for $205,000 a digester cover constructed in accordance with the plans and design specifications of the consulting engineer on the Madison project, CH2M-Hill (Hill). To achieve the desired gas operating pressure, the Hill design specified the use of traditional solid concrete ballast blocks together with an air-filled buoyancy ring constructed of steel.

For reasons not relevant here, Hill decided not to award the mechanical portion of the Madison project to any of the general contractor bidders. It instead scheduled a re-bid of this portion for May 8, 1980.

In the interim, Envirotech employees Cook and Brown conceived the hydroballaster invention and, in accordance with company policy, completed both an "invention record" and a "disclosure of invention." Both documents were stamped "confidential" and neither was sent outside the company. A May 6, 1980 letter from an Envirotech patent attorney to the inventors advised them of the receipt of their invention disclosure and said, "You mentioned that you were planning to bid and the bid would be the first offer for sale or public disclosure." Although Envirotech previously had described its idea for the hydroballaster to Hill in an April 9, 1980 meeting, it had kept the details of the design confidential. Two local concrete contractors in the Madison area were the only persons outside of Envirotech to know of the hydroballast block design: Envirotech had attached copies of a sketch of the blocks, marked "confidential," to April 28, 1980 letters seeking price quotations for block fabrication.

Sometime between May 5 and 8, 1980, Envirotech submitted its second proposal for the Madison project (the May 8 proposal) to all general contractors re-bidding the mechanical portion of the project. The proposal offered a "digester gas holder cover"--three times referencing the Hill specifications contained in the contract documents—for $134,000. When at the May 8 bid opening Hooper Construction Corporation (Hooper) appeared as the lowest responsive bidder, it accepted Envirotech's proposal.

Subsequently, on May 30, 1980, Envirotech disclosed a detailed description of its hydroballaster to Hill as part of a required pre-award submittal. Envirotech acknowledged that it had "suggested" its innovative approach to Hill "during the formative stages of this job" but now included as part of the submittal both a description and detailed drawings of the hydroballaster: how it would operate and be constructed as well as the advantages it possessed over the Hill design.

Before the consulting engineer Hill decided whether to approve Envirotech's proposed design substitution, Hooper placed a purchase order with an Envirotech salesman on June 24, 1980. The order required Envirotech to furnish a digester cover "in accordance with proposal # 45-0379"—the May 8 proposal—"and spec. section 11385"—the section of the contract documents specifying the Hill design. On August 25, 1980, Hooper sent a confirmation of this purchase order to Envirotech and again specified that Envirotech must "[f]urnish in strict accordance with the attached Section 11385 of the Specifications and Plan Sheet[ ] D-S-17 [showing the Hill design] ... one complete digester gasholder cover...." Hill did not approve Envirotech's proposed substitution of its hydroballaster until September 17, 1980; not until October 6, 1980 did Envirotech apprise Hooper that it would furnish a hydroballaster instead of a Hill-designed digester cover.

Cook and Brown applied for a patent on the hydroballaster on May 29, 1981. They subsequently assigned the invention and application to Envirotech which, as the owner of the Cook patent, brought suit for patent infringement against Westech Engineering Incorporated (Westech) in 1986. In a motion for partial summary judgment Westech asserted the patent was invalid because of an on sale bar. After hearing argument and with the consent of the parties, the court held an evidentiary hearing.

Based on that hearing, the court invalidated the patent. It held that "Envirotech's May 8th bid and proposal to sell the cover violated the statutory bar of 35 U.S.C. § 102(b) in that the invention was 'on sale' in this country more than one year before the application for a patent was filed." 713 F.Supp. at 377, . The court based this holding on the three ancillary conclusions that "[n]o later than May 8, 1980, Envirotech placed on sale its ballasting digester cover, which embodies the entire invention set out in the Cook patent, by bidding and proposing to sell it to Hooper for $134,000"; that the invention had been "sufficiently reduced to practice to be commercially marketable" by May 8; and that the May 8th bid was made primarily for commercial rather than experimental purposes. *Id.*, 713 F.Supp. at 377. Envirotech appeals.

Discussion

The party asserting the on sale bar must prove by "clear and convincing evidence," Buildex, Inc. v. Kason Industries, Inc., 849 F.2d 1461, 1463 (Fed.Cir.1988), "that there was a definite sale or offer to sell more than one year before the application for the subject patent, and that the subject matter of the sale or offer to sell fully anticipated the claimed invention or would have rendered the claimed invention obvious by its addition to the prior art." UMC Electronics Co. v. United States, 816 F.2d 647, 656, (Fed.Cir.1987). Whether an invention is on sale is a question of law, and no single finding or conclusion is a sine qua non to its resolution. Id. at 657. "[T]he totality of the circumstances must always be considered in order to ascertain whether an offer of the new invention was in fact made." King Instrument Corp. v. Otari Corp., 767 F.2d 853, 860 (Fed.Cir.1985). The totality of the circumstances approach is necessary because "the policies or purposes underlying the on sale bar, in effect, define it." RCA Corp. v. Data General Corp., 887 F.2d 1056, 1062 (Fed.Cir.1989). These policies include discouraging removal of inventions from the public domain that the public reasonably has come to believe are freely available; favoring the prompt and widespread disclosure of inventions; allowing the inventor a reasonable amount of time following sales activity to determine the potential economic value of a patent; and prohibiting the inventor from commercially exploiting his invention beyond the statutorily prescribed time. King Instrument, 767 F.2d at 860.

As implicated here, none of these policies supports the on sale bar. First, the "public," that is, Hooper and the other general contractors that received Envirotech's May 8 proposal, could not have come to believe that the hydroballaster was freely available based upon that proposal. The district court's finding that "Envirotech made its May 8th bid with the intent of exploiting the hydroballast invention and with knowledge of how the invention would perform, whether or not the engineers or Hooper had actual knowledge of it," 713 F.Supp. at 375 (emphasis added), suggests that neither Hill nor Hooper was sufficiently aware of the hydroballaster to justifiably believe that it was freely available. Moreover, because the court based its invocation of the on sale bar specifically on Envirotech's offer to sell the hydroballaster to Hooper, its finding that Envirotech had "described its idea" for the hydroballaster to the consulting engineer Hill prior to the critical date does not support its conclusion. Even if Hill had known how the invention would perform, in the absence of any relationship or evidence of communication between Hill and Hooper, that fact would be insufficient to establish that Envirotech offered the invention to Hooper.

Second, that Envirotech knew how the invention would perform is manifest but not dispositive. Knowing how an invention will perform is not the same as offering or intending to offer it for sale. The district court did not find that Envirotech either intended to or did offer the hydroballaster in its May 8 proposal. Citing testimony that Envirotech's bid strategy was to offer the Hill design and attempt later to substitute its patented invention, the court found instead that Envirotech bid with the intent of ultimately exploiting the hydroballaster on the Madison project. *Id.*, 713 F.Supp. at

373. The distinction is important because, while we agree that the policies underlying the on sale bar concentrate on the inventor's attempt to exploit his invention rather than the potential purchaser's cognizance of it, King Instrument, 767 F.2d at 860, the inventor's attempted exploitation must be objectively manifested as a definite sale or offer to sell the invention. The subjective, uncommunicated, and ultimate intention of the offeror, however clear, is not alone sufficient.

Here, the district court unduly focused on Envirotech's admitted motive. The record is clear that Envirotech neither definitely offered for sale nor otherwise exploited the Cook invention until after the critical date of May 29, 1980.

An internal Envirotech memorandum dated April 17, 1980 shows that Envirotech itself did not intend to offer the hydroballaster in its May 8 proposal. Regarding ballast, Hollie has a great idea to say in the proposal that we are providing precast ballast blocks that are included in our price. We should get a Salt Lake City quote without freight for Lynn Cook's [the patented] design and margin this at about ten (10%) percent with every intention of breaking this out to the contractor after we bid the job. This way, we won't tip our hand to our design. The district court agreed that this language showed "Envirotech planned to submit a proposal which would include 'precast ballast blocks' but would keep the design of the blocks confidential." 713 F.Supp. at 373. But because the court also found that Envirotech "intended to provide a hydroballast system for the Madison project," id. at 374, it viewed the May 8 proposal as sufficient to invoke the on sale bar. In this, it erred.

Envirotech freely admits that it decided, prior to submitting its May 8 proposal, to attempt to substitute its patented invention for the Hill design-- but only if it received the contract. Its internal price review meeting minutes and price estimate details prepared in anticipation of the May 8 bid clearly reflect that its strategy was to bid the Hill design but quote the lower hydroballaster price. But Envirotech's assuming the risk that Hill might disapprove its proposed substitution does not negate the fact that Envirotech remained obligated by the contract documents, incorporated into every proposal, to provide Hooper with a digester cover constructed according to the Hill design.

Contrary to Westech's assertions, the contract documents do not furnish the Hill design as an "example" of how to achieve the specified gas operating pressure. The design requirements contained in the documents are specific, not merely functional; Envirotech could not have bid its hydroballaster and met the requirements. The invitation to bid clearly requires all work to be done "as provided for in the Contract Documents," which include the drawings and specifications. The "general conditions" section of the documents states that the drawings "show the location, character, dimensions, and details of the work to be performed," and drawing D-S-17 clearly depicts the Hill design, with its traditional solid concrete ballast blocks and air-filled steel buoyancy chamber. The "summary of work" section of the documents similarly provides that "[d]etailed technical requirements for the work are stated in the applicable Specification sections and shown on the Drawings."

Furthermore, every bidder's proposal contained the proviso that "this Proposal is made according to the provisions and under the terms of the Contract Documents, which Documents are hereby made a part of this Proposal." Hooper's proposal in particular stated: "The Bidder further proposes to furnish and install in accordance with the Specifications, bound herewith, the items of equipment specified in section[ ] ... 11385." Neither Hooper in its proposal to Hill nor Envirotech in its proposal to Hooper noted any exceptions to the digester cover plans and specifications contained in the contract documents. Specification section 11385, entitled "Digester Gasholder Cover," is clear (emphasis added): This section covers the work necessary to furnish and install, complete, one steel digester gasholder cover to be installed on the 80-foot inner diameter Storage Tank No. 3, as shown on the Drawings.

* * * * * *

> "It is the intent of this Specification to functionally describe the gasholder cover, as well as establish design criteria. It shall be the responsibility of the cover supplier to design the cover to satisfy both functional and construction specifications and submit supporting data according to this Specification. This tank cover will require a ballast ring with a buoyant chamber in order to obtain the specified design pressure and relief pressure while maintaining a minimum rim submergence. Particular attention will be given to the submittal information describing the proposed method of attaining these design conditions."

The facts here thus differ markedly from those in *RCA*, which Westech relies on, and do not support an on sale bar. Here, the bid documents clearly specify the Hill design rather than the patented invention; there, they contained a technical description sufficient to identify the patented invention. 887 F.2d at 1060. Here, the district court found that Envirotech planned in its May 8 proposal to keep the patented design of its ballast blocks confidential, 713 F.Supp. at 373; there, testimonial evidence established that the offeror intended to offer the invention prior to the critical date. *RCA*, 887 F.2d at 1060.

Finally, as noted above, Hooper understood that Envirotech's May 8 proposal offered the Hill design. While there is no requirement that the purchaser have actual knowledge of the invention to invoke the on sale bar, King Instrument, 767 F.2d at 860, what the purchaser reasonably believes the inventor to be offering is relevant to whether, on balance, the offer objectively may be said to be of the patented invention. Here, the court recognized that Hooper lacked actual knowledge of the invention. 713 F.Supp. at 375. More importantly, Hooper objectively interpreted Envirotech's May 8 offer to be of the Hill design. In both its Sedimentation Order Transmittal of June 24, 1980 and its follow-up purchase order of August 25, 1980, Hooper stressed that

Envirotech must supply a digester cover in accordance with specification section 11385--the Hill design.

Other evidence the district court cites in support of its conclusion that Envirotech offered the Cook invention to Hooper prior to the critical date is unpersuasive. For instance, the fact that two Madison-area concrete contractors were shown sketches of the tub-shaped ballast blocks on April 28 for the purpose of providing price quotations is, given the lack of any evidence that the contractors shared their knowledge with Hooper, insufficient to establish that Envirotech similarly disclosed the invention to Hooper.

As for the May 6, 1980 letter from Envirotech's patent attorney to the two inventors, nothing in the record suggests that the attorney was familiar with the terms of Envirotech's May 8 offer. Yet the district court construed the reference in the letter to the "bid" that "would be the first offer for sale or public disclosure" as a reference to the actual Envirotech proposal instead of to the hydroballaster as identified in the invention disclosure--the document in reference to which the attorney wrote the letter. Moreover, because the district court did not find and the evidence does not suggest that the inventors themselves were responsible for formulating or submitting Envirotech's proposal, their knowledge of counsel's opinion is not evidence of whether Envirotech intended to offer the hydroballaster in its May 8 proposal. In fact, the district court found that "Envirotech planned to submit a proposal which would include 'precast ballast blocks' in the price but would keep the design of the blocks confidential." 713 F.Supp. at 373.

To be sure, the evidence amply supports the district court's conclusion that Envirotech intended ultimately to exploit the Cook invention on the Madison project. But it does not support the court's further conclusion that Envirotech offered the invention for sale prior to the critical date and, in particular, "[n]o later than May 8, 1980." Id. at 377. The totality of the circumstances does not support an on sale bar.[*]

Conclusion

Accordingly, the judgment of the district court is reversed and the case is remanded.

***.

REVERSED AND REMANDED.

PAGE 933. Add new note 5.

---

[*] Because we hold that Envirotech did not offer the hydroballaster for sale prior to the critical date, we need not address whether the inventors had sufficiently developed the invention as of the critical date.

A recent case very much like Elizabeth v. Pavement Co. is Manville Sales Corp. v. Paramount Systems, 917 F.2d 544 (Fed. Cir. 1990). The invention involved an outdoor lighting fixture for use at a highway rest stop in Wyoming. A previous light fixture had failed due to the rugged winter weather in Wyoming. The light fixture was installed at the site under express conditions of confidentiality, and ownership retained by the patent owner. The court held that the use was experimental.

PAGE 946. Add new note.

NOTE

The Uruguay Round Agreements Act, Pub. L. 103-465, Dec. 8, 1994, amended 35 U.S.C. § 104 to except from its provisions activity occurring in a NAFTA or WTO member country. Prior to this amendment U.S. patent law did not recognize inventions made outside the United States for purposes of determining priority. This was advantageous to inventors based in the United States and disadvantageous to inventors based outside the United States, but contrary to the principle of equal treatment in GATT TRIPS and NAFTA.

Given that the first-to-invent doctrine no longer operates in a manner that favors U.S. inventors, it seems more likely than before that the U.S. will eventually move from a first-to-invent to a first-to-file system, which is the international standard, and which avoids the complexities of proof involved in administration of the first-to-invent doctrine.

PAGE 947. Add new case.

SCOTT v. FINNEY
United States Court of Appeals for the Federal Circuit, 1994
34 F.3d 1058

RADER, Circuit Judge.

The Board of Patent Appeals and Interferences awarded priority in Interference No. 102,429 to the senior party, Dr. Roy P. Finney. The Board held that the junior party, Dr. F. Brantley Scott and John H. Burton, did not show a reduction to practice before Dr. Finney's date of invention. Because the Board imposed an overly strict requirement for testing to show reduction to practice, this court reverses and remands.

BACKGROUND

This interference involves Dr. Finney's United States Patent No. 4,791,917, which was accorded the benefit of its May 15, 1980 parent application, and the Scott and Burton application, Serial No. 07/241,826, which was accorded the benefit of its parent application Serial No. 06/264,202, filed May 15, 1981. Although the Scott and Burton application claims a joint invention of both applicants, Dr. Scott is the sole inventor of the subject matter in interference No. 102,429.

The invention is a penile implant for men unable to obtain or maintain an erection. The prosthetic device is a self-contained unit that permits the patient to simulate an erection. The implant contains two reservoirs connected through a valve. The invention operates by shifting the inflating liquid between the two reservoirs. When the penis is flaccid, the invention maintains inflating liquid in a reservoir at the base of the penis. A simulated erection occurs when the liquid shifts through the valve into the elongated reservoir implanted in the forward section of the penis.

Prior art devices fell into two categories: flexible rods and inflatable devices. Flexible rods had the disadvantage of making the penis permanently erect. The prior inflatable devices relied on fluid from a source and pump external to the body to inflate tubes implanted in the penis. These devices also had several disadvantages.

The Interference Count at issue states: An implantable penile prosthesis for implanting completely within a patient's penis comprising at least one elongated member having a flexible distal forward section for implantation within the pendulous penis, said forward section being constructed to rigidize upon being filled with pressuring fluid; a proximal, rearward section adapted to be implanted within the root end of the penis, said rearward section containing a fluid reservoir chamber, externally operable pump means in said member for transferring fluid under pressure to said flexible distal forward section of said member for achieving an erection; and valve means positioned within said member which open when said pump is operated so that fluid is forced from said pump through said valve means into said flexible distal forward section of said chamber.

The parties to this interference had contested related subject matter in an earlier interference, No. 101,149. The count of 101,149 was a species of the generic count in this interference. Dr. Scott won that earlier interference.

In this interference, No. 102,429, Dr. Finney's application has an earlier filing date than Scott's application. Dr. Scott still has, however, an earlier conception date. Dr. Scott did not present evidence of diligence after conception of his invention. See, e.g., Griffith v. Kanamaru, 816 F.2d 624, 626 (Fed.Cir.1987). Rather, Dr. Scott opted to show an actual reduction to practice before Dr. Finney's date of invention.

Before the Board, Dr. Scott's primary evidence of actual reduction to practice was a videotape. The videotape showed an operation where the surgeon inserted Dr. Scott's prototype device into the penis of an anesthetized patient. The videotape showed the surgeon manipulating the implanted device. Several times the device simulated an erection when the surgeon manipulated the valve. Several times the fluid filled the forward reservoir. Several times the surgeon returned the penis to a flaccid condition by draining the fluid back into the rear reservoir. The Board found: It is uncontested that the penile implant used in the in-and-out procedure did rigidify the penis by pressurization of the rear chamber and did produce an erection. After the device was actuated to form the erection, the valve mechanism was manipulated to allow the device to become flaccid.... Board opinion at 8-9.

Although not part of the count, the parties agree that the invention envisions implantation of two devices--one on either side of the penis. In the videotaped demonstration, the surgeon implanted only a single prosthesis into the patient. Although using only a single prosthesis, the videotape showed a penis with enough rigidity to produce an erection. After manipulating the implanted device through the skin to simulate having and losing an erection, the surgeon removed Dr. Scott's prototype and inserted a prior art external pump mechanism.

Dr. Scott supplied other evidence as well. He presented evidence of testing for leakage, disclosed that the fabrication material was common in implanted devices, and supplied the testimony of Dr. Drogo K. Montague, an expert in the field. Dr. Montague personally handled the device at issue and viewed the videotape. He testified that the video showed, even with only a single tube, sufficient rigidity for intercourse.

In opposition, Dr. Finney testified personally about the difficulty of determining sufficient rigidity for intercourse on the basis of insertion in an anesthetized patient. Both Drs. Finney and Montague agreed that insertion of two tubes would greatly enhance rigidity.

The Board discerned insufficient evidence to show reduction to practice. Specifically, the Board determined that Dr. Scott had not shown utility, i.e., that the device would successfully operate under actual use conditions for a reasonable length of time. Thus, the Board required "testing of an implantable medical device under actual use conditions or testing under conditions that closely simulate actual use conditions for an appropriate period of time." Board opinion at 8.

Because Dr. Scott had not tested his device in actual intercourse or in similar conditions to intercourse for a proper period of time, the Board determined that Dr. Scott had not reduced his invention to practice. The Board awarded the count to Dr. Finney. This appeal followed.

DISCUSSION

***.

The Scott and Burton application was copending with that of Dr. Finney. Consequently, as the junior party in this interference, Dr. Scott had the burden to show prior invention by a preponderance of evidence. ***. To show prior invention, the junior party must show reduction to practice of the invention before the senior party, or, if the junior party reduced to practice later, conception before the senior party followed by reasonable diligence in reducing it to practice. ***.

To show reduction to practice, the junior party must demonstrate that the invention is "suitable for its intended purpose." ***. When testing is necessary to show proof of actual reduction to practice, the embodiment relied upon as evidence of priority must actually work for its intended purpose. ***. Because Dr. Scott relied on such testing, this court must examine the quality and quantity of testing asserted to show a reduction to practice.

***.

All cases deciding the sufficiency of testing to show reduction to practice share a common theme. In each case, the court examined the record to discern whether the testing in fact demonstrated a solution to the problem intended to be solved by the invention. See, e.g., Farrand Optical Co. v. United States, 325 F.2d 328, 333 (2d Cir.1963) ("The essential inquiry here is whether the advance in the art represented by the invention ... was embodied in a *workable device* that demonstrated that it could do what it was claimed to be capable of doing.") (emphasis added). In tests showing the invention's solution of a problem, the courts have not required commercial perfection nor absolute replication of the circumstances of the invention's ultimate use. Rather, they have instead adopted a common sense assessment. This common sense approach prescribes more scrupulous testing under circumstances approaching actual use conditions when the problem includes many uncertainties. On the other hand, when the problem to be solved does not present myriad variables, common sense similarly permits little or no testing to show the soundness of the principles of operation of the invention.

In the prosthetic implants field, polyurethane materials and inflatable penile prostheses were old in the art. They were tested extensively. Only the insertion and hydraulics of a manipulable valve separating two implanted reservoirs were new. Thus, Dr. Scott had the burden to show that his novel valve and dual reservoir system would simulate an erection for sexual intercourse when manipulated through the skin. Consequently, the problem presented to Dr. Scott, when viewed from the vantage point of earlier proven aspects of penile implant technology, was relatively uncomplicated.

In the videotape presentation, Dr. Scott demonstrated sufficiently the workability of his invention to solve the problems of a wholly internal penile implant. The videotaped operation showed both rigidity for intercourse and operability of the valve to inflate and deflate the device through the skin. The use of materials previously shown to work in prosthetic implants over a reasonable period of time also showed the durability of the invention for its intended purpose. In sum, Dr. Scott showed sufficient testing to establish a reasonable expectation that his invention would work under normal conditions for its intended purpose, beyond a probability of failure.

The Board erred by setting the reduction to practice standard too high. The Board erroneously suggested that a showing of reduction to practice requires human testing in actual use circumstances for a period of time. See Engelhardt v. Judd, 369 F.2d 408, 410-11 (CCPA 1966) (human testing of antihistamine and antiserotonin unnecessary in light of tests on laboratory animals). Reduction to practice, however, does not require actual use, but only a reasonable showing that the invention will work to overcome the problem it addresses. The videotape showed the rigidity and manipulability of the valve through the skin necessary for actual use. Experts testified to the invention's suitability for actual use. In the context of this art and this problem, Dr. Scott made that reasonable showing.

The Board rejected these proofs because the device was not actually used during intercourse. In this instance of a solution to a relatively simple problem, the Board required more testing than necessary to show that the device would work for its intended purpose. Even accepting the Board's conclusion that the intended purpose is to facilitate normal sexual intercourse, prior art prosthetic devices had fully tested the workability of most features of Dr. Scott's invention. Dr. Scott used the same tested and workable materials and designs of prior art implants. Only the hydraulics of a fully self-contained internal prosthesis remained to be tested for workability. Dr. Scott adequately showed the workability of these features.

Testing for the full safety and effectiveness of a prosthetic device is more properly left to the Food and Drug Administration (FDA). Title 35 does not demand that such human testing occur within the confines of Patent and Trademark Office (PTO) proceedings. ***.

The Board's holding that Dr. Scott did not reduce his invention to practice before the May 15, 1980 filing date of Dr. Finney is reversed. Dr. Finney asserted that Dr. Scott abandoned, suppressed, or concealed the invention embodied by the count within the meaning of 35 U.S.C. § 102(g) (1988). The Board did not reach this issue in light of its holding that no reduction to practice occurred. Because the Board has not considered this issue, this court remands for a determination of whether Dr. Scott abandoned, suppressed, or concealed the invention within the meaning of 35 U.S.C. § 102(g).

PAGE 958. Add new section.

(2A) Conception

BURROUGHS WELLCOME CO. v. BARR LABORATORIES, INC.
United States Court of Appeals for the Federal Circuit, 1994
40 F.3d 1223, certiorari denied 116 S.Ct. 771 (1996)

MAYER, Circuit Judge.

Barr Laboratories, Inc., *** appeal[s] the order of the United States District Court for the Eastern District of North Carolina, Burroughs Wellcome Co. v. Barr Lab., Inc., 828 F.Supp. 1208 (E.D.N.C.1993), granting the motion of Burroughs Wellcome Co. for judgment as a matter of law that six United States patents were not invalid and were infringed. We affirm in part, vacate in part, and remand.

Background

Burroughs Wellcome Co. is the owner of six United States patents that cover various preparations of 3'-azidothymidine (AZT) and methods for using that drug in the treatment of persons infected with the human immunodeficiency virus (HIV). Each of these patents names the same five inventors--Janet Rideout, David Barry, Sandra Lehrman, Martha St. Clair, and Phillip Furman (Burroughs Wellcome inventors)--all of whom were employed by Burroughs Wellcome at the time the inventions were alleged to have been conceived. The defendants-appellants concede that all five are properly named as inventors on the patents.

Burroughs Wellcome's patents arise from the same parent application filed on September 17, 1985. Five of the patents relate to the use of AZT to treat patients infected with HIV or who have acquired immunodeficiency syndrome (AIDS). The other patent, the '750 patent, covers a method of using AZT to increase the T--lymphocyte count of persons infected with HIV.

In the early 1980s, scientists began to see patients with symptoms of an unknown disease of the immune system, now known as AIDS. The disease attacks and destroys certain white blood cells known as CD4 T-lymphocytes or T-cells, which form an important component of the body's immune system. The level of destruction eventually becomes so great that the immune system is no longer able to mount an effective response to infections that pose little threat to a healthy person.

In mid-1984, scientists discovered that AIDS was caused by a retrovirus, known as HTLV III or, more commonly today, HIV. After the identification of HIV, Burroughs Wellcome began to search for a cure, screening compounds for antiretroviral activity using two murine (or mouse) retroviruses, the Friend leukemia virus and the Harvey sarcoma virus.

At about this time, scientists at the National Institutes of Health (NIH), led by Samuel Broder, were looking for effective AIDS therapies as well. Unlike Burroughs Wellcome, Broder and his colleagues used live HIV, and were able to develop a test that could demonstrate a compound's effectiveness against HIV in humans using a unique line of T-cell clones (the ATH8 cell line). The NIH scientists began to seek compounds from private pharmaceutical companies for screening in their cell line.

After Burroughs Wellcome contacted Broder in the fall of 1984, he agreed to accept compounds from Burroughs Wellcome under code for testing against live HIV.

Burroughs Wellcome's Rideout selected AZT and a number of other compounds for testing in the murine screens on October 29, 1984. The tests, performed at Burroughs Wellcome facilities by St. Clair, showed that AZT had significant activity against both murine retroviruses at low concentrations. In light of these positive results, the Burroughs Wellcome inventors met on December 5, 1984, to discuss patenting the use of AZT in the treatment of AIDS. Burroughs Wellcome's patent committee thereafter recommended that the company prepare a patent application for future filing. By February 6, 1985, the company had prepared a draft application for filing in the United Kingdom. The draft disclosed using AZT to treat patients infected with HIV, and set out various pharmaceutical formulations of the compound in an effective dosage range to treat HIV infection.

Two days earlier, on February 4, 1985, Burroughs Wellcome had sent a sample of AZT, identified only as Compound S, to Broder at NIH. In an accompanying letter, Lehrman told Broder of the results of the murine retrovirus tests and asked that he screen the compound for activity against HIV in the ATH8 cell line. Another NIH scientist, Hiroaka Mitsuya, performed the test in mid-February 1985, and found that Compound S was active against HIV. Broder informed Lehrman of the results by telephone on February 20, 1985. Burroughs Wellcome filed its patent application in the United Kingdom on March 16, 1985.

After Burroughs Wellcome learned that AZT was active against HIV, it began the process of obtaining Food and Drug Administration (FDA) approval for AZT as an AIDS therapy. As a part of the clinical trials leading to FDA approval, Broder and another NIH scientist, Robert Yarchoan, conducted a Phase I human patient study which showed that treatment with AZT could result in an increase in the patient's T-cell count. Broder reported this result to Lehrman on July 23, 1985. In 1987, the FDA approved AZT for marketing by Burroughs Wellcome; Burroughs Wellcome markets the drug for treatment of HIV infection under the trademark Retrovir.

On March 19, 1991, Barr Laboratories, Inc. (Barr) sought FDA approval to manufacture and market a generic version of AZT by filing an Abbreviated New Drug Application (ANDA) pursuant to 21 U.S.C. § 355(j) (1988). As part of the process, Barr certified to the FDA that Burroughs Wellcome's patents were invalid or were not infringed by the product described in its ANDA. After Barr informed Burroughs Wellcome of its action, Burroughs Wellcome commenced this case for patent infringement against Barr on May 14, 1991, alleging technical infringement of its patents under 35 U.S.C. § 271(e)(2)(A) (1988).

Barr filed a counterclaim under 35 U.S.C. § 256 (1988) seeking correction of the patents to list Broder and Mitsuya as coinventors. Barr admitted that its AZT product would infringe the patents, but contended that it did not because Barr had obtained a license to manufacture and sell AZT from the government, which should be deemed the owner of the interest of coinventors Broder and Mitsuya in the AZT patents. Burroughs Wellcome denied that Broder and Mitsuya were coinventors and also responded that the assertion of any rights of Broder, Mitsuya, or the government in the patents was barred by laches, estoppel, and waiver.

***.

After more than three weeks of trial, while Burroughs Wellcome was still in the process of presenting its case, the district court granted Burroughs Wellcome's motion for judgment as a matter of law against all of the defendants, concluding that the Burroughs Wellcome inventors had conceived of the subject matter of the inventions at some time before February 6, 1985, without the assistance of Broder, Mitsuya, or Yarchoan. The court rejected the arguments of Barr *** that [it] *** should be allowed to present evidence that the Burroughs Wellcome inventors had no reasonable belief that the inventions would actually work--that AZT was in fact active against HIV--until they were told the results of the NIH testing.

The court also rejected *** [the] argument that the Burroughs Wellcome inventors had not conceived the invention of the '750 patent--the use of AZT to increase a patient's T-cell count--before July 23, 1985, when Broder reported the results of the NIH patient study to Lehrman. The court concluded that the increase in T-cell count was an obvious phenomenon known to the inventors that would result from administration of AZT. And the district court denied Barr's renewed motion for partial summary judgment on Burroughs Wellcome's equitable defenses to its counterclaim for correction of the patents under section 256.

Discussion

The arguments of Barr *** are directed to when the inventors conceived the invention. Burroughs Wellcome says it was before they learned the results of the NIH tests; Barr *** say[s] that confirmation of the inventions' operability, which came from the NIH tests, was an essential part of the inventive process. If Burroughs Wellcome is right, then the patents name the proper inventors, they are not invalid, and the appellants are liable for infringement. If Barr *** [is] correct, then Broder, Mitsuya, and Yarchoan should have been named as joint inventors and the resolution of Burroughs Wellcome's infringement suits is premature.

***.

Conception is the touchstone of inventorship, the completion of the mental part of invention. ***. It is "the formation in the mind of the inventor, of a definite and permanent idea of the complete and operative invention, as it is hereafter to be applied in practice." Hybritech Inc. v. Monoclonal Antibodies, Inc., 802 F.2d 1367, 1376 (Fed.Cir.1986) (citation omitted). Conception is complete only when the idea is so clearly defined in the inventor's mind that only ordinary skill would be necessary to reduce the invention to practice, without extensive research or experimentation. ***. Because it is a mental act, courts require corroborating evidence of a contemporaneous disclosure that would enable one skilled in the art to make the invention. ***.

Thus, the test for conception is whether the inventor had an idea that was definite and permanent enough that one skilled in the art could understand the invention; the inventor must prove his conception by corroborating evidence, preferably by showing a contemporaneous disclosure. An idea is definite and permanent when the inventor has a specific, settled idea, a particular solution to the problem at hand, not just a general goal or research plan he hopes to pursue. ***. The conception analysis necessarily turns on the inventor's ability to describe his invention with particularity. Until he can do so, he cannot prove possession of the complete mental picture of the invention. These rules ensure that patent rights attach only when an idea is so far developed that the inventor can point to a definite, particular invention.

But an inventor need not know that his invention will work for conception to be complete. ***. He need only show that he had the idea; the discovery that an invention actually works is part of its reduction to practice. ***.

Barr *** suggest[s] that the inventor's definite and permanent idea must include a reasonable expectation that the invention will work for its intended purpose. They argue that this expectation is of paramount importance when the invention deals with uncertain or experimental disciplines, where the inventor cannot reasonably believe an idea will be operable until some result supports that conclusion. Without some experimental confirmation, they suggest, the inventor has only a hope or an expectation, and has not yet conceived the invention in sufficiently definite and permanent form. But this is not the law. An inventor's belief that his invention will work or his reasons for choosing a particular approach are irrelevant to conception. ***.
***.

It is undoubtedly true that "[i]n some instances, an inventor is unable to establish a conception until he has reduced the invention to practice through a successful experiment." Amgen[, Inc. V. Chugai Pharmaceutical Co., 927 F.2d [1200] at 1206 [(Fed. Cir. 1993)]; Alpert v. Slatin, 305 F.2d 891, 894 (CCPA 1962) (no conception "where results at each step do not follow as anticipated, but are achieved empirically by what amounts to trial and error"). But in such cases, it is not merely because the field is unpredictable; the alleged conception fails because, as in Smith, it is incomplete. Then the event of reduction to practice in effect provides the only evidence to corroborate conception of the invention.

Under these circumstances, the reduction to practice can be the most definitive corroboration of conception, for where the idea is in constant flux, it is not definite and permanent. A conception is not complete if the subsequent course of experimentation, especially experimental failures, reveals uncertainty that so undermines the specificity of the inventor's idea that it is not yet a definite and permanent reflection of the complete invention as it will be used in practice. See Amgen, 927 F.2d at 1207 (no conception until reduction to practice where others tried and failed to clone gene using suggested strategy); Rey-Bellet v. Engelhardt, 493 F.2d 1380, 1387 (CCPA 1974) (focusing on nature of subsequent research as indicator that inventors encountered no perplexing intricate difficulties). It is this factual uncertainty, not the general uncertainty surrounding experimental sciences, that bears on the problem of conception.

*** .

We emphasize that we do not hold that a person is precluded from being a joint inventor simply because his contribution to a collaborative effort is experimental. Instead, the qualitative contribution of each collaborator is the key--each inventor must contribute to the joint arrival at a definite and permanent idea of the invention as it will be used in practice.

Nor do we suggest that a bare idea is all that conception requires. The idea must be definite and permanent in the sense that it involves a specific approach to the particular problem at hand. It must also be sufficiently precise that a skilled artisan could carry out the invention without undue experimentation. And, of course, the alleged conception must be supported by corroborating evidence. On the facts before us, it is apparent that the district court correctly ruled against Barr *** as to five of the patents, but that the court's judgment as to the sixth, the '750 patent, was premature.

The '232, '838, '130, '208, and '538 patents encompass compositions and methods of using AZT to treat AIDS. The Burroughs Wellcome inventors claim conception of these inventions prior to the NIH experiments, based on the draft British patent application. That document is not itself a conception, for conception occurs in the inventors' minds, not on paper. The draft simply corroborates the claim that they had formulated a definite and permanent idea of the inventions by the time it was prepared.

The Burroughs Wellcome inventors set out with the general goal of finding a method to treat AIDS, but by the time Broder confirmed that AZT was active against HIV, they had more than a general hope or expectation. They had thought of the particular antiviral agent with which they intended to address the problem, and had formulated the idea of the inventions to the point that they could express it clearly in the form of a draft patent application, which Barr *** concede[s] would teach one skilled in the art to practice the inventions. The draft expressly discloses the intended use of AZT to treat AIDS. It sets out the compound's structure, which, along with at least one method of preparation, was already well known. The draft also discloses in detail both how to prepare a pharmaceutical formulation of AZT and how to use it to treat a patient infected with HIV. The listed dosages, dose forms, and routes of administration conform to those eventually approved by the FDA. The draft shows that the idea was clearly defined in the inventors' minds; all that remained was to reduce it to practice--to confirm its operability and bring it to market. See Haskell v. Colebourne, 671 F.2d 1362, 1365-66 (CCPA 1982) (enabling draft patent application sufficient to corroborate conception).

An examination of the events that followed the preparation of Burroughs Wellcome's draft confirms the soundness of the conception. Broder and Mitsuya received from Burroughs Wellcome a group of compounds, known to Broder and Mitsuya only by code names, selected for testing by the Burroughs Wellcome inventors. They then tested those compounds for activity against HIV in their patented cell line. The test results revealed for the first time that one of the compounds, later revealed to be AZT, was exceptionally active against the virus.

Here, though, the testing was brief, simply confirming the operability of what the draft application disclosed. True, the science surrounding HIV and AIDS was unpredictable and highly experimental at the time the Burroughs Wellcome scientists made the inventions. But what matters for conception is whether the inventors had a definite and permanent idea of the operative inventions. In this case, no prolonged period of extensive research, experiment, and modification followed the alleged conception. By all accounts, what followed was simply the normal course of clinical trials that mark the path of any drug to the marketplace.

That is not to say, however, that the NIH scientists merely acted as a "pair of hands" for the Burroughs Wellcome inventors. Broder and Mitsuya exercised considerable skill in conducting the tests, using their patented cell line to model the responses of human cells infected with HIV. Lehrman did suggest initial concentrations to Broder, but she hardly controlled the conduct of the testing, which necessarily involved interpretation of results for which Broder and Mitsuya, and very few others, were uniquely qualified. But because the testing confirmed the operability of the inventions, it showed that the Burroughs Wellcome inventors had a definite and permanent idea of the inventions. It was part of the reduction to practice and inured to the benefit of Burroughs Wellcome.

Barr *** allege[s] error in the district court's refusal to hear their evidence of the poor predictive value of the murine retrovirus screens for activity against HIV. Regardless of the predictive value of the murine tests, however, the record shows that soon after those tests, the inventors determined, for whatever reason, to use AZT as a treatment for AIDS, and they prepared a draft patent application that specifically set out the inventions, including an enabling disclosure. Obviously, enablement and conception are distinct issues, and one need not necessarily meet the enablement standard of 35 U.S.C. § 112 to prove conception. See Fiers [v. Revel], 984 F.2d [1164] at 1169 [(Fed. Cir. 1993)]. But the enabling disclosure does suffice in this case to confirm that the inventors had concluded the mental part of the inventive process--that they had arrived at the final, definite idea of their inventions, leaving only the task of reduction to practice to bring the inventions to fruition.

The question is not whether Burroughs Wellcome reasonably believed that the inventions would work for their intended purpose, the focus of the evidence offered by Barr ***, but whether the inventors had formed the idea of their use for that purpose in sufficiently final form that only the exercise of ordinary skill remained to reduce it to practice. See MacMillan v. Moffett, 432 F.2d at 1239 (Inventor's "reasons or lack of reasons for including U-5008 are not relevant to the question of conception. The important thing is that he did think in definite terms of the method claimed."). Whether or not Burroughs Wellcome believed the inventions would in fact work based on the mouse screens is irrelevant.

We do not know precisely when the inventors conceived their inventions, but the record shows that they had done so by the time they prepared the draft patent application that thoroughly and particularly set out the inventions as they would later be used. The district court correctly ruled that on this record, the NIH scientists were not joint inventors of these inventions.

The '750 patent is another question. It claims "[a] method of increasing the number of T-lymphocytes in a human infected with the [HIV] virus comprising administering to said human an effective amount of" AZT. *** [It is] argue[d] that there is no evidence, under any test of inventorship, that the Burroughs Wellcome inventors conceived of this invention until after the Phase I patient study conducted by Broder and Yarchoan revealed that AZT could lead to increased levels of T-cells in AIDS patients.

*** [T]he record is devoid of any statement that the inventors thought AZT could raise a patient's T-cell levels, but evidence need not always expressly show possession of the invention to corroborate conception. The district court held that the record supported conception as a matter of law, concluding that "an increase in T-lymphocyte count was an 'obvious,' natural phenomenon known to the [Burroughs Wellcome] inventors that would result from the inhibition of a retrovirus." Burroughs Wellcome Co. v. Barr Lab., Inc., 828 F.Supp. at 1213. Burroughs Wellcome argues that this conclusion was proper because increased T-cell count is simply an obvious property or use of the greater discovery at issue here, the treatment of HIV infection with AZT. Because an increase in T-lymphocytes follows inevitably from treatment of AIDS patients with AZT, Burroughs Wellcome says, Broder and Yarchoan merely observed that the method invented by the Burroughs Wellcome inventors had qualities that the inventors failed to perceive. Burroughs Wellcome says this is not an inventive contribution to the claims of any of the AZT patents.

But even though all six patents arise from the same parent application and are subject to terminal disclaimers to avoid rejection for obviousness-type double patenting, each patent claims a different invention.[8] See In re Longi, 759 F.2d 887, 892 (Fed.Cir.1985) (inventor can get only one patent for any single invention). It is true that the Patent Office determined that the method of the '750 patent would have been obvious to those skilled in the art in light of the inventions claimed in the other patents. That is, however, irrelevant to the question whether the Burroughs Wellcome inventors had conceived of the invention before they learned the results of the Phase I trials. For conception, we look not to whether one skilled in the art could have thought of the invention, but whether the alleged inventors actually had in their minds the required definite and permanent idea. Cf. Bosies v. Benedict, 27 F.3d 539, 543 (Fed.Cir.1994) (testimony of noninventor as to noninventor's understanding of inventor's written formula insufficient to prove conception). The record does not now support resolution of this question as a matter of law.

The alleged conception is supported by testimony of Burroughs Wellcome's experts, Burroughs Wellcome's draft Phase I protocol, and the same draft patent application that corroborates conception of the other five inventions. The experts testified that those skilled in the art at the time expected increased immune function to accompany inhibition of HIV. The draft patent application discloses that HIV preferentially destroys T-cells, that AIDS is associated with progressive depletion of T-cells, and that AZT is an effective treatment for HIV infection. Finally, the draft protocol directs the administrators of the Phase I study to monitor patients' T-lymphocyte count. This evidence supports an inference that the Burroughs Wellcome inventors did have the necessary definite and permanent idea, for, given the virus' effect on T-lymphocytes, it seems logical to conclude that stopping the virus might reverse the process of T-cell destruction and restore the body's immune system to a pre-infection state. If this were the only evidence in the record, the court's judgment would be sustained.

But *** evidence [was offered] suggesting that one skilled in the art would not have expected T-cell count to rise. On deposition, Broder testified that prior to the first patient study, "no one knew whether there was such a thing as recovery" of T-cells, based on the NIH's experience with suramin, a drug that entered clinical trials before AZT. Although suramin showed some activity against HIV, inhibition of the retrovirus apparently was not accompanied by increases in T-cell count or restoration of immune functions. Of course, there might be any number of other explanations for the results of the suramin trials; but they might suggest that although those skilled in the art recognized the significance of T-lymphocyte levels in HIV infection and AIDS, they might have expected inhibition of the virus simply to halt the continuing destruction of

---

[8] We must assume for the purposes of this case that the '750 patent is drawn to an invention different from each of the other five patents. The parties do not ask us to decide whether claims drawn to an effect or mechanism of action of AZT--its ability to raise T-cell count--reach the same invention as (that is, are inherent in) claims drawn to use of the drug to treat HIV infection or AIDS, and we express no opinion on that. ***

T-cells, not to increase T-cell count and restore immune function. This could support an inference that the inventors themselves did not conceive the invention prior to the Phase I study.

*** [It is] also contend[ed] that Burroughs Wellcome prepared its Phase I protocol in collaboration with Broder and the NIH, possibly from a draft protocol prepared by Broder and Yarchoan pursuant to their study of suramin. These contentions are relevant to the conception inquiry for they tend to undermine the corroborative value of the draft protocol, and might even support joint inventorship based on that draft. See Coleman v. Dines, 754 F.2d [353] at 360 [(Fed. Cir. 1985)], (document's co-author cannot be considered sole inventor of invention disclosed in document without further proof). Because under Rule 50(a) all inferences must be taken against the moving party, the court's ruling on the '750 patent was inappropriate, and we vacate the judgment to that extent and remand for further proceedings.

Conclusion

Accordingly, the judgment of the United States District Court for the Eastern District of North Carolina is affirmed in part, vacated in part, and remanded.

PAGE 975. Add after note 1.

GLAXO INC. v. NOVOPHARM LTD.
United States Court of Appeals for the Federal Circuit, 1995.
52 F.3d 1043, certiorari denied 116 S.Ct. 516 (1995)

RICH, Circuit Judge.

Novopharm Ltd. (Novopharm) appeals the judgment of the United States District Court for the Eastern District of North Carolina, Glaxo, Inc. v. Novopharm Ltd., 830 F.Supp. 871 (E.D.N.C.1993), that United States Patent No. 4,521,431 was not invalid and was infringed, and enjoining Novopharm from the commercial manufacture or sale of the patented crystalline form of ranitidine hydrochloride. We affirm.

Background

Glaxo Inc. and Glaxo Group Ltd. (collectively Glaxo) are the owner and exclusive United States licensee, respectively, of United States Patent No. 4,521,431 ('431 patent). The '431 patent claims a specific crystalline form of the compound ranitidine hydrochloride, designated as "Form 2," which Glaxo markets as an antiulcer medication under the brand name Zantac.[1] The '431 patent issued on June 4, 1985.

In 1976, Glaxo chemists investigating potential antiulcer medications synthesized an aminoalkyl furan derivative, later named ranitidine, which proved to be a potent histamine blocker, inhibiting the secretion of stomach acid. Later that year, Glaxo filed an application for a patent on ranitidine in the United Kingdom. It followed with an application for a United States patent, which issued as No. 4,128,658 ('658 patent) on December 5, 1978. The '658 patent claims a number of structurally similar compounds, including ranitidine and its hydrochloride salt. It discloses one method for preparing ranitidine hydrochloride, set forth in the '658 patent as Example 32.[2]

Glaxo prepared large quantities of ranitidine hydrochloride between 1977 and 1980 for use in toxicology and clinical studies. Instead of using the process of Example 32, however, Glaxo's chemists prepared this material using a similar process that they labelled Process 3A. They later developed a more efficient method that they called Process 3B. Until April 15, 1980, both Process 3A and Process 3B yielded ranitidine hydrochloride identical in all respects to that originally produced using the Example 32 procedure.

On that date, however, Glaxo's Derek Crookes used Process 3B to prepare crystalline ranitidine hydrochloride that was visibly different from all previous batches of the salt. The difference was confirmed by infra-red (IR) spectroscopy and x-ray powder diffraction, which revealed that the new product was a crystalline form, or polymorph, of ranitidine hydrochloride that differed from the previously known form. Glaxo began to refer to this new polymorph as Form 2 ranitidine hydrochloride (designating the old polymorph as Form 1).

---

[1] Claims 1 and 2 of the '431 patent, in issue here, read: 1. Form 2 ranitidine hydrochloride characterised by an infra-red spectrum as a mull in mineral oil showing the following main peaks: [list of peaks] 2. Form 2 ranitidine hydrochloride according to claim 1 further characterised by the following x-ray powder diffraction pattern expressed in terms of "d" spacings and relative intensities (1) (s = strong, m = medium, w = weak, v = very, d = diffuse) and obtained by the Debye Scherrer method in a 114.6 mm diameter camera by exposure for 12 hours to CoK suba radiation and for 3 hours to CuK suba radiation: [table] The '431 patent also claims various pharmaceutical compositions and methods of using Form 2 ranitidine hydrochloride. These claims are not at issue in this case.

[2] Developed by Glaxo's David Collin in June 1977, that method involves dissolving ranitidine in industrial methylated spirit containing dissolved hydrogen chloride gas. Ethyl acetate is added to the solution, and ranitidine hydrochloride precipitates from solution as a crystalline solid characterized by a melting point of 133-134 degrees C.

Because Form 2 had better filtration and drying properties, making it better suited for commercial applications, Glaxo decided to proceed with commercialization of Form 2 rather than Form 1. Form 2 was hampered by poor flow properties, however, which made the material difficult to measure and dispense in its pure form. Accordingly, Glaxo scientists developed a novel azeotroping process[3] to granulate the Form 2 salt, which made it much easier to make into pharmaceutical compositions. This process was the subject of a British patent application that Glaxo eventually abandoned without disclosing the process to the public.

Glaxo filed a patent application covering Form 2 ranitidine hydrochloride in the United Kingdom on October 1, 1980. It filed a United States application thereon the next year, which eventually issued as the '431 patent in suit. When George Graham Brereton, Glaxo's patent officer initially charged with pursuing the United States application, learned of the azeotropic granulation process and Glaxo's desire to keep that process secret, he recommended that Glaxo not claim pharmaceutical compositions of the Form 2 salt for fear of violating the best mode requirement. Brereton apparently believed that disclosure of the azeotroping process would be necessary because it was the best way to make the Form 2 salt for use in preparing pharmaceutical compositions. He later moved to another position at Glaxo. The U.S. application was eventually amended to include pharmaceutical composition claims, but Glaxo did not amend the specification to disclose the azeotroping process.

On August 9, 1991, Novopharm Ltd. filed an Abbreviated New Drug Application (ANDA) with the Food and Drug Administration (FDA), seeking FDA approval to manufacture and sell a generic version of Form 2 ranitidine hydrochloride beginning December 5, 1995, the expiration date of the '658 patent, well before the expiration date of the '431 patent in 2002. Glaxo filed this suit for patent infringement on November 13, 1991, alleging technical infringement of claims 1 and 2 of the '431 patent by the ANDA filing as provided in 35 U.S.C. § 271(e)(2) (1988). Novopharm admitted infringement of the claims, but contended that the '431 patent was invalid because it was anticipated by the disclosure of the '658 patent.

Novopharm later amended its answer to add the defense of inequitable conduct arising from alleged false and misleading affidavits provided to the U.S. Patent and

---

[3] Azeotroping is a technique for separating a chemical mixture, the components of which would otherwise be difficult to separate because of the similarity of their boiling points. An additional substance is added to the mixture, selected for its ability to interact with a component of the original mixture to form an azeotrope--a mixture of substances "the composition of which does not change upon distillation." See McGraw-Hill Dictionary of Scientific and Technical Terms 162 (4th ed. 1989). If the proper substance is selected, the resulting azeotrope will have a boiling point that differs substantially from the desired component of the original mixture. The desired component can then be successfully separated from the azeotrope by distillation. See Hawley's Condensed Chemical Dictionary 109 (11th ed. 1987).

Trademark Office (PTO) during prosecution of the applications from which the '431 patent issued. Finally, on June 21, 1993, Novopharm sought summary judgment based on a third defense, Glaxo's alleged failure to disclose the best mode of practicing the claimed invention. The trial court denied the motion, and the case was tried to the court beginning on August 9, 1993.

On the question of anticipation, the court found that Novopharm had not carried its burden of proving by clear and convincing evidence that practice of Example 32 of the '658 patent always produced Form 2 ranitidine hydrochloride, so that Form 2 was not inherently disclosed by Example 32. As for inequitable conduct, the court agreed with Novopharm that the affidavits presented to the examiner were misleading and material, but it found that Novopharm had failed to prove any deceptive intent. The court also concluded that there was no violation of the best mode requirement because Novopharm had not proved that Crookes, the inventor, knew of the best mode, the statute and this court's precedent providing that knowledge by the inventor himself is required. Accordingly, the court held that the '431 patent was not invalid, was enforceable and infringed, and ordered that Novopharm refrain from commercial manufacture or sale of Form 2 ranitidine hydrochloride before the '431 patent expires. Novopharm appeals.

Discussion

I. Example 32, anticipation

[The court affirmed the district court's finding of no anticipation.]

* * *

II. Inequitable Conduct

[The court affirmed the district court's finding that Glaxo did not intend to deceive when it made misrepresentations to the patent office.]

* * *

III. Best Mode

Novopharm next asserts that Glaxo failed to disclose the best mode of practicing the invention, that is, the azeotroping process it uses to formulate the claimed Form 2 ranitidine hydrochloride into pharmaceutical compositions. The best mode defense arose little more than two months before trial just after Glaxo produced documents based on which Novopharm filed a motion for summary judgment of invalidity for failure to disclose the best mode. Less than a week before trial, the district court denied Novopharm's motion stating that "the court cannot hold as a matter of law that Dr. Crookes knew that the azeotroping process was the best mode of manufacturing ranitidine hydrochloride, and summary judgment must therefore be denied." Glaxo, Inc. v. Novopharm Ltd., 830 F.Supp. 869, 871 (E.D.N.C.1993). The district court further stated that it reserved for trial "ruling on the question of whether and to what extent the knowledge of other Glaxo employees and agents may be imputed to Dr. Crookes for purposes of finding a best mode analysis [sic, violation]." *Id.*

At trial, Novopharm produced evidence that officials at Glaxo knew of the azeotroping process and considered it to be the best mode of making Form 2 ranitidine hydrochloride into a pharmaceutical composition. Novopharm argued in district court, as it does here, that the knowledge of the azeotroping process by Glaxo officials should be imputed to inventor Crookes for purposes of finding a best mode violation.

The trial court found Novopharm's argument to have some "intuitive appeal" since Glaxo "has enjoyed the monopoly the issued patent provides." Glaxo, 830 F.Supp. 871, 881-82 (E.D.N.C.1993). Indeed, the trial court stated that if it were to impute the knowledge of others to the inventor of the '431 patent, "then clearly the court would be required to find a best mode violation." *Id.* at 882. The trial court concluded, however, that the statute, 35 U.S.C. § 112, first paragraph, and this court's holding in Texas Instruments, Inc. v. United States International Trade Commission, 871 F.2d 1054 (Fed.Cir.1989) do not permit using imputed knowledge in a best mode analysis. The district court concluded that Novopharm "as a matter of law ... failed to show the '431 patent should be invalidated based on a best mode violation." *Id.* at 882. On appeal, Novopharm asserts that the district court erred as a matter of law in holding that a best mode defense cannot be found in the absence of proof that the inventor knew of that mode.

The statutory provision at issue sets forth that:

The specification ... shall set forth the best mode contemplated by the inventor of carrying out his invention.

35 U.S.C. § 112, first paragraph (1988).

The statutory language could not be clearer. The best mode of carrying out an invention, indeed if there is one, to be disclosed is that "contemplated by the inventor." That the best mode "belongs" to the inventor finds consistent support in previous statutory language as well.[6] Additionally, the commentary on the 1952 Patent Act

---

[6] The 1793 Act stated: "in the case of any machine [the inventor] shall fully explain the principle, and the several modes in which he has contemplated the application of that principle or character, by which it may be distinguished from other inventions." Act of Feb. 21, 1793, ch. 11, § 3, 1 Stat. 318. The 1836 Act stated: "in case of any machine, [the inventor] shall fully explain the principle, and the several modes in which he has contemplated the application

states with respect to the best mode provision that "[t]his requirement, it should be noted, is not absolute, since it only requires disclosure of the best mode contemplated by the inventor, presumably at the time of filing the application." P.J. Federico, Commentary on the New Patent Act, 35 U.S.C.A. 1, 25 (1954).

In arguing that Glaxo did not comply with the best mode requirement of § 112, first paragraph, Novopharm relies on Amgen, Inc. v. Chugai Pharmaceutical Co., 927 F.2d 1200 (Fed.Cir.), cert. denied, 502 U.S. 856 (1991), for the proposition that the best mode requirement lies at the heart of the statutory quid pro quo of the patent system. This is true enough. However, *Amgen*, consistent with the statute, speaks of the best mode requirement in terms of the best mode contemplated by the inventor. Amgen, 927 F.2d at 1210 ("Our case law has interpreted the best mode requirement to mean that there must be no concealment of a mode *known by the inventor* to be better than that which is disclosed.") (emphasis added). In fact, as we have previously stated, the sole purpose of the best mode requirement "is to restrain *inventors* from applying for patents while at the same time concealing from the public preferred embodiments of their inventions which *they* have in fact conceived." Chemcast Corp. v. Arco Indus. Corp., 913 F.2d 923, 926 (Fed.Cir.1990) (emphasis added) (quoting In re Gay, 309 F.2d 769, 772 (CCPA 1962)); ***.

The best mode inquiry focuses on the inventor's state of mind at the time he filed his application, raising a subjective factual question. Chemcast, 913 F.2d at 926. The specificity of disclosure required to comply with the best mode requirement must be determined by the knowledge of facts within the possession of the inventor at the time of filing the application. Spectra-Physics, Inc. v. Coherent, Inc., 827 F.2d 1524, 1535 (Fed.Cir.), cert. denied, 484 U.S. 954 (1987).

That the best mode inquiry is grounded in knowledge of the inventor is even more evident upon contrasting the best mode requirement of § 112 with the enablement requirement of that section. Chemcast, 913 F.2d at 926. "Enablement looks to placing the subject matter of the claims generally in the possession of the public." Spectra-Physics, 827 F.2d at 1532. Best mode looks to whether specific instrumentalities and techniques have been developed by the inventor and known to him at the time of filing as the best way of carrying out the invention. *Id.*; Chemcast, 913 F.2d at 927-28. The enablement requirement, thus, looks to the objective knowledge of one of ordinary skill in the art, while the best mode inquiry is a subjective, factual one, looking to the state of the mind of the inventor. Indeed, recently this court in addressing whether an applicant's best mode had to be updated upon filing a continuation application affirmed that the best mode requirement "focuses on what the

---

of the principle or character by which it may be distinguished from other inventions." Act of July 4, 1836, ch. 357, § 6, 5 Stat. 117. The Act of 1870 changed the 'several modes' provision of the previous Acts to the present-day 'best mode.' Act of July 7, 1870, ch. 230, § 26, 16 Stat. 198.

inventor knows." Transco Prods. Inc. v. Performance Contracting, Inc., 38 F.3d 551, 558 (Fed.Cir.1994) (emphasis added), cert. denied, 115 S.Ct. 1102 (1995).

Based on the clear wording of the statute and our case law, the trial court properly rejected Novopharm's "imputed knowledge" best mode defense. As the trial court correctly noted, we held in Texas Instruments that there was no violation of the best mode requirement of § 112 by reason of knowledge of the purported best mode on the part of T.I. employees, other than the inventor, in the manufacturing group when the inventor did not know of or conceal this best mode. Texas Instruments, 871 F.2d at 1061.

There is simply no evidence in the record before us, indeed Novopharm points to none, that the inventor of the '431 patent knew of and concealed the azeotroping process when his application was filed. Inventor Crookes in a declaration in opposition to Novopharm's best mode summary judgment motion stated "I did not know of any azeotroping of ranitidine hydrochloride, or of its benefits, prior to commencement of this litigation. I did not--indeed, could not--consider the azeotrope process a 'best mode' of making ranitidine hydrochloride tablets at the time of filing any patent application." Crookes indicated that he worked in a different department than those who developed the azeotroping process.

As the district court observed, the record does indicate, however, that others at Glaxo knew of the azeotroping process and knew that this process would be used commercially to produce pharmaceutical forms of the claimed product.[7] The record also indicates that these individuals as well as their English patent agent were concerned that failure to disclose the azeotroping process may present a best mode problem. However, in neither instance did Glaxo nor its patent agent appropriately consider that inventor Crookes knew nothing of the azeotroping process. That Glaxo thought it may have a best mode problem either because of its incorrect or incomplete consideration of U.S. patent law does not make it so.

Novopharm maintains that Glaxo intentionally isolated Crookes from knowledge of the azeotroping process leaving "it to others to commercialize and reduce the invention to practice." Thus, Novopharm fears that Glaxo purposefully prevented the inventor from gaining knowledge of the most advantageous application for his invention, the azeotroping process, so that that process could be maintained as a trade secret. That fear does not equate with a best mode violation.

---

[7] The claims at issue are not directed to a pharmaceutical compound. Therefore, there may be a question whether the azeotroping process is indeed the best mode of carrying out the claimed invention. See Chemcast, 913 F.2d at 927. In view of our decision, however, it is not necessary for us to reach this issue.

In this case, Crookes was unconcerned with the commercialization of the claimed compound. It is undisputed that Crookes invented a compound and was not involved in whatever processes were to be used to commercially produce it. Therefore, whether Glaxo deliberately walled off the inventor is irrelevant to the issue of failure of his application to disclose the best mode known to him.

In arguing that Crookes was screened from knowledge, Novopharm relies on testimony of Glaxo's in-house patent agent that Crookes was not consulted "at any time" during the preparation of the application that matured into the '431 patent. This however, completely ignores the requirement that patents are applied for "in the name of the actual inventor or inventors" according to 37 C.F.R. § 1.41(a) (1983). The inventor(s) must submit an oath or declaration attesting that they have "reviewed and understand[ ] the contents of the specification" and believe "the named inventor or inventors to be the original and first inventor or inventors of the subject matter which is claimed and for which a patent is sought." 37 C.F.R. § 1.63(b)(1), (2) (1992); see also 37 C.F.R. § 1.51(a)(2) (1992). ***. Novopharm has not alleged that these requirements were violated.

It is therefore presumed that Crookes, the inventor and applicant, must have reviewed the specification and signed the required declaration before the application was filed. Without more, Novopharm is simply wrong when it alleges that Crookes had nothing to do with determining what needed to be disclosed in his patent application.

Novopharm additionally contends that looking solely to the inventor's knowledge in a best mode analysis "makes a mockery of the best mode requirement, and fosters a 'head in the sand' mentality for corporate applicants."

However, the practical reality is that inventors in most every corporate scenario cannot know all of the technology in which their employers are engaged. Therefore, whether intentionally or not, inventors will be effectively isolated from research no matter how relevant it is to the field in which they are working. Separating scenarios in which employers unintentionally isolate inventors from relevant research from instances in which employers deliberately set out to screen inventors from research, and finding a best mode violation in the latter case, would ignore the very words of § 112, first paragraph, and the case law as it has developed, which consistently has analyzed the best mode requirement in terms of knowledge of and concealment by the inventor. Congress was aware of the differences between inventors and assignees, see 35 U.S.C. §§ 100(d) and 152, and it specifically limited the best mode required to that contemplated by the inventor. We have no authority to extend the requirement beyond the limits set by Congress.

The dissent argues that imputing knowledge of others than the inventor to the inventor for purposes of considering what was "contemplated by the inventor" in a best mode analysis "may be necessary under appropriate circumstances, to protect the public's 'paramount interest in seeing that patent monopolies spring from backgrounds free from fraud or other inequitable conduct.'" The dissent contends that such knowledge can be imputed to the inventor under principles of agency law stating that, "[a]n agent's acts and knowledge can be imputed to the principal when necessary to protect the interests of others, so long as the acts or knowledge in question fall within the scope of the agent's authority," citing Restatement (Second) of Agency, § 261.

The Restatement defines agency as "the fiduciary relation which results from the manifestation of consent by one person to another that the other shall act on his behalf and subject to his control, and consent, by the other so to act." Restatement (Second) of Agency, § 1.

The flaw in the dissent's analysis is that a patent attorney does not enter into an agency relationship with the inventor for purposes of what is disclosed in the inventor's patent application. Simply, the inventor never authorizes his patent attorney to "act on his behalf" with respect to disclosing the invention. Or, in the terms used by the dissent, the scope of the patent attorney's authority does not include inventing, i.e., either supplementing or supplanting the inventor's knowledge of his own invention. Rather, the information disclosed in the inventor's patent application must be that which is actually known to him. The statute requires that he submit an oath to this effect. See 35 U.S.C. § 115 (1988).

An agency relationship may exist during prosecution before the PTO where the patent attorney is acting on the inventor's behalf. See 37 C.F.R. 1.56(a) (1992). An agency relationship does not exist, however, with respect to what an inventor must disclose in order to obtain a patent on his invention, which includes, of course, any best mode under § 112. Therefore, in addition to being inconsistent with § 112, as explained above, because an agency relationship does not exist for purposes of what is disclosed in a patent application, it would be improper to impute a patent attorney's knowledge of a best mode to the inventor for purposes of finding a best mode violation.

In any case, the dissent's application of general agency principles to the analysis of best mode disclosure under § 112 is an entirely new idea and is not existing law.

The trial court here correctly noted that this court has "found that the absence of a showing of *actual knowledge by the inventor* was dispositive of the defendant's best mode argument" and held that the law "does not permit using imputed knowledge" in a best mode defense. Glaxo, 830 F.Supp. at 881-82 (emphasis added). The district court therefore correctly rejected the best mode defense.

IV. Conclusion

Accordingly, the judgment of the United States District Court for the Eastern District of North Carolina is affirmed.

MAYER, Circuit Judge, dissenting.

With this case, the court blesses corporate shell games resulting from organizational gerrymandering and willful ignorance by which one can secure the monopoly of a patent while hiding the best mode of practicing the invention the law expects to be made public in return for its protection. Because I believe this is a perverse interpretation of the law, I dissent.

* * *

The problem is that Glaxo's version of best mode, which the court now adopts, would allow, if not encourage, employers to isolate their employee/inventors from research directed to finding the most advantageous applications for their inventions, knowledge that the inventors would probably have had but for the employer's efforts to keep the work secret. As a result, inventors may have only limited perspective on the real value of their inventions, and can accordingly share only this limited perspective with the public. All the while, the employer/assignee will have a view of the big picture, fully aware, through its other employees, of superior modes of practicing the invention. But the assignee will be under no obligation to disclose those modes to the public. This deliberate subversion of the statutory disclosure would deprive the public of the benefits of the best mode of practicing the invention. There is no reason why this court should condone such abuse of the public trust.

I would hold that if there truly was such a pattern of deliberate concealment of information that would otherwise have been known to the inventor, the knowledge of those who sought to conceal that information and who now attempt to enforce the patent may be imputed to the inventor. The district court can refuse to enforce the patent and should be given the opportunity to do so with a correct understanding of its powers.

NOTE

1. Wahl Instruments, Inc. v. Acvious, Inc., 950 F.2d 1575 (Fed. Cir. 1991), involved a patent on an egg-timer device made with plastic and thermochromic paint or ink. A thermochromic material is a material that changes color at a certain temperature. The patented device could be placed in the fluid being heated and would change color when the desired amount of heat had been applied. At the time of the application the inventor was involved in developing precise manufacturing techniques for commercial production, but he did not disclose the techniques in the patent. The district court entered summary judgment against the patent owner for failure to disclose his best mode. The Federal Circuit reversed on the ground that the undisclosed manufacturing procedures were simply routine manufacturing decisions involving techniques known to those with skill in the relevant arts. The court said:

> A description of particular materials or sources or of a particular method or technique selected for manufacture may or may not be required as part of a best mode disclosure respecting a device.

***. Thus, the particulars of making a prototype or even a commercial embodiment do not necessarily equate with the "best mode" of "carrying out" an invention. Indeed, the inventor's manufacturing materials or sources or techniques used to make a device may vary from wholly irrelevant to critical. For example, if the inventor develops or knows of a particular method of making which substantially improves the operation or effectiveness of his invention, failure to disclose such peripheral development may well lead to invalidation. ***. On the other hand, an inventor is not required to supply "production" specifications. *** Under our case law, there is no mechanical rule that a best mode violation occurs because the inventor failed to disclose particular manufacturing procedures beyond the information sufficient for enablement. One must look at the scope of the invention, the skill in the art, the evidence as to the inventor's belief, and all of the circumstances in order to evaluate whether the inventor's failure to disclose particulars of manufacture gives rise to an inference that he concealed information which one of ordinary skill in the art would not know. ***.

950 F.2d 1579-80.

PAGE 975. Add new note 3.

Amgen, Inc. v. Chugai Pharmaceutical Co., 927 F.2d 1200 (Fed. Cir. 1991), involved patent litigation over Erythropoietin (EPO), a protein which stimulates the production of red blood cells. It is used to treat anemias or other blood disorders characterized by low bone marrow production of red blood cells. The drug has been particularly useful for cancer or AIDS patients suffering from low red blood cell production as a result of other therapies. It has also been very profitable. The Amgen patent disclosed a method of producing EPO through use of biotechnology. The defendants argued that Amgen's disclosure of the best mode was inadequate because Amgen had not placed a sample of a key substance used in the process on deposit where competitors could obtain a sample. Amgen argued that the patent specification adequately disclosed how to make the substance. The court addressed these arguments as follows, Id. 1209-1212:

AMGEN, INC. v. CHUGAI PHARMACEUTICAL CO., LTD.
United States Court of Appeals for the Federal Circuit, 1991.
927 F. 2d 1200, certiorari denied 502 U.S. 856 (1991)

C. Best Mode

Defendants argue that the district court erred in failing to hold the '008 patent invalid under 35 U.S.C. § 112, asserting that Lin failed to disclose the best mammalian host cells known to him as of November 30, 1984, the date he filed his fourth patent application.

The district court found that the "best mode" of practicing the claimed invention was by use of a specific genetically-heterogeneous strain of Chinese hamster ovary (CHO) cells, which produced EPO at a rate greater than that of other cells. It further found that this strain was disclosed in Example 10 and that Lin knew of no better mode. GI argues that Lin's best mode was not adequately disclosed in Example 10 because one skilled in the art could not duplicate Lin's best mode without his having first deposited a sample of the specific cells in a public depository. The issue before us therefore is whether the district court erred in concluding that Example 10 of the '008 patent satisfied the best mode requirement as to the invention of the challenged claims and that a deposit of the preferred CHO cells was not necessary.

* * *

35 U.S.C. § 112 provides in relevant part: The specification shall contain a written description of the invention, and of the manner and process of making and using it, in such full, clear, concise, and exact terms as to enable any person skilled in the art to which it pertains, or with which it is most nearly connected, to make and use the same, and shall set forth *the best mode contemplated by the inventor of carrying out his invention.* (Emphasis added).

This court has recently discussed the best mode requirement, pointing out that its analysis has two components. Chemcast Corp. v. Arco Indus. Corp., 913 F.2d 923, 927 (Fed.Cir.1990). The first is a subjective one, asking whether, at the time the inventor filed his patent application, he contemplated a best mode of practicing his invention. If he did, the second inquiry is whether his disclosure is adequate to enable one skilled in the art to practice the best mode or, in other words, whether the best mode has been concealed from the public. The best mode requirement thus is intended to ensure that a patent applicant plays "fair and square" with the patent system. It is a requirement that the quid pro quo of the patent grant be satisfied. One must not receive the right to exclude others unless at the time of filing he has provided an adequate disclosure of the best mode known to him of carrying out his invention. Our case law has interpreted the best mode requirement to mean that there must be no concealment of a mode known by the inventor to be better than that which is disclosed. Hybritech Inc. v. Monoclonal Antibodies, Inc., 802 F.2d 1367, 1384-85 (Fed.Cir.1986), cert. denied, 480 U.S. 947 (1987). Section 282 imposes on those attempting to prove invalidity the burden of proof. We agree that the district court did not err in finding that defendants have not met their burden of proving a best mode violation.

As noted above, the district court found that the best mode of making the CHO cells was set forth in Example 10. As the district court stated, while it was not clear which of two possible strains Lin considered to be the best, the cell strain subjected to

1000 nanomolar MTX (methotrexate) or that subjected to 100 nanomolar MTX, the best mode was disclosed because both were disclosed.[6] Defendants argue that this disclosure is not enough, that a deposit of the cells was required.

Defendants contend that "[i]n the field of living materials such as microorganisms and cell cultures," we should require a biological deposit so that the public has access to exactly the best mode contemplated by the inventor. This presents us with a question of first impression concerning the best mode requirement for patents involving novel genetically-engineered biological subject matter.

For many years, it has been customary for patent applicants to place microorganism samples in a public depository when such a sample is necessary to carry out a claimed invention. This practice arose out of the development of antibiotics, when microorganisms obtained from soil samples uniquely synthesized antibiotics which could not be readily prepared chemically or otherwise. In re Argoudelis, 434 F.2d 1390 (CCPA 1970). Such a deposit has been considered adequate to satisfy the enablement requirement of 35 U.S.C. § 112, when a written description alone would not place the invention in the hands of the public and physical possession of a unique biological material is required. See, e.g., In re Wands, 858 F.2d 731, 735-36 (Fed.Cir.1988) ("Where an invention depends on the use of living materials ... it may be impossible to enable the public to make the invention (i.e., to obtain these living materials) solely by means of written disclosure."); In re Lundak, 773 F.2d 1216, 1220 (Fed.Cir.1985) ("When an invention relates to a new biological material, the material may not be reproducible even when detailed procedures and a complete taxonomic description are included in the specification."); see generally Hampar, Patenting of Recombinant DNA Technology: The Deposit Requirement, 67 J. Pat. & Trademark Off. Soc'y 569, 607 (1985) ("The deposit requirement is a nonstatutory mechanism for ensuring compliance with the 'enabling' provision under 35 U.S.C. § 112.").

The district court found that the claims at issue require the use of biological materials that were capable of being prepared in the laboratory from readily available biological cells, using the description in Example 10. The court also found that there were no starting materials that were not publicly available, that were not described, or that required undue experimentation for their preparation in order to carry out the best mode. The court noted that Lin testified that the isolation of the preferred strain was a "routine limited dilution cloning procedure" well known in the art. Dr. Simonsen,

---

[6] In its opinion, the district court stated that "the best way to express EPO was from mammalian cells ... and that a cell line derived from 11 possible clones from the CHO B11 3,.1 cell strain was to be used for Amgen's master working cell bank, which was expected to be started on November 26, 1984." 13 USPQ2d at 1772. At another point, the court stated that Amgen "did disclose the best mode in Example 10 of the invention, when it described the production rates of the 100 nanomolar- amplified cells (the B11 3,.1 cell strain) and one micromolar-treated cells." Id.

GI's own expert, testified that the disclosed procedures were "standard" and that: with the vectors and the sequences shown in Example 10, I have no doubt that someone eventually could reproduce--well, could generate cell lines [sic, strains] making some level of EPO, and they could be better, they could be worse in terms of EPO production. The district court relied on this testimony, and, upon review, we agree with its determination. The testimony accurately reflects that the invention, as it relates to the best mode host cells, could be practiced by one skilled in the art following Example 10. Thus, the best mode was disclosed and it was adequately enabled.

These materials are therefore not analogous to the biological cells obtained from unique soil samples. When a biological sample required for the practice of an invention is obtained from nature, the invention may be incapable of being practiced without access to that organism. Hence the deposit is required in that case. On the other hand, when, as is the case here, the organism is created by insertion of genetic material into a cell obtained from generally available sources, then all that is required is a description of the best mode and an adequate description of the means of carrying out the invention, not deposit of the cells. If the cells can be prepared without undue experimentation from known materials, based on the description in the patent specification, a deposit is not required. See Feldman v. Aunstrup, 517 F.2d 1351, 1354 (CCPA 1975), ("No problem exists when the microorganisms used are known and readily available to the public."), cert. denied, 424 U.S. 912 (1976). Since the court found that that is the case here, we therefore hold that there is no failure to comply with the best mode requirement for lack of a deposit of the CHO cells, when the best mode of preparing the cells has been disclosed and the best mode cells have been enabled, i.e., they can be prepared by one skilled in the art from known materials using the description in the specification.

Defendants also contend that the examiner's rejection of the application that matured into the '008 patent for failure to make a publicly accessible biological deposit supports its argument. U.S. Patent Application Serial No. 675,298, Prosecution History at 179 (First Rejection July 3, 1986). However, that rejection was withdrawn after an oral interview and a written argument that the invention did not require a deposit. *Id.* at 208.

We also note that the PTO has recently prescribed guidelines concerning the deposit of biological materials. See 37 C.F.R. § 1.802(b) (1990) (biological material need not be deposited "if it is known and readily available to the public or can be made or isolated without undue experimentation"). The PTO, in response to a question as to whether the deposit requirement is applicable to the best mode requirement, as distinct from enablement, said: The best mode requirement is a safeguard against the possible selfish desire on the part of some people to obtain patent protection without making a full disclosure. The requirement does not permit an inventor to disclose only what is known to be the second-best embodiment, retaining the best.... The fundamental issue that should be addressed is whether there was evidence to show that the quality of an applicant's best mode disclosure is so poor as to effectively result in concealment. In re Sherwood, 615 [613] F.2d 809, (CCPA 1980). If a deposit is the only way to comply with the best mode requirement then the deposit must be made. 52 Fed.Reg. 34080, 34086 (Sept. 8, 1987).

We see no inconsistency between the district court's decision, which we affirm here, and these guidelines.

Defendants also assert that the record shows that scientists were unable to duplicate Lin's genetically-heterogeneous best mode cell strain. However, we have long held that the issue is whether the disclosure is "adequate," not that an exact duplication is necessary. Indeed, the district court stated that [t]he testimony is clear that no scientist could ever duplicate exactly the best mode used by Amgen, but that those of ordinary skill in the art could produce mammalian host cell strains or lines with similar levels of production identified in Example 10. 13 USPQ2d at 1774. What is required is an adequate disclosure of the best mode, not a guarantee that every aspect of the specification be precisely and universally reproducible.
* * *.

PAGE 999. Add Note 4.

4. Article 28.1(b) of the GATT TRIPS provides: "where the subject matter of a patent is a process, [the patent owner shall have the exclusive right] to prevent third parties not having the owner's consent from the act of using the process, and from the acts of: using, offering for sale, selling, or importing for these purposes at least the product obtained directly by that process."

PAGE 1008. Add Note after *Paper Converting Machine Co. v. Magna-Graphics Corp.*

NOTE

In Joy Technologies v. Flakt Inc., 6 F.3d 770 (Fed. Cir. 1993), the district court enjoined the defendant from entering into any contracts for the sale of a machine to be used to practice a patented process prior to the end of the term on the process patent. The Federal Circuit reversed, distinguishing Magna-Graphics as follows:

> "*Paper Converting Machine* is easily distinguishable from the present case. In *Paper Converting Machine*, * * * we stated:
>> 'It is undisputed that [the defendant] intended to finesse [the patentee] out of the sale of a machine on which [the patentee] held a valid patent during the life of that patent.'
>
> While a method claim had been asserted along with the apparatus claims, the method claim was not discussed nor found infringed by the Fort Howard devices. The analysis focused solely on the patented machine, not on the process implemented by the machine.

In the present case, the patent contains only method claims, which, as discussed above, are directly infringed only when the method is practiced. Joy is basically seeking to convert its method claims into apparatus claims. The facts of *Paper Converting Machine* do not support the injunction in the present case."

PAGE 1025. Add to note 2.

On April 6, 1994 the Federal Trade Commission and the Department of Justice announced new antitrust guidelines for the licensing of intellectual property which establish a safety zone for intellectual property licensing arrangements among entities that collectively account for no more than 20 percent of each relevant market affected by the restraint when the restraint is not anticompetitive on its face. See 49 BNA Patent Trademark and Copyright Journal 703 (April 13, 1994).

PAGE 1037. Add to note 2.

The reverse doctrine of equivalents was applied in Scripps Clinic & Research Foundation v. Genentech, Inc., 927 F.2d 1565 (Fed. Cir. 1991). Scripps owned a patent on the product human blood Factor VIII:C, necessary for clotting, obtained through purification.. Genentech wished to make the same product through the use of recombinant DNA technology. The Scripps patents contained claims, obtained in a reissue proceeding, covering Factor VIII:C. Genentech argued that its Factor VIII:C did not infringe. The court addressed these arguments as follows, Id. at 1581-82:

**SCRIPPS CLINIC & RESEARCH FOUNDATION
v. GENENTECH, INC.**
United States Court of Appeals for the Federal Circuit, 1991.
927 F. 2d 1565

* * *

B

The so-called "reverse doctrine of equivalents" is an equitable doctrine invoked in applying properly construed claims to an accused device. Just as the purpose of the "doctrine of equivalents" is to prevent "pirating" of the patentee's invention, Graver Tank & Mfg. Co. v. Linde Air Prod. Co., 339 U.S. 605, 607, 608, reh'g denied, 340 U.S. 845 (1950), so the purpose of the "reverse" doctrine is to prevent unwarranted extension of the claims beyond a fair scope of the patentee's invention.

The reverse doctrine of equivalents flows from the Supreme Court's statement in Graver Tank that an accused article may avoid infringement, even if it is within the literal words of the claim, if it is "so far changed in principle from a patented article that it performs the same or a similar function in a substantially different way." 339 U.S. at 608-09. Application of the doctrine requires that facts specific to the accused device be determined and weighed against the equitable scope of the claims, which in turn is determined in light of the specification, the prosecution history, and the prior art.

The record contained evidence of the properties of plasma-derived and recombinantly produced VIII:C, which was presented primarily by Scripps in connection with its proofs of infringement. There was deposition testimony that there were differences between VIII:C from plasma and VIII:C obtained by recombinant techniques; a Scripps' witness described the products as "apples and oranges", referring specifically to stability and formulations. The parties disputed, in connection with the summary judgment motions, the capabilities of the respective processes in terms of the purity and specific activities that were enabled for the respective products. The record on this point is extensive.

Genentech argues that its product is equitably seen as changed "in principle", particularly when viewed in the context of the prior art. Genentech asserts that the specific activities and purity that are obtainable by recombinant technology exceed those available by the Scripps process; an assertion disputed by Scripps, but which if found to be correct could provide--depending on the specific facts of similarities and differences--sufficient ground for invoking the reverse doctrine. These aspects were not discussed by the district court.

The principles of patent law must be applied in accordance with the statutory purpose, and the issues raised by new technologies require considered analysis. Genentech has raised questions of scientific and evidentiary fact that are material to the issue of infringement. Consideration of extrinsic evidence is required, and summary judgment is inappropriate. See C.R. Bard, Inc. v. Advanced Cardiovascular Systems, Inc., 911 F.2d 670, 673 (Fed.Cir.1990).

The grant of summary judgment of infringement of claims 24, 25, 28, and 29 is reversed. The issue requires trial.

PAGE 1037. Add to note 5.

PENNWALT CORPORATION v. DURAND-WAYLAND, INC.
United States Court of Appeals for the Federal Circuit (in banc), 1987
833 F. 2d 931, certiorari denied 485 U.S. 961, 1009 (1988)

BISSELL, Circuit Judge.

This appeal and cross-appeal are from a judgment of the United States District Court for the Northern District of Georgia, 225 USPQ 558 (N.D.Ga.1984). The district court found that Durand-Wayland's accused devices do not infringe any claim, literally or under the doctrine of equivalents. Unable to view that finding as clearly erroneous under Fed.R.Civ.P. 52(a), we affirm the judgment of noninfringement and vacate, as moot, that part of the judgment concerning the validity of Pennwalt's patent.

BACKGROUND

Pennwalt sued Durand-Wayland for infringing claims 1, 2, 10 and 18 (claims-at-issue) of its U.S. Patent No. 4,106,628 (the '628 patent) on an invention of Aaron J. Warkentin and George A. Mills, entitled "Sorter for Fruit and the Like." Following a nonjury trial on the issues of patent infringement and validity, the district court, on March 22, 1984, issued an opinion concluding that (1) the claims-at-issue were not anticipated by the prior art, (2) the '628 patent had not run afoul of the "on sale" bar of 35 U.S.C. s 102(b) (1982), and (3) the accused devices did not infringe any of the claims-at-issue, either literally or under the doctrine of equivalents. In an unpublished supplemental order of April 26, 1984, the district court concluded as a matter of law that the claims-at-issue would not have been obvious in light of the prior art.

Pennwalt appeals from the district court's holding of noninfringement, both literally and under the doctrine of equivalents, and its award of costs against Pennwalt. Durand-Wayland appeals from the district court's validity holdings and its denial of Durand-Wayland's request for recovery of its attorney fees.

ISSUE

Our disposition of this appeal requires resolution of the single question of whether the district court's finding of no infringement was clearly erroneous.

OPINION

The '628 patent claims a sorter. The principal object of the invention is to provide a rapid means for sorting items, such as fruit, by color, weight, or a combination of these two characteristics. The sorter recited in claims 1 and 2 conveys items along a track having an electronic-weighing device that produces an electrical signal proportional to the weight of the item, along with signal comparison means, clock means, position indicating means, and discharge means, each of which performs specified functions. The specification describes the details of a "hard-wired" network consisting of discrete electrical components which perform each step of the claims, e.g., by comparing the signals from the weighing device to reference signals and sending an appropriate signal at the proper time to discharge the item into the container corresponding to its weight. The combined sorter of claims 10 and 18 is a multifunctional apparatus whereby the item is conveyed across the weighing device and also carried past an optical scanner that produces an electrical signal proportional to the color of the item. The signals from the weighing device and color sensor are combined and an appropriate signal is sent at the proper time to discharge the item into the container corresponding to its color and weight.

Durand-Wayland manufactures and sells two different types of sorting machines. The first accused device, the "Microsizer," sorts by weight only and employs software labeled either Version 2 or Version 5. The second accused device employs software labeled Version 6 and sorts by both color and weight through the use of the "Microsizer" in conjunction with a color detection apparatus called a "Microsorter."

A more complete description of the claimed invention and of the accused devices is set forth in the district court's opinion. Pennwalt, 225 USPQ at 559-60. The claims-at-issue are set forth in the district court's opinion. *Id.* at 564-65.

I.

Literal Infringement

Pennwalt asserts on appeal that all limitations set forth in claims 1 and 2 and some limitations set forth in claims 10 and 18 can be read literally on the accused devices. Pennwalt contends that the district court erred in interpreting the claims by going beyond the means-plus-function language of a claim limitation and comparing the structure in the accused devices with the structure disclosed in the specification. Such comparison allegedly resulted in the court's reading nonexistent structural limitations into the claims. Pennwalt relies on the statement in Graver Tank & Mfg. Co. v. Linde Air Prods. Co., 339 U.S. 605, 607 (1950): "If accused matter falls clearly within the claim, infringement is made out and that is the end of it." In view of the literal breadth of means-plus-function language in the claims, that "test" for literal infringement would encompass any means that performed the function of a claim element. 35 U.S.C. § 112 (1982). This is not the "test." The Graver Tank statement predated the inclusion in the 1952 Act of the provision specifically permitting "means" limitations, section 112, paragraph 6. See P. Federico, Commentary on the New Patent Law, 35 USCA 1, 25 (1954). As Judge Rich, one of the drafters of the statute, stated in a 1952 address explaining the import of section 112, paragraph 6: If you adopt this practice, that element or step is to be construed--shall be construed (it is mandatory)--to cover the corresponding structure, material or acts described in the specification and equivalents thereof. Address before the New York Patent Law Association (November 6, 1952), reprinted in R. Calvert, The Encyclopedia of Patent Practice and Invention Management 17, "Section 112--Means Claims" (1964).

Thus, section 112, paragraph 6, rules out the possibility that any and every means which performs the function specified in the claim literally satisfies that limitation. While encompassing equivalents of those disclosed in the specification, the provision, nevertheless, acts as a restriction on the literal satisfaction of a claim limitation. Data Line Corp. v. Micro Technologies, Inc., 813 F.2d 1196, 1201

(Fed.Cir.1987). If the required function is not performed exactly in the accused device, it must be borne in mind that section 112, paragraph 6, equivalency is not involved. Section 112, paragraph 6, plays no role in determining whether an equivalent function is performed by the accused device under the doctrine of equivalents.

Thus, it was not legal error (as Pennwalt asserts) for the district court to have made a comparison between Durand-Wayland's structure and the structure disclosed in the specification for performing a particular function. The statute means exactly what it says: To determine whether a claim limitation is met literally, where expressed as a means for performing a stated function, the court must compare the accused structure with the disclosed structure, and must find equivalent structure as well as identity of claimed function for that structure. * * *.

Where the issue is raised, it is part of the ultimate burden of proof of the patent owner to establish, with respect to a claim limitation in means- plus-function form, that the structure in the accused device which performs that function is the same as or an equivalent of the structure disclosed in the specification. In essence, Pennwalt erroneously argues that, if an accused structure performs the function required by the claim, it is *per se* structurally equivalent. That view entirely eliminates the section 112, paragraph 6, restriction and has been rejected in the above-cited precedent of this court.

We need not, and do not, determine whether the district court correctly found no equivalency in structure because the district court also found that the accused devices, in any event, did not perform the same functions specified in the claim. For example, the district court found that the accused devices had no position indicating means which tracked the location of the item being sorted. That finding negates the possibility of finding literal infringement.

II.

Infringement under the Doctrine of Equivalents

Under the doctrine of equivalents, infringement may be found (but not necessarily[7]) if an accused device performs substantially the same overall function or work, in substantially the same way, to obtain substantially the same overall result as the claimed invention. Perkin-Elmer Corp. v. Computervision Corp., 732 F.2d 888, 901-02 (Fed.Cir.), cert. denied, 469 U.S. 857 (1984); Graver Tank, 339 U.S. at 608. That formulation, however, does not mean one can ignore claim limitations. As this

---

[7] The doctrine of equivalents is limited in that the doctrine will not extend (1) to cover an accused device in the prior art, and (2) to allow the patentee to recapture through equivalence certain coverage given up during prosecution. Loctite Corp. v. Ultraseal Ltd., 781 F.2d 861, 870 (Fed.Cir.1985).

court recently stated in Perkin-Elmer Corp. v. Westinghouse Elec. Corp., 822 F.2d 1528 (Fed.Cir.1987):

> "One must start with the claim, and though a 'non-pioneer' invention may be entitled to some range of equivalents, a court may not, under the guise of applying the doctrine of equivalents, erase a plethora of meaningful structural and functional limitations of the claim on which the public is entitled to rely in avoiding infringement.... Though the doctrine of equivalents is designed to do equity, and to relieve an inventor from a semantic strait jacket when equity requires, it is not designed to permit wholesale redrafting of a claim to cover non-equivalent devices, i.e., to permit a claim expansion that would encompass more than an insubstantial change. (Citations omitted.) ... [I]n applying the doctrine of equivalents, each limitation must be viewed in the context of the entire claim.... 'It is ... well settled that each element of a claim is material and essential, and that in order for a court to find infringement, the plaintiff must show the presence of every element or its substantial equivalent in the accused device.' Lemelson v. United States, 752 F.2d 1538, 1551 (Fed.Cir.1985) (footnote omitted). To be a 'substantial equivalent,' the element substituted in the accused device for the element set forth in the claim must not be such as would substantially change the way in which the function of the claimed invention is performed." Id. at 1532-33.

Pennwalt argues that the "accused machines simply do in a computer what the patent illustrates doing with hard-wired circuitry," and asserts that "this alone is insufficient to escape infringement," citing Decca Ltd. v. United States, 544 F.2d 1070, 1080-81 (Ct. Cl. 1976). If Pennwalt was correct that the accused devices differ only in substituting a computer for hard-wired circuitry, it might have a stronger position for arguing that the accused devices infringe the claims. The claim limitations, however, require the performance of certain specified functions. Theoretically, a microprocessor could be programmed to perform those functions. However, the district court found that the microprocessor in the accused devices was not so programmed.

After a full trial, the district court made findings that certain functions of the claimed inventions were "missing" from the accused devices and those which were performed were "substantially different." *Pennwalt*, 225 USPQ at 572. The district court observed that "because the 'Microsizer' uses different elements and different operations (on the elements it does use) than the elements and operations disclosed in the patent-in-suit to achieve the desired results, infringement can only be found if the different elements and operations are the legal equivalents of those disclosed in the patent-in- suit." Id. It is clear from this that the district court correctly relied on an element-by-element comparison to conclude that there was no infringement under the doctrine of equivalents, because the accused devices did not perform substantially the same functions as the Pennwalt invention. For example, the district court found in part: The machine described in the patent-in-suit uses shift registers that respond to "clock pulses" in order to indicate the various positions of the items to be sorted before each item is discharged. The "Microsizer" does not have any "indicating means" to determine positions of the items to be sorted since the microprocessor stores weight and color data, not the positions of the items to be sorted. After a piece of fruit has been analyzed by the "Microsorter" and while it is in transit from the optical detection means to the weight scale, the color value determined by the "Microsorter" is sorted in a color value queue. A color value queue pointer (which changes in value) points to the location of the data corresponding to the next piece of fruit to reach the weight scale. A weight value queue pointer (which also changes in value) is used to correspond to the number of cups between the weight scale and the drop location. The microprocessor software utilizes a random access memory that stores the digital numbers which resulted from the conversion of the analog signals generated by the "Microsorter" and the weight scale, and the queue pointers (under clock control) point to the memory location that has the data about a piece of fruit. The data is never "shifted" around, but rather is just stored in memory until the software routines call for data to be utilized in subsequent portions of the program(s). Thus, the "Microsizer" has neither a "first position indicating means" nor a "second position indicating means." The machine described in the patent-in-suit produces signals that indicate where the fruit is, i.e. track the progression of each cup. The "Microsizer" does not. Id. at 569.

Pennwalt argues that the district court erred as a matter of law in interpreting the claims which led to these findings. Pennwalt asserts that the district court looked to the specification and compared the accused devices with the preferred embodiment. As indicated, under the section 112, paragraph 6, analysis, such comparison was entirely correct, but it is readily apparent that the court did not so limit its infringement analysis. The court also looked for equivalent functions.

* * *

Here, if the district court was not clearly erroneous in finding that even a single function required by a claim or an equivalent function is not performed by the Durand-Wayland sorters, the court's finding of no infringement must be upheld. * * *.

Pennwalt asks us to reweigh the testimony, urging that the testimony of the court-appointed expert, Dr. Vacroux, is so strongly supportive of the contrary finding of infringement under the doctrine of equivalents that the district court's finding of no infringement cannot stand. Pennwalt, however, misconstrues the effect of Dr. Vacroux's testimony. Dr. Vacroux was a technical, not a legal, expert. He was not expected to, and did not, analyze infringement under a legal standard. He was not concerned, for example, with the scope of equivalents to which the claims were entitled in view of the prosecution history. In this light, the reports and testimony of Dr.

Vacroux fully support the district court's finding of no infringement, rather than Pennwalt's position.

Pennwalt relies on the conclusory statement in Dr. Vacroux's initial written report in which he characterized the accused devices as "functionally equivalent" to the "invention." However, Dr. Vacroux also stated therein that "the new designs could be totally equivalent to those they replaced, although the components and methods used differed significantly." (Emphasis added.) Further, when Dr. Vacroux was called to testify, and, in response to detailed questioning by the court, Dr. Vacroux testified that the accused devices performed "some " of the same type of operations but "in a different way" from the claimed invention. Specifically, Dr. Vacroux answered a question by the court as follows: Dr. Vacroux: They [the accused and claimed devices] are *not equivalent,* but functionally the internal operations I would say internally are functionally equivalent because they perform some of the same type of operations. They compare, they shift, they add so we do have the same type of functions internally but done in a different way. [Emphasis added.]

Dr. Vacroux's statement that the accused devices performed only "some of the same type of operations" supports the court's finding that some were not. It does not conflict with any of his other testimony or with his written report. Thus, on the issue of whether the accused devices performed each of the functional limitations of the claim or its equivalent and, thus, operated in substantially the same way, the district court followed its expert precisely. The court cannot be faulted for finding no infringement where the expert's testimony as to facts negates a finding of equivalency under the correct legal standard. * * *.

With respect to the scope of equivalent functions, the court correctly limited the claims, based upon review of the prosecution history, stating that "the claims of the patent should be read in light of the careful phraseology [of functions] chosen by the inventors" because "the machine disclosed in the patent-in-suit was carefully described so that it did not read on the prior art." *Pennwalt,* 225 USPQ at 570. As the court correctly noted, the invention was not a pioneer, but an improvement in a crowded art. The claims are "broad" with respect to what type of product can be sorted, i.e., "items" and, thus, sorters of all types of "items" fall within the relevant prior art. The claims are narrow, however, with respect to how the claimed sorter operates. Originally, the claims contained no position indicating means element with its associated functional limitations. The addition of that element was crucial to patentability. A device that does not satisfy this limitation at least equivalently does not function in substantially the same way as the claimed invention. * * *.

The trial court found that the accused devices do not have any position indicating means to determine positions of the items to be sorted. Specifically with respect to claims 10 and 18, the court correctly held that "the microprocessor stores weight and color data, not the positions of the items to be sorted." *Pennwalt,* 225 USPQ at 569. Since each of the claims- at-issue requires a position indicating means and the same analysis applies to each, we set forth only the relevant language of claim 10: "first position indicating means responsive to a signal from said clock means and said signal from said second comparison means for continuously indicating the position of an item to be sorted while the item is in transit between said optical detection means and said electronic weighing means, second position indicating means responsive to the signal from said clock means, the signal from said first comparison means and said first position indicating means for generating a signal continuously indicative of the position of an item to be sorted after said item has been weighed."

The testimony of Dr. Alford, Durand-Wayland's expert, was that the accused machine had no component which satisfied either of the above limitations defining position indicating means, and Pennwalt has admitted that the accused machines do not sort by keeping track of the physical location of an item in transit, continuously or otherwise, as required by each of these limitations.

Pennwalt argues that there is a way to find out where an item is physically located on the track in the accused machine. Its witness, Dr. Moore, testified "you could find the location of a particular fruit as it moves from the scale to the drop by *counting the distance* from the stored value for that fruit back to the place the pointer is indicating at the start of the queue." (Emphasis added.) Dr. Alford, Durand-Wayland's expert, admitted this was possible. Thus, Pennwalt asserts that the accused devices have "position indicating means."

One need not explain the technology to understand the inadequacy of Dr. Moore's testimony. As Dr. Moore himself indicates, the accused machine simply does not do what he explains "could" be done. It is admitted that the physical tracking of fruit is not part of the way in which the Durand-Wayland sorter works, in contrast to the claimed sorter which requires some means for "continuously indicating the position of an item to be sorted." While a microprocessor theoretically could be programmed to perform that function, the evidence led the court to a finding that the Durand-Wayland machines performed a substantially different function from that which each of the claims requires.

With respect to the other limitations of claim 10, Pennwalt admits that the asserted "position indicating means" of Durand-Wayland does not meet the limitation that the means must be "responsive to ... said signal from said second comparison means" because no comparison is made on the Durand-Wayland machine before the discharge point. However, Pennwalt contends that Durand- Wayland "has merely changed the position of an operable element, but the operation and results achieved are the same as those claimed." Pennwalt's analysis is flawed in significant respects.

First, the claim requires that the "position indicating means" must be responsive to certain specified signals. Thus, finding some combination of components in the accused device that might also be labeled a "position indicating means" is a meaningless exercise when such combination is not responsive to the specified signal. * * * *.

Second, the district court correctly rejected Pennwalt's assertion that the memory component of the Durand-Wayland sorter which stores information as to weight and color of an item performed substantially the same functions as claimed for the position indicating means. The district court found that a memory function is not the same or substantially the same as the function of "continuously indicating" where an item is physically located in a sorter. On this point the record is indisputable that before the words "continuously indicating" were added as an additional limitation, the claim was unpatentable in view of prior art which, like the accused machines, stores the information with respect to sorting criteria in memories, but did not "continuously" track the location. See, e.g., U.S. Patent No. 3,289,832 issued to Ramsey.

Thus, the facts here do not involve later-developed computer technology which should be deemed within the scope of the claims to avoid the pirating of an invention. On the contrary, the inventors could not obtain a patent with claims in which the functions were described more broadly. Having secured claims only by including very specific functional limitations, Pennwalt now seeks to avoid those very limitations under the doctrine of equivalents. This it cannot do. * * * [cites]. Simply put, the memory components of the Durand-Wayland sorter were not programmed to perform the same or an equivalent function of physically tracking the items to be sorted from the scanner to the scale or from the scale to its appropriate discharge point as required by the claims.

Contrary to Pennwalt's arguments, the district court did not disregard the need to consider a range of equivalent functions under the doctrine of equivalents. Rather, upon evaluation of the evidence, the court concluded, as a fact, that no component in the Durand-Wayland devices performed a function within the permissible range of equivalents for the function of the first position indicating means. That function is required by all of the claims-at- issue. No means in the accused devices performs that function and thus there could be no literal infringement. No means with an equivalent function was substituted in the accused devices and thus there can be no infringement under the doctrine of equivalents. The district court's finding of no infringement is not clearly erroneous.

CONCLUSION

We affirm the judgment based on the finding of no infringement, the award of costs, and the denial of attorney fees to Durand-Wayland. There being no indication that Durand-Wayland's cross-appeal on validity extends beyond the litigated claims or the accused devices found to be noninfringing, we dismiss the cross-appeal as moot and vacate that part of the judgment concerning the validity of Pennwalt's patent.

NOTE

In Hilton Davis Chemical Co. v. Warner-Jenkinson Co., 62 F.3d 1512 (Fed. Cir. 1995), an en banc court reaffirmed traditional doctrine of equivalents doctrine. The court rejected the position, embraced by some panels of the court, that the doctrine was "equitable" and should not be available in every case. The court also reaffirmed that the doctrine of equivalents is part of the process by which a determination is made as to whether a patent has been infringed, that infringement is an issue of fact, and in a jury trial infringement is decided by the jury after instructions from the judge describing both infringement and the doctrine of equivalents in general terms. Several judges dissented and their opinions advanced the position, among others, that the issue of equivalents should be decided by the judge and that the doctrine is inconsistent with the statute, which provides that it is the claims that define the scope of the patent. The Supreme Court granted certiorari, Warner-Jenkinson Co., Inc. v. Hilton Davis Chemical Co., 116 S.Ct. 1014 (Feb 26, 1996) (No. 95-728).

There is a tension between the Federal Circuit's decision in Hilton-Davis and the decision of the Supreme Court in Markman v. Westview Instruments, Inc., 116 S.Ct. 1384 (1996). In that case the Supreme Court affirmed a decision of the Federal Circuit and held that issues of claim construction are issues of law, to be decided by the judge. Thus if the Supreme Court also affirms *Hilton Davis* the judge will decide what the claim means and the the jury will decide whether it was infringed, including deciding whether it was infringed under the doctrine of equivalents by conduct that did not actually fall within the claim as construed by the judge.

It is possible that the Supreme Court will hold that there is no doctrine of equivalents, which will be an interesting result since the United States has criticized the patent systems of other countries, particularly the Japanese, because the Japanese patent laws do not have a doctrine of equivalents. For an ambitious general study of these problems see T Takenaka XXXX.

In the past U.S. patent lawyers, relying on the doctrine of equivalents, have not been under pressure to draft claims with such words as "about" or "nearly" or "approximately" or "equivalently." If there were no doctrine of equivalents, the effective scope of presently issued patents would be narrowed. Can the use of such terms overcome its absence as to patents drafted in the future? Or would the use of such terms in patent claims violate § 112 ¶2 which provides that "The specification shall conclude with one or maore claims *particularly* pointing out and distinctly claiming the subject mattter which the applicant regards as his invention." If there were not doctrine of equivalents, would that cause patent applicants to draft their applications with many more claims?

M. An Overview.

The Future of Copyright and Patent

Professor J.H. Reichman has raised important questions about the future structure of intellectual property in J.R. Reichman, *Charting the Collapse of the Patent-Copyright Dichotomy: Premises for a Restructured International Intellectual Property System*, 13 CARDOZO ARTS & ENT. LAW J. 475 (1995). He takes particular note of the rise in importance of various forms of hybrid protection which are outside the traditional Berne and Paris Convention systems.